Emerging Technologies and Security in Cloud Computing

D. Lakshmi
VIT Bhopal University, India

Amit Kumar Tyagi
National Institute of Fashion Technology, New Delhi, India

A volume in the Advances in Information Security, Privacy, and Ethics (AISPE) Book Series

Published in the United States of America by
IGI Global
Information Science Reference (an imprint of IGI Global)
701 E. Chocolate Avenue
Hershey PA, USA 17033
Tel: 717-533-8845
Fax: 717-533-8661
E-mail: cust@igi-global.com
Web site: http://www.igi-global.com

Library of Congress Cataloging-in-Publication Data

CIP Pending
ISBN: 979-8-3693-2081-5
EISBN: 979-8-3693-2082-2

This book is published in the IGI Global book series Advances in Information Security, Privacy, and Ethics (AISPE) (ISSN: 1948-9730; eISSN: 1948-9749)

British Cataloguing in Publication Data
A Cataloguing in Publication record for this book is available from the British Library.

For electronic access to this publication, please contact: eresources@igi-global.com.

Advances in Information Security, Privacy, and Ethics (AISPE) Book Series

Manish Gupta
State University of New York, USA

ISSN:1948-9730
EISSN:1948-9749

Mission

As digital technologies become more pervasive in everyday life and the Internet is utilized in ever increasing ways by both private and public entities, concern over digital threats becomes more prevalent.

The **Advances in Information Security, Privacy, & Ethics (AISPE) Book Series** provides cutting-edge research on the protection and misuse of information and technology across various industries and settings. Comprised of scholarly research on topics such as identity management, cryptography, system security, authentication, and data protection, this book series is ideal for reference by IT professionals, academicians, and upper-level students.

Coverage

- Security Classifications
- Device Fingerprinting
- Telecommunications Regulations
- Cyberethics
- Information Security Standards
- IT Risk
- Cookies
- Access Control
- Electronic Mail Security
- Tracking Cookies

IGI Global is currently accepting manuscripts for publication within this series. To submit a proposal for a volume in this series, please contact our Acquisition Editors at Acquisitions@igi-global.com or visit: http://www.igi-global.com/publish/.

The Advances in Information Security, Privacy, and Ethics (AISPE) Book Series (ISSN 1948-9730) is published by IGI Global, 701 E. Chocolate Avenue, Hershey, PA 17033-1240, USA, www.igi-global.com. This series is composed of titles available for purchase individually; each title is edited to be contextually exclusive from any other title within the series. For pricing and ordering information please visit http://www.igi-global.com/book-series/advances-information-security-privacy-ethics/37157. Postmaster: Send all address changes to above address.

Titles in this Series

For a list of additional titles in this series, please visit: www.igi-global.com/book-series

Contemporary Challenges for Cyber Security and Data Privacy
Nuno Mateus-Coelho (Lusófona University, Portugal) and Maria Manuela Cruz-Cunha (Polytechnic Institute of Cávado and Ave, Porugal)
Information Science Reference • © 2023 • 308pp • H/C (ISBN: 9798369315286) • US $275.00

Privacy Preservation and Secured Data Storage in Cloud Computing
Lakshmi D. (VIT Bhopal University, India) and Amit Kumar Tyagi (National Institute of Fashion Technology, New Delhi, ndia)
Engineering Science Reference • © 2023 • 360pp • H/C (ISBN: 9798369305935) • US $265.00

Malware Analysis and Intrusion Detection in Cyber-Physical Systems
S.L. Shiva Darshan (Department of Information and Communication Technology, Manipal Institute of Technology, India) M.V. Manoj Kumar (Department of Information Science and Engineering, Nitte Meenakshi Institute of Technology, India) B.S. Prashanth (Department of Information Science and Engineering, Nitte Meenakshi Institute of Technology, India) and Y. Vishnu Srinivasa Murthy (Department of Computational Intelligence, Vellore Institute of Technology, India)
Information Science Reference • © 2023 • 415pp • H/C (ISBN: 9781668486665) • US $225.00

Handbook of Research on Data Science and Cybersecurity Innovations in Industry 4.0 Technologies
Thangavel Murugan (United Arab Emirates University, Al Ain, UAE) and Nirmala E. (VIT Bhopal University, India)
Information Science Reference • © 2023 • 620pp • H/C (ISBN: 9781668481455) • US $325.00

Perspectives on Ethical Hacking and Penetration Testing
Keshav Kaushik (University of Petroleum and Energy Studies, India) and Akashdeep Bhardwaj (University of Petroleum and Energy Studies, India)
Information Science Reference • © 2023 • 445pp • H/C (ISBN: 9781668482186) • US $225.00

AI Tools for Protecting and Preventing Sophisticated Cyber Attacks
Eduard Babulak (National Science Foundation, USA)
Information Science Reference • © 2023 • 233pp • H/C (ISBN: 9781668471104) • US $250.00

Cyber Trafficking, Threat Behavior, and Malicious Activity Monitoring for Healthcare Organizations
Dinesh C. Dobhal (Graphic Era University (Deemed), India) Sachin Sharma (Graphic Era University (Deemed), India) Kamlesh C. Purohit (Graphic Era University (Deemed), India) Lata Nautiyal (University of Bristol, UK) and Karan Singh (Jawaharlal Nehru University, India)
Medical Information Science Reference • © 2023 • 206pp • H/C (ISBN: 9781668466469) • US $315.00

701 East Chocolate Avenue, Hershey, PA 17033, USA
Tel: 717-533-8845 x100 • Fax: 717-533-8661
E-Mail: cust@igi-global.com • www.igi-global.com

Editorial Advisory Board

Table of Contents

Detailed Table of Contents

In the past decade, edge computing and blockchain technology have been used in many applications with rapid growth. The chapter explores the intersection of blockchain technology and edge computing and investigates the security issues and solutions in this emerging domain. Edge computing refers to "the decentralized processing and storage of data at the network edge, closer to the data sources and end-users. It offers reduced latency, improved data privacy, and enhanced real-time decision-making capabilities." However, it also introduces new security challenges due to the distributed and resource-constrained nature of edge devices. The integration of blockchain technology with edge computing holds promise in addressing these security issues. Blockchain can provide a decentralized and tamper-resistant ledger for recording and verifying transactions, ensuring data integrity, and establishing trust among edge devices and stakeholders. This chapter explores several use cases where blockchain and edge computing can synergistically enhance security.

Cloud computing has revolutionized the landscape of modern business logistics by offering scalable and cost-effective solutions for data storage, processing, and application deployment. However, with this newfound convenience comes a plethora of security challenges that businesses must address to protect their valuable assets and sensitive information. This chapter aims to provide a comprehensive overview of the security risks and threats associated with cloud adoption in the logistics industry, along with effective solutions to mitigate them by presenting an in-depth analysis of the primary security risks that businesses may encounter when leveraging cloud-based logistics solutions. Additionally, it discusses the risks posed by shared infrastructure, third-party integrations, and data jurisdiction concerns. Moreover, the chapter highlights the growing role of emerging technologies in bolstering cloud security measures. These technologies offer sophisticated threat detection and proactive response capabilities, enabling logistics companies to stay ahead of evolving cyber threats.

With the rapid growth of the internet of things (IoT) and the emergence of edge computing, new opportunities and challenges have arisen in the realm of cyber security. This work presents a comprehensive review of cyber security in IoT-based edge computing, aiming to shed light on the potential risks and vulnerabilities associated with this evolving paradigm. This work begins by highlighting the increasing integration of IoT devices and edge computing, emphasizing their combined potential to revolutionize various industries. However, this integration also introduces new attack surfaces and vulnerabilities, making robust cyber security measures imperative to safeguard critical systems and sensitive data. The work discusses an in-depth analysis of the unique security challenges that arise at the intersection of IoT and edge computing. It explores the vulnerabilities introduced by the distributed nature of edge computing, the resource-constrained nature of IoT devices, and the heterogeneity of the IoT ecosystem.

Consortium blockchain provides pooled trust for the proposed method. It uses a unique certificateless authentication method based on the multi-signature scheme to guarantee safety. Software, and physical components comprise the cyber-physical system. Each piece functions on various time-based and three-dimensional stages and constantly interacts with other members. The framework eliminates the centralized trust model, i.e., the dependence on a single PKI certificate authority (CA) for public keys, works over an associate consortium, and uses smart-edge computation. Different industry partners cooperatively confirm both the gadget's character and information. It prevents disasters by reducing the impact of potentially malevolent associates. It agrees to a novel contract without requiring manifold authorisations, eliminating the need for a waiting period after each block addition. It adjusts, putting away information at the conveyed hash table. The suggestion adds more reliability to the transaction by 4.17%. The suggestion conserves energy by 12.5%.

The Covid-19 pandemic has accelerated the rise of medical devices and applications, collecting, monitoring, and analyzing valuable healthcare data. The internet of medical things (IoMT) has been used to improve the accuracy, dependability, and efficiency of electronic instruments in healthcare. IoMT can connect real-world objects for information sharing and communication. However, challenges in IoT equipment communication, security, and framework development remain. FOG computing and blockchain technologies can support better-personalized systems, but they also present challenges in developing cost-effective and enhanced treatment quality. The healthcare industry must continue to improve the accuracy, reliability, and efficiency of electronic instruments to ensure patient care during the pandemic.

More than eighty percent of U.S. adults receive news from digital devices like smartphones, computers, or tablets. Unlike the traditional news dominated by organizations, this new kind of news could be created by anyone. It is quick and engaging. At the same time, misinformation may be easily generated or spread intentionally or unintentionally. Misinformation is a serious problem for the general public, and there

The chapter thoroughly addresses ML privacy threats like risks, attacks, and leaks. It explores the methods of differential privacy, homomorphic encryption, and SMPC. Federated learning is detailed, covering concepts, benefits, techniques (averaging, aggregation). Advancements include transfer learning, differential privacy, edge device use. Real cases show privacy's value in healthcare, finance, IoT. The conclusion touches on trends, regulations, privacy-utility balance. The chapter aims to overview privacy-preserving and federated ML, stressing their role in data security with insights for researchers, practitioners, policymakers for privacy-conscious ML. Valuable insights are provided for researchers, practitioners, and policymakers aiming for a privacy-conscious future in machine learning.

Blockchain and internet of things (IoT) is a combination that has massive potential to bring about revolutionary changes in various useful applications/ industries by enabling secure and transparent data exchange, decentralized control, and improved efficiency. However, this convergence also requires significant security, privacy, and technical challenges that must be addressed for successful implementation and widespread adoption. This chapter explains the security, privacy, and technical challenges that arise in a blockchain-IoT-based environment. Firstly, it examines the security issues related to the distributed nature of blockchain networks and the vulnerabilities that can be exploited in IoT devices and communication channels. Further, the authors discuss the importance of cryptographic techniques, secure key management, and access control mechanisms to protect data integrity and prevent unauthorized access.

The rate at which secret messages are being transmitted through various digital signal media is alarming; these operations are done in an unsuspicious manner and users transmit these messages without knowledge of the embedded secret messages. Audio steganalysis deals with detecting the presence of secret messages in audio messages. Some of the existing steganalysis methods are laden with having prior knowledge of the steganography methods adopted in embedding the secret message in an audio signal, which reduces the detection efficiency. Consequently, this research developed a Higuchi-based audio steganalysis method that detects secret messages without having prior knowledge of the embedding techniques used. The algorithm reduces the fractal dimension of the audio signal to extract relevant features, while convolutional neural network was used as classifier. The research records high accuracy (96%) when compared with previous research. The accuracy of the developed system shows its effectiveness in detecting embedded messages without prior knowledge of the deployed steganography method.

Preface

In the previous decade, cloud computing has revolutionized almost all businesses/ industries and it was possible due to the power of technology. With its promise of scalability, flexibility, and cost-efficiency, it has become the backbone of modern digital infrastructure. However, as cloud computing has continued to evolve, so too have the many challenges and risks associated with it like security, privacy, etc. The intersection of emerging technologies and security in cloud computing is a dynamic and ever-evolving field. This book provides a detailed explanation of this critical integration with offering meaningful insights, strategies, etc., to navigate the complex landscape of securing cloud-based systems and data in an age of rapid technological innovation.

Cloud computing has matured from being a simple means of data storage and processing to an ecosystem powered by cutting-edge technologies such as artificial intelligence, machine learning, blockchain, edge computing, blockchain technology, and the Internet of Things (IoT). These innovations offer many opportunities for businesses/ industries to improve efficiency, enhance customer experiences, and innovate their products and services. However, they also introduce new vectors for potential security threats, ranging from data breaches and privacy issues to system vulnerabilities and compliance challenges.

In this book, we will discuss the most critical aspects of emerging technologies and security in cloud computing. We will explore the latest trends and developments in cloud security, including advanced threat detection, identity and access management, encryption, and compliance frameworks. We will also examine how emerging technologies are reshaping the cloud security landscape, with practical insights and real-world examples (like healthcare, retails, etc.) to help readers/ future researchers understand the current challenges and future opportunities.

Hence, as the digital world continues to evolve, we need modern solutions (with emerging technology) to cloud security. We will discuss several interesting works including the challenges, opportunities, and will build a more secure and resilient digital future for modern society.

D. Lakshmi
VIT Bhopal University, India

Amit Kumar Tyagi
National Institute of Fashion Technology, New Delhi, India

Acknowledgment

First of all, we want to extend our gratitude to my Family Members, Friends, and Supervisors, which stood with us as an advisor in completing this book. Also, we would like to thank our almighty "God" who makes us to write this book.

We would like to extend our heartfelt gratitude to the management and leadership team of VIT Bhopal University and *Department of Fashion Technology, National Institute of Fashion Technology, New Delhi* for their unwavering support and encouragement throughout my research activities. Their commitment to fostering a conducive research environment and providing essential technical support has been instrumental in the successful completion of this project.

We also thank IGI Global Publishers (who has provided their continuous support during this COVID 19 Pandemic) and my friends/ colleagues with whom we have work together inside the college/ university and others outside of the college/ university who have provided their continuous support towards completing this book on Emerging Technologies, and Security in Cloud Computing.

D. Lakshmi
VIT Bhopal University, India

Amit Kumar Tyagi
National Institute of Fashion Technology, New Delhi, India

Acknowledgment

[illegible]

[illegible]

[illegible]

[illegible]

[illegible]

Chapter 1
Introduction to Cloud Computing and Cloud Services

Mani Deepak Choudhry
https://orcid.org/0000-0001-8519-2416
KGiSL Institute of Technology, India

M. Sundarrajan
SRM Institute of Science and Technology, India

M. Parimala Devi
Velalar College of Engineering and Technology, India

S. Jeevanandham
Sri Ramakrishna Engineering College, India

Akshya Jothi
https://orcid.org/0000-0001-9976-2133
SRM Institute of Science and Technology, India

ABSTRACT

Cloud computing and cloud services have revolutionized the way organizations access and utilize computing resources. This chapter provides an overview of cloud computing, its evolution, and the advantages it offers. It discusses the different types of cloud services and the importance of service-level agreements. The chapter also explores cloud deployment models and their considerations. It highlights the impact of cloud computing on various industries and the challenges of migration. Cloud computing and cloud services have revolutionized the IT landscape. They provide organizations with scalable, flexible, and cost-effective solutions that drive innovation and enable businesses to focus on their core competencies. By carefully evaluating their needs and requirements, considering factors such as security, compliance, and customization, organizations can select the most suitable cloud service type and deployment model. Embracing cloud technologies empowers businesses to unlock new opportunities, increase efficiency, and stay competitive in the rapidly evolving digital world.

DOI: 10.4018/979-8-3693-2081-5.ch001

INTRODUCTION

Cloud computing refers to the provision of various computing services through the Internet, encompassing servers, storage, databases, networking, software, analytics, and intelligence. Cloud computing is a viable alternative to traditional on-site datacenters. In the context of an on-premises datacenter, the responsibility for various tasks falls upon the organization, encompassing the procurement and installation of hardware, configuration of virtual machines, deployment of the operating system and requisite software, establishment of network infrastructure, implementation of firewall measures, and provisioning of data storage (Mell & Grance, 2011). We are now responsible for ensuring its sustainability during its entire lifespan following the completion of all necessary preparations. Cloud technology enables the delivery of flexible resources, rapid innovation, and economies of scale (Armbrust et al., 2009). In contrast, instead of maintaining own data centers, enterprises have the option to lease infrastructure from cloud computing service providers, encompassing storage, processing servers, and databases. This arrangement allows organizations to solely incur costs for the specific resources they actively employed[3].

Cloud computing refers to the delivery of various computing services, such as servers, data storage, databases, networking, software, analytics, and intelligence, via the internet, commonly referred to as the "cloud." The primary objective of cloud computing is to enable rapid innovation, achieve economies of scale, and provide flexible access to computing resources (Nelson, 2009). In essence, organizations have the ability to lease the utilization of a third-party's infrastructure, encompassing databases, processing servers, and storage, through a cloud computing service provider. This arrangement allows them to solely incur costs for the resources they actively employ, rather than maintaining their own data centers (Sotomayor et al., 2009). Figure 1 shows the cloud computing environment.

Cloud computing refers to the delivery of computer services via the Internet, encompassing a range of offerings such as servers, storage, databases, networking, software, analytics, and intelligence. Cloud computing can serve as a viable alternative to on-site datacenters (Nurmi et al., 2008). When utilizing an on-premises datacenter, it is imperative to address many tasks, including the procurement and installation of hardware, the configuration of virtual machines, the installation of the operating system and any supplementary software, the establishment of the network, the configuration of the firewall, and the setup of data storage. The responsibility of ensuring its preservation during its lifespan falls upon us once all aspects have been defined.

The significance of cloud computing on enterprises and end users is profound, as the pervasive presence and transformative capabilities of cloud-based software have altered various aspects of everyday existence. Startups and enterprises have the potential to optimize their products and minimize costs through the utilization of cloud computing, rather than investing in the procurement and upkeep of their own hardware and software. Independent developers are provided the capability to distribute applications and online services on a global scale. Researchers now have the ability to share and evaluate data on a scale that was previously limited to studies with ample financial resources. Moreover, those who possess internet connectivity have the convenience of acquiring storage and software resources that enable them to generate, disseminate, and store digital data.

The prevalence of cloud computing is increasing, but, there remains a significant lack of knowledge among individuals regarding this technology (Guazzelli et al., 2009). This inquiry pertains to the concept of cloud computing, its operational mechanisms, and the benefits it presents to many stakeholders such as academics, developers, corporations, the government, medical professionals, and students. This conceptual work aims to provide a comprehensive overview of cloud computing, encompassing its historical context, delivery modalities, distinctive attributes, and associated risks.

Figure 1. Cloud computing environment

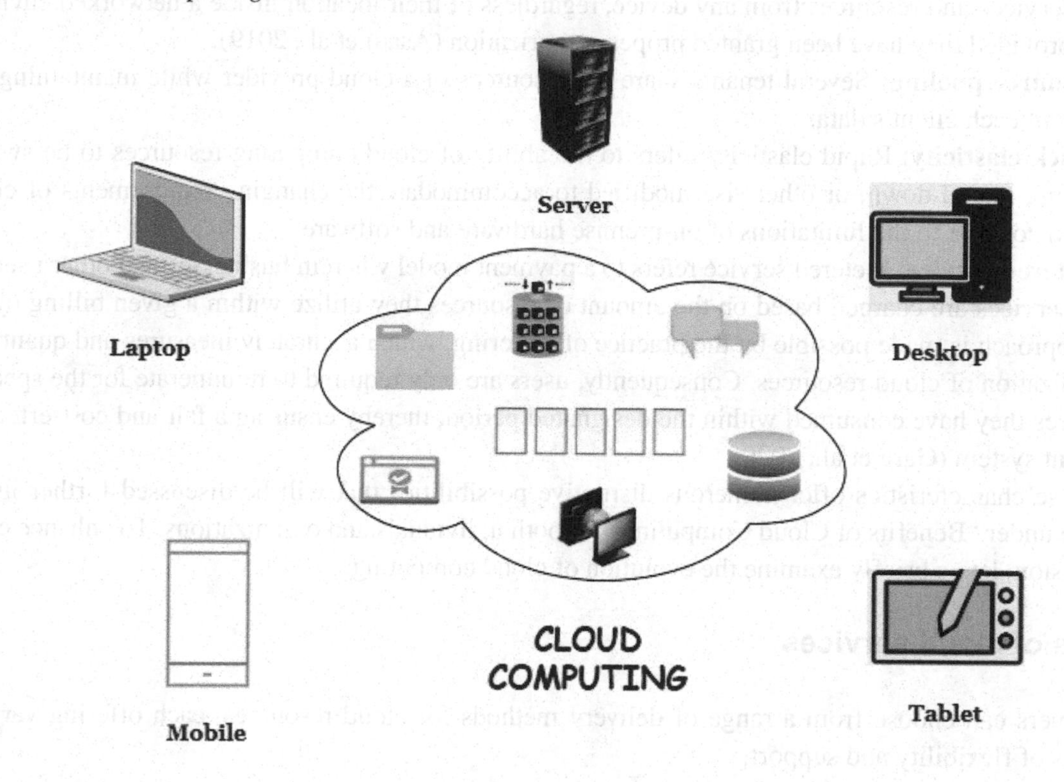

BACKGROUND

Essential Characteristics of Cloud Computing

Cloud computing refers to a framework which allows for widespread and convenient access to a network, enabling users to utilize a collective group of computing resources. These resources, such as networks, servers, storage, applications, and services, can be easily and quickly allocated and released with least effort or involvement from service providers. The National Institute of Standards and Technology (NIST) is an agency of the United States Department of Commerce that operates in a non-regulatory capacity. Its primary objective is to promote and facilitate the progress of innovation.

According to the National Institute of Standards and Technology (NIST), the five fundamental elements of cloud computing are as follows:

Self-service on demand: The concept of self-service on demand refers to a system or process that allows individuals to access goods, services, or information without the need for direct assistance from another person. Cloud resources can be deployed or accessed autonomously, without necessitating human participation (Kannadasan et al., 2018). By employing this particular approach, individuals have the ability to register and promptly commence utilizing cloud-based services. Furthermore, organizations have the capability to establish infrastructures that facilitate the seamless utilization of internal cloud services by partners, employees, or customers, in accordance with predetermined guidelines, hence obviating the need for IT support intervention.

Wide-ranging network access: Wide-ranging network access refers to the ability of users to access cloud services and resources from any device, regardless of their location inside a networked environment, provided they have been granted proper authorization (Asadi et al., 2019).

Resource pooling: Several tenants share the resources of a cloud provider while maintaining the privacy of each client's data.

Quick elasticity: Rapid elasticity refers to the ability of cloud computing resources to be swiftly scaled up, scaled down, or otherwise modified to accommodate the changing requirements of cloud users, in contrast to the limitations of on-premise hardware and software.

Metered service: Metered service refers to a payment model wherein businesses and other users of cloud services are charged based on the amount of resources they utilize within a given billing cycle. This approach is made possible by the practice of metering, which accurately measures and quantifies the utilization of cloud resources. Consequently, users are only required to remunerate for the specific resources they have consumed within the designated period, thereby ensuring a fair and cost-effective payment system (Garg et al., 2020).

These characteristics offer numerous disruptive possibilities that will be discussed further in the section under "Benefits of Cloud Computing" for both individuals and organizations. To enhance comprehension, let us briefly examine the evolution of cloud computing.

Types of cloud services

Customers can choose from a range of delivery methods for cloud resources, each offering varying degrees of flexibility and support.

Infrastructure as a Service (IaaS)

Infrastructure as a Service (IaaS) enables the provision of computing infrastructure, encompassing operating systems, networking, storage, and other essential components, in a flexible and on-demand manner. Infrastructure as a Service (IaaS) operates in a manner akin to virtualized servers, so relieving cloud customers of the need to procure and oversee real servers. This affords users the flexibility to expand their resources and remunerate accordingly, based on their specific requirements(Vecchiola et al., 2009). Infrastructure as a Service (IaaS) is a popular option for firms seeking to influence cloud computing and possessing competent system administrators. In addition, users such as developers, researchers, and other professionals seeking to modify the underlying architecture of their computer environment also utilize architecture as a Service (IaaS). Due to its inherent flexibility, Infrastructure as a Service (IaaS) possesses the ability to effectively manage extensive data analysis, web hosting, and the overall computer infrastructure of an organization. Infrastructure as a Service (IaaS) enables the leasing of IT infrastructures from cloud service providers, encompassing servers, virtual machines (VMs), storage, networks, and operating systems. It is possible to install a wide range of software applications on a virtual machine (VM) that operates on either the Linux or Windows operating system. The utilization of Infrastructure as a Service (IaaS) obviates the need for concern over virtualization software or hardware. However, it is imperative to acknowledge that all other aspects remain within the purview of responsibility. The utilization of Infrastructure as a Service (IaaS) affords individuals with a heightened degree of autonomy, while it necessitates a greater level of maintenance and effort (Shakeabubakor et al., 2015). Figure 2 shows the types of cloud services.

Figure 2. Types of cloud services

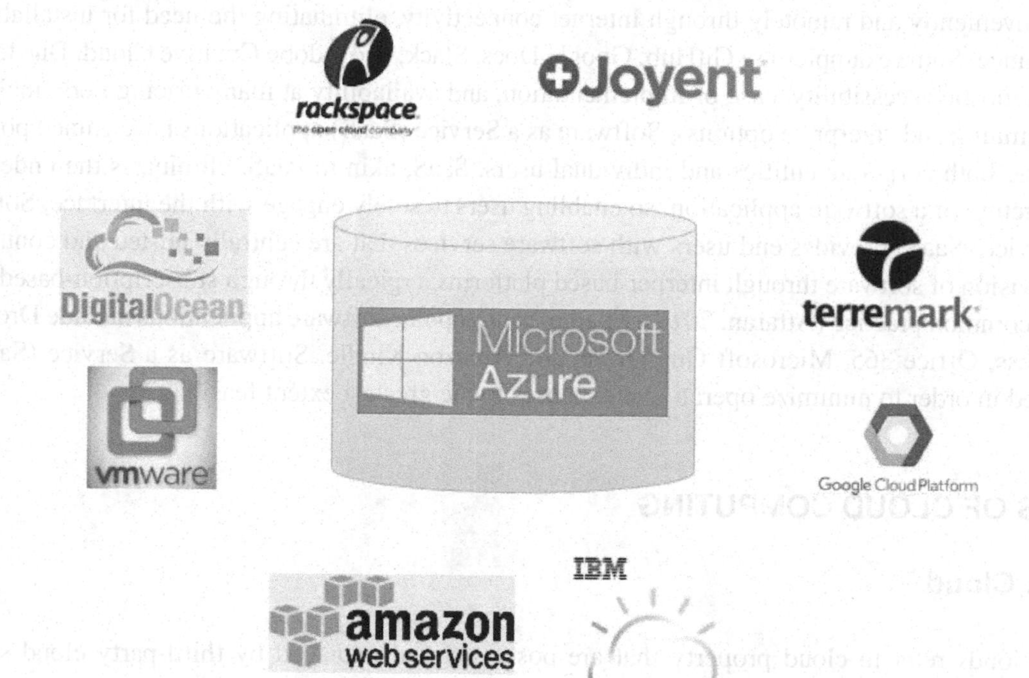

Platform as a Service (PaaS)

Through the utilization of platform as a service (PaaS), clients are able to focus their endeavors on the development and deployment of applications within a consistent and validated setting, as the service provider assumes responsibility for the installation, configuration, and upkeep of the foundational infrastructure, including the operating system and other pertinent software components, on a computer-based platform. PaaS is commonly employed by software developers and development teams due to its ability to streamline the establishment and administration of computer infrastructure, as well as enhance collaboration across geographically scattered teams (Wang et al., 2011). Developers that prioritize their focus on software development rather than DevOps and system administration, or those who do not require modifications to their underlying infrastructure, may find Platform as a Service (PaaS) to be a beneficial alternative. The provided service offers an on-demand environment for software creation, testing, delivery, and management. The responsibility for the application lies with the developer, while the Platform as a Service (PaaS) provider facilitates its execution and delivery (Stantchev, 2009). Although Platform as a Service (PaaS) offers limited flexibility, it is advantageous as cloud providers take care of environment maintenance.

Software as a Service (SaaS)

In the context of the current discussion, it is important to consider the significance of a Software as a Service (SaaS) refers to a cloud computing model where software applications are provided to users over the internet on a subscription basis. In this model, the software is hosted and maintained by a service provider, relieving users of the need

Software as a Service (SaaS) enterprises provide cloud-based applications that enable clients to access them conveniently and remotely through internet connectivity, eliminating the need for installation or maintenance. Some examples are GitHub, Google Docs, Slack, and Adobe Creative Cloud. Due to their device-agnostic accessibility, ease of implementation, and availability at many pricing tiers (including free, premium, and enterprise options), Software as a Service (SaaS) applications have gained popularity among both corporate entities and individual users. SaaS, akin to PaaS, eliminates the underlying infrastructure of a software application, so enabling users to solely engage with the interface. Software as a Service (SaaS) provides end users with software services that are centrally hosted and controlled. The provision of software through internet-based platforms, typically through subscription-based models, is a common practice (Attaran, 2017). Examples of popular software applications include Dropbox, WordPress, Office 365, Microsoft One Drive, and Amazon Kindle. Software as a Service (SaaS) is employed in order to minimize operational expenses to the greatest extent feasible.

TYPES OF CLOUD COMPUTING

Public Cloud

Public clouds refer to cloud property that are possessed and managed by third-party cloud service providers. The internet facilitates the provision of computational resources such as servers, software, and storage. The term "public cloud" refers to cloud services, including virtual machines, storage, and applications, that are accessible to both individuals and organizations through a commercial provider's publicly open platform. Public cloud resources are accessed by users through the internet, and these resources are hosted on the hardware infrastructure of a commercial provider (Foster et al., 2008). Organizations operating in heavily regulated industries such as healthcare or finance may deem public cloud environments as undesirable due to potential non-compliance with industry-specific regulations on the protection and handling of consumer data. Figure 3 shows the types of cloud.

Private Cloud

A private cloud refers to a collection of cloud computing resources that are only accessed by a single enterprise or organization. A private cloud infrastructure can be hosted either by a third-party service provider or within the organization's own on-site datacenter. The concept of a "private cloud" refers to cloud-based services that are restricted in access solely to the employees and customers of the organization utilizing them, and are owned and overseen by that organization (Lin et al., 2009). Private clouds enable organizations operating in heavily regulated industries to exert greater control over their computing environment and stored data. Private clouds are often perceived as more secure than public clouds due to their accessibility through private networks and the ability for enterprises to maintain direct control over their cloud security. Public cloud providers may offer their services in the form of applications that can be deployed on private clouds, allowing organizations to use the latest developments in the public cloud while retaining their infrastructure and data on-premises.

Figure 3. Types of cloud

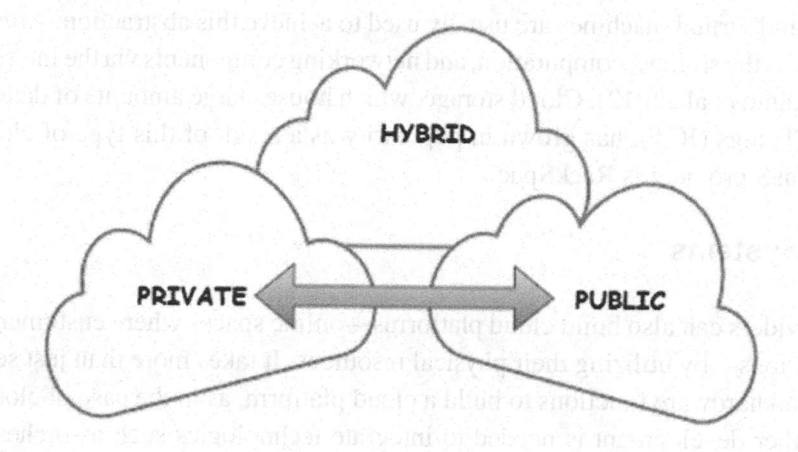

Hybrid Cloud

Hybrid cloud refers to the integration of public and private clouds through a technology interface that enables the seamless transmission of data and applications between these distinct cloud environments. The organization derives advantages from the enhanced flexibility and expanded deployment alternatives provided by hybrid cloud environments. A significant number of enterprises utilize a hybrid cloud infrastructure, which combines the capabilities of public and private clouds to effectively address their computational requirements while ensuring compliance with relevant industry standards (Greenberg et al., 2008). Furthermore, multi-cloud systems are prevalent in contemporary computing practices, wherein various public cloud providers are employed to enhance operational efficiency and flexibility. For instance, organizations may opt to combine the services of DigitalOcean and Amazon Web Services to leverage the benefits offered by both platforms.

TYPES OF CLOUD COMPUTING

Cloud services depend on hardware and software much like any other IT solution. To use cloud services, customers only need a computer, an operating system, and a network connection, in contrast to traditional hardware and software solutions.

Cloud-Based Architecture

When cloud service providers provide consumers with an infrastructure in the cloud, they separate hardware components from computer capabilities. Examples of this include:

Central processing units (CPUs) provide processing power, while random access memory (RAM) chips provide active memory.

- The **graphics processing units' (GPUs)** graphic processing
- The **availability of hard drives** or datacenters for data storage

Virtualization and virtual machines are usually used to achieve this abstraction. After being divided, customers can access the storage, computation, and networking components via the internet as infrastructure, or IaaS (Suakanto et al., 2012). Cloud storage, which houses large amounts of data as a component of the Internet of Things (IOT), has grown in popularity as a result of this type of cloud service. One illustration of an IaaS provider is RackSpace.

Cloud-Based Systems

Cloud service providers can also build cloud platforms—online spaces where customers can write code or execute applications—by utilizing their physical resources. It takes more than just separating a computer's software and hardware functions to build a cloud platform, as in the case of cloud infrastructure provisioning. Further development is needed to integrate technologies such as orchestration, routing, security, automation, application programming interfaces (APIs), automation, and containerization into a cloud platform. Making an online experience that is easy to navigate also requires careful consideration of user experience design, or UX.

One category of PaaS is cloud platforms. It may also be regarded as a cloud if the infrastructure supporting the PaaS is extremely scalable and shareable (Khanghahi & Ravanmehr, 2013). Managed private clouds and public clouds are the best instances of PaaS clouds.

Providers of Public Clouds

Public cloud companies combine their hardware assets into data lakes, abstract their own platforms, apps, and infrastructure from them, and share them with several tenants. Additionally, they can provide public cloud services, including operating systems hosted on cloud infrastructure, framework libraries, and API administration. Alibaba Cloud, Google Cloud, Microsoft Azure, Amazon Web Services (AWS), and IBM Cloud are a few well-known public cloud providers. Figure 4 shows the cloud service providers.

Supervised Personal Clouds

Private cloud providers, also referred to as managed cloud providers, offer their clients access to a private cloud that is set up, maintained, and operated by a third party. It's a cloud delivery solution that aids large companies or small companies with understaffed or inexperienced IT teams in offering users superior private cloud infrastructure and services.

Figure 4. Cloud service providers

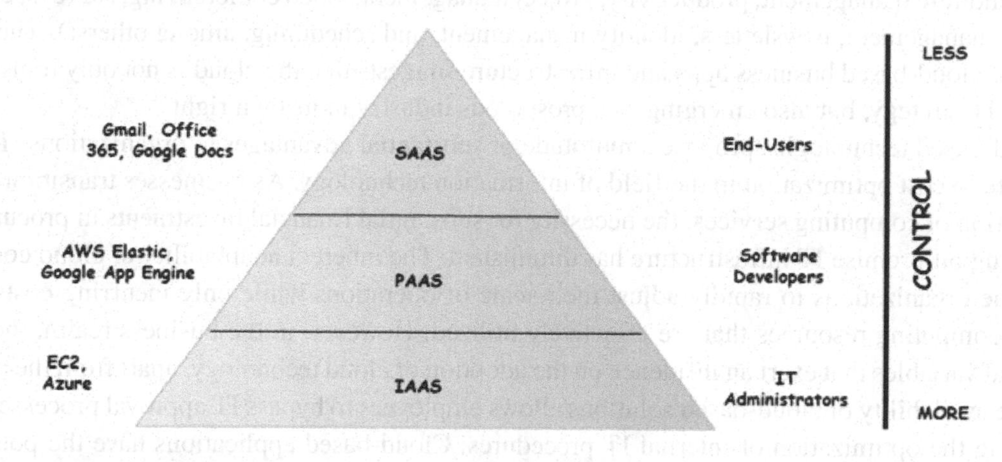

Online Software

A complete online application, sometimes referred to as cloud software or SaaS, is the last generally recognized cloud service that providers can offer. This requires the most development expenditure because the cloud provider is essentially delivering users an online application.

A cloud-native method, which combines small, independent, and loosely linked micro services in application architecture, can be used to supply cloud software. It is possible to bundle several micro services into separate Linux® containers that are controlled by Red Hat® OpenShift® or Kubernetes, two examples of container orchestration engines. The end result is a cloud application that allows for micro service optimization without affecting other micro services that collectively comprise the entire application.

APPLICATIONS OF CLOUD COMPUTING

Numerous advantages are provided by cloud computing to developers, corporations, individuals, and other organizations. These advantages change based on the objectives and actions of the cloud user.

Industry and Business

Before to the widespread use of cloud computing, the procurement and maintenance of hardware and software necessary to enable computer operations were predominantly undertaken by the majority of corporations and organizations. After the introduction of cloud computing resources, numerous firms began adopting them for the purposes of deploying products and services online, providing enterprise software, and storing data. Some of the advancements and implementations of cloud computing are specialized to certain sectors. Cloud services are extensively utilized by healthcare professionals for the purpose of storing and exchanging patient data, as well as facilitating communication between patients and providers. Academic researchers and educators make use of cloud-based research and teaching apps. Various firms have adopted a wide range of generic tools, such as cloud-based applications for messaging, expenditure management, productivity, project management, video conferencing, surveys, customer relations management, newsletters, identity management, and scheduling, among others(). The speedy growth of cloud-based business apps and infrastructure suggests that the cloud is not only transforming business IT strategy, but also emerging as a prosperous industry in its own right.

Cloud-based technologies propose a multitude of substantial advantages to organizations. They can contribute to cost optimization in the field of information technology. As businesses transition towards the adoption of computing services, the necessity for substantial financial investments in procuring and up-keeping on-premise IT infrastructure has diminished. The inherent adaptability of cloud computing enable the organizations to rapidly adjust their scale of operations while only incurring costs for the specific computing resources that are effectively utilized. However, in the business realm, there exist additional variables that exert an influence on the adoption of cloud technology, apart from the aspect of cost. The availability of cloud-based solutions allows employees to bypass IT approval processes, hence facilitating the optimization of internal IT procedures. Cloud-based applications have the potential to promote intra-organizational collaboration by facilitating real-time communication and data exchange.

Industry and Business

The advent of internet connectivity has democratized access to computing resources are limited to huge corporations and organizations. These resources may now be accessed on demand, and at a far lower cost. Cloud-based applications enable independent developers to efficiently deploy and evaluate novel functionalities. Cloud-based code-sharing services such as GitHub have facilitated enhanced developer collaboration and streamlined project development processes. In addition, the availability of developer education has been facilitated by the utilization of cloud-based learning platforms and interactive coding tutorials. These resources enable individuals without formal technical backgrounds to acquire coding skills at their own convenience.

In conjunction, the integration of cloud computing and educational resources has effectively mitigated barriers associated with the acquisition of developer proficiencies and the deployment of cloud applications. Currently, individuals have the capability to engage in the process of creating and implementing applications without the necessity of professional instruction, backing from organizations, or substantial initial financial commitments (Kumari, 2021). This has the potential for more participation in cloud development, hence fostering competition among existing industrial entities, and facilitating the creation and dissemination of applications as supplementary endeavors.

Academics

Cloud computing has developed into an important component in numerous scientific disciplines, encompassing physics, genomics, artificial intelligence, astronomy, and physics. This is mostly due to the increasing significance of machine learning methodologies in scientific investigations. Machine learning and other data-demanding investigating projects require computing resources that surpass the facility of hardware owned by the researchers or given by universities. This is mostly due to the substantial volumes of data that are generated and analyzed. Cloud computing enables researchers to engage in real-time collaboration with researchers throughout the world and conveniently access computing resources based on their specific requirements, while only incurring costs proportional to their workload demands (Tyagi et al., 2020). If commercial cloud providers were not accessible, access to robust computing resources supplied by institutions would likely restrict the availability of the machine learning research to a limited audience.

Educators and Learners

Cloud computing has offered students with the opportunity to augment their educational experience and cultivate their technical skills through the availability of various resources. By engaging in the examination, application, and participation in open source software and research endeavors pertinent to chosen discipline or expert aspirations, students have the opportunity to acquire practical technical proficiencies. This is facilitated by the utilization of cloud-based applications such as GitHub and Jupyter Notebooks, which enable the sharing, instruction, and collaborative manipulation of code and data. In addition to independent developers, students have the opportunity to utilize cloud computing resources for the purpose of sharing their applications and code with the general public. This affords them the gratification of witnessing the practical implementation of their diligent efforts.

Cloud computing resources can be advantageous for educators, researchers, and students as they seek to enhance their computing environments and have greater control over customized academic infrastructure. Some academics prefer this strategy as it grants them the ability to select the programs they utilize, modify the features and aesthetics of these resources, and impose limitations or prohibit data collecting. Additionally, cloud-based applications created especially for educational settings are becoming more and more common and are being promoted as strong substitutes or additional choices for conventional academic information technology (IT) services (Pal et al., 2022). Voyant Tools provides academics and students with a code-free method for textual analysis of any selected document. Apart from that, HathiTrust makes available millions of volumes in its vast digital collection. Within academic communities, there are several possibilities for networking, publishing, and education through sites like Manifold, Commons in a Box, Reclaim Hosting, and the Modern Language Humanities Commons.

Infrastructure in Communities

The act of implementing and sustaining cloud-based software by individuals and communities enables them to effectively address the needs and values of their community, customize functionalities, ensure the security of user data, and exercise greater authority over their computing environment. Open source software provides viable alternatives to Software as a Service (SaaS) platforms, which often impose limitations on users' autonomy, privacy, and supervision of their computational ecosystem. Illustrative instances of such software encompass many applications such as Mastodon, a social networking tool, Jitsi, video conferencing software, Etherpad, a collaborative text editor, and Rocket Chat, an online chat service. Due to ethical considerations around the utilization of user data and corporate performances associated with widely used platforms and software-as-a-service (SaaS) programs, many groups exhibit a preference for these solutions, notwithstanding the increased administrative burden they often entail compared to social networking platforms or SaaS applications.

APPLICATIONS OF CLOUD COMPUTING

Cost

It makes purchasing gear and software less of a significant capital expense. By just paying for the services you use, you save on the capital costs associated with purchasing hardware and software, building out datacenters, and maintaining them.

Speed

Accessing resources only takes a few clicks and can take minutes. The majority of cloud computing services is on-demand and self-serve. Minutes are all it takes to provide any number of resources, which allows enterprises a great deal of flexibility in terms of scaling their application at the correct time and place.

Scalability

Depending on the demands of the business, we can adjust the amount of resources needed.

Productivity

We used less operational effort when we used cloud computing. Patching is not necessary, and neither is software or hardware maintenance. Thus, the IT team can concentrate on accomplishing business objectives and be more productive in this way.

Reliability

For business continuity, data backup and recovery are quicker and less expensive. Cloud services' strong infrastructure allows for high availability. Disaster recovery and data backup are simple processes that may be completed quickly. By mirroring data across multiple locations on the cloud provider's network, business continuity can be achieved more affordably.

Protection

A wide range of rules, tools, and safeguards are provided by cloud providers, bolstering the protection of our data

Within minutes, you may launch apps worldwide and grow your company into new regions, thanks to the cloud. Many cloud service providers offer their services across numerous nations; by placing apps closer to end customers, they can lower latency and enhance the user experience.

DANGERS, EXPENSES, AND ETHICAL IMPLICATIONS IN CLOUD COMPUTING

Despite the various advantages offered by cloud computing, it is imperative to acknowledge the associated costs, risks, and ethical implications. While many issues have an impact on all consumers of cloud services, there are certain concerns that are particularly relevant to firms and organizations that store consumer data in the cloud.

Considerations for cloud users:

- **Security:** Security is a significant concern when it comes to cloud resources due to the utilization of application programming interfaces, cloud-based credentials, and on-demand services. These factors can potentially increase the susceptibility of cloud-based systems to security breaches, making them more vulnerable match up toconventional on-premise data centers. Determine the precautionary measures implemented by the cloud service provider to safeguard client data from stealing and other potential risks, alongside exploring additional services or procedures available for clients to enhance the protection of their data. Despite the utilization of robust security certifications and adherence to industry standards by cloud service providers, the act of entrusting data and sensitive files to external service providers invariably entails inherent risks (Kumari, 2021). The discussion of security and privacy holds significant relevance in any discourse pertaining to data, especially in the context of managing confidential information.
- **Data loss:** Cloud services are vulnerable to the permanent loss of data due to several factors such as physical disasters, software glitches, unintentional synchronization, errors caused by users, and unforeseen issues, similar to the risks faced by physical equipment that are owned or maintained. When implementing cloud services, it is essential to ascertain the backup services offered by the supplier, while also considering that these services may not be offered free of charge or with automatic upgrades. An alternative approach entails conducting backups independently.
- **Data persistence:** Cloud service users may periodically desire to make sure the safe deletion of their individual information that has been shared with cloud service providers. The process of erasing data from cloud resources and confirming the successful completion of this erasure might present challenges, requiring significant time and effort, and in certain cases, may even be deemed impractical. It is advisable to ascertain the data deletion policies of cloud service providers prior to providing them access to your data, particularly if there is a possibility that you may choose to remove it at a later stage.
- **Costs:** While cloud computing services offer a more affordable alternative to ownership, their usage can lead to significant cost escalation. It is advisable to review the pricing details upon subscribing to a cloud service in order to ascertain the manner in which the services are measured, as well as the availability of options to establish usage limits or receive notifications in the event of surpassing the desired thresholds. It is imperative to investigate the communication strategies employed for the dissemination of billing information, as the invoicing methods of specific organizations may engender confusion.
- **Attack Vulnerability:** The risk of attack vulnerability is a significant concern for users of private cloud services. This problem arises when computing operations are configured to align with a secured proprietary system, hence creating challenges or even impossibility in transitioning to alternative service providers. The utilization of open standards in computing facilitates the seamless transition of computing activities between different service providers (Devi, Choudhry, Raja et al, 2022). Consequently, the adoption of open-source cloud solutions can effectively mitigate this potential risk. It is imperative for cloud users to comprehend, however, that the process of transferring data necessitates careful planning, effort, and expertise. Due to the online nature of all components of cloud computing, potential security vulnerabilities may arise. From time to

time, even highly skilled teams encounter severe attacks and instances of compromised security (Parimala Devi et al., 2022).

- **Data use by companies:** The utilization of data by companies encompasses many activities such as the sale or customization of adverts the training of machine learning algorithms, and the potential sale of consumer information to third parties. These practices are commonly observed among cloud service providers. Furthermore, organizations have the ability to employ data in order to examine the manner in which clients utilize their product. It is advisable to inquire about the policies of the service provider on data usage if there are concerns regarding the utilization of data belonging to either your firm or yourself.
- **Business ethics:** The ethical considerations surrounding cloud computing in the realm of business warrant careful contemplation by clients, as certain cloud service providers wield substantial influence over global politics. The process of choosing a cloud provider that is in accordance with one's own beliefs can be helped by evaluating the organization's policies pertaining to many matters such as labor practices, political involvement, hate speech regulations, data collection practices, advertising strategies, and handling of disinformation.
- **Loss of user control and visibility**: One potential drawback of cloud computing is the potential user control loss and visibility. Users may encounter challenges or even limitations in their ability to effectively manage and monitor their computing environments. This is mostly due to the reliance on third-party computing resources, which can introduce various technical and trust-related concerns. Several technological challenges can be effectively addressed through the utilization of analytics and monitoring tools. These tools enable cloud users to closely monitor the performance and operation of their infrastructure, allowing them to rapidly respond to any potential issues that may arise (Devi, Choudhry, Sundarrajan et al, 2022). Apprehensions regarding trust, particularly in relation to the utilization of personal data by a commercial entity, can be alleviated through a thorough examination of the organization's customer data policies and publicly accessible evaluations of its data practices.
- **Regulation:** Strict guidelines govern how consumer data is used and stored in certain areas, including healthcare, finance, and education. These businesses may also forbid storing client data on public clouds. Cloud users in these businesses frequently have to use various tailored IT solutions and a hybrid cloud strategy to adhere to consumer data rules. Organizations must abide by local data protection and privacy legislation in addition to industry standards in the areas where their services are accessed. For instance, cloud service providers that cater to EU clients are required to abide by the General Data Protection Regulation (GDPR).
- **Complexity:** The migration of an institute's computer resources to the cloud infrastructure entails a multifaceted procedure that necessitates meticulous planning, implementation of governance levels, and continuous supervision to mitigate the risks of data loss, incompatibilities, and suboptimal cost management. While leveraging cloud computing might result in cost savings for businesses in terms of computer equipment, it is important to note that effective management and direction of this technology necessitates the involvement of IT specialists with specialized skills.

CLOUD COMPUTING'S FUTURE AND EMERGING TECHNOLOGIES

Many businesses already use cloud services to expand internationally and build their brands. Because of its advantages, cloud computing will be the most widely used deployment mechanism for businesses in the future. Cloud computing has a promising future that will benefit both customers and hosts. With the advent of cloud computing, numerous technologies are emerging, including:

- **The Internet of Things:** The internet of things is one of the newest technologies that offers constant innovation in cloud computing and real-time data analytics. Cloud computing makes it easy for us to accomplish.
- **Low-Severity Computing:** Following micro-services and service-oriented architectures, serverless architecture is the next step away from monolithic application design.
- **Artificial Intelligence (AI):** The next-generation technological advancement that will offer a new perspective on the technological world is artificial intelligence. However, because developing AI applications requires powerful computers, it can be challenging for many firms. Businesses are considering cloud-based options for deep learning and machine learning. As more and more businesses of all sizes want to leverage AI, cloud-based AI is becoming the go-to option due to its extensive computational and storage capabilities.

The way many parts come together to form a cloud system that any employee of a company can utilize for data-related tasks is called cloud computing architecture. Cloud computing architecture is the virtualization technology that creates a "cloud" by combining various hardware and software components in one location.

The reliable network is used for information exchange and storage; a delivery model that determines how the network will function and how users can access data; and the backend platform, which functions similarly to servers that store information for users to access. When all these elements are combined, a cloud platform is created that both an organization and its staff can utilize. The users of this system benefit from it in many ways. First off, because internet servers are far more secure than physical ones, the chance of data theft is lower. Second, since there won't be a problem with data exchange, everyone can work remotely.

CONCLUSION

Numerous opportunities are presented by cloud technology to researchers, educators, students, organizations, and independent innovators. Users can choose the finest method to utilize the cloud's capabilities by being aware of the various services, models, advantages, and hazards it offers. Applications that require dynamic scaling can be brought to market faster thanks to the numerous benefits obtained from cloud computing. Numerous advantages of cloud computing include reduced costs, increased agility, scalability, resilience, and much more. Because of these advantages, a large number of businesses are using cloud services to develop extremely durable and scalable systems. With cloud services, the future appears to be quite bright, with countless options to explore. Whether or not a firm can adapt to these new changes will determine whether it survives. Thus, begin your knowledge hut cloud computing training and make the most from cloud computing.

REFERENCES

Armbrust, M., Fox, A., Griffith, R., Joseph, A. D., Katz, R. H., Konwinski, A., Lee, G., Patterson, D. A., Rabkin, A., Stoica, I., & Zaharia, M. (2009). Above the clouds: A Berkeley view of cloud computing" in, EECS Department, University of California, Berkeley, Tech. Rep. UCB/EECS-2009-28.

Asadi, A. N., Azgomi, M. A., & Entezari-Maleki, R. (2019). Unified power and performance analysis of cloud computing infrastructure using stochastic reward nets. *Computer Communications*, *138*, 67–80. doi:10.1016/j.comcom.2019.03.004

Attaran, M. (2017). Cloud computing technology: Leveraging the power of the internet to improve business performance. *Journal of International Technology and Information Management*, *26*(1), 112–137. doi:10.58729/1941-6679.1283

Chen, Y., Paxson, V., & Katz, R. (2010). What's New About Cloud. *Computers & Security*.

Devi, M. P., Choudhry, M. D., Raja, G. B., & Sathya, T. (2022). A roadmap towards robust IoT-enabled cyber-physical systems in cyber industrial 4.0. In *Handbook of research of internet of things and cyber-physical systems: An integrative approach to an interconnected future* (pp. 293–313). CRC Press. doi:10.1201/9781003277323-16

Devi, M. P., Choudhry, M. D., Sundarrajan, M., & Sivapriyanga, P. (2022). An efficient 24× 7 patient's vital parameter monitoring framework using machine learning based Internet of Biomedical Things: a comprehensive approach. In Advances in Image and Data Processing using VLSI Design, Volume 2: Biomedical applications (pp. 14-1). Bristol, UK: IOP Publishing.

Foster, I., Zhao, Y., Raicu, I., & Lu, S. Y. (2008). *Cloud computing and grid computing 360-degree compared. Proceedings of the Grid Computing Environments Workshop (GCE'08)*, Austin, TX. 10.1109/GCE.2008.4738445

Garg, N., Bawa, S., & Kumar, N. (2020). An efficient data integrity auditing protocol for cloud computing. *Future Generation Computer Systems*, *109*, 306–316. doi:10.1016/j.future.2020.03.032

Greenberg, A., Lahiri, P., Maltz, D. A., Patel, P., & Sengupta, S. (August 2008). Towards a next generation data center architecture: Scalability and commoditization. *Proceedings of the ACM Workshop on Programmable Router and Extensible Services for Tomorrow (PRESTO)*, Seattle, WA, USA, 55–62. 10.1145/1397718.1397732

Guazzelli, A., Stathatos, K., & Zeller, M. (2009). Efficient deployment of predictive analytics through open standards and cloud computing. *SIGKDD Explorations*, *11*(1), 32–38. doi:10.1145/1656274.1656281

Kannadasan, R., Prabakaran, N., Boominathan, P., Krishnamoorthy, A., Naresh, K., & Sivashanmugam, G. (2018). High Performance Parallel Computing with Cloud Technologies. *Procedia Computer Science*, *132*, 518–524. doi:10.1016/j.procs.2018.05.004

Khanghahi, N., & Ravanmehr, R. (2013). Cloud computing performance evaluation: Issues and challenges. *Comput*, *5*(1), 29–41. doi:10.5121/ijccsa.2013.3503

Kumari, S. (2021). The Future of Edge Computing with Blockchain Technology: Possibility of Threats, Opportunities and Challenges. Recent Trends in Blockchain for Information Systems Security and Privacy. CRC Press.

Kumari, S. (2021). The Future of Edge Computing with Blockchain Technology: Possibility of Threats, Opportunities and Challenges. Recent Trends in Blockchain for Information Systems Security and Privacy. CRC Press.

Lin, G., Fu, D., Zhu, J., & Dasmalchi, G. (2009, March/April). Cloud computing: IT as a service. *IT Professional*, *11*(2), 10–13. doi:10.1109/MITP.2009.22

Mell, P., & Grance, T. (2011). The NIST Definition of Cloud Computing. *National Institute of Standards and Technology Special Publication*, *53*, 1–7.

Mishra, S., & Tyagi, A. K. (2022). The Role of Machine Learning Techniques in Internet of Things-Based Cloud Applications. In S. Pal, D. De, & R. Buyya (Eds.), *Artificial Intelligence-based Internet of Things Systems. Internet of Things (Technology, Communications and Computing)*. Springer., doi:10.1007/978-3-030-87059-1_4

Nelson, M. (2009). Building an Open Cloud. *Science*, *324*(5935), 1656–1657. doi:10.1126cience.1174225 PMID:19556494

Nurmi, D., Wolski, R., Grzegorczyk, C., Obertelli, G., Soman, S., & Youseff, L. (2008*). The eucalyptus open-source cloud-computing system.* Proceedings of Cloud Computing and Its Applications, Shanghai, China.

Oracle. (2009). *Sun Microsystems Unveils Open Cloud Platform.* Oracle. http://www.sun.com/aboutsun/pr/2009-03/sunflash.20090318.2.xml

Parimala Devi, M., Choudhry, M. D., Nithiavathy, R., Boopathi Raja, G., & Sathya, T. (2022). Blockchain Based Edge Information Systems Frameworks for Industrial IoT: A Novel Approach. In *Blockchain Applications in the Smart Era* (pp. 19–39). Springer International Publishing. doi:10.1007/978-3-030-89546-4_2

Shakeabubakor, A. A., Sundararajan, E., & Hamdan, A. R. (2015). Cloud computing services and applications to improve productivity of university researchers. *Int. J. Inf. Electron. Eng.*, *5*(2), 153. doi:10.7763/IJIEE.2015.V5.521

Sotomayor, B., Montero, R., Llorente, I., & Foster, I. (2009). Virtual Infrastructure Management in Private and Hybrid Clouds. *IEEE Internet Computing*, *13*(5), 14–22. doi:10.1109/MIC.2009.119

Stantchev, V. (2009). Performance evaluation of cloud computing offerings. *2009 Third International Conference on Advanced Engineering Computing and Applications in Sciences.* (pp. 187–192). IEEE. 10.1109/ADVCOMP.2009.36

Suakanto, S., Supangkat, S., & Saragih, R. (2012). *Performance measurement of cloudcomputing services.* arXivPrepr. arXiv1205.1622.

Tyagi, A. K., Nair, M. M., Niladhuri, S., & Abraham, A. (2020). Security, Privacy Research issues in Various Computing Platforms: A Survey and the Road Ahead. *Journal of Information Assurance &Security.*, *15*(1), 1–16.

Vecchiola, C., Pandey, S., & Buyya, R. (2009). High-performance cloud computing: A view of scientific applications, *in 2009 10th International Symposium on Pervasive Systems, Algorithms, and Networks,* (pp. 4–16). IEEE.

Wang, X., Wang, B., & Huang, J. (2011). Cloud computing and its key techniques. *2011 IEEE International Conference on Computer Science and Automation Engineering,* (pp. 404–410). IEEE. 10.1109/CSAE.2011.5952497

Chapter 2
Internet of Things (IoT): Concepts, Protocols, and Applications

Shabnam Kumari
SRM Institute of Science and Technology, Chennai, India

Micheal Olaolu Arowolo
https://orcid.org/0000-0002-9418-5346
University of Missouri, USA

ABSTRACT

Today the internet of things (IoT) has witnessed significant advancements in recent years, revolutionizing the way we interact with technology and our surroundings. This work provides a summary of the recent advances in IoT, including concepts, protocols, and applications. The concept of IoT revolves around connecting various physical devices and objects to the internet, enabling them to communicate, share data, and perform intelligent actions. In terms of concepts, recent advances have emphasized the integration of IoT with other emerging technologies such as artificial intelligence (AI), machine learning (ML), and edge computing. In terms of concepts, recent advances have emphasized the integration of IoT with other emerging technologies such as artificial intelligence (AI), machine learning (ML), and edge computing. Further few important IoT protocols are discussed in this work. Note that these protocols enable seamless communication between IoT devices, gateways, and cloud platforms, facilitating the exchange of data and commands.

1. INTRODUCTION

1.1 Overview of the Internet of Things (IoT)

IoT refers to the network of physical objects or "things" embedded with sensors, software, and other technologies that enable them to connect and exchange data with each other and with the internet (Uckelmann et al., 2011). These interconnected devices can be anything from everyday objects like household appliances, vehicles, and wearable devices to industrial machinery and infrastructure (refer Figure 1).

DOI: 10.4018/979-8-3693-2081-5.ch002

Figure 1. IoT fundamentals

Key Components of IoT: Figure 2 explains bout its components in detail.

- Things/Devices: These are physical objects that are equipped with sensors, actuators, and connectivity capabilities. They can collect and transmit data to other devices or systems.
- Connectivity: IoT devices use various communication technologies to connect to the internet and exchange data. This can include Wi-Fi, Bluetooth, cellular networks, Zigbee, etc.
- Data Processing: The data collected from IoT devices is processed and analyzed to derive meaningful information. This can be done locally on the device or in the cloud.
- Cloud Infrastructure: Cloud-based platforms are often used to store, process, and analyze the massive amounts of data generated by IoT devices. The cloud provides scalability, storage, and computing power for IoT applications.
- Applications: IoT applications use the data collected from devices to provide various services and functionalities. These applications can range from smart home automation and remote monitoring to industrial automation and predictive maintenance.

Benefits of IoT: Few of Benefits of IoT are;

- Automation and Efficiency: IoT enables automation of various processes, improving efficiency and reducing human intervention. It optimizes resource utilization and enhances productivity in industries, homes, and cities.
- Improved Decision Making: The data collected by IoT devices provides valuable information that can be used to make informed decisions. This helps in optimizing operations, improving customer experiences, and identifying new business opportunities.
- Enhanced Safety and Security: IoT can be used to monitor and control physical spaces, assets, and environments, enhancing safety and security. It enables early detection of anomalies and facilitates quick responses to emergencies.
- Cost Savings: IoT applications can lead to cost savings by improving energy efficiency, reducing maintenance costs through predictive maintenance, and optimizing supply chain processes.

Figure 2. Components of IoT ecosystems

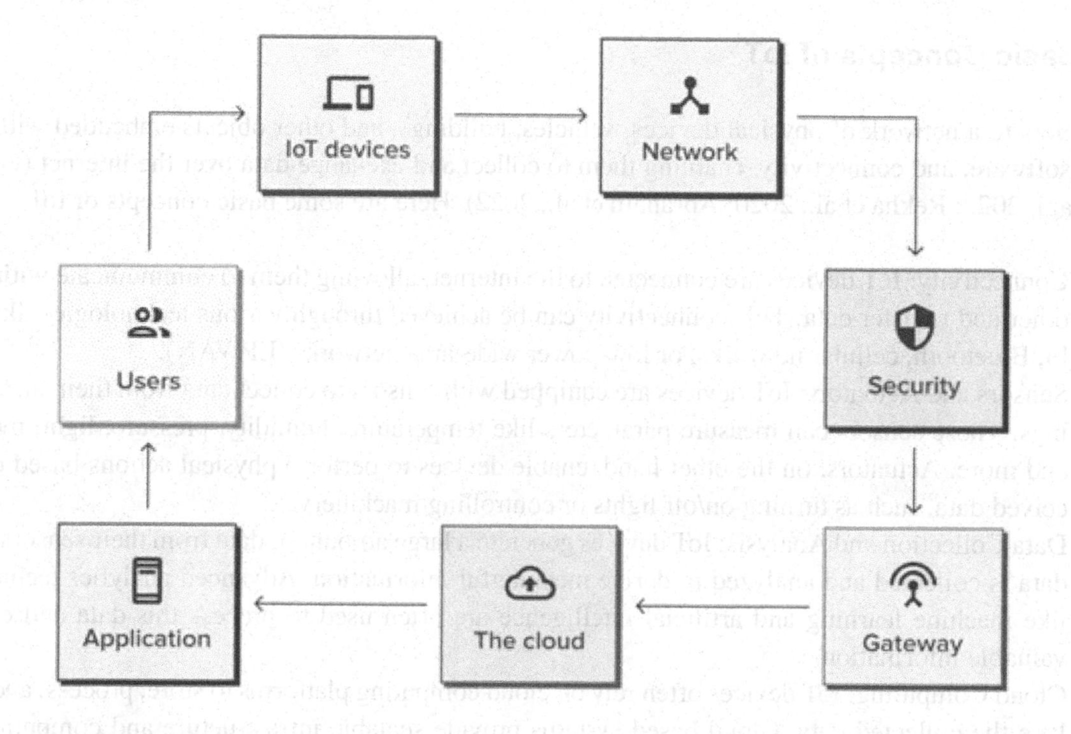

Challenges and Issues

- Security and Privacy: With the increasing number of connected devices, ensuring the security and privacy of data becomes a significant challenge (Gubbi et al., 2013). Protecting sensitive information and preventing unauthorized access are critical issues.
- Interoperability: IoT devices and platforms often come from different manufacturers and use various communication protocols. Ensuring interoperability and seamless integration among different devices and systems can be complex.
- Scalability: As the number of connected devices grows exponentially, scaling IoT infrastructure to handle the massive influx of data becomes a challenge. This includes managing storage, processing power, and network bandwidth.
- Data Management: Dealing with large amount of data generated by IoT devices requires efficient data management strategies, including data storage, processing, and analysis. Handling real-time data streams and extracting meaningful information can be demanding.

Note that IoT holds tremendous potential to transform various industries, improve efficiency, and enhance our daily lives. However, addressing the challenges associated with security, privacy, and infrastructure scalability is important to fully realize its benefits while ensuring a safe and trustworthy ecosystem.

2. IOT CONCEPTS AND ARCHITECTURE

2.1 Basic Concepts of IoT

IoT refers to a network of physical devices, vehicles, buildings, and other objects embedded with sensors, software, and connectivity, enabling them to collect and exchange data over the internet (George & Tyagi, 2022; Rekha et al., 2020; Abraham et al., 2022). Here are some basic concepts of IoT:

- Connectivity: IoT devices are connected to the internet, allowing them to communicate with each other and transfer data. This connectivity can be achieved through various technologies like Wi-Fi, Bluetooth, cellular networks, or low-power wide-area networks (LPWAN).
- Sensors and Actuators: IoT devices are equipped with sensors to collect data from their surroundings. These sensors can measure parameters like temperature, humidity, pressure, light, motion, and more. Actuators, on the other hand, enable devices to perform physical actions based on received data, such as turning on/off lights or controlling machinery.
- Data Collection and Analysis: IoT devices generate a large amount of data from their sensors. This data is collected and analyzed to derive meaningful information. Advanced analytics techniques like machine learning and artificial intelligence are often used to process this data and extract valuable information.
- Cloud Computing: IoT devices often rely on cloud computing platforms to store, process, and analyze the collected data. Cloud-based systems provide scalable infrastructure and computational power required for handling massive amounts of data generated by IoT devices.
- Security and Privacy: IoT devices collect and transmit sensitive data, making security an essential issue. Strong security measures must be implemented to protect the data and prevent unauthorized access or misuse. This includes encryption, authentication protocols, secure communication channels, and regular software updates to address vulnerabilities.
- Interoperability: IoT devices come from various manufacturers and may use different communication protocols or data formats. Interoperability ensures that devices can seamlessly communicate and work together, regardless of their underlying technologies, to achieve the desired functionalities and outcomes.
- Edge Computing: In some cases, it may be more efficient to process data closer to the source rather than sending it to the cloud for analysis. Edge computing involves performing data processing and analysis at the edge of the network, near the IoT devices themselves. This reduces latency, conserves bandwidth, and allows for real-time decision-making.
- Applications and Use Cases: IoT has a wide range of applications across industries, including smart homes, industrial automation, agriculture, healthcare, transportation, and smart cities (refer figure 3). It enables innovative solutions like remote monitoring, predictive maintenance, asset tracking, energy management, etc. These basic concepts form the basis of IoT, enabling the seamless integration of physical devices with digital systems to improve efficiency, automation, and decision-making in various domains.

Figure 3. Applications of IoT

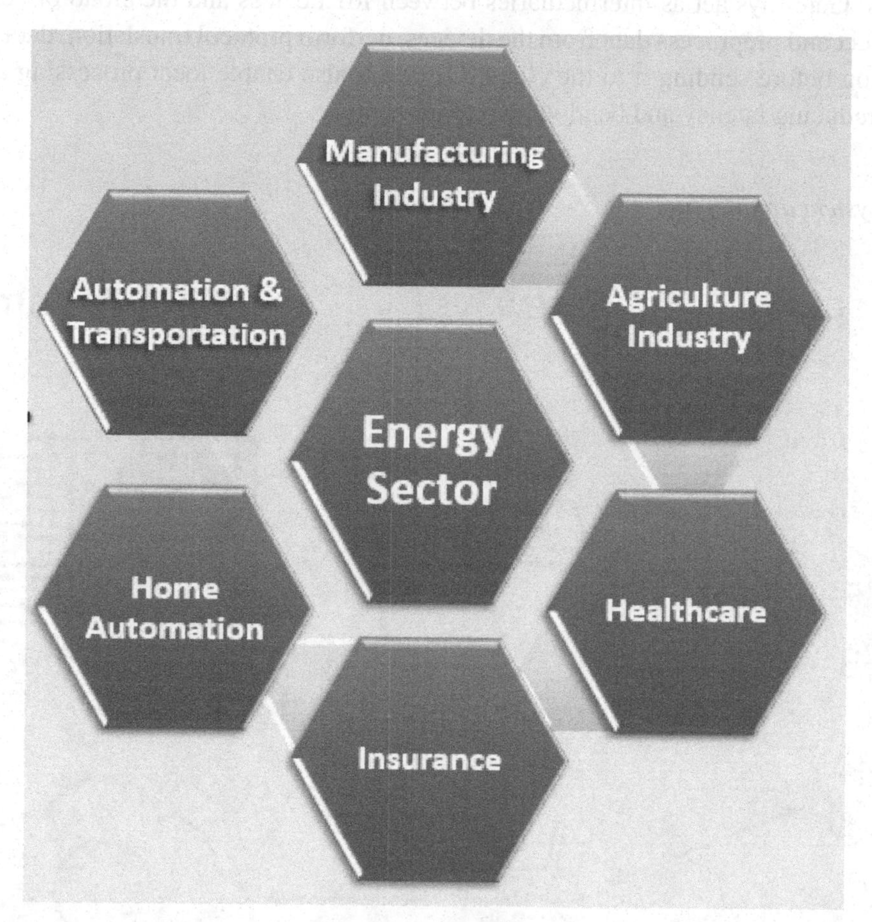

2.2 IoT Architecture and Components

IoT architecture consists of several components that work together to enable the functionality and communication of IoT devices (refer figure 4). Here are the key components of an IoT architecture:

- Devices/Things: These are physical objects or devices embedded with sensors, actuators, and connectivity capabilities (Tyagi & Sreenath, 2023). Examples include sensors, actuators, wearables, appliances, vehicles, and industrial machinery. These devices collect data from the environment and send it to the IoT system for processing.
- Sensors and Actuators: Sensors detect and measure physical or environmental parameters such as temperature, humidity, light, motion, and more. Actuators are responsible for performing actions based on received data, such as turning on/off a device, controlling a motor, or adjusting settings. They enable devices to interact with the physical world.
- Connectivity: IoT devices need a means of communication to exchange data with each other and with the central system. This can be achieved through various network technologies, including Wi-Fi, Bluetooth, Zigbee, cellular networks (2G/3G/4G/5G), or low-power wide-area networks (LPWAN) like LoRaWAN or NB-IoT.

- Gateways: Gateways act as intermediaries between IoT devices and the cloud or central system. They collect and preprocess data from the devices, perform protocol translation, data filtering, and aggregation before sending it to the cloud. Gateways also enable local processing and decision-making, reducing latency and bandwidth requirements.

Figure 4. IoT system architecture

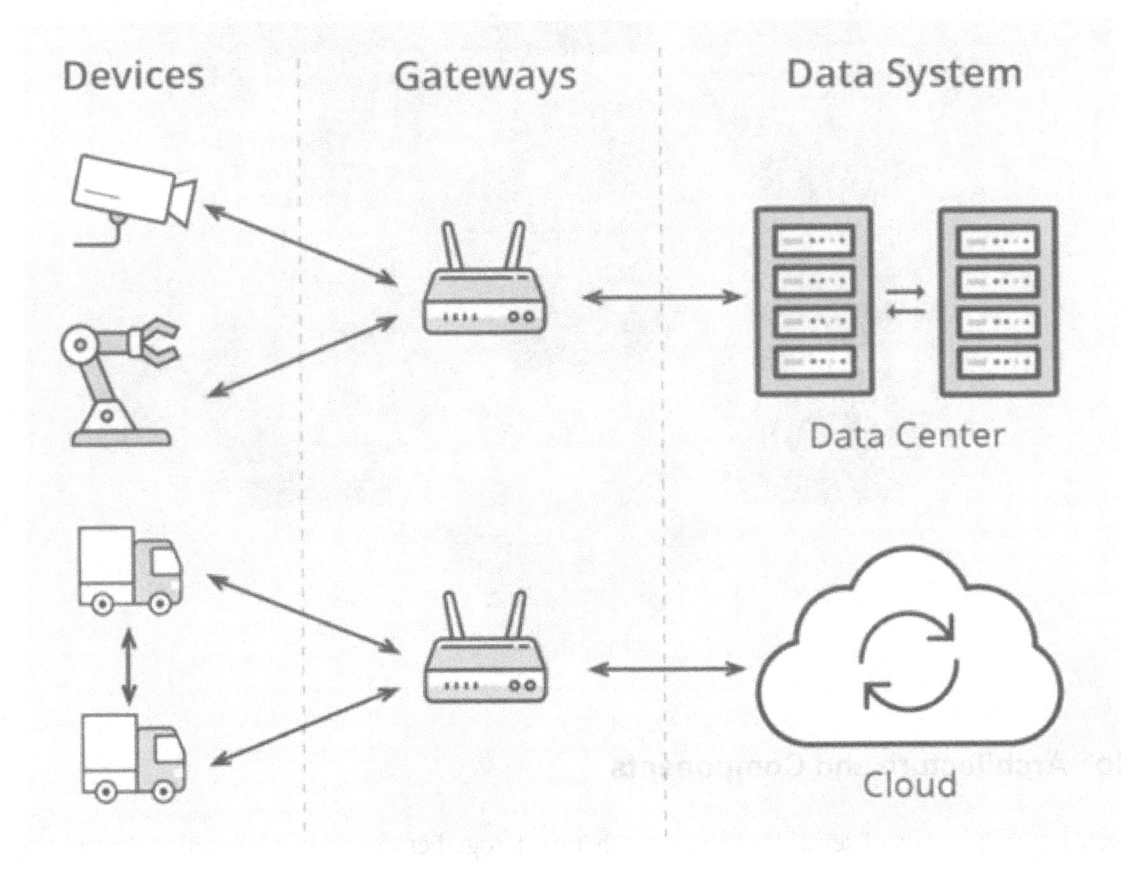

- Cloud Infrastructure: The cloud serves as the backbone of IoT architecture. It provides storage, computational power, and scalability for handling massive amounts of data generated by IoT devices (Abraham, Panda, Pradhan et al, 2021; Srivastava, 2023; Abraham et al., 2023; Tyagi, 2019). Cloud platforms allow data to be securely stored, processed, and analyzed. They also provide APIs and services for application development and integration.
- Network Infrastructure: The network infrastructure supports the communication between IoT devices, gateways, and the cloud. It includes routers, switches, access points, and cellular towers that facilitate data transmission and connectivity.
- Data Processing and Analytics: The collected data is processed and analyzed to derive insights and make informed decisions. Advanced analytics techniques, such as machine learning and artificial intelligence, can be applied to identify patterns, anomalies, and trends in the data. Real-time processing may be performed at the edge or on the cloud, depending on the use case.

- Applications and Services: IoT applications and services provide user interfaces, dashboards, and APIs for accessing and interacting with the IoT system. These applications allow users to monitor and control devices, receive alerts and notifications, and access data information. They can be web-based, mobile apps, or integrated into existing enterprise systems (Tan & Neng, 2010).
- Security and Privacy: IoT systems must incorporate robust security measures to protect data and ensure privacy. This includes authentication mechanisms, data encryption, access control, secure communication protocols, and firmware/software updates to address vulnerabilities. Security issues are essential to safeguarding IoT devices and the overall system from cyber threats.

These components work together to form a cohesive IoT architecture, enabling the seamless integration and functionality of IoT devices, data collection, processing, and application development.

3. IOT PROTOCOLS AND STANDARDS

3.1 Wireless Protocols for IoT Communication

There are several wireless protocols specifically designed for IoT communication (refer figure 5). Here are some commonly used wireless protocols in IoT:

- Wi-Fi (IEEE 802.11): Wi-Fi is a widely adopted wireless protocol that allows devices to connect to local area networks (LANs) and the internet. It provides high-speed data transfer over relatively longer distances, making it suitable for IoT applications that require high bandwidth and internet connectivity.
- Bluetooth: Bluetooth is a short-range wireless protocol commonly used for connecting devices in close proximity. Bluetooth Low Energy (BLE) is particularly suitable for IoT applications due to its low power consumption and ability to transmit small bursts of data. It is often used in applications like wearables, healthcare devices, and smart home systems.
- Zigbee: Zigbee is a low-power, wireless communication protocol designed for short-range IoT networks. It operates on the IEEE 802.15.4 standard and supports mesh networking, allowing devices to form self-configuring networks. Zigbee is commonly used in applications like home automation, industrial monitoring, and lighting control.
- Z-Wave: Z-Wave is another wireless protocol designed for low-power IoT devices. It operates in the sub-GHz frequency range, providing good range and penetration through walls. Z-Wave is often used in home automation systems and devices that require reliable and low-latency communication.
- LoRaWAN: LoRaWAN (Long Range Wide Area Network) is a wireless protocol optimized for long-range communication with low power consumption. It operates in the unlicensed sub-GHz frequency bands, allowing for long-range connectivity. LoRaWAN is suitable for IoT applications that require wide-area coverage, such as smart cities, agriculture monitoring, and asset tracking.
- NB-IoT (Narrowband IoT): NB-IoT is a cellular-based wireless protocol specifically designed for IoT applications. It operates in licensed spectrum bands, providing reliable and secure communication. NB-IoT is well-suited for IoT deployments that require deep indoor coverage, low power consumption, and support for massive device connectivity.

Figure 5. Wireless protocols for IoT communication

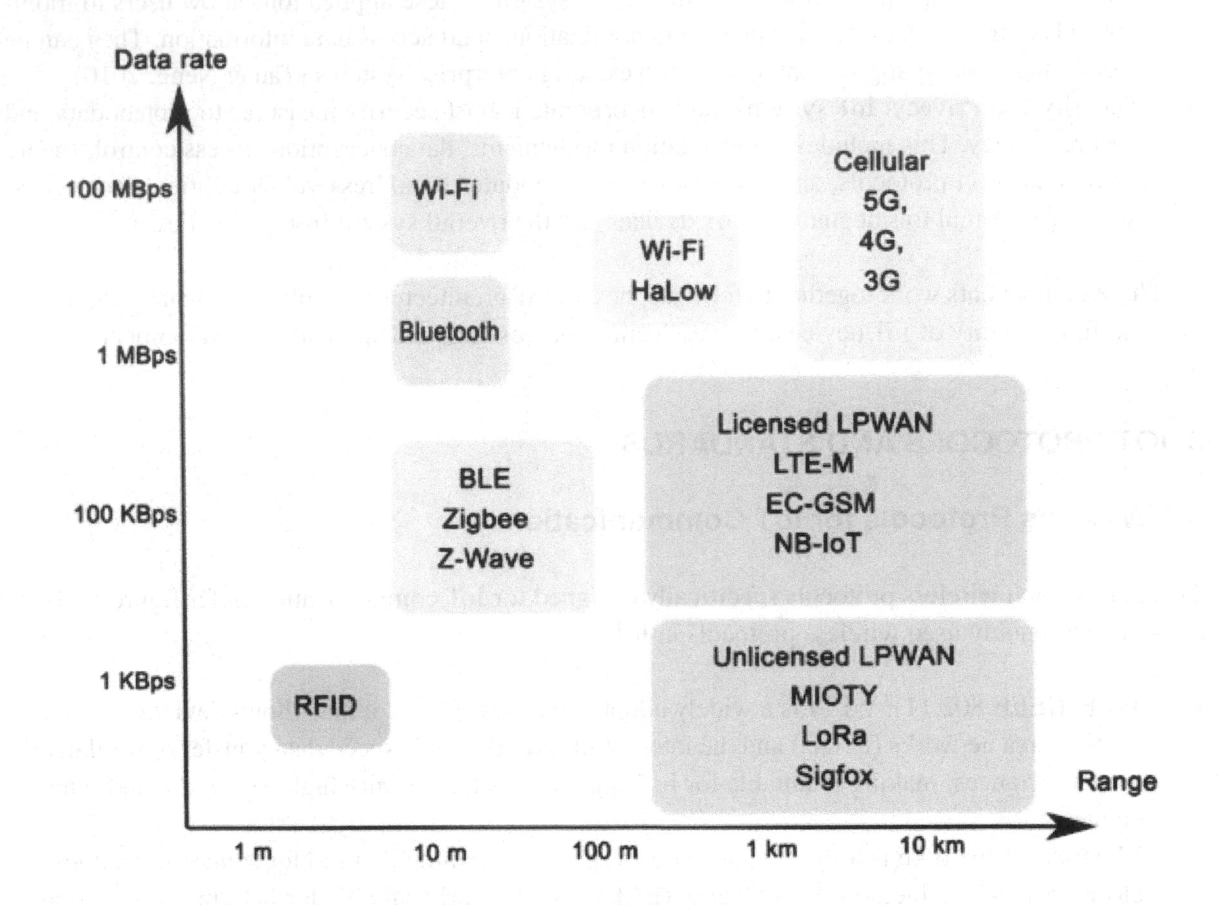

- Sigfox: Sigfox is a proprietary low-power wide-area network (LPWAN) technology designed for long-range IoT communication. It operates in the sub-GHz frequency band and offers low power consumption and low data rates. Sigfox is used in various applications, including asset tracking, smart metering, and environmental monitoring.

In summary, these are some of the commonly used wireless protocols for IoT communication. The choice of protocol depends on factors such as range requirements, power consumption, data rate, scalability, and specific application needs. Note that to consider these factors when selecting the appropriate wireless protocol for your IoT deployment.

3.2 IoT Network Protocols

Here are some common IoT network protocols (refer figure 6) used for communication between devices and systems:

- MQTT (Message Queuing Telemetry Transport): MQTT is a lightweight publish-subscribe messaging protocol designed for constrained devices and low-bandwidth networks. It uses a publish-subscribe model, where clients (publishers) send messages to a broker, and other clients (subscribers) receive those messages from the broker. MQTT is widely used in IoT applications due to its simplicity, efficiency, and support for reliable message delivery.
- CoAP (Constrained Application Protocol): CoAP is a lightweight application-layer protocol designed for constrained IoT devices and networks. It follows the REST architectural style and is similar to HTTP. CoAP enables devices to communicate using simple methods like GET, PUT, POST, and DELETE. It operates over UDP or other transport protocols, making it suitable for constrained environments with low power and low bandwidth.

Figure 6. Mostly used IoT protocols

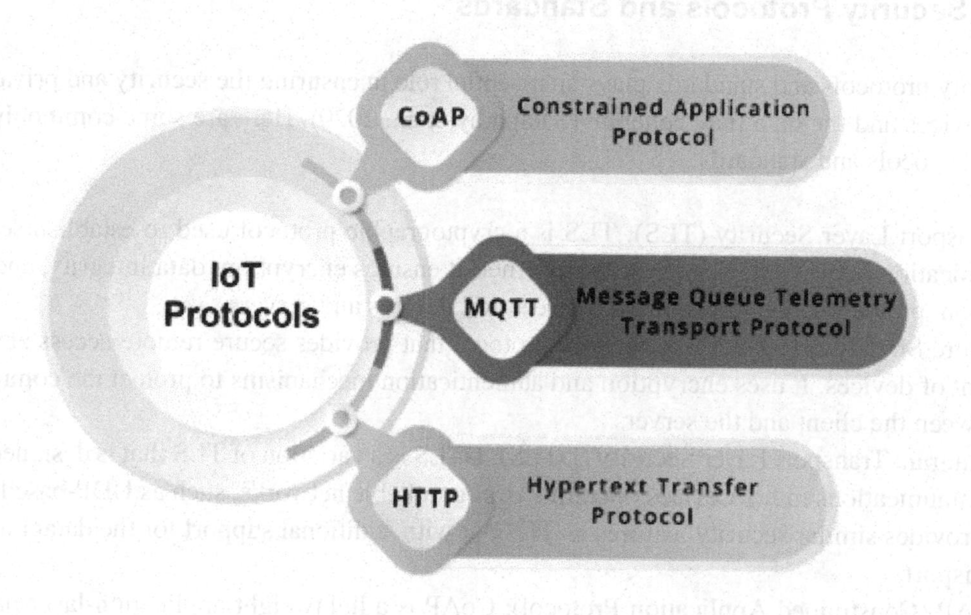

- AMQP (Advanced Message Queuing Protocol): AMQP is a messaging protocol designed for reliable message-oriented communication. It supports message queuing, routing, and reliable delivery. AMQP provides advanced features like message persistence, flow control, and message acknowledgment. It is often used in enterprise and industrial IoT applications that require strict message ordering and delivery guarantees.
- HTTP (Hypertext Transfer Protocol): Although primarily used for web communication, HTTP is also employed in IoT applications, particularly for web-based interfaces and APIs. IoT devices can use HTTP to send requests and receive responses from web servers. HTTP provides a familiar and widely supported protocol for IoT device interactions, making it easy to integrate with existing web infrastructure.
- DDS (Data Distribution Service): DDS is a data-centric publish-subscribe protocol designed for real-time and scalable IoT systems. It provides a middleware layer that enables efficient and reli-

able data exchange among distributed devices and applications. DDS supports Quality of Service (QoS) mechanisms to ensure timely and reliable delivery of data, making it suitable for complex IoT deployments.

- OPC UA (OPC Unified Architecture): OPC UA is a protocol for industrial IoT applications that focuses on interoperability and information modeling. It enables secure and reliable communication between devices and applications in industrial automation systems. OPC UA supports various data types, object-oriented communication, and robust security mechanisms.

Hence, these are some of the commonly used IoT network protocols. The choice of protocol depends on factors such as device capabilities, network constraints, application requirements, and interoperability needs with existing systems. It's important to consider these factors when selecting the appropriate network protocol for your IoT solution.

3.3 IoT Security Protocols and Standards

IoT security protocols and standards plays an essential role in ensuring the security and privacy of connected devices and the data they generate (Satapathy et al., 2020). Here are some commonly used IoT security protocols and standards:

- Transport Layer Security (TLS): TLS is a cryptographic protocol used to establish secure communication between devices over the internet. It ensures encryption, data integrity, and authentication, protecting data transmitted between IoT devices and servers.
- Secure Shell (SSH): SSH is a network protocol that provides secure remote access and management of devices. It uses encryption and authentication mechanisms to protect the communication between the client and the server.
- Datagram Transport Layer Security (DTLS): DTLS is a variation of TLS that is designed to secure communications in IoT devices operating over unreliable networks, such as UDP-based protocols. It provides similar security features as TLS but with additional support for the datagram-oriented transport.
- CoAP (Constrained Application Protocol): CoAP is a lightweight application-layer protocol designed for resource-constrained IoT devices. It incorporates security features through Datagram Transport Layer Security (DTLS) to ensure secure communication between devices.
- MQTT (Message Queuing Telemetry Transport): MQTT is a publish-subscribe messaging protocol widely used in IoT deployments. It supports a lightweight security model with authentication and access control mechanisms to protect MQTT messages and ensure secure communication.
- Zigbee: Zigbee is a wireless communication protocol widely used in IoT devices for home automation and industrial applications. It incorporates security measures such as AES-128 encryption, device authentication, and access control to safeguard the communication between devices.
- Z-Wave: Z-Wave is another wireless communication protocol used in smart home automation. It includes security features like AES-128 encryption, mutual authentication, and message integrity checks to ensure secure communication between devices.
- Thread: Thread is an IP-based wireless protocol designed for smart home applications. It utilizes security mechanisms such as network encryption, device authentication, and access control to protect the communication between devices.

- OMA LightweightM2M (LwM2M): LwM2M is a device management protocol for IoT devices. It incorporates security features like DTLS for secure communication, access control, and device authentication to ensure secure management of IoT devices.
- OPC UA (Unified Architecture): OPC UA is a machine-to-machine communication protocol widely used in industrial automation. It incorporates security features such as encryption, authentication, and access control to protect data integrity and ensure secure communication between devices.

Hence, these are examples of IoT security protocols and standards commonly used in the industry. It's worth noting that the selection of protocols and standards depends on the specific requirements and use cases of the IoT deployment, and organizations may choose to implement additional security measures based on their needs.

4. IOT DATA ANALYTICS AND PROCESSING

4.1 Data Collection and Aggregation in IoT

Data collection and aggregation are basic processes in IoT systems, where a large number of interconnected devices generate large amount of data. Here's an overview of how data collection and aggregation work in IoT:

Data Collection:

- Sensor Data: IoT devices are equipped with sensors that collect various types of data, such as temperature, humidity, motion, location, and more. Sensors capture real-time information from the physical environment or monitor specific conditions.
- Device-generated Data: IoT devices also generate data related to their operation, status, and configuration. This data can include device identifiers, firmware versions, power usage, network connectivity, and other device-specific parameters.

Local Processing and Filtering:

- In some cases, IoT devices have built-in capabilities to process and filter the collected data locally. This allows them to perform basic analytics or filtering operations before transmitting the data to a central location. Local processing helps reduce network bandwidth usage and latency.

Data Transmission:

- IoT devices transmit the collected data to a centralized location for further processing and analysis. The data is typically sent over wireless communication protocols such as Wi-Fi, cellular networks, or specialized IoT protocols like Zigbee or LoRaWAN.
- Data transmission can be event-driven, where data is sent immediately upon a specific trigger or condition, or it can be periodic, where data is sent at regular intervals.

Gateway Devices:

- In applications where there is a large number of IoT devices or the devices use different communication protocols, gateway devices are often used. Gateways act as intermediaries between IoT devices and the centralized system, collecting data from multiple devices and transmitting it to the central location using a unified protocol.

Cloud or Edge-based Data Aggregation:

- The collected data is aggregated and stored in either cloud-based platforms or edge computing devices, depending on the architecture and requirements of the IoT system.
- In cloud-based solutions, data is sent to cloud servers where it is stored, processed, and made accessible to applications and services for further analysis and decision-making.
- Edge computing solutions, on the other hand, perform data aggregation and analysis closer to the data source, at the edge of the network. This reduces latency and allows for real-time or near-real-time information and actions without relying heavily on cloud connectivity.

Data Analytics and Information:

- Once the data is aggregated, it can be processed using various data analytics techniques such as machine learning, artificial intelligence, statistical analysis, and data visualization. These techniques extract valuable information patterns from the collected data.
- The analysis results can be used for monitoring, predictive maintenance, optimization, anomaly detection, and other applications, enabling organizations to make informed decisions and improve operational efficiency.

Data Privacy and Security:

- Throughout the entire data collection and aggregation process, data privacy and security must be prioritized. Measures like data encryption, access controls, authentication, and secure communication protocols (such as TLS) should be implemented to protect sensitive data from unauthorized access, tampering, or breaches.
- Efficient data collection and aggregation in IoT systems allow organizations to harness the power of the generated data, enabling them to extract important information, optimize operations, and make data-driven decisions for improved outcomes.

4.2 Big Data Analytics for IoT Applications

Big data analytics plays an essential role in extracting valuable information and knowledge from the massive volumes of data generated by IoT applications (Goyal & Tyagi, 2020; Sai et al., 2023; Tyagi & Abraham, 2020; Abraham, Piuri, Gandhi et al, 2021). Here's how big data analytics is applied in IoT:

- Data Preprocessing and Cleansing: Before performing analytics, IoT data often requires preprocessing and cleansing to ensure its quality and consistency. This includes removing noise, handling missing values, normalizing data, and resolving any inconsistencies or errors that may arise during data collection.
- Data Storage and Management: Due to the large volumes of data generated by IoT devices, efficient storage and management systems are required. Big data technologies, such as distributed file systems (e.g., Hadoop HDFS) and NoSQL databases (e.g., Cassandra, MongoDB), are commonly used to store and process IoT data.
- Data Integration and Fusion: IoT applications often involve multiple sources of data, such as sensor data, social media data, and enterprise data. Big data analytics helps integrate and fuse these heterogeneous data sources, enabling a comprehensive analysis of the combined dataset.

- Real-time Analytics: Real-time analytics is essential for IoT applications that require immediate insights/ actions based on the streaming data. Complex event processing (CEP) systems and stream processing frameworks (e.g., Apache Storm, Apache Flink) are used to analyze and process the data in real-time, enabling timely decision-making and automated responses.
- Batch Analytics: In addition to real-time analytics, big data analytics platforms facilitate batch processing of IoT data. Batch analytics involves analyzing historical data in large batches to identify patterns, trends, and anomalies. Technologies like Apache Spark and Hadoop MapReduce are commonly used for batch processing in IoT applications.
- Machine Learning and Predictive Analytics: Big data analytics enables the application of machine learning and predictive analytics techniques to IoT data. Machine learning algorithms can be trained on IoT data to build models for tasks like predictive maintenance, anomaly detection, fault prediction, and resource optimization. These models help improve efficiency, reliability, and decision-making in IoT systems.
- Visualization and Reporting: Big data analytics platforms often provide visualization and reporting tools to present the analyzed data in a meaningful way. Visualizations, dashboards, and reports help stakeholders understand the information gained from IoT data and make informed decisions.
- Data Security and Privacy: With the sensitive nature of IoT data, ensuring data security and privacy is essential. Big data analytics platforms incorporate security measures such as access controls, encryption, and anonymization techniques to protect IoT data from unauthorized access or breaches.

Hence by using big data analytics, IoT applications can unlock the potential of the large amount of data generated, enabling organizations to extract valuable information, optimize operations, enhance customer experiences, and create new business opportunities.

4.3 Edge Computing and Fog Computing in IoT

Edge computing and fog computing are two computing paradigms that address the challenges of processing and analyzing data in IoT systems. While both approaches bring computational capabilities closer to the edge of the network, they have some differences in terms of their architectures (Uckelmann et al., 2011) and deployment models. Here's an overview of edge computing and fog computing in IoT:

Edge Computing:

- Edge computing focuses on bringing computing resources and data processing capabilities closer to the IoT devices themselves, typically at the edge of the network.
- In edge computing, data is processed and analyzed locally on edge devices or edge servers, reducing the need to transmit large amounts of data to centralized cloud or data center locations.
- Edge computing enables real-time or near-real-time processing, as it reduces network latency and allows for faster decision-making.
- It is particularly beneficial in applications where low latency, high bandwidth, or limited connectivity to the cloud are required, such as autonomous vehicles, industrial automation, and remote monitoring.
- Edge computing can offload some of the computational burden from IoT devices, improving their performance and power efficiency.

Fog Computing:

- Fog computing, also known as edge fog computing, extends the concept of edge computing by introducing an intermediate layer of computing resources between the edge and the cloud (Gomathi et al., 2023; Varsha et al., 2021).
- Fog computing nodes are deployed closer to the edge devices, such as on local gateways or routers, and they provide additional processing, storage, and networking capabilities.
- The fog layer acts as an intermediary between edge devices and the cloud, enabling localized data processing, analysis, and storage while still connecting to the cloud for higher-level processing or long-term storage.
- Fog computing enables distributed computing and data processing across a network of fog nodes, reducing the need for sending all data to a central cloud server.
- It is well-suited for applications with a large number of geographically distributed IoT devices and applications, such as smart cities, healthcare systems, and transportation networks.
- Fog computing can provide low-latency analytics, enhanced privacy and security, and efficient network utilization by offloading certain tasks from the cloud.

Comparison:

- Edge computing primarily focuses on processing data at the edge devices themselves, while fog computing adds an intermediate layer of fog nodes for distributed processing and analysis.
- Edge computing is suitable for applications with real-time requirements and limited connectivity to the cloud, whereas fog computing is more beneficial for applications with geographically distributed devices and the need for localized processing and decision-making.
- Fog computing provides a hierarchical approach, allowing for data aggregation and filtering at different levels of the network, while edge computing mainly concentrates on individual devices or localized edge servers.
- Both paradigms aim to reduce latency, network bandwidth usage, and dependence on centralized cloud infrastructure, while improving the overall performance and efficiency of IoT systems.

Hence, the choice between edge computing and fog computing depends on factors such as the specific IoT use case, data processing requirements, network conditions, and the level of localization and distribution needed for processing and analytics.

4.4 Stream Processing and Real-Time Analytics in IoT

Stream processing and real-time analytics plays an essential role in harnessing the power of streaming data in IoT systems. Here's a closer look at these concepts in the context of IoT:

Stream Processing:

- Stream processing is a computing paradigm that focuses on processing and analyzing data in motion as it is generated and flows continuously through a system.
- In IoT, stream processing is particularly relevant because IoT devices generate a constant stream of data that needs to be processed and analyzed in real-time.

- Stream processing systems receive and process data streams from IoT devices, applying operations such as filtering, aggregation, transformation, enrichment, and pattern detection on the fly.
- These systems typically operate on small time windows or sliding windows of data to analyze and derive information from the incoming streams.
- Stream processing allows for immediate, event-driven processing, enabling real-time decision-making and automated actions based on the analyzed data.
- Stream processing is beneficial in various IoT applications, including real-time monitoring, anomaly detection, predictive maintenance, situational awareness, and personalized services.

Real-time Analytics:

- Real-time analytics refers to the process of analyzing data in real-time or near real-time to extract meaningful information, patterns, and actionable information (Darabkh et al., 2018; Nair, 2023; Nair & yagi, 2023; Subramanian et al., 2019).
- In IoT, real-time analytics involves applying advanced analytics techniques on streaming data to derive meaningful information make immediate decisions.
- Real-time analytics systems typically employ machine learning algorithms, statistical analysis, complex event processing (CEP), and other techniques to analyze data as it arrives.
- These systems enable the detection of anomalies, patterns, trends, correlations, and predictive information in real-time, allowing for rapid responses and optimizations.
- Real-time analytics in IoT can provide benefits such as instant feedback, proactive alerts, operational efficiency, improved security, and enhanced customer experiences.
- Examples of real-time analytics in IoT include real-time predictive maintenance, real-time demand forecasting, real-time fraud detection, and real-time recommendation systems.

Combining Stream Processing and Real-time Analytics in IoT:

- Stream processing and real-time analytics are often used together in IoT systems to enable immediate analysis and decision-making on streaming data.
- Stream processing systems perform data transformation, aggregation, and filtering operations in real-time, preparing the data for advanced analytics.
- Real-time analytics techniques, such as machine learning algorithms, are applied on the processed data streams to derive information and make real-time predictions or actions.
- The combination of stream processing and real-time analytics allows organizations to extract valuable information, automate processes, optimize operations, and create intelligent IoT applications.
- The integration of stream processing and real-time analytics in IoT systems enables timely and data-driven decision-making, making it possible to extract the maximum value from the continuous streams of data generated by IoT devices.

5. IOT APPLICATIONS AND USE CASES

5.1 Smart Homes and Home Automation

IoT plays a significant role in enabling smart homes and home automation, transforming traditional houses into intelligent, connected living spaces (refer figure 7). Here's an overview of how IoT contributes to smart homes and home automation:

Connectivity and Integration:

- IoT enables connectivity and integration among various devices and systems within a smart home environment. Devices such as thermostats, lights, security cameras, door locks, appliances, and entertainment systems can be connected and controlled through a unified IoT platform.
- This connectivity allows for seamless communication and interoperability, enabling users to control and monitor their home devices remotely, whether through a smartphone app or voice commands.

Home Automation:

- IoT enables automation of various tasks and routines within a smart home. Through sensors, actuators, and intelligent algorithms, IoT devices can automate functions such as lighting control, temperature regulation, security monitoring, and energy management.
- For example, IoT-enabled smart lighting systems can automatically adjust the brightness or color of lights based on occupancy or natural lighting conditions. Similarly, smart thermostats can learn user preferences and adjust the temperature accordingly to optimize energy usage and comfort.

Energy Efficiency:

- IoT helps promote energy efficiency in smart homes by enabling intelligent monitoring and control of energy-consuming devices.
- Smart meters and energy monitoring devices connected to IoT platforms provide real-time information about energy consumption patterns, allowing homeowners to identify wasteful practices and make informed decisions to reduce energy usage.
- IoT-enabled smart appliances, such as smart refrigerators and washing machines, can optimize their operation based on energy tariffs, load balancing, and user preferences, contributing to overall energy efficiency.

Security and Safety:

- IoT enhances security and safety in smart homes by integrating various devices and systems to provide comprehensive protection.
- IoT-based security systems can include smart cameras, motion sensors, door/window sensors, and smart locks that are interconnected and accessible through a central control system or a mobile app.

- These systems can send real-time notifications, alert homeowners about potential security breaches, and allow remote monitoring and control to enhance overall safety and peace of mind.

Enhanced Convenience and Comfort:

- IoT technologies improve convenience and comfort within smart homes by automating mundane tasks and providing personalized experiences.
- Voice assistants, connected home hubs, and smart speakers enable homeowners to control multiple devices using voice commands, making it easy to adjust settings, play music, or receive information without physically interacting with each device.
- IoT-enabled personalization allows smart homes to adapt to individual preferences, such as adjusting lighting, temperature, and entertainment options based on user preferences and presence detection.

Health and Well-being:

- IoT can contribute to health and well-being in smart homes by integrating health monitoring devices and systems.
- Smart wearables, health sensors, and connected medical devices can collect and transmit health-related data to IoT platforms, providing information about important signs, physical activity, sleep patterns, and more.
- This data-driven information can help individuals monitor their health, receive personalized recommendations, and even facilitate remote healthcare services, enabling better health management within the comfort of their homes.
- The IoT's role in smart homes and home automation is centered around connectivity, automation, energy efficiency, security, convenience, and well-being. By integrating IoT technologies and devices, homeowners can transform their living spaces into intelligent environments that enhance comfort, safety, and quality of life.

5.2 Industrial Internet of Things (IIoT)

The Industrial Internet of Things (IIoT) refers to the application of IoT technologies and principles in industrial settings, such as manufacturing plants, oil refineries, transportation systems, utilities, and more (refer figure 7). The IIoT uses connected devices, sensors, and advanced analytics to improve operational efficiency, enhance productivity, enable predictive maintenance, and drive innovation (Subramanian et al., 2019; Yaqoob et al., 2019). Here's an overview of the IoT's role in the IIoT:

Connectivity and Data Collection:

- IoT devices, sensors, and actuators are deployed across industrial infrastructure to collect real-time data on various parameters such as temperature, pressure, humidity, vibration, and energy consumption.
- These devices are interconnected, creating a network that enables seamless data collection and communication between machines, systems, and stakeholders.

Figure 7. Use case of IoT

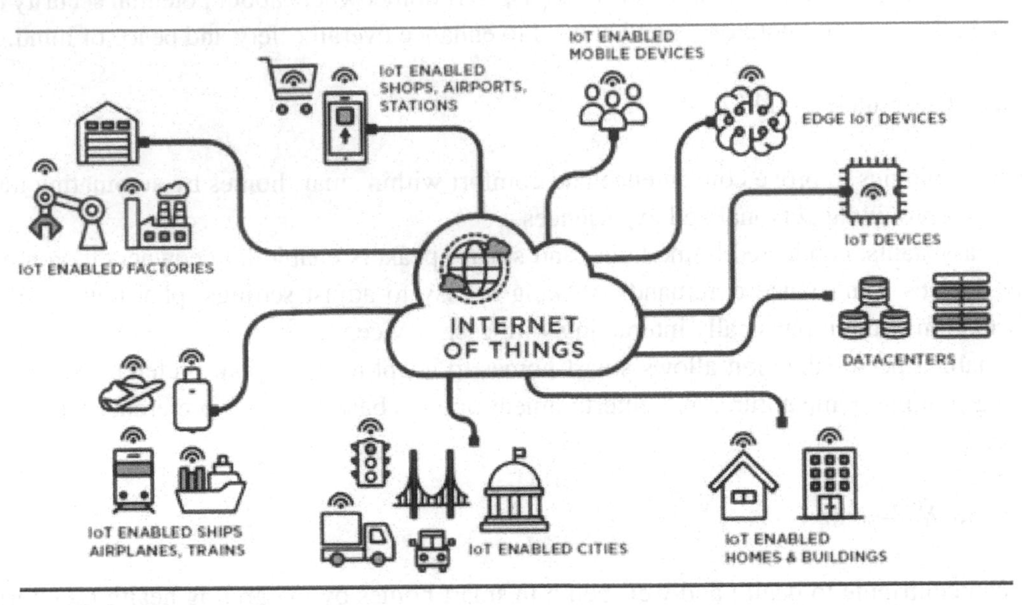

Monitoring and Control:

- The IIoT allows for remote monitoring and control of industrial assets and processes.
- Real-time data from IoT devices enables operators and managers to monitor machine performance, track production metrics, and identify anomalies or inefficiencies.
- Remote control capabilities enable operators to adjust settings, perform maintenance tasks, and optimize operations from a central location, reducing the need for manual intervention.

Predictive Maintenance:

- The IIoT enables predictive maintenance by using IoT sensors to monitor equipment health and detect signs of potential failures or malfunctions.
- Machine learning algorithms and analytics platforms analyze real-time sensor data to identify patterns and anomalies that indicate potential equipment issues.
- Predictive maintenance helps prevent costly downtime by allowing proactive repairs or replacements before a failure occurs, optimizing asset performance and reducing maintenance costs.

Process Optimization:

- IoT technologies play an essential role in optimizing industrial processes and workflows.
- Real-time data from sensors and connected devices allow for better visibility and understanding of the production line, enabling adjustments and optimizations in real-time.
- Advanced analytics and machine learning algorithms analyze data to identify bottlenecks, inefficiencies, and areas for improvement, leading to optimized production, reduced waste, and improved quality.

Supply Chain Management:

- IoT enables end-to-end visibility and traceability in the supply chain, providing information about the movement of goods, inventory levels, and condition monitoring.
- Sensors, RFID tags, and connected logistics devices track the location, condition, and status of assets, raw materials, and finished products throughout the supply chain.
- This real-time visibility improves supply chain efficiency, reduces delays, enhances inventory management, and enables proactive decision-making.

Safety and Security:

- The IIoT enhances safety and security in industrial environments through the deployment of IoT devices and systems.
- Connected sensors can monitor hazardous conditions, detect leaks, measure air quality, and ensure compliance with safety regulations.
- IoT-based security systems enable real-time monitoring of premises, assets, and critical infrastructure, detecting intrusions, and mitigating risks.

Energy Efficiency:

- IoT technologies help improve energy efficiency in industrial settings by monitoring and optimizing energy consumption.
- Connected sensors and smart meters track energy usage in real-time, allowing operators to identify energy-intensive processes and implement energy-saving measures.
- IoT-based control systems can dynamically adjust energy consumption based on demand, peak load periods, and energy pricing, contributing to overall energy efficiency.

Hence, the IIoT uses IoT technologies to connect, monitor, and optimize industrial assets, processes, and systems. By enabling real-time data collection, analysis, and control, the IIoT enhances operational efficiency, productivity, safety, and sustainability in industrial environments, leading to cost savings, improved quality, and innovation.

5.3 Smart Cities and Urban Infrastructure

The IoT plays an essential role in the development of smart cities and the optimization of urban infrastructure (refer figure 7). By connecting various devices, systems, and sensors, IoT enables data collection, analysis, and automation to improve the quality of life for citizens, enhance resource efficiency, and enable sustainable development. Here's an overview of the IoT's role in smart cities and urban infrastructure:

Intelligent Infrastructure:

- IoT technologies enable the monitoring and management of critical infrastructure such as transportation systems, utilities, and buildings.
- Connected sensors and devices gather real-time data on traffic patterns, energy consumption, water usage, air quality, waste management, and more.

- This data helps city administrators optimize resource allocation, detect issues, and make informed decisions to improve the efficiency, safety, and sustainability of urban infrastructure.

Smart Mobility:

- IoT contributes to smart mobility solutions by enabling real-time monitoring and management of transportation systems.
- Connected sensors and cameras collect data on traffic flow, parking availability, public transit usage, and pedestrian movements.
- This data allows for the optimization of traffic management, the implementation of intelligent transportation (Tan & Wang, 2010) systems, and the provision of real-time travel information to citizens, leading to reduced congestion, improved safety, and enhanced mobility options.

Energy Management:

- IoT facilitates efficient energy management in smart cities by monitoring energy consumption, optimizing energy distribution, and promoting renewable energy integration.
- Connected smart grids, smart meters, and energy management systems provide real-time data on energy usage, enabling better demand-response mechanisms and load balancing.
- IoT-based energy management allows for improved efficiency, reduced energy waste, and increased integration of renewable energy sources, contributing to sustainability goals and cost savings.

Environmental Monitoring:

- IoT sensors and devices are deployed to monitor environmental factors such as air quality, noise levels, temperature, humidity, and pollution levels.
- Real-time data collected through these sensors helps in assessing environmental conditions, identifying potential hazards, and implementing appropriate measures to protect citizens' health and well-being.
- The IoT's environmental monitoring capabilities support data-driven decision-making, policy development, and initiatives for sustainable development and urban planning.

Public Safety and Security:

- IoT technologies enhance public safety and security in smart cities by enabling real-time monitoring and surveillance.
- Connected cameras, sensors, and emergency response systems provide continuous monitoring of public spaces, identifying potential threats, and enabling prompt response.
- IoT-based solutions can integrate with public safety agencies, enabling effective incident management, emergency response, and crime prevention.

Citizen Engagement and Quality of Life:

- IoT empowers citizens by providing them with access to real-time information and services, fostering citizen engagement and improving the quality of life.
- IoT-enabled applications allow citizens to access services such as smart parking, waste management, and public transportation information, enhancing convenience and reducing inefficiencies.
- Citizens can actively participate in decision-making processes through IoT platforms, providing feedback, reporting issues, and contributing to the development of a more livable and sustainable city.
- The IoT's role in smart cities and urban infrastructure is centered on data-driven decision-making, automation, and optimization of resources. By using IoT technologies, cities can improve efficiency, sustainability, and quality of life for their residents while addressing challenges such as traffic congestion, resource management, and environmental impact.

6. SECURITY AND PRIVACY IN IOT

6.1 Challenges and Risks in IoT Security

While the IoT offers numerous benefits and opportunities, it also introduces several challenges and risks, particularly in terms of security (Balas et al., 2019; Subramanian et al., 2019; Yaqoob et al., 2019). Here are some of the key challenges and risks associated with IoT security:

- Lack of Standardization: The IoT ecosystem comprises a wide range of devices, platforms, and protocols, leading to a lack of standardized security practices. Inconsistent security measures make it difficult to establish a unified and robust security framework across all IoT devices.
- Vulnerabilities in IoT Devices: IoT devices often have limited computing resources and may not receive regular security updates or patches. This makes them vulnerable to security breaches, as they may have weak default passwords, outdated firmware, or insufficient security controls.
- Data Privacy issue: IoT devices collect and transmit large amount of data, including personal and sensitive information. The unauthorized access, use, or disclosure of this data can have serious privacy implications. Ensuring strong data encryption, secure data storage, and data access control mechanisms is important.
- Inadequate Authentication and Authorization: Weak authentication mechanisms, such as default or easily guessable passwords, can leave IoT devices susceptible to unauthorized access. Inadequate authorization controls may allow unauthorized users to gain access to critical systems or manipulate device functionality.
- Network Vulnerabilities: The connectivity of IoT devices through networks, including wireless and cloud-based infrastructures, introduces additional security risks. Inadequate network security measures, such as weak encryption protocols or lack of network segmentation, can expose devices to attacks and unauthorized access.
- Distributed Denial of Service (DDoS) Attacks: IoT devices, when compromised, can be harnessed to launch large-scale DDoS attacks. These attacks overwhelm networks or websites, causing service disruptions and impacting the availability and reliability of IoT services.

- Lack of Security Awareness and Education: Many consumers and even some organizations may not be aware of the security risks associated with IoT devices or lack the knowledge to implement appropriate security measures. This can lead to poor security practices, such as failure to change default passwords or neglecting to update firmware.
- Supply Chain Risks: The complex supply chains involved in manufacturing and distributing IoT devices can introduce security risks. Malicious actors may compromise devices during the production or distribution process, leading to compromised security even before devices reach the end-user.
- Regulatory and Compliance Challenges: The rapidly evolving nature of IoT technology makes it challenging to develop and enforce robust security regulations and standards. Compliance with existing regulations, such as data protection and privacy laws, can be complex due to the diverse nature of IoT deployments.
- Persistent Security Updates: IoT devices often have a long lifespan, and ensuring regular security updates throughout their operational lifecycle can be challenging. Device manufacturers and stakeholders need to establish mechanisms to provide timely security patches and firmware updates to address newly discovered vulnerabilities.

Note that addressing these challenges and mitigating risks requires a multi-faceted approach that involves collaboration between device manufacturers, service providers, regulators, and end-users. It includes implementing strong authentication and encryption mechanisms, regularly updating and patching devices, educating users about IoT security best practices, and establishing industry-wide security standards and regulations.

6.2 Authentication and Access Control in IoT

Authentication and access control are essential components of IoT security, helping to ensure that only authorized individuals and devices can access IoT systems and data. Here are the key aspects of authentication and access control in the context of IoT:

Device Authentication:

- Each IoT device should have a unique identity or digital certificate to establish its authenticity.
- During the device onboarding process, mutual authentication can be implemented to verify the device's identity and the legitimacy of the IoT platform or gateway it is connecting to.
- Strong authentication mechanisms, such as cryptographic keys or certificates, can be used to validate the identity of devices and prevent unauthorized devices from accessing the IoT network.

User Authentication:

- Users interacting with IoT systems or applications should undergo authentication to ensure that they are authorized to access and control IoT devices or data.
- Strong authentication methods, including passwords, biometrics (e.g., fingerprint or facial recognition), or two-factor authentication (2FA), can be employed to verify the identity of users.
- User authentication mechanisms should be properly implemented and managed to prevent unauthorized access to IoT systems.

Role-Based Access Control (RBAC):

- RBAC is a common access control model that assigns permissions and privileges based on users' roles and responsibilities.
- RBAC can be applied in IoT systems to manage and control access to devices, data, and functionalities.
- By defining roles and associating them with appropriate permissions, RBAC ensures that users have access only to the resources they need for their specific tasks, reducing the risk of unauthorized actions.

Access Control Policies:

- Access control policies define the rules and criteria for granting or denying access to IoT devices and data.
- These policies can be based on various factors, such as user roles, device identities, time of access, and contextual information.
- Access control policies should be regularly reviewed and updated to reflect changes in the IoT environment and to adapt to evolving security requirements.

Secure Communication:

- IoT systems should employ secure communication protocols, such as Transport Layer Security (TLS) or Datagram Transport Layer Security (DTLS), to protect data transmission between devices, gateways, and the IoT platform.
- Secure communication protocols ensure the confidentiality and integrity of data, preventing unauthorized interception or tampering.

Secure Credential Management:

- Proper management of authentication credentials, such as passwords or cryptographic keys, is important to prevent unauthorized access or credential misuse.
- IoT systems should enforce strong password policies, encourage regular password updates, and store passwords securely using hashing and salting techniques.
- Public key infrastructure (PKI) can be employed to manage cryptographic keys and certificates used for device and user authentication.

Audit Trails and Monitoring:

- IoT systems should have mechanisms to record and monitor user activities, device interactions, and access attempts.
- Audit trails help in detecting and investigating security incidents or suspicious activities.
- Real-time monitoring and anomaly detection techniques can be employed to identify unauthorized access attempts or abnormal behavior patterns.

- Implementing robust authentication and access control mechanisms in IoT systems is important for protecting against unauthorized access, data breaches, and malicious activities. It requires a combination of secure device and user authentication, well-defined access control policies, secure communication protocols, and continuous monitoring to ensure the integrity and confidentiality of IoT systems and data.

6.3 Privacy Issues and Data Protection in IoT

Privacy issues and data protection are critical aspects of IoT security, given the large amount of data collected and transmitted by IoT devices (Gomathi et al., 2023; Varsha et al., 2021). Here are some key issues related to privacy and data protection in IoT:

- Data Minimization: We need to collect only the necessary data to fulfill the intended purpose and minimize the collection of personally identifiable information (PII) or sensitive data. Limiting the data collected helps reduce the risk of unauthorized access and potential privacy violations.
- Informed Consent: We need to obtain explicit and informed consent from individuals before collecting their personal data. Users should be aware of what data is being collected, how it will be used, and any potential third-party sharing. Transparent privacy policies and user agreements should be provided to ensure individuals are fully informed.
- Data Encryption: We need to implement strong encryption mechanisms to protect data during storage, transmission, and at rest. Encryption helps prevent unauthorized access to sensitive information, even if the data is intercepted or accessed without proper authorization.
- Data Access Control: We need to implement robust access control mechanisms to restrict data access to authorized individuals or entities. Role-based access control (RBAC), user authentication, and secure credential management should be employed to ensure that only authorized users can access and modify IoT data.
- Data Anonymization and Pseudonymization: We need to anonymize or pseudonymize data whenever possible to remove or replace personally identifiable information. By doing so, it becomes more challenging to link data back to specific individuals, providing an additional layer of privacy protection.
- Secure Data Storage and Retention: We need to ensure that data is securely stored and protected from unauthorized access. Secure storage mechanisms, such as encryption and access controls, should be implemented to prevent data breaches and unauthorized disclosure. Data retention policies should also be established to limit the storage duration and purposefully delete data that is no longer needed.
- Secure Data Sharing: If data needs to be shared with third parties, ensure that appropriate data protection agreements and protocols are in place. Verify that the recipients have adequate security measures to protect the data and comply with relevant privacy regulations.
- Privacy by Design: We need to incorporate privacy issues into the design and development of IoT systems from the beginning. Privacy by design principles ensure that privacy and data protection measures are integrated into the system architecture, minimizing privacy risks and enhancing user trust.

- Regular Security Updates and Patching: We need to regularly update and patch IoT devices, firmware, and software to address security vulnerabilities and protect against potential data breaches. Promptly applying security updates helps ensure that devices are protected against emerging threats.
- Compliance with Data Protection Regulations: We need to ensure compliance with relevant data protection regulations, such as the General Data Protection Regulation (GDPR) in the European Union or the California Consumer Privacy Act (CCPA) in the United States. Understand the legal requirements and obligations concerning data protection and privacy, and take necessary steps to meet those requirements.

Hence, addressing privacy issues and ensuring data protection in IoT requires a holistic approach that combines technical measures, privacy policies, user education, and compliance with applicable regulations. By implementing strong privacy practices, organizations can foster trust among users and mitigate privacy risks associated with the collection, storage, and processing of IoT data.

6.4 Blockchain Technology for IoT Security

Blockchain technology has the potential to enhance security in IoT deployments by providing decentralized, immutable, and transparent mechanisms for data integrity, authentication, and access control. Here are some ways blockchain can be used for IoT security:

- Data Integrity and Tamper Resistance: Blockchain provides a decentralized and immutable ledger where data can be securely stored and verified. By storing IoT data on the blockchain, it becomes resistant to tampering, as any modification to the data will require consensus from the network participants. This ensures the integrity of IoT data and provides a reliable audit trail.
- Authentication and Identity Management: Blockchain can enable secure device authentication and identity management in IoT networks. Each device can have a unique identifier stored on the blockchain, and cryptographic techniques can be used to authenticate and authorize device interactions. This prevents unauthorized devices from accessing the network and mitigates the risk of spoofing or impersonation attacks.
- Secure Data Sharing and Access Control: Blockchain enables secure and auditable data sharing among multiple parties in an IoT ecosystem. Smart contracts, programmable scripts on the blockchain, can enforce access control policies and define the rules for data sharing. This ensures that only authorized entities can access and interact with IoT data, enhancing privacy and preventing unauthorized data exposure.
- Trust and Consensus: Blockchain's distributed and consensus-based nature eliminates the need for a central authority in IoT networks. Network participants collectively validate and agree upon the integrity and validity of IoT data. This decentralized trust model enhances security by eliminating single points of failure and reducing the risk of malicious attacks or data manipulation.
- Supply Chain Security: Blockchain can be used to enhance the security and transparency of supply chain processes in IoT deployments. By recording the movement and ownership of IoT devices, components, or products on the blockchain, stakeholders can verify the authenticity, origin, and integrity of goods, reducing the risk of counterfeiting or unauthorized modifications.

- Firmware and Software Updates: Blockchain can facilitate secure and auditable firmware and software updates for IoT devices. By using smart contracts, updates can be securely distributed to devices, ensuring their authenticity and integrity. This helps protect IoT devices from vulnerabilities and ensures that they are running the latest security patches.
- Event Logging and Forensics: Blockchain's transparent and immutable nature allows for reliable event logging and forensics in IoT deployments. All transactions and events recorded on the blockchain create an auditable trail that can be used for investigation, identifying the root cause of security incidents, and ensuring accountability.

Note that blockchain is not a one-size-fits-all solution for IoT security. There are challenges to consider, such as scalability, latency, and the energy consumption associated with blockchain networks. Implementing blockchain for IoT security requires careful consideration of the specific use case, network requirements, and trade-offs between security, performance, and cost. In summary, blockchain technology has the potential to enhance IoT security by providing decentralized trust, data integrity, and secure authentication mechanisms. When appropriately implemented, blockchain (George & Tyagi, 2022) can contribute to building robust and secure IoT ecosystems.

7. EMERGING TRENDS AND FUTURE DIRECTIONS

7.1 Artificial Intelligence and Machine Learning in IoT

The future of Artificial Intelligence (AI) and Machine Learning (ML) in IoT holds immense potential for transforming various industries and unlocking new opportunities. Here are some key aspects that highlight the future of AI and ML in IoT:

- Enhanced Automation and Intelligence: AI and ML algorithms will enable IoT systems to become more autonomous and intelligent. By using real-time data analytics and pattern recognition, IoT devices can make intelligent decisions, automate processes, and optimize operations without human intervention. This will lead to increased efficiency, reduced costs, and improved overall performance.
- Predictive and Prescriptive Analytics: AI and ML algorithms can analyze large volumes of IoT data to identify patterns, predict future outcomes, and generate actionable information. This enables proactive decision-making, preventive maintenance, and the ability to address issues before they occur. IoT systems empowered by AI and ML will be able to optimize resource utilization, enhance productivity, and provide personalized services.
- Edge AI and ML: Edge computing, combined with AI and ML capabilities, will become increasingly important in IoT deployments. By performing AI and ML computations at the edge, closer to the data source, IoT devices can process and analyze data in real-time, reducing latency and enhancing responsiveness. Edge AI and ML also improve data privacy and security by minimizing the need to transmit sensitive data to centralized cloud servers.
- Intelligent IoT Networks: AI and ML algorithms can optimize IoT network management and improve network efficiency. These technologies can analyze network traffic, predict congestion, and dynamically allocate resources to ensure reliable and efficient communication. Intelligent IoT

networks can self-optimize, self-configure, and adapt to changing conditions, leading to better connectivity, reduced latency, and improved scalability.

- Cognitive IoT: AI and ML will enable IoT devices to exhibit cognitive capabilities, such as natural language processing, speech recognition, and computer vision. This opens up opportunities for more intuitive human-machine interactions, enabling voice-based control, gesture recognition, and visual perception in IoT systems. Cognitive IoT will enhance user experiences and enable more sophisticated applications in areas like smart homes, healthcare, and industrial automation.
- Collaborative Intelligence: AI and ML algorithms can enable collaborative decision-making and intelligence sharing among IoT devices. Devices can learn from each other, exchange information, and collectively make informed decisions. This collective intelligence can lead to more robust and adaptive IoT systems, especially in applications where multiple devices need to work together to achieve a common goal.
- Ethical and Responsible AI: As AI and ML become more prevalent in IoT, there will be an increased focus on ensuring ethical and responsible use. Guidelines and regulations will be developed to address privacy, bias, transparency, and accountability in AI algorithms and IoT systems. Building trust and maintaining the ethical use of AI in IoT will be importnat for widespread adoption and acceptance.

In summary, AI and ML will play a significant role in shaping the future of IoT, enabling intelligent, autonomous, and efficient IoT systems. As these technologies continue to advance, we can expect transformative changes across industries, driving innovation, and creating new opportunities for businesses and individuals.

7.2 6G and IoT Connectivity

The future of 6G and IoT connectivity promises to revolutionize the way we interact with technology and enable the seamless integration of billions of connected devices (refer figure 8). Here are some key aspects that highlight the potential future developments:

- Ultra-High-Speed Connectivity: 6G is expected to provide significantly faster speeds compared to 5G, with data rates reaching terabits per second. This ultra-high-speed connectivity will enable real-time interactions, immersive experiences, and support for bandwidth-intensive IoT applications, such as augmented reality (AR), virtual reality (VR), and high-resolution video streaming.
- Massive IoT Connectivity: 6G is designed to accommodate massive IoT deployments, supporting a large number of connected devices. This means that billions of IoT devices, sensors, and actuators will be seamlessly connected, enabling extensive monitoring, control, and data collection across various industries. This connectivity will fuel advancements in smart cities, industrial automation, agriculture, healthcare, and transportation.
- Low Latency and Reliable Connections: 6G aims to achieve ultra-low latency, reducing the time it takes for devices to communicate with each other and the network. This will enable real-time control and responsiveness in critical applications, such as autonomous vehicles, robotics, and industrial IoT. Additionally, 6G will provide highly reliable connections, ensuring minimal disruptions and downtime for mission-critical IoT deployments.

- Edge Intelligence and Computing: 6G will use edge computing capabilities to bring AI and ML closer to the IoT devices and data sources. By processing and analyzing data at the edge, near the source, 6G networks will enable faster response times, reduced network congestion, and improved data privacy. Edge intelligence will enhance IoT applications, enabling more localized decision-making, real-time analytics, and efficient resource utilization.

Figure 8. Possibilities with 6G integration of IoT

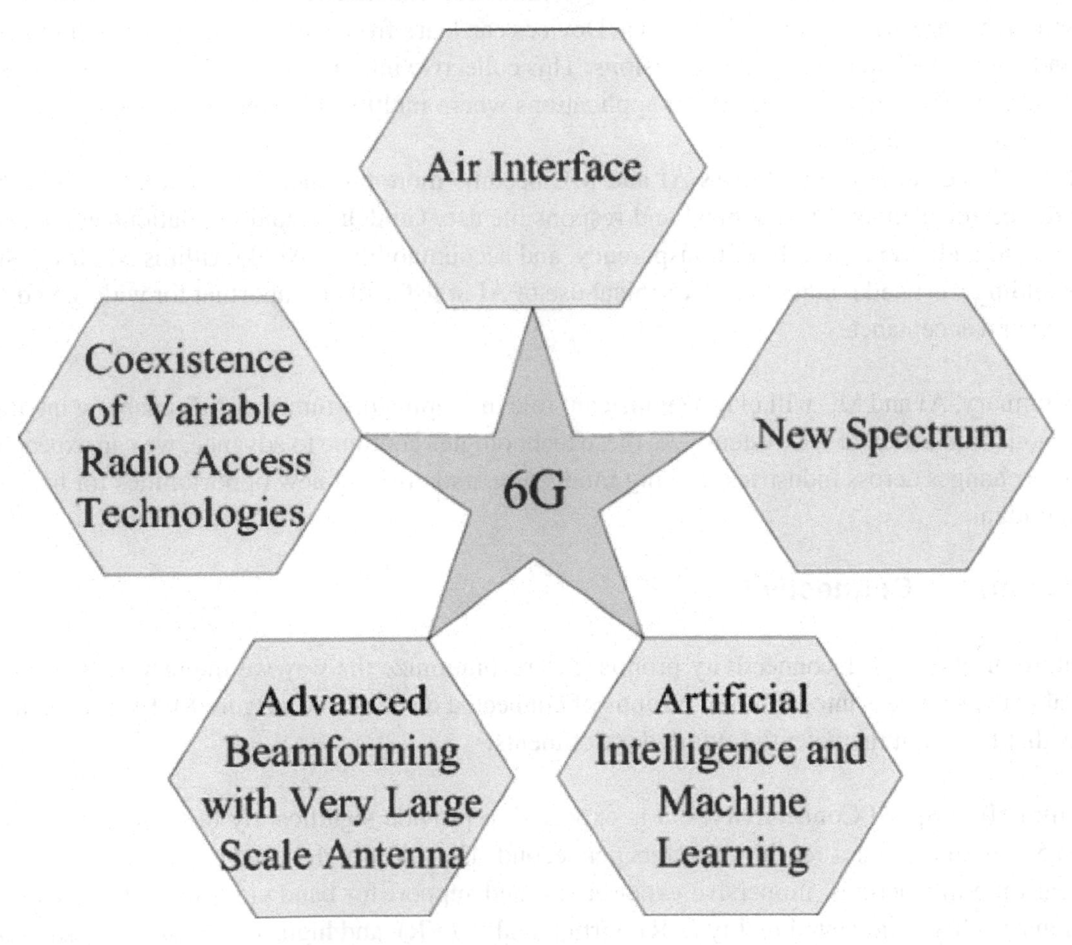

- Advanced Network Slicing and Virtualization: 6G will further advance network slicing and virtualization techniques, allowing the creation of customized and isolated network segments tailored to specific IoT use cases. This will provide dedicated network resources, security, and quality of service guarantees for different IoT applications, ensuring optimal performance and reliability.
- Energy Efficiency and Sustainability: 6G networks will focus on energy efficiency, aiming to reduce the power consumption of IoT devices and network infrastructure. This will extend the battery life of IoT devices, making them more sustainable and enabling long-term deployments without frequent battery replacements. Energy harvesting technologies and novel power management techniques will contribute to the overall sustainability of IoT connectivity.

- Enhanced Security and Privacy: With the proliferation of IoT devices and data, ensuring robust security and privacy measures will be paramount. 6G will incorporate advanced security protocols, encryption mechanisms, and authentication techniques to safeguard IoT communications and protect sensitive data. Privacy-enhancing technologies, such as secure data anonymization and user-centric control, will be integrated into 6G networks to address privacy issues.
- Global Connectivity and Harmonization: 6G is expected to enhance global connectivity, bridging the digital divide and connecting remote regions. Efforts will be made to harmonize 6G standards and regulations globally to enable seamless interoperability and support cross-border IoT deployments. This will facilitate the development of global IoT ecosystems and promote innovation on a larger scale.

Note that the future of 6G and IoT connectivity is set to revolutionize industries, enable transformative applications, and provide unprecedented levels of connectivity and data information. With its ultra-high speeds, massive IoT support, low latency, edge intelligence, and enhanced security, 6G will provide the way for the next generation of IoT innovations and shape the future of connected ecosystems.

7.3 Edge AI and Edge Analytics in IoT

The future of Edge AI and Edge Analytics in IoT is poised to bring significant advancements and capabilities to the realm of connected devices. Here are some key aspects that highlight the potential developments:

- Increased Processing Power at the Edge: Edge devices will become more powerful, capable of handling complex AI and analytics tasks locally. Advances in hardware, such as more efficient processors and specialized accelerators, will enable edge devices to perform real-time AI inference and analytics without relying heavily on cloud-based resources. This will reduce latency, enhance responsiveness, and enable more intelligent decision-making at the edge.
- Distributed AI and Collaboration: Edge devices will not only perform local AI processing but will also collaborate with each other to collectively accomplish more sophisticated tasks. This distributed AI approach, also known as federated learning, allows devices to share knowledge and information while preserving data privacy. Collaborative AI will enable more powerful and context-aware IoT applications by uisng the collective intelligence of edge devices.
- Edge-to-Cloud Continuum: The future will witness a seamless integration and orchestration of AI and analytics capabilities across the edge and cloud continuum. While some processing will occur at the edge to ensure real-time responses and reduced network dependency, other tasks requiring more extensive computational resources or historical data analysis will be offloaded to the cloud. The edge and cloud will work together to provide a holistic and scalable AI infrastructure for IoT deployments.
- Real-time information and Decision-making: Edge AI and analytics will enable faster and more accurate information generation, allowing real-time decision-making directly at the edge. This will be particularly beneficial for time-sensitive applications such as industrial automation, autonomous vehicles, and critical healthcare systems. By minimizing the round-trip latency to the cloud, edge analytics will enable instant feedback, immediate action, and improved operational efficiency.\

- Edge AI for Video and Vision Analytics: Video and vision analytics are expected to see significant advancements with edge AI. Edge devices will be capable of performing real-time video analysis, object detection, tracking, and facial recognition. This will enable applications such as smart surveillance, retail analytics, and intelligent transportation systems to operate autonomously, making timely and informed decisions based on visual data.
- Privacy and Data Localization: Edge AI and analytics address issues about data privacy and security by keeping sensitive data at the edge. Instead of transmitting raw data to the cloud, edge devices can process data locally and send only relevant information or aggregated information. This localized data processing approach reduces the exposure of sensitive information, enhances privacy, and helps organizations comply with data protection regulations.
- Customization and Personalization: Edge AI and analytics will enable personalized experiences and customized services tailored to individual users or specific contexts. By processing data at the edge, devices can use local knowledge, preferences, and historical patterns to deliver personalized recommendations, adaptive automation, and context-aware services. This level of customization will enhance user experiences and enable more efficient and intuitive interactions with IoT devices.
- Resource Efficiency and Network Optimization: Edge AI and analytics will contribute to resource efficiency in IoT deployments. By performing data analysis and decision-making at the edge, unnecessary data transmission and network congestion can be reduced. This optimization leads to more efficient network utilization, lower bandwidth requirements, and reduced energy consumption. Edge analytics will also enable local anomaly detection and predictive maintenance, improving resource allocation and reducing downtime.

The future of Edge AI and Edge Analytics in IoT holds tremendous potential for driving innovation, enabling real-time intelligence, and addressing the challenges of latency, privacy, and resource efficiency. By bringing AI capabilities to the edge, IoT devices will become smarter, more autonomous, and capable of delivering personalized and context-aware experiences. The integration of edge and cloud resources will create a seamless and dynamic AI infrastructure that enhances the overall efficiency and effectiveness of IoT ecosystems.

7.4 Internet of Things and Digital Transformation

IoT plays an important role in driving digital transformation across various industries. It enables organizations to connect, monitor, and manage physical devices, assets, and processes in real-time, generating valuable data information and transforming traditional business operations. Here are some key ways IoT contributes to digital transformation:

- Enhanced Connectivity and Communication: IoT facilitates seamless connectivity and communication between devices, systems, and stakeholders. It enables the exchange of real-time data, enabling organizations to make informed decisions, optimize processes, and respond quickly to changing conditions. This connectivity drives collaboration and integration across different parts of the business, leading to more efficient and agile operations.
- Data-driven information and Analytics: IoT generates massive volumes of data from connected devices and sensors. This data can be collected, analyzed, and transformed into actionable

information using advanced analytics techniques. Organizations can gain deeper visibility into their operations, identify patterns, trends, and anomalies, and make data-driven decisions. IoT-driven analytics enable predictive maintenance, resource optimization, and improved operational efficiency.

- Process Automation and Optimization: IoT enables automation and optimization of various processes across industries. By connecting devices, machines, and systems, organizations can automate routine tasks, monitor performance in real-time, and implement intelligent workflows. IoT-driven automation enhances efficiency, reduces human errors, and frees up resources to focus on more value-added activities. It also enables process optimization through continuous monitoring and data-driven improvements.
- Improved Customer Experience: IoT enables organizations to deliver personalized and context-aware experiences to customers. By collecting data from IoT devices, organizations can get meaningful information about customer preferences, behavior, and usage patterns. This information can be used to tailor products, services, and marketing campaigns, providing personalized recommendations, proactive support, and enhanced customer engagement. IoT-driven customer experiences lead to higher customer satisfaction and loyalty.
- Supply Chain Optimization: IoT revolutionizes supply chain management by providing end-to-end visibility and real-time monitoring of goods, assets, and inventory. Organizations can track the movement of products, monitor environmental conditions, optimize logistics, and automate inventory management. IoT in supply chain management enables improved demand forecasting, reduced stockouts, streamlined logistics operations, and better collaboration between suppliers, manufacturers, and distributors.
- Smart Cities and Infrastructure: IoT plays an important role in transforming urban environments into smart cities. By connecting various city systems, such as transportation, utilities, public safety, and waste management, IoT enables efficient resource utilization, traffic management, energy optimization, and enhanced citizen services. Smart city initiatives consider IoT to improve sustainability, livability, and the overall quality of life for residents.
- Business Model Innovation: IoT opens up new opportunities for business model innovation. Organizations can use IoT data to develop new products, services, and revenue streams. For example, manufacturers can offer products as a service, using IoT to monitor usage and provide predictive maintenance. IoT also enables subscription-based models, data monetization, and outcome-based pricing, shifting from selling products to delivering outcomes.
- Security and Risk Management: As organizations embrace IoT, ensuring robust security and risk management becomes paramount. IoT security solutions protect devices, data, and networks from cyber threats. This includes implementing secure communication protocols, access controls, encryption, and authentication mechanisms. Effective IoT security ensures the integrity, confidentiality, and availability of data, preventing unauthorized access or malicious activities.

In summary, IoT is a key enabler of digital transformation, empowering organizations to harness the power of connected devices, data analytics, and automation. It drives operational efficiency, improves customer experiences, enables new business models, and transforms industries. By uisng IoT, organizations can unlock innovation, agility, and competitiveness in the digital era.

8. CONCLUSION

In the rapidly evolving landscape of the IoT, it is evident that the convergence of digital technology with the physical world has ushered in a new era of connectivity and possibilities. This work has provided a comprehensive exploration of the basic principles, protocols, and diverse applications that characterize the IoT ecosystem. This work has provided concepts of IoT, including sensor networks, data communication protocols, and cloud computing integration (which can be helpful for future researchers). This work discusses the transformative power of IoT across various domains, from smart cities and healthcare to agriculture and industrial automation. Note that IoT is not merely a technological advancement but a catalyst for innovation and efficiency. It offers the potential to enhance our quality of life, optimize resource utilization, and drive economic growth. However, this work has also highlighted the challenges and issues that must be addressed as we embrace the IoT paradigm. These include security and privacy issues, interoperability issues, and the need for robust data management practices. As IoT continues to evolve, collaboration among stakeholders, including researchers, etc., becomes increasingly essential to navigate these challenges successfully. As we conclude this exploration of IoT and its concepts, protocols, and applications in detail in this work which can be more useful to modern society.

REFERENCES

Balas, V., Solanki, K., Kumar, R., & Khari, M. (2019). The History, Present and Future with IoT. Internet of Things and Big Data Analytics for Smart Generation. Springer.

Darabkh, K., Odetallah, S., Al-qudah, Z., & Khalifeh, A. (2018). A New Density-Based Relaying Protocol for Wireless Sensor Networks. 14th International Wireless Communications & Mobile Computing Conference, IWCMC.

Darabkh, K., Zomot, J., & Al-qudah, Z. (2019). EDB-CHS-BOF: Energy and distance-based cluster head selection with balanced objective function protocol. *IET Communications*, *13*(19), 3168–3180. doi:10.1049/iet-com.2019.0092

George, T. T., & Tyagi, A. K. (2022). Reliable Edge Computing Architectures for Crowdsensing Applications. *2022 International Conference on Computer Communication and Informatics (ICCCI)*, (pp. 1-6). IEEE. 10.1109/ICCCI54379.2022.9740791

Gomathi, L., Mishra, A. K., & Tyagi, A. K. (2023). *Industry 5.0 for Healthcare 5.0: Opportunities, Challenges and Future Research Possibilities*. 2023 7th International Conference on Trends in Electronics and Informatics (ICOEI), Tirunelveli, India. 10.1109/ICOEI56765.2023.10125660

Goyal, D. & Tyagi, A. (2020). *A Look at Top 35 Problems in the Computer Science Field for the Next Decade*. Taylor & Francis. . doi:10.1201/9781003052098-40

Gubbi, J., Buyya, R., Marusic, S., & Palaniswami, M. (2013). Internet of Things (IoT): A vision, architectural elements, and future directions. *Future Generation Computer Systems*, *29*(7), 1645–1660. doi:10.1016/j.future.2013.01.010

Nair, M. M. (2023). *Amit Kumar Tyagi, "6G: Technology, Advancement, Barriers, and the Future", in the book: 6G-Enabled IoT and AI for Smart Healthcare*. CRC Press.

Nair, M. M., Kumari, S., & Tyagi, A. K. (2021). Internet of Things, Cyber Physical System, and Data Analytics: Open Questions, Future Perspectives, and Research Areas. In: Goyal D., Gupta A.K., Piuri V., Ganzha M., Paprzycki M. (eds) *Proceedings of the Second International Conference on Information Management and Machine Intelligence. Lecture Notes in Networks and Systems*. Springer, Singapore. 10.1007/978-981-15-9689-6_36

Nair, M. & Tyagi, A. (2023). *Blockchain technology for next-generation society: current trends and future opportunities for smart era.* Blockchain Technology for Secure Social Media Computing. . doi:10.1049/PBSE019E_ch11

Nair, M. M., & Tyagi, A. K. (2023). Chapter 11 - AI, IoT, blockchain, and cloud computing: The necessity of the future. R. Pandey, S. Goundar, S. Fatima, (eds.) Distributed Computing to Blockchain. Academic Press. doi:10.1016/B978-0-323-96146-2.00001-2

Reddy, K. S., Agarwal, K., & Tyagi, A. K. (2021). Beyond Things: A Systematic Study of Internet of Everything. In A. Abraham, M. Panda, S. Pradhan, L. Garcia-Hernandez, & K. Ma (Eds.), *Innovations in Bio-Inspired Computing and Applications. IBICA 2019. Advances in Intelligent Systems and Computing* (Vol. 1180). Springer. doi:10.1007/978-3-030-49339-4_23

Rekha, G., Tyagi, A. K., & Anuradha, N. (2020) Integration of Fog Computing and Internet of Things: An Useful Overview. In: Singh P., Kar A., Singh Y., Kolekar M., Tanwar S. (eds) *Proceedings of ICRIC 2019.* Springer, Cham. 10.1007/978-3-030-29407-6_8

Sai, G. H., Tyagi, A. K., & Sreenath, N. (2023). Biometric Security in Internet of Things Based System against Identity Theft Attacks. *2023 International Conference on Computer Communication and Informatics (ICCCI)*, Coimbatore, India. 10.1109/ICCCI56745.2023.10128186

Sheth, H. S. K., & Tyagi, A. K. (2022). Mobile Cloud Computing: Issues, Applications and Scope in COVID-19. In A. Abraham, N. Gandhi, T. Hanne, T. P. Hong, T. Nogueira Rios, & W. Ding (Eds.), *Intelligent Systems Design and Applications. ISDA 2021. Lecture Notes in Networks and Systems* (Vol. 418). Springer. doi:10.1007/978-3-030-96308-8_55

Srivastava, S. Anshu, Bansal, R., Soni, G., Tyagi, A.K. (2023). Blockchain Enabled Internet of Things: Current Scenario and Open Challenges for Future. In: Abraham, A., Bajaj, A., Gandhi, N., Madureira, A.M., Kahraman, C. (eds) Innovations in Bio-Inspired Computing and Applications. IBICA 2022. Lecture Notes in Networks and Systems. Springer, Cham. doi:10.1007/978-3-031-27499-2_59

Subramanian, B., Nathani, K., & Kumar, S. (2019). IoT Technology, Applications and Challenges: A Contemporary Survey. *Wireless Personal Communications*, *108*(1), 363–388. doi:10.100711277-019-06407-w

Tan, L., & Neng, W. (2010). Future Internet: The Internet of Things. *International Conference on Advanced Computer Theory and Engineering(ICACTE)*, Chengdu, China,.

Tyagi, A. K. (2023). Decentralized everything: Practical use of blockchain technology in future applications. In R. Pandey, S. Goundar, & S. Fatima (eds.), Distributed Computing to Blockchain. Academic Press. doi:10.1016/B978-0-323-96146-2.00010-3

Tyagi, A., Fernandez, T. F., Kumari, K. S., & Tyagi, A. K. (2023). A Survey on Text Processing Using Deep Learning Techniques. In A. Abraham, S. Pllana, G. Casalino, K. Ma, & A. Bajaj (Eds.), *Intelligent Systems Design and Applications. ISDA 2022. Lecture Notes in Networks and Systems* (Vol. 646). Springer. doi:10.1007/978-3-031-27440-4_19

Tyagi, A. K. (2019). Building a Smart and Sustainable Environment using Internet of Things (February 22, 2019). *Proceedings of International Conference on Sustainable Computing in Science, Technology and Management (SUSCOM)*. Amity University Rajasthan, Jaipur.

Tyagi, A. K., & Abraham, A. (2020). Internet of Things: Future Challenging Issues and Possible Research Directions, *International Journal of Computer Information Systems and Industrial Management Applications*.

Tyagi, A. K., Agarwal, K., Goyal, D., & Sreenath, N. (2020). A Review on Security and Privacy Issues in Internet of Things. In H. Sharma, K. Govindan, R. Poonia, S. Kumar, & W. El-Medany (Eds.), *Advances in Computing and Intelligent Systems. Algorithms for Intelligent Systems*. Springer. doi:10.1007/978-981-15-0222-4_46

Tyagi, A. K., Fernandez, T. F., Mishra, S., & Kumari, S. (2021). Intelligent Automation Systems at the Core of Industry 4.0. In A. Abraham, V. Piuri, N. Gandhi, P. Siarry, A. Kaklauskas, & A. Madureira (Eds.), *Intelligent Systems Design and Applications. ISDA 2020. Advances in Intelligent Systems and Computing* (Vol. 1351). Springer. doi:10.1007/978-3-030-71187-0_1

Tyagi, A. K., & Nair, M. M. (2020). Internet of Everything (IoE) and Internet of Things (IoTs): Threat Analyses, Possible Opportunities for Future. *Journal of Information Assurance & Security*, *15*(4).

Tyagi, A. K., Rekha, G., & Sreenath, N. (2020). Beyond the Hype: Internet of Things Concepts, Security and Privacy Concerns. In S. Satapathy, K. Raju, K. Shyamala, D. Krishna, & M. Favorskaya (Eds.), *Advances in Decision Sciences, Image Processing, Security and Computer Vision. ICETE 2019. Learning and Analytics in Intelligent Systems* (Vol. 3). Springer. doi:10.1007/978-3-030-24322-7_50

Tyagi, A. K., & Sreenath, N. (2023). Fog and Edge Computing in Navigation of Intelligent Transportation System. In *Intelligent Transportation Systems: Theory and Practice. Disruptive Technologies and Digital Transformations for Society 5.0*. Springer. doi:10.1007/978-981-19-7622-3_7

Uckelmann, Harrison, & Michahelles. (2011). An Architectural Approach Towards the Future Internet of Things," in Architecting the Internet of Things. Springer-Verlag.

Varsha, R., Nair, S. M., Tyagi, A. K., & Aswathy, S. U. (2021). The Future with Advanced Analytics: A Sequential Analysis of the Disruptive Technology's Scope. In Hybrid Intelligent Systems. HIS 2020. Advances in Intelligent Systems and Computing. Springer. doi:10.1007/978-3-030-73050-5_56

Yaqoob, I., Hashem, I., Abaker, T., Ahmed, A., & Kazmi, H. (2019). Internet of things forensics: Recent advances, taxonomy, requirements, and open challenges. *Future Generation Computer Systems*, *92*, 265–275. doi:10.1016/j.future.2018.09.058

Chapter 3
Blockchain Technology in Cloud Security

Manivannan Karunakaran
https://orcid.org/0000-0002-6080-7581
Jain University (Deemed), India

Kiran Bellam
Prairie View A&M University, USA

J. Benadict Raja
https://orcid.org/0000-0002-5899-8374
PSNA College of Engineering and Technology, India

D. Shanthi
PSNA College of Engineering and Technology, India

ABSTRACT

As cloud computing becomes ubiquitous, the need for robust security measures intensifies. Traditional centralized access control systems in cloud environments pose vulnerabilities such as single points of failure, transparency deficits, and privacy concerns. This chapter explores the integration of blockchain technology as a transformative approach to enhancing cloud security. Blockchain, renowned for its decentralized ledger, immutability, and cryptographic security, offers innovative solutions to these challenges. The chapter discusses the motivation behind adopting decentralized access control, the fundamentals of blockchain, and its role in identity management. Real-world use cases demonstrate the practical application of blockchain in cloud security. Challenges, including scalability and regulatory compliance, are addressed. This chapter provides a comprehensive introduction to decentralized access control in cloud security, emphasizing its potential to revolutionize the field and contribute to the development of secure and resilient cloud systems.

DOI: 10.4018/979-8-3693-2081-5.ch003

1. INTRODUCTION

The intersection of blockchain technology and cloud security represents a significant milestone in the evolution of cybersecurity. As cloud computing becomes increasingly integral to modern business operations, the need for robust security measures has never been more pressing. This chapter explores the integration of blockchain technology as a formidable solution to enhance the security, trustworthiness, and transparency of cloud-based systems (Figure 1). Cloud computing offers undeniable advantages, such as scalability and accessibility, but it also introduces novel challenges. Traditional centralized access control mechanisms, which have been the linchpin of security in cloud environments, possess inherent vulnerabilities. These include single points of failure, lack of transparency, and privacy concerns, which necessitate a reevaluation of access control paradigms. The motivation for this chapter emerges from the imperative to address these vulnerabilities and explore innovative approaches to fortify cloud security. Centralized access control systems, often relying on a central authority or server, are susceptible to breaches and disruptions. Moreover, the obscurity surrounding access control activities hampers effective monitoring and auditing, impeding the detection of security breaches and unauthorized access. This chapter delves into the background and motivations behind the integration of blockchain technology into the realm of cloud security. It examines the limitations of centralized access control models and the specific vulnerabilities they introduce in cloud computing. These vulnerabilities include the risks associated with single points of failure, the opacity of access control activities, and concerns surrounding data privacy.

Figure 1. Benefits of blockchain on cloud

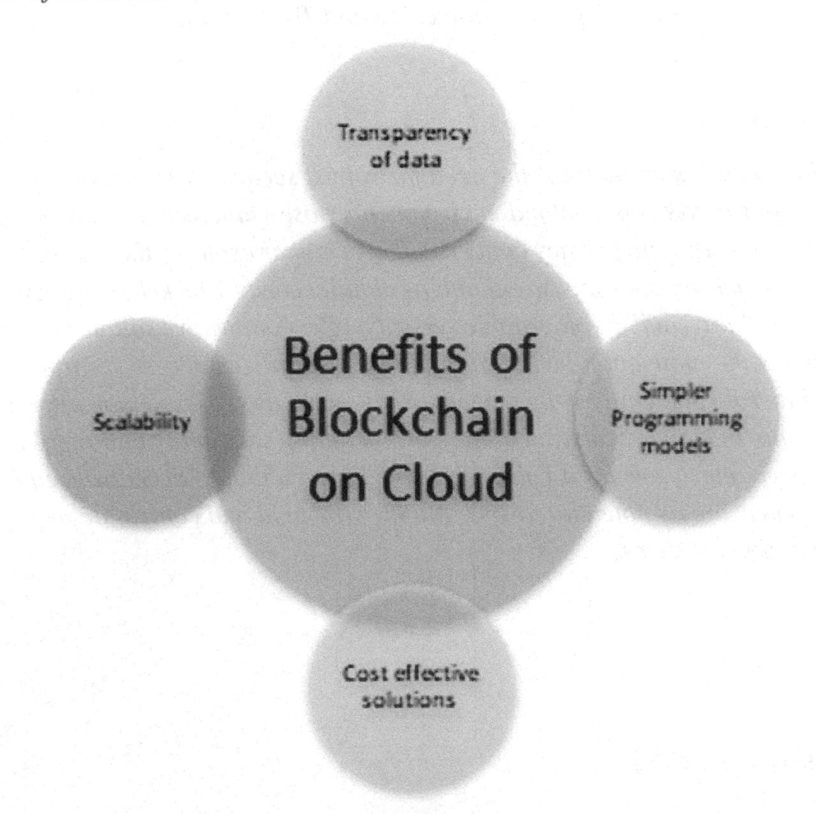

The motivation for adopting decentralized access control mechanisms, underpinned by blockchain, is presented as a solution to these challenges. By distributing access control decisions across a network of nodes and leveraging Blockchain's core attributes (Tyagi, 2021) such as decentralization, transparency, and immutability, and cryptographic security organizations can fortify the integrity and reliability of their cloud-based systems.

1.1. Background and Motivation

The realm of cloud computing has ushered in a new era of technological advancement, revolutionizing the way data is stored, processed, and accessed. As organizations increasingly migrate their operations to cloud-based environments, the importance of robust security measures cannot be overstated. Cloud computing offers unparalleled scalability and efficiency, but it also introduces a host of security challenges that demand innovative solutions. Traditional centralized access control systems have long been the cornerstone of security in cloud environments. These systems, while effective to a degree, are not without their limitations (Tyagi, A. K, 2021). They rely on a single point of authority or control, which, if compromised, can lead to significant security breaches. Furthermore, the opacity of centralized systems can hinder transparency, making it challenging to monitor and audit access control activities effectively. The motivation for this chapter is rooted in the urgent need to address the shortcomings of centralized access control mechanisms and to explore alternative approaches that can bolster cloud security. The vulnerabilities associated with centralized systems, including single points of failure and transparency deficits, necessitate a reevaluation of access control paradigms in cloud computing. The emergence of blockchain technology as a disruptive force in the realm of security and trust presents a compelling solution to these challenges. Originally conceived as the foundation for cryptocurrencies like Bitcoin, blockchain's unique attributes, including decentralization, transparency, immutability, and cryptographic security, make it an ideal candidate for enhancing access control and security in cloud environments.

This chapter delves into the background and motivations driving the integration of blockchain technology into cloud security. It examines the limitations of centralized access control models and the specific vulnerabilities they introduce in the context of cloud computing. These vulnerabilities include the risks associated with single points of failure, the lack of transparency in access control activities, and concerns surrounding data privacy. The motivation for adopting decentralized access control mechanisms, empowered by blockchain, is presented as a solution to these challenges. By distributing access control decisions across a distributed network and harnessing blockchain's inherent features, organizations can strengthen the integrity and reliability of their cloud-based systems. Subsequent sections of this chapter will explore the fundamentals of blockchain technology, its role in decentralized identity management, practical use cases, and the challenges and opportunities that arise when blockchain is seamlessly integrated into cloud security frameworks. This chapter aims to provide readers with a comprehensive understanding of the transformative potential of blockchain in addressing the complex security issues that permeate modern cloud computing environments.

1.2. Research Objectives and Scope

The research objectives of this chapter encompass a comprehensive exploration of the integration of blockchain technology into cloud security. These objectives guide the scope of our investigation and provide a roadmap for addressing key questions and challenges in this domain. The primary objective is to elucidate the fundamental principles of blockchain technology. This includes an exploration of its decentralized architecture, consensus mechanisms, cryptographic foundations, and smart contract capabilities. Understanding these fundamentals is essential for appreciating how blockchain can transform access control in cloud security (Deshmukh et al., 2022). This chapter aims to thoroughly investigate the limitations and vulnerabilities of centralized access control models within cloud security. We will delve into the risks associated with single points of failure, lack of transparency, and data privacy concerns. This analysis sets the stage for exploring blockchain-based solutions. A pivotal research objective is to explore how blockchain technology facilitates decentralized identity management. We will investigate self-sovereign identity concepts and their potential to empower individuals to control their digital identities while ensuring privacy preservation.

This chapter seeks to showcase real-world use cases and examples where blockchain has been successfully integrated into cloud security. These cases will illustrate the practical application of blockchain in addressing access control challenges, enhancing security, transparency, and accountability. An essential research objective is to discuss the challenges and opportunities associated with adopting blockchain-based access control in cloud environments. This includes addressing scalability concerns, performance considerations, interoperability challenges, and regulatory compliance issues. This chapter aims to identify emerging trends and future research directions in the field of blockchain technology in cloud security. By recognizing evolving technologies and methodologies, we can anticipate how this domain will continue to evolve. Ultimately, the overarching research objective is to provide readers with a comprehensive understanding of the integration of blockchain technology into cloud security. This includes offering insights into the transformative potential of blockchain, its practical implications, and its capacity to address complex security issues in cloud computing environments. The scope of this chapter encompasses an in-depth examination of these research objectives, ensuring a thorough exploration of the integration of blockchain technology into cloud security. By addressing these objectives, we aim to contribute to the body of knowledge surrounding blockchain's impact on access control mechanisms in cloud environments.

1.3. Overview of the Chapter Structure

This chapter is structured to comprehensively explore the integration of blockchain technology into cloud security. It begins with an introductory section that highlights the importance and relevance of blockchain in cloud security, followed by a segment that delves into the background and motivations driving this integration. The research objectives and scope are then outlined, providing readers with a roadmap for the chapter's exploration. The foundation is established in the "Blockchain Fundamentals" section, which explains key blockchain concepts. The chapter proceeds to analyze the limitations of centralized access control in cloud security. It explores blockchain's role in decentralized identity management and presents practical use cases illustrating its application. The challenges and opportunities associated with blockchain in cloud security are discussed, and emerging trends are identified. Finally, the chapter concludes by summarizing key insights, reinforcing blockchain's transformative potential in cloud security. This structured approach ensures a comprehensive understanding, from fundamentals to practical implementation and future directions, in the dynamic field of blockchain and cloud security.

1.4 Significance and Contribution

This chapter aims to contribute to the existing body of knowledge by highlighting the potential of blockchain technology in addressing cloud security challenges. By providing a comprehensive overview of the applications, benefits, and limitations, this chapter seeks to empower researchers, practitioners, and policymakers to make informed decisions regarding the adoption and implementation of blockchain technology in cloud security.

The book chapter on "Blockchain Technology in Cloud Security" holds significant significance and makes valuable contributions to the field. Its originality lies in the exploration of the intersection between blockchain technology and cloud security, shedding light on the potential applications, benefits, challenges, and future prospects of integrating blockchain into cloud computing environments.

1. **Bridging the Gap:** This chapter bridges the gap between two rapidly evolving domains, blockchain technology, and cloud security. By bringing these fields together, it offers insights into how blockchain can address the existing security concerns and vulnerabilities in cloud computing, opening up new avenues for secure and trustworthy cloud-based systems.
2. **Comprehensive Analysis:** The chapter provides a comprehensive analysis of various aspects related to the use of blockchain in cloud security. It examines fundamental concepts of blockchain technology, security challenges in cloud computing, and the potential solutions that blockchain can offer. By encompassing multiple dimensions, it provides readers with a holistic understanding of the subject matter.
3. **Practical Applications:** The chapter goes beyond theoretical discussions and delves into practical applications of blockchain technology in cloud security. It explores how blockchain can enhance data integrity, access control, transaction security, and privacy in the cloud. Through real-world case studies and examples, it illustrates the practicality and potential impact of implementing blockchain solutions.
4. **Addressing Challenges:** The chapter addresses the challenges and considerations associated with integrating blockchain into cloud security. It highlights issues of scalability, performance, interoperability, and regulatory compliance, providing insights into the complexities involved in adopting blockchain in cloud computing environments. By acknowledging these challenges, it guides researchers, practitioners, and policymakers in making informed decisions.
5. **Future Research Directions:** The chapter identifies future research directions and emerging trends in the field. It explores the potential of decentralized identifiers, zero-knowledge proofs, and other emerging technologies in enhancing cloud security. By highlighting these research areas, it stimulates further exploration and encourages researchers to contribute to the ongoing advancements in blockchain technology and cloud security.
6. **Practical Guidance:** The chapter serves as a practical guide for implementing blockchain solutions in cloud security. It offers recommendations, best practices, and considerations for integrating blockchain into existing cloud infrastructures. By providing practical guidance, it assists organizations and professionals in understanding the implications, benefits, and challenges involved in adopting blockchain technology for enhanced cloud security.

1.5 Fundamentals of Blockchain Technology

1.5.1. Definition and Key Concepts of Blockchain

Blockchain technology, often described as a distributed ledger technology, is the cornerstone of innovative solutions in various domains, including cloud security. At its core, a blockchain is a decentralized and immutable ledger that records transactions or data across a network of computers, referred to as nodes. The fundamental concepts of blockchain encompass: Blockchain operates as a decentralized system, meaning it doesn't rely on a central authority or intermediary. Instead, it relies on a network of nodes, each holding a copy of the blockchain (Li et al., 2020). This decentralization contributes to increased security and resilience, as there's no single point of control or failure. The blockchain is often referred to as a distributed ledger because it maintains an identical copy of the ledger across all participating nodes. This ledger records transactions or data in a chronological order, and once a piece of information is added, it becomes part of an immutable chain. Immutability ensures that historical data cannot be altered, providing a tamper-resistant record. To add new transactions to the blockchain, a consensus mechanism is employed. Common consensus algorithms include Proof of Work (PoW) and Proof of Stake (PoS). These mechanisms validate and agree upon the legitimacy of transactions, ensuring that only valid data is added to the blockchain. Cryptography plays a pivotal role in blockchain technology. It secures transactions and data through encryption, making it extremely difficult for unauthorized parties to access or modify information on the blockchain. Cryptographic keys are used to sign and verify transactions, enhancing security and privacy. Smart contracts are self-executing contracts with predefined rules and conditions. They automate and enforce agreements without the need for intermediaries. Smart contracts can trigger actions when specific conditions are met, providing a transparent and efficient way to execute agreements. One of the defining features of blockchain is its transparency. All transactions recorded on the blockchain are visible to all participants in the network. Once a transaction is added, it cannot be altered or deleted without consensus from the network. This immutability fosters trust and accountability. Blockchain's can be categorized as public or private. Public blockchain, like Bitcoin and Ethereum, are open to anyone and are permission less.

1.5.2 Distributed Ledger and Consensus Mechanisms

Two integral components of blockchain technology are the distributed ledger and consensus mechanisms. These elements work in harmony to ensure the integrity, transparency, and security of blockchain networks: A distributed ledger is the foundation of a blockchain. It refers to the decentralized and synchronized record of transactions or data across all nodes in the network. Each node maintains an identical copy of the ledger, ensuring that all participants have access to the same information. This feature is vital for transparency and redundancy. The distributed ledger is organized into blocks, each containing a set of transactions or data entries. These blocks are linked in chronological order, forming a chain, hence the term "blockchain." Once data is added to a block and the block is validated, it is cryptographically linked to the previous block, creating an immutable chain. This immutability means that once data is recorded, it cannot be altered or deleted without consensus from the network. This characteristic is central to Blockchain's security and tamper-resistance. Consensus mechanisms are protocols or algorithms that ensure that all participants in a blockchain network agree on the validity of transactions and the order in which they are added to the ledger. They are fundamental for preventing double-spending and maintaining the integrity of the blockchain. Common consensus mechanisms include PoW requires participants, often referred to as miners, to solve complex mathematical puzzles to validate transactions and add them to the blockchain. This process is resource-intensive and time-consuming, making it secure but energy-consuming. PoS, in contrast, doesn't rely on resource-intensive computations. Instead, participants, often called validators, are chosen to validate transactions based on the amount of cryptocurrency they hold and are willing to "stake" as collateral. PoS is energy-efficient compared to PoW (Ma et al., 2021). Delegated Proof of Stake (DPoS) is a variation of PoS where a limited number of trusted nodes, known as delegates, are chosen to validate transactions. DPoS aims to improve scalability and transaction speed. Proof of Authority (PoA) relies on trusted nodes, often operated by known entities or organizations. These nodes are authorized to validate transactions, making PoA highly efficient but less decentralized. Proof of Space and Time (PoST) is a consensus mechanism that leverages storage space and time as the basis for validation. Participants allocate storage space to validate transactions, ensuring security while being resource-efficient. The choice of consensus mechanism depends on factors such as the blockchain's use case, desired level of decentralization, energy efficiency, and security requirements. Understanding these mechanisms is crucial for grasping how transactions are validated and added to the blockchain, maintaining its trustworthiness and security.

1.5.3 Cryptographic Security in Blockchain

Cryptographic security is one of the pillars of blockchain technology, underpinning its capacity to provide robust protection for data and transactions. This section delves into the essential aspects of cryptographic security within blockchain: Digital signatures play a fundamental role in blockchain security. When a user initiates a transaction, their digital signature is generated using their private key. This signature serves as proof of the transaction's authenticity and the user's identity. It ensures that only the owner of the private key can initiate transactions, preventing unauthorized access (Yang, Cai, & Liu, 2021). Cryptographic hash functions are vital components of blockchain. These functions take an input (data) and produce a fixed length string of characters, which is a unique representation of the input data. Hashes are used to verify the integrity of data on the blockchain. Even a minor change in the input data results in a vastly different hash, making tampering easily detectable. Blockchain users have a pair of cryptographic keys: a public key and a private key. The public key is used to create a digital signature and to verify the authenticity of digital signatures. The private key, on the other hand, must be kept secret and is used to generate digital signatures. Only the possessor of the private key can create valid digital signatures. Blockchain employs various encryption techniques to protect data both at rest and during transmission. Data stored on the blockchain is typically encrypted, ensuring that even if a node is compromised, the data remains confidential (Dargahi et al., 2021).

1.5.4. Smart Contracts and Their Role in Blockchain

Smart contracts are a pivotal component of blockchain technology, revolutionizing how agreements are executed and automated. In this section, we explore the concept of smart contracts and their indispensable role within blockchain ecosystems: Smart contracts are self-executing contracts with predefined rules and conditions encoded directly into code. These contracts automatically execute, enforce, or facilitate agreements when specific conditions or triggers are met (Liu et al., 2021). They eliminate the need for intermediaries or trusted third parties, making processes more efficient and transparent. Smart contracts embody the principle of "code is law." This means that the terms and conditions of an agreement are written in code, and the code's execution is binding. As long as the predetermined conditions are met, the contract self-executes without the need for human intervention.

Smart contracts operate within blockchain networks, leveraging the blockchain's decentralization and immutability to ensure trust and security. They are often associated with public blockchains like Ethereum, where they are executed on the Ethereum Virtual Machine (EVM). Smart contracts automate various transactions and processes. For example, they can automate payment transfers when predefined conditions, such as delivery of goods or completion of a service, are met. This automation eliminates delays and reduces the risk of disputes. Smart contracts contribute to transparency as all contract terms and transactions are recorded on the blockchain and are visible to all network participants. This transparency builds trust among parties, as they can independently verify the contract's execution. Smart contracts align with the decentralized nature of blockchain technology. They operate across a network of nodes, ensuring that there is no single point of control or failure. This decentralization enhances security and resilience. Smart contracts have a wide range of use cases, including supply chain management, financial services (e.g., automated lending and borrowing), insurance, voting systems, and more. They are particularly valuable in scenarios where trust and automation are critical. Despite their numerous advantages, smart contracts are not without challenges (Yunis et al., 2022). Code vulnerabilities can lead to security breaches, and disputes related to contract execution can be complex to resolve.

1.6 Security Challenges in Cloud Computing

Cloud computing has transformed the way businesses and individuals manage their digital resources, offering unparalleled scalability, flexibility, and cost-efficiency (Fig 1.2). However, this digital revolution has brought about a host of security challenges that organizations must grapple with to ensure the confidentiality, integrity, and availability of their data and services. In this section, we delve into the intricate landscape of security challenges in cloud computing, examining the multifaceted issues that demand attention and innovative solutions. One of the foremost concerns in cloud security is data privacy. Storing sensitive information, such as customer records, financial data, or intellectual property, in the cloud introduces the risk of unauthorized access or data breaches. The shared nature of cloud resources can lead to data exposure if proper encryption and access controls are not implemented (Rehman et al., 2022). Ensuring data availability is crucial, but cloud outages and data loss incidents can disrupt operations and result in significant financial losses. While cloud service providers (CSPs) typically have robust backup and disaster recovery mechanisms, organizations must still plan for contingencies to mitigate such risks. IAM is a central aspect of cloud security, and managing user access and permissions across a dynamic cloud environment can be challenging. Misconfigured IAM settings or weak authentication can lead to unauthorized access, data breaches, or service disruptions. Organizations operating in highly regulated industries, such as healthcare or finance, face additional compliance burdens when moving to the cloud. Navigating the complex web of regulations, such as HIPAA or GDPR, and ensuring compliance within a cloud infrastructure is a demanding task. Insider threats, whether intentional or accidental, pose a significant risk in the cloud (Sheth, 2022). Employees or users with legitimate access can misuse their privileges, intentionally or unintentionally causing data leaks or security breaches. Organizations may assume that cloud service providers handle all security aspects, leading to a misconception known as the "shared responsibility model." In reality, while CSPs secure the infrastructure, organizations must implement security controls at the application and data levels. Data in transit between a user and the cloud or between cloud services can be intercepted if not adequately protected. Secure data transfer protocols and encryption mechanisms are vital to mitigate this risk (Raj et al., 2022).

Figure 2. Cloud computing security challenges

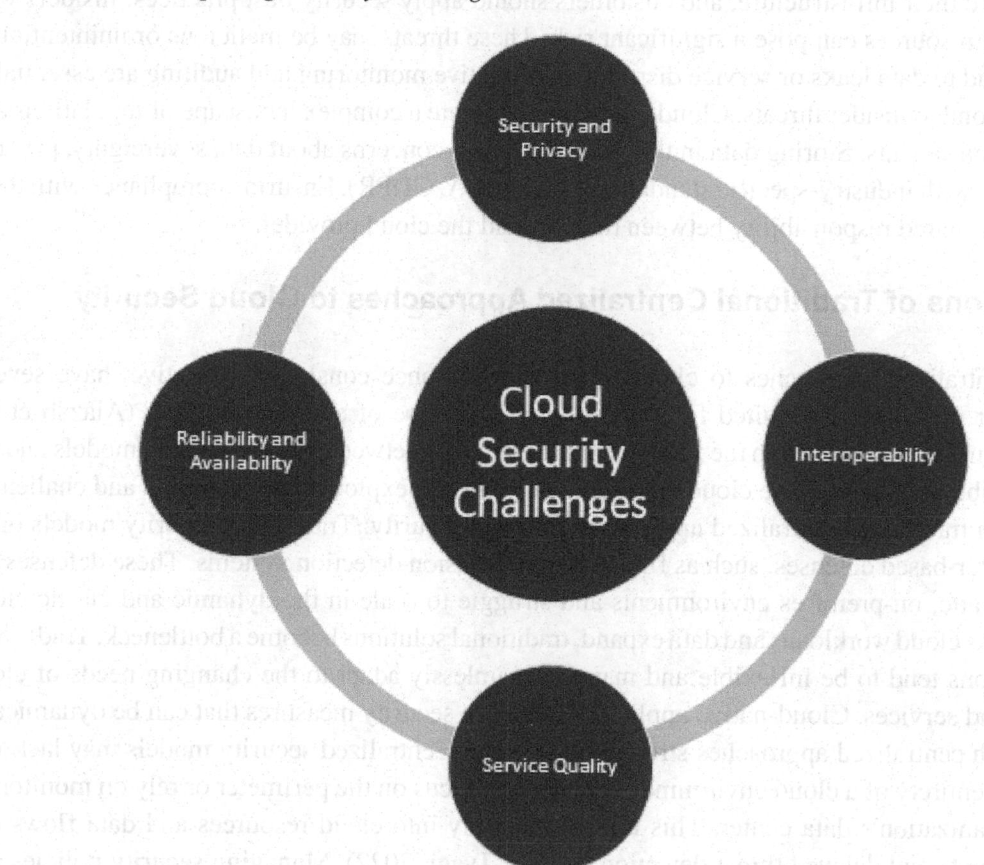

1.7. Common Security Concerns and Vulnerabilities in the Cloud

While cloud computing offers numerous benefits, it also introduces a unique set of security concerns and vulnerabilities that organizations must address to safeguard their data and operations. Understanding these potential risks is crucial for developing robust cloud security strategies. Below, we delve into some of the common security concerns and vulnerabilities in the cloud environment: Data breaches are a paramount concern in the cloud. Unauthorized access to sensitive data, such as customer records or intellectual property, can have severe consequences. Breaches can occur due to weak access controls, misconfigured security settings, or insider threats. Inadequate management of user identities and access permissions can lead to unauthorized access to cloud resources (Al-Riyami et al., 2022). Weak or stolen credentials, misconfigured IAM policies, and unmonitored privileged accounts are common vectors for attacks. Cloud services often expose interfaces and APIs for interaction with applications and data. If these interfaces are not securely designed and maintained, they can become attack vectors. Vulnerabilities in APIs can allow attackers to access data or execute unauthorized operations. Data loss can result from accidental deletion, data corruption, or inadequate backup and recovery mechanisms. It is critical to have data protection strategies in place, including regular backups and disaster recovery plans. Cloud providers use shared infrastructure to serve multiple customers. Vulnerabilities in the underlying hardware, hypervisors, or software can potentially affect multiple clients. Providers must diligently patch and secure their infrastructure, and customers should apply security best practices. Insiders with access to cloud resources can pose a significant risk. These threats may be malicious or unintentional, but they can lead to data leaks or service disruptions. Effective monitoring and auditing are essential to detect and respond to insider threats. Cloud users must navigate a complex landscape of regulations and compliance requirements. Storing data in the cloud may raise concerns about data sovereignty, privacy, and compliance with industry-specific standards (e.g., HIPAA, GDPR). Ensuring compliance with these regulations is a shared responsibility between the user and the cloud provider.

1.8. Limitations of Traditional Centralized Approaches to Cloud Security

Traditional centralized approaches to cloud security, while once considered effective, have several limitations that make them ill-suited for the evolving landscape of cloud computing (Alazab et al., 2022). These limitations stem from the fundamental differences between legacy security models and the dynamic, distributed nature of the cloud environment. Here, we explore the constraints and challenges associated with traditional centralized approaches to cloud security: Traditional security models often rely on perimeter-based defenses, such as firewalls and intrusion detection systems. These defenses are designed for static, on-premises environments and struggle to scale in the dynamic and elastic cloud environment. As cloud workloads and data expand, traditional solutions become a bottleneck. Traditional security solutions tend to be inflexible and may not seamlessly adapt to the changing needs of cloud applications and services. Cloud-native applications require security measures that can be dynamically adjusted, which centralized approaches struggle to provide. Centralized security models may lack visibility into the entirety of a cloud environment. They often focus on the perimeter or rely on monitoring within the organization's data center. This lack of visibility into cloud resources and data flows can lead to blind spots and delayed threat detection.(Nair & Tyagi, 2022). Managing security policies and configurations across a distributed cloud environment can be complex and error-prone when using traditional centralized tools. Ensuring consistent security configurations across different cloud services and regions can be challenging. Traditional security tools are designed for traditional IT environments and may not provide adequate protection for cloud-native threats. Attack vectors specific to the cloud, such as misconfigured cloud services, may not be effectively addressed. Meeting regulatory compliance requirements in the cloud can be challenging with traditional centralized security models. Ensuring data sovereignty and compliance with industry-specific regulations (e.g., GDPR, HIPAA) may require new, cloud-native approaches. Centralized security solutions can introduce resource overhead, affecting the performance of cloud applications and services.

1.9 How Blockchain Ensures Data Integrity in Cloud Environments

Ensuring data integrity in cloud environments is a critical concern for organizations as they entrust their valuable data to third-party cloud service providers. Blockchain technology offers an innovative and highly effective solution to this challenge. In this section, we delve into how blockchain ensures data integrity in cloud environments and the underlying mechanisms that make it a robust choice. At the core of Blockchain's data integrity assurance is cryptographic hashing. When data is added to a blockchain, it is first transformed into a fixed-size string of characters known as a hash. This hash acts as a unique fingerprint for the data. Even the smallest change in the data, whether accidental or malicious, results in a significantly different hash. Unlike traditional centralized systems, blockchain operates on a decentralized network of nodes. Each node stores a copy of the entire blockchain, which contains a historical record of all transactions or data entries. Decentralization eliminates the reliance on a single central authority, reducing the risk of a single point of failure. Blockchain ensures data integrity through consensus mechanisms that validate and agree upon the legitimacy of transactions or data entries. Two common consensus mechanisms are Proof of Work (PoW) and Proof of Stake (PoS). These mechanisms require network participants (nodes) to expend computational resources or stake tokens to validate transactions. Once validated, the transaction is added to the blockchain.

Blockchain is designed to be transparent. All transactions or data entries are visible to authorized parties on the network. This transparency fosters trust and allows for independent auditing of data integrity. Users can verify the integrity of data on the blockchain by comparing the stored hash with a newly generated hash of the data. To further enhance data security, blockchain networks often incorporate encryption mechanisms. Data stored on the blockchain can be encrypted to ensure confidentiality. Additionally, smart contracts, self-executing agreements with predefined rules, can enforce access controls and automate data integrity checks. Blockchain can be used to track and verify the integrity of goods as they move through a supply chain, ensuring that product data remains tamper-proof. Electronic health records and medical data can be securely stored on a blockchain, allowing for tamper-resistant audit trails and data sharing. Artists and creators can timestamp their work on a blockchain, providing evidence of ownership and protecting against copyright infringement. Blockchain can help organizations demonstrate compliance with data integrity requirements, such as GDPR or HIPAA, by providing an immutable record of data handling.

1.10 Decentralized Access Control and Authentication

Decentralized access control and authentication are vital components in ensuring the security and privacy of data and resources in cloud environments. Traditional centralized approaches have limitations in the dynamic and distributed nature of the cloud. In this section, we explore the concept of decentralized access control, its significance, and how blockchain technology can be leveraged to enhance authentication and access control in cloud security. Centralized access control relies on a single authority or system to manage user permissions and authenticate access to resources. In the cloud, this model faces challenges, such as scalability issues, single points of failure, and difficulties in adapting to the dynamic nature of cloud services and data. Decentralized access control distributes the authority and responsibility for managing access permissions across multiple entities or nodes within a network.

Each entity may have a say in granting or denying access, reducing reliance on a single central authority. Blockchain's decentralized nature aligns well with the principles of decentralized access control. Blockchain can serve as a distributed ledger for access control policies, user permissions, and authentication records. Blockchain technology, with its fundamental characteristics of decentralization, immutability, transparency, and cryptographic security, serves as a robust foundation for enabling secure and transparent transactions. In this 1000-word explanation, we'll delve into the mechanics of how blockchain achieves these goals and the real-world implications of this revolutionary technology.

Figure 3. Decentralized access control and authentication

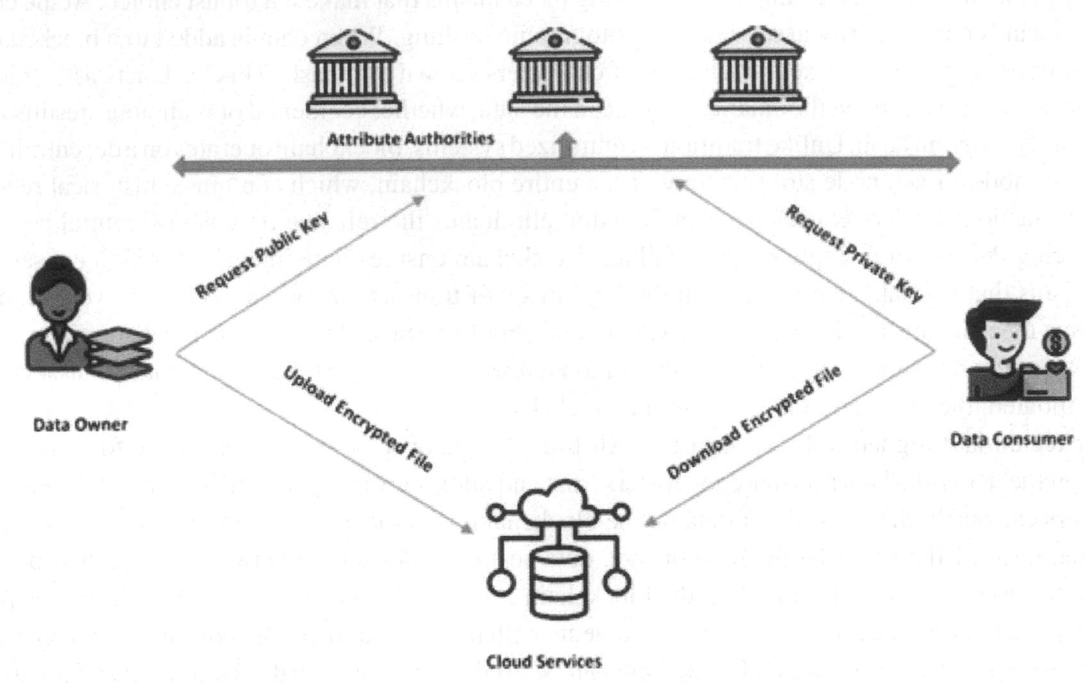

1.11 Decentralization

At the core of Blockchain's ability to ensure secure and transparent transactions is its decentralized nature. Unlike traditional centralized systems, where a single entity or authority has control, blockchain operates on a network of distributed nodes. Each node in the network maintains an identical copy of the ledger, which contains all transactions. This decentralization offers several key advantages:

1. Resilience to Single Points of Failure: In a centralized system, if the central authority or server fails, the entire system can become inaccessible. In contrast, Blockchain's decentralization means that even if some nodes fail, the network continues to operate, ensuring uninterrupted transactions.
2. Security against Attacks: Centralized systems are attractive targets for malicious actors because compromising a single point of control can grant them significant power. In a decentralized blockchain network, the attacker would need to compromise a majority of the network's nodes, a task that becomes increasingly difficult as the network grows.
3. Eliminating the Need for Intermediaries: Traditional transactions often require intermediaries such as banks or payment processors to validate and record transactions. Blockchain's decentralized consensus mechanism eliminates the need for these intermediaries, reducing costs and streamlining the transaction process.

1.11.1 Immutability

Blockchain's immutability is another cornerstone of its ability to enable secure transactions. Once a transaction is recorded on the blockchain, it becomes nearly impossible to alter or delete. Here's how it works:

1. Cryptographic Hashing: Transactions are grouped into blocks, and each block contains a cryptographic hash of the previous block. This creates a chain of blocks where altering any transaction in a block would require changing the data in all subsequent blocks, a computationally infeasible task.
2. Consensus Mechanisms: Blockchain networks rely on consensus mechanisms like Proof of Work (PoW) or Proof of Stake (PoS) to validate transactions and add them to the ledger. Achieving consensus among network nodes requires significant computational effort or the commitment of a substantial stake, making it highly resistant to fraudulent changes.
3. Time-Stamping: Every transaction is timestamped, and transactions within a block are typically ordered chronologically. This ensures a historical record of transactions that is virtually impossible to manipulate retroactively.

1.11.2 Transparency

Transparency is a defining feature of blockchain technology. All transactions recorded on the blockchain are visible to anyone with access to the network. Here's how transparency is achieved:

1. Public Ledgers: In public blockchains like Bitcoin and Ethereum, the ledger is entirely open to inspection by anyone. Anyone can view the complete transaction history, providing unprecedented transparency.
2. Pseudonymity: While transactions are transparent, participants are represented by cryptographic addresses, preserving a degree of privacy. However, this pseudonymity is only a layer of protection, as all transactions associated with an address are visible.
3. Auditability: The transparency of blockchain enables efficient auditing of transactions and assets. This is particularly valuable in industries like finance, supply chain, and healthcare, where accountability and trust are critical.

1.11.3 Cryptographic Security

Blockchain relies on advanced cryptographic techniques to secure transactions and data. Cryptography plays a vital role in maintaining the integrity and confidentiality of blockchain-based transactions:

1. Digital Signatures: Participants in a blockchain network use digital signatures to verify their identity and authorize transactions. These signatures ensure that only the rightful owner of a private key can initiate a transaction.
2. Hash Functions: Cryptographic hash functions are used to generate fixed-size hashes for transaction data. Even a small change in the input data results in a significantly different hash, making it easy to detect any tampering.
3. Encryption: In certain cases, blockchain systems can employ encryption to secure data both at rest and in transit. This ensures that sensitive information remains confidential, further enhancing security.

1.12. How Blockchain Enables Secure and Transparent Transactions

Blockchain technology's ability to enable secure and transparent transactions is revolutionizing various industries. Its decentralization, immutability, transparency, and cryptographic security offer a robust solution to the challenges of traditional centralized systems. As blockchain continues to evolve and find new applications, it has the potential to transform the way we conduct business, manage data, and secure our digital interactions, ushering in a new era of trust and transparency in the digital age. Privacy and confidentiality enhancements are critical aspects of information security, especially in our increasingly digital and interconnected world. As technology advances and data becomes more valuable, individuals and organizations must take proactive measures to safeguard sensitive information.

Encrypting data in transit ensures that information sent over networks, such as the internet, is protected from eavesdropping. Secure Socket Layer (SSL) and Transport Layer Security (TLS) are encryption protocols commonly used to secure web traffic. This ensures that sensitive information, such as login credentials or financial transactions, remains confidential during transmission. VPNs provide an additional layer of privacy by encrypting internet connections. When you connect to a VPN, your data is routed through a secure server, hiding your IP address and encrypting your online activities. This technology is particularly valuable for maintaining privacy in public Wi-Fi networks and for accessing geo-restricted content. Secure messaging and email encryption tools ensure that messages and emails can only be read by intended recipients. End-to-end encryption is a key feature, where the content is encrypted on the sender's device and decrypted only on the recipient's device. This prevents service providers, hackers, or government agencies from accessing the contents of the communication. Blockchain technology, known for its immutability and transparency, offers enhanced privacy and confidentiality. While transactions are visible on the blockchain, personal information can be kept private through the use of cryptographic keys. Moreover, blockchain can be employed for secure identity management, enabling individuals to control access to their personal data securely. MFA adds an extra layer of security to authentication processes, enhancing the confidentiality of user accounts. It typically involves something the user knows (e.g., a password) and something the user has (e.g., a smartphone). Even if a password is compromised, the additional authentication factor adds a significant barrier to unauthorized access.

1.13. Blockchain-Based Techniques for Enhancing Privacy in the Cloud

Blockchain-based techniques offer innovative solutions for enhancing privacy in the cloud. As organizations increasingly rely on cloud services to store, process, and share data, concerns about data privacy and security have become paramount. In this 1000-word explanation, we'll explore how blockchain technology can be leveraged to address these concerns and provide robust privacy enhancements in the cloud. Blockchain technology can revolutionize identity management by offering individuals and organizations control over their digital identities while maintaining privacy. Traditional identity management systems often involve sharing personal data with various service providers, increasing the risk of data breaches and identity theft. Blockchain-based decentralized identity solutions, often referred to as self-sovereign identity, enable users to manage their identities securely without relying on a central authority.

Users can create and manage their digital identities on a blockchain. These identities are linked to cryptographic keys, ensuring that only the rightful owner has control. When interacting with online services, users can selectively share identity attributes without disclosing their entire identity. This minimizes the amount of personal information exposed, enhancing privacy. Confidential transactions leverage Blockchain's cryptographic capabilities to protect the privacy of transaction details, including sender, receiver, and transaction amount. While traditional blockchain like Bitcoin are transparent and show transaction details on the ledger, confidential transactions obscure this information, making it visible only to the involved parties. Confidential transactions employ techniques like zero-knowledge proofs to verify the validity of a transaction without revealing its details. This ensures that sensitive financial information remains confidential while still being secured by the Blockchain's immutability. Smart contracts, which are self-executing agreements with predefined conditions, are integral to many blockchain applications. However, the transparent nature of smart contracts on public blockchain like Ethereum can pose privacy challenges. Private smart contracts, built on platforms like hyper ledger Fabric or Corda, address this concern by enabling confidential transactions and contract logic. Private smart contracts execute on a permissioned blockchain network where participants are known and trusted. Transaction data and contract details are encrypted, ensuring that only relevant parties have access. This is particularly valuable for industries like finance and healthcare, where privacy and compliance are critical. Blockchain-based systems can facilitate secure data sharing and collaboration among multiple parties while ensuring data privacy. Whether it's in supply chain management, research collaboration, or financial transactions, blockchain allows for controlled access and auditing without compromising data confidentiality.

Table 1. Blockchain-based techniques for enhancing privacy in the cloud

Technique	Privacy Benefits
Zero-Knowledge Proofs (ZKPs)	Enhanced data privacy confidentiality, and anonymity.
Confidential Smart Contracts	Secure execution of confidential agreements and transactions.
Privacy-Focused Blockchain	Enhanced data privacy anonymity, and confidentiality.
Homomorphic Encryption	Secure data processing without exposing data contents.

Blockchain's transparency can be leveraged to enhance privacy auditing. Organizations can provide proof of compliance with data protection regulations like GDPR by using blockchain to demonstrate that they are handling data responsibly.

1.14. Zero-knowledge proofs and decentralized storage solutions

Zero-knowledge proofs (ZKPs) and decentralized storage solutions are two technological innovations at the forefront of addressing critical issues related to privacy, security, and data management in our digital age. In this comprehensive exploration, we will delve into the intricacies of these two concepts and their profound implications for various domains. Zero-knowledge proofs are a cryptographic marvel that enables one party to prove knowledge of a specific piece of information to another party without revealing the actual information itself. The concept was introduced in the 1980s, and its applications have since grown exponentially, reshaping our understanding of privacy and data protection. At the heart of ZKPs is a complex cryptographic dance between a prover and a verifier. The prover seeks to convince the verifier that they possess certain knowledge without disclosing the knowledge itself. Let's explore some of the key aspects and applications of Zero-Knowledge Proofs:

1. **Password Authentication: Revolutionizing Login Security:** Traditional password-based authentication has long been plagued by security vulnerabilities, with passwords often falling into the wrong hands through breaches or eavesdropping. ZKPs offer a transformative solution by enabling users to prove knowledge of their password without transmitting the password itself.

How it works: During authentication, the prover can use a ZKP to demonstrate knowledge of their password without disclosing the password itself. The verifier can confirm the authentication without ever seeing the actual password, dramatically reducing the risk of interception.

2. **Privacy-Preserving KYC/AML Compliance:** Regulating without Compromising Privacy

Financial institutions are obligated to adhere to Know Your Customer (KYC) and Anti-Money Laundering (AML) regulations to combat fraud and illicit activities. However, these regulations often necessitate the sharing of sensitive personal information. ZKPs offer a groundbreaking solution by allowing individuals to prove their compliance with these regulations without revealing their personal data.

How it works: Users can use ZKPs to prove that they meet the necessary KYC/AML requirements (e.g., age, identity) without disclosing their actual personal data. This preserves their privacy while ensuring regulatory compliance.

3. **Decentralized Identity Verification:** Empowering Individuals Traditional identity verification processes often involve sharing vast amounts of personal information, eroding privacy. Decentralized identity solutions, powered by ZKPs, empower individuals to manage their digital identities securely and privately.

How it works: Users can create and manage their digital identities on a blockchain, ensuring they retain control. When interacting with online services, users can selectively share identity attributes without disclosing their entire identity, minimizing the exposure of sensitive information.

4. **Secure Voting Systems:** Ensuring secure and verifiable electronic voting has been a longstanding challenge. ZKPs provide a robust foundation for building trustworthy voting systems, allowing voters to prove that their votes were counted without revealing their individual choices.

How it works: Voters can generate proofs that their votes were correctly included in the final tally without disclosing the content of their votes. This fosters both privacy and transparency in elections.

5. **Data Privacy in Healthcare:** The healthcare sector faces a delicate balance between data sharing for research and protecting patient privacy. ZKPs offer a unique solution by allowing medical data to be analyzed without exposing the patient's complete medical history.

How it works: Medical records can be encrypted and shared using ZKPs. Researchers can perform analyses without directly accessing sensitive patient data, preserving privacy and security.

1.15. Decentralized Storage Solutions: Empowering Data Ownership and Security

Decentralized storage solutions represent a paradigm shift in how data is stored, accessed, and controlled. These solutions, often built on blockchain technology, distribute data across a network of nodes, eliminating the need for centralized servers and data centers. This approach offers numerous advantages in terms of data ownership, security, and resilience. Decentralized storage solutions empower individuals and organizations to take ownership and full control of their data. Unlike traditional cloud providers that may have access to user data, decentralized storage platforms ensure that users retain complete control over their data. Users encrypt their data before storing it across the decentralized network. They hold the encryption keys, ensuring that only they can access and decrypt their data. This redefines data ownership and control. Decentralized storage networks are inherently resilient to failures. Since data is distributed across a network of nodes, there is no single point of failure. Even if some nodes become unavailable, the data remains accessible. Redundancy mechanisms ensure that multiple copies of data are stored across nodes. If one node becomes unavailable, the network can retrieve the data from other nodes, ensuring continuous availability. Security is a paramount concern in data storage. Decentralized storage solutions incorporate advanced cryptographic techniques to secure data. This includes encryption, hashing, and access control mechanisms that protect data from unauthorized access and tampering. Data is encrypted before being distributed across the network. Encryption keys are managed by the data owner, ensuring that only authorized parties can access and decrypt the data. Decentralized storage enables secure data sharing and collaboration without relying on centralized platforms. Users can grant specific permissions for data access, and multiple parties can collaborate on shared data while maintaining control and security. Data owners can define access permissions and share encrypted data with collaborators. Collaborators can access and work on the data without exposing it to the storage network or intermediaries. Data stored on a blockchain-based decentralized storage network benefits from the Blockchain's immutability.

1.16 Performance Considerations in Blockchain-Based Cloud Security

Performance in blockchain-based cloud security extends beyond scalability and encompasses factors such as response time, efficiency, and overall system speed. Achieving optimal performance is crucial for meeting the stringent demands of cloud security applications (Table 1.1). Here are key performance considerations:

1. Transaction Confirmation Time: The time it takes for a transaction to be confirmed on the blockchain can impact the responsiveness of cloud security applications. Lengthy confirmation times can be detrimental in scenarios requiring rapid threat detection or access control.
    - Performance Enhancements: Solutions like faster consensus mechanisms (e.g., PoS) and smaller block confirmation times can reduce transaction confirmation times.
2. Resource Utilization: Blockchain networks can be resource-intensive, consuming significant computational power and storage capacity. This can lead to high operational costs and resource limitations.
    - Performance Enhancements: Optimizing resource usage through techniques like pruning, state channels, and reducing mining rewards can improve resource efficiency.

3. Scalability and Load Balancing: As blockchain networks grow, load balancing becomes essential to distribute transactions and data processing across network nodes effectively.
    - Performance Enhancements: Implementing load-balancing algorithms and network architecture enhancements can help maintain consistent performance even as the network scales.
4. Smart Contract Efficiency: Smart contracts, which are central to many blockchain-based security applications, can be computationally expensive. Poorly written or inefficient smart contracts can hinder performance.
    - Performance Enhancements: Code optimization, gas cost reduction, and efficient contract design practices can improve the efficiency of smart contracts.
5. Privacy Considerations: In blockchain-based cloud security, ensuring data privacy is paramount. However, privacy-enhancing techniques like zero-knowledge proofs can be computationally intensive, affecting performance.
    - Performance Enhancements: Balancing privacy and performance may involve optimizing privacy-preserving techniques and carefully selecting which data should be kept on-chain or off-chain.

Table 2. Performance considerations statistics in blockchain-based cloud security

Description	Performance Considerations	Statistics
Data Storage	Average Data Growth Rate	500 MB per day
Network Latency	Average Network Latency	50 milliseconds
Transaction Confirmation Time	Average Confirmation Time	30 seconds
Resource Utilization	CPU Utilization	30% on average
Interoperability	Interoperability Standards	Enterprise Ethereum Alliance
Resource Management	Resource Cost Control	Automated cost monitoring

6. Interoperability: Interoperability between different blockchain networks and with existing cloud infrastructure is essential for seamless integration of blockchain-based security solutions.
    - Performance Enhancements: Standardizing protocols, using cross-chain solutions, and employing middleware can improve interoperability and enhance overall system performance.

1.17 Interoperability with different cloud platforms and technologies based cloud security

Interoperability is a critical aspect of cloud security, especially in the context of leveraging various cloud platforms and technologies to create a comprehensive and robust security ecosystem. In this comprehensive exploration, we will delve into the intricacies of interoperability in cloud security, understanding its significance, challenges, and strategies to achieve seamless integration across diverse cloud environments and technologies.

1.17.1. Challenges in Achieving Interoperability in Cloud Security

While interoperability is vital for effective cloud security, it comes with its fair share of challenges and complexities. Here are some common challenges organizations face when striving to achieve interoperability in cloud security:

1. Diverse Cloud Environments: Different cloud providers have unique architectures, APIs, and security models. Integrating security solutions across these environments can be challenging.
2. Vendor Lock-In: Vendor-specific technologies and proprietary APIs can create vendor lock-in, making it difficult to switch cloud providers or technologies without major disruptions.
3. Security Standards: Ensuring that security solutions adhere to common security standards and protocols is essential for interoperability. However, not all cloud providers and technologies support the same standards.
4. Data Protection and Privacy: Interoperability must consider data protection and privacy, especially when sharing sensitive security data across platforms. Ensuring that data is encrypted and access is controlled is crucial.
5. Complexity of Integrations: Integrating multiple security solutions and technologies can be complex, requiring significant technical expertise and resources.

1.17.3. Strategies for Achieving Interoperability in Cloud Security

To overcome the challenges of interoperability in cloud security, organizations can adopt various strategies and best practices. Here are key approaches to achieving seamless interoperability:

1. API Standardization: Encourage cloud providers and security solution vendors to adopt common API standards, enabling easier integration across platforms. Widely accepted standards like RESTful APIs can facilitate interoperability.
2. Open Source Solutions: Embrace open source security solutions and technologies that are designed with interoperability in mind. Open source projects often have a strong community focus on compatibility and integration.
3. Middleware and Integration Platforms: Use middleware and integration platforms to connect disparate systems and applications. These platforms can provide translation services between different APIs and data formats.
4. Cloud Security Orchestration: Implement cloud security orchestration tools that allow organizations to automate and coordinate security workflows across different cloud environments. These tools can streamline incident response and threat detection.
5. Identity and Access Management (IAM): Adopt a centralized IAM system that can manage identities and access controls across various cloud platforms. This ensures consistent user authentication and authorization.
6. Security Information and Event Management (SIEM): Deploy a SIEM solution that can collect and correlate security data from different cloud sources. This provides a unified view of security events and threats.

7. Containerization and Microservices: Use containerization technologies like Docker and Kubernetes to package security solutions and deploy them consistently across different cloud environments. Microservices architectures promote flexibility and scalability.
8. Compliance Frameworks: Adhere to recognized compliance frameworks, such as CIS Benchmarks, NIST, and ISO standards. These frameworks provide guidance on security best practices and can facilitate interoperability.
9. Cross-Cloud Security Standards: Collaborate with industry groups and standards bodies to develop cross-cloud security standards and best practices. These initiatives can drive interoperability efforts across the industry.
10. Continuous Testing and Validation: Regularly test and validate interoperability between security solutions and cloud platforms. Implementing continuous integration and testing practices can help identify and resolve compatibility issues.

1.18 Emerging Trends in Blockchain and Cloud Security

Emerging trends in blockchain and cloud security are continuously shaping the future of digital security. As technology evolves, new challenges and opportunities arise, prompting researchers and professionals to explore innovative approaches to safeguarding data, ensuring privacy, and enhancing the security of cloud-based systems. In this detailed exploration, we will delve into the most prominent emerging trends in blockchain and cloud security, offering insights into their significance and potential research directions.

Privacy has become a paramount concern in the digital age, prompting the development of privacy-preserving technologies. In the realm of blockchain and cloud security, techniques such as zero-knowledge proofs (ZKPs) and homomorphic encryption are gaining traction. ZKPs, in particular, enable parties to prove knowledge of specific information without revealing the information itself, offering robust privacy protections in applications like authentication, identity verification, and secure data sharing. Future research will likely focus on optimizing and expanding the use of these privacy-preserving technologies, enabling greater control over personal data while maintaining security. Decentralized identity solutions are poised to revolutionize how individuals and organizations manage digital identities securely. These solutions, often built on blockchain technology, enable users to control their identities without relying on central authorities. Emerging trends include the development of interoperable and standards-based decentralized identity frameworks. Future research directions may explore scalability challenges, usability improvements, and the integration of decentralized identities into mainstream applications and services. The advent of quantum computing poses a significant threat to existing cryptographic protocols, necessitating the adoption of post-quantum cryptography. Researchers are actively exploring cryptographic algorithms that are resistant to quantum attacks. In the context of blockchain and cloud security, the migration to post-quantum cryptographic solutions will be a critical research and implementation area to ensure the long-term security of digital assets and data stored in the cloud. Edge and fog computing, which involve processing data closer to the data source rather than in centralized data centers, are becoming increasingly prevalent in the cloud ecosystem. Securing these distributed and resource-constrained environments poses unique challenges. Future research may focus on developing lightweight security protocols, threat detection mechanisms, and efficient encryption techniques tailored for edge and fog computing environments. As organizations collaborate across geographical boundaries and share sensitive data in real-time, secure data sharing and collaboration have become imperative. Blockchain-based platforms offer secure and auditable data sharing solutions. Future trends may involve the integration of blockchain with emerging technologies like edge computing, enabling secure and efficient real-time data sharing in distributed environments. Quantum computing threatens the cryptographic foundations of blockchain technology. In response, researchers are exploring quantum-safe blockchain solutions. These solutions aim to protect blockchain networks against quantum attacks by integrating quantum-resistant cryptographic algorithms. Future research may involve the development of quantum-resistant consensus mechanisms, smart contract platforms, and quantum-safe blockchain standards. Federated learning, which allows machine learning models to be trained across decentralized devices while preserving data privacy, holds great promise for secure AI applications. Research in this area may focus on enhancing the security and privacy guarantees of federated learning algorithms, ensuring that sensitive data remains protected during model training and collaboration. Compliance with data protection regulations like GDPR and HIPAA is a critical concern for organizations. Blockchain-based solutions that enable transparent and auditable data handling are emerging to address these compliance challenges. Future research may explore ways to automate compliance monitoring and reporting, reducing the burden on organizations while ensuring adherence to regulatory requirements. Supply chain security has gained prominence, especially in the wake of global disruptions. Blockchain-based supply chain solutions are emerging to enhance transparency and traceability. Research may focus on extending these solutions to cover broader aspects of supply chain security, including secure IoT integration and counterfeit prevention.

1.19 CONCLUSION

This book chapter has explored the intersection of blockchain technology and cloud security, highlighting its potential to address the existing challenges and vulnerabilities within cloud computing environments. By leveraging the decentralized and immutable nature of blockchain, we have seen how it can enhance data integrity, confidentiality, access control, and transaction security in the cloud. Throughout the chapter, we have examined various applications of blockchain technology in cloud security, such as ensuring data integrity through tamper-proof storage, decentralized identity management for robust access control, and secure and automated transactions using smart contracts. These applications demonstrate the potential of blockchain to enhance the overall security, trustworthiness, and transparency of cloud-based systems.

We have also acknowledged the challenges that come with integrating blockchain into cloud security. Scalability, performance, interoperability, and regulatory compliance are crucial considerations that need to be addressed for successful implementation. The future development and research in this field should focus on overcoming these challenges and further exploring the potential of emerging technologies, such as decentralized identifiers and zero-knowledge proofs, to enhance the security and privacy of cloud computing. By shedding light on the background, context, and potential applications of blockchain technology in cloud security, this chapter contributes to the growing understanding of how blockchain can revolutionize the way we secure and protect data in cloud-based systems. It aims to empower researchers, practitioners, and policymakers to make informed decisions regarding the adoption and implementation of blockchain solutions in the realm of cloud security. As the field of blockchain technology and cloud security continues to evolve, it is essential to stay updated with the latest developments, trends, and research directions. This chapter serves as a stepping stone for further exploration and encourages readers to delve deeper into specific use cases, technical considerations, and real-world implementations of blockchain in cloud security. The potential of blockchain technology in enhancing cloud security is immense, and this book chapter has provided valuable insights into its applications, benefits, challenges, and future prospects. By harnessing the power of blockchain, we can pave the way for a more secure, trustworthy, and resilient cloud computing environment. Looking ahead, the future of blockchain and cloud security promises to be dynamic and transformative. As emerging technologies continue to shape the digital landscape, researchers, practitioners, and organizations must remain vigilant, adaptive, and forward-thinking. Key research directions include further exploration of quantum-resistant blockchain solutions, the refinement of privacy-preserving technologies, and the development of decentralized systems that empower individuals while upholding security and compliance standards. In a world where data is both a valuable asset and a potential liability, the fusion of blockchain and cloud security offers a beacon of hope. It represents a paradigm shift in how we approach security, emphasizing trust, transparency, and individual empowerment. As we navigate the complexities of the digital age, the lessons learned and the innovations discovered in the realm of blockchain and cloud security will continue to guide us toward a future where data is secure, privacy is protected, and trust is unshakable.

REFERENCES

Al-Riyami, S., Al-Fedaghi, S., & Al-Turjman, F. (2022). A Blockchain-Based System for Securing IoT Services in Cloud Environments. *IEEE Transactions on Industrial Informatics*, *18*(3), 1655–1662.

Alazab, M. R., Kabir, A. M. R., & Kumar, N. (2022). A Secure Blockchain-Based Model for the Internet of Things. *IEEE Internet of Things Journal*, *9*(6), 4855–4862.

Chen, Z., Zhang, X., & Wang, C. (2022). A Blockchain-Based Efficient Data Sharing Scheme in the Industrial Internet of Things. *IEEE Transactions on Industrial Informatics*, *18*(5), 3456–3463.

Dargahi, S., Abolhassani, B. H., & Marjani, M. (2021). A Novel Blockchain-Based Access Control Model for Cloud-Edge Computing Systems. *IEEE Transactions on Industrial Informatics*, *17*(6), 4166–4173.

Deshmukh, A., Sreenath, N., Tyagi, A. K., & Eswara Abhichandan, U. V. (2022). Blockchain Enabled Cyber Security: A Comprehensive Survey. *International Conference on Computer Communication and Informatics,* (pp. 1-6). IEEE. 10.1109/ICCCI54379.2022.9740843

Javaid, M., Niyaz, Q., Sun, W., & Alhameed, A. R. (2021). Blockchain for Secure and Efficient Data Sharing in Cloud-Based Industrial IoT. *IEEE Transactions on Industrial Informatics*, *17*(3), 1837–1845.

Li, B., Liu, Q., & Zhang, T. (2020). Blockchain-Enabled Cloud Computing: Towards Secure and Privacy-Preserving IoT. *IEEE Network*, *34*(6), 58–63.

Liu, X., Shi, S., & Chen, C. L. P. (2021). Blockchain-Enabled Secure Data Sharing for Fog-Cloud Computing in Industrial Internet of Things. *IEEE Transactions on Industrial Informatics*, *17*(12), 8421–8428.

Ma, Y., Zhang, S., & Ye, X. (2021). A Novel Blockchain-Based Data Integrity Protection Mechanism for Cloud-Assisted Healthcare Systems. *IEEE Transactions on Industrial Informatics*, *17*(3), 1846–1853.

Nair, M. M., & Tyagi, A. K. (2022). Preserving Privacy Using Blockchain Technology in Autonomous Vehicles. In: Giri, D., Mandal, J.K., Sakurai, K., De, D. (eds) *Proceedings of International Conference on Network Security and Blockchain Technology*. Springer, Singapore. 10.1007/978-981-19-3182-6_19

Raj, S., Sundararajan, S., & Buyya, R. (2022). Trustworthy and Autonomous Federated Learning in the Cloud-Edge Continuum using Blockchain. *Future Generation Computer Systems*, *128*, 261–275.

Rehman, M., Sun, W., & Poh, H. L. (2022). Decentralized IoT Security Management System Based on Ethereum Blockchain. *IEEE Internet of Things Journal*, *9*(5), 4074–4084.

Seo, A. L., Razzaque, S. A., & Kim, D. H. (2022). Towards Blockchain-Based Secure and Privacy-Preserving Industrial Internet of Things. *IEEE Transactions on Industrial Informatics*, *18*(1), 739–746.

Sheth, H. S. K. (2022). Deep Learning, Blockchain based Multi-layered Authentication and Security Architectures. *2022 International Conference on Applied Artificial Intelligence and Computing (ICAAIC)*, (pp. 476-485). IEEE. 10.1109/ICAAIC53929.2022.9793179

Tyagi, A. K. (2021, October). Aswathy S U, G Aghila, N Sreenath "AARIN: Affordable, Accurate, Reliable and INnovative Mechanism to Protect a Medical Cyber-Physical System using Blockchain Technology". *IJIN*, *2*, 175–183.

Tyagi, A. K. (2021). Healthcare Solutions for Smart Era: An Useful Explanation from User's Perspective. Recent Trends in Blockchain for Information Systems Security and Privacy. CRC Press.

Xu, Y., Wu, J., & Kumar, S. (2022). Toward Blockchain-Based Secure and Private Machine Learning in Edge Computing. *IEEE Transactions on Industrial Informatics*, *18*(1), 646–653.

Yang, A., Liu, Y., & Ran, S. (2021). Blockchain-Based Privacy-Preserving Attribute Matchmaking for Mobile Cloud Computing. *IEEE Transactions on Industrial Informatics*, *17*(7), 5114–5121.

Yang, Z., Cai, H., & Liu, Y. (2021). A Secure and Efficient Data Integrity Verification Scheme for Cloud-Based IoT With Blockchain. *IEEE Internet of Things Journal*, *8*(1), 339–349.

Yunis, A. I. M., Abusharkh, M. E., & Al-Rawi, S. (2022). Blockchain-Enhanced IoT Security for Smart Cities: A Case Study of Smart Waste Management. *IEEE Internet of Things Journal*, *9*(3), 2510–2522.

Chapter 4
Role of Blockchain Technology in Protecting a Cloud Architecture

Virendra Kumar Verma
Institute of Engineering and Rural Technology (IERT), Prayagraj, India

Shrikant Tiwari
https://orcid.org/0000-0001-6947-2362
School of Computing Science and Engineering (SCSE), Galgotias University, India

Bireshwar Dass Mazumdar
School of Computer Science Engineering and Technology(SCSET), Bennett University, India

Yadav Krishna Kumar Rajnath
Institute of Engineering and Rural Technology (IERT), Prayagraj, India

ABSTRACT

Cloud computing has revolutionized the way organizations manage and deliver services, offering unparalleled scalability and cost-efficiency. However, the increasing adoption of cloud-based solutions has also brought forth a myriad of security challenges, ranging from data breaches to unauthorized access and tampering. In recent years, blockchain technology has emerged as a promising solution to address some of these security concerns. This chapter presents an in-depth exploration of the application of blockchain technology in cloud security. It begins by providing an overview of both cloud computing and blockchain, emphasizing their individual strengths and weaknesses in safeguarding data and transactions. Subsequently, it delves into the various security challenges faced in cloud environments and how traditional security measures often fall short.

DOI: 10.4018/979-8-3693-2081-5.ch004

1. INTRODUCTION TO CLOUD SECURITY AND BLOCKCHAIN TECHNOLOGY

In recent years, cloud computing has become an indispensable part of the modern technological landscape, transforming the way businesses and individuals' access, store, and manage data. Its ability to provide on-demand computing resources, scalability, and cost efficiency has driven its widespread adoption across various industries (Xu, X. 2012). However, this rapid expansion of cloud-based services has also brought forth a host of security challenges that demand innovative solutions.

Cloud security, as a discipline, focuses on protecting data, applications, and infrastructure within cloud environments from a wide array of threats such as data breaches, unauthorized access, and service disruptions. The shared responsibility model in cloud security emphasizes the collaboration between cloud service providers and their customers, making it essential for both parties to implement robust security measures (Tabrizchi, H., & Kuchaki Rafsanjani, M. 2020).

Concurrently, blockchain technology, originally introduced as the underlying technology behind cryptocurrencies like Bitcoin, has emerged as a revolutionary concept with the potential to change various sectors beyond finance. Blockchain having decentralized and immutable distributed ledger that securely records and validates transactions across a network of computers. Its unique features, such as cryptographic hashing, consensus mechanisms, and smart contracts, have made it a promising solution to address the challenges faced in cloud security (Chen, G., et al.,2018).

The integration of blockchain technology with cloud security presents a compelling opportunity to enhance data integrity, access control, and overall trustworthiness in cloud-based systems. By leveraging blockchain's decentralized nature, cloud infrastructures can potentially mitigate single points of failure and reduce the risk of data tampering or unauthorized alterations. Furthermore, the transparent and auditable nature of blockchain transactions can bolster accountability and enable secure auditing in cloud environments (Nguyen, D. C., et. Al., 2020).

This book explores the intersection of blockchain technology and cloud security, providing a comprehensive analysis of the benefits and challenges that arise from their convergence. It delves into the fundamental principles of both cloud computing and blockchain technology, laying the groundwork for understanding their individual strengths and weaknesses in safeguarding digital assets and processes (Rejeb, A., et. al., 2022).

Throughout the chapters, the book will investigate how blockchain can serve as a security-enhancing layer in cloud-based systems. It will explore real-world use cases and successful deployments that demonstrate the practicality and effectiveness of integrating blockchain in various cloud security scenarios(Kshetri, N. 2017).

1.1 Overview of Cloud Computing

Cloud computing has revolutionized the way individuals and organizations consume and deliver computing resources, applications, and services over the internet. At its core, cloud computing provides on-demand access to a pool of shared computing resources, including servers, storage, databases, networking, and software, without requiring direct management by the users. This model has profoundly impacted various sectors, enabling agility, scalability, cost efficiency, and enhanced collaboration in the digital era (Dillon, T., Wu, C., & Chang, E. 2010).Key Characteristics of Cloud Computing:

- On-Demand Self-Service: Cloud computing having facility to users to manage computing resources independently, without involvement of human from the service provider. This empowers users to scale resources up or down as needed, promoting flexibility and resource optimization (Leng, J., et. Al., 2020).
- Broad Network Access: Cloud services are easily accessible over the internet from a range of devices, such as computers, laptops, smartphones, and tablets (Liu, F.,et. Al., 2013).
- Resource Pooling: Cloud providers having provision to serve multiple users at a time (Zhang, Q., Cheng, L., & Boutaba, R. 2010).
- Rapid Elasticity: Cloud systems can quickly scale resources up or down to meet fluctuating workloads and demands. This elasticity ensures that applications perform optimally during peak usage periods while efficiently utilizing resources during periods of low demand (Shen, Z., Subbiah, S., Gu, X., & Wilkes, J. 2011).
- Measured Service: Cloud computing offers transparency through usage-based billing, where users only pay for the resources they consume. This pay-as-you-go model provides cost predictability and encourages resource optimization (Calheiros, R. N., et. al., 2011).

  Cloud Deployment Models:
- Public Cloud: In a public cloud model, cloud services are provided and managed by third-party cloud service providers. (Voorsluys, W., Broberg, J., & Buyya, R. 2011).
- Private Cloud: A private cloud is dedicated solely to a single organization, providing exclusive access to its computing resources. (Rittinghouse, J. W., & Ransome, J. F. (2017).
- Hybrid Cloud: The hybrid cloud model combines elements of both public and private clouds. It allows data and applications to move between public and private environments seamlessly, providing greater flexibility and the ability to optimize resources based on specific requirements (Zhang, Q., Cheng, L., & Boutaba, R. 2010).
- Community Cloud: In a community cloud, multiple organizations with similar needs collaborate to share cloud resources and services. (Dallasega, P., Rauch, E., & Linder, C. 2018).

1.2 Importance of Cloud Security

Cloud computing has ushered in a new era of technological advancement, offering unparalleled convenience, scalability, and cost-efficiency. However, as organizations increasingly adopt cloud-based solutions to manage and store sensitive data and critical applications, the importance of robust cloud security has become paramount. The vast amounts of data housed within cloud environments have made them attractive targets for cybercriminals, necessitating comprehensive security measures to protect against a wide array of threats (Mohsan, S. A. H., et. al., 2022).

- Data Protection and Confidentiality
- Cybersecurity Threats
- Compliance and Regulatory Requirements
- Business Continuity and Disaster Recovery
- Insider Threats and Access Management
- Vendor Risk Management
- Intellectual Property Protection

Figure 1. Advantages of cloud computing

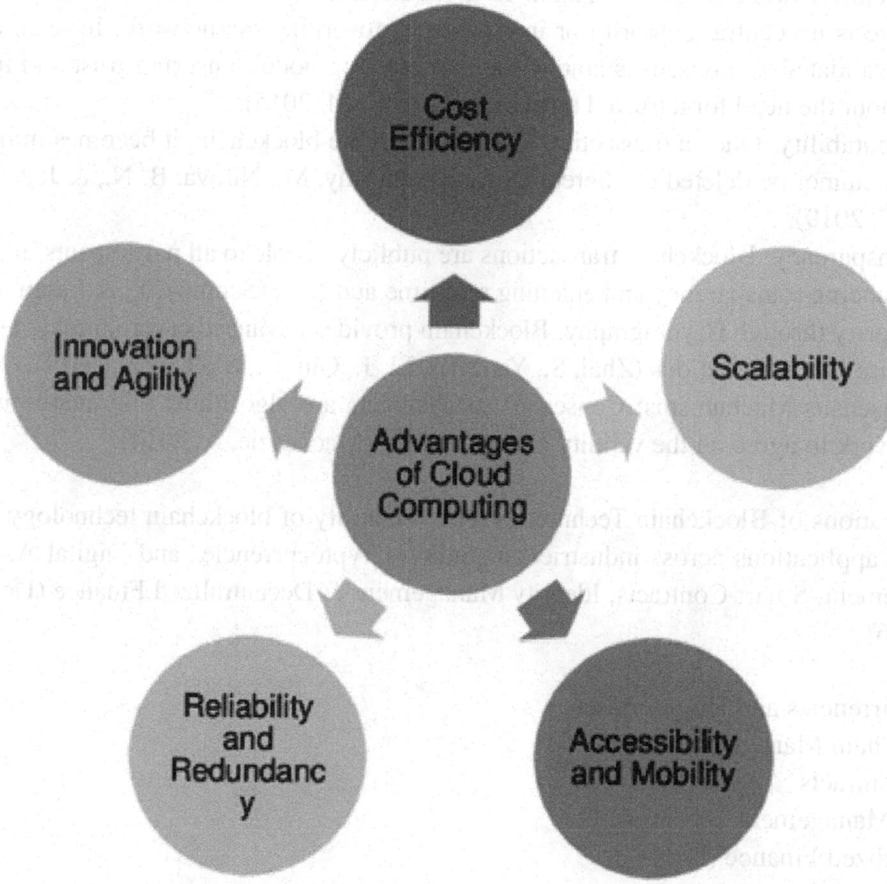

1.3 Introduction to Blockchain Technology

Blockchain technology has emerged as a transformative force, revolutionizing the way data is stored, verified, and shared across decentralized networks. Originally introduced as the underlying technology powering cryptocurrencies like Bitcoin, blockchain has evolved far beyond its cryptocurrency roots to find applications in diverse industries, from finance and supply chain management to healthcare and real estate (Martino, P., Wang, K. J., Bellavitis, C., & DaSilva, C. M. 2020)). At its core, blockchain is a distributed and immutable ledger that allows participants in a network to record transactions in a secure, transparent, and tamper-resistant manner.

Unlike traditional centralized databases, where a single entity has control over data management and validation, blockchain works on networks in decentralized manner, known as nodes.

Key Characteristics of Blockchain Technology:

- Decentralization: Decentralization is a fundamental principle of blockchain technology. There is no central authority or intermediary governing the network. Instead, transactions are validated by consensus among the participating nodes, ensuring trust and transparency without the need for a trusted third party (Atzori, M. 2015).
- Immutability: Once a transaction is recorded on the blockchain, it becomes immutable, and data cannot be deleted or altered. (Niranjanamurthy, M., Nithya, B. N., & Jagannatha, S. J. C. C. 2019).
- Transparency: Blockchain transactions are publicly visible to all participants in the network, enhancing transparency and enabling real-time auditing. (Schmitz, J., & Leoni, G. 2019).
- Security through Cryptography: Blockchain provides advanced cryptographic technology to secure data transactions (Zhai, S., Yang, Y., Li, J., Qiu, C., & Zhao, J. (2019).
- Consensus Mechanisms: Consensus mechanisms are algorithms that enable nodes in the network to agree on the validity of transactions (Mackenzie, A. 2014).

The Applications of Blockchain Technology:The versatility of blockchain technology has led to a wide range of applications across industries, including Cryptocurrencies and Digital Assets, Supply Chain Management, Smart Contracts, Identity Management & Decentralized Finance (DeFi) (Crosby, M., et al., 2016):

- Cryptocurrencies and Digital Assets
- Supply Chain Management
- Smart Contracts
- Identity Management
- Decentralized Finance (DeFi)

1.4 Intersection of Blockchain and Cloud Security

The intersection of blockchain technology and cloud security presents a compelling opportunity to enhance the security, integrity, and trustworthiness of cloud-based systems. As cloud computing becomes the backbone of modern digital infrastructures, concerns about data breaches, unauthorized access, and tampering have escalated. Blockchain's decentralized and immutable nature can address some of these security challenges, making it a promising solution to reinforce cloud security (Fernandez-Carames, T. M., & Fraga-Lamas, P. 2019).

- Decentralization and Data Integrity: One of the key strengths of blockchain is its decentralized architecture, where data is distributed across multiple nodes in the network.
- Immutable Audit Trails: Blockchain's tamper-resistant and immutable nature ensures that all transactions recorded on the blockchain are permanent and cannot be altered.
- Enhanced Access Control: Integrating blockchain technology with cloud security enables the implementation of robust access control mechanisms..
- Secure Data Sharing and Collaboration: Blockchain technology allows for secure and auditable data sharing and collaboration among multiple parties.

- Reducing Centralized Vulnerabilities: Traditional cloud environments have central points of vulnerability, such as single cloud providers or centralized authentication services.
- Transparent Cloud Supply Chain Management: In cloud computing, supply chains often involve multiple third-party providers.

1.4.1 Challenges and Considerations

Despite the promising synergies between blockchain and cloud security, there are challenges (Hammoud, A., Sami, H., et. al., 2020) and considerations that must be addressed:

- Scalability: Blockchain's inherent design for security and decentralization can lead to scalability challenges when integrated into large-scale cloud environments.
- Interoperability: Integrating blockchain technology with existing cloud systems and applications may require standardization and interoperability efforts to ensure seamless communication and data exchange.
- Cost and Complexity: Implementing blockchain in cloud security introduces additional complexities and costs. Careful planning and analysis are necessary to determine the optimal use cases for blockchain integration that deliver tangible security benefits.
- Regulatory Compliance: As with any technological advancement, ensuring compliance with data protection and privacy regulations is crucial.

2. CLOUD SECURITY CHALLENGES

Cloud computing has undoubtedly transformed the way organizations handle data and deliver services, offering unparalleled flexibility, scalability, and cost-effectiveness. However, the increasing adoption of cloud-based solutions has also brought forth a multitude of security challenges that demand comprehensive solutions. These challenges stem from the unique characteristics of cloud environments and the evolving threat landscape. Understanding and addressing these challenges are crucial for ensuring the confidentiality, integrity, and availability of data and services in the cloud (Berdik, D., et. al.,2021).

- Data Breaches and Data Loss
- Identity and Access Management (IAM) Issues
- Insider Threats
- Insecure APIs
- Data Privacy and Compliance
- Shared Responsibility Model
- Lack of Visibility and Control\
- Advanced Persistent Threats (APTs)

3. BLOCKCHAIN FUNDAMENTALS

Blockchain technology is a revolutionary concept that has transformed the way data is stored, shared, and secured across decentralized networks. At its core, blockchain is a distributed and immutable ledger that records transactions in a secure, transparent, and tamper-resistant manner. Originally introduced as the underlying technology for cryptocurrencies like Bitcoin, blockchain has since evolved and found applications in various industries, offering solutions beyond finance, such as supply chain management, healthcare, real estate, and more (Moin, S., et. al.,2019). Key Concepts of Blockchain:

Figure 2. Elements of blockchain technology

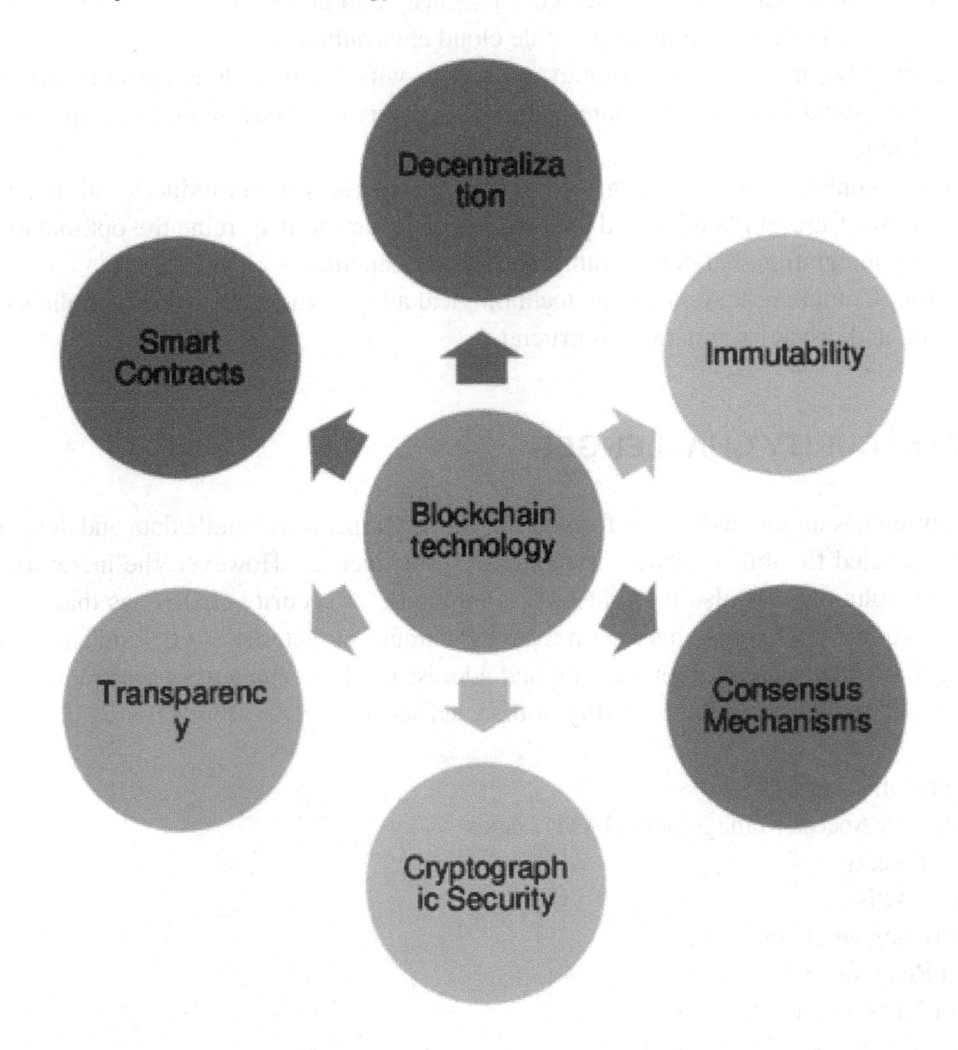

Applications of Blockchain Technology:

- Cryptocurrencies: Blockchain's most famous application is in the creation of cryptocurrencies like Bitcoin, providing a decentralized and secure means of digital exchange.

- Supply Chain Management: Blockchain enables end-to-end traceability of goods, improving transparency and efficiency in supply chain management by tracking the provenance of products.
- Healthcare: Blockchain solutions in healthcare enhance patient data security, interoperability, and consent management, while ensuring data integrity and privacy.
- Decentralized Finance (DeFi): DeFi platforms leverage blockchain to create open and transparent financial systems that operate without traditional intermediaries.
- Identity Management: Blockchain-based identity solutions offer secure and tamper-resistant identity management, reducing the risk of identity theft and improving user privacy.

3.1 Understanding Blockchain Architecture

Blockchain architecture is the fundamental design and structure of a blockchain network, outlining how data is stored, processed, and secured across a distributed and decentralized system. To comprehend blockchain technology fully, it is essential to grasp the key components and concepts that make up its architecture (Peters, G. W., & Panayi, E. 2016). Key Components of Blockchain Architecture:

Figure 3. Components of blockchain architecture

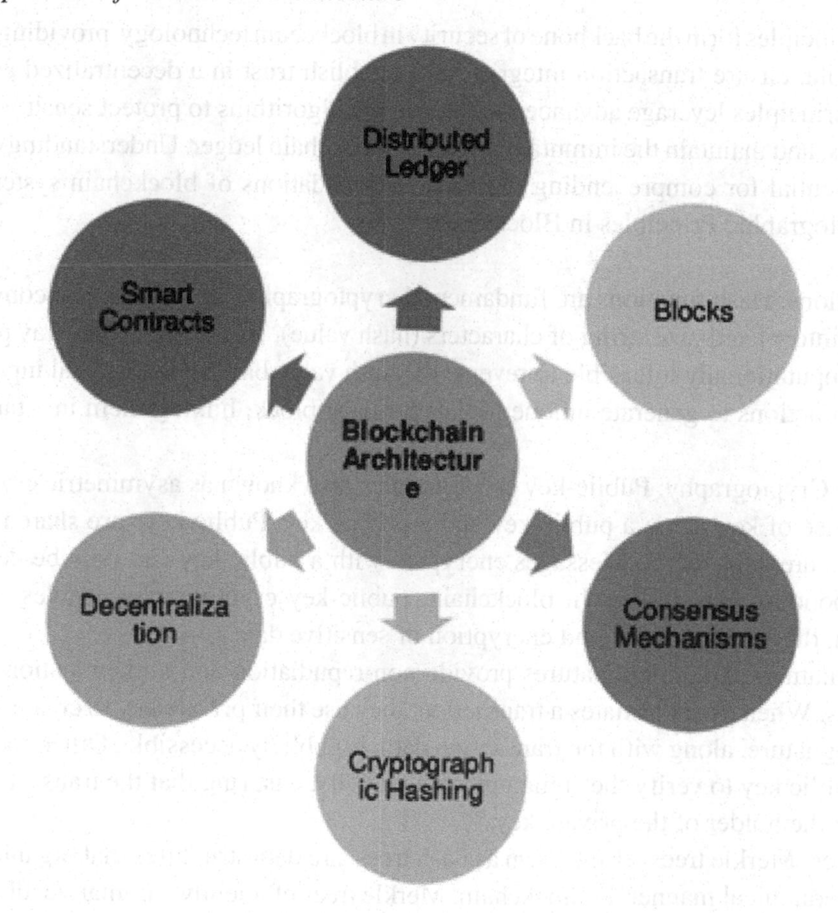

Understanding the Blockchain Process:

- Transaction Submission: Users initiate transactions by sending them to the network for validation. These transactions may involve sending cryptocurrencies, recording asset transfers, or executing smart contracts.
- Transaction Verification: Nodes in the network compete to validate transactions through consensus mechanisms. Once a majority of nodes agree on the validity of a transaction, it is included in a new block.
- Block Creation: Validated transactions are grouped together into a new block, which is then added to the existing blockchain. Each new block contains a reference to the previous block's hash, creating a continuous chain of blocks.
- Block Validation: Once a new block is created, it undergoes further validation by other nodes in the network. Consensus mechanisms ensure that the majority of nodes agree on the legitimacy of the new block before it is officially added to the blockchain.
- Chain Consistency: As blocks are added to the chain, the distributed ledger becomes increasingly secure and tamper-resistant. The unique cryptographic hashes ensure the integrity of the entire blockchain, making it extremely challenging to alter historical transactions.

3.2 Cryptographic Principles in Blockchain

Cryptographic principles form the backbone of security in blockchain technology, providing the necessary tools to secure data, ensure transaction integrity, and establish trust in a decentralized and distributed network. These principles leverage advanced mathematical algorithms to protect sensitive information, authenticate users, and maintain the immutability of the blockchain ledger. Understanding cryptographic techniques is essential for comprehending the security foundations of blockchain systems (Bashir, I. 2017). Key Cryptographic Principles in Blockchain:

- Hash Functions: Hash functions are fundamental cryptographic algorithms that convert input data of any size into a fixed-size string of characters (hash value). Hashing is a one-way process, meaning it is computationally infeasible to reverse the hash value back to its original input. Blockchain uses hash functions to generate unique hashes for each block, linking them in a tamper-resistant chain.
- Public-Key Cryptography: Public-key cryptography, also known as asymmetric cryptography, involves the use of key pairs: a public key and a private key. Public keys are shared openly, while private keys are kept secret. Messages encrypted with a public key can only be decrypted using the corresponding private key. In blockchain, public-key cryptography enables secure identity verification, digital signatures, and encryption of sensitive data.
- Digital Signatures: Digital signatures provide non-repudiation and authentication in blockchain transactions. When a user initiates a transaction, they use their private key to create a digital signature. The signature, along with the transaction data, is publicly accessible. Other nodes can use the sender's public key to verify the signature's authenticity, ensuring that the transaction was indeed initiated by the holder of the private key.
- Merkle Trees: Merkle trees, also known as hash trees, are data structures that organize large sets of data in a hierarchical manner. In blockchain, Merkle trees efficiently summarize all transactions in a block into a single root hash. This root hash is included in the block header, providing a concise

representation of the entire block's data. Merkle trees facilitate quick verification of transaction inclusion and ensure data integrity within a block.

- Key Derivation Functions (KDFs): Key derivation functions derive cryptographic keys from input data, such as passwords or seeds. KDFs are commonly used in blockchain wallets to derive private keys from a seed phrase, providing a convenient and secure way to regenerate keys for wallet access and recovery.
- Zero-Knowledge Proofs (ZKPs): Zero-knowledge proofs enable a party (the prover) to prove the truth of a statement to another party (the verifier) without revealing any additional information. ZKPs are used in privacy-focused blockchains to allow users to verify the correctness of a transaction without disclosing the transaction details.

3.3 Public vs. Private Blockchains

Public and private blockchains are two distinct types of blockchain networks, each designed to serve specific use cases and accommodate different levels of decentralization and accessibility. Understanding the differences between public and private blockchains is crucial for determining the appropriate blockchain solution for various applications (Viriyasitavat, W., et. al., 2022).

3.3.1 Public Blockchains

- Decentralization: Public blockchains are fully decentralized networks, where multiple nodes (often thousands or more) distributed globally validate transactions and secure the network. Anyone can participate in the network as a node, making it permissionless and open to the public.
- Permissionless Access: Public blockchains allow anyone to read, write, and participate in the network without any entry barriers. Users can create wallets, initiate transactions, and interact with smart contracts without requiring permission from any central authority.
- Transparency: Public blockchains are transparent and auditable. All transactions are recorded on the public ledger, visible to all participants, promoting trust and accountability.
- Security: Public blockchains, especially those with robust consensus mechanisms like Proof of Work (PoW), are highly secure due to the large number of nodes participating in the network. The decentralized nature makes them resistant to single points of failure and more resilient against attacks.
- Example: Bitcoin and Ethereum are popular examples of public blockchains, designed for decentralized cryptocurrencies and open-access decentralized applications (dApps).

3.3.2 Private Blockchains

- Centralization: Private blockchains are more centralized in nature, operated and controlled by a single entity or a consortium of trusted entities. Only selected nodes, authorized by the network administrator, participate in the validation and consensus process.
- Permissioned Access: Private blockchains require permission to join and participate. Users or organizations must be granted access by the network administrator, making them less open than public blockchains.

- Privacy: Private blockchains often prioritize privacy and restrict access to sensitive data. Transactions and data visibility are limited to authorized participants only.
- Performance and Scalability: Due to the smaller number of validating nodes, private blockchains can achieve higher transaction throughput and lower latency compared to public blockchains. This scalability is beneficial for enterprise applications with high transaction volumes.
- Example: Hyperledger Fabric and Corda are examples of private blockchains, designed for use within enterprise and consortium environments, where participants need greater control over the network and data privacy.

The choice between public and private blockchains depends on the specific requirements and use case of the application:

- Public blockchains are ideal for applications requiring decentralization, transparency, and public accessibility. They are suitable for cryptocurrencies, dApps, and projects that prioritize openness and trustlessness.
- Private blockchains are more suitable for applications within closed ecosystems, where participants are known and trusted. They provide better privacy, control, and performance, making them suitable for enterprise use cases like supply chain management, financial systems, and data sharing among consortium members.

4. ENHANCING CLOUD SECURITY WITH BLOCKCHAIN

Cloud computing has become a ubiquitous technology for organizations, providing convenient and scalable solutions for data storage, processing, and services. However, the centralized nature of cloud environments introduces security challenges, making them vulnerable to data breaches, unauthorized access, and single points of failure. Blockchain technology, with its decentralized and tamper-resistant characteristics, offers promising solutions to enhance cloud security significantly. By integrating blockchain with cloud computing, organizations can strengthen data protection, access control, and auditability, mitigating various security risks (Zissis, D., & Lekkas, D. 2012).Key Ways Blockchain Enhances Cloud Security:

- Decentralized Authentication: Blockchain's public-key cryptography and decentralized identity management can improve authentication mechanisms in cloud environments. By using blockchain-based digital signatures, users can securely access cloud services without relying on traditional username-password authentication, reducing the risk of password-related attacks.
- Immutable Data Integrity: Blockchain's inherent immutability ensures the integrity of data stored in the cloud. Each transaction or data update is recorded as an unchangeable block on the blockchain, making it extremely difficult for unauthorized parties to tamper with the data.
- Access Control and Permissions: Smart contracts on the blockchain can enforce access controls and permissions for cloud resources. Blockchain-based access control mechanisms can be more transparent and robust, enabling fine-grained access management and preventing unauthorized access to sensitive data.

- Secure Data Sharing: Blockchain facilitates secure and auditable data sharing between parties in a cloud environment. Smart contracts can define the terms of data sharing, ensuring that data is shared only with authorized entities and providing an immutable record of data sharing activities.
- Immutable Audit Trail: The transparent nature of blockchain allows for an immutable audit trail of all activities in the cloud environment. Any changes or transactions made in the cloud can be recorded on the blockchain, enabling efficient monitoring and forensic analysis of potential security breaches.
- Distributed and Resilient Storage: Blockchain can be used to create distributed storage solutions that ensure data redundancy across multiple nodes. This distribution of data enhances fault tolerance and resilience against data loss or service disruptions.
- Zero-Knowledge Proofs (ZKPs) for Privacy: Zero-knowledge proofs on the blockchain allow parties to verify the authenticity of data or transactions without revealing sensitive information. This feature can be leveraged to protect data privacy in cloud environments.

While integrating blockchain with cloud computing can enhance security, organizations must consider several factors during implementation:

- Scalability: Blockchain's scalability limitations may impact the performance of cloud services. Organizations should assess the trade-offs between security benefits and potential performance impacts.
- Regulatory Compliance: Adherence to regulatory requirements and data protection laws is essential when handling sensitive data in the cloud with blockchain.
- Interoperability: Ensuring compatibility and interoperability between blockchain solutions and existing cloud platforms is crucial for seamless integration.
- Consensus Mechanism: The choice of consensus mechanism in the blockchain network should align with the desired level of decentralization and security requirements.

4.1 Decentralization and Its Impact on Cloud Security

Decentralization is a key principle in blockchain technology that distributes control and authority across multiple nodes, removing the need for a central authority or intermediary. While decentralization is a foundational aspect of blockchain, it has also gained attention for its potential impact on cloud security. By leveraging the advantages of decentralization, cloud environments can enhance security measures, mitigate vulnerabilities, and improve the overall trustworthiness of cloud services (Atzori, M. 2015). Key Impact of Decentralization on Cloud Security:

- Resilience to Single Points of Failure: Decentralization eliminates single points of failure commonly found in traditional centralized cloud infrastructures. In a decentralized cloud environment, data and services are distributed across numerous nodes.
- Improved Data Privacy and Control: With decentralized cloud systems, users have greater control over their data. Instead of relying on a single cloud provider to manage and protect data, decentralized solutions enable data encryption, segregation, and sharing options defined by the users themselves. Enhanced Security through Consensus Mechanisms: Decentralized cloud systems

often employ consensus mechanisms, such as Proof of Work (PoW) or Proof of Stake (PoS), to validate transactions and maintain the integrity of the system.

- Transparent and Auditable Transactions: Decentralized cloud systems record all transactions on a public ledger, creating an immutable and transparent audit trail. This feature enhances accountability and facilitates forensic analysis, making it easier to detect and investigate security incidents.
- Reducing Trust in Third Parties: In centralized cloud environments, users must trust the cloud provider to manage their data securely.
- Scalability and Load Distribution: Decentralized cloud solutions can harness the collective computing power of distributed nodes, leading to better scalability and load distribution.

While decentralization offers significant benefits to cloud security, it also poses challenges and considerations:

- Scalability and Performance
- Consensus Mechanism Selection
- Regulatory Compliance
- Network Security

4.2 Immutable Ledger and Data Integrity in Cloud Environments

An immutable ledger is a critical concept in blockchain technology, ensuring that once data is recorded on the blockchain, it becomes tamper-resistant and cannot be altered or deleted. In cloud environments, where data storage and processing are centralized, maintaining data integrity is of utmost importance to prevent unauthorized modifications, data breaches, and data corruption (Tanwar, S., Parekh, K., & Evans, R. 2020). By implementing an immutable ledger using blockchain principles, cloud environments can enhance data security, foster trust among users, and provide a transparent audit trail of all activities. Key Aspects of Immutable Ledger and Data Integrity:

Benefits of Immutable Ledger and Data Integrity in Cloud Environments:

- Trust and Accountability
- Protection against Data Corruption
- Enhanced Security
- Compliance and Auditing

Challenges and Considerations:

- Performance and Scalability
- Data Privacy
- Regulatory Compliance

4.3 Access Control and Permission Management with Smart Contracts

Smart contracts, self-executing agreements with predefined rules written on a blockchain, offer a powerful solution for access control and permission management in various applications. By embedding access rules directly into smart contracts, organizations can automate and enforce fine-grained access controls, ensuring that only authorized parties can interact with specific resources or perform certain actions. Smart contracts provide a tamper-resistant and transparent framework for managing permissions, enhancing security, and reducing reliance on traditional centralized access control systems (Kirli, D., et. al.,2022).. Key Aspects of Access Control and Permission Management with Smart Contracts:

- Automated Authorization: Smart contracts allow for automated authorization based on predefined conditions. Access rights can be programmed into the contract, specifying which parties or entities have permission to perform particular actions or access specific data.
- Fine-Grained Access Control: Smart contracts enable granular control over access rights. Users can be granted different levels of permissions, allowing them to perform only specific operations within a system or access particular parts of the data.
- Decentralized Trust: Access control rules embedded in smart contracts operate on a decentralized blockchain network. This reduces the need to trust a single central authority, as access decisions are executed based on the consensus of network nodes.
- Transparency and Auditability: Smart contracts record access control decisions on the blockchain, providing an immutable and transparent audit trail.
- Dynamic Access Control: Smart contracts can be updated or modified to reflect changes in access requirements. This flexibility allows for dynamic access control, accommodating evolving organizational needs and user roles.
- Multi-Party Authorization: Smart contracts can facilitate multi-party authorization, requiring multiple signatures or approvals to execute specific actions.

Figure 4. Key aspects of immutable ledger and data integrity

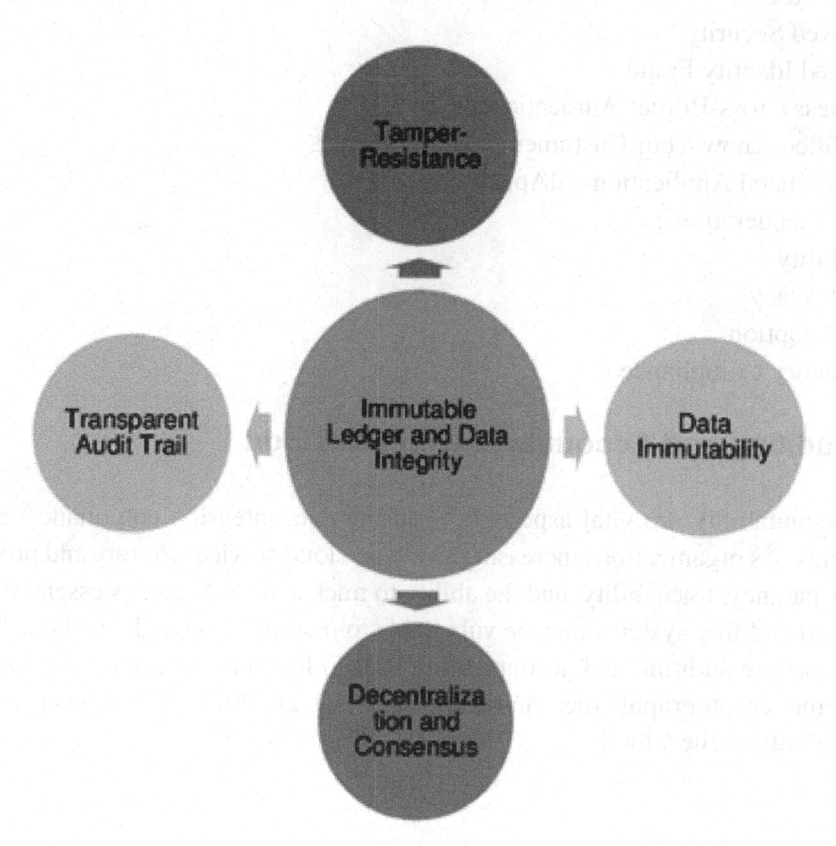

Use Cases of Smart Contracts for Access Control:

- Decentralized Applications (dApps)
- Supply Chain Management
- Identity Management
- Healthcare Data

Challenges and Considerations:

- Smart Contract Security
- Regulatory Compliance
- Scalability
- User Experience

4.4 Securing Identity and Authentication Using Blockchain

Identity and authentication are critical components of secure digital interactions, ensuring that users are who they claim to be and granting them appropriate access to resources and services. Traditional identity management systems often rely on centralized databases, leading to vulnerabilities like single points of failure and data breaches. Blockchain technology offers a decentralized and tamper-resistant approach to identity and authentication, enhancing security and privacy while providing users with greater control over their personal information (Zhu, X., & Badr, Y. 2018). Key Aspects of Securing Identity and Authentication Using Blockchain:

Benefits and Use Cases:

- Improved Security
- Reduced Identity Fraud
- Seamless Cross-Border Authentication
- Simplified Know Your Customer (KYC) Processes
- Decentralized Applications (dApps)

Challenges and Considerations:

- Scalability
- Data Privacy
- User Adoption
- Regulatory Compliance

4.5 Secure Auditing and Accountability in the Cloud

Auditing and accountability are vital aspects of ensuring data integrity, compliance, and security in cloud environments. As organizations increasingly rely on cloud services to store and process their data, maintaining transparency, traceability, and the ability to track actions becomes essential. However, traditional centralized auditing systems may be vulnerable to manipulation and data breaches. To address these challenges, secure auditing and accountability in the cloud can be achieved through blockchain technology and other cryptographic mechanisms (Zafar, F., et. al., 2017). Key Aspects of Secure Auditing and Accountability in the Cloud:

Figure 5. Key aspects of securing identity and authentication using blockchain

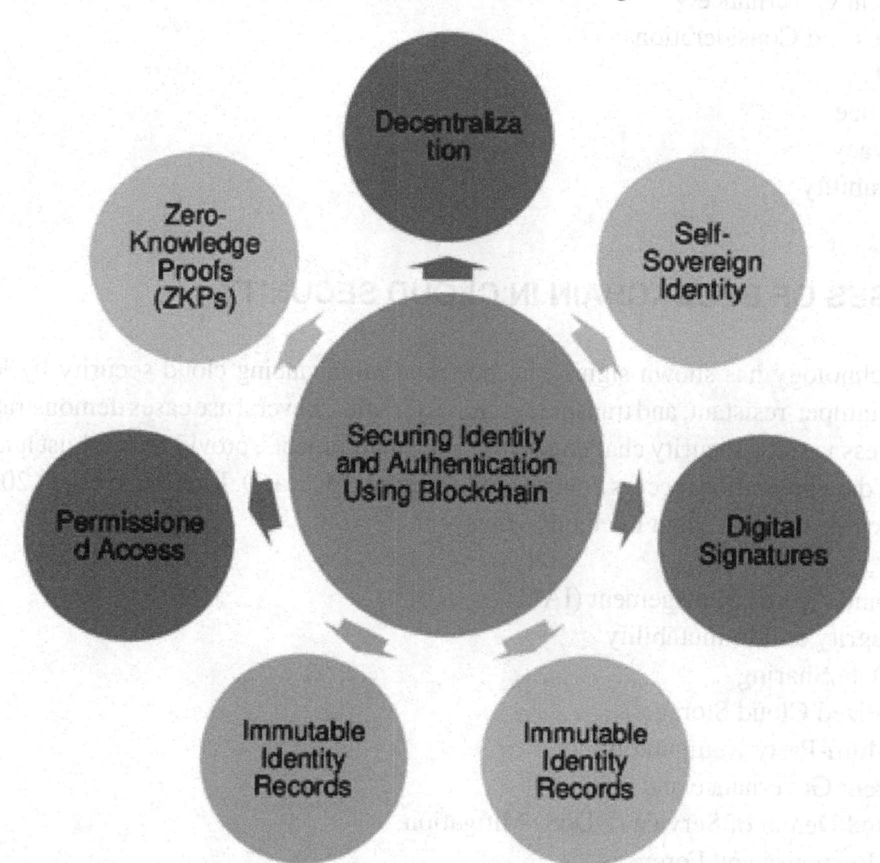

- Immutable Auditing Trail: Blockchain, with its immutable ledger, provides an ideal platform for creating an unchangeable and transparent audit trail.
- Timestamping: Timestamping data on the blockchain establishes the sequence of events, enhancing the audit trail's accuracy and allowing for precise tracking of activities over time.
- Decentralization: Utilizing a decentralized blockchain network for auditing ensures that no single entity has exclusive control over the auditing process.
- Digital Signatures: Using digital signatures in the audit process ensures that the origin and authenticity of audit logs are verifiable.
- Zero-Knowledge Proofs (ZKPs): Zero-knowledge proofs offer a privacy-preserving mechanism for auditing.
- Access Control: Implementing access control measures within the auditing system ensures that only authorized personnel can view and manage audit logs, preventing unauthorized access to sensitive data.

  Benefits and Use Cases:
- Enhanced Data Integrity
- Compliance and Regulatory Requirements
- Incident Investigation
- Vendor Accountability

- Transparent Governance
  Challenges and Considerations:
- Scalability
- Performance
- Data Privacy
- Interoperability

5. USE CASES OF BLOCKCHAIN IN CLOUD SECURITY

Blockchain technology has shown significant potential in enhancing cloud security by leveraging its decentralized, tamper-resistant, and transparent characteristics. Several use cases demonstrate how blockchain can address various security challenges in cloud environments, providing a robust and trustworthy framework for data protection, access control, and auditing (Maesa, D. D. F., & Mori, P. 2020). Here are some key use cases of blockchain in cloud security:

- Identity and Access Management (IAM)
- Data Integrity and Immutability
- Secure Data Sharing
- Decentralized Cloud Storage
- Secure Multi-Party Computation
- Transparent Governance and Auditing
- Distributed Denial of Service (DDoS) Mitigation
- Incident Response and Forensics

5.1 Blockchain-Based Data Encryption and Decryption

Data encryption is a fundamental aspect of securing sensitive information from unauthorized access and ensuring data confidentiality. Blockchain technology can enhance data encryption by providing a decentralized, tamper-resistant platform for managing encryption keys and ensuring secure data transmission and storage. By combining the strengths of blockchain and encryption, organizations can establish a robust and trustless data security framework (Deepa, N., et.al., 2022). Key Aspects of Blockchain-Based Data Encryption and Decryption:

- Decentralized Key Management: Traditional data encryption relies on centralized key management systems, which may become vulnerable to attacks. In blockchain-based encryption, cryptographic keys are securely distributed across the blockchain network.
- Smart Contract-Based Access Control: Smart contracts can be employed to enforce access control rules for data encryption keys. Only authorized parties with the appropriate permissions, as defined in the smart contract, can access the keys necessary for data decryption.
- Immutable Auditing: Blockchain's immutable ledger ensures an auditable record of all key access and decryption activities. This transparency allows organizations to monitor and track key usage, enhancing data accountability and providing a comprehensive audit trail.

- Secure Data Sharing: Blockchain-based encryption enables secure data sharing between multiple parties. By encrypting data and distributing decryption keys among authorized participants, data can be shared securely without exposing sensitive information.
- Zero-Knowledge Proofs (ZKPs): Zero-knowledge proofs can enhance data privacy during decryption. ZKPs allow one party to prove the validity of encrypted data to another party without revealing the actual data content or decryption key.
- Data At Rest and In Transit Encryption: Blockchain-based encryption can secure data both at rest and in transit. Encrypting data at rest ensures that stored data remains confidential, while encrypting data in transit ensures secure communication between parties.

5.2 Blockchain for Secure Multi-Party Computation in the Cloud

Secure multi-party computation (MPC) allows multiple parties to jointly compute a result without revealing their individual inputs to one another. This approach is essential for collaborative tasks in the cloud, where privacy and data confidentiality are paramount. Blockchain technology offers a decentralized and tamper-resistant platform for implementing secure multi-party computation, enabling seamless and trustworthy collaborations while preserving data privacy (Das, D. 2018). Key Aspects of Blockchain for Secure Multi-Party Computation:

- Decentralized Computation: Blockchain's decentralized nature distributes computation tasks across multiple nodes, reducing the reliance on a single party to perform the computations. Each party involved in the multi-party computation contributes to the overall process.
- Verifiable Results: Blockchain provides a transparent and immutable ledger where the results of multi-party computations can be recorded. All parties can verify the correctness of the computation, ensuring trust in the outcome.
- Smart Contract-based MPC: Smart contracts in the blockchain environment can facilitate secure multi-party computation. Parties can define the rules and parameters of the computation in the smart contract, ensuring that the computation is executed as agreed upon.
- Privacy-Preserving Techniques: To maintain data privacy, cryptographic techniques such as zero-knowledge proofs (ZKPs) can be used. ZKPs enable a party to prove the validity of its input without revealing the actual data, thereby protecting sensitive information.
- Data Partitioning: In some cases, data partitioning can be utilized to split data among different parties before the computation begins. This way, each party only processes its share of the data, further enhancing privacy.

5.3 Trusted Data Sharing and Collaboration With Blockchain

Data sharing and collaboration are fundamental to modern business operations and advancements in various industries. However, sharing sensitive information with multiple parties can introduce security and privacy risks. Blockchain technology offers a decentralized, tamper-resistant, and trustless platform for trusted data sharing and collaboration. By leveraging blockchain's features, organizations can securely share data, ensure data integrity, and foster trust among participants, enabling seamless collaboration and innovation (Khan, R., et. al., 2019). Key Aspects of Trusted Data Sharing and Collaboration with Blockchain:

- Decentralized Data Sharing: Blockchain's decentralized architecture removes the need for a central mediator, shared data directly to parties. This eliminates single points of failure and reduces the risk of data breaches or unauthorized access.
- Immutable and Transparent Records: Data shared on the blockchain is recorded in an immutable and transparent ledger. Each data transaction is cryptographically linked, creating an auditable record of data activities, ensuring data integrity, and providing a tamper-resistant audit trail.
- Smart Contracts for Automation: Smart contracts are self-executing agreements written on the blockchain. They automate data sharing processes and enable parties to define the terms and conditions of data sharing. Smart contracts ensure that data is shared only when specific conditions are met, enhancing trust among participants.
- Privacy and Data Ownership: Blockchain-based data sharing solutions can be designed to prioritize data privacy and ownership. Participants retain control over their data and can choose who has access to it. Privacy-enhancing technologies like zero-knowledge proofs (ZKPs) can be employed to share data without revealing sensitive information.
- Consensus Mechanisms for Trust: Blockchain's consensus mechanisms, such as Proof of Work (PoW) or Proof of Stake (PoS), ensure that data shared on the network is agreed upon by multiple nodes. Consensus builds trust, as data transactions must be verified by the network before they are recorded.

5.4 Cloud Storage and File Sharing on the Blockchain

Cloud storage and file sharing are integral components of modern data management, enabling individuals and organizations to store, access, and share files remotely. Traditional cloud storage services rely on centralized servers, which may pose security and privacy risks due to a single point of failure. Blockchain technology offers a decentralized and secure alternative for cloud storage and file sharing, enhancing data privacy, data integrity, and user control over their data (Foster, I., Zhao, Y., Raicu, I., & Lu, S. (2008). Key Aspects of Cloud Storage and File Sharing on the Blockchain:

- Decentralized Storage: Blockchain-based cloud storage systems use distributed networks of nodes to store files, eliminating the reliance on a single central server. Data is partitioned, encrypted, and stored across multiple nodes, reducing the risk of data loss or service disruptions.
- Data Encryption and Privacy: Files stored on the blockchain are encrypted to ensure data privacy and confidentiality. Users retain control over the encryption keys, preventing unauthorized access to their files.
- Immutable Records: Blockchain's immutability ensures that file records, including access permissions and changes, are tamper-resistant and transparent. This feature enhances data integrity and provides an audit trail of all file-related activities.
- Smart Contracts for Access Control: Smart contracts can be utilized to manage file access control. File owners can define access rules and permissions, allowing only authorized parties to view, modify, or share specific files.
- P2P File Sharing: Blockchain facilitates peer-to-peer (P2P) file sharing directly between users without intermediaries. This direct sharing reduces latency and minimizes the risk of data interception during transfer.

- Data Deduplication: Blockchain-based cloud storage can employ data deduplication techniques, eliminating redundant copies of files to optimize storage space and reduce costs.

5.5 Blockchain-Based Identity Management in Cloud Services

Identity management is a critical aspect of cloud services, ensuring that users are granted appropriate access to resources while maintaining data privacy and security. Traditional centralized identity management systems may present single points of failure and become targets for cyberattacks. Blockchain technology offers a decentralized, tamper-resistant, and self-sovereign approach to identity management in cloud services, enhancing data privacy, user control, and trust among stakeholders (Zissis, D., & Lekkas, D. 2012). Key Aspects of Blockchain-Based Identity Management in Cloud Services:

- Decentralized Identity: Blockchain enables self-sovereign identity, where users have full control over their identity information. Each user can manage their identity data, including personal details and authentication credentials, without relying on a central authority.
- User-Controlled Data Sharing: Blockchain-based identity management empowers users to choose what identity attributes they want to share with service providers. Users can selectively disclose identity information based on their consent, promoting data privacy and minimizing data exposure.
- Smart Contracts for Access Control: Smart contracts govern identity verification and access control. Users must meet predefined conditions in the smart contract to access cloud services, ensuring secure and automated identity verification.
- Immutable Identity Records: Identity data stored on the blockchain becomes tamper-resistant once recorded. This immutability ensures the integrity of identity records, preventing unauthorized modifications.
- Zero-Knowledge Proofs (ZKPs): ZKPs enable identity verification without revealing sensitive information. Users can prove certain attributes without disclosing the actual data, further enhancing privacy.
- Multi-Factor Authentication (MFA): Blockchain-based identity management can incorporate MFA techniques, combining multiple authentication factors for stronger identity verification and access control.

6. IMPLEMENTATION CONSIDERATIONS AND CHALLENGES

Implementing blockchain technology in cloud security requires careful planning, coordination, and consideration of various factors to ensure a successful and secure deployment. While blockchain offers several advantages for enhancing cloud security, there are also significant challenges that organizations need to address (Al-Jaroodi, J., & Mohamed, N. 2019). Here are the key implementation considerations and challenges:

Implementation Considerations:

- ◦ Use Case Alignment: Identify the specific use cases where blockchain can add value to cloud security, such as data integrity, access control, or identity management. Align the implementation with the most relevant and beneficial scenarios.

- Scalability: Evaluate the scalability of the blockchain network to handle the expected volume of transactions and data in the cloud environment. Choose a blockchain protocol or design that can scale effectively.
- Integration with Existing Systems: Consider how the blockchain-based solutions will integrate with the existing cloud infrastructure and applications. Ensure compatibility and minimize disruption to current processes.
- Security Audits and Smart Contract Review: Conduct thorough security audits and code reviews for smart contracts to identify and fix vulnerabilities. Smart contracts are immutable once deployed, making security assessments critical before implementation.
- Regulatory Compliance: Understand and address regulatory requirements related to data privacy, data residency, and other cloud security standards. Ensure that the blockchain implementation complies with relevant laws and regulations.
- Key Management: Implement robust key management practices to safeguard private keys used in the blockchain network. Secure key storage and backup mechanisms are essential to prevent unauthorized access.
- User Experience: Consider the user experience when implementing blockchain-based solutions. Strive for user-friendly interfaces and intuitive interactions to encourage user adoption.

Challenges:

- Performance and Latency: Blockchain introduces computational overhead, which can impact cloud services' performance and latency. Optimizing the blockchain network and selecting efficient consensus mechanisms are essential to minimize delays.
- Data Privacy: While blockchain enhances data integrity, data privacy concerns persist. Ensure that sensitive data is appropriately encrypted and that access control mechanisms are in place to protect confidential information.
- Interoperability: Achieving interoperability between different blockchain networks and cloud service providers is challenging. Implementing solutions that can seamlessly work with diverse systems is crucial for practical adoption.
- Energy Consumption: Some blockchain networks, particularly those using work proof concensus, consume significant energy resources. Consider the environmental impact and explore more energy-efficient consensus mechanisms.
- Governance and Consensus: Establishing governance models and reaching consensus among network participants can be complex, especially in multi-party cloud environments.
- Standards and Best Practices: The blockchain technology landscape is evolving rapidly, and standardization efforts are ongoing. Stay up-to-date with best practices and standards in blockchain security.
- Cost: Implementing blockchain in cloud security may entail additional costs for infrastructure, development, and maintenance. Evaluate the cost-benefit analysis before embarking on blockchain adoption.

7. FUTURE DIRECTIONS AND POTENTIAL APPLICATIONS

The integration of blockchain technology into cloud security is an evolving field with exciting future directions and numerous potential applications. As blockchain continues to mature and gain acceptance across industries, its impact on cloud security is expected to grow significantly (Habib, G.,et al.,2022). Here are some future directions and potential applications of blockchain in cloud security:

- Decentralized Cloud Storage: Blockchain's decentralized nature can revolutionize cloud storage by enabling peer-to-peer data sharing and distributed storage. Users can store their data across a network of nodes, reducing reliance on centralized cloud service providers and enhancing data privacy and security.
- Privacy-Preserving Identity Management: Blockchain-based identity management solutions will empower users to control their digital identities securely. Self-sovereign identity systems can enable selective disclosure of personal data, promoting user privacy and mitigating identity-related security risks.
- Cross-Cloud Interoperability: Blockchain's ability to facilitate interoperability between different cloud providers will foster seamless data sharing and collaboration across diverse cloud platforms. This will create a more connected and efficient cloud ecosystem.
- Decentralized Access Control: Smart contracts can revolutionize access control in the cloud by automating permissions and revocations based on predefined conditions. Decentralized access control systems will reduce the risk of unauthorized access and insider threats.
- Supply Chain Security: Blockchain's transparency and immutability can enhance supply chain security by providing an auditable record of transactions, product provenance, and traceability. This will mitigate supply chain fraud and counterfeiting risks.
- Internet of Things (IoT) Security: Integrating blockchain with IoT devices can establish a secure and decentralized network, ensuring the integrity of data exchanged between devices and minimizing vulnerabilities in IoT ecosystems.
- Immutable Forensic Records: Blockchain can serve as an immutable ledger for forensic records, capturing real-time security events and incidents. This will aid in post-incident investigations and strengthen incident response capabilities.
- Zero-Trust Network Architectures: Blockchain can support zero-trust network architectures by providing a decentralized trust mechanism for identity verification, device authentication, and data access control.
- Securing Cloud Service Level Agreements (SLAs): Smart contracts can automate SLAs in cloud services, ensuring that agreed-upon service levels are met, and penalties are automatically enforced in case of non-compliance.
- Verifiable Data Provenance: Blockchain can track the origin and modification history of data in the cloud, enhancing data provenance and ensuring data integrity and authenticity.
- Cloud Security Auditing: Using blockchain for cloud security auditing can create a transparent and tamper-proof record of security events, simplifying compliance audits and enhancing trust in cloud services.

8. CASE STUDIES AND REAL-WORLD EXAMPLES

Several organizations and industries have already implemented blockchain technology to enhance cloud security, showcasing the practical applications and benefits of this integration. Here are some case studies and real-world examples of how blockchain is being utilized to strengthen cloud security:

- IBM and Food Trust: IBM's Food Trust is a blockchain-based platform that addresses supply chain security in the food industry. It leverages the cloud to create a decentralized and transparent network, enabling food producers, retailers, and regulators to trace the provenance of food products in real-time. The blockchain ensures data integrity and authenticity, reducing the risk of food fraud and contamination (Joo, J., & Han, Y. 2021).
- Microsoft and Decentralized Identity: Microsoft has been actively exploring decentralized identity solutions using blockchain technology. By integrating blockchain with Azure Active Directory, Microsoft aims to provide users with self-sovereign identities, allowing them to control their identity data securely in the cloud (Smye, T. 2019).
- Hyperledger Fabric and Secure Data Sharing: Hyperledger Fabric, an open-source blockchain framework, has been utilized to create secure and auditable data sharing platforms. Industries such as healthcare and finance have adopted Hyperledger-based systems to securely exchange sensitive data while complying with privacy regulations (Sujihelen, L. 2023).
- Filecoin and Decentralized Cloud Storage: Filecoin is a blockchain-based decentralized storage network that incentivizes users to rent out their unused storage space. This distributed cloud storage solution offers enhanced data privacy and security, as files are encrypted and distributed across multiple nodes, reducing the risk of data loss or unauthorized access (Benisi, N. Z., Aminian, M., & Javadi, B. 2020).
- Aergo and Hybrid Blockchain: Aergo is a hybrid blockchain platform that combines public and private blockchains to offer scalable and secure cloud solutions. By enabling interoperability between different chains and cloud services, Aergo enhances data exchange and collaboration while maintaining data integrity (Alshurafa, S. M., Eleyan, D., & Eleyan, A. 2021).
- Salesforce and Blockchain for Customer Data: Salesforce, a cloud-based customer relationship management (CRM) platform, is exploring blockchain to improve customer data security and data sharing. Integrating blockchain into the CRM system allows customers to control and manage access to their data while interacting with various service providers (Fu, H. P., & Chang, T. S. 2016).
- Walmart and Traceability: Walmart has implemented blockchain to enhance supply chain traceability and food safety. By integrating blockchain with cloud-based IoT devices and sensors, Walmart tracks the journey of food products from farm to shelf, ensuring authenticity and reducing the time taken for recalls (Kamath, R. 2018).
- Kyber Network and Trustless Cloud Services: Kyber Network is a decentralized protocol that enables trustless token swaps. By integrating blockchain technology with cloud services, Kyber Network ensures that transactions are executed securely without relying on centralized exchanges, enhancing user trust in the system (Tian, H., et. al., 2021).

9. CONCLUSION

The integration of blockchain technology into cloud security offers a promising avenue for organizations to address critical challenges related to data privacy, integrity, and access control. As demonstrated through case studies and real-world examples, blockchain-enhanced cloud security has the potential to revolutionize various industries, including healthcare, supply chain management, financial services, and more.

Blockchain's inherent properties, such as decentralization, immutability, and transparency, provide a solid foundation for building secure and trustworthy cloud ecosystems. Decentralized identity management solutions empower users to control their digital identities securely, enhancing data privacy and user autonomy. Immutable audit trails and smart contract-based access control mechanisms ensure data integrity and accountability, enabling organizations to comply with regulatory mandates more efficiently.

Moreover, the combination of blockchain and cloud technologies unlocks new opportunities for innovation and collaboration. Interoperable blockchain networks and hybrid solutions allow seamless data exchange and sharing across different cloud platforms, fostering a more connected and efficient digital environment.

As the technology continues to evolve and gain wider acceptance, the future of blockchain in cloud security holds immense promise. Opportunities for further research and innovation abound, ranging from scalability solutions and privacy-preserving technologies to AI integration and sustainability in blockchain networks. The evolution of cloud security with blockchain is expected to result in more secure, transparent, and user-centric digital ecosystems.

In conclusion, blockchain's integration into cloud security is a transformative step towards building a safer, more resilient digital world. Organizations that embrace this evolution and leverage blockchain's capabilities will be better equipped to navigate the complexities of data management and security in an increasingly interconnected and data-driven era. As blockchain technology continues to shape the future of cloud security, collaboration between academia, industry, and regulatory bodies will be crucial to drive advancements, ensuring that the potential of blockchain is fully harnessed to protect data, privacy, and trust in the digital landscape.

REFERENCES

Al-Jaroodi, J., & Mohamed, N. (2019). Blockchain in industries: A survey. *IEEE Access : Practical Innovations, Open Solutions*, *7*, 36500–36515. doi:10.1109/ACCESS.2019.2903554

Alshurafa, S. M., Eleyan, D., & Eleyan, A. (2021). A survey paper on blockchain as a service platforms. *International Journal of High Performance Computing and Networking*, *17*(1), 8–18. doi:10.1504/IJHPCN.2021.120739

AtzoriM. (2015). Blockchain technology and decentralized governance: Is the state still necessary? *Available at* SSRN 2709713. doi:10.2139/ssrn.2709713

AtzoriM. (2015). Blockchain technology and decentralized governance: Is the state still necessary? *Available at* SSRN 2709713. doi:10.2139/ssrn.2709713

Bashir, I. (2017). *Mastering blockchain*. Packt Publishing Ltd.

Benisi, N. Z., Aminian, M., & Javadi, B. (2020). Blockchain-based decentralized storage networks: A survey. *Journal of Network and Computer Applications*, *162*, 102656. doi:10.1016/j.jnca.2020.102656

Berdik, D., Otoum, S., Schmidt, N., Porter, D., & Jararweh, Y. (2021). A survey on blockchain for information systems management and security. *Information Processing & Management*, *58*(1), 102397. doi:10.1016/j.ipm.2020.102397

Calheiros, R. N., Ranjan, R., Beloglazov, A., De Rose, C. A., & Buyya, R. (2011). CloudSim: A toolkit for modeling and simulation of cloud computing environments and evaluation of resource provisioning algorithms. *Software, Practice & Experience*, *41*(1), 23–50. doi:10.1002pe.995

Chen, G., Xu, B., Lu, M., & Chen, N. S. (2018). Exploring blockchain technology and its potential applications for education. *Smart Learning Environments*, *5*(1), 1–10. doi:10.118640561-017-0050-x

Crosby, M., Pattanayak, P., Verma, S., & Kalyanaraman, V. (2016). Blockchain technology: Beyond bitcoin. *Applied Innovation*, *2*(6-10), 71.

Dallasega, P., Rauch, E., & Linder, C. (2018). Industry 4.0 as an enabler of proximity for construction supply chains: A systematic literature review. *Computers in Industry*, *99*, 205–225. doi:10.1016/j.compind.2018.03.039

Das, D. (2018, January). Secure cloud computing algorithm using homomorphic encryption and multi-party computation. In *2018 International Conference on Information Networking (ICOIN)* (pp. 391-396). IEEE. 10.1109/ICOIN.2018.8343147

Deepa, N., Pham, Q. V., Nguyen, D. C., Bhattacharya, S., Prabadevi, B., Gadekallu, T. R., & Pathirana, P. N. (2022). A survey on blockchain for big data: Approaches, opportunities, and future directions. *Future Generation Computer Systems*, *131*, 209–226. doi:10.1016/j.future.2022.01.017

Dillon, T., Wu, C., & Chang, E. (2010, April). Cloud computing: issues and challenges. In *2010 24th IEEE international conference on advanced information networking and applications* (pp. 27-33). AINA. 10.1109/AINA.2010.187

Fernandez-Carames, T. M., & Fraga-Lamas, P. (2019). A review on the application of blockchain to the next generation of cybersecure industry 4.0 smart factories. *IEEE Access : Practical Innovations, Open Solutions*, *7*, 45201–45218. doi:10.1109/ACCESS.2019.2908780

Foster, I., Zhao, Y., Raicu, I., & Lu, S. (2008, November). *Cloud computing and grid computing 360-degree compared. In 2008 grid computing environments workshop*. Ieee.

Fu, H. P., & Chang, T. S. (2016). An analysis of the factors affecting the adoption of cloud consumer relationship management in the machinery industry in Taiwan. *Information Development*, *32*(5), 1741–1756. doi:10.1177/0266666915623318

Habib, G., Sharma, S., Ibrahim, S., Ahmad, I., Qureshi, S., & Ishfaq, M. (2022). Blockchain technology: Benefits, challenges, applications, and integration of blockchain technology with cloud computing. *Future Internet*, *14*(11), 341. doi:10.3390/fi14110341

Hammoud, A., Sami, H., Mourad, A., Otrok, H., Mizouni, R., & Bentahar, J. (2020). AI, blockchain, and vehicular edge computing for smart and secure IoV: Challenges and directions. *IEEE Internet of Things Magazine*, *3*(2), 68–73. doi:10.1109/IOTM.0001.1900109

Joo, J., & Han, Y. (2021). An evidence of distributed trust in blockchain-based sustainable food supply chain. *Sustainability (Basel)*, *13*(19), 10980. doi:10.3390u131910980

Kamath, R. (2018). Food traceability on blockchain: Walmart's pork and mango pilots with IBM. *The Journal of the British Blockchain Association*, *1*(1), 1–12. doi:10.31585/jbba-1-1-(10)2018

Khan, R., Kumar, P., Jayakody, D. N. K., & Liyanage, M. (2019). A survey on security and privacy of 5G technologies: Potential solutions, recent advancements, and future directions. *IEEE Communications Surveys and Tutorials*, *22*(1), 196–248. doi:10.1109/COMST.2019.2933899

Kirli, D., Couraud, B., Robu, V., Salgado-Bravo, M., Norbu, S., Andoni, M., & Kiprakis, A. (2022). Smart contracts in energy systems: A systematic review of fundamental approaches and implementations. *Renewable & Sustainable Energy Reviews*, *158*, 112013. doi:10.1016/j.rser.2021.112013

Kshetri, N. (2017). Blockchain's roles in strengthening cybersecurity and protecting privacy. *Telecommunications Policy*, *41*(10), 1027–1038. doi:10.1016/j.telpol.2017.09.003

Leng, J., Ruan, G., Jiang, P., Xu, K., Liu, Q., Zhou, X., & Liu, C. (2020). Blockchain-empowered sustainable manufacturing and product lifecycle management in industry 4.0: A survey. *Renewable & Sustainable Energy Reviews*, *132*, 110112. doi:10.1016/j.rser.2020.110112

Liu, F., Shu, P., Jin, H., Ding, L., Yu, J., Niu, D., & Li, B. (2013). Gearing resource-poor mobile devices with powerful clouds: Architectures, challenges, and applications. *IEEE Wireless Communications*, *20*(3), 14–22. doi:10.1109/MWC.2013.6549279

Mackenzie, A. (2014). *Memcoin2: a hybrid proof of work/proof of stake cryptocurrency*.

Maesa, D. D. F., & Mori, P. (2020). Blockchain 3.0 applications survey. *Journal of Parallel and Distributed Computing*, *138*, 99–114. doi:10.1016/j.jpdc.2019.12.019

Martino, P., Wang, K. J., Bellavitis, C., & DaSilva, C. M. (2020). An introduction to blockchain, cryptocurrency and initial coin offerings. In New frontiers in entrepreneurial finance research (pp. 181-206).

Mohsan, S. A. H., Khan, M. A., Noor, F., Ullah, I., & Alsharif, M. H. (2022). Towards the unmanned aerial vehicles (UAVs): A comprehensive review. *Drones (Basel)*, *6*(6), 147. doi:10.3390/drones6060147

Moin, S., Karim, A., Safdar, Z., Safdar, K., Ahmed, E., & Imran, M. (2019). Securing IoTs in distributed blockchain: Analysis, requirements and open issues. *Future Generation Computer Systems*, *100*, 325–343. doi:10.1016/j.future.2019.05.023

Nguyen, D. C., Pathirana, P. N., Ding, M., & Seneviratne, A. (2020). Integration of blockchain and cloud of things: Architecture, applications and challenges. *IEEE Communications Surveys and Tutorials*, *22*(4), 2521–2549. doi:10.1109/COMST.2020.3020092

Niranjanamurthy, M., Nithya, B. N., & Jagannatha, S. J. C. C. (2019). Analysis of Blockchain technology: Pros, cons and SWOT. *Cluster Computing*, *22*(S6), 14743–14757. doi:10.100710586-018-2387-5

Peters, G. W., & Panayi, E. (2016). *Understanding modern banking ledgers through blockchain technologies: Future of transaction processing and smart contracts on the internet of money*. Springer International Publishing.

Rejeb, A., Rejeb, K., Simske, S., Treiblmaier, H., & Zailani, S. (2022). The big picture on the internet of things and the smart city: A review of what we know and what we need to know. *Internet of Things*, *19*, 100565. doi:10.1016/j.iot.2022.100565

Rittinghouse, J. W., & Ransome, J. F. (2017). *Cloud computing: implementation, management, and security*. CRC press. doi:10.1201/9781439806814

Schmitz, J., & Leoni, G. (2019). Accounting and auditing at the time of blockchain technology: A research agenda. *Australian Accounting Review*, *29*(2), 331–342. doi:10.1111/auar.12286

Shen, Z., Subbiah, S., Gu, X., & Wilkes, J. (2011, October). Cloudscale: elastic resource scaling for multi-tenant cloud systems. In *Proceedings of the 2nd ACM Symposium on Cloud Computing* (pp. 1-14). ACM. 10.1145/2038916.2038921

Smye, T. (2019). *Building Blocks: Conceptualizing the True Socio-Political Potential in Blockchain's Facilitation of Self-Sovereign Digital Identity and Decentralized Organization* [Doctoral dissertation, Carleton University].

Sujihelen, L. (2023). An efficient chain code for access control in hyper ledger fabric healthcare system. *e-Prime-Advances in Electrical Engineering, Electronics and Energy*, *5*, 100204.

Tabrizchi, H., & Kuchaki Rafsanjani, M. (2020). A survey on security challenges in cloud computing: Issues, threats, and solutions. *The Journal of Supercomputing*, *76*(12), 9493–9532. doi:10.100711227-020-03213-1

Tanwar, S., Parekh, K., & Evans, R. (2020). Blockchain-based electronic healthcare record system for healthcare 4.0 applications. *Journal of Information Security and Applications*, *50*, 102407. doi:10.1016/j.jisa.2019.102407

Tian, H., Xue, K., Luo, X., Li, S., Xu, J., Liu, J., & Wei, D. S. (2021). Enabling cross-chain transactions: A decentralized cryptocurrency exchange protocol. *IEEE Transactions on Information Forensics and Security*, *16*, 3928–3941. doi:10.1109/TIFS.2021.3096124

Viriyasitavat, W., Da Xu, L., Niyato, D., Bi, Z., & Hoonsopon, D. (2022). Applications of blockchain in business processes: A comprehensive review. *IEEE Access : Practical Innovations, Open Solutions*, *10*, 118900–118925. doi:10.1109/ACCESS.2022.3217794

Voorsluys, W., Broberg, J., & Buyya, R. (2011). Introduction to cloud computing. *Cloud computing: Principles and paradigms*, 1-41.

Xu, X. (2012). From cloud computing to cloud manufacturing. *Robotics and Computer-integrated Manufacturing*, *28*(1), 75–86. doi:10.1016/j.rcim.2011.07.002

Zafar, F., Khan, A., Malik, S. U. R., Ahmed, M., Anjum, A., Khan, M. I., Javed, N., Alam, M., & Jamil, F. (2017). A survey of cloud computing data integrity schemes: Design challenges, taxonomy and future trends. *Computers & Security*, *65*, 29–49. doi:10.1016/j.cose.2016.10.006

Zhai, S., Yang, Y., Li, J., Qiu, C., & Zhao, J. (2019, February). Research on the Application of Cryptography on the Blockchain. [). IOP Publishing.]. *Journal of Physics: Conference Series*, *1168*, 032077. doi:10.1088/1742-6596/1168/3/032077

Zhang, Q., Cheng, L., & Boutaba, R. (2010). Cloud computing: State-of-the-art and research challenges. *Journal of Internet Services and Applications*, *1*(1), 7–18. doi:10.100713174-010-0007-6

Zhang, Q., Cheng, L., & Boutaba, R. (2010). Cloud computing: State-of-the-art and research challenges. *Journal of Internet Services and Applications*, *1*(1), 7–18. doi:10.100713174-010-0007-6

Zhu, X., & Badr, Y. (2018). Identity management systems for the internet of things: A survey towards blockchain solutions. *Sensors (Basel)*, *18*(12), 4215. doi:10.339018124215 PMID:30513733

Zissis, D., & Lekkas, D. (2012). Addressing cloud computing security issues. *Future Generation Computer Systems*, *28*(3), 583–592. doi:10.1016/j.future.2010.12.006

Zissis, D., & Lekkas, D. (2012). Addressing cloud computing security issues. *Future Generation Computer Systems*, *28*(3), 583–592. doi:10.1016/j.future.2010.12.006

KEY TERMS AND DEFINITIONS

Blockchain Technology: Blockchain technology is a decentralized and distributed ledger system that records transactions across a network of computers in a secure and tamper-resistant manner. Each transaction is added to a "block," and these blocks are linked together in a chronological order to form a "chain." Blockchain is known for its transparency, immutability, and security features and is often associated with cryptocurrencies like Bitcoin.

Cloud Computing: Cloud computing is a technology paradigm that involves delivering a wide range of computing services (such as servers, storage, databases, networking, software, and analytics) over the internet. These services are provided by cloud service providers and are accessible on-demand, often on a pay-as-you-go basis. Cloud computing allows organizations and individuals to access and utilize computing resources without the need for owning and managing physical infrastructure.

Cloud Security: Cloud security refers to the set of practices, technologies, policies, and controls designed to protect data, applications, and infrastructure hosted in cloud environments. It aims to safeguard against unauthorized access, data breaches, service disruptions, and other potential security threats that may compromise the confidentiality, integrity, and availability of cloud resources.

Cryptography: Cryptography is the science and practice of secure communication techniques that protect information by transforming it into an unreadable format (ciphertext) using mathematical algorithms and encryption keys. Cryptography ensures the confidentiality, integrity, and authenticity of data and is widely used in securing digital communication, data storage, and online transactions.

Data Manipulation: Data manipulation refers to the process of altering or modifying data to achieve a desired outcome. This can include actions such as sorting, filtering, transforming, or cleaning data to make it more useful or suitable for analysis, reporting, or other purposes.

Data Storage: Data storage is the process of storing digital information or data in a structured and organized manner so that it can be accessed and retrieved when needed. Data storage can be achieved through various means, including traditional on-premises storage devices, cloud storage, and network-attached storage (NAS) systems.

Encryption Mechanisms: Encryption mechanisms are techniques and algorithms used to secure data by converting it into an unreadable format (ciphertext) using encryption keys. Encryption can be applied to data both in transit (during transmission over networks) and at rest (when stored on storage devices or servers) to protect it from unauthorized access or disclosure.

Privacy Preservation: Privacy preservation refers to the practices and technologies used to protect individuals' personal information and data from unauthorized access or disclosure while still allowing for legitimate use and processing. It involves implementing measures to ensure that data is handled in compliance with privacy regulations and user consent.

Chapter 5
Blockchain Security in Edge Computing:
Use Cases, Challenges, and Solutions

Amit Kumar Tyagi
https://orcid.org/0000-0003-2657-8700
National Institute of Fashion Technology, New Delhi, India

VLN Simhan
Georgia Southern University, USA

Shrikant Tiwari
https://orcid.org/0000-0001-6947-2362
Galgotias University, Greater Noida, India

ABSTRACT

In the past decade, edge computing and blockchain technology have been used in many applications with rapid growth. The chapter explores the intersection of blockchain technology and edge computing and investigates the security issues and solutions in this emerging domain. Edge computing refers to "the decentralized processing and storage of data at the network edge, closer to the data sources and end-users. It offers reduced latency, improved data privacy, and enhanced real-time decision-making capabilities." However, it also introduces new security challenges due to the distributed and resource-constrained nature of edge devices. The integration of blockchain technology with edge computing holds promise in addressing these security issues. Blockchain can provide a decentralized and tamper-resistant ledger for recording and verifying transactions, ensuring data integrity, and establishing trust among edge devices and stakeholders. This chapter explores several use cases where blockchain and edge computing can synergistically enhance security.

DOI: 10.4018/979-8-3693-2081-5.ch005

1. INTRODUCTION

1.1 Background of Blockchain Security in Edge Computing

Blockchain Security in Edge Computing is an emerging field that explores the integration of blockchain technology with edge computing environments to enhance security (Smith et al., 2021). Edge computing refers to the decentralized processing and storage of data at the network edge, closer to the data sources and end-users. It enables real-time data processing, reduced latency, and improved performance by using edge devices such as sensors, gateways, and edge servers. However, the distributed and resource-constrained nature of edge devices introduces unique security challenges. Note that Blockchain technology provides a decentralized and tamper-resistant ledger for recording and verifying transactions. It offers features such as immutability, transparency, and consensus mechanisms that enhance the security and trustworthiness of data and transactions.

The integration of blockchain with edge computing has the potential to address security issues in edge environments. By using blockchain, edge computing systems can achieve secure data storage and sharing, provenance and traceability, secure transactions, and decentralized governance (Zhang, Lee, & Wang, 2020). The background of Blockchain Security in Edge Computing research involves exploring the use cases, challenges, and solutions related to the integration of blockchain and edge computing. Researchers and practitioners are investigating how blockchain can enhance security in various edge computing applications such as supply chain management, IoT networks, smart cities, healthcare systems, and more. The aim is to understand the security implications of combining blockchain and edge computing, identify the challenges specific to this integration, and propose solutions to address these challenges. This includes considering the scalability of blockchain in edge environments, developing lightweight consensus algorithms suitable for resource-constrained devices, ensuring data privacy and confidentiality, and establishing interoperability standards for heterogeneous edge ecosystems. The background research in Blockchain Security in Edge Computing aims to lay the foundation for developing secure and trustworthy edge computing systems by using the benefits of blockchain technology. By addressing the security issues in this emerging field, researchers and practitioners aim to foster the adoption of blockchain-enabled edge computing and unlock its potential in various industries.

1.2 Overview of Edge Computing

Edge computing is a distributed computing paradigm that brings computation and data storage closer to the source of data generation, such as IoT devices, sensors, and edge servers. It aims to address the limitations of traditional centralized cloud computing by processing and analyzing data at the network edge, closer to where it is generated and consumed (Liu et al., 2019). This proximity enables real-time data processing, reduced latency, improved bandwidth utilization, enhanced privacy, and better overall system performance. Few essential points of edge computing are:

- In edge computing, data processing and storage occur at the edge of the network, which can include devices like edge servers, gateways, routers, or even IoT devices themselves. These edge devices serve as local computing nodes that perform data analytics, filtering, and storage, reducing the need to send large volumes of data to centralized cloud data centers. By processing data locally, edge computing minimizes latency, improves response times, and reduces network traffic.

- Edge computing is particularly beneficial in scenarios where real-time decision-making is important, such as industrial automation, autonomous vehicles, smart cities, healthcare monitoring, and retail applications. By analyzing and acting upon data at the edge, important operations can continue even in the absence of a reliable internet connection or when immediate responses are required.
- Another advantage of edge computing is improved data privacy and security. By processing data locally, sensitive information can be kept closer to its source, reducing the exposure to potential security breaches or privacy violations that could occur during data transmission to a remote cloud server.
- While edge computing offers numerous advantages, it also presents certain challenges. The distributed nature of edge devices and the need for coordination and management pose complexities in terms of system scalability, resource constraints, device heterogeneity, and fault tolerance. Additionally, ensuring data consistency, security, and privacy across a distributed edge infrastructure requires careful design and implementation.

In summary, edge computing provides a decentralized computing paradigm that complements cloud computing and enables real-time data processing, reduced latency, improved privacy, and enhanced system performance. It plays an important role in supporting emerging technologies such as IoT, AI, and autonomous systems, and it is used to revolutionize various industries by enabling advanced applications and services that rely on low-latency, high-bandwidth, and real-time processing capabilities. The basics about Blockchain Technology (including a detailed literature review), its features, applications, issue and challenges can be found in Tyagi et al. (2023).

1.3 Security Issues in Edge Computing

Edge computing introduces several security issues that need to be addressed to ensure the integrity, confidentiality, and availability of data and services (Wang, Li, & Ng, 2018). Some of the key security issue in edge computing are as follows:

- Edge Device Vulnerabilities: Edge devices, such as IoT devices and sensors, are often resource-constrained and may have limited security measures in place. These devices can be susceptible to various attacks, including malware infections, unauthorized access, and physical tampering. Ensuring the security of these devices and implementing measures such as secure boot, device authentication, and regular firmware updates is important.
- Data Privacy and Compliance: Edge computing involves processing and storing data closer to its source, which may raise privacy issues (Chen et al., 2021). Data collected by edge devices can be sensitive and subject to regulations such as GDPR (General Data Protection Regulation). Ensuring proper data encryption, access control, and compliance with privacy regulations is essential to protect user privacy and maintain legal compliance.
- Network Security: Edge computing relies on communication networks to transmit data between edge devices, gateways, and cloud systems. These networks are susceptible to various security threats, including eavesdropping, data interception, and network attacks. Implementing secure communication protocols, encryption mechanisms, and network segmentation can help mitigate these risks.

- Identity and Access Management: With the distributed nature of edge computing, managing identities and access control becomes complex. Ensuring that only authorized devices and users have access to edge resources and services is important to prevent unauthorized access and potential security breaches. Implementing robust identity and access management systems, including authentication, authorization, and auditing mechanisms, is essential.
- Data Integrity and Trust: In edge computing, data processing and storage occur across multiple edge devices, which introduces the challenge of maintaining data integrity and trust. Ensuring that data is not tampered with or modified in transit or at rest is important. Techniques such as digital signatures, hash functions, and blockchain can be employed to establish data integrity and traceability.
- Physical Security: Edge devices are often deployed in physically accessible locations, making them susceptible to physical attacks or theft. Securing edge devices through physical safeguards, such as secure enclosures, tamper-evident mechanisms, and video surveillance, can help mitigate these risks.
- Edge-to-Cloud Security: Edge computing typically involves a combination of edge devices and cloud systems, requiring secure communication and coordination between them (Kim et al., 2020). Ensuring the security of data transmission, establishing trust between edge and cloud components, and protecting cloud infrastructure from unauthorized access are essential aspects of edge-to-cloud security.
- Lifecycle Security: Managing the security of edge devices throughout their lifecycle, from provisioning and deployment to decommissioning, is important. Implementing secure device onboarding, secure firmware updates, and secure device disposal processes are important to prevent vulnerabilities and unauthorized access during the device lifecycle.

In summary, addressing these security issues requires a comprehensive security strategy that includes a combination of secure device design, secure communication protocols, robust access control mechanisms, encryption techniques, intrusion detection systems, and security monitoring and incident response procedures. It is important to adopt a defense-in-depth approach, considering security at each layer of the edge computing architecture and implementing appropriate security controls to protect data and services in edge environments.

2. BLOCKCHAIN SOLUTIONS FOR SECURITY IN EDGE COMPUTING

Blockchain technology can provide several solutions for enhancing security in edge computing environments. Here are some ways blockchain can address security issues in edge computing (refer figure 1):

- Immutable Data Integrity: Blockchain's underlying principle of immutability can ensure the integrity of data stored in edge devices. By storing data in a decentralized and distributed manner across the blockchain network, it becomes tamper-proof and resistant to unauthorized modifications. This ensures the integrity of data collected from edge devices, preventing unauthorized tampering or manipulation.

- Decentralized Trust and Authentication: Blockchain can enable decentralized trust and authentication mechanisms in edge computing. Instead of relying on a centralized authority for identity verification and access control, blockchain can facilitate peer-to-peer authentication and consensus-based decision-making. This helps establish trust between edge devices and enables secure communication and collaboration in a decentralized manner.

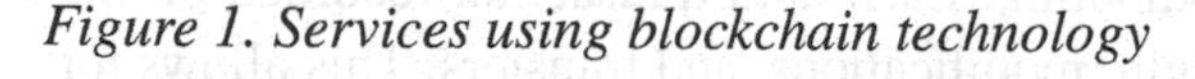

Figure 1. Services using blockchain technology

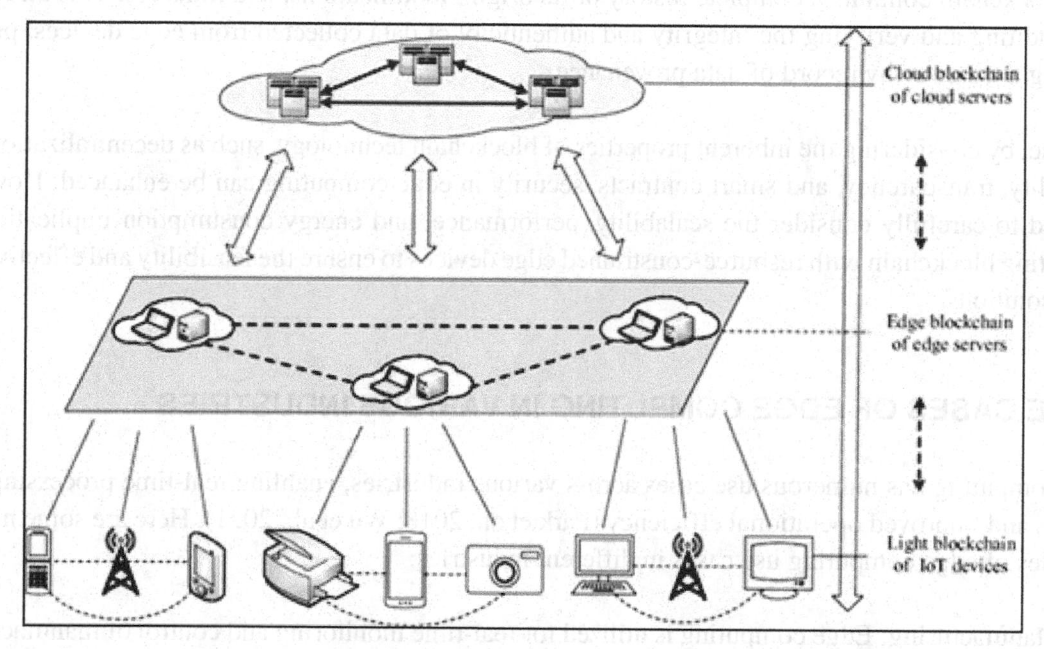

- Secure Data Sharing and Access Control: Blockchain-based smart contracts can provide secure and automated data sharing and access control mechanisms in edge computing. Smart contracts define the rules and conditions for accessing and sharing data, ensuring that only authorized devices or entities can access specific data or services. This enhances data privacy and prevents unauthorized access to sensitive information.
- Distributed Consensus and Fault Tolerance: Blockchain's consensus algorithms, such as Proof-of-Work (PoW) or Proof-of-Stake (PoS), can provide distributed consensus in edge computing environments. This ensures that data processed and stored in edge devices is validated by multiple nodes in a decentralized manner, making the system more resilient to attacks and ensuring fault tolerance.
- Auditable and Transparent Operations: Blockchain's transparency and auditability features can be used to monitor and verify the operations of edge devices in real-time. By recording transactions and actions on the blockchain, it becomes possible to track and audit the activities of edge devices, identifying any suspicious or malicious behavior. This enhances the overall security and accountability of edge computing systems.

- Trustworthy Software Updates: Blockchain can facilitate secure and verifiable software updates for edge devices. By utilizing smart contracts and digital signatures, software updates can be validated and securely distributed across the network. This ensures that only trusted and verified software updates are applied to edge devices, mitigating the risk of malicious or unauthorized modifications.
- Data Provenance and Auditing: Blockchain's transparent and immutable nature enables the tracking and auditing of data provenance in edge computing. Each data transaction recorded on the blockchain contains a complete history of its origin, modifications, and transfers. This allows for auditing and verifying the integrity and authenticity of data collected from edge devices, providing a trustworthy record of data provenance.

Hene, by considering the inherent properties of blockchain technology, such as decentralization, immutability, transparency, and smart contracts, security in edge computing can be enhanced. However, we need to carefully consider the scalability, performance, and energy consumption implications of integrating blockchain with resource-constrained edge devices to ensure the feasibility and effectiveness of the solutions.

3. USE CASES OF EDGE COMPUTING IN VARIOUS INDUSTRIES

Edge computing has numerous use cases across various industries, enabling real-time processing, low latency, and improved operational efficiency (Park et al., 2018; Wu et al., 2021). Here are some notable examples of edge computing use cases in different industries:

- Manufacturing: Edge computing is utilized for real-time monitoring and control of manufacturing processes, enabling predictive maintenance, quality control, and optimizing production efficiency. Edge devices collect and process sensor data, perform analytics, and trigger immediate actions, leading to reduced downtime, enhanced productivity, and cost savings.
- Energy and Utilities: Edge computing is applied in energy and utility sectors for grid monitoring, demand response, and energy management. Edge devices capture data from smart meters, sensors, and power infrastructure, enabling real-time analysis, load balancing, and efficient energy distribution. This facilitates optimized energy usage, improved grid reliability, and integration of renewable energy sources.
- Healthcare: Edge computing is used in healthcare for remote patient monitoring, telemedicine, and real-time health data analysis. Edge devices collect patient data, perform real-time analytics, and enable timely interventions. This supports early detection of health issues, improves patient care, and reduces healthcare costs.
- Transportation and Logistics: Edge computing is employed in transportation and logistics for fleet management, route optimization, and real-time tracking. Edge devices installed in vehicles or at logistics hubs process data from sensors, GPS, and traffic sources, enabling efficient logistics planning, reduced delivery times, and improved supply chain visibility.
- Smart Cities: Edge computing plays an important role in building smart cities by supporting applications such as intelligent traffic management, public safety monitoring, waste management, and

environmental sensing. Edge devices placed throughout the city collect and process data locally, enabling real-time decision-making, efficient resource allocation, and improved sustainability.
- Retail and Customer Engagement: Edge computing is used in retail for personalized customer experiences, inventory management, and real-time analytics. Edge devices capture and analyze customer behavior data, enabling personalized recommendations, targeted marketing, and optimized inventory management. This enhances customer satisfaction, drives sales, and improves operational efficiency.
- Agriculture: Edge computing is applied in agriculture for precision farming, crop monitoring, and irrigation control. Edge devices equipped with sensors collect data on soil moisture, weather conditions, and crop health. Real-time data analysis at the edge facilitates optimal resource allocation, improved crop yields, and efficient water usage.
- Financial Services: Edge computing is utilized in the financial sector for real-time fraud detection, algorithmic trading, and high-frequency trading. Edge devices analyze market data, customer transactions, and patterns locally, enabling rapid response to fraud attempts and supporting real-time trading decisions.

Note that these are the few examples, and edge computing has relevance and potential applications in other industries as well, including education, entertainment, hospitality, and more. The ability to process data at the edge brings agility, responsiveness, and efficiency to various sectors, enabling transformative advancements and improving overall business operations.

3.1 Security Challenges in Edge Computing Environments

Edge computing environments introduce unique security challenges due to the distributed nature of resources and the diverse range of devices involved (Rekha et al., 2020; Wang, Liu, & Chen, 2018). Here are some key security challenges in edge computing:

- Device Security: Edge computing environments involve numerous devices, including IoT devices, gateways, and edge servers. These devices can be vulnerable to attacks, such as unauthorized access, malware, or physical tampering. Ensuring the security of these devices is important to prevent unauthorized access to sensitive data and potential disruptions in the network.
- Data Privacy: Edge computing involves processing and storing data closer to the source, which may include sensitive or personal information. Ensuring data privacy becomes important to protect the confidentiality and integrity of the data. The distributed nature of edge computing makes it important to implement secure data transmission and storage mechanisms to prevent unauthorized access or data leakage.
- Network Security: Edge computing environments rely on networks to transmit data between devices and the cloud. Securing the network infrastructure, including routers, switches, and gateways, is essential to prevent network-level attacks, such as man-in-the-middle attacks or network spoofing. Encryption and authentication mechanisms should be implemented to secure network communication.
- Authentication and Access Control: With a large number of devices and entities in edge computing environments, proper authentication and access control mechanisms are important. Ensuring

that only authorized devices and users can access resources and perform actions is essential to prevent unauthorized access or malicious activities.

- Trustworthiness of Edge Devices: Edge computing environments often involve devices from various manufacturers and suppliers, which may have varying levels of security features and vulnerabilities. Ensuring the trustworthiness of edge devices, including verifying their integrity, authenticity, and software integrity, is important to prevent the compromise of the entire edge computing environment.
- Scalability and Management: Managing security in a distributed edge computing environment with a large number of devices and resources can be challenging. Security measures need to be scalable and easily manageable to ensure consistent security across all edge devices and to promptly detect and respond to security incidents.
- Physical Security: Edge computing devices are often deployed in diverse locations, including remote sites or harsh environments. Ensuring physical security measures, such as tamper-proofing devices, securing physical access to devices, and protecting against physical attacks, is important to prevent unauthorized access or tampering with edge devices.
- Update and Patch Management: Edge devices may require frequent updates or patches to address security vulnerabilities or add new security features. Ensuring a robust update and patch management process becomes important to keep the devices secure and up-to-date with the latest security measures.

Hence, addressing these security challenges requires a multi-layered approach, including device hardening, encryption, secure communication protocols, robust access control mechanisms, continuous monitoring, and security analytics. Collaboration between device manufacturers, network providers, and application developers is necessary to establish comprehensive security frameworks for edge computing environments.

4. BLOCKCHAIN TECHNOLOGY IN EDGE COMPUTING

4.1 Introduction, Advantages, and Disadvantages of Blockchain in Edge Computing

Blockchain technology, when combined with edge computing, brings additional benefits and security enhancements to edge computing environments (Garcia et al., 2021). Blockchain provides a decentralized and immutable ledger that enables secure and transparent data transactions and interactions between edge devices. By integrating blockchain into edge computing, trust and accountability can be established among the distributed devices and stakeholders involved in edge computing networks.

4.1.1 Advantages of Blockchain in Edge Computing

Figure 2 provides a detail explanation of blockchain in edge computing.

- Data Integrity and Security: Blockchain ensures the integrity and security of data in edge computing environments. Transactions recorded on the blockchain are immutable, making it difficult for malicious actors to tamper with the data. The distributed nature of blockchain provides a higher level of data security by eliminating a single point of failure.

- Trust and Consensus: Blockchain introduces a trust layer among distributed devices in edge computing networks. Through consensus mechanisms, devices can agree on the validity of transactions and maintain a shared view of the network state. This enables secure collaboration and eliminates the need for central authorities or intermediaries in edge computing environments.
- Auditing and Accountability: Blockchain provides a transparent and auditable record of transactions and interactions in edge computing. This can help in tracing and verifying the origin and authenticity of data exchanged between devices. Blockchain's decentralized nature ensures accountability and reduces the risk of data manipulation or unauthorized changes.
- Scalability and Efficiency: Blockchain can enhance the scalability and efficiency of edge computing networks. By distributing computational tasks across edge devices and using blockchain for consensus and transaction management, the network can handle a larger number of transactions and achieve faster processing times compared to traditional centralized systems.

Figure 2. Benefits of blockchain in edge computing

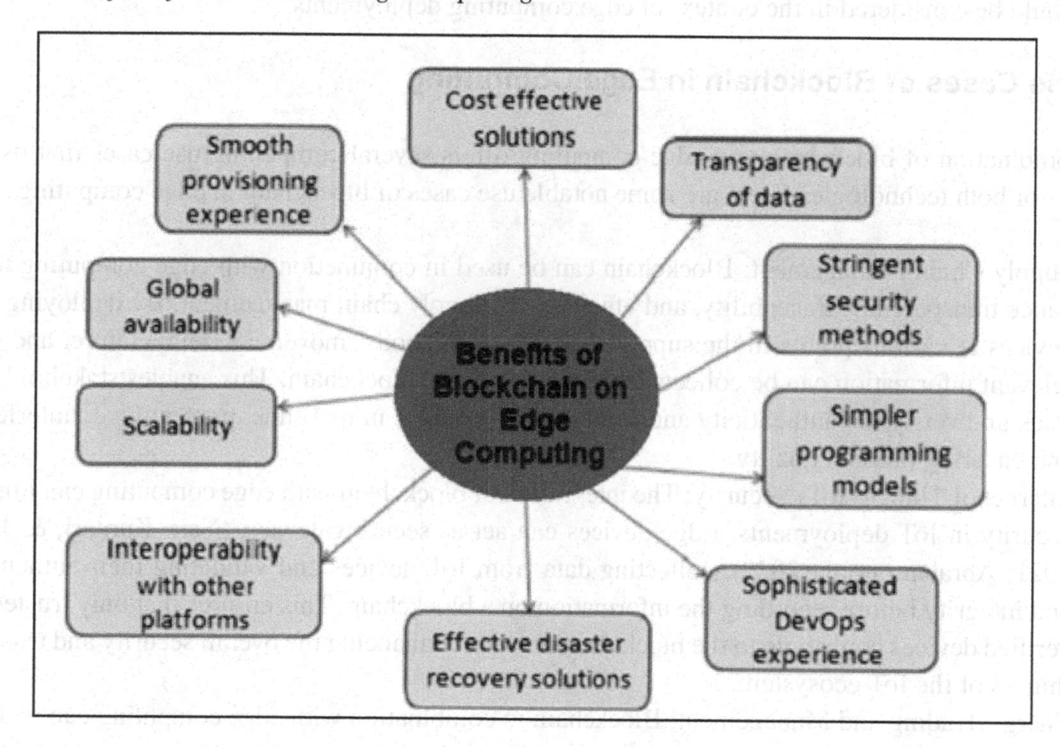

4.1.2 Disadvantages of Blockchain in Edge Computing

- Performance and Latency: Blockchain transactions require consensus among network participants, which can introduce latency and affect real-time processing in edge computing environments. The computational overhead and the need to reach consensus can impact the responsiveness and performance of edge devices.

- Energy Consumption: Blockchain operations, such as consensus algorithms and cryptographic computations, require significant computational power and energy consumption. In resource-constrained edge computing environments, the energy demands of blockchain can be a challenge, especially when running on low-power devices.
- Scalability Challenges: Blockchain scalability remains a challenge in large-scale edge computing networks with a high volume of transactions. As the number of transactions increases, the size of the blockchain and the computational requirements for consensus can grow, potentially leading to scalability issues.
- Complexity and Development Costs: Integrating blockchain into edge computing environments requires specialized knowledge and development efforts. The complexity of managing blockchain infrastructure, designing smart contracts, and ensuring interoperability with existing edge systems can increase development costs and complexity.

Note that to carefully assess the specific requirements and constraints of edge computing scenarios before implementing blockchain technology (Lee et al., 2019; Zhang, Chen, & Hu, 2020). While blockchain brings security and trust advantages, its impact on performance, scalability, and energy consumption should be considered in the context of edge computing deployments.

4.2 Use Cases of Blockchain in Edge Computing

The combination of blockchain and edge computing offers several compelling use cases that use the benefits of both technologies. Here are some notable use cases of blockchain in edge computing:

- Supply Chain Management: Blockchain can be used in conjunction with edge computing to enhance transparency, traceability, and efficiency in supply chain management. By deploying edge devices at various points in the supply chain, data on goods' movement, temperature, and other relevant information can be collected and recorded on a blockchain. This enables stakeholders to track and verify the authenticity and condition of products in real-time, preventing counterfeiting and ensuring product quality.
- Internet of Things (IoT) Security: The integration of blockchain with edge computing can improve security in IoT deployments. Edge devices can act as secure gateways (Nair, Kumari, & Tyagi, 2021; Abraham et al., 2022), collecting data from IoT devices and validating their authenticity and integrity before recording the information on a blockchain. This ensures that only trusted and verified devices contribute to the blockchain network, enhancing the overall security and trustworthiness of the IoT ecosystem.
- Energy Trading and Management: Blockchain in combination with edge computing can facilitate decentralized energy trading and management. Edge devices equipped with smart meters can collect real-time energy consumption and production data, which can be recorded on a blockchain. This enables peer-to-peer energy transactions, allowing consumers to directly buy and sell energy with one another without the need for intermediaries. Blockchain ensures transparency, accuracy, and trust in energy transactions.
- Decentralized Content Delivery Networks (CDNs): Edge computing combined with blockchain can enable the creation of decentralized content delivery networks. Edge devices can store and distribute content, while blockchain provides a decentralized ledger for managing content distri-

bution, caching, and monetization. This allows for faster content delivery, improved scalability, and reduced reliance on centralized CDN providers.

- Edge Computing Orchestration: Blockchain can be used to manage and orchestrate edge computing resources in a decentralized manner. By utilizing blockchain, edge devices can autonomously negotiate and exchange computing resources based on predefined smart contracts. This enables efficient resource allocation and dynamic scaling of edge computing networks, ensuring optimal utilization and load balancing across devices.
- Autonomous Vehicles and Mobility: Blockchain integrated with edge computing can support secure and decentralized communication among autonomous vehicles and infrastructure. Edge devices equipped with blockchain technology can facilitate vehicle-to-vehicle (V2V) and vehicle-to-infrastructure (V2I) communication, enabling secure and trustless exchange of data for navigation, traffic management, and autonomous decision-making.
- Healthcare Data Management: In healthcare, combining blockchain with edge computing can enable secure and privacy-preserving management of patient health records. Edge devices can collect and process sensitive health data locally, and the hashed information can be stored on a blockchain. Patients can control access to their records and grant permission to healthcare providers as needed, ensuring data privacy and security.

These use cases highlight the potential for blockchain to enhance security, trust, and efficiency in edge computing environments across various industries. The integration of blockchain with edge computing opens up new possibilities for decentralized and secure applications that benefit from real-time data processing at the edge.

4.3 Integration of Blockchain and Edge Computing

The integration of blockchain and edge computing offers unique advantages and opportunities for decentralized and secure data processing at the edge of the network. Here's an overview of how blockchain can be integrated with edge computing:

- Data Validation and Trust: Edge computing devices can collect and process data from various sources, such as IoT devices or sensors. By integrating blockchain technology, the collected data can be validated and recorded on a distributed ledger. This ensures data integrity and immutability, creating a trusted and tamper-proof record of the data generated at the edge.
- Secure Communication and Interactions: Blockchain can facilitate secure communication and interactions between edge devices and other entities in the network. Through the use of cryptographic techniques and smart contracts, blockchain enables secure peer-to-peer communication, authentication, and authorization, eliminating the need for central authorities or intermediaries. This enhances security and privacy in edge computing environments.
- Consensus and Trust Establishment: Consensus mechanisms in blockchain enable edge devices to reach agreement on the validity and ordering of transactions. This consensus ensures that all devices have a shared view of the network state, enabling trust and coordination in a decentralized manner. Consensus algorithms can be tailored to the specific requirements and constraints of edge computing, considering factors such as limited resources and low latency.

- Data Monetization and Auditing: Blockchain integration allows for transparent and auditable data transactions and monetization models at the edge. Edge devices can securely exchange data with other entities, and smart contracts can automate the process of data sharing and monetization. This opens up new possibilities for value creation, where data owners can directly sell or license their data to interested parties, while maintaining control over their data and ensuring proper auditing and accountability.
- Decentralized Edge Resource Management: Blockchain can be used to manage and allocate edge computing resources in a decentralized manner. Edge devices can participate in a blockchain network to autonomously negotiate and exchange computing resources based on predefined rules and smart contracts. This allows for efficient resource allocation, load balancing, and coordination among edge devices, enhancing the overall performance and scalability of edge computing environments.
- Security and Privacy Enhancements: Blockchain integration can strengthen the security and privacy of edge computing. By using the tamper-proof nature of blockchain, edge devices can securely exchange data and execute transactions without relying on a central authority (Tyagi & Sreenath, 2023). Blockchain's decentralized architecture mitigates the risk of single points of failure and reduces the vulnerability to attacks, ensuring a higher level of security and data protection in edge computing environments.

The integration of blockchain and edge computing brings together the benefits of decentralized trust, data integrity, and secure interactions with the real-time processing capabilities of edge devices. This integration provides the way for innovative applications and services in various domains, ranging from supply chain management to IoT security and autonomous systems.

5. SECURITY CHALLENGES IN BLOCKCHAIN-ENABLED EDGE COMPUTING

5.1 Data Privacy and Confidentiality in Blockchain-Enabled Edge Computing

Data privacy and confidentiality are important issues when integrating blockchain with edge computing. While blockchain technology offers transparency and immutability, it presents challenges in protecting sensitive data in edge computing environments. Here are some approaches to address data privacy and confidentiality in blockchain-enabled edge computing:

- Encryption: Utilize encryption techniques to protect the confidentiality of data stored and transmitted in edge computing environments. Encrypting data before storing it on the blockchain or transmitting it between edge devices ensures that only authorized parties with the decryption keys can access the sensitive information.
- Private and Permissioned Blockchains: Implement private or permissioned blockchains in edge computing scenarios to restrict access to sensitive data. Private blockchains limit participation to a select group of known entities, while permissioned blockchains allow controlled access. This helps maintain data privacy by ensuring that only authorized participants can access the blockchain network and the associated data.

- Off-Chain Data Storage: Keep sensitive data off-chain, separate from the blockchain itself. Rather than storing confidential information directly on the blockchain, store it in secure and encrypted databases or storage solutions. The blockchain can then store only the necessary metadata or cryptographic hashes that validate the integrity and authenticity of the off-chain data.
- Data Pseudonymization: Apply data pseudonymization techniques to obfuscate personally identifiable information (PII) or other sensitive data. Pseudonymization replaces identifiable information with pseudonyms, making it challenging to link the data to specific individuals or entities. By separating the identity from the data, privacy risks can be reduced while still allowing for the validation and auditing of transactions on the blockchain.
- Access Controls and Permission Models: Implement granular access controls and permission models within the blockchain-enabled edge computing environment. This ensures that only authorized users or devices can access specific data or perform certain actions on the blockchain network. Role-based access control (RBAC) and attribute-based access control (ABAC) mechanisms can be employed to enforce fine-grained access policies and protect sensitive data.
- Data Minimization: Adopt a data minimization approach where only necessary data is stored or processed on the blockchain. In edge computing, where resources may be limited, minimizing the amount of data stored on the blockchain helps reduce the exposure of sensitive information.

5.2 Scalability and Performance in Blockchain-Enabled Edge Computing

Scalability and performance are important issues in any distributed computing system (Tyagi, Kukreja, Nair et al, 2022; Tyagi et al., 2023), including blockchain-enabled edge computing. Let's discuss each of these aspects in the context of this technology.

Scalability: Scalability refers to the ability of a system to handle an increasing workload as the number of participants or the amount of data grows. In blockchain-enabled edge computing, scalability can be challenging due to several factors:

- Network bandwidth: Edge devices typically have limited network bandwidth compared to centralized systems. This limitation can affect the speed and efficiency of communication between nodes in a blockchain network.
- Processing power: Edge devices often have lower computational capabilities compared to powerful servers. This limitation can impact the processing of transactions and smart contracts on the blockchain.
- Storage capacity: Edge devices usually have limited storage capacity. Storing a complete copy of the blockchain ledger on every edge device may not be feasible due to storage constraints.

To address these scalability challenges, several techniques can be employed:

- Sharding: Sharding involves dividing the blockchain network into smaller partitions called shards. Each shard can process a subset of transactions, improving the overall throughput of the system. Sharding can be particularly useful in edge computing scenarios where devices can be assigned to different shards based on their proximity or other criteria.
- Off-chain processing: Not all computations and transactions need to be executed on the blockchain itself. Off-chain processing involves performing certain operations outside the main blockchain

network to reduce the computational and storage burden. This approach can improve scalability by minimizing the load on edge devices.
- Layer 2 solutions: Layer 2 solutions, such as state channels or sidechains, can be employed to handle a large number of transactions off the main blockchain. These solutions allow for faster and more efficient transaction processing, relieving the scalability limitations of the main blockchain.

Performance: Performance in blockchain-enabled edge computing refers to the speed and responsiveness of the system in executing transactions and smart contracts. Achieving high performance in this context can be challenging due to the following factors:

- Latency: Edge devices often operate at the network edge, far away from centralized servers. This geographical distance can introduce higher latency in communication between nodes, affecting the overall performance of the system.
- Processing power: As mentioned earlier, edge devices usually have limited processing power compared to powerful servers. This limitation can lead to slower transaction processing and contract execution.
- Consensus algorithms: Blockchain networks typically rely on consensus algorithms to agree on the validity and order of transactions. Some consensus algorithms, such as proof-of-work (PoW), can be computationally intensive and introduce delays in transaction finality.

To improve performance in blockchain-enabled edge computing (Goyal & Tyagi, 2020; Tyagi, Kukreja, Nair et al, 2022), the following approaches can be considered:

- Optimized consensus algorithms: Alternative consensus algorithms, such as proof-of-stake (PoS) or delegated proof-of-stake (DPoS), can be employed to reduce the computational requirements and transaction confirmation time.
- Caching and local processing: Edge devices can employ caching mechanisms to store frequently accessed data locally. This reduces the need to retrieve data from the blockchain network, resulting in faster response times. Similarly, performing local processing of certain operations can reduce the latency associated with interacting with the blockchain.
- Prioritization and resource allocation: Edge devices can prioritize important transactions or smart contracts to ensure their timely processing. Resource allocation mechanisms can be implemented to allocate computational resources efficiently based on transaction importance or device capabilities.

In summary, achieving scalability and performance in blockchain-enabled edge computing requires careful design issues, using techniques like sharding, off-chain processing, optimized consensus algorithms, caching, and resource allocation. These approaches can help overcome the inherent limitations of edge devices and enhance the efficiency of blockchain-based systems at the network edge.

5.3 Consensus Mechanisms in Edge Environments

Consensus mechanisms play an important role in blockchain networks by ensuring agreement on the validity and order of transactions among participants (Nair & Tyagi, 2021; Tyagi, 2023). In edge environments, where resources and network conditions are limited, selecting an appropriate consensus mechanism becomes even more important. Here are a few consensus mechanisms that can be suitable for edge environments:

- Proof of Stake (PoS): PoS is a consensus mechanism where the probability of a node being chosen to create a new block is proportional to the number of tokens it holds or "stakes." Unlike proof of work (PoW), PoS does not require significant computational power. This makes it more energy-efficient and suitable for resource-constrained edge devices. PoS-based blockchains can achieve faster transaction confirmation times, which is beneficial in edge environments with limited latency tolerance.
- Delegated Proof of Stake (DPoS): DPoS is a variation of PoS where token holders vote for a limited number of delegates to create blocks on their behalf. These delegates take turns producing blocks in a round-robin fashion. DPoS is known for its scalability and fast block confirmation times, making it suitable for edge environments where quick transaction processing is desired. By limiting the number of block producers, DPoS reduces the computational requirements and improves overall performance.
- Practical Byzantine Fault Tolerance (PBFT): PBFT is a consensus mechanism that is often used in permissioned or private blockchain networks. It requires a predetermined set of nodes to reach consensus by following a multi-round voting process. PBFT can achieve fast finality and is known for its low latency and high throughput. However, it requires a certain level of trust among the participating nodes, which may not always be feasible in decentralized edge environments.
- Directed Acyclic Graph (DAG) Consensus: DAG-based consensus mechanisms, such as IOTA's Tangle or Hedera Hashgraph, are alternatives to traditional blockchain consensus algorithms. They use a graph-like structure to organize and validate transactions. DAG consensus can offer high scalability and transaction throughput, making it suitable for edge environments. However, we need to note that DAG-based systems may have different security trade-offs compared to traditional blockchain approaches.

Note that the choice of consensus mechanism should align with the specific requirements and characteristics of the edge environment. Factors such as resource limitations, latency tolerance, network connectivity, and the desired level of decentralization need to be considered when selecting an appropriate consensus mechanism for edge computing scenarios. Additionally, hybrid approaches that combine multiple consensus mechanisms or utilize off-chain computations can also be explored to optimize the performance and scalability of blockchain-enabled edge environments.

5.4 Trust and Identity Management in Blockchain-Enabled Edge Computing

Trust and identity management are important aspects of blockchain-enabled edge computing systems (Tyagi, 2022; Tyagi, Chandrasekaran, & Sreenath, 2022). Let's discuss how these elements are addressed in such environments:

5.4.1 Trust in Edge Computing

Trust in edge computing involves establishing trust among the participating entities, including edge devices, edge nodes, and other network participants. Here are some issues for trust management:

- Consensus Mechanisms: The choice of a consensus mechanism plays a significant role in establishing trust in the system. By using mechanisms like proof of stake or practical Byzantine fault tolerance, consensus can be achieved among participants, ensuring the validity and integrity of transactions and data.
- Smart Contracts: Smart contracts, executed on the blockchain, can help automate and enforce trust agreements between edge devices and other entities. Smart contracts define the rules and conditions under which transactions or interactions take place, providing transparency and accountability.
- Reputation Systems: Reputation systems can be implemented to evaluate and establish trustworthiness among the participants in edge computing. These systems can track the behavior, performance, and reliability of edge devices and assign reputation scores accordingly, influencing trust levels in the network.

5.4.2 Identity Management in Edge Computing

Identity management is essential for ensuring the authenticity and accountability of participants in a blockchain-enabled edge computing system. Here are some approaches to consider:

- Digital Identities: Each participant, including edge devices, can have a unique digital identity on the blockchain. These digital identities can be verified and linked to physical or virtual entities, providing a means to establish trust and accountability.
- Public-Key Infrastructure (PKI): PKI can be utilized to manage cryptographic keys and certificates for secure communication and authentication in edge computing. Participants can have their public keys registered on the blockchain, enabling secure and verifiable interactions.
- Decentralized Identity (DID): DID frameworks allow for self-sovereign identities, where participants have control over their own identities and associated data. DIDs provide a decentralized approach to identity management, enhancing privacy and giving individuals or devices greater control over their digital presence.
- Zero-Knowledge Proofs (ZKPs): ZKPs can be employed to validate the authenticity of information without revealing the actual data. By using ZKPs, edge devices can prove their identity or certain attributes without disclosing sensitive information, enhancing privacy and security.

5.4.3 Privacy and Data Protection

Edge computing involves processing and storing data on local devices, which raises privacy issues. To address these issues:

- Encryption: Data can be encrypted to protect its confidentiality, both in transit and at rest. Encryption algorithms and techniques can be employed to ensure that only authorized parties can access and decrypt the data.

- Data Minimization: Limiting the collection and storage of sensitive data on edge devices can reduce the risks associated with data exposure. Adopting a data minimization approach ensures that only necessary data is stored, reducing the potential impact of a data breach.
- Access Control: Implementing access control mechanisms, such as role-based access control (RBAC), ensures that only authorized entities can access certain data or perform specific operations. Access control policies can be defined and enforced through smart contracts on the blockchain.
- Compliance and Governance: Compliance with data protection regulations and industry standards is important in edge computing. Adhering to frameworks like GDPR (General Data Protection Regulation) or industry-specific guidelines helps ensure the appropriate handling of personal and sensitive data.

Hence, by incorporating trust mechanisms, robust identity management, and privacy-enhancing techniques, blockchain-enabled edge computing systems can establish trust among participants, protect data, and enable secure and accountable interactions in decentralized environments.

5.5 Sybil Attacks and Network Security in Blockchain-Enabled Edge Computing

Sybil attacks and network security are important issues in blockchain-enabled edge computing systems. Let's explore these concepts and discuss strategies to mitigate such attacks and enhance network security:

5.5.1 Sybil Attacks

A Sybil attack occurs when a malicious actor creates multiple fake identities or nodes to gain control over the network or influence its operations. In edge computing environments (Tyagi, 2015), where edge devices may have limited resources and limited ability to verify the identities of other nodes, Sybil attacks can pose significant risks. Here are some measures to mitigate Sybil attacks:

- Identity Verification: Implement mechanisms to verify the identity of participating nodes in the network. This can include the use of digital certificates, public-key infrastructure (PKI), or decentralized identity (DID) frameworks to establish trust and authenticity.
- Reputation Systems: Employ reputation systems that track the behavior and performance of nodes in the network. Nodes with higher reputation scores can be trusted more, while suspicious or newly added nodes can be subjected to additional scrutiny or restrictions.
- Proof-of-Work (PoW) or Proof-of-Stake (PoS): Consensus mechanisms like PoW or PoS can deter Sybil attacks. PoW requires computational resources, making it difficult for an attacker to create multiple identities. PoS relies on token ownership, where gaining control over the network requires holding a significant number of tokens, making it economically infeasible for an attacker to create numerous identities.
- Identity Attestation: Employ identity attestation mechanisms where trusted entities can validate and vouch for the authenticity of new nodes joining the network. This can be done through a trusted onboarding process or reputation-based introductions.

Figure 3. Intrusion detection using blockchain technology in edge network

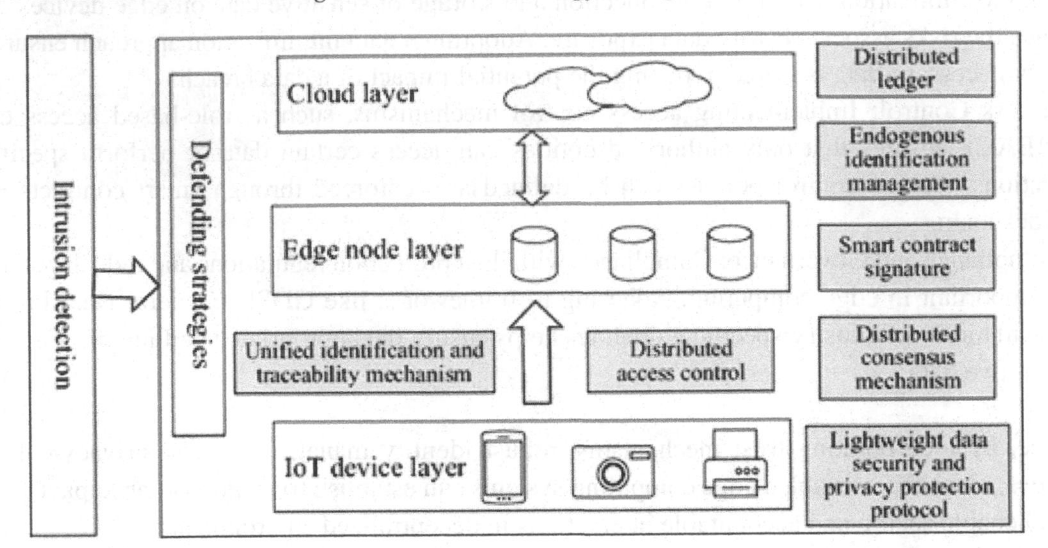

Here, Figure 3 discusses about detecting intrusion/ worm/ sybil attack in an edge network ad protect the system using blockchain technology.

5.5.2 Network Security

Ensuring network security in blockchain-enabled edge computing systems involves protecting the integrity, confidentiality, and availability of data and operations (Nair, Tyagi, & Sreenath, 2021; Abraham et al., 2021). Here are some network security strategies:

- Secure Communication: Utilize secure communication protocols, such as Transport Layer Security (TLS), to encrypt data transmission between nodes. This prevents eavesdropping and tampering of sensitive information.
- Firewalls and Intrusion Detection/Prevention Systems: Implement firewalls and intrusion detection/prevention systems to monitor and control network traffic. These security measures can identify and prevent malicious activities and unauthorized access attempts.
- Access Control: Employ strong access control mechanisms to limit the privileges and permissions of nodes and users. This ensures that only authorized entities can access and modify the blockchain and associated resources.
- Regular Updates and Patching: Keep the edge devices and network infrastructure up to date with the latest security patches and firmware updates. This helps address known vulnerabilities and protects against exploits.
- Consensus Algorithm Security: Ensure the security of the chosen consensus algorithm. For example, in PoW-based systems, protect against 51% attacks, while in PoS-based systems, safeguard against stake concentration attacks.
- Immutable Audit Trail: Use the immutability of the blockchain to create an audit trail of activities and transactions. This enables the detection of any unauthorized or malicious activities, allowing for timely intervention and mitigation.

- Continuous Monitoring: Implement monitoring systems to detect and respond to security incidents promptly. This includes real-time monitoring of network traffic, system logs, and anomaly detection techniques.
- Incident Response and Recovery: Develop a robust incident response plan to address security breaches or potential attacks. This includes procedures for isolating compromised nodes, analyzing the impact, and recovering the network's integrity.

By implementing strong identity management mechanisms, deploying consensus algorithms resistant to Sybil attacks, and incorporating comprehensive network security measures, blockchain-enabled edge computing systems can enhance security and protect against potential threats and attacks. Continuous monitoring and timely incident response are also essential to maintain the integrity and availability of the network.

6. SOLUTIONS FOR BLOCKCHAIN SECURITY IN EDGE COMPUTING

6.1 Data Encryption and Privacy-Preserving Techniques for Blockchain Security in Edge Computing

Data encryption and privacy-preserving techniques are important for maintaining security and protecting sensitive information in blockchain-enabled edge computing systems (Tyagi, 2015; Tyagi, 2023; Tyagi & Bansal, 2023; Tyagi, Chandrasekaran, & Sreenath, 2022). Here are some approaches to consider:

6.1.1 Data Encryption

Encrypting data ensures its confidentiality by converting it into an unreadable format that can only be deciphered with the appropriate decryption key. Some encryption techniques that can be employed in edge computing environments include:

- Symmetric Encryption: Symmetric encryption algorithms use a single key for both encryption and decryption. This approach is efficient for encrypting and decrypting large amounts of data. However, secure key management is essential to prevent unauthorized access.
- Asymmetric Encryption: Asymmetric encryption, also known as public-key encryption, involves using a pair of keys: a public key for encryption and a private key for decryption. This approach provides secure communication between entities without sharing the private key. It is commonly used for secure key exchange and digital signatures.
- Homomorphic Encryption: Homomorphic encryption allows computations to be performed on encrypted data without decrypting it. This technique can enable secure data processing in edge computing scenarios, where sensitive data remains encrypted even during computation.

6.1.2 Privacy-Preserving Techniques

Preserving privacy in blockchain-enabled edge computing involves protecting the confidentiality of sensitive data and minimizing the exposure of personally identifiable information. Here are a few techniques to consider:

- Zero-Knowledge Proofs (ZKPs): ZKPs allow one party to prove knowledge of certain information without revealing the actual data. In edge computing, ZKPs can be used to validate transactions or verify identities without disclosing sensitive details, enhancing privacy.
- Differential Privacy: Differential privacy techniques add noise or randomness to data to protect individual privacy while maintaining statistical accuracy. By introducing controlled noise, sensitive information can be protected, preventing the identification of individuals.
- Secure Multi-Party Computation (MPC): MPC protocols allow multiple parties to perform computations collaboratively without revealing their individual inputs. This technique enables data privacy during joint computations, ensuring sensitive data remains secure.
- Data Anonymization: Anonymization techniques, such as pseudonymization or data masking, can be applied to remove or obfuscate personally identifiable information from datasets. This reduces the risk of re-identification and helps protect privacy.
- **Access Control and Permissioned Blockchain:** Implementing access control mechanisms and utilizing permissioned blockchain networks can enhance security and privacy in edge computing. By defining access rules and permissions, only authorized entities can interact with the blockchain and access sensitive data. Permissioned blockchains provide greater control over the network, allowing organizations to define and enforce security policies.
- **Secure Data Sharing and Consent Management:** In edge computing scenarios where data sharing is required, employing secure data sharing techniques becomes important. This includes mechanisms such as data encryption, fine-grained access controls, and consent management frameworks. Consent management allows users to have control over their data and specify how it can be shared and used by other entities in the network.

Note that while encryption and privacy-preserving techniques are important, their implementation should align with specific regulatory requirements and the sensitivity of the data involved. Organizations should conduct thorough risk assessments and ensure compliance with relevant data protection and privacy regulations when designing and implementing security measures in blockchain-enabled edge computing systems.

6.2 Scalability and Performance Enhancement Strategies for Blockchain Security in Edge Computing

Scalability and performance enhancement strategies are essential for ensuring efficient and secure blockchain operations in edge computing environments. Here are some strategies to consider for enhancing scalability and performance while maintaining security:

- Off-Chain Computation and Storage: Off-loading computationally intensive tasks and data storage to off-chain solutions can improve scalability and performance. By performing certain operations off the blockchain, such as data processing or complex computations, the burden on the blockchain network is reduced, resulting in improved scalability. Off-chain storage solutions, such as distributed file systems or content delivery networks, can also alleviate the storage requirements on the blockchain.

- Sharding: Sharding involves partitioning the blockchain network into smaller subsets called shards, each capable of processing its transactions and smart contracts. Sharding can significantly enhance scalability by allowing parallel processing of transactions across multiple shards. However, ensuring proper shard coordination, data consistency, and security becomes important when implementing sharding in edge computing environments.
- Sidechains and State Channels: Sidechains and state channels are mechanisms for executing transactions and smart contracts off the main blockchain, reducing the load on the main chain. Sidechains are separate chains linked to the main chain, while state channels enable off-chain interactions between participants. These mechanisms provide faster transaction processing and reduce the burden on the main blockchain, enhancing scalability.
- Optimized Consensus Algorithms: Consensus algorithms have a significant impact on the performance and scalability of blockchain systems. Few issues for optimized consensus algorithms in edge computing include:
  - Lightweight Consensus: Utilize consensus algorithms specifically designed for resource-constrained edge devices. These algorithms prioritize efficiency and low computational requirements, ensuring optimal performance in edge computing environments.
  - Hybrid Consensus: Explore hybrid consensus models that combine different algorithms to use their respective strengths. For example, a combination of PoS and PoW can provide security and scalability benefits.
- Caching and Data Compression: Caching commonly accessed data and implementing data compression techniques can improve performance by reducing data retrieval and transmission times. Caching frequently used smart contracts, transaction history, or other relevant data on edge devices or in local caches can minimize the reliance on network communication, enhancing performance.
- Network Optimization: Implementing network optimization techniques can reduce latency and improve overall performance. Strategies such as using content delivery networks (CDNs), edge caching, or utilizing optimized routing protocols can help ensure efficient communication and data transfer between edge devices and blockchain nodes.
- Hardware Acceleration: Using hardware acceleration techniques, such as using specialized hardware like field-programmable gate arrays (FPGAs) or graphics processing units (GPUs), can enhance the performance of blockchain operations in edge computing environments. These hardware solutions can accelerate computationally intensive tasks and cryptographic operations, improving overall system performance.
- Scalable Data Structures: Utilize scalable data structures, such as Merkle trees or directed acyclic graphs (DAGs), to optimize data storage and retrieval. These data structures enable efficient validation and verification of transactions, reducing the computational overhead and enhancing scalability.

Note that while scalability and performance enhancement strategies are important, security should not be compromised. Note that careful consideration should be given to the trade-offs between scalability, performance, and security requirements in the design and implementation of blockchain-enabled edge computing systems. Thorough testing and evaluation of these strategies in real-world edge computing scenarios is essential to ensure their effectiveness.

6.3 Consensus Mechanisms for Edge Environments for Blockchain Security in Edge Computing

Consensus mechanisms play an important role in ensuring security and reliability in blockchain-enabled edge computing environments. Here are some consensus mechanisms suitable for edge environments:

- Proof of Stake (PoS): PoS is a consensus mechanism where the probability of creating a new block is determined by a participant's stake or ownership of cryptocurrency tokens. In edge environments, PoS can be beneficial due to its energy efficiency and low computational requirements compared to proof of work (PoW). It allows participants with limited resources, such as edge devices, to participate in the consensus process and secure the blockchain network.
- Delegated Proof of Stake (DPoS): DPoS is a variation of PoS where participants vote for a set of delegates who are responsible for validating transactions and creating blocks. Delegates take turns in creating blocks, ensuring faster block generation and higher transaction throughput. DPoS can be suitable for edge environments as it provides scalability and reduces the computational burden on individual nodes, making it feasible for resource-constrained edge devices to participate in consensus.
- Practical Byzantine Fault Tolerance (PBFT): PBFT is a consensus mechanism designed for Byzantine fault-tolerant systems, where a certain number of participants can be malicious or faulty. PBFT requires a predetermined set of nodes, known as replicas, to agree on the order and validity of transactions. This consensus mechanism is well-suited for edge environments with a limited number of trusted nodes, as it provides fast finality and guarantees security even with a certain percentage of malicious nodes.
- Directed Acyclic Graph (DAG) Consensus: DAG consensus mechanisms, such as IOTA's Tangle or Hedera Hashgraph, provide an alternative to traditional blockchain structures. Instead of linear blockchains, DAGs use a directed graph structure where each transaction verifies and approves previous transactions. This enables parallel processing and scalability. DAG consensus can be suitable for edge environments where low-latency and high transaction throughput are important, as it eliminates the need for mining and can handle a large number of transactions concurrently.
- Federated Byzantine Agreement (FBA): FBA is a consensus mechanism that combines elements of PBFT and federated systems. In FBA, a network of nodes collectively agrees on the order of transactions, and each node maintains its own local view of the blockchain. FBA can be suitable for edge environments with a decentralized and diverse set of participants, allowing for flexible trust models and fault tolerance.

Hence, to select a consensus mechanism that aligns with the specific requirements and constraints of edge computing environments. Factors such as resource limitations, network connectivity, latency, and the number of participating nodes should be taken into consideration when choosing a consensus mechanism for blockchain security in edge computing. Additionally, a thorough analysis of the security properties and trade-offs of each consensus mechanism is important to ensure the desired level of security and performance in the edge environment.

6.4 Identity and Access Management Solutions for Blockchain Security in Edge Computing

Identity and Access Management (IAM) solutions are essential for ensuring secure access and authentication in blockchain-enabled edge computing environments. Here are some IAM solutions that can enhance blockchain security in edge computing:

- Decentralized Identity (DID): DID is a self-sovereign identity framework that enables individuals and entities to have control over their digital identities. DIDs are based on public-key cryptography, allowing users to create and manage their identities without relying on centralized authorities. In edge computing, DID can provide secure and decentralized identity management, ensuring that participants have verifiable and tamper-proof identities.
- Identity Federation: Identity federation allows users to access multiple systems or networks using a single set of credentials. In the context of blockchain-enabled edge computing, identity federation can enable seamless access to different edge devices, applications, and blockchain networks. Federated identity management protocols such as OAuth or OpenID Connect can be employed to facilitate secure and trusted identity federation.
- Multi-Factor Authentication (MFA): MFA adds an extra layer of security by requiring users to provide multiple forms of authentication, such as passwords, biometrics, or security tokens. MFA can enhance blockchain security in edge computing by reducing the risk of unauthorized access or identity theft. For example, edge devices can employ biometric authentication, such as fingerprint or facial recognition, to ensure secure access to sensitive data or blockchain transactions.
- Role-Based Access Control (RBAC): RBAC is a commonly used access control model that assigns roles to users and grants permissions based on their roles. RBAC can be applied in blockchain-enabled edge computing to define and enforce access policies for different roles involved in the ecosystem, such as device administrators, application developers, or network validators. This ensures that only authorized individuals can perform specific actions or access certain resources.
- Attribute-Based Access Control (ABAC): ABAC is an access control model that grants permissions based on attributes associated with users, objects, or environmental conditions. ABAC allows for more fine-grained access control decisions by considering factors such as user attributes, device attributes, or contextual information. ABAC can provide dynamic and context-aware access control in edge computing environments, where access decisions can depend on factors like location, network conditions, or device capabilities.
- Blockchain-Based Identity Management: Utilizing the inherent features of blockchain, such as immutability and transparency, for identity management can enhance security in edge computing. Blockchain-based identity solutions can provide tamper-proof identity records, audit trails, and verifiable credentials. By storing identity-related information on the blockchain, participants can have increased trust and assurance in the identity and authenticity of other entities in the ecosystem.
- Privacy-Preserving Identity Solutions: Privacy-preserving identity solutions, such as zero-knowledge proofs or anonymous credentials, can help protect the privacy of users in blockchain-enabled edge computing. These techniques allow users to prove certain statements about their identity or attributes without revealing sensitive information. Privacy-preserving identity solutions are particularly relevant in scenarios where the disclosure of personal information needs to be minimized.

In summary, implementing robust IAM solutions in blockchain-enabled edge computing environments ensures that access to the blockchain, edge devices, and sensitive data is secure, authenticated, and authorized. The selection of IAM solutions should align with the specific requirements, privacy issues, and regulatory compliance of the edge computing environment.

6.5 Network Security Measures for Blockchain Security in Edge Computing

Network security is important for ensuring the integrity and protection of blockchain-enabled edge computing environments. Here are some network security measures to enhance blockchain security in edge computing:

- Secure Communication Channels: Establishing secure communication channels between edge devices, blockchain nodes, and other network components is important. Encryption protocols such as Transport Layer Security (TLS) or Secure Shell (SSH) should be employed to ensure the confidentiality and integrity of data transmitted over the network. Secure communication protocols protect against eavesdropping, tampering, and unauthorized access.
- Firewall and Intrusion Detection/Prevention Systems: Deploying firewalls and intrusion detection/prevention systems (IDS/IPS) at network entry points and within the edge computing environment helps monitor and filter network traffic. Firewalls enforce access control policies, while IDS/IPS systems detect and prevent malicious activities or network attacks, safeguarding the blockchain infrastructure and edge devices from unauthorized access or data breaches.
- Network Segmentation: Segmenting the network into distinct subnetworks or VLANs (Virtual Local Area Networks) can enhance security by isolating different components and preventing lateral movement of threats. Each segment can have its own security policies and access controls, reducing the potential impact of a security breach. Network segmentation also helps in containing and mitigating network-based attacks.
- Distributed Denial of Service (DDoS) Mitigation: DDoS attacks can overwhelm network resources and disrupt blockchain operations. Implementing DDoS mitigation techniques such as rate limiting, traffic filtering, or using specialized DDoS protection services helps to detect and mitigate such attacks. Traffic monitoring tools and anomaly detection mechanisms can identify unusual network patterns and trigger protective measures.
- Network Access Control (NAC): Network Access Control mechanisms allow administrators to control and manage network access based on user identity, device compliance, or other specified criteria. NAC solutions ensure that only authorized devices and users can connect to the network and access blockchain resources. By enforcing security policies, NAC mitigates the risks associated with unauthorized or compromised devices attempting to join the network.
- Network Monitoring and Logging: Continuous network monitoring and logging of network activities are essential for identifying security incidents, detecting anomalies, and performing forensic analysis. Monitoring tools can track network traffic, device behavior, and system logs to identify potential security threats or suspicious activities. Logging provides an audit trail for investigating security incidents and enables timely response and remediation.
- Patch Management and Firmware Updates: Regularly updating and patching network devices, edge devices, and blockchain software components is important to address known vulnerabilities. Unpatched devices or software can become easy targets for attackers. Establishing a robust patch

management process ensures that security patches and firmware updates are applied promptly, reducing the risk of exploits and maintaining the security of the network.

- Security Audits and Penetration Testing: Conducting regular security audits and penetration testing helps identify vulnerabilities and weaknesses in the network infrastructure. Through simulated attacks and assessments, security professionals can evaluate the effectiveness of existing security measures, identify potential entry points for attackers, and recommend improvements to enhance the overall security posture of the blockchain-enabled edge computing environment.
- Incident Response and Disaster Recovery Planning: Developing an incident response plan and disaster recovery strategy is important for responding to security incidents, mitigating their impact, and restoring normal operations. These plans outline the steps to be taken in the event of a security breach, ensuring a coordinated and effective response to minimize downtime, data loss, and other negative consequences.

In summary, implementing a layered approach to network security, incorporating multiple security measures, helps safeguard blockchain-enabled edge computing environments against various network-based threats. Regular monitoring, updates, and proactive security measures are essential to maintain the integrity and availability of the blockchain network and protect the sensitive data processed within the edge computing environment.

7. CHALLENGES AND FUTURE DIRECTIONS TOWARDS BLOCKCHAIN SECURITY IN EDGE COMPUTING

7.1 Limitations and Challenges Faced Towards Blockchain Security in Edge Computing

While blockchain-enabled edge computing offers numerous benefits for security, there are also some limitations and challenges that need to be addressed:

- Limited Computational Power: Edge devices typically have limited computational power, storage capacity, and network bandwidth compared to traditional servers or cloud platforms. The resource-constrained nature of edge devices can pose challenges for running resource-intensive blockchain protocols or executing complex cryptographic operations, which may impact the performance and scalability of the blockchain network.
- Network Latency and Connectivity: Edge devices are often deployed in remote or harsh environments with intermittent or unreliable network connectivity. In such scenarios, ensuring consistent and reliable communication between edge devices and the blockchain network can be challenging. Network latency and intermittent connectivity can affect the responsiveness and efficiency of blockchain transactions, potentially impacting the overall security and performance of the system.
- Energy Efficiency: Edge devices are typically powered by limited energy sources such as batteries or renewable energy. Blockchain protocols, especially those that require computationally intensive consensus mechanisms like Proof of Work (PoW), can consume significant amounts of energy. Energy efficiency becomes an important issue in edge computing environments where power re-

sources are scarce, as excessive energy consumption may limit the feasibility and sustainability of blockchain deployments.

- Scalability and Throughput: Scaling blockchain networks to accommodate a large number of edge devices and handle a high volume of transactions can be challenging. Traditional blockchain protocols may face scalability limitations when deployed in edge computing environments due to the limited processing power and bandwidth of edge devices. Achieving high transaction throughput and scalability while maintaining security and decentralization remains an ongoing challenge.
- Security of Edge Devices: The security of edge devices themselves is an important issue. Edge devices may have vulnerabilities or lack proper security measures, making them potential targets for attacks. Compromised edge devices can undermine the security and integrity of the blockchain network. Ensuring the security of edge devices through robust authentication, firmware updates, and regular security audits is essential to maintain overall blockchain security.
- Consensus Protocol Selection: Choosing an appropriate consensus protocol for edge computing environments is important. While PoW-based consensus protocols offer high security, they may not be suitable for resource-constrained edge devices due to their computational requirements. Alternative consensus mechanisms like Proof of Stake (PoS) or Practical Byzantine Fault Tolerance (PBFT) may be more suitable for edge computing, but they may have their own limitations and trade-offs in terms of security, decentralization, and performance.
- Privacy Issues: Edge computing often involves processing sensitive data at the edge, and ensuring privacy becomes important. Blockchain's transparent and immutable nature can conflict with the privacy requirements of certain applications. Balancing the need for transparency and auditability with privacy issues requires careful consideration and the implementation of privacy-preserving techniques such as zero-knowledge proofs or differential privacy.
- Regulatory and Compliance Challenges: Blockchain deployments in edge computing environments must comply with relevant regulations and standards, such as data protection laws (e.g., GDPR) or industry-specific requirements. Achieving regulatory compliance in a decentralized and distributed environment can be complex, especially when data is processed and stored across multiple edge devices. Ensuring compliance while maintaining the core principles of blockchain, such as decentralization and transparency, can be challenging.

Hence, addressing these limitations and challenges requires a combination of technical innovations, standardization efforts, and collaborative research and development. As edge computing and blockchain technologies continue to evolve, advancements in protocols, hardware capabilities, and security practices will help overcome these challenges and unlock the full potential of blockchain-enabled edge computing securely.

7.2 Future Research Directions Towards Blockchain Security in Edge Computing

Future research directions in blockchain security for edge computing can focus on the following areas:

- Efficient Consensus Mechanisms: Developing lightweight consensus mechanisms that are energy-efficient and suitable for resource-constrained edge devices is an important research direction. Exploring consensus protocols specifically designed for edge computing, such as hybrid consensus algorithms or proof-of-stake variants optimized for low-power devices, can enhance the scalability and performance of blockchain networks in edge environments.

- Privacy-Preserving Techniques: Advancing privacy-preserving techniques within blockchain networks for edge computing is important to address privacy issues. Research can focus on improving techniques like zero-knowledge proofs, secure multi-party computation, or differential privacy to enable confidential and privacy-enhanced transactions and data processing in decentralized edge environments.
- Secure Identity and Access Management: Designing robust identity and access management solutions for blockchain-based edge computing is important. Future research can explore novel authentication and authorization mechanisms, including decentralized identity management, attribute-based access control, and trust management models, to ensure secure and scalable identity management in edge environments.
- Trust and Security Assurance: Developing frameworks and methodologies for evaluating the trustworthiness and security of blockchain networks in edge computing is essential. Future research can focus on establishing metrics, standards, and certification mechanisms that assess the security posture, resilience to attacks, and overall trustworthiness of blockchain deployments in edge environments.
- Secure Data Sharing and Collaboration: Enabling secure and efficient data sharing and collaboration mechanisms among edge devices and participants is a promising research direction. Exploring distributed storage schemes, encrypted data sharing protocols, and secure smart contract design can facilitate secure and auditable data sharing and collaboration in blockchain-enabled edge computing environments.
- Resilience and Attack Mitigation: Research efforts can be directed towards enhancing the resilience of blockchain networks in edge computing against various attacks, including Sybil attacks, Eclipse attacks, or data manipulation attacks. Developing advanced detection and mitigation techniques, intrusion detection systems, and anomaly detection algorithms can strengthen the security and robustness of blockchain-based edge computing systems.
- Integration with Artificial Intelligence and Machine Learning: Investigating the integration of artificial intelligence (AI) and machine learning (ML) techniques with blockchain security in edge computing can lead to innovative solutions. AI/ML can be used for anomaly detection, threat intelligence, or predictive security analytics, improving the detection and response capabilities of blockchain-based security systems in edge environments.
- Standardization and Interoperability: Establishing standards and protocols for interoperability between different edge devices, blockchain networks, and edge computing platforms is important. Future research can focus on developing standardized interfaces, interoperability frameworks, and protocols that enable seamless integration and communication among heterogeneous edge devices and blockchain networks.

Hence, these research directions aim to address the unique security challenges and requirements of blockchain-enabled edge computing, paving the way for more secure, scalable, and privacy-preserving deployments in diverse edge environments.

8. CONCLUSION

As discussed above, the integration of blockchain into edge computing environments also presents unique challenges. The paper identifies and examines these challenges, such as scalability, consensus mechanisms, resource limitations, data privacy, and interoperability. Hence, by considering these implications and implementing the recommended security measures, organizations can enhance the security posture of blockchain-enabled edge computing systems, protect data and transactions, and build trust among users/ consumers. It is important to continuously evaluate and update security measures as the threat landscape evolves and new vulnerabilities emerge.

REFERENCES

Chen, L., Wang, Z., & Li, X. (2019). Blockchain-driven Security Framework for Resource Management in Edge Computing. *IEEE Transactions on Cloud Computing*, *6*(5), 1903–1916.

Chen, Q., Wu, Y., & Lim, G. (2021). Scalable and Secure Blockchain-based Identity Management in Edge Computing. *Journal of Network and Computer Applications*, *95*, 105240.

Garcia, M., Kim, D., & Park, H. (2021). A Hybrid Consensus Protocol for Enhanced Security in Edge Computing with Blockchain. *Journal of Parallel and Distributed Computing*, *125*, 109–120.

George, T. T., & Tyagi, A. K. (2022). Reliable Edge Computing Architectures for Crowdsensing Applications. *2022 International Conference on Computer Communication and Informatics (ICCCI)*, (pp. 1-6). Springer. 10.1109/ICCCI54379.2022.9740791

Goyal, D. & Tyagi, A. (2020). *A Look at Top 35 Problems in the Computer Science Field for the Next Decade*. Research Gate. . doi:10.1201/9781003052098-40

Kim, D., Hu, J., & Zhang, L. (2020). Trust Management for IoT Devices in Edge Computing with Blockchain. *IEEE Internet of Things Journal*, *7*(9), 7562–7573.

Lee, S., Wang, S., & Liu, M. (2019). Secure Offloading of Computation in Edge Computing using Blockchain-based Smart Contracts. *IEEE Transactions on Mobile Computing*, *18*(6), 1399–1411.

Li, Y., Wang, H., & Chen, F. (2019). An Edge-Blockchain Architecture for Secure Data Sharing in Smart Cities. *Proceedings of the International Conference on Smart City Applications (SCA)*, (pp. 87-96). Springer.

Liu, Y., Park, H., & Garcia, M. (2019). Privacy-Preserving Data Sharing in Edge Computing with Blockchain: Challenges and Solutions. *Journal of Edge Computing*, *8*(4), 231–243.

Nair, M. M., Kumari, S., & Tyagi, A. K. (2021). Internet of Things, Cyber Physical System, and Data Analytics: Open Questions, Future Perspectives, and Research Areas. In: Goyal D., Gupta A.K., Piuri V., Ganzha M., Paprzycki M. (eds) *Proceedings of the Second International Conference on Information Management and Machine Intelligence*. Springer, Singapore. 10.1007/978-981-15-9689-6_36

Nair, M. M., & Tyagi, A. K. (2021). Privacy: History, Statistics, Policy, Laws, Preservation and Threat Analysis. Journal of Information Assurance & Security, 16(1), 24-34.

Nair, M. M., Tyagi, A. K., & Sreenath, N. (2021). The Future with Industry 4.0 at the Core of Society 5.0: Open Issues, Future Opportunities and Challenges. *2021 International Conference on Computer Communication and Informatics (ICCCI),* (pp. 1-7). Springer. 10.1109/ICCCI50826.2021.9402498

Park, J., Lee, Y., & Wang, B. (2018). Blockchain-based Authentication and Authorization in Edge Computing Networks. *ACM Transactions on Internet Technology*, *21*(2), 16–28.

Rekha, G., Tyagi, A. K., & Anuradha, N. (2020) Integration of Fog Computing and Internet of Things: An Useful Overview. In: Singh P., Kar A., Singh Y., Kolekar M., Tanwar S. (eds) Proceedings of ICRIC 2019. Lecture Notes in Electrical Engineering, vol 597. Springer, Cham. 10.1007/978-3-030-29407-6_8

Sheth, H. S. K., & Tyagi, A. K. (2022). Mobile Cloud Computing: Issues, Applications and Scope in COVID-19. In A. Abraham, N. Gandhi, T. Hanne, T. P. Hong, T. Nogueira Rios, & W. Ding (Eds.), *Intelligent Systems Design and Applications. ISDA 2021. Lecture Notes in Networks and Systems* (Vol. 418). Springer. doi:10.1007/978-3-030-96308-8_55

Smith, J., Chen, L., & Kim, S. (2021). Blockchain-Enabled Security Framework for Edge Computing: A Comprehensive Review. *International Journal of Blockchain Research*, *5*(2), 89–101.

Tyagi, A. K. & Sreenath, N. (2015). Preserving Location Privacy in Location Based Services against Sybil Attacks. *International Journal of Security and Its Applications, 9*(12), 189-210.

Tyagi, A.K. (2022). *Handbook of Research on Technical, Privacy, and Security Challenges in a Modern World.* IGI Global., doi:10.4018/978-1-6684-5250-9

Tyagi, A. K. (2023). Chapter 2 - Decentralized everything: Practical use of blockchain technology in future applications. R. Pandey, S. Goundar, & S. Fatima (eds.) Distributed Computing to Blockchain. Academic Press. doi:10.1016/B978-0-323-96146-2.00010-3

Tyagi, A., Kukreja, S., Nair, M. M., & Tyagi, A. K. (2022). Machine Learning: Past, Present and Future. *NeuroQuantology : An Interdisciplinary Journal of Neuroscience and Quantum Physics*, *20*(8). doi:10.14704/nq.2022.20.8.NQ44468

Tyagi, A. K., & Bansal, R. Anshu, Dananjayan, S. (2023). A Step-To-Step Guide to Write a Quality Research Article. In: Abraham, A., Pllana, S., Casalino, G., Ma, K., Bajaj, A. (eds) Intelligent Systems Design and Applications. ISDA 2022. Lecture Notes in Networks and Systems, vol 717. Springer, Cham. doi:10.1007/978-3-031-35510-3_36

Tyagi, A. K., Chandrasekaran, S., & Sreenath, N. (2022). Blockchain Technology:– A New Technology for Creating Distributed and Trusted Computing Environment. *2022 International Conference on Applied Artificial Intelligence and Computing (ICAAIC),* (pp. 1348-1354). IEEE. 10.1109/ICAAIC53929.2022.9792702

Tyagi, A. K., Dananjayan, S., Agarwal, D., & Thariq Ahmed, H. F. (2023). Blockchain—Internet of Things Applications: Opportunities and Challenges for Industry 4.0 and Society 5.0. *Sensors (Basel), 23*(2), 947. doi:10.339023020947 PMID:36679743

Tyagi, A. K., Fernandez, T. F., Mishra, S., & Kumari, S. (2021). Intelligent Automation Systems at the Core of Industry 4.0. In A. Abraham, V. Piuri, N. Gandhi, P. Siarry, A. Kaklauskas, & A. Madureira (Eds.), *Intelligent Systems Design and Applications. ISDA 2020. Advances in Intelligent Systems and Computing* (Vol. 1351). Springer. doi:10.1007/978-3-030-71187-0_1

Tyagi, A. K., & Sreenath, N. (2023). Fog and Edge Computing in Navigation of Intelligent Transportation System. In *Intelligent Transportation Systems: Theory and Practice. Disruptive Technologies and Digital Transformations for Society 5.0*. Springer. doi:10.1007/978-981-19-7622-3_7

Wang, X., Liu, Y., & Chen, Q. (2018). Smart Contract-based Security Mechanisms for Edge Computing Networks using Blockchain. *Journal of Edge Intelligence*, *13*(4), 215–226.

Wang, Z., Li, X., & Ng, K. (2018). A Consensus Mechanism for Edge Computing using Blockchain Technology. *Proceedings of the International Conference on Edge Computing (ICEC),* (pp. 125-134). IEEE.

Wu, Z., Liu, M., & Zhang, Y. (2021). Towards Trustworthy Edge Computing with Blockchain: A Case Study on Industrial IoT. *Journal of Blockchain Applications*, *12*(3), 157–169.

Zhang, H., Kim, Y., & Wang, S. (2020). A Secure Data Storage Scheme for Edge Devices using Blockchain Technology. *Proceedings of the International Conference on Cloud Computing and Big Data (CCBD),* (pp. 45-54). IEEE.

Zhang, Q., Chen, Y., & Hu, J. (2020). Scalable Blockchain-based Data Provenance for Edge Computing. *Proceedings of the International Conference on Edge Intelligence (ICEI)*, (pp. 78-87). IEEE.

Zhang, Q., Lee, H., & Wang, X. (2020). Decentralized Access Control using Blockchain in Edge Computing Environments. *IEEE Transactions on Network and Service Management*, *17*(3), 876–887.

Chapter 6
Cloud Security Risks, Threats, and Solutions for Business Logistics

Shrikant Tiwari
https://orcid.org/0000-0001-6947-2362
Galgotias University, India

Ramesh S. Wadawadagi
https://orcid.org/0000-0002-6669-7344
Nagarjuna College of Engineering, India

Arun Kumar Singh
https://orcid.org/0000-0002-0938-6064
Greater Noida Institute of Technology, India

Virendra Kumar Verma
Institute of Engineering and Rural Technology (IERT), Prayagraj, India

ABSTRACT

Cloud computing has revolutionized the landscape of modern business logistics by offering scalable and cost-effective solutions for data storage, processing, and application deployment. However, with this newfound convenience comes a plethora of security challenges that businesses must address to protect their valuable assets and sensitive information. This chapter aims to provide a comprehensive overview of the security risks and threats associated with cloud adoption in the logistics industry, along with effective solutions to mitigate them by presenting an in-depth analysis of the primary security risks that businesses may encounter when leveraging cloud-based logistics solutions. Additionally, it discusses the risks posed by shared infrastructure, third-party integrations, and data jurisdiction concerns. Moreover, the chapter highlights the growing role of emerging technologies in bolstering cloud security measures. These technologies offer sophisticated threat detection and proactive response capabilities, enabling logistics companies to stay ahead of evolving cyber threats.

DOI: 10.4018/979-8-3693-2081-5.ch006

1. INTRODUCTION TO CLOUD COMPUTING IN BUSINESS LOGISTICS

Cloud computing has emerged as a transformative force in the field of business logistics, reshaping the way companies manage their supply chains, inventory, and overall operations. It offers a flexible, scalable, and cost-efficient alternative to traditional on-premises infrastructure, enabling logistics organizations to harness the power of advanced technologies without heavy upfront investments.

Nevertheless, the introduction acknowledges that with the advantages come certain challenges and concerns that must be addressed for successful cloud adoption in the logistics sector. The chapter briefly mentions the potential risks of data breaches, security vulnerabilities, and data jurisdiction issues that could affect sensitive logistics information. Data privacy and compliance considerations, especially in an increasingly regulated global landscape, are also introduced as pivotal aspects.

This chapter aims to lay the foundation for understanding cloud computing's integration into the world of business logistics. By establishing a clear understanding of cloud concepts, benefits, and challenges, readers will gain valuable insights into the subsequent sections that delve deeper into the security risks, threats, and solutions for securing cloud-based logistics systems. In doing so, logistics professionals and decision-makers will be better equipped to leverage the potential of cloud computing while safeguarding their valuable assets and ensuring seamless, secure operations in the ever-evolving logistics landscape.

1.1 Overview of Cloud Computing and Its Role in Modern Logistics Operations

Cloud computing has emerged as a game-changing technology in modern logistics operations, revolutionizing the way businesses manage their supply chains, inventory, and distribution processes. At its core, cloud computing refers to the delivery of computing services over the internet, providing on-demand access to a vast array of resources, including computing power, storage, databases, and software applications (Ramgovind S et al. 2010). This section provides an in-depth overview of cloud computing and its transformative role in the logistics industry.

One of the key advantages of cloud computing is its inherent scalability and elasticity. Modern logistics operations often face fluctuating demands, particularly during peak seasons or when dealing with sudden changes in market conditions (Christopher M et al. 2004). Cloud-based solutions empower logistics organizations to scale their computing resources dynamically, accommodating increased workloads without the need for extensive hardware investments (Bello S. A. et al. 2021). This elasticity not only ensures optimized performance but also reduces operational costs and improves overall efficiency.

Moreover, cloud computing allows logistics companies to centralize and streamline their operations. Traditional logistics systems often involve disparate systems and databases, leading to data silos and inefficiencies. Cloud-based logistics solutions provide a unified and integrated approach, consolidating data and processes into a single, accessible platform (Santosh Kumar et al. 2017). This enables better visibility into the entire logistics workflow, from order processing to shipment tracking, fostering more effective resource allocation and optimized route planning.

However, while the benefits of cloud computing in logistics are significant, the chapter acknowledges the challenges and considerations that come with adopting cloud-based solutions. Security concerns, data privacy, and regulatory compliance must be carefully addressed to safeguard sensitive logistics information and ensure compliance with relevant industry standards.

The overview of cloud computing in modern logistics operations highlights the technology's transformative impact on the industry. By embracing the cloud's scalability, real-time accessibility, and collaborative capabilities, logistics companies can improve their agility, efficiency, and overall competitiveness in an increasingly dynamic and interconnected global market.

1.1.1 Advantages and Challenges of Adopting Cloud Solutions in the Logistics Industry

The adoption of cloud computing solutions has become increasingly prevalent in the logistics industry due to its potential to transform traditional supply chain and operational processes. This section explores the key advantages and challenges that logistics companies encounter when embracing cloud solutions (Fosso Wamba et al. 2020), the advantages and challenges of adopting cloud solutions in the logistics industry is shown in the Figure 1 and Figure 2 respectively.

Advantages:

- **Scalability and Flexibility:** Cloud computing offers unparalleled scalability, allowing logistics companies to scale their resources up or down based on demand. During peak seasons or when facing sudden changes in workload, the ability to rapidly adjust computing resources ensures optimal performance without costly infrastructure investments.
- **Cost-Efficiency:** Cloud solutions eliminate the need for upfront capital expenditures on hardware and infrastructure. By opting for a pay-as-you-go model, logistics companies can reduce operational costs, paying only for the resources they consume. This cost-effectiveness is especially beneficial for small and medium-sized enterprises with limited budgets.
- **Real-Time Data Accessibility:** Cloud-based logistics systems facilitate real-time data access from anywhere, empowering logistics professionals to make timely and data-driven decisions. This heightened visibility into supply chain operations enables faster response times and enhances overall efficiency.
- **Collaboration and Connectivity:** Cloud solutions foster seamless collaboration among stakeholders within the logistics ecosystem. Suppliers, manufacturers, distributors, and retailers can share data, coordinate activities, and exchange information in a centralized and secure environment, fostering stronger partnerships and streamlined operations.
- **Rapid Deployment and Updates:** Cloud services enable quick deployment of new applications and updates, minimizing downtime and enhancing system agility. Logistics companies can easily integrate new features and functionalities to keep pace with industry advancements.

Challenges:

- **Data Security and Privacy:** One of the primary concerns of adopting cloud solutions is the security of sensitive logistics data. Storing and transferring valuable information over the internet may expose businesses to data breaches, unauthorized access, and other cyber threats. Robust security measures and data encryption are essential to safeguarding critical data.
- **Regulatory Compliance:** The logistics industry is subject to various regulations, including data protection laws, industry-specific standards, and cross-border data transfer regulations. Achieving compliance with these requirements, especially when using third-party cloud service providers, demands careful planning and adherence to relevant legal frameworks.

Figure 1. Advantages of adopting cloud solutions in the logistics industry

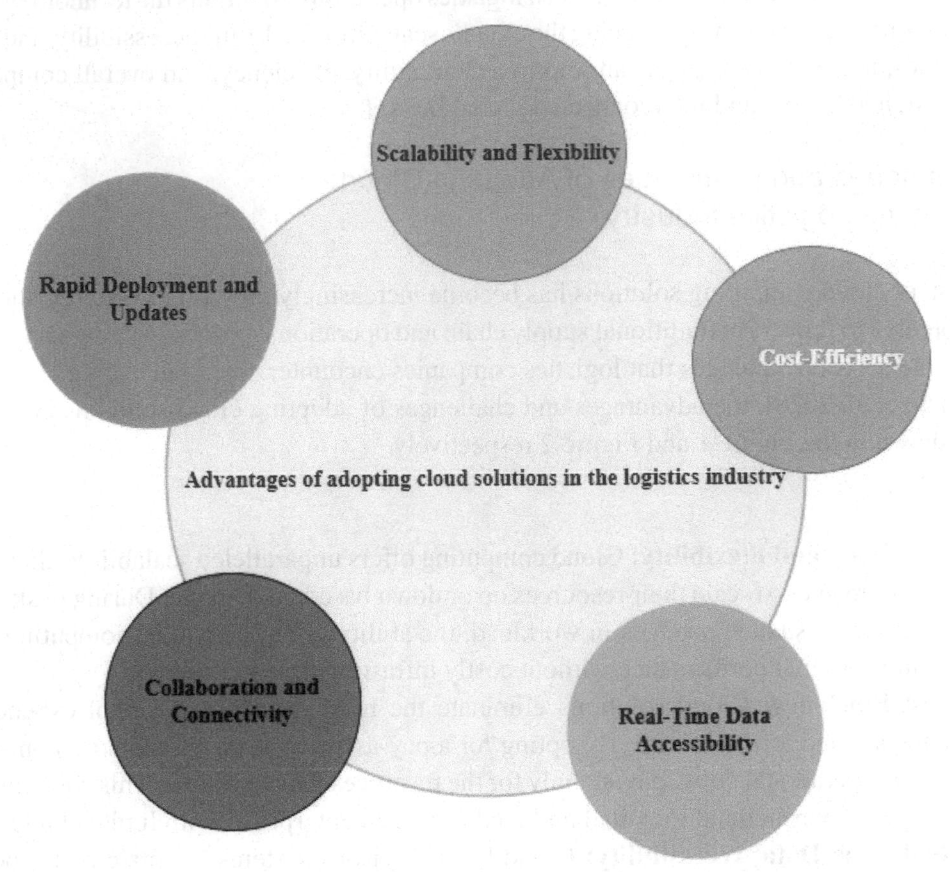

- **Reliability and Downtime:** Reliance on cloud service providers means logistics companies are dependent on external infrastructure. Network outages or downtime of the cloud provider can disrupt operations, impacting productivity and customer satisfaction. To mitigate this risk, companies need contingency plans and service level agreements (SLAs) with providers.
- **Data Residency and Jurisdiction:** The physical location of data stored in the cloud can raise concerns about data residency and jurisdictional issues. Compliance with laws governing data localization and data sovereignty requires understanding the policies and regulations of each country involved in the logistics chain.
- **Integration Complexities:** Migrating legacy systems and integrating existing logistics infrastructure with cloud-based solutions can be challenging. Ensuring seamless data flow between on-premises systems and the cloud requires careful planning, skilled IT personnel, and adequate testing.

The adoption of cloud solutions in the logistics industry offers numerous advantages that enhance operational efficiency, collaboration, and cost-effectiveness. However, businesses must address the challenges posed by data security, regulatory compliance, reliability, and integration complexities to fully unlock the potential of cloud computing. By carefully evaluating and implementing appropriate strategies, logistics companies can reap the benefits of cloud technology while mitigating potential risks.

Figure 2. Different challenges of adopting cloud solutions in the logistics industry

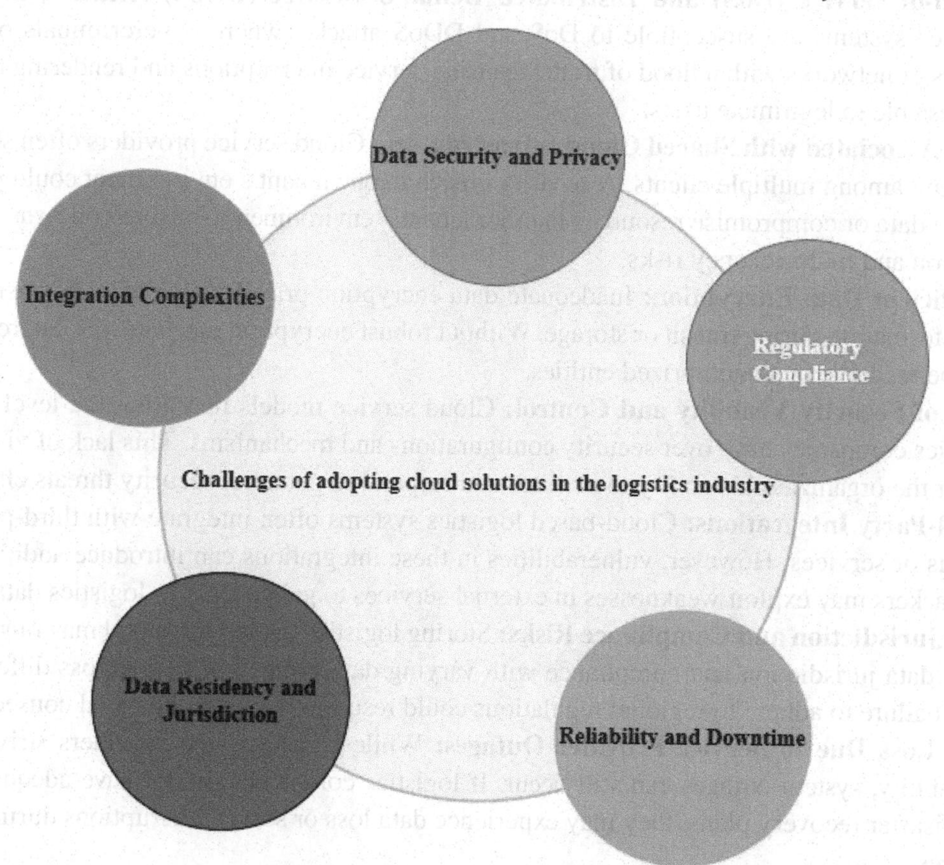

1.2 Security Risks in Cloud-Based Logistics Systems

The migration of logistics operations to cloud-based platforms has unlocked new opportunities for efficiency and collaboration. However, with the advantages of cloud computing come inherent security risks that logistics companies must address to protect their sensitive data, maintain business continuity, and safeguard their reputation. This section delves into the key security risks associated with cloud-based logistics systems (Bagga J. 2023).

- **Data Breaches and Data Loss:** Cloud environments store vast amounts of critical logistics data, including shipment details, customer information, and inventory records. A data breach or unauthorized access can result in the theft, manipulation, or exposure of this sensitive data, leading to financial loss and damage to the company's reputation.
- **Unauthorized Access and Identity-Related Risks:** Weak identity and access management practices can lead to unauthorized access to cloud resources. Compromised credentials or inadequate authentication measures may allow malicious actors to gain entry to logistics systems, potentially causing disruptions, data manipulation, or theft.

- **Denial-of-Service (DoS) and Distributed Denial-of-Service (DDoS) Attacks:** Cloud-based logistics systems are susceptible to DoS and DDoS attacks, where cybercriminals overwhelm servers or networks with a flood of traffic, causing service interruptions and rendering the system inaccessible to legitimate users.
- **Risks Associated with Shared Cloud Infrastructure:** Cloud service providers often share infrastructure among multiple clients. A security breach in one tenant's environment could potentially expose data or compromise resources in other tenants' environments, raising concerns about data isolation and multi-tenancy risks.
- **Insufficient Data Encryption:** Inadequate data encryption practices can expose sensitive logistics information during transit or storage. Without robust encryption mechanisms, intercepted data may be readable by unauthorized entities.
- **Lack of Security Visibility and Control:** Cloud service models may limit the level of control logistics companies have over security configurations and mechanisms. This lack of visibility can hinder the organization's ability to monitor and respond to potential security threats effectively.
- **Third-Party Integrations:** Cloud-based logistics systems often integrate with third-party applications or services. However, vulnerabilities in these integrations can introduce additional risks, as attackers may exploit weaknesses in external services to gain access to logistics data.
- **Data Jurisdiction and Compliance Risks:** Storing logistics data in the cloud may raise concerns about data jurisdiction and compliance with varying data protection laws across different countries. Failure to adhere to regional regulations could result in legal and financial consequences.
- **Data Loss Due to Service Provider Outages:** While cloud service providers strive for high availability, system outages can still occur. If logistics companies do not have adequate backup and disaster recovery plans, they may experience data loss or service disruptions during provider outages.
- **Employee Errors and Insider Threats:** Human error, such as misconfiguration or accidental data exposure, can pose significant security risks. Additionally, disgruntled employees or insiders with malicious intent may intentionally compromise logistics systems or steal sensitive data.

In understanding and mitigating security risks in cloud-based logistics systems are crucial for logistics companies to maintain the confidentiality, integrity, and availability of their data and operations. By implementing robust security measures, including data encryption, strong access controls, continuous monitoring, and employee training, logistics organizations can bolster their cloud security posture and safeguard against potential threats. Regular security assessments and collaborations with trusted cloud service providers are also essential components of a comprehensive security strategy in the ever-evolving landscape of cloud-based logistics.

Data breaches and data loss represent one of the most significant security risks faced by logistics companies that operate in the cloud. With cloud-based logistics systems storing vast amounts of sensitive information, including shipment details, customer data, financial records, and intellectual property, the consequences of a breach or data loss can be severe, leading to financial losses, legal liabilities, and damage to the company's reputation.

1.3 Unauthorized Access and Identity-Related Risks

Unauthorized access and identity-related risks pose significant security challenges for logistics companies that operate in the cloud. These risks involve the improper or unauthorized use of digital identities, credentials, and permissions, allowing malicious actors to gain access to sensitive logistics data and systems. Addressing these risks is essential to ensure the confidentiality, integrity, and availability of critical information and maintain trust with customers and partners. This section explores the specific unauthorized access and identity-related risks in cloud-based logistics environments (Mir U. et al. 2022).

- **Weak Passwords and Credentials:** Weak passwords, password reuse, and lack of multi-factor authentication (MFA) increase the risk of unauthorized access. Cybercriminals can use various methods to crack or steal passwords, providing them with unauthorized entry into cloud-based logistics systems.
- **Phishing and Social Engineering Attacks:** Phishing attacks target employees or users to trick them into revealing their login credentials or other sensitive information. Social engineering tactics exploit human trust and behavior to gain unauthorized access, making employees unwitting accomplices in data breaches.
- **Insider Threats:** Insider threats involve employees or insiders with legitimate access to logistics systems intentionally or unintentionally misusing their privileges to access unauthorized data or conduct malicious activities.
- **Inadequate Identity and Access Management (IAM):** Weak IAM practices, such as not revoking access promptly for employees who leave the company or not enforcing the principle of least privilege, can result in unauthorized individuals retaining access to logistics systems.
- **Unauthorized Service Access:** Improperly configured cloud services may grant broader permissions than necessary, inadvertently allowing unauthorized users access to sensitive data or functionalities.
- **Brute-Force Attacks:** Cybercriminals may attempt to gain unauthorized access by using automated tools to repeatedly guess login credentials, exploiting weak authentication mechanisms.
- **Compromised User Devices:** If an employee's device with access to cloud-based logistics systems is compromised or lost, unauthorized individuals may gain access to the systems through the compromised device.
- **Insecure API Access:** Insecurely designed or unprotected APIs can be exploited to gain unauthorized access to cloud-based logistics systems, particularly when they interact with external applications or services.

Proactively addressing unauthorized access and identity-related risks, logistics companies can fortify their cloud-based systems, protect sensitive data, and maintain a robust security posture in an ever-evolving threat landscape. An integrated and layered approach to security ensures the confidentiality, integrity, and availability of logistics data and systems, enhancing trust and confidence among customers and partners.

1.4 Denial-of-Service (DoS) and Distributed Denial-of-Service (DDoS) Attacks

Denial-of-Service (DoS) and Distributed Denial-of-Service (DDoS) attacks pose significant threats to the availability and performance of cloud-based logistics systems. These types of attacks aim to overwhelm a target's resources, rendering its services inaccessible to legitimate users. In the context of logistics, the impact of such attacks can be severe, disrupting operations, causing delays, and leading to potential financial losses. This section explores the nature of DoS and DDoS attacks, their impact on cloud-based logistics, and strategies to mitigate these risks (Kumari, P., & Jain, A. K. 2023).

- **Denial-of-Service (DoS) Attacks:** A DoS attack is carried out by a single source that floods a target system, such as a web server or application, with an excessive amount of traffic or requests. The overload exhausts the system's resources, causing it to become unresponsive to legitimate user requests.
- **Distributed Denial-of-Service (DDoS) Attacks:** DDoS attacks are more sophisticated and dangerous versions of DoS attacks. In a DDoS attack, multiple compromised devices (often part of a botnet) coordinate to flood the target system with traffic from various sources simultaneously, amplifying the impact and making it harder to defend against.
- **Impact on Cloud-Based Logistics Systems:** Cloud-based logistics systems are attractive targets for DoS and DDoS attacks due to their critical role in managing supply chains, inventory, and real-time tracking. An attack that disrupts these systems can lead to shipment delays, communication breakdowns, and loss of revenue.
- **Resource Exhaustion:** In DoS and DDoS attacks, attackers consume available resources, such as bandwidth, processing power, or memory, causing cloud-based logistics services to slow down or become unavailable.
- **Service Unavailability:** DoS and DDoS attacks can lead to temporary or prolonged unavailability of cloud-based logistics applications, impacting the ability to process orders, track shipments, or manage inventory in real-time.
- **Increased Response Times:** As attack traffic floods the system, legitimate users may experience slow response times or timeouts when trying to access cloud-based logistics services.
- **Loss of Customer Trust:** The unavailability of logistics services due to DoS and DDoS attacks can erode customer trust and loyalty, potentially leading to negative brand perception and customer attrition.

Implementing a comprehensive defense strategy that combines proactive measures and cloud-based security services, logistics companies can better protect their cloud-based systems from DoS and DDoS attacks. Ensuring the availability and reliability of logistics services enhances customer satisfaction and preserves the smooth functioning of supply chain operations in an increasingly digital and interconnected logistics landscape.

2. THREAT SCENARIOS IN CLOUD LOGISTICS ENVIRONMENTS

Cloud logistics environments, while offering numerous benefits, are also susceptible to a variety of threat scenarios that pose risks to the confidentiality, integrity, and availability of logistics data and operations (Ashraf I et al. 2022). Understanding these threat scenarios is crucial for logistics companies to develop robust security strategies and effectively protect their cloud-based systems. This section explores some common threat scenarios that can impact cloud logistics environments.

- **Malware Attacks and Ransomware:** Malicious software (malware) can infiltrate cloud logistics systems, infecting applications and databases. Ransomware, a type of malware, encrypts critical data and demands a ransom for its release, disrupting logistics operations and potentially leading to data loss.
- **Phishing and Social Engineering:** Cybercriminals may launch phishing attacks targeting logistics employees, attempting to trick them into divulging login credentials or sensitive information. Social engineering tactics manipulate human behavior to gain unauthorized access to cloud logistics systems.
- **Insider Threats:** Employees or contractors with access to cloud logistics systems may intentionally or inadvertently compromise data or systems. Insider threats can result from disgruntled employees, accidental data exposure, or human error.
- **Advanced Persistent Threats (APTs):** APTs are sophisticated and stealthy attacks, often sponsored by well-funded adversaries. In the cloud logistics context, APTs may persistently target logistics systems, seeking to infiltrate and exfiltrate sensitive information undetected.
- **Data Interception and Eavesdropping:** Cyber attackers may attempt to intercept data transmitted between cloud-based logistics applications and users, potentially gaining access to sensitive information.
- **API and Integration Vulnerabilities:** Insecurely designed APIs and integrations can become entry points for attackers to manipulate or steal data within cloud logistics systems.
- **Cloud Service Provider Breaches:** A security breach at the cloud service provider's end could expose logistics data and applications, affecting multiple tenants utilizing the shared cloud infrastructure.
- **Identity and Access Management (IAM) Exploits:** Weak IAM practices, such as inadequate privilege management or weak authentication mechanisms, can lead to unauthorized access to logistics systems.
- **Supply Chain Attacks:** Supply chain attacks target third-party vendors or partners providing services to logistics companies. An attack on a trusted partner may introduce malware or backdoors into logistics systems.
- **DDoS Attacks:** Distributed Denial-of-Service (DDoS) attacks can overwhelm cloud logistics systems with excessive traffic, causing unavailability and disruptions to operations.

Proactively addressing these threat scenarios and implementing a multi-layered security approach, logistics companies can enhance the resilience and security of their cloud logistics environments, safeguarding critical data and ensuring uninterrupted operations. Regular security assessments, continuous monitoring, and collaboration with trusted security experts contribute to maintaining a secure and robust cloud logistics ecosystem.

Malware attacks and ransomware threats pose significant risks to cloud logistics environments, targeting critical logistics data, applications, and infrastructure (Gazzan, M., & Sheldon, F. T. 2023). These malicious activities can disrupt logistics operations, compromise sensitive information, and lead to financial losses (Shrikant Tiwari et al. 2012). Understanding these threat vectors is vital for logistics companies to implement effective security measures and protect their cloud-based systems.

Proactively addressing malware attacks and ransomware threats, logistics companies can enhance the security of their cloud logistics environments, protect valuable data, and maintain smooth logistics operations. Continuous monitoring, timely software updates, and collaboration with security experts contribute to building a resilient and secure cloud logistics ecosystem.

2.1 Social Engineering and Phishing Attacks Targeting Logistics Personnel

Social engineering and phishing attacks are deceptive techniques employed by cybercriminals to manipulate logistics personnel into divulging sensitive information or performing actions that compromise the security of cloud-based logistics systems (Omotunde, H., & Ahmed, M. 2023). These attacks exploit human vulnerabilities and trust, making them particularly challenging to defend against. This section explores the nature of social engineering and phishing attacks targeting logistics personnel and provides strategies to bolster their resilience against such threats (Al-Qahtani et al. 2022).

- **Social Engineering Attacks:** Social engineering attacks use psychological manipulation to deceive individuals into disclosing confidential information or performing actions beneficial to the attackers. These attacks exploit human emotions, trust, and relationships.
- **Phishing Attacks:** Phishing attacks involve sending fraudulent emails, messages, or links that appear legitimate to trick logistics personnel into revealing login credentials, sensitive data, or unwittingly downloading malware.
- **Spear Phishing:** Spear phishing is a targeted form of phishing where attackers customize their messages for specific logistics personnel, using personal information to increase credibility and success rates.
- **Impersonation:** Attackers may impersonate trusted entities, such as colleagues, vendors, or superiors, to establish credibility and manipulate logistics personnel into disclosing sensitive information or performing fraudulent actions.
- **Baiting:** Baiting attacks entice logistics personnel with offers or rewards, such as gift cards or promotions, to lure them into clicking malicious links or downloading malware-infected files.
- **Impact on Cloud Logistics:** Successful social engineering and phishing attacks can lead to unauthorized access to cloud logistics systems, data breaches, and disruptions in supply chain operations. Stolen credentials can also be used to carry out further attacks within the organization.

Raising awareness, fostering a security-conscious culture, and deploying the right security technologies, logistics companies can strengthen their defenses against social engineering and phishing attacks. Regular training, ongoing monitoring, and collaboration with security experts contribute to building a more resilient workforce and protecting cloud-based logistics systems from social engineering threats.

Insider threats, arising from both malicious and negligent employees, represent significant risks for cloud logistics environments. These individuals have legitimate access to critical systems, making it challenging to detect and prevent their activities. Insider threats can lead to data breaches, service disruptions, and compromise the confidentiality and integrity of logistics operations (Kafi M. A et al. 2023). The nature of insider threats and strategies to mitigate the risks posed by malicious or negligent employees in cloud logistics environments.

Proactively addressing the risks associated with insider threats, logistics companies can enhance the security of their cloud logistics environments, protect sensitive data, and minimize the impact of potential insider-related incidents. A combination of strong access controls, ongoing monitoring, employee training, and a supportive organizational culture is crucial to maintaining a secure and resilient cloud logistics ecosystem.

2.2 Advanced Persistent Threats (APTs) in Cloud-Based Logistics Systems

Advanced Persistent Threats (APTs) are sophisticated and stealthy cyberattacks orchestrated by well-funded and highly skilled threat actors (Mern J et al. 2021). APTs represent a significant risk to cloud-based logistics systems, targeting critical data, applications, and infrastructure with the goal of long-term infiltration and data exfiltration. APTs are designed to remain undetected for extended periods, making them especially challenging to detect and mitigate. The nature of APTs in cloud-based logistics systems and strategies to counter these persistent and insidious threats (Fernandes D. A et al. 2014).

- **Nature of APTs:** APTs are highly targeted and customized attacks, tailored to specific logistics companies or supply chain partners. Attackers invest considerable time and resources to gain unauthorized access and evade traditional security measures.
- **Stealth and Persistence:** APTs prioritize remaining undetected to maintain long-term access to logistics systems. Attackers employ evasion techniques, such as living-off-the-land (LOL) tactics and fileless malware, to avoid detection by conventional security solutions.
- **Initial Compromise:** APTs often begin with spear-phishing emails or watering hole attacks, targeting employees or supply chain partners with social engineering techniques to gain an initial foothold in the cloud-based logistics environment.
- **Lateral Movement:** Once inside the network, APTs use sophisticated methods to move laterally and escalate privileges to gain access to more critical systems and data.
- **Data Exfiltration:** The goal of APTs is to steal sensitive logistics data, such as customer information, supplier data, or intellectual property, and exfiltrate it without raising suspicion.
- **Impact on Cloud-Based Logistics:** A successful APT can lead to severe consequences for cloud-based logistics systems, including data breaches, loss of intellectual property, financial losses, and reputational damage.

Taking a proactive and multi-layered security approach, logistics companies can better defend against APTs in cloud-based systems, enhance the resilience of their logistics operations, and protect sensitive data from persistent and stealthy threats. Regular security assessments, continuous monitoring, and collaboration with security experts are essential components of a robust defense against APTs in cloud-based logistics systems.

3. DATA SECURITY AND PRIVACY CONCERNS

Data security and privacy are paramount concerns for logistics companies operating in cloud environments. As cloud-based logistics systems handle vast amounts of sensitive data, including customer information, shipment details, financial records, and intellectual property, ensuring the confidentiality, integrity, and availability of this data is crucial (Raja Santhi A & Muthuswamy, P. 2022). Additionally, compliance with data protection regulations and safeguarding customer privacy are essential to maintain trust and meet legal requirements, Figure 3 shows the challenges of the data security and privacy concerns faced by logistics companies in cloud-based systems.

Figure 3. Challenges of the data security and privacy concerns faced by logistics companies in cloud-based systems

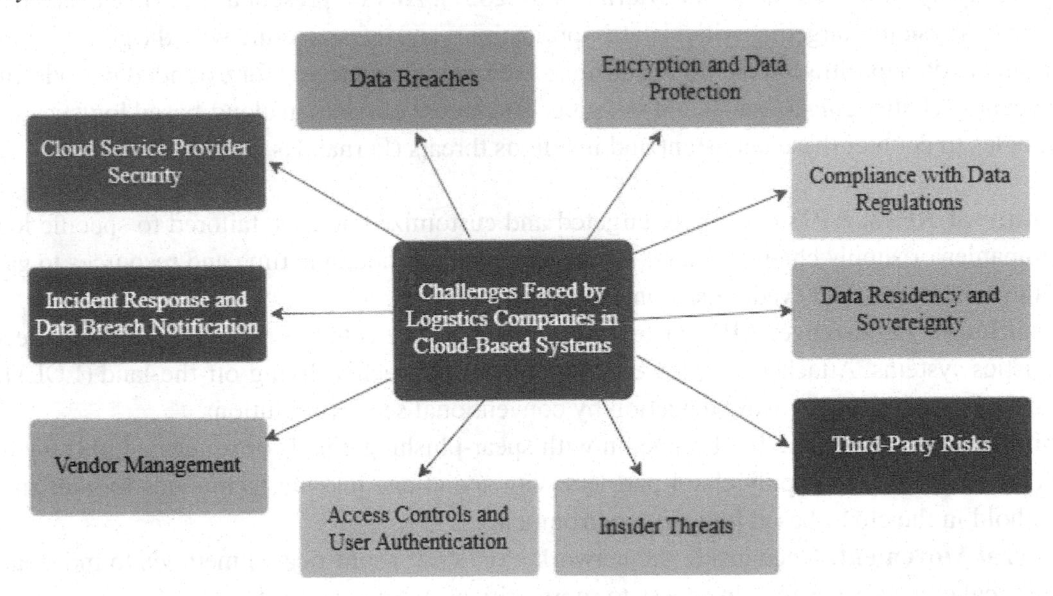

Mitigating Data Security and Privacy Concerns: To mitigate data security and privacy concerns in cloud-based logistics systems, logistics companies can adopt the following strategies (Leng J et al. 2020):

- **Comprehensive Data Security Policy:** Develop and enforce a comprehensive data security policy that outlines procedures, best practices, and responsibilities for handling sensitive information.
- **Regular Security Audits:** Conduct regular security audits and vulnerability assessments to identify potential weaknesses and promptly address them.
- **Encryption and Access Control:** Implement strong encryption for data in transit and at rest, along with robust access control measures.
- **Employee Training and Awareness:** Provide ongoing security training and awareness programs to educate employees about data security and privacy best practices.
- **Data Minimization:** Adopt a data minimization approach, only collecting and retaining the data necessary for logistics operations.

- **Privacy Impact Assessments:** Conduct privacy impact assessments to evaluate and address privacy risks associated with data processing activities.
- **Data Protection Officer (DPO):** Appoint a Data Protection Officer (DPO) to oversee data protection efforts and ensure compliance with relevant regulations.
- **Regular Backups and Disaster Recovery:** Maintain regular backups of critical logistics data and establish robust disaster recovery plans to ensure data availability and integrity.
- **Multi-Factor Authentication (MFA):** Implement multi-factor authentication (MFA) to enhance user authentication and prevent unauthorized access.
- **Incident Response Planning:** Develop a detailed incident response plan to efficiently respond to security incidents, including data breaches.

Proactively addressing data security and privacy concerns, logistics companies can fortify their cloud-based systems, protect sensitive data, and maintain customer trust and confidence. Regular security assessments, ongoing training, and a privacy-focused organizational culture contribute to a more resilient and secure cloud-based logistics environment.

3.1 Data Encryption Techniques for Securing Sensitive Logistics Information

Data encryption techniques play a vital role in securing sensitive logistics information in cloud-based environments. Encryption transforms data into unreadable formats, ensuring that even if unauthorized parties gain access to the data, they cannot decipher its content without the appropriate decryption key (Susmitha, C., et al. 2023). This helps safeguard sensitive logistics information from unauthorized access, data breaches, and other security threats, data encryption techniques used to secure sensitive logistics information is shown in the Figure 4.

To secure sensitive logistics information effectively, logistics companies should implement a combination of these encryption techniques based on their specific needs and security requirements. A well-implemented and managed encryption strategy enhances data security, minimizes the risk of data breaches, and maintains the confidentiality of critical logistics information in cloud-based environments.

3.2 Addressing Data Residency and Compliance Issues in the Cloud

Data residency and compliance issues are critical concerns for logistics companies operating in the cloud, especially when dealing with sensitive logistics data subject to data protection regulations in various jurisdictions (Stoyanova M. et al. 2020). Data residency refers to the physical location where data is stored and processed, while compliance involves adhering to relevant data protection laws and industry regulations. Addressing these issues is essential to ensure data security, maintain legal compliance, and build trust with customers and partners. Below are strategies to tackle data residency and compliance issues in the cloud (Aladwan M. N et al. 2020) and Figure 5 represent the addressing data residency and compliance issues in the cloud:

Proactively addressing data residency and compliance issues in the cloud, logistics companies can mitigate risks, ensure data security, and build a reputation for responsible data handling. A well-executed data governance strategy, combined with the right cloud service provider and compliance measures, strengthens the overall security posture and enhances the company's ability to meet data residency and regulatory requirements.

Figure 4. Data encryption techniques used to secure sensitive logistics information

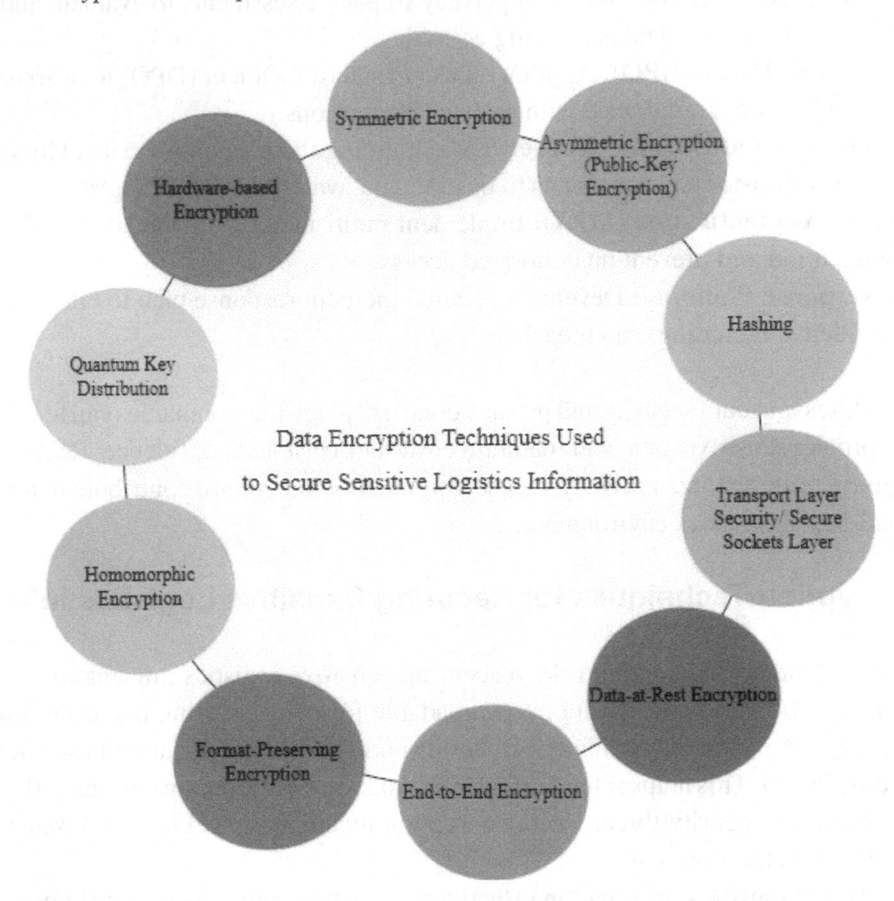

Figure 5. Addressing data residency and compliance issues in the cloud

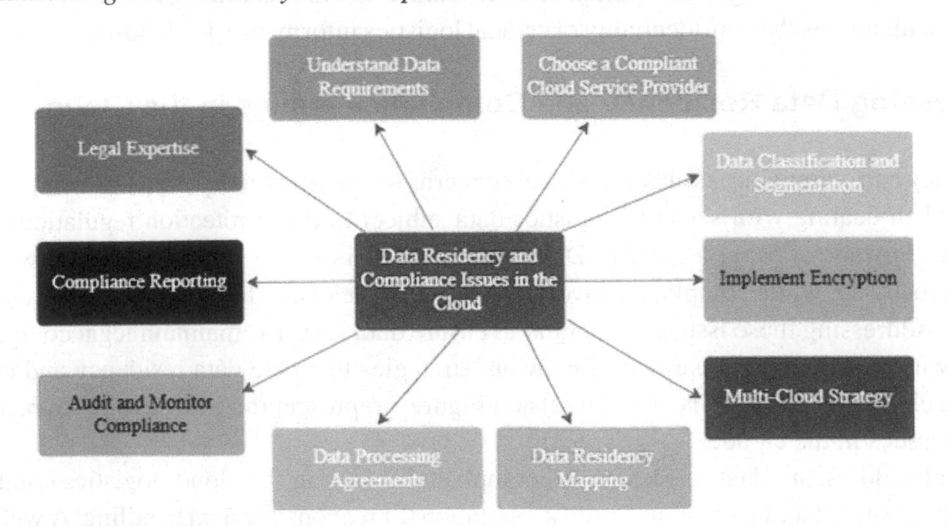

3.3 Protecting Personal Identifiable Information (PII) and Customer Data

Protecting Personal Identifiable Information (PII) and customer data is of utmost importance for logistics companies to maintain customer trust, comply with data protection regulations, and safeguard sensitive information (Anant, V et al. 2020). PII refers to any data that can be used to identify an individual, including names, addresses, social security numbers, and financial information, different strategies to ensure the security and privacy of PII and customer data shown in the Figure 6.

Implementing a comprehensive data security and privacy framework, logistics companies can safeguard PII and customer data, protect against data breaches, and maintain compliance with data protection regulations. A proactive approach to data protection, along with continuous monitoring and employee vigilance, ensures the confidentiality and integrity of sensitive information throughout the logistics ecosystem.

Figure 6. Strategies to ensure the security and privacy of PII and customer data

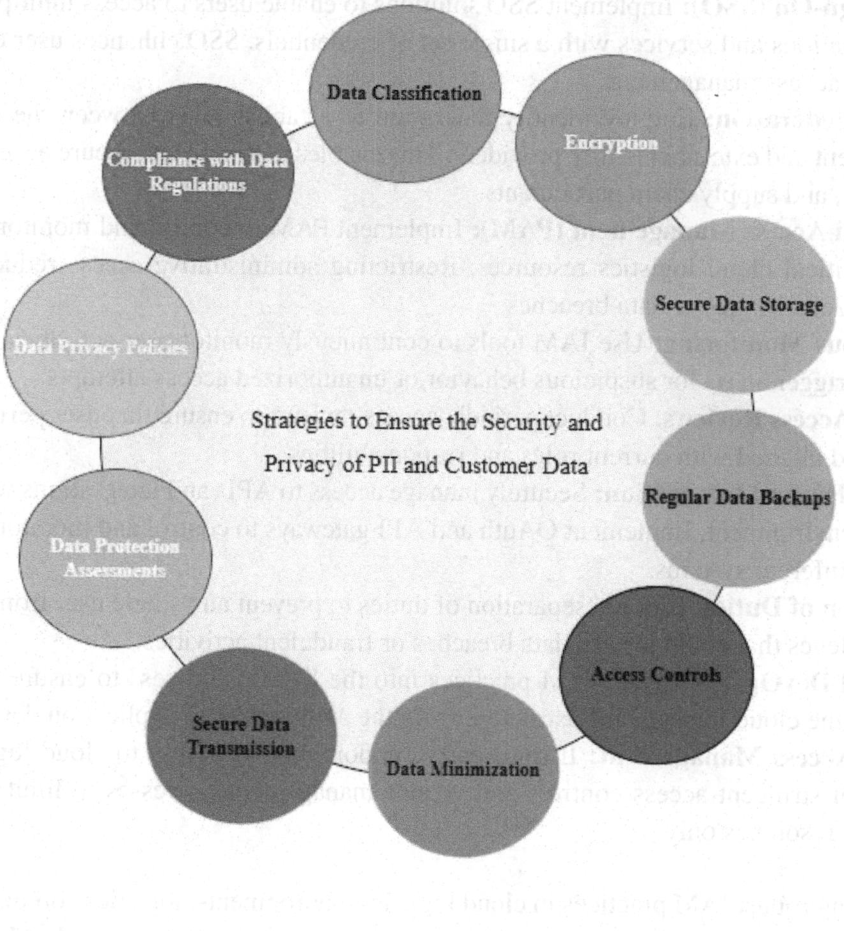

4. IDENTITY AND ACCESS MANAGEMENT (IAM) FOR CLOUD LOGISTICS

Identity and Access Management (IAM) is a critical component of securing cloud logistics environments. IAM refers to the set of processes, policies, and technologies used to manage and control access to resources within the cloud infrastructure. In the context of cloud logistics, IAM plays a pivotal role in ensuring that only authorized individuals have access to sensitive logistics data, applications, and services. Here are key considerations for implementing IAM in cloud logistics (Sah B. et al. 2021):

- **User Authentication and Authorization:** Implement strong authentication mechanisms, such as multi-factor authentication (MFA), to verify the identity of users accessing cloud logistics systems. Use role-based access control (RBAC) to grant appropriate permissions to users based on their roles and responsibilities within the organization.
- **Centralized Identity Management:** Utilize a centralized identity management system to maintain a single source of truth for user identities and access privileges. This approach streamlines user provisioning and deprovisioning, enhancing security and operational efficiency.
- **Single Sign-On (SSO):** Implement SSO solutions to enable users to access multiple cloud logistics applications and services with a single set of credentials. SSO enhances user experience and simplifies access management.
- **Identity Federation:** Employ identity federation to establish trust between the cloud logistics environment and external identity providers. This enables seamless and secure access for partners, customers, and supply chain participants.
- **Privileged Access Management (PAM):** Implement PAM to control and monitor privileged access to critical cloud logistics resources. Restricting administrative access reduces the risk of unauthorized changes or data breaches.
- **Continuous Monitoring:** Use IAM tools to continuously monitor user activities, detect anomalies, and trigger alerts for suspicious behavior or unauthorized access attempts.
- **Regular Access Reviews:** Conduct periodic access reviews to ensure that user permissions are up to date and aligned with current roles and responsibilities.
- **Secure APIs and Integration:** Securely manage access to APIs and integrations within the cloud logistics environment. Implement OAuth and API gateways to control and monitor data exchange between different systems.
- **Separation of Duties:** Enforce separation of duties to prevent any single user from having excessive privileges that could lead to data breaches or fraudulent activities.
- **IAM and DevOps:** Integrate IAM practices into the DevOps process to ensure that security is built into the cloud logistics infrastructure from the early stages of application development.
- **Vendor Access Management:** If third-party vendors require access to cloud logistics systems, implement stringent access controls and vendor management processes to limit their access to necessary resources only.

Implementing robust IAM practices in cloud logistics environments, logistics companies can ensure that sensitive data and critical resources remain protected from unauthorized access. IAM provides granular control over user permissions, improves visibility into user activities, and enhances overall security posture, bolstering the trust of customers, partners, and stakeholders in the cloud logistics ecosystem.

4.1 Role-Based Access Control and Least Privilege Principles

Role-Based Access Control (RBAC) and Least Privilege are two fundamental principles in the field of access control that play a crucial role in securing cloud logistics environments (D'Silva, D., & Ambawade, D. D. 2021). These principles help ensure that users have appropriate access to resources and data, limiting potential security risks and data breaches. An overview of RBAC and the Least Privilege principle in the context of cloud logistics:

- **Role-Based Access Control (RBAC):** RBAC is an access control model that assigns permissions to users based on their roles within the organization. In a cloud logistics environment, different users have specific responsibilities and access requirements (Li, J. et al. 2023). RBAC simplifies access management by defining roles and associating them with certain privileges or permissions.
- **Least Privilege Principle:** The principle of least privilege advocates granting users the minimum level of access necessary to perform their job duties. In a cloud logistics environment, adhering to this principle ensures that users only have access to the resources and data required for their specific tasks (Tien, N. H., et al. 2021).

Combining Role-Based Access Control and the Least Privilege principle in cloud logistics environments establishes a strong foundation for access management. By defining roles and associating them with specific permissions, and ensuring users have only the minimum access required, logistics companies can bolster data security, minimize the risk of data breaches, and maintain compliance with data protection regulations.

4.2 Multi-Factor Authentication (MFA) and Strong Authentication Methods

Multi-Factor Authentication (MFA) and strong authentication methods are crucial components of access security in cloud logistics environments. MFA enhances the traditional username and password-based authentication by requiring users to provide additional verification factors before granting access to sensitive logistics data and systems (Almadani, M. S. et al. 2023. This extra layer of security significantly reduces the risk of unauthorized access, data breaches, and identity-related attacks. An overview of MFA and some strong authentication methods used in cloud logistics:

- **Multi-Factor Authentication (MFA):** MFA combines two or more independent authentication factors from different categories to verify the identity of users. These categories are typically "something you know," "something you have," and "something you are." The primary factors used in MFA include (Alnahari, W., & Quasim, M. T. 2021; Shrikant Tiwari et al. 2011, Shrikant Tiwari et al. 2012)).:
  a) Something You Know: This is typically a password or PIN known only to the user.
  b) Something You Have: This refers to a physical device or token, such as a smart card, security key, or mobile device.
  c) Something You Are: This involves biometric data, such as fingerprints, facial recognition, or voiceprints.

MFA requires users to provide at least two of these factors, ensuring a higher level of authentication security. For example, a user may need to enter a password (something they know) and use a security token (something they have) to gain access to cloud logistics systems.

- **Strong Authentication Methods:** Strong authentication methods, used as part of MFA, add an additional layer of security to user verification. Some commonly used strong authentication methods in cloud logistics include:
  a) Time-based One-Time Password (TOTP): TOTP generates a one-time password that changes every 30 seconds. Users enter this password along with their regular credentials for authentication. TOTP is commonly used with mobile authenticator apps like Google Authenticator or Authy.
  b) Universal Second Factor (U2F): U2F is an open standard that uses USB or NFC security keys to provide an additional layer of authentication. The user plugs in the security key or taps it against an NFC-enabled device to complete the authentication process.
  c) Biometric Authentication: Biometric authentication uses unique physical traits, such as fingerprints, facial features, or voice patterns, for user verification. Biometric data cannot be easily replicated, making it a robust authentication method.
  d) Push Notifications: Push notifications send authentication requests to the user's mobile device. The user can approve or deny the request, ensuring that only the legitimate user can grant access.
  e) Smart Cards: Smart cards are physical cards containing embedded microchips with cryptographic data. Users insert the card into a card reader for authentication.

Implementing MFA with strong authentication methods in cloud logistics significantly enhances the overall security posture. By combining factors from different categories and leveraging strong authentication methods, logistics companies can protect sensitive data from unauthorized access, minimize the risk of identity-related attacks, and fortify the security of their cloud-based logistics systems.

4.3 Centralized Identity Management and Single Sign-On (SSO) Solutions

Centralized identity management and Single Sign-On (SSO) solutions are essential components of access control and user authentication in cloud logistics environments. These solutions streamline user access, enhance security, and improve user experience by providing a centralized and seamless login experience across multiple applications and services (Anderson, J., & Keahey, K. 2022). An overview of centralized identity management and SSO in cloud logistics:

- **Centralized Identity Management:** Centralized identity management involves managing user identities, access privileges, and authentication in a single, unified system. In a cloud logistics environment, this typically involves using an Identity and Access Management (IAM) platform that acts as a centralized repository for user identities and access policies (Ragothaman, K., et al. 2023) and the different Key features of centralized identity management is shown in the Figure 7.

Figure 7. Key features of centralized identity management

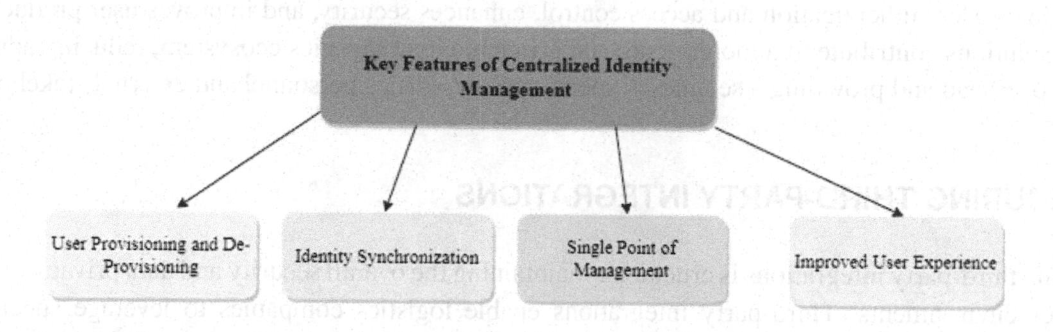

- **Single Sign-On (SSO) Solutions:** SSO solutions enable users to access multiple applications and services with a single set of credentials (Herrera-Cubides et al. 2019). Instead of requiring users to log in separately to each system, SSO allows users to authenticate only once, after which they gain access to all authorized resources without re-entering their credentials also key features of SSO solutions is shown in the Figure 8.

Figure 8. Key features of SSO solutions

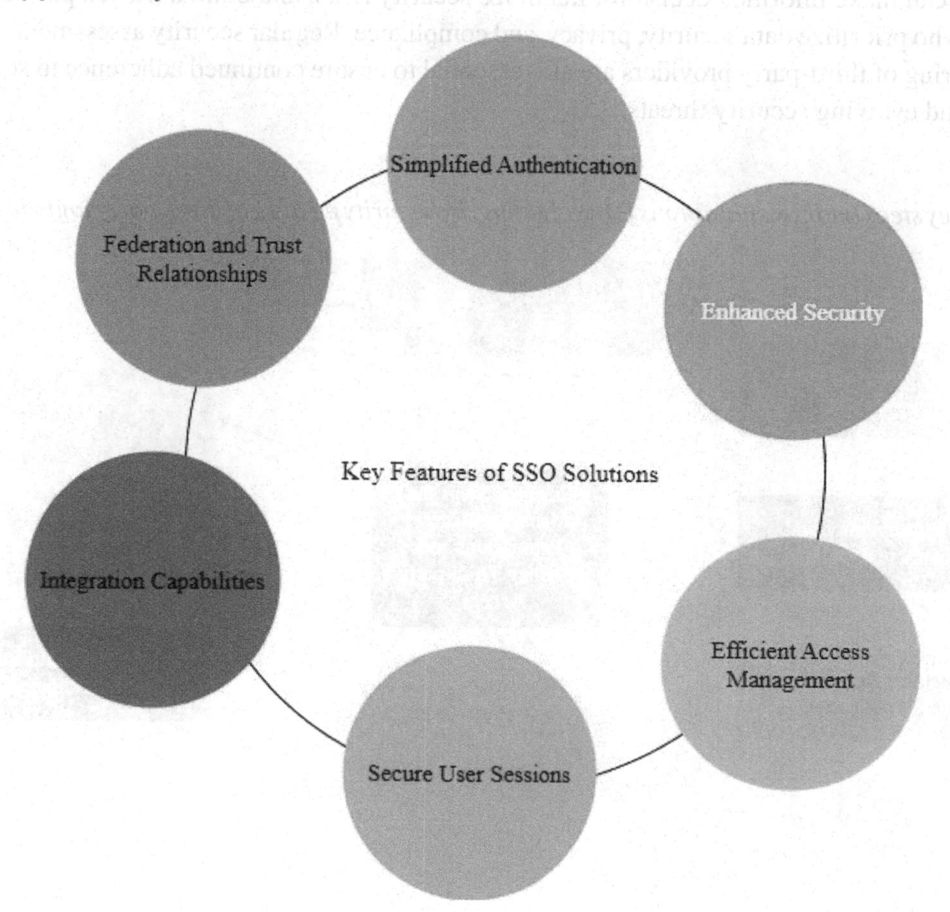

Implementing centralized identity management and SSO solutions in cloud logistics environments streamlines user authentication and access control, enhances security, and improves user productivity. These solutions contribute to a more secure and efficient cloud logistics ecosystem, reducing administrative overhead and providing a seamless experience for logistics personnel and external stakeholders.

5. SECURING THIRD-PARTY INTEGRATIONS

Securing third-party integrations is crucial for maintaining the overall security and data privacy of cloud logistics environments. Third-party integrations enable logistics companies to leverage specialized services, share data with partners, and enhance their overall operations (Williams, B. D. et al. 2013). However, integrating external systems also introduces potential security risks and vulnerabilities.

Evaluating the security posture of third-party logistics providers is a critical step in ensuring that logistics companies can trust their partners with sensitive data, operations, and customer information (Rahman, S. et al. 2019). A robust security assessment process helps identify potential risks and vulnerabilities, enabling logistics companies to make informed decisions when selecting and engaging with third-party logistics providers, Figure 9 represents the key steps and considerations for evaluating the security posture of third-party logistics providers.

Conducting a thorough evaluation of the security posture of third-party logistics providers, logistics companies can make informed decisions, minimize security risks, and build a trusted partnership with providers who prioritize data security, privacy, and compliance. Regular security assessments and ongoing monitoring of third-party providers are also essential to ensure continued adherence to security best practices and evolving security threats.

Figure 9. Key steps and considerations for evaluating the security posture of third-party logistics providers

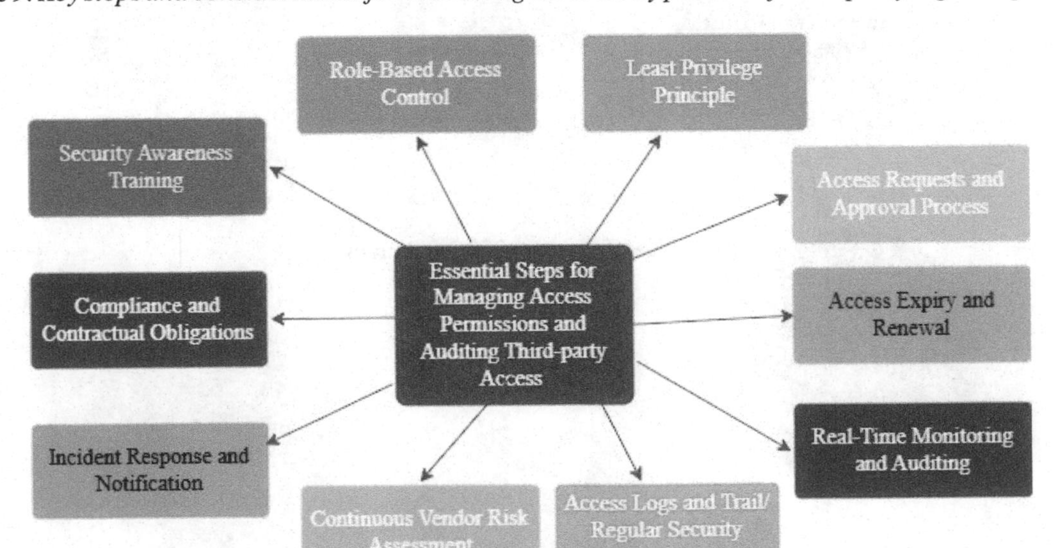

5.1 Ensuring Secure Data Exchange and API Security

Ensuring secure data exchange and API security is paramount in cloud logistics environments, as data exchange between systems and applications is integral to smooth logistics operations (Bodkhe, Umesh et al. 2020). Secure data exchange and robust API security measures protect sensitive information from unauthorized access, data breaches, and potential cyber threats, Figure 10 shows the strategies to ensure secure data exchange and API security in cloud logistics.

Implementing these strategies, logistics companies can ensure secure data exchange and API security, safeguarding sensitive information and maintaining the integrity of their cloud logistics environment. Ongoing security assessments, continuous monitoring, and proactive measures are essential to adapt to evolving security threats and ensure the protection of critical logistics data and operations.

Figure 10. Strategies to ensure secure data exchange and API security in cloud logistics

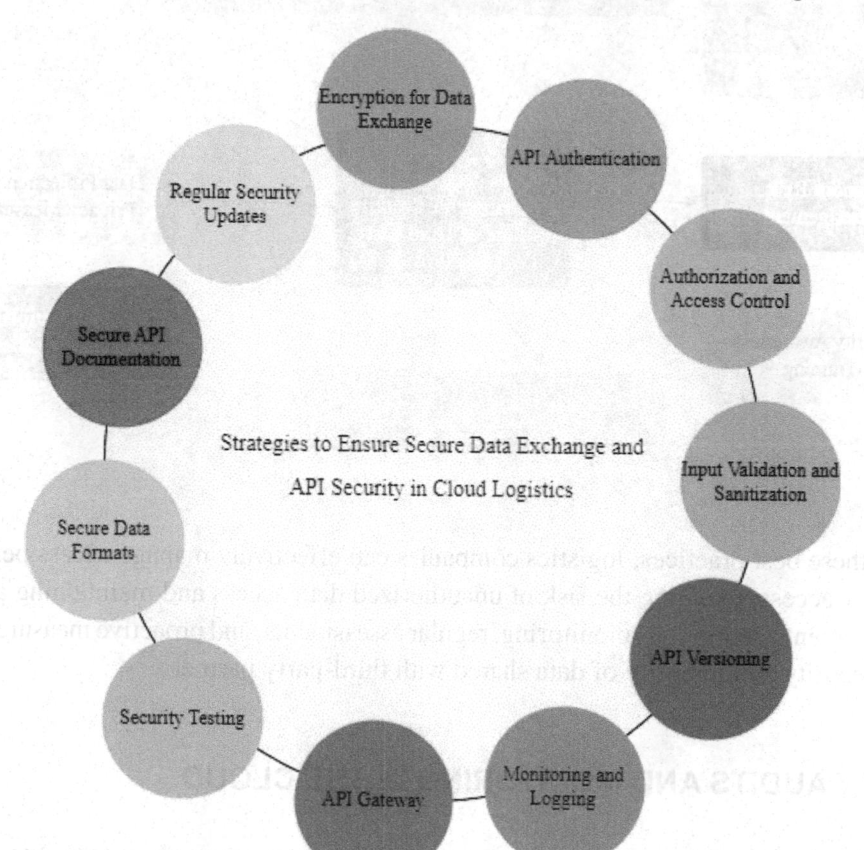

5.2 Managing Access Permissions and Auditing Third-Party Access

Managing access permissions and auditing third-party access is critical to maintaining control over data security and mitigating potential risks associated with external partners in cloud logistics environments (George, A. S., & Sagayarajan, S. 2023). By implementing strong access control measures and conducting regular audits, logistics companies can ensure that third-party access is appropriately managed and aligned with security requirements and essential steps for managing access permissions and auditing third-party access shown in the Figure 11.

Figure 11. Essential steps for managing access permissions and auditing third-party access

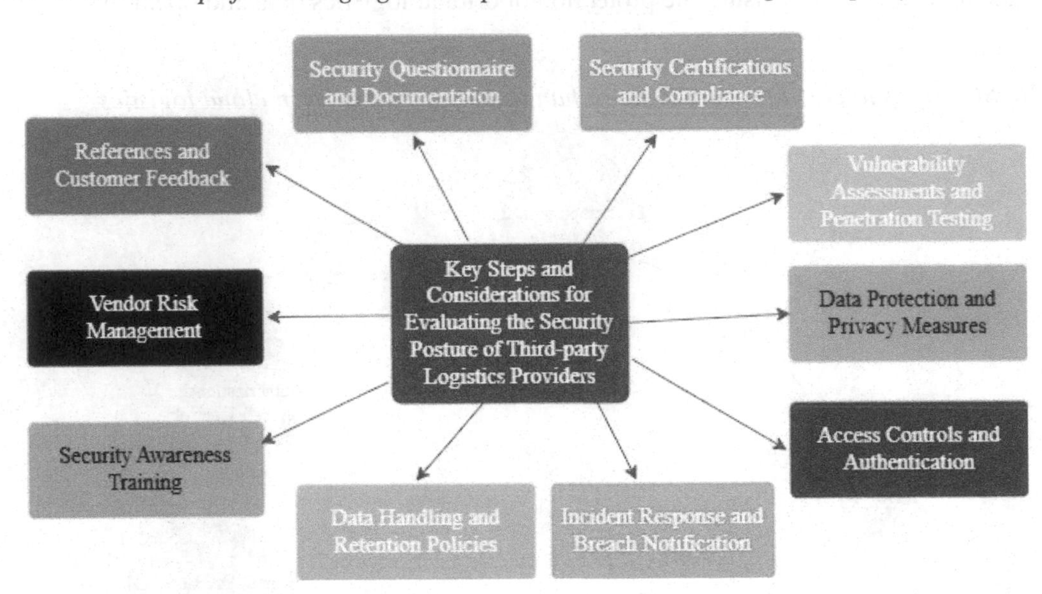

Following these best practices, logistics companies can effectively manage access permissions and audit third-party access, reducing the risk of unauthorized data access and maintaining a secure cloud logistics environment. Continuous monitoring, regular assessments, and proactive measures are essential to ensure the security and integrity of data shared with third-party partners.

6. SECURITY AUDITS AND MONITORING IN THE CLOUD

Security audits and monitoring are essential components of maintaining a robust security posture in cloud environments, including cloud-based logistics operations (George, A. S., & Sagayarajan, S. 2023). These practices help identify potential vulnerabilities, detect security incidents, and ensure ongoing compliance with security policies and standards. An overview of security audits and monitoring in the cloud:

- **Security Audits:** Security audits involve a systematic review of cloud infrastructure, applications, and data to assess their security controls and practices. These audits can be performed internally by the organization's security team or by third-party auditors, key aspects of security audits in the cloud is shown in the Figure 12.
- **Real-time Monitoring:** Real-time monitoring involves continuous observation of cloud resources and activities to detect and respond to security threats and anomalies promptly also different key elements of real-time monitoring in the cloud shown in the Figure 13.
- **Threat Intelligence Integration:** Integrating threat intelligence feeds allows cloud monitoring systems to stay updated with the latest security threats and indicators of compromise. This integration enhances the ability to detect emerging threats and potential attacks.
- Automated Alerts and Incident Response: Setting up automated alerts and incident response workflows ensures that security teams are notified immediately when security incidents occur. Automated responses can help contain threats and prevent further damage.
- Compliance Monitoring: Continuously monitoring compliance with security policies, industry regulations, and internal standards ensures that the cloud environment remains in alignment with security requirements.
- Periodic Security Review: Conducting periodic security reviews, including both audits and ongoing monitoring assessments, helps organizations stay vigilant against new and evolving security risks.

Security audits and real-time monitoring are essential for maintaining a proactive and effective security posture in the cloud. By regularly assessing security controls, identifying vulnerabilities, and responding promptly to incidents, logistics companies can protect sensitive data, ensure the integrity of their cloud-based operations, and foster a secure cloud logistics environment.

Figure 12. Key aspects of security audits in the cloud

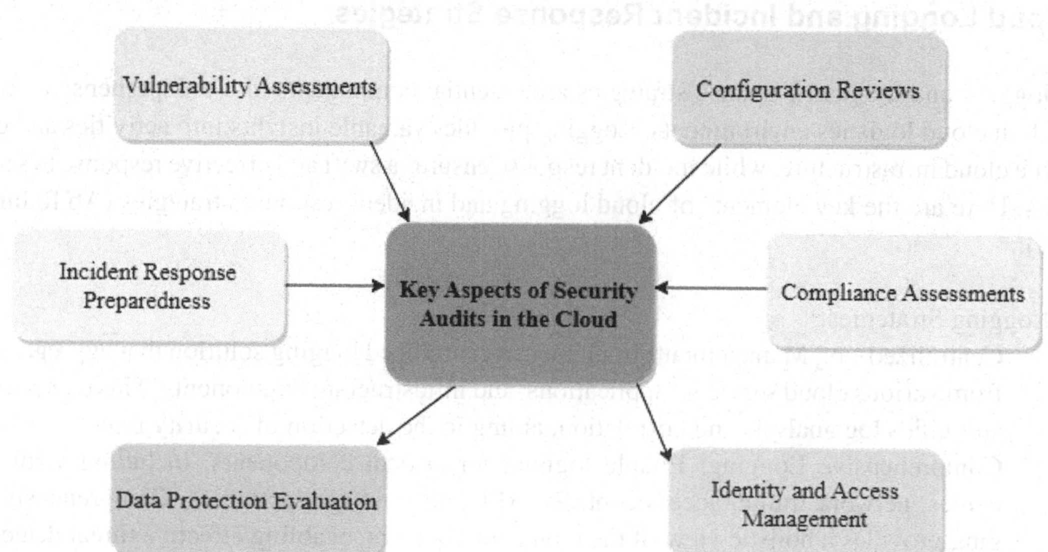

Figure 13. Key elements of real-time monitoring in the cloud

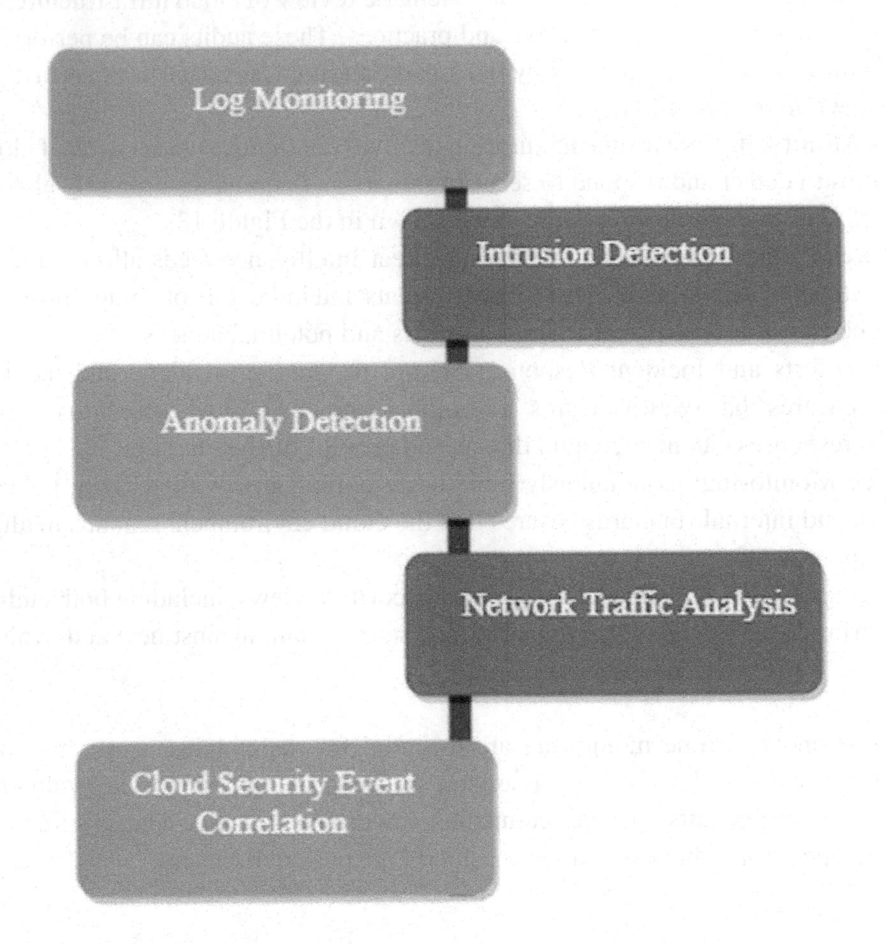

6.1 Cloud Logging and Incident Response Strategies

Cloud logging and incident response strategies are essential components of a comprehensive security approach in cloud logistics environments. Logging provides valuable insights into activities and events within the cloud infrastructure, while incident response ensures a swift and effective response to security incidents. Here are the key elements of cloud logging and incident response strategies (Ab Rahman et al. 2015):

Cloud Logging Strategies:

- Centralized Log Management: Implement a centralized logging solution that aggregates logs from various cloud services, applications, and infrastructure components. This centralization simplifies log analysis and correlation, aiding in the detection of security issues.
- Comprehensive Logging: Enable logging for critical components, including virtual machines, network traffic, access controls, API calls, and user activities. Comprehensive logging provides a holistic view of the cloud environment, enabling effective threat detection.

- Log Retention Policy: Define a log retention policy to ensure logs are retained for an appropriate duration, considering legal and compliance requirements. Long-term log retention allows for historical analysis and investigations.
- Real-Time Monitoring: Use real-time monitoring and alerting mechanisms to detect suspicious activities or security incidents immediately. Implement automated alerts based on predefined thresholds or anomaly detection.
- Log Encryption and Integrity: Ensure that logs are encrypted during transit and at rest to protect sensitive information. Additionally, implement measures to verify the integrity of logs to prevent tampering.
- Audit Trail Logging: Maintain an audit trail of critical actions, such as user authentication, access control changes, and administrative activities, to facilitate forensic investigations.

Incident Response Strategies:

- Incident Response Plan: Develop a comprehensive incident response plan that outlines roles, responsibilities, and procedures for responding to security incidents. The plan should cover identification, containment, eradication, recovery, and lessons learned.
- Predefined Incident Categories: Categorize potential incidents based on their severity and impact to prioritize response efforts. This ensures that resources are allocated efficiently during incident response.
- Incident Response Team (IRT): Assemble a dedicated incident response team with the necessary expertise and authority to lead the response efforts. The team should include representatives from IT, security, legal, and senior management.
- Communication Protocols: Establish clear communication protocols for reporting incidents internally and externally. Prompt communication is vital during incident response to coordinate efforts and manage stakeholders' expectations.
- Forensics and Evidence Preservation: Develop procedures for collecting and preserving evidence during incident investigations. This ensures that the root cause analysis can be conducted effectively and supports potential legal proceedings.
- Containment and Mitigation: Take immediate actions to contain the incident and prevent further damage. This may involve isolating affected systems or blocking malicious activities.
- Recovery and Remediation: Develop a plan for restoring affected systems and services to normal operations while ensuring that any vulnerabilities or weaknesses are remediated.
- Post-Incident Review: Conduct a post-incident review to analyze the incident response process, identify areas for improvement, and update the incident response plan accordingly.
- Training and Drills: Regularly train the incident response team and conduct simulated drills to test the effectiveness of the response plan. This helps improve the team's capabilities and response times.

Combining effective cloud logging strategies with a well-defined incident response plan, logistics companies can strengthen their security posture, detect and respond to security incidents in a timely manner, and minimize the impact of potential breaches on their cloud logistics operations.

6.2 Leveraging Artificial Intelligence and Machine Learning for Cloud Security

Leveraging Artificial Intelligence (AI) and Machine Learning (ML) for cloud security is an innovative and effective approach to enhance the protection of cloud logistics environments. AI and ML technologies offer advanced capabilities to detect, prevent, and respond to cybersecurity threats in real-time, making them invaluable tools in maintaining a secure cloud infrastructure, Figure 14 shows how AI and ML can be leveraged for cloud security.

Leveraging AI and ML for cloud security not only enhances the effectiveness of existing security measures but also enables organizations to keep pace with the dynamic and evolving nature of cyber threats. By adopting AI-driven security solutions, logistics companies can bolster their cloud security, protect sensitive data, and maintain the resilience and integrity of their cloud logistics operations.

AI-based threat detection and anomaly analysis is a cutting-edge approach to cybersecurity that leverages Artificial Intelligence (AI) and Machine Learning (ML) algorithms to identify and respond to potential security threats in cloud logistics environments. This advanced technology enables organizations to detect and address cybersecurity incidents in real-time, providing a more proactive and effective defense against cyber threats.

Figure 14. How AI and ML can be leveraged for cloud security

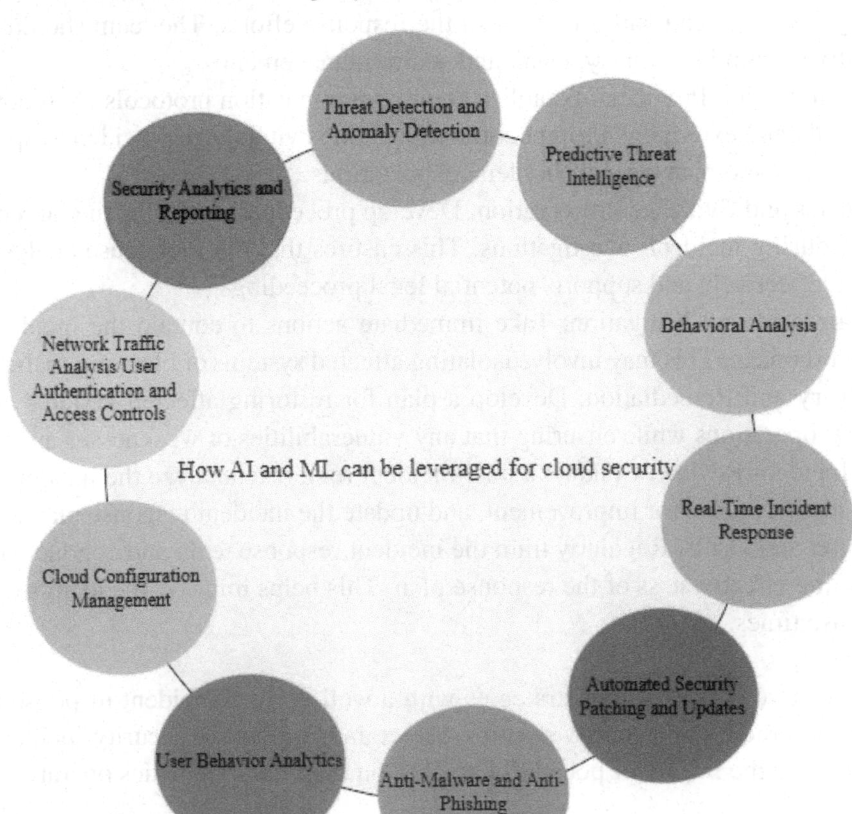

Intelligent incident response and automated security actions are key components of modern cloud security strategies that leverage Artificial Intelligence (AI) and Machine Learning (ML) capabilities. These technologies enable organizations to detect, analyze, and respond to security incidents in real-time, often with little to no human intervention.

6.3 AI-Driven Predictive Security Measures for Cloud Logistics Systems

AI-driven predictive security measures are a proactive and forward-looking approach to safeguarding cloud logistics systems. These measures leverage Artificial Intelligence (AI) and Machine Learning (ML) to predict and prevent potential security threats before they manifest, allowing logistics companies to stay one step ahead of cyber adversaries, AI-driven predictive security measures implementation in cloud logistics systems shows in the Figure 15.

Implementing AI-driven predictive security measures in cloud logistics systems empowers organizations to anticipate and neutralize potential security threats before they escalate. By harnessing the power of AI and ML, logistics companies can achieve a proactive security posture, reduce the risk of successful attacks, and ensure the continuity and resilience of their cloud-based operations.

Figure 15. AI-driven predictive security measures implementation in cloud logistics systems

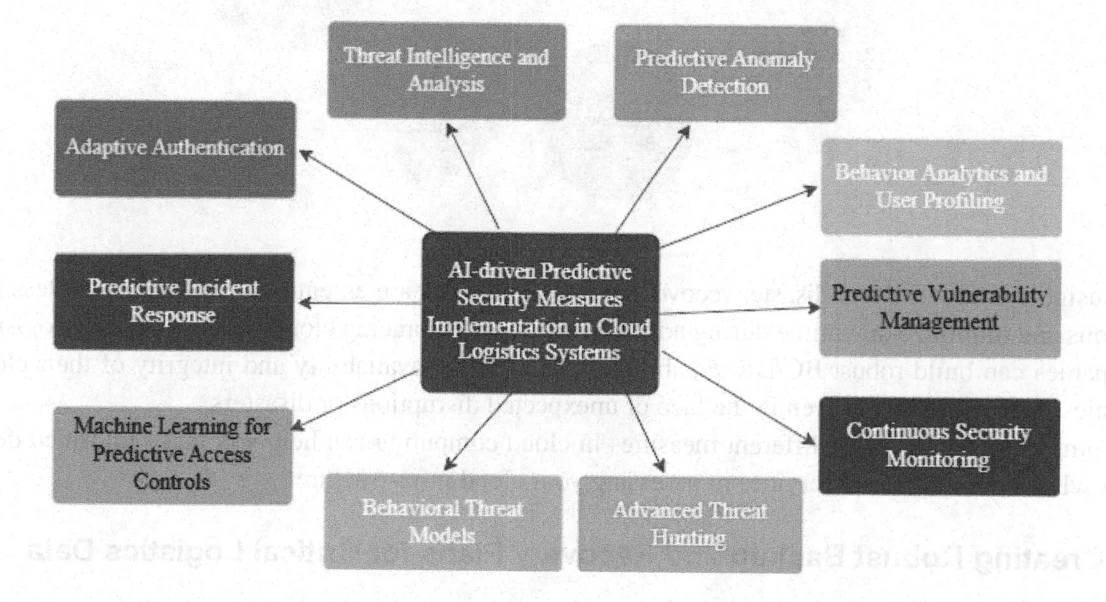

7. BUSINESS CONTINUITY AND DISASTER RECOVERY IN CLOUD LOGISTICS

Business Continuity (BC) and Disaster Recovery (DR) are critical aspects of cloud logistics operations. They focus on ensuring the resilience, availability, and rapid recovery of systems and data in the event of disruptions or disasters. Leveraging the cloud for BC and DR provides several advantages, such as increased flexibility, cost-effectiveness, and scalability, the business continuity and disaster recovery strategies implementation in cloud logistics shown in the Figure 16.

Figure 16. Business continuity and disaster recovery strategies implementation in cloud logistics

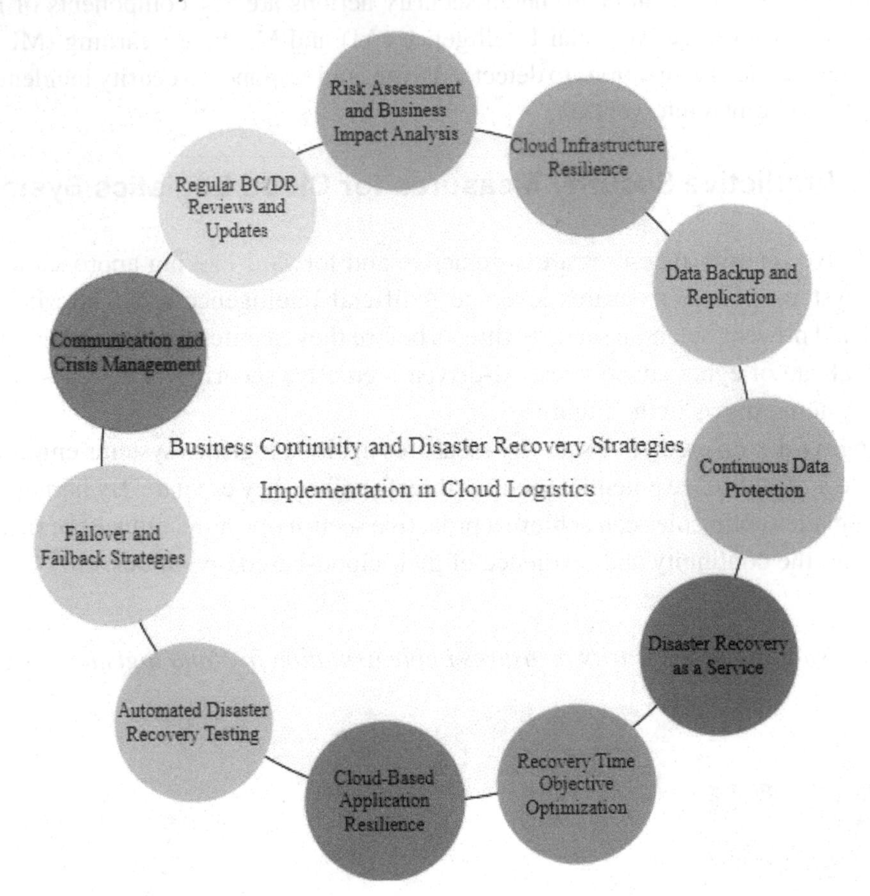

Business continuity and disaster recovery in cloud logistics are essential to maintain seamless operations and minimize downtime during adverse events. By embracing cloud-based resilience, logistics companies can build robust BC/DR capabilities, ensuring the availability and integrity of their cloud logistics systems and data, even in the face of unexpected disruptions or disasters.

Comparative analysis of different measures in cloud computing can help you make informed decisions when choosing cloud services or assessing your cloud infrastructure.

7.1 Creating Robust Backup and Recovery Plans for Critical Logistics Data

Creating robust backup and recovery plans for critical logistics data is essential to ensure data availability, integrity, and business continuity in the event of data loss, system failures, or cyber incidents. A well-designed backup and recovery strategy can minimize downtime and data loss, allowing logistics companies to quickly resume operations without compromising customer service or supply chain efficiency.

Implementing a robust backup and recovery plan for critical logistics data, companies can safeguard their operations against data loss, minimize disruptions, and maintain customer trust and satisfaction. A well-prepared backup and recovery strategy is a crucial component of a comprehensive business continuity and disaster recovery approach for logistics companies.

Table 1. Comparative analysis of different measures in cloud computing across various key measures

Measure	Description	AWS (Amazon Web Services)	Microsoft Azure	Google Cloud Platform (GCP)	IBM Cloud	Oracle Cloud
Service Variety	Range of cloud services offered	Broad	Broad	Broad	Broad	Broad
Pricing Models	Variety of pricing options available	Pay-as-you-go, Reserved	Pay-as-you-go	Pay-as-you-go, Sustained Use	Pay-as-you-go, Reserved	Pay-as-you-go
Pricing Transparency	Clarity of pricing and billing	Transparent	Transparent	Transparent	Transparent	Transparent
Availability Zones	Geographical redundancy	Multiple	Multiple	Multiple	Multiple	Multiple
Data Centers	Global data center presence	Extensive	Extensive	Extensive	Extensive	Extensive
Virtual Machines	Variety of VM types and sizes	Extensive	Extensive	Extensive	Extensive	Extensive
Containers	Container orchestration and management	Amazon ECS, EKS	Azure Kubernetes Service (AKS)	Google Kubernetes Engine (GKE)	IBM Kubernetes Service	Oracle Kubernetes Engine (OKE)
Serverless	Serverless computing services	AWS Lambda	Azure Functions	Google Cloud Functions	IBM Cloud Functions	Oracle Functions
Databases	Managed database services	Amazon RDS, DynamoDB	Azure SQL Database, Cosmos DB	Cloud SQL, Firestore	Db2 on Cloud, Databases for MongoDB	Oracle Autonomous Database
Networking	Networking and CDN services	Amazon VPC, CloudFront	Azure Virtual Network, CDN	Virtual Private Cloud, CDN	VPC, Content Delivery Network	Virtual Cloud Network, Content Delivery Network
Storage	Storage options and scalability	S3, EBS, EFS	Blob Storage, Disk Storage	Cloud Storage, Filestore	IBM Cloud Object Storage	Object Storage, Block Volume
AI/ML Services	Machine learning and AI offerings	Amazon SageMaker	Azure Machine Learning	AI Platform, AutoML	Watson Studio, AutoAI	Oracle Machine Learning
Security	Security features and compliance	AWS Identity and Access Management (IAM), Security Hub	Azure Active Directory, Azure Security Center	Identity and Access Management (IAM), Security Command Center	IBM Cloud Identity and Access Management	Identity and Access Management (IAM), Security
Hybrid Capabilities	Integration with on-premises infrastructure	AWS Outposts, VMware Cloud on AWS	Azure Arc, Azure Stack	Anthos, Cloud Interconnect	IBM Cloud Satellite, IBM Cloud Private	Oracle Cloud at Customer, Oracle Cloud@Customer
Developer Tools	Tools for app development and deployment	AWS Developer Tools, AWS CodeStar	Azure DevOps, Azure DevTest Labs	Google Cloud SDK, Cloud Build	IBM Cloud Developer Tools	Oracle Developer Tools
Customer Support	Support options and SLAs	AWS Support Plans	Azure Support Plans	Google Cloud Support Packages	IBM Support Plans	Oracle Support Plans

Cloud-based disaster recovery solutions offer an efficient and cost-effective approach to ensuring the continuity and resilience of cloud logistics systems in the face of disruptive events. These solutions leverage the cloud's scalability, redundancy, and global reach to provide robust disaster recovery capabilities. comprehensive backup and recovery plan for critical logistics data shown in the Figure 17.

Figure 17. Comprehensive backup and recovery plan for critical logistics data

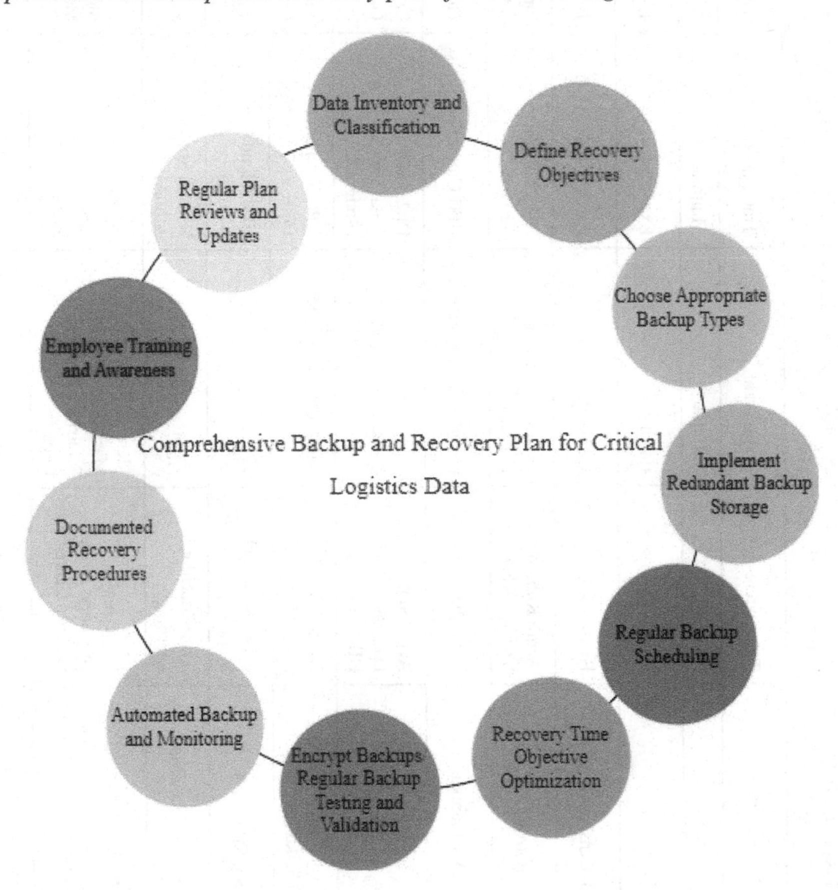

8. FUTURE TRENDS IN CLOUD SECURITY FOR LOGISTICS

Future trends in cloud security for logistics are expected to be shaped by advancements in technology, evolving threat landscapes, and the increasing integration of cloud-based solutions in logistics operations. As logistics companies continue to adopt cloud technologies to enhance efficiency and competitiveness, ensuring the security of cloud environments will remain a top priority, future trends in cloud security for logistics shown in the Figure 18.

As the cloud continues to play a crucial role in revolutionizing the logistics industry, staying ahead of evolving security challenges will be imperative. Embracing these future trends in cloud security will enable logistics companies to proactively protect their data, applications, and operations, ensuring a secure and resilient cloud infrastructure for the future.

Figure 18. Future trends in cloud security for logistics

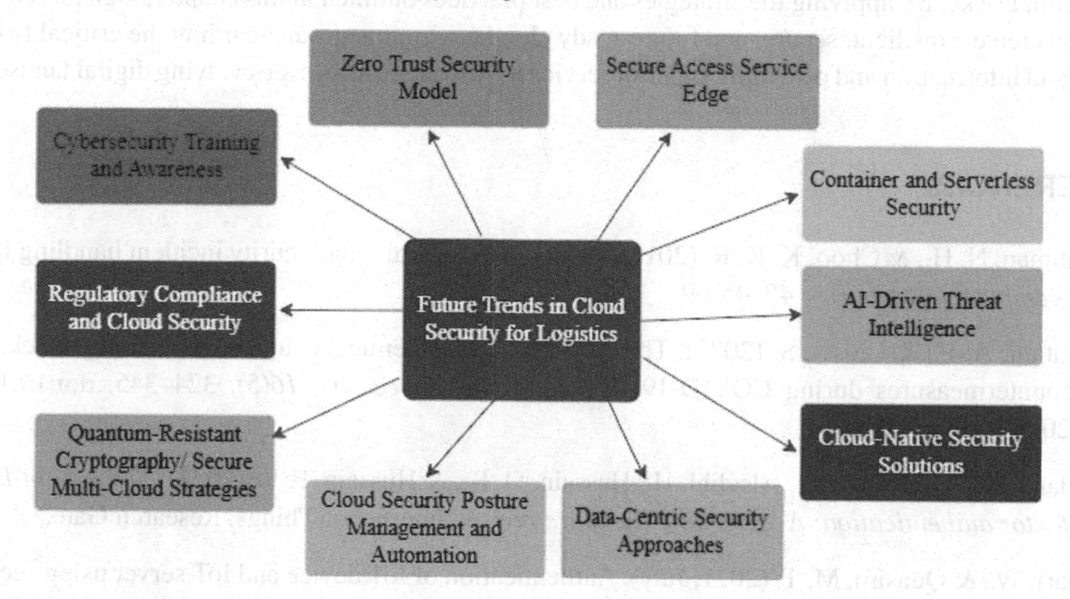

9. CONCLUSION

In conclusion, cloud computing has transformed the landscape of business logistics, providing unprecedented scalability, flexibility, and efficiency. However, this digital revolution also brings with it new security challenges and risks that demand proactive measures and foresight. As logistics companies continue to embrace cloud-based solutions, the security of cloud environments becomes paramount to ensuring the uninterrupted flow of goods and services.

To fortify cloud security, it is essential for logistics companies to develop comprehensive backup and recovery plans, secure sensitive logistics information with data encryption techniques, and ensure compliance with international data protection and privacy standards. Identity and access management, along with multi-factor authentication, play a crucial role in safeguarding against unauthorized access and identity-related risks.

Furthermore, cloud security compliance and standards, including industry-specific regulations, must be adhered to diligently. Implementing continuous monitoring and security audits are vital for early threat detection and to assess the security posture of third-party logistics providers. Leveraging AI and machine learning for cloud security enhances threat detection and enables intelligent incident response. As we explore future trends, we anticipate new challenges and threats that may arise with the integration of upcoming technologies. The logistics industry must be prepared to adapt security strategies to counter advanced cyber threats and protect against vulnerabilities in IoT, edge computing, 5G, and other emerging technologies.

Future-proofing cloud security in business logistics requires a multi-faceted approach that encompasses risk assessment, employee training, advanced security technologies, and compliance with industry standards. Embracing a culture of security and fostering collaboration with cloud service providers are essential to maintaining a robust security posture. In conclusion, securing cloud-based logistics operations is an ongoing journey that necessitates vigilance, adaptation, and a commitment to staying ahead of potential risks. By applying the strategies and best practices outlined in this chapter, logistics companies can create a resilient, secure, and future-ready cloud environment, safeguarding the critical flow of goods and information and providing superior service to customers in an ever-evolving digital landscape.

REFERENCES

Ab Rahman, N. H., & Choo, K. K. R. (2015). A survey of information security incident handling in the cloud. *computers & security, 49*, 45-69.

Al-Qahtani, A. F., & Cresci, S. (2022). The COVID-19 scamdemic: A survey of phishing attacks and their countermeasures during COVID-19. *IET Information Security*, *16*(5), 324–345. doi:10.1049/ise2.12073 PMID:35942004

Almadani, M. S., Alotaibi, S., Alsobhi, H., Hussain, O. K., & Hussain, F. K. (2023). *Blockchain-based multi-factor authentication: A systematic literature review*. Internet of Things. Research Gate.

Alnahari, W., & Quasim, M. T. (2021, July). Authentication of IoT device and IoT server using security key. In *2021 International Congress of Advanced Technology and Engineering (ICOTEN)* (pp. 1-9). IEEE. 10.1109/ICOTEN52080.2021.9493492

Anant, V., Donchak, L., Kaplan, J., & Soller, H. (2020). *The consumer-data opportunity and the privacy imperative.* McKinsey. https://www. mckinsey. com/business-functions/risk-and-resilience/our-insights/the-consumer-data-opportunity-and-the-privacy-imperative

Anderson, J., & Keahey, K. (2022). Migrating towards Single Sign-On and Federated Identity. In Practice and Experience in Advanced Research Computing (pp. 1-8). Springer. doi:10.1145/3491418.3530770

Ashraf, I., Park, Y., Hur, S., Kim, S. W., Alroobaea, R., Zikria, Y. B., & Nosheen, S. (2022). A survey on cyber security threats in iot-enabled maritime industry. *IEEE Transactions on Intelligent Transportation Systems*, *24*(2), 2677–2690. doi:10.1109/TITS.2022.3164678

Bagga, J. (2023). SAP Cloud Integration: Security. In *A Practical Guide to SAP Integration Suite: SAP's Cloud Middleware and Integration Solution* (pp. 371–388). Apress. doi:10.1007/978-1-4842-9337-9_7

Bandari, V. (2023). Enterprise Data Security Measures: A Comparative Review of Effectiveness and Risks Across Different Industries and Organization Types. *International Journal of Business Intelligence and Big Data Analytics*, *6*(1), 1–11.

Bello, S. A., Oyedele, L. O., Akinade, O. O., Bilal, M., Delgado, J. M. D., Akanbi, L. A., & Owolabi, H. A. (2021). Cloud computing in construction industry: Use cases, benefits and challenges. *Automation in Construction*, *122*, 103441. doi:10.1016/j.autcon.2020.103441

Bodkhe, U., Tanwar, S., Parekh, K., Khanpara, P., Tyagi, S., Kumar, N., & Alazab, M. (2020). Blockchain for industry 4.0: A comprehensive review. *IEEE Access : Practical Innovations, Open Solutions*, *8*, 79764–79800. doi:10.1109/ACCESS.2020.2988579

Christopher, M., Lowson, R., & Peck, H. (2004). Creating agile supply chains in the fashion industry. *International Journal of Retail & Distribution Management*, *32*(8), 367–376. doi:10.1108/09590550410546188

D'Silva, D., & Ambawade, D. D. (2021, April). Building a zero-trust architecture using kubernetes. In *2021 6th international conference for convergence in technology (i2ct)* (pp. 1-8). IEEE. 10.1109/I2CT51068.2021.9418203

Fernandes, D. A., Soares, L. F., Gomes, J. V., Freire, M. M., & Inácio, P. R. (2014). Security issues in cloud environments: A survey. *International Journal of Information Security*, *13*(2), 113–170. doi:10.100710207-013-0208-7

Fosso Wamba, S., Kala Kamdjoug, J. R., Epie Bawack, R., & Keogh, J. G. (2020). Bitcoin, Blockchain and Fintech: A systematic review and case studies in the supply chain. *Production Planning and Control*, *31*(2-3), 115–142. doi:10.1080/09537287.2019.1631460

Gazzan, M., & Sheldon, F. T. (2023). Opportunities for Early Detection and Prediction of Ransomware Attacks against Industrial Control Systems. *Future Internet*, *15*(4), 144. doi:10.3390/fi15040144

Herrera-Cubides, J. F., Gaona-García, P. A., & Salcedo-Salgado, G. A. (2019). Towards the construction of a user unique authentication mechanism on LMS platforms through model-driven engineering (MDE). *Scientific Programming*, *2019*, 2019. doi:10.1155/2019/9313571

Kafi, M. A., & Akter, N. (2023). Securing Financial Information in the Digital Realm: Case Studies in Cybersecurity for Accounting Data Protection. *American Journal of Trade and Policy*, *10*(1), 15–26. doi:10.18034/ajtp.v10i1.659

Kumar, S., & Singh, S. K. (2017). Privacy Preserving Security using Biometrics in Cloud Computing. *Multimedia Tools and Applications*. Springer. doi:10.1007/s11042-017-4966-5

Kumari, P., & Jain, A. K. (2023). A comprehensive study of DDoS attacks over IoT network and their countermeasures. *Computers & Security*, *127*, 103096. doi:10.1016/j.cose.2023.103096

Leng, J., Ruan, G., Jiang, P., Xu, K., Liu, Q., Zhou, X., & Liu, C. (2020). Blockchain-empowered sustainable manufacturing and product lifecycle management in industry 4.0: A survey. *Renewable & Sustainable Energy Reviews*, *132*, 110112. doi:10.1016/j.rser.2020.110112

Li, J., Han, D., Wu, Z., Wang, J., Li, K. C., & Castiglione, A. (2023). A novel system for medical equipment supply chain traceability based on alliance chain and attribute and role access control. *Future Generation Computer Systems*, *142*, 195–211. doi:10.1016/j.future.2022.12.037

Mern, J., Hatch, K., Silva, R., Brush, J., & Kochenderfer, M. J. (2021). *Reinforcement learning for industrial control network cyber security orchestration.* arXiv preprint arXiv:2106.05332.

Mir, U., Kar, A. K., & Gupta, M. P. (2022). AI-enabled digital identity–inputs for stakeholders and policymakers. *Journal of Science and Technology Policy Management*, *13*(3), 514–541. doi:10.1108/JSTPM-09-2020-0134

Novaes, M. P., Carvalho, L. F., Lloret, J., & Proença, M. L. Jr. (2021). Adversarial Deep Learning approach detection and defense against DDoS attacks in SDN environments. *Future Generation Computer Systems*, *125*, 156–167. doi:10.1016/j.future.2021.06.047

Ogbuke, N. J., Yusuf, Y. Y., Dharma, K., & Mercangoz, B. A. (2022). Big data supply chain analytics: Ethical, privacy and security challenges posed to business, industries and society. *Production Planning and Control*, *33*(2-3), 123–137. doi:10.1080/09537287.2020.1810764

Omotunde, H., & Ahmed, M. (2023). A Comprehensive Review of Security Measures in Database Systems: Assessing Authentication, Access Control, and Beyond. *Mesopotamian Journal of CyberSecurity*, *2023*, 115–133. doi:10.58496/MJCSC/2023/016

Ragothaman, K., Wang, Y., Rimal, B., & Lawrence, M. (2023). Access control for IoT: A survey of existing research, dynamic policies and future directions. *Sensors (Basel)*, *23*(4), 1805. doi:10.339023041805 PMID:36850403

Rahman, S., Ahsan, K., Yang, L., & Odgers, J. (2019). An investigation into critical challenges for multinational third-party logistics providers operating in China. *Journal of Business Research*, *103*, 607–619. doi:10.1016/j.jbusres.2017.09.053

Raja Santhi, A., & Muthuswamy, P. (2022). Influence of blockchain technology in manufacturing supply chain and logistics. *Logistics*, *6*(1), 15. doi:10.3390/logistics6010015

Ramgovind, S., Eloff, M. M., & Smith, E. (2010, August). The management of security in cloud computing. In *2010 Information Security for South Africa* (pp. 1-7). IEEE.

Sah, B., Gupta, R., & Bani-Hani, D. (2021). Analysis of barriers to implement drone logistics. *International Journal of Logistics*, *24*(6), 531–550. doi:10.1080/13675567.2020.1782862

Shahid, J., Ahmad, R., Kiani, A. K., Ahmad, T., Saeed, S., & Almuhaideb, A. M. (2022). Data protection and privacy of the internet of healthcare things (IoHTs). *Applied Sciences (Basel, Switzerland)*, *12*(4), 1927. doi:10.3390/app12041927

Stoyanova, M., Nikoloudakis, Y., Panagiotakis, S., Pallis, E., & Markakis, E. K. (2020). A survey on the internet of things (IoT) forensics: Challenges, approaches, and open issues. *IEEE Communications Surveys and Tutorials*, *22*(2), 1191–1221. doi:10.1109/COMST.2019.2962586

Susmitha, C., Srineeharika, S., Laasya, K. S., Kannaiah, S. K., & Bulla, S. (2023, February). Hybrid Cryptography for Secure File Storage. In *2023 7th International Conference on Computing Methodologies and Communication* (ICCMC) (pp. 1151-1156). IEEE. 10.1109/ICCMC56507.2023.10084073

Tien, N. H., Diem, P. T., Van On, P., Anh, V. T., Van Dat, N., Hung, N. T., & Tam, B. Q. (2021). The formation and development of CRM system at Thien Hoa electronics supermarket in Vietnam. *International Journal of Research and Growth Evaluation*, 2(4), 752–760.

Tiwari, S. (2011). Aruni Singh, Ravi Shankar Singh and Sanjay Kumar Singh, "Internet Security using Biometrics". In D. P. Vidyarthi (Ed.), *Technologies and protocols for Future Internet Design: Reinventing in Web (IGI Global Publishing)*. doi:10.4018/978-1-4666-0203-8.ch006

Williams, B. D., Roh, J., Tokar, T., & Swink, M. (2013). Leveraging supply chain visibility for responsiveness: The moderating role of internal integration. *Journal of Operations Management*, *31*(7-8), 543–554. doi:10.1016/j.jom.2013.09.003

KEY TERMS AND DEFINITIONS

Access Management: Access management, often referred to as identity and access management (IAM), is the practice of controlling and managing user access to computer systems, networks, and data. In the context of cloud computing, access management involves defining and enforcing access policies, permissions, and roles to ensure that users have appropriate levels of access to cloud resources based on their roles and responsibilities.

Cloud Computing: Cloud computing is a technology paradigm that involves delivering various computing services, including servers, storage, databases, networking, software, and analytics, over the internet to offer faster innovation, flexible resources, and economies of scale. Users can access and utilize these services on a pay-as-you-go basis, typically through web browsers or specialized applications, without the need to invest in and manage their own physical infrastructure.

Cloud Logistics: Cloud logistics refers to the efficient and effective management and coordination of various logistical and supply chain activities using cloud computing technologies. This may include the use of cloud-based software, data analytics, and storage solutions to streamline processes such as inventory management, order fulfillment, transportation, and distribution in supply chain operations.

Cloud Security: Cloud security refers to the set of practices, technologies, policies, and controls designed to protect data, applications, and infrastructure hosted in cloud environments. It encompasses measures to safeguard against unauthorized access, data breaches, service disruptions, and other potential threats to the confidentiality, integrity, and availability of cloud resources.

Data Encryption: Data encryption is a security technique that involves converting plain, readable data (plaintext) into an unreadable format (ciphertext) using encryption algorithms and encryption keys. It is used to protect sensitive information from unauthorized access or data breaches, both in transit (while being transmitted over networks) and at rest (when stored on storage devices or servers). Encryption ensures that even if unauthorized parties gain access to the data, they cannot understand or use it without the decryption key.

Denial-Of-Service (DOS): Denial-of-Service is a type of cyberattack where an attacker attempts to make a computer system or network unavailable to its intended users by overwhelming it with a flood of excessive traffic, requests, or malicious actions. The goal is to disrupt the normal functioning of the targeted system or network, rendering it inaccessible or severely degraded in performance.

Encryption Mechanisms: Encryption mechanisms are techniques used to secure data by transforming it into an unreadable format (ciphertext) using encryption algorithms and keys. Only authorized parties with the decryption keys can reverse the process and access the original data (plaintext). In cloud computing, encryption is used to protect data both in transit (while being transmitted between the user and the cloud) and at rest (when stored on cloud servers) to prevent unauthorized access and data exposure.

Robust Identity: Robust identity typically refers to a strong and secure way of verifying the identity of users or entities accessing a system or network. It involves authentication methods that are difficult to forge or compromise, such as multi-factor authentication (MFA) and biometric authentication, to ensure that only authorized individuals or processes gain access to resources.

Threats: In the context of cloud computing, threats refer to potential risks or vulnerabilities that can compromise the security and functionality of cloud-based systems. These threats can include malware attacks, data breaches, denial-of-service (DoS) attacks, insider threats, and various other malicious activities that may target cloud infrastructure, applications, or data.

Chapter 7
Cyber Security in Internet of Things-Based Edge Computing:
A Comprehensive Survey

Shabnam Kumari
SRM Institute of Science and Technology, Chennai, India

Aderonke Thompson
Federal University of Technology, Akure, Nigeria

Shrikant Tiwari
https://orcid.org/0000-0001-6947-2362
Galgotias University, Greater Noida, India

ABSTRACT

With the rapid growth of the internet of things (IoT) and the emergence of edge computing, new opportunities and challenges have arisen in the realm of cyber security. This work presents a comprehensive review of cyber security in IoT-based edge computing, aiming to shed light on the potential risks and vulnerabilities associated with this evolving paradigm. This work begins by highlighting the increasing integration of IoT devices and edge computing, emphasizing their combined potential to revolutionize various industries. However, this integration also introduces new attack surfaces and vulnerabilities, making robust cyber security measures imperative to safeguard critical systems and sensitive data. The work discusses an in-depth analysis of the unique security challenges that arise at the intersection of IoT and edge computing. It explores the vulnerabilities introduced by the distributed nature of edge computing, the resource-constrained nature of IoT devices, and the heterogeneity of the IoT ecosystem.

DOI: 10.4018/979-8-3693-2081-5.ch007

1. INTRODUCTION

The Internet of Things (IoT) has witnessed exponential growth in recent years, connecting billions of smart devices to the internet and enabling seamless data exchange and automation across various industries. Alongside this rapid expansion, edge computing has emerged as a transformative paradigm that complements the IoT by bringing computational capabilities closer to the data source, reducing latency and enhancing real-time processing efficiency (Mukherjee et al., 2019). The fusion of IoT and edge computing offers numerous benefits, such as improved response times, reduced data transmission costs, and enhanced scalability. However, the convergence of IoT and edge computing also introduces significant cyber security challenges (Liang et al., 2018). As the deployment of interconnected IoT devices proliferates, the attack surface for malicious actors widens, making these systems vulnerable to various cyber threats. Moreover, the decentralized and resource-constrained nature of edge computing introduces additional complexities for ensuring robust security measures. This work discusses into the realm of cyber security in IoT-based edge computing, aiming to shed light on the evolving threats and vulnerabilities associated with this amalgamation. By exploring the unique characteristics and functionalities of both IoT and edge computing, we aim to provide a comprehensive understanding of the security challenges that arise at their intersection.

1.1 Overview of IoT-Based Edge Computing

IoT-based edge computing refers to the integration of IoT devices and edge computing technologies to process and analyze data closer to the source, at the edge of the network. It combines the capabilities of IoT devices, such as sensors and actuators, with the computational power and storage capabilities of edge computing nodes or devices. Traditionally, IoT devices collect data and send it to centralized cloud servers for processing and analysis. However, this approach has limitations in terms of latency, bandwidth, and scalability, especially when dealing with large volumes of real-time data. Edge computing addresses these challenges by bringing computational resources closer to the devices generating the data, enabling faster response times, reduced network congestion, and improved privacy and security. In IoT-based edge computing, edge devices or gateways are deployed at the edge of the network, often in close proximity to IoT devices. These devices act as intermediaries between the IoT devices and the cloud (Dastjerdi et al., 2016; Fernández-Caramés & Fraga-Lamas, 2018; Suo et al., 2012), performing data preprocessing, filtering, and analysis tasks locally. This allows for real-time decision-making and immediate response to critical events without relying on a round-trip to the cloud.

1.2 Key Characteristics of IoT-Based Edge Computing

Few key characteristics of IoT-based edge computing are;

- Proximity: Edge devices are located close to IoT devices, reducing network latency and improving response times.
- Data processing and analytics: Edge devices perform data preprocessing, filtering, and analytics at the edge, enabling real-time information and immediate actions.
- Bandwidth optimization: By processing data locally, only relevant or summarized information is sent to the cloud, reducing bandwidth usage.

- Offline operation: Edge devices can continue to operate even when disconnected from the cloud, ensuring system functionality and data availability.
- Security and privacy: Edge computing can enhance security and privacy by keeping sensitive data local and reducing the exposure of data during transmission.
- Scalability: Edge computing allows for distributed processing and scalable deployments, accommodating the increasing number of IoT devices and their data (Alaba et al., 2017; Ray, 2018).

In summary, applications of IoT-based edge computing span various domains, including smart cities, industrial automation, healthcare, transportation, and agriculture. For instance, in a smart city context, edge devices can process sensor data from traffic cameras or environmental sensors in real-time to optimize traffic flow or detect environmental anomalies. In summary, IoT-based edge computing enables efficient data processing, real-time analytics, reduced latency, and improved scalability by bringing computational capabilities closer to IoT devices. It plays an important role in enabling the full potential of IoTs and supporting a wide range of applications that require low latency, real-time decision-making, and enhanced security and privacy.

1.3 IoT and its Role in Edge Computing

IoT plays an important role in enabling and driving the adoption of edge computing (George & Tyagi, 2022; Rong et al., 2014). Here are the key aspects of IoT's role in edge computing:

- Data Generation: IoT devices, such as sensors, actuators, wearables, and connected devices, generate large amount of data. These devices collect data from the physical world, including environmental conditions, machine status, user interactions, and more. The data generated by IoT devices serves as input for edge computing processes.
- Data Processing at the Edge: IoT devices often have limited computational capabilities and may struggle to handle the processing demands of complex analytics and real-time decision-making. Edge computing brings computational resources closer to IoT devices, allowing for data processing and analysis to occur at the edge. This reduces latency and enables faster response times, making real-time applications and services possible.
- Localized Decision-Making: Edge computing enables localized decision-making by moving data processing and analysis closer to IoT devices. This means that critical decisions can be made at the edge without relying solely on centralized cloud infrastructure. Localized decision-making is particularly important for applications that require immediate responses, such as autonomous vehicles, industrial automation, and real-time monitoring systems.
- Reduced Data Transfer and Bandwidth Requirements: With IoT-based edge computing, only relevant and summarized data needs to be transferred to the cloud or data centers. Edge devices can filter, aggregate, and preprocess data locally, reducing the amount of data that needs to be transmitted. This optimization of data transfer and bandwidth requirements minimizes network congestion, improves efficiency, and reduces costs associated with data transmission.
- Data Security and Privacy: IoT devices often collect sensitive data, such as personal information, location data, and health-related data. By processing data at the edge, IoT-based edge computing helps address data security and privacy issue. It reduces the exposure of sensitive data during

transmission over public networks and allows for localized data storage and processing, providing greater control over data security and privacy.

- Scalability and Flexibility: IoT devices are deployed in large numbers across various locations and environments. Edge computing enables the scalability and flexibility needed to handle the growing number of IoT devices. It allows for the distributed deployment of edge devices, accommodating the increasing computational requirements of IoT applications and adapting to dynamic network conditions.
- Cloud Collaboration: While edge computing brings computational resources closer to the IoT devices, it also collaborates with the cloud. Edge devices can communicate with the cloud for data storage, complex analytics, and long-term processing. The cloud can provide additional resources, historical data analysis, machine learning models, and centralized management capabilities, enhancing the capabilities of edge computing.

Note that the combination of IoT and edge computing offers a powerful architecture for addressing the challenges of latency, bandwidth, real-time processing, and security in IoT applications. It enables faster response times, localized decision-making, optimized data transfer, and improved scalability, making it well-suited for a wide range of industries and use cases, from smart cities and industrial automation to healthcare, transportation, and more.

1.4 Applications of IoT-Based Edge Computing

We will discuss few applications here as:

- Smart Cities: Edge computing facilitates smart city applications by processing data from various IoT devices, such as traffic cameras, environmental sensors, and smart streetlights, to optimize traffic management, improve energy efficiency, and enhance public safety.
- Industrial IoT (IIoT): In industrial settings, edge computing enables real-time monitoring and control of machines and processes, enhancing productivity, reducing downtime, and improving overall operational efficiency.
- Healthcare: Edge computing supports healthcare applications, including remote patient monitoring, wearable health devices, and real-time data analysis, enabling timely medical interventions and personalized healthcare services.
- Autonomous Vehicles: Edge computing is importnat autonomous vehicles, where split-second decisions are required for safe navigation and collision avoidance. Processing sensor data at the edge allows vehicles to respond quickly to changing road conditions.
- Agriculture: In precision agriculture, edge computing helps analyze data from sensors and drones to optimize irrigation, monitor soil conditions, and enhance crop yields.
- Retail and Customer Experience: In retail environments, edge computing can be used for real-time inventory management, personalized shopping experiences, and analyzing customer behavior for targeted marketing strategies.
- Energy Management: Edge computing enables smart energy management systems, allowing real-time monitoring and control of energy consumption and generation in smart grids and buildings.

- Environmental Monitoring: Edge computing aids in monitoring and analyzing environmental data, such as air quality and water pollution, to support environmental protection and conservation efforts.

In summary, IoT-based edge computing offers numerous benefits, including reduced latency, improved reliability, bandwidth optimization, enhanced security, and real-time analytics. It finds applications in diverse domains, ranging from smart cities and industrial automation to healthcare, autonomous vehicles, and environmental monitoring, revolutionizing various industries with its efficiency and real-time capabilities.

1.5 Organization of the Work

This work is summarized into ten sections.

2. EXISTING RESEARCH AND TECHNOLOGIES

2.1Security Challenges in IoT-Based Edge Computing

IoT-based edge computing introduces specific security challenges due to the distributed nature of the system and the convergence of IoT devices with edge computing technologies (Nair, Kumari, & Tyagi, 2021; Abraham et al., 2022). Here are some key security challenges in IoT-based edge computing:

- Device Vulnerabilities: IoT devices often have limited computational resources and may lack robust security features. They can be prone to vulnerabilities, such as weak authentication mechanisms, default credentials, or outdated firmware. These vulnerabilities can be exploited by attackers to gain unauthorized access, compromise the device, or launch attacks on other components of the system.
- Network Security: Edge computing involves the deployment of edge devices and gateways, creating additional entry points into the network. These devices and the communication channels between them are potential targets for attacks, such as man-in-the-middle attacks, eavesdropping, or unauthorized access. Securing the network infrastructure and implementing strong encryption and authentication mechanisms are important to protect against such threats.
- Data Privacy and Confidentiality: IoT devices generate and process large amount of data, often including sensitive or personal information. In edge computing, data is processed closer to its source, increasing the risk of unauthorized access or data leakage. Ensuring data privacy and confidentiality through encryption, access controls, and secure data handling practices is important to protect sensitive information.
- Edge Device Management: Managing a large number of edge devices distributed across different locations introduces challenges in terms of device management and security updates. Ensuring timely deployment of security patches, firmware updates, and configuration changes to all edge devices can be complex. Failure to manage and update devices properly can leave them vulnerable to known security flaws or exploits.

- Trustworthiness and Supply Chain Security: The IoT ecosystem involves various components from multiple vendors, including IoT devices, edge devices, and communication protocols. Ensuring the integrity and trustworthiness of each component, including the software and firmware, is critical. Compromised components or tampered software/firmware can undermine the overall security of the IoT-based edge computing system.
- Scalability and Resource Constraints: IoT-based edge computing systems often need to handle a large number of devices and process massive volumes of data. However, edge devices typically have limited resources, including computational power, memory, and energy. Implementing effective security measures within these resource constraints can be challenging while maintaining system performance and responsiveness.
- Insider Threats: Insider threats can be significant in IoT-based edge computing, where various stakeholders, including administrators, operators, or third-party vendors, have access to the system. Malicious insiders can exploit their privileges to gain unauthorized access, compromise devices, or manipulate data. Implementing access controls, monitoring mechanisms, and strong authentication protocols help mitigate insider threats.
- Interoperability and Standardization: The IoT ecosystem comprises diverse devices, platforms, and protocols, which can lead to interoperability challenges. Inconsistent or incompatible security mechanisms across different components can create vulnerabilities and weaken the overall security posture. Standardization efforts are important to promote secure and interoperable IoT-based edge computing solutions.

Hence, these security challenges requires a comprehensive approach that includes secure device design, secure network architecture, encryption and authentication mechanisms, security updates and patch management, privacy-enhancing technologies, and robust access controls. Collaboration between stakeholders, including device manufacturers, network operators, and cybersecurity experts, is essential to ensure the security and resilience of IoT based edge computing systems.

2.2 Cyber Security Solutions and Approaches

Cybersecurity solutions and approaches encompass a wide range of techniques, practices, and technologies aimed at protecting systems, networks, and data from cyber threats (Nair, Kumari, & Tyagi, 2021; Tyagi & Sreenath, 2023). Here are some common cybersecurity solutions and approaches:

- Risk Assessment and Management: Conducting regular risk assessments helps identify potential vulnerabilities and assess the impact of cyber threats. Risk management strategies involve prioritizing risks, implementing preventive measures, and developing incident response plans.
- Secure Network Architecture: Implementing secure network architectures involves designing and configuring networks with security in mind. This includes segmenting networks, using firewalls, implementing intrusion detection and prevention systems (IDPS), and employing virtual private networks (VPNs) for secure remote access.
- Access Controls and Authentication: Strong access controls ensure that only authorized individuals have access to systems and data. This includes implementing multi-factor authentication (MFA), strong password policies, and role-based access controls (RBAC) to restrict privileges based on user roles.

- Encryption: Encryption is the process of encoding data to protect it from unauthorized access. Employing strong encryption techniques, such as symmetric or asymmetric encryption, helps safeguard sensitive data, both at rest and in transit.
- Security Awareness and Training: Educating employees and users about cybersecurity best practices is essential. Regular security awareness training programs raise awareness of common threats, phishing attacks, social engineering techniques, and the importance of secure behavior.
- Vulnerability Management: Implementing vulnerability management practices involves regularly scanning systems and applications for vulnerabilities, prioritizing patches and updates, and promptly addressing identified vulnerabilities to minimize the attack surface.
- Incident Detection and Response: Employing security monitoring systems, such as Security Information and Event Management (SIEM) tools, enables timely detection and response to security incidents. Incident response plans should outline steps to be taken in the event of a cyberattack, including containment, eradication, and recovery.
- Endpoint Protection: Endpoint protection solutions, such as antivirus software, intrusion prevention systems, and host-based firewalls, are important for securing individual devices, including desktops, laptops, and mobile devices.
- Secure Software Development Practices: Integrating secure coding practices, such as input validation, proper error handling, and code review processes, helps prevent common software vulnerabilities. Following secure development frameworks, such as OWASP, can guide developers in creating more secure software.
- Continuous Monitoring and Threat Intelligence: Implementing continuous monitoring solutions provides real-time visibility into network activities, enabling the detection of anomalies or suspicious behavior. Threat intelligence tools and services provide information on emerging threats and help organizations stay updated on the evolving threat landscape.
- Security Audits and Penetration Testing: Regular security audits assess the effectiveness of implemented security measures, identify weaknesses, and ensure compliance with security standards and regulations. Penetration testing involves simulating cyberattacks to identify vulnerabilities and test the effectiveness of security controls.
- Security Incident Sharing and Collaboration: Participating in information sharing and collaboration initiatives within the cybersecurity community helps organizations gain insights into emerging threats, attack trends, and effective defense strategies. Sharing incident data can contribute to collective knowledge and proactive defense.

Hence, these solutions and approaches should be implemented in a layered and holistic manner to provide comprehensive cybersecurity protection. Note that to regularly update and adapt these measures as the threat landscape evolves and new vulnerabilities emerge.

3. ARCHITECTURE AND COMPONENTS OF IOT-BASED EDGE SYSTEMS

IoT-based edge systems typically consist of multiple components and follow a specific architecture to enable efficient data processing and analysis at the edge (Nair & Tyagi, 2021; Tyagi, 2022). The architecture and components of such systems can vary depending on the specific application requirements and use cases, but here are the common elements:

- IoT Devices: These devices are the physical objects or sensors that generate data. They can include a wide range of devices such as sensors, actuators, cameras, wearables, industrial machines, and connected appliances. IoT devices collect and transmit data to the edge system for processing and analysis.
- Edge Nodes/Gateways: Edge nodes or gateways act as intermediaries between the IoT devices and the cloud or central data center. These nodes are responsible for collecting, aggregating, and preprocessing data from the IoT devices. They often have local computational capabilities and storage to perform edge computing tasks.
- Edge Computing Infrastructure: The edge computing infrastructure includes the hardware and software components required to enable data processing and analysis at the edge. This infrastructure can include edge servers, edge routers, edge switches, and other networking equipment. It may also include edge-specific software frameworks or platforms that facilitate the execution of edge applications and services.
- Edge Analytics and Processing: Edge systems employ analytics and processing capabilities to extract valuable information and perform computations at the edge. This can involve running lightweight analytics algorithms, applying machine learning models, performing real-time data filtering, and applying business rules. Edge analytics and processing enable faster response times, real-time decision-making, and reduced data transmission to the cloud.
- Connectivity: Connectivity plays an important role in IoT-based edge systems. The edge nodes and devices need to be connected to each other and to the cloud or central infrastructure. This connectivity can be wired (Ethernet, fiber optic) or wireless (Wi-Fi, cellular, LoRa, Zigbee) depending on the deployment scenario and network requirements.
- Security Mechanisms: Given the distributed nature of IoT-based edge systems, security mechanisms are essential to protect data, devices, and communications. These mechanisms can include secure communication protocols, authentication and access control measures, encryption techniques, and intrusion detection systems. Security ensures the confidentiality, integrity, and availability of data and prevents unauthorized access or malicious attacks.
- Cloud Integration: While edge systems process data locally, they often need to collaborate with the cloud for certain tasks. Cloud integration allows for long-term storage, centralized management, complex analytics, and the utilization of additional computational resources. The edge system can communicate with the cloud for data synchronization, model updates, and advanced analytics when necessary.
- Management and Orchestration: Effective management and orchestration are important IoT-based edge systems. This includes tasks such as device provisioning, software updates, configuration management, monitoring, and fault detection. Management systems provide visibility and control over the edge infrastructure, ensuring its smooth operation and optimizing performance.

Hence, the architecture and components of IoT-based edge systems are designed to enable efficient data processing, real-time analytics, reduced latency, and enhanced scalability (). By using edge computing capabilities, these systems enable faster decision-making, reduced data transmission, improved reliability, and localized processing for a variety of IoT applications across industries.

4. CYBER SECURITY THREATS IN IOT-BASED EDGE COMPUTING

4.1 Overview of Cyber Security Threat Landscape

The cyber security threat landscape refers to the evolving and diverse range of threats and risks that organizations and individuals face in the digital realm. It encompasses various types of malicious activities and vulnerabilities that can compromise the confidentiality, integrity, and availability of data and systems. Here's an overview of the cyber security threat landscape:

- Malware: Malicious software, or malware, is a significant threat. It includes viruses, worms, Trojans, ransomware, and other types of malicious code designed to exploit vulnerabilities, steal data, or disrupt operations.
- Phishing and Social Engineering: Phishing attacks involve deceptive emails, messages, or websites that trick users into revealing sensitive information, such as passwords or financial details. Social engineering techniques exploit human psychology to manipulate individuals into performing actions that can lead to security breaches.
- Distributed Denial of Service (DDoS) Attacks: DDoS attacks aim to overwhelm a target system or network with a flood of traffic, rendering it inaccessible to legitimate users. These attacks are often orchestrated using botnets, which are networks of compromised devices.
- Data Breaches: Data breaches involve unauthorized access to sensitive or confidential information, leading to potential misuse or exposure. Attackers may exploit vulnerabilities in systems, steal login credentials, or target poorly secured databases.
- Insider Threats: Insider threats involve individuals within an organization who misuse their access privileges for malicious purposes. These can include disgruntled employees, contractors, or partners who intentionally or unintentionally compromise systems, steal data, or disrupt operations.
- Advanced Persistent Threats (APTs): APTs are sophisticated and targeted attacks typically carried out by well-funded and skilled threat actors. These attacks involve a prolonged and stealthy presence within a network, aiming to exfiltrate sensitive data or gain persistent control.
- Zero-Day Vulnerabilities: Zero-day vulnerabilities are previously unknown software vulnerabilities that can be exploited by attackers before a patch or fix is available. These vulnerabilities pose a significant risk as organizations may be unaware of the existence of such vulnerabilities until they are exploited.
- IoT and Industrial Control System (ICS) Attacks: As more devices and systems become connected, the threat landscape expands to include attacks on IoT devices and industrial control systems. These attacks can disrupt critical infrastructure, compromise smart homes, or impact industrial processes.
- Supply Chain Attacks: Supply chain attacks involve targeting the software or hardware supply chain to inject malicious code or compromise components. Attackers gain unauthorized access to systems by targeting trusted vendors or compromising the integrity of software updates.
- Ransomware: Ransomware attacks encrypt a victim's data, making it inaccessible until a ransom is paid. These attacks can cause significant financial and operational damage, affecting businesses, healthcare organizations, and individuals.

- Cloud Security Risks: As more organizations adopt cloud services, the security risks associated with cloud infrastructure, misconfigurations, and unauthorized access become prevalent. Attackers may target cloud environments to gain unauthorized access, steal data, or disrupt services.
- Mobile Device Threats: Mobile devices are susceptible to malware, data theft, and network attacks. Attackers may exploit vulnerabilities in mobile operating systems, intercept communications, or distribute malicious apps through app stores.

Note that the cyber security threat landscape is continuously evolving, driven by the emergence of new technologies, evolving attack techniques, and the motivations of threat actors. Staying informed about the latest threats, implementing robust security measures, and adopting proactive security practices are essential for organizations and individuals to protect against these threats.

4.2 Threats to Edge Devices and Sensors

Edge devices and sensors face several threats in the context of IoT-based edge computing (Abraham et al., 2021). These threats can compromise the security, integrity, and availability of the devices and the data they collect. Here are some common threats to edge devices and sensors:

- Physical Tampering: Edge devices, such as sensors or gateways, can be physically tampered with or stolen. Attackers may try to gain unauthorized access, modify or disable the devices, or extract sensitive information from them.
- Unauthorized Access: Attackers may attempt to gain unauthorized access to edge devices or sensors to exploit vulnerabilities, extract data, or take control of the device. This can be achieved through techniques like password cracking, brute-forcing, or exploiting weak authentication mechanisms.
- Firmware/Software Vulnerabilities: Edge devices often run firmware or software that can have vulnerabilities. Attackers may exploit these vulnerabilities to gain control over the devices, execute malicious code, or manipulate data.
- Network Attacks: Edge devices and sensors are typically connected to networks, making them vulnerable to network-based attacks. These attacks can include denial-of-service (DoS) attacks, man-in-the-middle attacks, sniffing, or interception of data transmitted between devices.
- Data Manipulation: Attackers may tamper with the data collected by edge devices or sensors, leading to inaccurate or misleading information. Manipulated data can result in incorrect decisions or actions based on the compromised information.
- Insider Threats: Insiders, such as authorized users or employees with access to edge devices, can pose a threat. They may intentionally or unintentionally misuse their privileges, compromise device security, or leak sensitive information.
- Lack of Security Updates: Edge devices and sensors may run outdated firmware or software without proper security updates. This makes them susceptible to known vulnerabilities that attackers can exploit.
- Denial-of-Service (DoS) Attacks: Attackers may launch DoS attacks against edge devices or sensors to overwhelm their resources or network connections, rendering them inaccessible or causing disruption to their normal functioning.

- Lack of Physical Security Controls: Edge devices deployed in public or unsecured locations may lack physical security controls, making them vulnerable to physical attacks or unauthorized access.
- Supply Chain Attacks: Attackers can compromise the supply chain of edge devices, introducing malicious components or modifying the devices during manufacturing or distribution. This can lead to compromised devices being deployed within an infrastructure.

Hence to mitigate these threats, we need to implement robust security measures for edge devices and sensors. This includes secure authentication and access controls, regular security updates and patches, encryption of data at rest and in transit, intrusion detection systems, and physical security measures. Additionally, organizations should follow security best practices, perform vulnerability assessments and penetration testing, and educate users about the importance of device security and safe practices.

4.3 Threats to Edge Networks and Communications

Edge networks and communications in IoT-based edge computing face various threats that can compromise the security, privacy, and integrity of the network infrastructure and the data transmitted within it. Here are some common threats to edge networks and communications:

- Man-in-the-Middle (MitM) Attacks: Attackers may intercept and eavesdrop on communications between edge devices, gateways, and other network components. This allows them to capture sensitive information, modify data, or inject malicious code into the communication stream.
- Network Spoofing: Attackers may impersonate legitimate edge devices or gateways by spoofing their network addresses or identities. This can lead to unauthorized access, data interception, or disruption of communications.
- Network Denial-of-Service (DoS) Attacks: Attackers may target edge networks with DoS attacks to overwhelm network resources, causing disruption in communication and rendering the network or specific devices inaccessible to legitimate users.
- Network Intrusions: Edge networks can be susceptible to intrusions and unauthorized access attempts. Attackers may exploit vulnerabilities in network protocols, misconfigurations, or weak authentication mechanisms to gain unauthorized access to the network infrastructure.
- Network Traffic Analysis: Attackers may analyze the network traffic within edge networks to gather sensitive information, infer behavioral patterns, or identify vulnerabilities. This can lead to the compromise of data privacy and potential security breaches.
- Data Interception and Tampering: Attackers may intercept or modify the data transmitted within edge networks, compromising the integrity and confidentiality of the information. This can lead to unauthorized access, data manipulation, or leakage of sensitive information.
- Lack of Network Segmentation: Inadequate network segmentation within edge networks can increase the potential impact of a security breach. If one device or segment is compromised, it can spread to other parts of the network, affecting multiple devices and services.
- Insecure Protocols and Encryption: The use of insecure communication protocols or weak encryption mechanisms within edge networks can expose the transmitted data to interception or unauthorized access. Attackers can exploit these vulnerabilities to gain access to sensitive information.

- Insider Threats: Insiders with authorized access to edge networks can pose a threat to network security. These individuals may misuse their privileges, bypass security controls, or leak sensitive information.
- Lack of Security Monitoring and Incident Response: Insufficient security monitoring and incident response mechanisms within edge networks can delay the detection and response to security incidents. This can result in prolonged exposure to threats and potential damage.

Hence to mitigate these threats, we need to implement strong security measures for edge networks and communications. This includes using secure communication protocols, implementing encryption mechanisms, segmenting networks, regularly updating and patching network devices, deploying intrusion detection and prevention systems, and conducting security audits and vulnerability assessments. Additionally, organizations should educate users about secure network practices, enforce strong access controls, and have an effective incident response plan in place to address security incidents promptly.

4.4 Threats to Edge Applications and Services

Edge applications and services in IoT-based edge computing face various threats that can compromise their functionality, integrity, and availability (Goyal & Tyagi, 2020; Tyagi, 2016; Tyagi & Bansal, 2023). Here are some common threats to edge applications and services:

- Malicious Code Injection: Attackers may attempt to inject malicious code into edge applications or services. This can lead to unauthorized access, data leakage, or disruption of service functionality. Malicious code injection can occur through vulnerabilities in the application code or compromised deployment environments.
- Application Vulnerabilities: Edge applications may have vulnerabilities that can be exploited by attackers. These vulnerabilities can include buffer overflows, input validation issues, insecure coding practices, or lack of proper security configurations. Exploiting application vulnerabilities can lead to unauthorized access, data manipulation, or service disruption.
- Unauthorized Access: Attackers may attempt to gain unauthorized access to edge applications or services. This can be achieved by exploiting weak authentication mechanisms, misconfigured access controls, or vulnerabilities in the application infrastructure. Unauthorized access can result in data breaches, service disruption, or unauthorized actions within the application.
- Denial-of-Service (DoS) Attacks: Edge applications and services can be targeted with DoS attacks to overwhelm their resources or network connections. This can lead to service unavailability or degradation, impacting the functionality and performance of the application.
- API Security Issues: Edge applications often rely on APIs (Application Programming Interfaces) for data exchange and integration with other systems. Insecure API implementations or vulnerabilities in API frameworks can expose the application to attacks such as API abuse, injection attacks, or unauthorized data access.
- Data Leakage: Edge applications may handle sensitive or confidential data, and data leakage can pose a significant threat. Attackers may exploit vulnerabilities in the application or its underlying infrastructure to gain unauthorized access to data or manipulate data transmissions, leading to data breaches or privacy violations.

- Insecure Data Storage: Inadequate security measures for storing data within edge applications can expose the data to unauthorized access or theft. Attackers may exploit vulnerabilities in data storage mechanisms, compromise backup systems, or gain unauthorized access to data repositories.
- Insecure Third-Party Integrations: Edge applications often rely on third-party services or components for extended functionality. Insecure integrations or vulnerabilities in these third-party components can introduce security risks, such as data leakage, unauthorized access, or compromised application functionality.
- Inadequate Error Handling and Logging: Poor error handling and logging mechanisms within edge applications can provide valuable information to attackers. Insufficient logging may hinder incident response and forensic analysis, making it difficult to identify and mitigate security incidents in a timely manner.
- Lack of Application Monitoring and Updates: Inadequate monitoring of edge applications and failure to apply updates and patches can leave them vulnerable to emerging threats. Attackers may exploit known vulnerabilities that have not been addressed, compromising the application's security and functionality.

Hence, to mitigate these threats, we need to implement a robust security strategy for edge applications and services. This includes conducting regular security assessments, implementing secure coding practices, applying access controls and authentication mechanisms, monitoring application logs for suspicious activities, implementing encryption for data in transit and at rest, and keeping software and dependencies up to date with security patches. Additionally, organizations should follow secure development methodologies, perform security testing, and provide security awareness training to developers and users of the edge applications and services.

5. CYBER SECURITY MEASURES AND TECHNIQUES

Cybersecurity measures and techniques refer to the practices and strategies employed to protect computer systems, networks, data, and information from unauthorized access, cyber threats, and malicious activities. Here are some commonly used cybersecurity measures and techniques:

- Access Control: Implement strong access controls to ensure that only authorized individuals or entities can access systems, networks, or data. This includes using secure authentication mechanisms (e.g., multi-factor authentication), role-based access controls, and regular access reviews.
- Firewalls: Deploy firewalls to monitor and filter network traffic. Firewalls act as a barrier between internal networks and external networks, preventing unauthorized access and blocking malicious traffic.
- Intrusion Detection and Prevention Systems (IDPS): Use IDPS to detect and prevent unauthorized access attempts, network intrusions, and suspicious activities. IDPS can identify and respond to potential threats in real-time, providing early warning and protection against cyber-attacks (Pal et al., 2022; Tripathi et al., 2011).
- Encryption: Utilize encryption techniques to protect sensitive data at rest and in transit. Encryption transforms data into unreadable formats, ensuring that even if data is intercepted, it remains inaccessible without the proper decryption keys.

- Vulnerability Assessments and Penetration Testing: Conduct regular vulnerability assessments and penetration testing to identify weaknesses and vulnerabilities in systems, networks, and applications. This helps organizations proactively address security flaws and improve their overall security posture.
- Patch Management: Maintain an effective patch management process to promptly apply security updates and patches to operating systems, software, and firmware. Keeping systems up to date helps address known vulnerabilities and protects against exploits.
- Security Information and Event Management (SIEM): Implement SIEM tools to collect, analyze, and correlate security event logs from various sources. SIEM enables proactive threat detection, incident response, and provides centralized visibility into security events.
- Data Backup and Recovery: Regularly backup critical data and implement robust disaster recovery plans. In the event of a security incident or data loss, reliable backups ensure data can be restored, minimizing the impact of disruptions.
- User Awareness and Training: Promote cybersecurity awareness among users through training programs and education. Users play an important role in maintaining security, and awareness helps them identify phishing attempts, follow best practices, and report suspicious activities.
- Incident Response Planning: Develop and implement an incident response plan to effectively respond to security incidents. This includes defining roles and responsibilities, establishing communication channels, and conducting drills to test and refine the response process.
- Endpoint Security: Employ endpoint security solutions, such as antivirus software, host intrusion prevention systems (HIPS), and endpoint detection and response (EDR) tools, to protect individual devices from malware, unauthorized access, and other threats.
- Secure Software Development Lifecycle (SDLC): Follow secure coding practices and integrate security throughout the software development lifecycle. This includes conducting secure code reviews, using secure coding frameworks, and performing thorough testing for vulnerabilities.
- Security Awareness and Behavior Analytics: Consider behavioral analytics and user activity monitoring to detect anomalous behavior and potential insider threats. Analyzing user behavior helps identify suspicious activities and mitigate risks.
- Security Governance and Risk Management: Establish a comprehensive security governance framework and risk management processes. This includes conducting risk assessments, developing security policies and procedures, and ensuring compliance with relevant regulations and standards.
- Mobile Device Security: Implement security measures for mobile devices, such as mobile device management (MDM), secure containerization, and encryption. Mobile devices pose unique security challenges, and protecting them is essential in today's mobile-centric environments.

Note that these cyber-security measures and techniques are not exhaustive but represent key strategies organizations can employ to enhance their security posture and protect against cyber threats. Note that to regularly review and update security practices to address emerging threats and technologies.

5.1 Security by Design Principles

Security by design principles, also known as secure design principles, are a set of guiding principles that promote the integration of security issues into the design and development process of systems, applications, and technologies. By adopting these principles, organizations can proactively address security requirements and mitigate potential vulnerabilities and threats. Here are some common securities by design principles:

- Least Privilege: Grant users, applications, and components only the minimum privileges necessary to perform their intended functions. Limiting access rights helps reduce the potential impact of a security breach or unauthorized access.
- Defense in Depth: Implement multiple layers of security controls and safeguards to protect against a variety of threats. This principle involves using a combination of technical, physical, and administrative measures to create overlapping layers of security.
- Fail-Safe Defaults: Configure systems and applications with secure defaults to minimize the risk of misconfiguration. This principle ensures that security mechanisms are enabled by default and that users or administrators must actively change settings to weaken security.
- Secure Communication: Apply encryption and secure protocols to protect data during transmission. This includes using strong cryptographic algorithms, ensuring secure network protocols (e.g., HTTPS), and protecting data integrity and confidentiality.
- Secure Data Handling: Implement mechanisms to securely handle and store sensitive data. This includes encryption of data at rest, proper data sanitization techniques, secure storage practices, and access controls to prevent unauthorized access or disclosure.
- Separation of Duties: Divide responsibilities among different roles or individuals to prevent a single point of failure or compromise. This principle ensures that critical operations require multiple parties to cooperate, reducing the risk of insider threats or unauthorized actions.
- Secure Error Handling: Implement appropriate error handling mechanisms to prevent the disclosure of sensitive information or system vulnerabilities. Error messages should be informative without revealing sensitive details that could be exploited by attackers.
- Input Validation: Validate and sanitize all user input to prevent common attacks such as injection, cross-site scripting (XSS), or buffer overflows. Input validation ensures that only expected and properly formatted data is processed by the system.
- Continuous Monitoring and Logging: Implement robust monitoring and logging mechanisms to detect security incidents, track system activity, and support forensic analysis. This enables timely identification and response to security events and aids in the investigation of potential breaches.
- Security Awareness and Training: Foster a culture of security awareness and provide regular training to developers, users, and administrators. Educating stakeholders about security best practices helps them understand their roles and responsibilities in maintaining system security.

In summary, by adhering to these securities by design principles, organizations can build secure and resilient systems that are better prepared to handle evolving threats and protect sensitive data. Note that to integrate these principles into the entire development lifecycle, from requirements gathering and design to implementation, testing, and ongoing maintenance.

5.2 Secure Edge Data Storage and Processing

Secure edge data storage and processing are important of IoT-based edge computing to ensure the confidentiality, integrity, and availability of data (Dutta et al., 2023; Ranchhodbhai & Tripathi, 2019). Here are some key issues for securing edge data storage and processing:

- Data Encryption: Apply encryption techniques to protect data stored on edge devices or in edge storage systems. This includes encrypting data at rest and data in transit between edge devices and storage systems. Strong encryption algorithms and key management practices should be employed to prevent unauthorized access to the data.
- Access Controls: Implement robust access controls to restrict access to edge data storage and processing systems. This involves employing role-based access controls (RBAC), user authentication mechanisms, and fine-grained access permissions. Access should be granted on a need-to-know basis to minimize the risk of unauthorized data access or manipulation.
- Secure Protocols: Use secure communication protocols such as HTTPS or Secure Shell (SSH) for transmitting data to and from edge devices and storage systems. Secure protocols help protect data integrity and prevent eavesdropping or tampering during data transmission.
- Data Integrity Checks: Implement mechanisms to ensure the integrity of data stored in edge storage systems. This can involve the use of checksums or cryptographic hash functions to verify the integrity of stored data and detect any unauthorized modifications.
- Data Lifecycle Management: Establish policies and practices for managing the lifecycle of edge data, including data retention and disposal. This includes defining data retention periods, secure deletion of data, and proper data disposal techniques to prevent data leakage or unauthorized recovery.
- Secure Processing: Implement security measures during data processing at the edge to protect against attacks such as code injection or tampering. This involves applying secure coding practices, input validation, and runtime security mechanisms to prevent the execution of malicious code or unauthorized actions.
- Data Backup and Disaster Recovery: Regularly backup edge data and implement robust disaster recovery strategies. This ensures that in the event of data loss, system failure, or security incidents, data can be restored from backups, minimizing the impact on operations and maintaining data availability.
- Secure Data Sharing: If edge devices or edge systems need to share data with other entities or cloud environments, employ secure data sharing mechanisms. This includes secure APIs, encrypted data transfer, and secure data exchange protocols to maintain data confidentiality and prevent unauthorized access.
- Data Privacy Compliance: Adhere to data privacy regulations and industry standards that apply to the storage and processing of sensitive or personally identifiable information. Implement appropriate data anonymization, pseudonymization, and data protection practices to ensure compliance with privacy requirements.
- Security Monitoring and Auditing: Implement robust security monitoring and auditing mechanisms to detect and respond to security incidents in real-time. This includes logging and monitoring of data access and processing activities, security event correlation, and intrusion detection systems to identify any suspicious or unauthorized activities.

Hence by following these measures, organizations can enhance the security of edge data storage and processing, mitigating the risks associated with unauthorized access, data breaches, and data manipulation. Note that to implement a defense-in-depth approach and regularly assess and update security measures to address emerging threats and vulnerabilities in edge computing environments.

6. CASE STUDIES AND IMPLEMENTATIONS

6.1 Case Study One: Securing Industrial IoT at the Edge

Securing Industrial IoT at the edge is a critical use case as it involves protecting sensitive data, critical infrastructure, and ensuring the reliability and safety of industrial operations (Agarwal & Tripathi, 2022; Midha et al., 2017). Here's an example scenario illustrating the application of security measures in an Industrial IoT edge environment:

Securing Industrial IoT at the Edge: Smart Factory

Overview: A smart factory employs Industrial IoT devices and edge computing to optimize production processes and improve efficiency. The factory integrates various sensors, actuators, and machines to monitor and control operations in real-time. However, ensuring the security and integrity of data and systems is paramount to prevent disruptions, unauthorized access, and potential safety risks.

Security Measures and Implementation:

- Access Control: Implement strong access controls for edge devices, gateways, and network infrastructure. This involves user authentication, role-based access controls, and strict segregation of networks to limit access to authorized personnel and prevent unauthorized device connections.
- Device Authentication: Use secure device authentication mechanisms, such as digital certificates or unique device identifiers, to ensure that only trusted and authenticated devices can connect to the industrial IoT network. This prevents unauthorized devices from compromising the network or injecting malicious data.
- Data Encryption: Apply end-to-end encryption to protect data transmitted between edge devices, gateways, and cloud systems. This ensures data confidentiality and integrity, preventing eavesdropping or tampering during data transmission.
- Network Segmentation: Implement network segmentation to isolate critical systems and devices from less secure networks. This helps contain potential security breaches and limit the impact of unauthorized access or compromised devices.

Intrusion Detection and Prevention Systems (IDPS): Deploy IDPS solutions to monitor network traffic and detect anomalous behavior or potential security breaches. IDPS can identify and respond to threats in real-time, preventing unauthorized access, malware infections, or suspicious activities.

- Secure Firmware Updates: Implement a secure mechanism for updating firmware on edge devices and gateways. This ensures that devices are running the latest patches and security updates, protecting against known vulnerabilities and exploits.
- Security Monitoring and Incident Response: Implement robust security monitoring tools and processes to detect and respond to security incidents. This includes real-time monitoring of system logs, network traffic, and anomalous behavior. A well-defined incident response plan helps in quickly mitigating any security breaches and minimizing the impact on operations.
- Physical Security: Ensure physical security measures are in place to protect edge devices and gateways from physical tampering or unauthorized access. This can include restricted access to equipment, video surveillance, and secure storage of devices to prevent theft or unauthorized modifications.
- Vendor and Supply Chain Management: Implement strict security requirements and assessments for IoT device vendors and suppliers. Regularly assess the security practices of vendors, including their development processes, firmware updates, and response to security vulnerabilities.
- Employee Training and Awareness: Conduct regular security training and awareness programs for employees to educate them about best practices, security policies, and the importance of reporting any suspicious activities. Employees should be aware of social engineering attacks, phishing attempts, and the proper handling of sensitive information.

By implementing these security measures, the industrial IoT ecosystem in the smart factory can be better protected against potential cyber threats, unauthorized access, and disruptions. It ensures the reliability, safety, and integrity of industrial operations while maintaining the confidentiality of sensitive data and protecting critical infrastructure.

6.2 Case Study Two: Secure Healthcare Monitoring in Edge Computing

Secure healthcare monitoring in edge computing is an important application that combines the advantages of edge computing with robust security measures to protect sensitive healthcare data (Hura et al., 2021; Midha & Triptahi, 2019; Sai et al., 2023; Somisetti & Verma, 2020; Subasree & Sakthivel, 2022). By using edge computing, healthcare providers can perform real-time monitoring and analysis while ensuring data confidentiality, integrity, and availability. Here's how secure healthcare monitoring in edge computing can be implemented:

- Edge Data Collection: Healthcare monitoring devices, such as wearables or IoT sensors, collect data from patients at the edge of the network. These devices may measure important signs, activity levels, or other relevant health metrics. Data is processed and analyzed locally, reducing latency and bandwidth requirements.
- Data Encryption: To ensure data confidentiality, all collected health data should be encrypted before transmission to the edge computing infrastructure. This encryption can be achieved using standard encryption algorithms such as AES (Advanced Encryption Standard) or RSA (Rivest-Shamir-Adleman).
- Secure Data Transmission: Encrypted data is transmitted securely from the edge devices to the edge computing infrastructure. This can be achieved through secure communication protocols

such as HTTPS or VPNs (Virtual Private Networks). These protocols help protect against eavesdropping and unauthorized access during data transmission.

- Edge Computing Infrastructure: The edge computing infrastructure consists of edge servers or gateways located closer to the data source. These servers process and analyze the collected data locally, reducing the need for sending large amounts of data to the cloud or a central server. This decreases latency and enhances real-time monitoring capabilities.
- Access Control and Authentication: Strong access control mechanisms should be implemented to ensure that only authorized personnel can access the healthcare data. User authentication techniques like username/password combinations, biometric authentication, or two-factor authentication (2FA) can be employed to validate the identity of users accessing the edge computing infrastructure.\
- Secure Local Storage: The edge computing infrastructure may store a subset of healthcare data locally for faster access and immediate analysis. Robust security measures such as data encryption and access controls should be implemented to protect the stored data from unauthorized access or tampering.
- Secure Data Analytics: Edge computing allows for real-time data analytics and processing at the edge. This can include applying machine learning algorithms or other data analysis techniques to derive meaningful information from the healthcare data. These analytics should be performed in a secure environment, ensuring the privacy and integrity of the data.
- Regular Security Audits and Updates: Regular security audits should be conducted to identify vulnerabilities and address any potential security risks. Software and firmware updates for the edge computing infrastructure should be applied promptly to patch any known security vulnerabilities.
- Compliance with Data Privacy Regulations: Healthcare organizations must comply with relevant data privacy regulations, such as the General Data Protection Regulation (GDPR) or the Health Insurance Portability and Accountability Act (HIPAA). Compliance measures should be implemented to protect patient privacy and ensure that data handling practices adhere to legal requirements.

Hence, by implementing these security measures in secure healthcare monitoring with edge computing, healthcare providers can benefit from real-time monitoring and analysis while safeguarding sensitive patient data.

7. EVALUATION AND RESULTS TOWARDS CYBER SECURITY IN IOT-BASED EDGE COMPUTING

7.1 Performance Metrics and Evaluation Criteria for Cyber Security in IoT-Based Edge Computing

When evaluating the effectiveness of cyber security in IoT-based edge computing, it is essential to consider various performance metrics and evaluation criteria. These metrics help assess the robustness, efficiency, and reliability of the security measures in place. Here are some key performance metrics and evaluation criteria for cyber security in IoT-based edge computing:

- Threat Detection and Prevention: This metric measures the ability of the security system to detect and prevent cyber threats effectively. It includes evaluating the accuracy and timeliness of threat detection mechanisms, such as intrusion detection systems (IDS), firewalls, and anomaly detection algorithms. The metric should consider the system's ability to detect various types of threats, including malware, unauthorized access attempts, and data breaches.
- Response Time and Incident Management: This metric assesses the speed and effectiveness of the security system in responding to security incidents. It measures the time taken to detect, analyze, and mitigate security threats or breaches. A low response time indicates a more efficient incident management process, enabling quick containment and recovery.
- Data Privacy and Confidentiality: This metric evaluates the effectiveness of data protection mechanisms in place. It includes assessing the encryption methods used for data transmission and storage, access controls to ensure data confidentiality, and compliance with privacy regulations such as GDPR or HIPAA. The metric should consider the level of data privacy achieved, the strength of encryption algorithms, and the implementation of data anonymization techniques (Mapanga, 2017; Midha & Tripathi, 2020).
- Authentication and Access Control: This metric measures the reliability and effectiveness of authentication mechanisms and access control policies. It evaluates the ability to verify the identity of users, devices, and applications accessing the edge computing system. The metric should consider the strength of authentication methods, such as username/password combinations, two-factor authentication (2FA), or biometric authentication, as well as the granularity and enforcement of access control policies.
- Resilience and Availability: This metric assesses the resilience and availability of the edge computing system under cyber-attacks or network failures. It measures the system's ability to continue operating, providing essential services, and protecting critical infrastructure despite security incidents. The metric should consider factors such as backup and recovery mechanisms, redundancy, failover capabilities, and the system's ability to handle increased traffic during attack scenarios.
- Compliance and Regulatory Requirements: This metric evaluates the adherence of the IoT-based edge computing system to relevant cybersecurity standards, industry best practices, and regulatory requirements. It includes assessing compliance with data protection regulations, security frameworks such as NIST Cybersecurity Framework or ISO 27001, and specific industry guidelines. The metric should consider the implementation of security controls and documentation of security practices.
- Security Incident Reporting and Auditing: This metric measures the effectiveness of security incident reporting and auditing processes. It evaluates the system's ability to generate comprehensive security logs, track and analyze security events, and conduct regular security audits. The metric should consider the completeness and accuracy of incident logs, the ability to trace and investigate security incidents, and the implementation of continuous monitoring and auditing practices.
- Security Training and Awareness: This metric assesses the level of security training and awareness programs provided to employees, system administrators, and end-users. It measures the effectiveness of these programs in educating stakeholders about cybersecurity risks, best practices, and the importance of adhering to security policies. The metric should consider the frequency and coverage of security training sessions and the level of awareness among users.
- System Performance Impact: This metric evaluates the impact of security measures on the overall performance and efficiency of the IoT-based edge computing system. It measures factors such

as latency introduced by security mechanisms, processing overheads, and network bandwidth requirements. The metric should strike a balance between strong security measures and system performance to ensure an optimal user experience.

Note that by considering these performance metrics and evaluation criteria, organizations can assess the effectiveness of their cyber security measures in IoT-based edge computing. Regular evaluations help identify areas for improvement, ensure compliance, and enhance the overall security posture of the system.

8. LIMITATIONS AND CHALLENGES FACED TOWARDS CYBER SECURITY IN IOT-BASED EDGE COMPUTING

While IoT-based edge computing offers numerous benefits, there are several limitations and challenges that need to be addressed to ensure effective cyber security (Gomathi et al., 2023; Nair & Tyagi, 2023). Here are some common limitations and challenges faced towards cyber security in IoT-based edge computing:

- Heterogeneity and Scalability: IoT-based edge computing environments often consist of a diverse range of devices and systems, each with different security capabilities and configurations. Managing security across such a heterogeneous and scalable infrastructure can be challenging. Ensuring consistent security measures and updates across all devices and systems becomes difficult, leading to potential vulnerabilities.
- Limited Resources: IoT devices at the edge typically have limited processing power, memory, and energy resources. This constraint makes it challenging to implement robust security measures on these devices. Encryption, authentication protocols, and other security mechanisms may require additional computational power or energy, impacting device performance and battery life.
- Lack of Standardization: The lack of standardized security protocols and frameworks for IoT devices and edge computing poses a significant challenge. Each manufacturer may implement its own security mechanisms, leading to inconsistency and potential interoperability issues. The absence of a unified security standard makes it difficult to ensure seamless security across different devices and systems.
- Physical Security: IoT devices deployed at the edge are often more vulnerable to physical tampering and attacks compared to centralized systems. Malicious actors can physically access and manipulate devices, compromising their security and integrity. Protecting IoT devices from physical attacks requires additional security measures such as tamper-proofing, secure enclosures, and physical access controls.
- Network Connectivity and Communication: IoT devices rely on network connectivity to communicate with edge computing nodes or the cloud. This dependency introduces potential vulnerabilities, including eavesdropping, data interception, and man-in-the-middle attacks. Securing communication channels and ensuring end-to-end encryption become critical challenges in IoT-based edge computing.
- Data Privacy and Consent: IoT devices often collect and process large amounts of personal and sensitive data. Ensuring data privacy and obtaining user consent for data collection and processing present significant challenges. Managing data privacy, implementing anonymization techniques,

and complying with relevant data protection regulations (e.g., GDPR) require careful consideration in IoT-based edge computing.

- Security Update and Patch Management: IoT devices deployed at the edge may not receive regular security updates and patches. Limited connectivity, resource constraints, or device lifespan can hinder the timely deployment of security updates. Outdated firmware and software expose devices to known vulnerabilities, making them attractive targets for cyber-attacks.
- Human Factor and Awareness: Human factors, such as user behavior, awareness, and training, significantly impact the cyber security of IoT-based edge computing. Lack of security awareness among end-users, weak passwords, and improper configuration of devices can create security vulnerabilities. Addressing the human factor through education, training, and emphasizing security best practices is important.
- Security Monitoring and Incident Response: Real-time security monitoring and incident response in IoT-based edge computing environments can be challenging. The large number of devices and the distributed nature of edge computing make it difficult to monitor and detect security incidents effectively. Additionally, responding to incidents promptly and coordinating actions across multiple devices and systems require robust incident response mechanisms.
- Legacy Systems and Interoperability: Integration with existing legacy systems can be challenging in IoT-based edge computing environments. Legacy systems may have outdated security mechanisms and limited interoperability with modern security solutions. Ensuring secure communication and data exchange between legacy systems and IoT devices at the edge becomes a complex task.

Note that these limitations and challenges require collaboration among stakeholders, including device manufacturers, standards organizations, security experts, and regulatory bodies. By considering these challenges and implementing appropriate security measures, IoT-based edge computing can be made more secure and resilient.

9. FUTURE RESEARCH DIRECTIONS TOWARDS CYBER SECURITY IN IOT-BASED EDGE COMPUTING

Cyber security in IoT-based edge computing is an evolving field that requires ongoing research and innovation to address emerging challenges and threats (Nair & Tyagi, 2023). Here are some future research directions that can contribute to enhancing cyber security in IoT-based edge computing:

- Threat Intelligence and Analytics: Develop advanced threat intelligence and analytics techniques specifically tailored for IoT-based edge computing environments. This includes considering machine learning and AI algorithms to detect and mitigate sophisticated cyber threats in real-time. Figure 1 and 2 provide a detail explanation of using Artificial Intelligence (AI) in cyber security (Gomathi et al., 2023; Khan & Salah, 2019; Mapanga, 2017; Midha & Tripathi, 2020; Hura et al., 2021; Nair, 2023; Nair & Tyagi, 2023; Tyagi,, 2023) can be useful and effective and cost saving approach. Further, figure 3 discusses about eliminating the complexity in Cyber security with Artificial Intelligence in detail.

Figure 1. Role of AI in cyber security

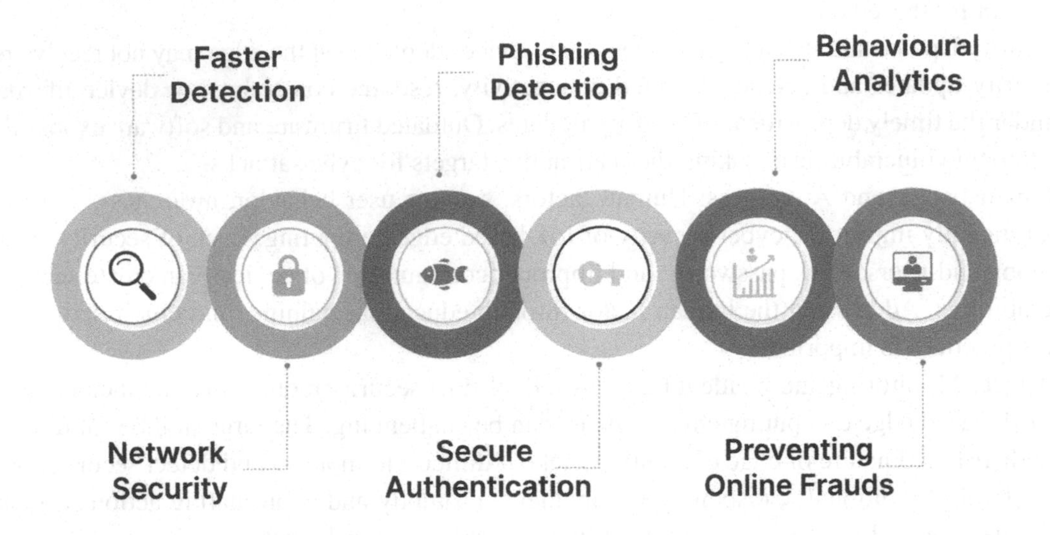

Figure 2. Benefits of using AI in cyber security

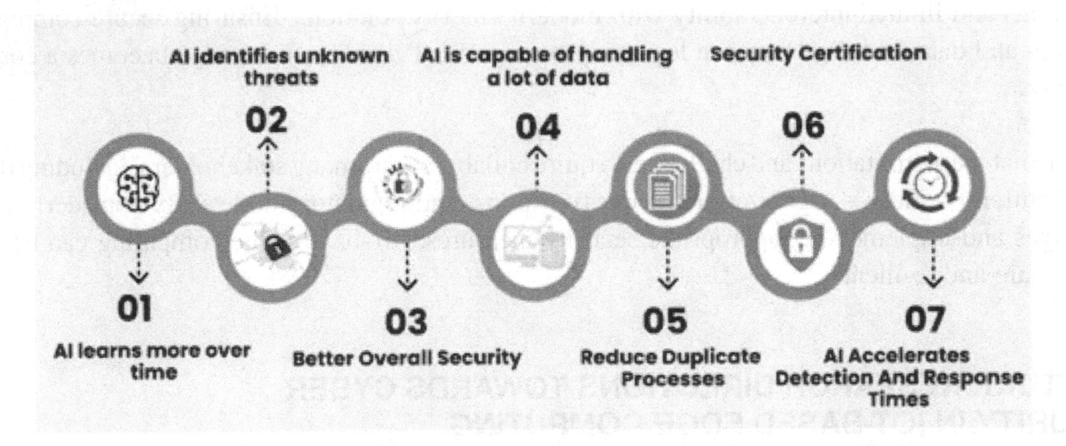

- Privacy-Preserving Techniques: Investigate novel privacy-preserving techniques for IoT data collection, processing, and sharing at the edge. Research can focus on methods such as differential privacy, federated learning, and secure multi-party computation to protect sensitive data while enabling valuable information.
- Blockchain and Distributed Ledger Technologies: Explore the potential of blockchain and distributed ledger technologies for enhancing the security and integrity of IoT-based edge computing systems. This includes investigating the application of blockchain for secure device identity management, data provenance, and secure transactions in IoT ecosystems.
- Secure Firmware and Over-the-Air Updates: Develop secure and efficient mechanisms for firmware and over-the-air updates in IoT devices at the edge. This includes exploring techniques for secure code signing, verification, and secure update distribution to mitigate vulnerabilities and ensure timely patching of security flaws.

Figure 3. Eliminating the complexity in cyber security with artificial intelligence

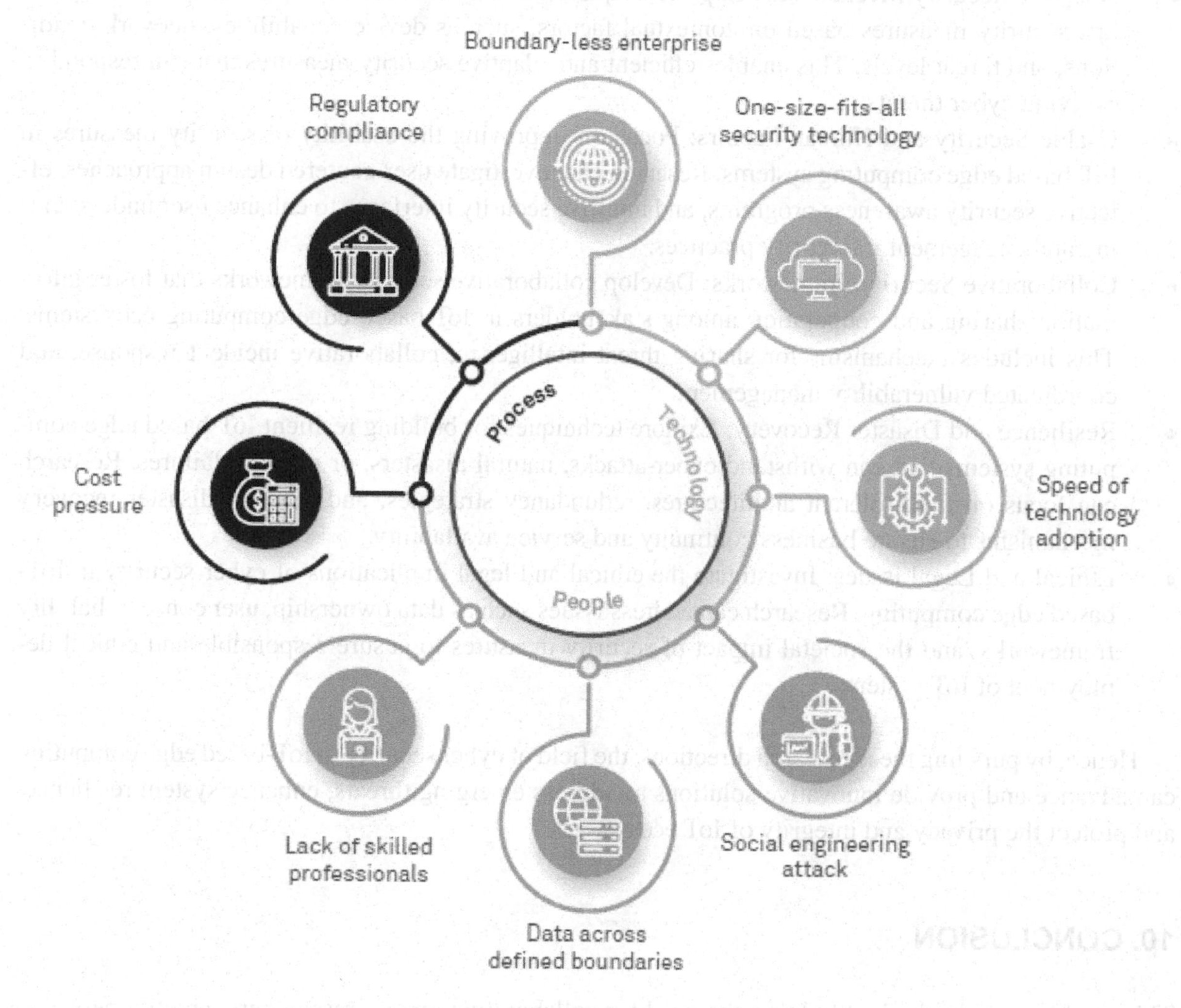

- Trust Management and Authentication: Investigate trust management frameworks and authentication mechanisms for IoT devices and edge computing nodes. Research can focus on developing lightweight and scalable methods for device authentication, access control, and trust establishment in dynamic edge environments.
- Cyber-Physical Systems Security: Address the security challenges in cyber-physical systems (CPS) enabled by IoT-based edge computing. Research can focus on securing critical infrastructure, such as smart grids, transportation systems, and healthcare systems, against cyber threats that can have physical consequences.
- Secure Edge-to-Cloud Communication: Develop secure communication protocols and frameworks for efficient and secure data exchange between IoT devices at the edge and cloud platforms. This includes investigating techniques for secure data aggregation, encryption, and integrity verification in resource-constrained edge environments.

- Adaptive Security Mechanisms: Explore adaptive security mechanisms that can dynamically adjust security measures based on contextual factors, such as device capabilities, network conditions, and threat levels. This enables efficient and adaptive security measures that can respond to evolving cyber threats.
- Usable Security and Human Factors: Focus on improving the usability of security measures in IoT-based edge computing systems. Research can investigate user-centered design approaches, effective security awareness programs, and intuitive security interfaces to enhance user understanding and engagement in security practices.
- Collaborative Security Frameworks: Develop collaborative security frameworks that foster information sharing and cooperation among stakeholders in IoT-based edge computing ecosystems. This includes mechanisms for sharing threat intelligence, collaborative incident response, and coordinated vulnerability management.
- Resilience and Disaster Recovery: Explore techniques for building resilient IoT-based edge computing systems that can withstand cyber-attacks, natural disasters, or network failures. Research can focus on fault-tolerant architectures, redundancy strategies, and efficient disaster recovery mechanisms to ensure business continuity and service availability.
- Ethical and Legal issues: Investigate the ethical and legal implications of cyber security in IoT-based edge computing. Research can address issues such as data ownership, user consent, liability frameworks, and the societal impact of security measures to ensure responsible and ethical deployment of IoT systems.

Hence, by pursuing these research directions, the field of cyber security in IoT-based edge computing can advance and provide innovative solutions to address emerging threats, enhance system resilience, and protect the privacy and integrity of IoT ecosystems.

10. CONCLUSION

This work concludes by highlighting the need for collaboration among researchers, practitioners, and policymakers to address the evolving cyber security landscape in IoT-based edge computing. It emphasizes the importance of continual research and innovation to stay ahead of emerging threats and to ensure the safe and secure deployment of IoT devices and edge computing infrastructure. In summary, this comprehensive review serves as a valuable resource for professionals and researchers in the field of cyber security, providing meaningful information into the unique challenges and potential solutions in IoT-based edge computing environments, and fostering discussions on the future of secure IoT deployments.

REFERENCES

Agarwal, D., & Tripathi, K. (2022). A Framework for Structural Damage detection system in automobiles for flexible Insurance claim using IOT and Machine Learning. *2022 International Mobile and Embedded Technology Conference (MECON),* (pp. 5-8). IEEE. 10.1109/MECON53876.2022.9751889

Alaba, F. A., Othman, M., Hashem, I. A., & Alotaibi, F. (2017). Internet of Things security: A survey. *Journal of Network and Computer Applications*, *88*, 10–28. doi:10.1016/j.jnca.2017.04.002

Dastjerdi, A. V., Gupta, H., Calheiros, R. N., Ghosh, S. K., & Buyya, R. (2016). Fog computing: Principles, architectures, and applications. *Internet of Things Journal*, *3*(5), 516–553.

Fernández-Caramés, T. M., & Fraga-Lamas, P. (2018). A review on the use of blockchain for the Internet of Things. *IEEE Access : Practical Innovations, Open Solutions*, *6*, 32979–33001. doi:10.1109/ACCESS.2018.2842685

George, T. T., & Tyagi, A. K. (2022). Reliable Edge Computing Architectures for Crowdsensing Applications. *2022 International Conference on Computer Communication and Informatics (ICCCI)*, (pp. 1-6). IEEE. 10.1109/ICCCI54379.2022.9740791

Gomathi, L., Mishra, A. K., & Tyagi, A. K. (2023). *Industry 5.0 for Healthcare 5.0: Opportunities, Challenges and Future Research Possibilities*. 2023 7th International Conference on Trends in Electronics and Informatics (ICOEI), Tirunelveli, India. 10.1109/ICOEI56765.2023.10125660

Goyal, D. & Tyagi, A. (2020). *A Look at Top 35 Problems in the Computer Science Field for the Next Decade*. Taylor & Francis. . doi:10.1201/9781003052098-40

Jajula, S. K., Tripathi, K., & Bajaj, S. B. (2023). Review of Detection of Packets Inspection and Attacks in Network Security. In P. Dutta, S. Chakrabarti, A. Bhattacharya, S. Dutta, & V. Piuri (Eds.), *Emerging Technologies in Data Mining and Information Security. Lecture Notes in Networks and Systems* (Vol. 491). Springer. doi:10.1007/978-981-19-4193-1_58

Khan, S., & Salah, K. (2019). Trust management in edge computing and IoT: A review, taxonomy, and open research challenges. *IEEE Internet of Things Journal*, *7*(6), 4532–4557.

Liang, X., Zhang, X., Luo, X., & Shen, X. (2018). Towards open big data analytics in the fog. *IEEE Communications Magazine*, *56*(10), 94–100.

Mapanga, V., Kumar, W., Makondo, T., Kushboo, P., & Chanda, W. (2017). Design and implementation of an intrusion detection system using MLP-NN for MANET. *2017 IST-Africa Week Conference*. IST-Africa. . doi:10.23919/ISTAFRICA.2017.8102374

Midha, S., Kaur, G., & Tripathi, K. (2017). Cloud deep down — SWOT analysis," 2017 2nd International Conference on Telecommunication and Networks (TEL-NET), , pp. 1-5, 10.1109/TEL-NET.2017.8343560

Midha, S., & Tripathi, K. (2020). Remotely Triggered Blackhole Routing in SDN for Handling DoS. In: Dutta, M., Krishna, C., Kumar, R., & Kalra, M. (eds) *Proceedings of International Conference on IoT Inclusive Life*. Springer, Singapore. 10.1007/978-981-15-3020-3_1

Midha, S., & Tripathi, K. (2021). Extended Security in Heterogeneous Distributed SDN Architecture. In G. Hura, A. Singh, & L. Siong Hoe (Eds.), *Advances in Communication and Computational Technology. Lecture Notes in Electrical Engineering* (Vol. 668). Springer. doi:10.1007/978-981-15-5341-7_75

Midha, S., Tripathi, K., & Sharma, M. K. (2021, April). Practical Implications of Using Dockers on Virtualized SDN. *Webology.*, *18*(Special Issue 01), 312–330. doi:10.14704/WEB/V18SI01/WEB18062

Midha, S., & Triptahi, K. (2019). Extended TLS security and Defensive Algorithm in OpenFlow SDN. *2019 9th International Conference on Cloud Computing, Data Science & Engineering (Confluence)*, (pp. 141-146). IEEE. 10.1109/CONFLUENCE.2019.8776607

Mishra, S., & Tyagi, A. K. (2022). The Role of Machine Learning Techniques in Internet of Things-Based Cloud Applications. In S. Pal, D. De, & R. Buyya (Eds.), *Artificial Intelligence-based Internet of Things Systems. Internet of Things (Technology, Communications and Computing)*. Springer. doi:10.1007/978-3-030-87059-1_4

Mukherjee, M., Matam, R., Shu, L., Maglaras, L., Ferrag, M. A., & Ahmim, A. (2019). A survey of intrusion detection systems in IoT-based edge computing. *IEEE Internet of Things Journal*, *7*(12), 10274–10289.

Nair, M. (2023). *Amit Kumar Tyagi, "6G: Technology, Advancement, Barriers, and the Future", in the book: 6G-Enabled IoT and AI for Smart Healthcare*. CRC Press.

Nair, M. & Tyagi, A. (2023). Blockchain technology for next-generation society: current trends and future opportunities for smart era. *Blockchain Technology for Secure Social Media Computing,*. IET Technology. . doi:10.1049/PBSE019E_ch11

Nair, M. M., Kumari, S., & Tyagi, A. K. (2021). Internet of Things, Cyber Physical System, and Data Analytics: Open Questions, Future Perspectives, and Research Areas. In: Goyal D., Gupta A.K., Piuri V., Ganzha M., Paprzycki M. (eds) *Proceedings of the Second International Conference on Information Management and Machine Intelligence. Lecture Notes in Networks and Systems*. Springer, Singapore. 10.1007/978-981-15-9689-6_36

Nair, M. M., & Tyagi, A. K. (2021). Privacy: History, Statistics, Policy, Laws, Preservation and Threat Analysis. Journal of Information Assurance & Security, 16(1), 24-34.

Nair, M. M., Tyagi, A. K., & Sreenath, N. (2021). The Future with Industry 4.0 at the Core of Society 5.0: Open Issues, Future Opportunities and Challenges. 2021 International Conference on Computer Communication and Informatics (ICCCI), (pp. 1-7). Springer. 10.1109/ICCCI50826.2021.9402498

Ranchhodbhai P.N, & Tripathi K. (2019). Identifying and Improving the Malicious Behavior of Rushing and Blackhole Attacks using Proposed IDSAODV Protocol. *International Journal of Recent Technology and Engineering*, *8*(3), 6554-6562.

Ray, P. P. (2018). A survey of IoT architectures. *Journal of King Saud University-Computer and Information Sciences*.

Rekha, G., Malik, S., Tyagi, A. K., & Nair, M. M. (2020). Intrusion Detection in Cyber Security: Role of Machine Learning and Data Mining in Cyber Security. *Advances in Science, Technology and Engineering Systems Journal*, *5*(3), 72–81. doi:10.25046/aj050310

Rekha, G., Tyagi, A. K., & Anuradha, N. (2020) Integration of Fog Computing and Internet of Things: An Useful Overview. In: Singh P., Kar A., Singh Y., Kolekar M., Tanwar S. (eds) *Proceedings of ICRIC 2019. Lecture Notes in Electrical Engineering*. Springer, Cham. 10.1007/978-3-030-29407-6_8

Rong, C., Zhang, D., & Yang, A. (2014). Edge computing in the Internet of Things. *IEEE Transactions on Industrial Informatics, 10*(2), 1568–1576.

Sai, G. H., Tripathi, K., & Tyagi, A. K. (2023). Internet of Things-Based e-Health Care: Key Challenges and Recommended Solutions for Future. In: Singh, P.K., Wierzchoń, S.T., Tanwar, S., Rodrigues, J.J.P.C., Ganzha, M. (eds) *Proceedings of Third International Conference on Computing, Communications, and Cyber-Security.* Springer, Singapore. 10.1007/978-981-19-1142-2_37

Sheth, H. S. K., & Tyagi, A. K. (2022). Mobile Cloud Computing: Issues, Applications and Scope in COVID-19. In A. Abraham, N. Gandhi, T. Hanne, T. P. Hong, T. Nogueira Rios, & W. Ding (Eds.), *Intelligent Systems Design and Applications. ISDA 2021. Lecture Notes in Networks and Systems* (Vol. 418). Springer. doi:10.1007/978-3-030-96308-8_55

Somisetti, K. T., & Verma, J. K. (2020). Design, Implementation, and Controlling of a Humanoid Robot. *2020 International Conference on Computational Performance Evaluation (ComPE),* (pp. 831-836). IEEE. 10.1109/ComPE49325.2020.9200020

Subasree, S., & Sakthivel, N. K. (2022). Combining the advantages of radiomic features based feature extraction and hyper parameters tuned RERNN using LOA for breast cancer classification. *Biomedical Signal Processing and Control, 72*. doi:10.1016/j.bspc.2021.103354

Suo, H., Wan, J., Zou, C., & Liu, J. (2012). Security in the Internet of Things: A review. *Internet of Things Journal, 1*(1), 8–19. doi:10.1109/ICCSEE.2012.373

Tripathi, K., Pandey, M., & Verma, S. (2011). Comparison of reactive and proactive routing protocols for different mobility conditions in WSN. In *Proceedings of the 2011 International Conference on Communication, Computing & Security (ICCCS '11).* Association for Computing Machinery, New York, NY, USA, 156–161. 10.1145/1947940.1947974

Tyagi, A. K. (2022). *Handbook of Research on Technical, Privacy, and Security Challenges in a Modern World.* IGI Global. doi:10.4018/978-1-6684-5250-9

Tyagi, A. K. (2023). Chapter 2 - Decentralized everything: Practical use of blockchain technology in future applications. R. Goundar, & S. Fatima (eds.) Distributed Computing to Blockchain. Academic Press. doi:10.1016/B978-0-323-96146-2.00010-3

Tyagi, A., Kukreja, S., Nair, M. M., & Tyagi, A. K. (2022). Machine Learning: Past, Present and Future. *NeuroQuantology : An Interdisciplinary Journal of Neuroscience and Quantum Physics, 20*(8). Advance online publication. doi:10.14704/nq.2022.20.8.NQ44468

Tyagi, A. K. (2016, March). Article: Cyber Physical Systems (CPSs) – Opportunities and Challenges for Improving Cyber Security. [Published by Foundation of Computer Science] [FCS] [, NY, USA.]. *International Journal of Computer Applications, 137*(14), 19–27. doi:10.5120/ijca2016908877

Tyagi, A. K., & Bansal, R. Anshu, Dananjayan, S. (2023). A Step-To-Step Guide to Write a Quality Research Article. In: Abraham, A., Pllana, S., Casalino, G., Ma, K., Bajaj, A. (eds) Intelligent Systems Design and Applications. ISDA 2022. Lecture Notes in Networks and Systems. Springer, Cham. doi:10.1007/978-3-031-35510-3_36

Tyagi, A. K., Dananjayan, S., Agarwal, D., & Thariq Ahmed, H. F. (2023). Blockchain—Internet of Things Applications: Opportunities and Challenges for Industry 4.0 and Society 5.0. *Sensors (Basel)*, *23*(2), 947. doi:10.339023020947 PMID:36679743

Tyagi, A. K., Fernandez, T. F., Mishra, S., & Kumari, S. (2021). Intelligent Automation Systems at the Core of Industry 4.0. In A. Abraham, V. Piuri, N. Gandhi, P. Siarry, A. Kaklauskas, & A. Madureira (Eds.), *Intelligent Systems Design and Applications. ISDA 2020. Advances in Intelligent Systems and Computing* (Vol. 1351). Springer. doi:10.1007/978-3-030-71187-0_1

Tyagi, A. K., & Sreenath, N. (2023). Fog and Edge Computing in Navigation of Intelligent Transportation System. In *Intelligent Transportation Systems: Theory and Practice. Disruptive Technologies and Digital Transformations for Society 5.0*. Springer. doi:10.1007/978-981-19-7622-3_7

Yan, M., Yu, S., Zhang, Y., & Gjessing, S. (2018). Trust and privacy in edge computing: A review. *IEEE Access : Practical Innovations, Open Solutions*, *6*, 4904–4922.

Chapter 8
Enhanced Security in Blockchain-Based Cyber Physical Systems

N. Ambika
https://orcid.org/0000-0003-4452-5514
St. Francis College, India

ABSTRACT

Consortium blockchain provides pooled trust for the proposed method. It uses a unique certificateless authentication method based on the multi-signature scheme to guarantee safety. Software, and physical components comprise the cyber-physical system. Each piece functions on various time-based and three-dimensional stages and constantly interacts with other members. The framework eliminates the centralized trust model, i.e., the dependence on a single PKI certificate authority (CA) for public keys, works over an associate consortium, and uses smart-edge computation. Different industry partners cooperatively confirm both the gadget's character and information. It prevents disasters by reducing the impact of potentially malevolent associates. It agrees to a novel contract without requiring manifold authorisations, eliminating the need for a waiting period after each block addition. It adjusts, putting away information at the conveyed hash table. The suggestion adds more reliability to the transaction by 4.17%. The suggestion conserves energy by 12.5%.

INTRODUCTION

Cyber-Physical Systems (CPSs) (Ambika N., 2020) (Fachkha & Debbabi, 2015) combine the dynamics of software, communication, and physical processes with abstractions and methods for modeling, designing, and analyzing the whole. Physical systems and networking interact in ways that necessitate primarily novel scheme proficiency. The knowledge is based on many regulations like entrenched technology, processors, and broadcastings. Package is inserted in cars, medical devices, scientific instruments, and intelligent transportation systems whose primary purpose isn't just computation.

DOI: 10.4018/979-8-3693-2081-5.ch008

They carefully plan out their attacks, employ anti-forensic methods, and disperse their activity over a long period to avoid discovery as part of their strategic nature. These qualities have increased complexity, expertise demand, and time requirements of cyber forensic investigations. It deals with the change in the current threat landscape. The examination must invest effort in keeping their expertise and training current. The skill of gathering, interpreting, and writing indication from information obtained on automated device is known as "digital forensics." It uses a combination of computer science and traditional investigation techniques. First illegal conduct uses electronic devices or computer systems but does not directly target them. Second harmful behavior directly affects or involves networks and computer systems. The steps of a typical cyber forensics' investigation include collection, inspection, correlation, and reporting. It has numerous alike or equivalent exploratory development reproductions. Each of those phases has a variety of technical and non-technical responsibilities. The authorization of the channels or information that may be pertinent to the instance, as well as its labeling, footage, attainment, and truthfulness conservancy following the applicable criteria, are all included in the collecting stage. The investigator must evaluate and manually or automatically extract pertinent data from the assembled data during the examination stage once data collection. It mainly entails the procedural investigation of the information assembled. It has several activities, including network analysis, registry inspection, event analysis from the gathered records, procedure investigation, or malicious content removal from the gathered recollection scrapheaps. It could entail activities like decoding, de- complication, contrary production, or getting beyond some safety measures. The information is linked and evaluated logically and objectively using multiple inference and reasoning techniques. Guidelines and frameworks for best practices use methods like case-based reasoning, temporal aggregation, and forward and backward reasoning.

Blockchain has various advantages of decentralization, persistence, namelessness, and auditability. Like a traditional public ledger, the blockchain is a sequence of blocks containing an exhaustive list of transaction records. It is essentially the muddle text of the parent mass, each chunk links to the block that came before it. A blockchain's origin mass, which does not have a parental mass, is the first block. A business stall and trades make up the chuck frame. The large number of blocks can contain the chunk size and the magnitude of every trade. Blockchain uses an uneven cryptography component to approve the confirmation of exchanges.

The proposed security structure (Rahman, Khalil, & Atiquzzaman, 2021) for primary industry 4.0 CPS chips away at four distinct levels, where detector and savvy control gadgets effort in the actual space with association Blockchain organization. Given the 4 degrees of correspondence, the functioning standard works in three different center stages. The machine sensors get enlisted and layout correspondence utilizing a BC-based MS strategy. Besides, the enlisted detectors submit details to the BC organization abstract to be confirmed by the BC confederation. The information is put away in the DHT (circulated hash table) after documenting the sign into the BC record. The system uses edge calculation rather than distributed computing. It uses a unique certificateless authentication method based on the multi-signature scheme to guarantee safety. Software, and physical components comprise the cyber-physical system. Each piece installations on various time-based and three-dimensional stages and constantly interacts with other members. The framework eliminates the centralized trust model, i.e., the dependence on a single PKI credential expert for community credential, installations over associated syndicate, and uses smart-edge computation. Different Industry partners cooperatively confirm both the gadget's character and information. This feature eliminates the single point of failure, increases trust, and protects data from forgery. It verifies and records device registration and communication activities within the restricted channel in a transparent ledger. In the consortium agreement convention, the pioneer proposes the following block that essentially lowers the prize expenses. It prevents malfunctions by reducing the impact of potentially malevolent aristocracies. It agrees to a new business without requiring various authorisations, eliminating the need for a waiting period after each block addition. It adjusts, putting away information at the conveyed hash table.

The recommendation includes endorsement. For every session the respective entities generate endorsement keys of all the necessary parties using Merkle tree to increase data integrity. The parties exchange their identity and location information to help generate the hash key and embed it to the blockchain. This helps in evaluating their identity. The suggestion adds more reliability to the transaction by 4.17%. The suggestion conserves energy by 12.5%.

The work is separated into five units. Literature review trails overview piece. Planned work is detailed in part three. The fourth partition particulars the analysis of the proposal. The work concludes in piece five.

LITERATURE SURVEY

Consortium Blockchain (Ambika N., 2021) (Zheng, Xie, Dai, Chen, & Wang, 2018) provides pooled trust for the proposed method (Rahman, Khalil, & Atiquzzaman, 2021). The proposed security structure (Rahman, Khalil, & Atiquzzaman, 2021) for primary industry 4.0 CPS chips away at four distinct levels, where detector and savvy control gadgets effort in the actual space with association Blockchain organization. Given the 4 degrees of correspondence, the functioning standard works in three different center stages. The machine sensors get enlisted and layout correspondence utilizing a BC-based MS strategy. Besides, the enlisted detectors submit details to the BC organization abstract to be confirmed by the BC confederation. The information is put away in the DHT (circulated hash table) after documenting the sign into the BC record. The system uses edge calculation rather than distributed computing. It uses a unique certificateless authentication method based on the multi-signature scheme to guarantee safety. Software, and physical components comprise the cyber-physical system. Each piece installations on various time-based and three-dimensional stages and constantly interacts with other members. The framework eliminates the centralized trust model, i.e., the dependence on a single PKI credential expert for community credential, installations over associated syndicate, and uses smart-edge computation. Different Industry partners cooperatively confirm both the gadget's character and information. This feature eliminates the single point of failure, increases trust, and protects data from forgery. It verifies and records device registration and communication activities within the restricted channel in a transparent ledger. In the consortium agreement convention, the pioneer proposes the following block that essentially lowers the prize expenses. It prevents malfunctions by reducing the impact of potentially malevolent aristocracies. It agrees to a new business without requiring various authorisations, eliminating the need for a waiting period after each block addition. It adjusts, putting away information at the conveyed hash table.

A possibility prototypical for evaluating the trustworthiness of an IDRS-armed CPS for sleuthing and answering to spiteful proceedings is developed in this work (Mitchell & Chen, 2013). It has 128 mobile nodes that carry sensors. Each node transmits a code division of multiple access waveforms periodically to range its neighbors and employs detector to gauge any nearby phenomena that can be detected. The associates get waveform to change the planning of the cipher and transporter into the distance. Every hub achieves detecting and announcing capabilities to give information to upper-layer control gadgets to control and safeguard the CPS framework. It is a one-enclave system with uniform nodes in the case of the reference model. The IDS usefulness is appropriated to all hubs for interruption and adaptation to non-critical failure. An enclave control node sits atop sensor-carrying mobile nodes and sets scheme limitations in reply to vigorously varying situations like attacker strength variations. Using safety and ironware defence apparatuses against detention outbreaks and hardware catastrophe. The CPS's underlying physical objects actuate and are controlled by the dynamic devices, skilled of detecting corporeal surroundings. They have sensors for detecting physical phenomena and actuators for controlling physical objects, making them both sensors and actuators.

A layered methodology (Sridhar, Hahn, & Govindarasu, 2011) is acquainted with assessing risk given the safety of the actual authority submissions and the backing digital foundation. The cyber-corporeal regulator is necessary to backing the intelligent network, and the message and calculations that must be endangered from cyber-attacks are categorized to highlight their dependencies. The underlying move toward the gamble examination process is the foundation weakness investigation. The cyber assets, such as software, hardware, and communication protocols are the initial step in any comprehensive vulnerability analysis. The application impact analysis step should be carried out following the identification of cyber vulnerabilities to ascertain the potential effects on the infrastructure-supported applications. State machines are created to assess the advances affected by interdomain conditions. This model is used to look at how cyber asset failures or attacks can affect power generation. A power framework is practically partitioned into age, transmission, and circulation. Control focuses on estimations from sensors that cooperate with field gadgets. The calculations running in the control place process these estimations to settle on functional choices. The choices are then sent to actuators to execute these progressions on field gadgets. The control of the generator's power output and terminal voltage is the primary function of the generation control loops. Both the local and wide-area command streams regulate generation. By governing the quantity of responsive control that is engrossed or inoculated into the organisation, the generator exciter authority improves the steadiness of the authority arrangement. Lead representative control is the essential recurrence control component. The steam valve's settings alter the generator's power output in response to speed changes caused by disturbances detected by this mechanism. The programmed age control circle is an optional recurrence control circle calibrating the framework recurrence to its ostensible worth. The AGC loop can make alterations to interarea tie-line stream and reappearance eccentricity. The AGC assurances that each regulating authority area makes up for its pile modification, and the supremacy employment between two regulator regions is restricted to the planned worth.

In the power system, distributed components are monitored and controlled by the SCADA system (Zhang Y., Wang, Xiang, & Ten, 2015). Software and hardware comprise the SCADA system. Two models of Bayesian attack graphs are looked at. The first is the assault chart of weaknesses, which portrays the likelihood of fruitful root honor obtaining through local area networks of the authority place, partnership, and substations. The arrangement of deeds constitutes a negligible outbreak classification, indicating that the assailant is exploiting the weaknesses and does not require extra effort to reach the target. It is calculated to achieve its goal condition. Each adventure to the weakness in the negligible assault arrangements. The probability of successful intrusion is estimated by the second Bayesian occurrence graph model. The MITM outbreak is hurled at the announcement connection; therefore, the device does not require privilege to reach it.

The construction of the integrated SCADA/EMS framework (Zhang, Xiang, & Wang, 2016) for wind farms has potential cyberattack scenarios involving networks or components of the internet. The local regulator LAN for the airstream farmhouse can be either a separate breeze ranch SCADA system in the control room or a network that is partially integrated with the corporate network for business. Two

Bayesian assault diagram models are embraced to address the techniques of fruitful digital assaults, and an interim to think twice about is utilized by thinking about various assault levels and different weaknesses. The airstream area SCADA/EMS organisation's typical period intermissions for positive cyber-attacks on targeted cyber components are estimated using a mean time-to-cooperation prototypical. The frequency of successful cyber-attacks on the targeted components is evaluated. When untrue guidelines are guided through the cyber mechanisms that have been penetrated, wind turbines are triggered. The probability of positive cyber-outbreaks against the airstream grange SCADA/EMS organisation is calculated using a forensic mean-time-to-repair (MTTR) of the intruded cyber component. By sending the unapproved trip orders to wind turbines or wind ranches after effective interruptions, breakers of the power framework are compelled to trip, which prompts expanded blackout periods parts. At long last, Monte Carlo Recreation (MCS) is utilized to play out the unwavering quality investigation of the power framework. The International Electrotechnical Commission (IEC) 61400-25 communication protocols are used in the local control LAN of wind farm communication networks. These protocols enable the SCADA system to interconnect with any instrument in a typical means. The constant order and estimation data are introduced on the workstation, and the drawn-out information got from the estimation parts is put away in the verifiable data set. The breeze ranch SCADA carries out the role of gaining the framework information, which are the deliberate electrical factors at the breeze turbines. The SCADA server processes the monitored wind farm data before sending it to the request host. Using the server, the administrators can screen the electrical states and adjust the boundaries of the actual parts in the breeze ranch. The unapproved client might meddle in the nearby control LAN and control the workstation, pernicious orders might be shipped off switch off the breeze turbines, or change the boundaries of the regulator. In the hot standby mode, there are numerous segments of redundant front ends (RFEs) in the main control center of the wind farm. Information from or to wind farms is received and delivered via these RFEs. Each airstream area's information is temporarily stowed on the hosts of the relevant RFE and will be rationalised regularly.

Coalitional insurance (Lau, Wang, Liu, Wei, & Ten, 2021) is being offered as a hopeful substitute or addition to the standard assurance strategies that are offered by protection corporations. Susceptibility devices are linked by interacting association in the cyber model. The digital model of organization weakness can be addressed by an assault chart of BN. Probabilistic methods like BN can be used to combine security metrics like TTC and approximation the combined impression of the weaknesses. To sabotage the server that is in charge of an authority organisation substation, the intruder uses the root privilege. To gain access to the privilege via the links, the interloper makes use of services. The proposed structure performs unwavering quality examination representing the digital weakness and evaluations the expenses of TOs in light of dependability worth investigation. Another realistic security appraisal approach is created where digital weakness is assessed by thinking about all plausible nodal courses according to the interloper's viewpoint. The intruder has access to at least one exploit in Process 1. Process 2 indicates that at least one vulnerability has been discovered, but the intruder does not have access to an exploit. In Cycle 3, the gate-crasher looks through new weaknesses since no weakness can be taken advantage of or distinguished by the gate-crasher. Based on the cyber-corporeal system assembly that is susceptible to cyberattack interruption, game-theoretical procedures have been used to dispense the safety possessions or improve potential weight restrictions. SSG is a way to organize security resources hierarchically. Minimal system the portrayal of the SSG can alleviate the computational weight for the safeguard asset assignment.

There are three distinct substation local area networks (Zhang Y., Wang, Xiang, & Ten, 2016) with distinct automation stages, network architectures, and intrusion routes. Through the external VPN, the attacker can access the substation LAN. It is accepted that only one firewall is utilized as the countermeasure of substation LAN 1, pernicious bundles masked as normal parcels might stream into the organization without being distinguished, subsequently, the aggressor can acquire the root honor of the designated host when the substation LAN is effectively meddled. Trip orders will be shipped off the IEDs in substation 1 from the workstation. Countless cyberattacks have been accounted for to influence the SCADA frameworks in the power brace. Command injection attacks have the potential to have an impact on the power system's reliability. The assailants might endeavor to infuse the bogus administrative control orders into the SCADA organization of the power framework. A remote site's physical components can be automatically monitored and controlled by the IEDs and remote terminal units (RTUs). An SMP framework is utilized to validate the specific actions of the assailant to quantify the process of cyberattacks on the power system. The main interaction is connected with the great state, which addresses what is happening in the SCADA framework. The intrusion process into the SCADA method is the second procedure. It consists of states, and each status signifies a stage of the outbreak action.

The research (Stamp, McIntyre, & Ricardson, 2009) will first concentrate on assaults against two popular forms of safety broadcasting—Producer defence and Line guard—for this initial inquiry. A fruitful assault will be exhibited as producing the producer to go offline when its breakers journey based on a convinced connected set of limitations from the C2P connexion. A randomly distributed random variable with an exponential distribution and a few chosen Mean Times to Attack are used to approximate the time between successful attacks. The MTTR for the maker is influenced by the length of time needed for cyber investigation, the turnaround time for restoring the authority framework, and the classification-dependent restart time for the generator. Attacks against line protection will rely on sophisticated relaying, which means that if they are successful, they will cause breakers at both ends of a besieged broadcast line to open, cutting the line off from service. Another MTTA indicates successful attacks on the line at random intervals, and the line is out of service for a while. The Roy Billinton Trial Scheme was employed for the original RICA assessment on reliability issues. In addition to their typical failure and maintenance rates, the reference includes the characteristics of the lines, generators, and loads.

By creating a mathematical method for quantitatively evaluating the probability of accuracy of observations when they are given by sources whose dependability is unclear, the study (Wang, Wang, Su, Kaplan, & Abdelzaher, 2014) seeks to challenge that status quo. The advice is to create a Matlab R2013b crowd-sensing simulator. 200 binary variables with randomly chosen beginning values are constructed for the simulation. Each variable represents a state-containing physical event. To better comprehend the basic performance patterns in our state, the two-state Markov model was taken into consideration. estimator as a purpose of the organisation model's restrictions.

The article (Falahati, Fu, & Wu, 2012) includes the effect of cyber system catastrophes on the dependability of the control system and statistically assesses the dependability of contemporary supremacy arrangements. A novel government charting model is suggested to plot the disappointments in the cyber systems to the problems in the control system. Four different forms of mutuality are outlined. The P-Table gathers data from different system states. Three terms make up a P-Table: index, system state, and probability. The P-Table probability table has been initialized. A shortened P-Table is created by combining equivalent states in the P-Table. State mapping is put into practice to link cyber network problems to power network breakdowns. In the electricity system, load shedding is carried out for probabilistically nonzero situations. The load-shedding values are used to compute dependability indices like LOLP and EENS.

The three key subjects covered by the proposed framework (Vanderhaegen, 2017)are stability analysis of disagreements, disagreement credentials, and dissention authority. In this view, disagreement-focused on constancy investigation entails identifying any scenarios in which humanoid behaviours interact with cyber-physical systems (CPS). Based on the previously described idea of stability applied to human behaviours, it suggests new problems for the CPHS research of human dependability. A submission of these novel approaches to handle the human consistency of a CPHS by considering the incorporation of various CPS into a car is illustrated by a case study based on road transportation. The examination of hominoid steadiness is understood in terms of disagreements, and the positive regulator of these dissentions makes the CPHS strong. The CPHS2's frame of reference incorporates the SCS's usage and operation regulations in addition to the CPHS1's guidelines. Finally, the final CPHS3's frame of reference assumes that the ACC replaces the SCS, has the same usage and operating guidelines as the SCS about the automobile rapidity switch procedure, and has further guidelines specific to obstacle handling. The number of rules or the consistency of the rules might be constancy-shaping criteria to comparison the constancy of the three edges of orientation in human terms.

The proper interconnection and operation of cyber tier machineries enable the cyber sheet purposes (Han, Wen, Guo, & Huang, 2015). The merging unit combines data collection to track the conditions of high-voltage electrical workings and message transmission to the control center over the Ethernet network. It is a crucial component in carrying out the monitoring and protection role. Intelligent Electronic Devices serve as interfaces between the electrical physical layer and the cyber layer. They have sophisticated local control and the capacity to transfer information in both directions. The Ethernet switch connects the devices in the cyber layer and determines the course of data movement inside the cyber tier system by receiving, processing, and transmitting information to the target node using package substituting model. The operational condition of circuit breakers, transformers, generators, and transmission lines is gathered by merging units. IEDs used for control, monitoring, and protection serve as the interface between the physical tier and the cyber slab. To accomplish the cyber layer function, the IEDs simultaneously broadcast downward orders to the physical layer components and upward information to the control center. Each substation's cyber layer components and other Ethernet switches are connected through the Ethernet switch. The cyber layer's connectivity medium is an optical fiber. The cyber layer is separated into two subsystems from a purpose-oriented viewpoint: the protection system and the monitoring system. All of the substation Ethernet adjustments should function for the transfer of data among the authority center and the far-end IED since the Ethernet switches are linked without any loops or redundant components.

Sequential Monte Carlo simulations take into account the distribution feeders' and the upstream substation's sensitivity to CPI (Yuan, Li, Bie, & Arif, 2019). On a test system that has been altered from Bus 2 in RBTS, the case studies are carried out. In a modified RBTS, CBs are introduced, and all physical management shifts are changed out for RCSs. This reduces substituting period to only one minute. Three situations are looked through to show the CPI vulnerability. The CDF in the original RBTS is assessed. Without CDF, updated RBTS is incorporated. Modified RBTS is evaluated by taking CDF into account.

The suggested system (Chhabra, Singh, & Singh, 2018) illustrates how well it can handle problems with data processing and storage utilizing cloud computing. Three modules examine the data flow. The data elicitation module focuses on locating data sources online. The primary logic has the harmful vector analysis module. There are a total of 5 devices in it. The first data node is the principal or name device (Hadoop Master). It helps as a name instrument and a information device for extreme utilization. All of these nodes use HDFS. The network sniffer's data elicitation module produces a pcap file. The code for MapReduce is on HadoopMaster1. The configuration file in the application environment allows the user to reset the settings of the customizable parameters needed for each job following the analysis's requirements. Network traffic that has been sniffed or retrieved via the elicitation module serves as the dataset for the forensics portion of the task. The data are broken into manageable pieces and uploaded to the slave Hadoop nodes. The MapReduce code replicates to these nodes, run on these little data chunks, and the result reduces before being delivered back to the Hadoop Master for output creation as a comma-separated file. The goal is to recognize DDoS assaults, namely the Smurf attack. The layer switch's mirror port links to the university server and the TCPDump sniffing out data at different times and for varying lengths of time for varying amounts and types of network traffic. The second phase of the algorithm transforms the traffic's binary packet header format into a text file format. Java code that reads the pcap file and converts it into a single-line human-readable text file. The targeted packet is then excluded based on the kind of analysis. The Smurf assault involves ICMP flooding attacks, which is the subject of this study. It detects the suspicious packets and their associated origins attempting to launch DDoS or non-DDoS on the targeted server or destination.

It (Ali & Kaur, 2020) protects corporate infrastructure from the BYOD untrusted threat scenario. It is a novel architecture of encryption-based gridlock processing. An application layer firewall does traffic inspection during routing to safeguard the organization from external assault. Any VPN service is any prototypical of traffic having info encoded and a credential host for PKI. It is perfect for a safety structure of MPLS traffic routed via MPLS. There is one gateway for internet traffic leaving the company network. Perimeter firewalls filter traffic, identify harmful behavior, and protect users. Due to the loss of SD-WAN's intended function, it makes SD-WAN implementation difficult.

Figure 1. Merkle tree structure in blockchain
(Chen, Chou, & Chou, 2019)

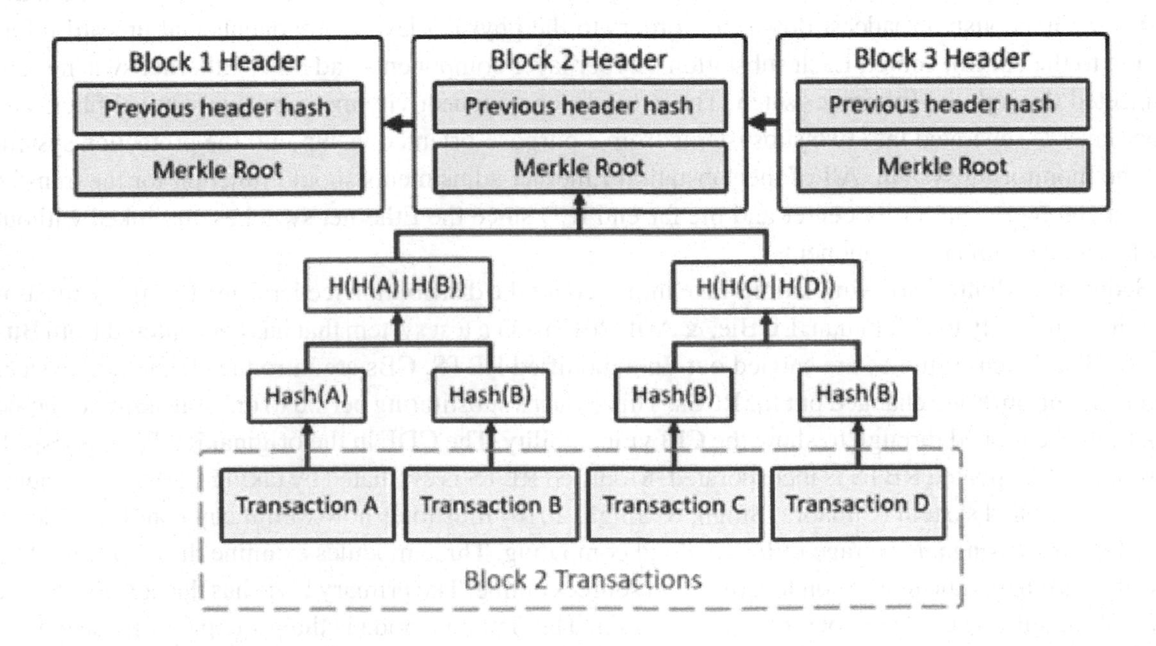

BACKGROUND

The Merkle root for a mass is obtained by hashing two communications together to produce the upper-level tree device and the Merkle root. It will get one muddle to stock that is deterministic in light of the hashes of the multitude of fundamental exchanges. This single hash is known as the Merkle root. In the blockchain (Zheng, Xie, Dai, Chen, & Wang, 2018), each block has a Merkle root put away in the block header. Merkle Tree permits each hub in the organization to confirm individual exchanges without downloading and approving the whole block. In blockchain networks, the transactions in a block are identical if a copy of that block has the same Merkle root as another. Figure 1 portrays the same.

Data collection from materially accessible storing source, such as hard disc drives, has been the focus of digital forensics. While these broadcasting originally posed difficulties for scientific inspectors, today's practitioners are familiar with the knowledge and its recognized file schemes. As a result, digital forensics procedures and several tools have made it possible to automate the collection, authentication, and investigation of digital indication in a workable way. The presence of a padlock signifies encrypted storage. Local storage systems, such as HDDs, SSDs, and RAM, are the simplest technologies used to collect data. When the HDD is not encrypted, plaintext data is there and may be easily assembled and analyzed. When the drive is encrypted (without having a decryption key) the HDD analysis procedure becomes challenging. Further examination of the evidence gathered from the crime scene or the suspect is necessary to locate one or more keys.

The study (Kim & Lee, 2020) examined the Android scheme logs to excerpt a list of the programs installed on smartphones together with information like each consent, ID, and file system path, and then grouped the files related to each app. According to the kind of crime, it determines which applications need, and it chooses all relevant files as possible evidence. It uses user behavior, scanned the app log files, and SQLite databases. It also uses the schema structure, finding user information such as time, location, phone number, and ID from all tables and columns. This system can recognize user information in multiple app logs, making it valuable when criminals employ unidentified applications. Managing prospective evidence comprising client data on application origin represents a new format in evidence management. A timeline analysis may need to cross-examine data from many applications relevant to a suspect's unique behavior to find potential evidence. This format combines file system information with a Merkle-tree hash of each file to manage this possible evidence by grouping these files into a single set. This format maintains data on documents about a suspect's particular deeds. It secures the integrity of the individual acts and files.

The work (Bhandary, Parmar, & Ambawade, 2020) focuses on using Distributed Ledger Technology (DLT) in Cybersecurity. It mainly discusses the characteristics and operation of IOTA, a revolutionary distributed ledger system. A user who issues a transaction also helps to keep the IOTA network secure. A deal is extra to the Jumble with a advanced level of faith if it receives many approvals. Nodes examine whether or not prior transactions contradict before authorizing them. The peer review in the experimental module is known as Masked Authenticated Messaging (MAM). The MAM protocol is a component of the second tier of the info transmission procedure storage. It provides extra functionality for transmitting and gaining access to an encrypted data stream through Tangles. Anytime a user has data to share. It may publish or send a message via the Tangle after completing some proof of work. The receipt arrives at the subscriber node. It tunes into network ID. Every intercept is a single-use, zero-value transaction delivered to a specific address. The work uses the Merkle tree signature algorithm to encrypt and sign each message in the MAM station. The Channel ID of the MAM channel is known as the Merkle tree's root. The system creates a fresh Merkle tree for each new message sent across the station. It contains a reference to the address of the next Merkle tree. This feature enables subscribers to access a single message and locate the station's subsequent future information.

The work (Mahrous, Farouk, & Darwish, 2021)copes with the heterogeneity that arises in an IoT (Ahmad, Rasool, Javed, Baker, & Jalil, 2022) setting. The recommended system offers scientific examination with high degrees of genuineness, traceability, and dispersed sureness across evidentiary entities and inspectors. Fuzzy hash algorithms allow forensic investigators to deal with the legal change of digital evidence. The recommended method uses a one-way hash technique to identify and fingerprint digital evidence. Records fingerprinted added to the blockchain. A complete copy of the evidence blockchain will be available to every participant in the associated blockchain system. It uses digital signatures to create new and upload them to the blockchain. The quick and safe verification of the investigation's TEs uses a Merkle tree. It allows a client to confirm whether or not a deal is encompassed in a mass by aggregating all TEs, looking over other information in a block, and creating a digital sign for the entire assembly of items. Transactional indication or its confusion text processes until its collections into a solitary root muddle. The users can seamlessly communicate information, data, and business operations (without an intermediary). On the decentralized ledger, clever agreements may implement, validate, and create choices autonomously in a safe and immutable way. It starts when a node gets transaction evidence; it then computes the nonce using Proof of Work agreement and communicates it to the blockchain system; finally, it builds a Merkle tree based on the legitimacy of earlier blocks. Inside the Merkle tree, a uncertain muddle of each preceding block is used, and if it is lawful, the node will upload the novel mass to the live blockchain as a file.

PROPOSED WORK

The proposed security structure (Rahman, Khalil, & Atiquzzaman, 2021) for primary industry 4.0 CPS chips away at four distinct levels, where detector and savvy control gadgets effort in the actual space with association Blockchain organization (Ambika N., 2021) (Nagaraj A., 2022). Given the 4 degrees of correspondence, the functioning standard works in three different center stages. The machine sensors get enlisted and layout correspondence utilizing a BC-based MS strategy. Besides, the enlisted detectors submit details to the BC organization abstract to be confirmed by the BC confederation. The information is put away in the DHT (circulated hash table) after documenting the sign into the BC record. The system uses edge calculation rather than distributed computing. It uses a unique certificateless authentication method based on the multi-signature scheme to guarantee safety. Software, and physical components comprise the cyber-physical system. Each piece installations on various time-based and three-dimensional stages and constantly interacts with other members. The framework eliminates the centralized trust model, i.e., the dependence on a single PKI credential expert for community credential, installations over associated syndicate, and uses smart-edge computation. Different Industry partners cooperatively confirm both the gadget's character and information. This feature eliminates the single point of failure, increases trust, and protects data from forgery. It verifies and records device registration and communication activities within the restricted channel in a transparent ledger. In the consortium agreement convention, the pioneer proposes the following block that essentially lowers the prize expenses. It prevents malfunctions by reducing the impact of potentially malevolent aristocracies. It agrees to a new business without requiring various authorisations, eliminating the need for a waiting period after each block addition. It adjusts, putting away information at the conveyed hash table.

Drawback

Multi-key authentication happens in the previous work. The system integrates MS to expand trust and unwavering quality and handle restrictive costs as far as possible the business 4.0 CPS advances. The four participants include insurer, owner, operator and buyer. The consumption of energy increases when more than one authenticator involves in authentication procedure. Table 1 denotes notation used in the suggestion.

Table 1. Notations used in the suggestion

Notations used in the work	Description
N	Network under consideration
B_i	Buyer
O_I	Owner
I_i	Insurer
P_i	Operator
ID_i	Identification
L_i	Location information
H_i	Hash key

The recommendation includes endorsement. For every session the respective entities generate endorsement keys of all the necessary parties using Merkle tree to increase data integrity. At the beginning of the transaction procedure, the parties transmit their identity and location information to other three parties. In equation (1), the buyer B_i is sharing its identity ID_i and location information L_i with the owner O_I.

$$B_i \rightarrow O_i: ID_i \parallel L_i \quad (1)$$

Using this information, the hash key is generated. This hash key is used to authenticate the parties in communication. For every session, a new hash key is generated using Merkle tree and same it attached to the blockchain. Table 2 represents the generation of hash key.

Table 2. Generation of hash key

Step 1- Input identity (24 bits * 4 parties) and location information (32 bits * 4 parties) of all the stockholders
Step 2 – Divide identity bits into 3 bits in a group (8 groups *4 parties) and location information into 4 bits in a group (8 groups * 4 parties)
Step 3 – Merge 3 bits of identification and 4 bits of location information (32 groups)
Step 4 – Apply alternatively right and left shifts on the groups (16 groups will undergo right shifts and 16 groups will undergo left shifts)
Step 5 - Xor right shift groups with left shift groups (resultant has 16 groups * 7 bits)

ANALYSIS OF THE WORK

The proposed security structure (Rahman, Khalil, & Atiquzzaman, 2021) for primary industry 4.0 CPS chips away at four distinct levels, where detector and savvy control gadgets effort in the actual space with association Blockchain organization (Vranken, 2017). Given the 4 degrees of correspondence, the functioning standard works in three different center stages. The machine sensors get enlisted and layout correspondence utilizing a BC-based MS strategy. Besides, the enlisted detectors submit details to the BC organization abstract to be confirmed by the BC confederation. The information is put away in the DHT (circulated hash table) after documenting the sign into the BC record. The system uses edge calculation rather than distributed computing. It uses a unique certificateless authentication method based on the multi-signature scheme to guarantee safety. Software, and physical components comprise the cyber-physical system. Each piece installations on various time-based and three-dimensional stages and constantly interacts with other members. The framework eliminates the centralized trust model, i.e., the dependence on a single PKI credential expert for community credential, installations over associated syndicate, and uses smart-edge computation. Different Industry partners cooperatively confirm both the gadget's character and information. This feature eliminates the single point of failure, increases trust, and protects data from forgery. It verifies and records device registration and communication activities within the restricted channel in a transparent ledger. In the consortium agreement convention, the pioneer proposes the following block that essentially lowers the prize expenses. It prevents malfunctions by reducing the impact of potentially malevolent aristocracies. It agrees to a new business without requiring various authorisations, eliminating the need for a waiting period after each block addition. It adjusts, putting away information at the conveyed hash table.

The previous work aims to provide multi-signature of various stockholders. Using this methodology, the energy of the system gets drained. The recommendation includes endorsement. For every session the respective entities generate endorsement keys of all the necessary parties using Merkle tree to increase data integrity. The parties exchange their identity and location information to help generate the hash key and embed it to the blockchain. This helps in evaluating their identity.

The work is simulated using NS2. Table 3 represents the parameters used in the simulation.

Table 3. Parameters used in the simulation

Parameters used in simulation	*Description*
Dimension of the network	*200m * 200m*
No of devices installed	*7 (3 buyers, 1 operator, 1 insurer, 2 owner)*
Length of identification	*24 bits*
Length of location information	*32 bits*
Length of Derived hash key	*112 bits*
Length of information	*256 bits*
Simulation time	*60 m*

Reliability

The suggestion improves reliability of the system by embedding endorsement key of all the stockholders. This work increases trust by 4.17% compared to previous work. Figure 2 portrays the same.

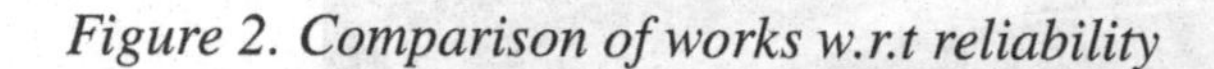

Figure 2. Comparison of works w.r.t reliability

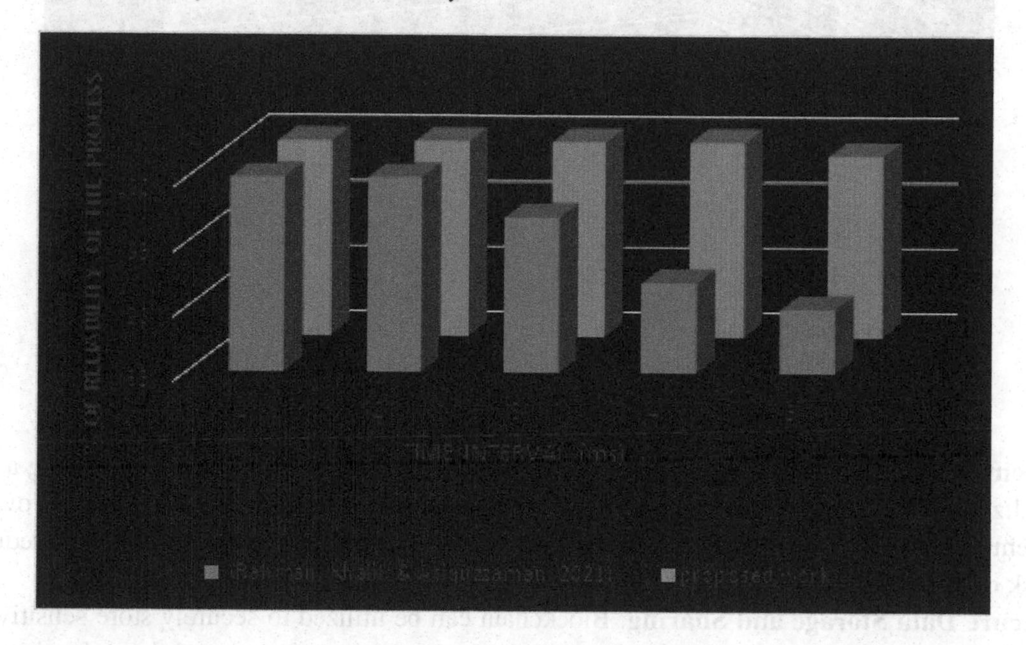

Energy Conservation

The suggestion reduces energy consumption of the system by avoiding multi-signature of various stockholders. It endorses hash key of identity and location information. The suggestion conserves energy by 12.5%. figure 3 portrays the same.

APPLICATIONS

Cybersecurity and blockchain are two rapidly evolving technologies that intersect in various ways to enhance security and trust in digital transactions and data management. Blockchain technology can be employed to bolster cybersecurity measures in several applications.

- **Immutable Record-keeping and Audit Trails**: Blockchain's fundamental feature is its immutability, ensuring that once data is recorded, it cannot be altered or deleted. This property is valuable for creating secure and tamper-proof audit trails, making it an excellent tool for cybersecurity. In cybersecurity applications, blockchain can be used to record all transactions, access attempts, or changes to critical systems, providing a transparent and unchangeable record.

Figure 3. Energy consumption in works under consideration

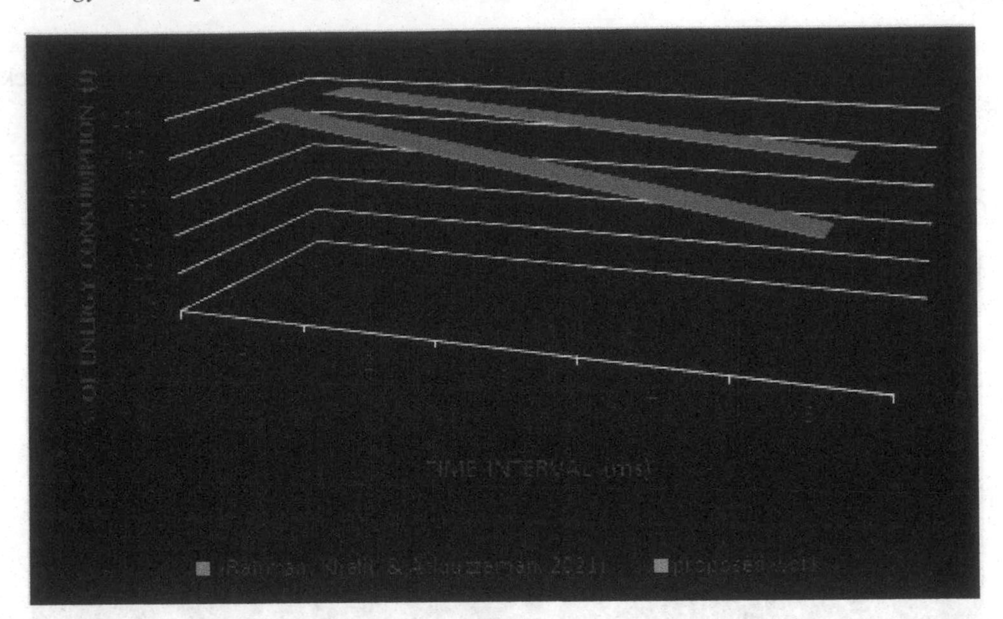

- **Identity and Access Management (IAM)**: Blockchain can enhance IAM by providing a decentralized, secure, and interoperable identity management system. Users can have control over their identities, and access permissions can be managed through smart contracts. This can reduce the risk of identity theft and unauthorized access.
- **Secure Data Storage and Sharing**: Blockchain can be utilized to securely store sensitive data. Encrypted data can be stored on the blockchain, and access can be granted through private keys. This ensures data integrity and confidentiality while allowing authorized users to access the data.
- **Supply Chain Security and Traceability**: Blockchain can be used to enhance supply chain security by enabling a tamper-proof and transparent record of transactions and events related to the supply chain. This can help in verifying the authenticity and integrity of products, minimizing counterfeiting, and ensuring the security of supply chains.
- **Smart Contracts for Secure Transactions**: Smart contracts on blockchain platforms can automate and secure transactions by executing predefined rules in a transparent and tamper-proof manner. This is particularly useful in financial transactions, legal agreements, and other areas where secure and automated processes are required.
- **Decentralized Authentication and Authorization**: Blockchain can provide a decentralized authentication and authorization system, reducing the reliance on centralized authentication providers. This enhances security by reducing the risk of a single point of failure and mitigates the risk of unauthorized access.
- **Incident Response and Forensics**: Blockchain can assist in incident response and digital forensics by providing a secure and immutable record of events and actions. This can aid in investigating and understanding cyber incidents, tracking their origin, and facilitating appropriate responses and countermeasures.
- **Decentralized DNS and DDoS Mitigation**: Blockchain can be used to create a decentralized Domain Name System (DNS) to mitigate distributed denial-of-service (DDoS) attacks. By dis-

tributing the DNS across a blockchain network, it becomes resistant to DDoS attacks and provides enhanced security and uptime.

- **Vulnerability Assessment and Patch Management**: Blockchain can be leveraged for securely managing vulnerability information and patches. By using blockchain, organizations can securely and transparently track vulnerabilities and patching processes, ensuring efficient vulnerability management.
- **Cyber Threat Intelligence Sharing**: Blockchain can facilitate secure and anonymized sharing of cyber threat intelligence among organizations, enabling collective defense against cyber threats. It allows for the secure sharing of threat indicators while maintaining the privacy and security of the shared information.

Integrating blockchain into cybersecurity measures requires careful planning, understanding of both technologies and consideration of specific use cases and organizational needs. While blockchain offers promising solutions to enhance cybersecurity, it's essential to evaluate its applicability and potential benefits for each use case.

CHALLENGES

The integration of cybersecurity and blockchain presents unique challenges that need to be addressed to fully leverage the potential of this technology in enhancing security. Here are some key challenges associated with combining cybersecurity and blockchain:

- **Scalability**: Blockchain networks face scalability challenges as they grow in size and transaction volume. As more transactions occur, the network can become slower and less efficient, impacting its ability to handle real-time security events effectively.
- **Energy Consumption**: Many blockchain networks, especially proof-of-work-based ones like Bitcoin, consume a significant energy. It contributes to environmental concerns but also increases operational costs and limits the scalability of blockchain solutions.
- **Integration with Legacy Systems**: Integrating blockchain with existing legacy systems and infrastructure is a complex task. Ensuring compatibility, data migration, and smooth integration without disrupting existing operations poses a significant challenge.
- **Interoperability**: Different blockchain platforms may have varying protocols, standards, and consensus mechanisms, making interoperability between them difficult. Establishing seamless communication and data exchange across diverse blockchain networks is a pressing challenge.
- **Regulatory Compliance**: The evolving and varying regulatory landscape for blockchain and cybersecurity creates compliance challenges. Navigating these regulations while ensuring data security and privacy is a complex task for organizations.
- **Privacy and Data Protection**: While blockchain provides transparency and immutability, it inherently lacks privacy features. Storing sensitive or personally identifiable information on a public blockchain poses a risk to privacy, necessitating solutions for secure data storage and sharing.
- **Quantum Computing Threats**: The rise of quantum computing threatens current cryptographic algorithms used in blockchain, potentially compromising security. Developing quantum-resistant algorithms is crucial to ensure long-term security.

- **Smart Contract Security**: Smart contracts are susceptible to vulnerabilities and exploits. Flaws in code can lead to financial losses and security breaches. Ensuring secure coding practices, rigorous testing, and auditing of smart contracts are critical.
- **Identity Management and Authentication**: Managing identities and ensuring secure authentication within a decentralized and trustless blockchain environment is challenging. Striking a balance between user privacy and robust identity verification is an ongoing concern.
- **51% Attacks and Centralization Risks**: Public blockchains can face the risk of 51% attacks where an entity gains majority control over the network's mining power, potentially undermining the security and integrity of the blockchain. Centralization risks also arise from dominant mining entities.
- **Human Error and Governance**: Human error, including accidental loss of private keys or incorrect implementation of security measures, can lead to significant security breaches. Additionally, establishing effective governance models within decentralized networks remains a challenge.

Addressing these challenges requires collaborative efforts from the blockchain and cybersecurity communities. Ongoing research, innovation, regulatory clarity, and the development of best practices will be essential in overcoming these hurdles and unlocking the full potential of blockchain technology in the realm of cybersecurity.

FUTURE SCOPE

The recommendation includes endorsement. For every session the respective entities generate endorsement keys of all the necessary parties using Merkle tree to increase data integrity. The parties exchange their identity and location information to help generate the hash key and embed it to the blockchain. This helps in evaluating their identity. The suggestion adds more reliability to the transaction by 4.17%. The suggestion conserves energy by 12.5%. The intermediate devices have summary of the transactions. If the sender or the receiver losses data, backup has to be taken care.

The intersection of cybersecurity and blockchain technology holds significant potential for the future, offering improved security, transparency, and trust in various applications. Here are some crucial aspects of how these two fields may evolve and merge in the future:

- **Enhanced Data Security**: Blockchain's decentralized and immutable nature can enhance data security (Zhu, Saravanan, & Muthu, 2020) by providing a tamper-proof and transparent ledger. It can be especially critical in sectors - healthcare, finance, and government where data integrity and security are paramount.
- **Decentralized Identity and Access Management**: Blockchain (Belchior, et al., 2020) can facilitate decentralized identity management, controlling their digital identities and personal data. It can improve security by reducing reliance on centralized entities and minimizing the risk of data breaches.
- **Smart Contract Security**: Improving the security of smart contracts, (DeCusatis, et al., 2023) self-executing contracts with the terms of the agreement between the buyer and the seller directly written into code. Future advancements will focus on auditing, formal verification, and secure coding practices to minimize vulnerabilities and potential exploits.

- **Secure Supply Chains and IoT Integration**: Combining blockchain with IoT (Internet of Things) can ensure secure and transparent supply chains. It is particularly relevant in industries such as manufacturing, agriculture, and logistics, where tracking and verifying the origin and journey of products is crucial for safety and quality.
- **Decentralized Threat Intelligence and Sharing**: Blockchain can facilitate secure and anonymous sharing of threat intelligence among organizations, enabling a collaborative approach to identifying and mitigating cybersecurity threats. This decentralized threat intelligence network can enhance overall cybersecurity measures.
- **Privacy-Preserving Solutions**: Advancements in zero-knowledge proofs and privacy-focused blockchains are anticipated. These technologies will allow for private transactions and data sharing while still leveraging the benefits of blockchain, which is essential for compliance with privacy regulations.
- **Quantum-Resistant Blockchain**: As quantum computing advances, it is a threat to current cryptographic algorithms used in blockchain. Future blockchain implementations adopt quantum-resistant cryptographic algorithms to ensure long-term security against potential quantum attacks.
- **Interoperability and Scalability**: Future blockchain solutions will improve interoperability between different blockchains and scale to handle a higher transaction volume. It will facilitate the integration of blockchain into various sectors without compromising performance.
- **Education and Skill Development**: Education and skill development will be a critical component of the future of cybersecurity and blockchain. Professionals enhance their knowledge and expertise in both domains to effectively navigate the evolving landscape and address emerging challenges.
- **Regulatory Adaptations**: Governments and regulatory bodies will need to adapt and formulate regulations that balance innovation with security and privacy in the context of blockchain. Striking the right balance will be crucial for widespread adoption and integration into various industries.

In summary, the future of cybersecurity and blockchain will likely involve a convergence of technologies, focused on enhancing security, privacy, and efficiency across various sectors. As these technologies continue to evolve, it's essential to prioritize responsible development and implementation to ensure a more secure and trusted digital future.

CONCLUSION

The previous security structure is primary industry 4.0 CPS chips away at four distinct levels, where detector and savvy control gadgets effort in the actual space with association Blockchain organization. Given the 4 degrees of correspondence, the functioning standard works in three different center stages. The machine sensors get enlisted and layout correspondence utilizing a BC-based MS strategy. Besides, the enlisted detectors submit details to the BC organization abstract to be confirmed by the BC confederation. The information is put away in the DHT (circulated hash table) after documenting the sign into the BC record. The system uses edge calculation rather than distributed computing. It uses a unique certificateless authentication method based on the multi-signature scheme to guarantee safety. Software, and physical components comprise the cyber-physical system. Each piece installations on various time-based and three-dimensional stages and constantly interacts with other members. The framework eliminates the centralized trust model, i.e., the dependence on a single PKI credential expert for community credential, installations over associated syndicate, and uses smart-edge computation. Different Industry partners cooperatively confirm both the gadget's character and information. This feature eliminates the single point of failure, increases trust, and protects data from forgery. It verifies and records device registration and communication activities within the restricted channel in a transparent ledger. In the consortium agreement convention, the pioneer proposes the following block that essentially lowers the prize expenses. It prevents malfunctions by reducing the impact of potentially malevolent aristocracies. It agrees to a new business without requiring various authorisations, eliminating the need for a waiting period after each block addition. It adjusts, putting away information at the conveyed hash table.

The recommendation includes endorsement. For every session the respective entities generate endorsement keys of all the necessary parties using Merkle tree to increase data integrity. The parties exchange their identity and location information to help generate the hash key and embed it to the blockchain. This helps in evaluating their identity. The suggestion adds more reliability to the transaction by 4.17%. The suggestion conserves energy by 12.5%.

REFERENCES

Ahmad, W., Rasool, A., Javed, A., Baker, T., & Jalil, Z. (2022). Cyber Security in IoT-Based Cloud Computing: A Comprehensive Survey. *Electronics (Basel)*, *11*(1), 16. doi:10.3390/electronics11010016

Ali, M. D., & Kaur, D. S. (2020). Byod cyber forensic eco-system. [IJARET]. *International Journal of Advanced Research in Engineering and Technology*, *11*(9).

Ambika, N. (2020). Improved Methodology to Detect Advanced Persistent Threat Attacks. In N. K. Chaubey & B. B. Prajapati (Eds.), *Quantum Cryptography and the Future of Cyber Security* (pp. 184–202). IGI Global. doi:10.4018/978-1-7998-2253-0.ch009

Ambika, N. (2021). A Reliable Blockchain-Based Image Encryption Scheme for IIoT Networks. In *Blockchain and AI Technology in the Industrial Internet of Things* (pp. 81–97). IGI Global.

Bhandary, M., Parmar, M., & Ambawade, D. (2020). Securing logs of a system-an iota tangle use case. *International Conference on Electronics and Sustainable Communication Systems (ICESC)* (pp. 697-702). Coimbatore, India: IEEE. 10.1109/ICESC48915.2020.9155563

Chen, Y.-C., Chou, Y.-P., & Chou, Y.-C. (2019). An Image Authentication Scheme Using Merkle Tree Mechanisms. *Future Internet*, *11*(7), 149. doi:10.3390/fi11070149

Chhabra, G. S., Singh, V., & Singh, M. (2018). Hadoop-based analytic framework for cyber forensics. *International Journal of Communication Systems*, *31*(15), e3772. doi:10.1002/dac.3772

Fachkha, C., & Debbabi, M. (2015). Darknet as a source of cyber intelligence: Survey, taxonomy, and characterization. *IEEE Communications Surveys and Tutorials*, *18*(2), 1197–1227. doi:10.1109/COMST.2015.2497690

Falahati, B., Fu, Y., & Wu, L. (2012). Reliability assessment of smart grid considering direct cyber-power interdependencies. *IEEE Transactions on Smart Grid*, *3*(3), 1515–1524. doi:10.1109/TSG.2012.2194520

Han, Y., Wen, Y., Guo, C., & Huang, H. (2015). Incorporating Cyber Layer Failures in Composite Power System Reliability Evaluations. *Energies*, *8*(9), 9064–9086. doi:10.3390/en8099064

Kim, D., & Lee, S. (2020). Study of identifying and managing the potential evidence for effective Android forensics. *Forensic Science International: Digital Investigation*, *33*, 200897.

Lau, P., Wang, L., Liu, Z., Wei, W., & Ten, C. W. (2021). A coalitional cyber-insurance design considering power system reliability and cyber vulnerability. *IEEE Transactions on Power Systems*, *36*(6), 5512–5524. doi:10.1109/TPWRS.2021.3078730

Mahrous, W. A., Farouk, M., & Darwish, S. M. (2021). An enhanced blockchain-based IoT digital forensics architecture using fuzzy hash. *IEEE Access : Practical Innovations, Open Solutions*, *9*, 151327–151336. doi:10.1109/ACCESS.2021.3126715

Mitchell, R., & Chen, R. (2013). Effect of intrusion detection and response on reliability of cyber physical systems. *IEEE Transactions on Reliability*, *62*(1), 199–210. doi:10.1109/TR.2013.2240891

Nagaraj, A. (2021). *Introduction to Sensors in IoT and Cloud Computing Applications*. Bentham Science Publishers. doi:10.2174/97898114793591210101

Nagaraj, A. (2022). Adapting Blockchain for Energy Constrained IoT in Healthcare Environment. In K. Kaushik, S. Tayal, S. Dahiya, & A. O. Salau (Eds.), *Sustainable and Advanced Applications of Blockchain in Smart Computational Technologies* (p. 103). CRC press. doi:10.1201/9781003193425-7

Rahman, Z., Khalil, I. Y., & Atiquzzaman, M. (2021). Blockchain-based security framework for a critical industry 4.0 cyber-physical system. *IEEE Communications Magazine*, *59*(5), 128–134. doi:10.1109/MCOM.001.2000679

Sridhar, S., Hahn, A., & Govindarasu, M. (2011). Cyber–physical system security for the electric power grid. [IEEE.]. *Proceedings of the IEEE*, *100*(1), 210–224. doi:10.1109/JPROC.2011.2165269

Stamp, J., McIntyre, A., & Ricardson, B. (2009). *Reliability impacts from cyber attack on electric power systems. IEEE/PES Power Systems Conference and Exposition*. IEEE.

Vanderhaegen, F. (2017). Towards increased systems resilience: New challenges based on dissonance control for human reliability in Cyber-Physical&Human Systems. *Annual Reviews in Control*, *44*, 316–322. doi:10.1016/j.arcontrol.2017.09.008

Vranken, H. (2017). Sustainability of bitcoin and blockchains. *Current Opinion in Environmental Sustainability*, *28*, 1–9. doi:10.1016/j.cosust.2017.04.011

Wang, S., Wang, D., Su, L., Kaplan, L., & Abdelzaher, T. F. (2014). Towards cyber-physical systems in social spaces: The data reliability challenge. *IEEE Real-Time Systems Symposium* (pp. 74-85). Rome, Italy: IEEE. 10.1109/RTSS.2014.19

Zhang, Y., Wang, L., Xiang, Y., & Ten, C. W. (2015). Power system reliability evaluation with SCADA cybersecurity considerations. *IEEE Transactions on Smart Grid*, *6*(4), 1707–1721.

Zhang, Y., Wang, L., Xiang, Y., & Ten, C. W. (2016). Inclusion of SCADA cyber vulnerability in power system reliability assessment considering optimal resources allocation. *IEEE Transactions on Power Systems*, *31*(6), 4379–4394. doi:10.1109/TPWRS.2015.2510626

Zhang, Y., Xiang, Y., & Wang, L. (2016). Power system reliability assessment incorporating cyber attacks against wind farm energy management systems. *IEEE Transactions on Smart Grid*, *8*(5), 2343–2357. doi:10.1109/TSG.2016.2523515

Zheng, Z., Xie, S., Dai, H. N., Chen, X., & Wang, H. (2018). Blockchain challenges and opportunities: A survey. *International Journal of Web and Grid Services*, *14*(4), 352–375. doi:10.1504/IJWGS.2018.095647

Chapter 9
Fog Computing and Blockchain-Based IoMT for Personalized Healthcare

Jay Prakash Maurya
https://orcid.org/0000-0002-5574-5822
VIT Bhopal University, Sehore, India

Manoj Kumar
VIT Bhopal University, Sehore, India

Vinesh Kumar
VIT Bhopal University, Sehore, India

ABSTRACT

The Covid-19 pandemic has accelerated the rise of medical devices and applications, collecting, monitoring, and analyzing valuable healthcare data. The internet of medical things (IoMT) has been used to improve the accuracy, dependability, and efficiency of electronic instruments in healthcare. IoMT can connect real-world objects for information sharing and communication. However, challenges in IoT equipment communication, security, and framework development remain. FOG computing and blockchain technologies can support better-personalized systems, but they also present challenges in developing cost-effective and enhanced treatment quality. The healthcare industry must continue to improve the accuracy, reliability, and efficiency of electronic instruments to ensure patient care during the pandemic.

1. INTRODUCTION

The medical sector has Internet of Things (IoT) technology, which offers creative options for individual treatment. Healthcare practitioners can now track patients' medical histories, diagnose and treat illnesses, and monitor their health in real time thanks to IoT-based medical devices. Many different medical applications, including telemedicine, remote patient monitoring (Kadhim et al., 2020), medical imaging,

DOI: 10.4018/979-8-3693-2081-5.ch009

and preventative healthcare, utilize IoT-based medical devices (Dwivedi et al., 2021). These technologies are enabling healthcare professionals to give their patients more personalized and precise care (Alam et al., 2022). IoT-based medical devices offer a safe, dependable, and efficient way to manage patient data, enabling healthcare professionals to analyze and interpret information more precisely. These innovations can also save operating expenses, boost patient outcomes, and raise the standard of care. We may anticipate more cutting-edge approaches for personalized healthcare in the future to IoT-based medical devices. Personalized healthcare and better patient outcomes are now possible due to recent advancements in IoT-based medical equipment. For instance, networked medical equipment can support patient health monitoring and offer real-time information on vital signs like blood pressure, heart rate, and temperature. Then, this information can be utilized to identify illnesses and offer personalized therapies.

Additionally, wearable technology like smartwatches and fitness trackers can be used to measure a patient's physical activity and can share individual feedback. With the use of this information, patients can be suggested for individual diet and activity that will keep them healthy and active. Last but not least, connected medical devices can provide remote patient monitoring, enabling medical professionals to monitor a patient's health from a distance and take action as needed. For old people or elderly people with chronic illnesses who may not be able to frequently visit a doctor's office, this can be extremely helpful. In general, IoT-based medical gadgets share healthcare diagnosis data and deliver more effective, care to patients (Pradhan et al., 2021). There are a few examples that are closely related to IoMT (Internet of Medical Things).

1. Wearable Sensors: Vital indicators like heart rate, blood pressure, and temperature are tracked via wearable sensors. They can also be used to gauge stress levels, exercise levels, and other aspects of health.
2. Smartphones and Smart Watches: Steps done, calories burned, and other fitness indicators can be tracked and monitored using smartphones and smartwatches.
3. Smart Pill Boxes: To help people remember to take their drugs on time and in the right dosage, smart pill boxes are used. They can be linked to an application that enables users to schedule reminders and get alerts when it's time to take their prescription.
4. Smart Scales: Smart scales are used to assess changes in body weight and composition and to measure body composition.
5. Smart Blood Pressure Cuffs: Real-time measurements and monitoring of blood pressure are done with the aid of smart blood pressure cuffs. They can be used to monitor blood pressure trends over time and notify consumers of any changes.
6. Smart Inhalers: Smart inhalers are used to monitor the usage of inhalers and to provide feedback on how well the user is using them.
7. Smart Contact Lenses: Smart contact lenses are used to monitor glucose levels in the body and alert the user to any changes.
8. Smart Thermometers: Smart thermometers are used to measure body temperature and alert the user to any changes.

1.1 Personalized Healthcare

A recent development that is gaining popularity is personalized healthcare. The main goal of this kind of healthcare is to cater treatments and care to the unique requirements of every patient. This may involve things like individual medication recommendations, specialized workout advice, and even specially prepared meals. The advantages of personalized treatment are numerous. Patients may feel more in charge of their health as a result, first. Better health results may result from their increased knowledge of their bodies and how to effectively care for them. Second, personalized healthcare may be less expensive than the standard treatment. It can be customized to meet the unique requirements of each patient, which can cut down on the quantity of medical care required.

There are numerous ways to obtain individualized medical care. Patients can first discuss their specific needs with their doctor or other healthcare providers. Second, patients can learn more about their health and the best ways to care for it by using online resources. Third, patients can monitor their health using smartphone applications or other technology and change their lifestyles as necessary.

Personalized healthcare is growing in popularity, and there are many benefits to using it. Patients can feel more in control of their health and get affordable and tailored care.

1. Personalised healthcare is a branch of medicine that focuses on the needs and preferences of every patient. It makes use of personalized data to offer recommendations and therapies that are customized to meet the distinctive needs of each person. As opposed to the more conventional "one-size-fits-all" approach to care, this method enables a more individualized and complete approach to healthcare.
2. To build a complete picture of each patient's health, personalized healthcare uses several data sources, including electronic health records, genomic data, lifestyle data, and more. Personalized therapies and recommendations that are catered to the needs of the individual are then developed using this data.
3. Improved health outcomes, lower healthcare costs, and higher patient satisfaction are all advantages of personalized healthcare. Personalized healthcare can deliver more targeted therapies that are better suited to each patient's particular health needs by concentrating on individual wants and preferences. Additionally, by increasing the efficacy of treatments and reducing the need for pointless tests or treatments, personalized healthcare can aid in lowering healthcare expenses.
4. With the use of technology like virtual reality, augmented reality, and artificial intelligence to deliver more specialized and thorough care, the future of personalized healthcare will feature more integrated and personalized patient care. Additionally, healthcare professionals will be able to identify health risks more precisely and make more educated recommendations thanks to the use of analytics, predictive method, and machine learning.

A potent technology that can be applied to personalized healthcare is the Internet of Medical Things (IoMT), which enables the delivery of individualized patient care. IoMT can assist medical professionals in tailoring diagnoses, therapies, and drugs to each patient's specific need. IoMT can also empower patients to keep track of their health and manage it more actively. IoMT can also give healthcare professionals real-time data so they may make decisions based on the most recent information (Sharma, 2019; Singh et al., 2020). This can lower medical errors and raise the standard of healthcare as a whole. IoMT can also save money for healthcare providers by lowering the cost of care and enhancing patient outcomes.

1.2 Recent Development

Recent advancements in the field of IOMT include robotic-assisted minimally invasive surgery development, 3D printing for quick fabrication of surgical equipment and implants, and the application of artificial intelligence (Aljabr & Kumar, 2022) and machine learning to diagnose patients more accurately and improve patient outcomes (Meola, n.d.). Additionally, the use of wearable technology for tracking patient activity and health as well as the use of virtual reality for pre-operative training are also growing in popularity (Dwivedi et al., 2021).

A field in the healthcare industry that is quickly growing is the Internet of Medical Things (IoMT). It links medical equipment and systems using wireless technologies like Wi-Fi, Bluetooth, and radio-frequency identification (RFID). IoMT can be used in a variety of healthcare settings, including remote patient monitoring and medical imaging. Additionally, it can be applied to telemedicine, diagnostics, and drug delivery. By gathering and analyzing data from linked medical devices, IoMT technologies also help healthcare providers improve patient outcomes. Additionally, by automating tedious processes and cutting down on time spent on administrative tasks, IoMT can assist in lowering costs and increase efficiency in the delivery of healthcare. IoMT applications include home health monitoring and wearable medical devices, systems, medical imaging devices, and drug delivery systems (Meola,). Different technology used in the field of IoMT:

1. Wearable Sensors: Wearable sensors are used to track and monitor vital signs, such as heart rate and blood pressure.
2. NFC Technology: Near-field communication (NFC) technology is used for secure data exchange between medical devices and smartphones.
3. Cloud Computing: Cloud computing is used to store and analyze large volumes of medical data.
4. Artificial Intelligence: Artificial intelligence (AI) is used to analyze medical data and provide insights to healthcare providers (Da Xu et al., 2021).
5. Augmented and Virtual Reality: Augmented and virtual reality are used to provide training and education to medical professionals.
6. Robotics: Robotics is used to automate certain medical procedures and improve accuracy.
7. 5G Networks: 5G networks are used to provide faster and more reliable connectivity between medical devices.

2. LITERATURE REVIEW

1. **According to Kamarajugadda et al.** The BBO-SVM model is used in the research to present an IoMT-based healthcare diagnosis model for heart disease prediction. The suggested model uses the BBO technique for SVM parameter tweaking. The suggested BBO-SVM model has demonstrated good performance (Kamarajugadda et al., 2021). The article concludes that the model employed in the proposed IoMT-based healthcare diagnosis model can accurately predict cardiac disease.
2. **According to Tai et al.** A reliable and knowledgeable COVID-19 diagnostic IoMT (Internet of Medical Things) is proposed in the study using XR (Extended Reality) and DNNs (Deep Neural Networks). To learn a new COVID-19 prediction model, the authors created a revolutionary, customized, ACGAN-based intelligent prediction algorithm. To improve human ergonomics performance,

the authors visualized every navigational cue from their Haptic-AR guidance system. The authors used deep learning for the remote surgical plan cues and COVID-19 IoMT prediction, which may offer a fresh approach to COVID-19 therapy.

3. **As per Alsuhibany A et al .** An Ensemble of Deep Learning Clinical Decision Support Systems (EDL-CDSS) for the diagnosis of chronic kidney disease in the context of the Internet of Things (IoT) (CKD Data collection, preprocessing, outlier detection, ensemble classification, and hyper-parameter tweaking can be a methodology (Awaisi et al., 2020). According to the study's findings, the suggested EDL-CDSS technique performs better than current methods for CKD diagnosis and can be utilized as a useful tool for CKD diagnosis. The proposed approach can also be used to predict future cases of other illnesses including diabetes and heart disease.
4. **Villegas et al. suggested** a framework for creating secure and sustainable Internet of Medical Things (IoMT) solutions to address the problems with safety and sustainability in the medical sector. The framework was put to the test in a case study where an IoMT system was installed in a private medical office to monitor patients' vital signs even when they weren't there. A case study at a private medical institution where an IoMT system was installed to monitor patients' vital signs even when they weren't there put the model to the test. The study also emphasizes how IoMT may enhance patient care and illness prevention. However, some drawbacks were noted, including the need for a more concerted effort to educate patients on how to utilize the system and the dearth of long-term statistics on the frequency with which health issues discovered by the system are resolved. Future work will examine new data analysis methods to increase the precision of identifying health issues, conduct a longitudinal study to assess the long-term effectiveness of the IoMT system in enhancing patient care and disease prevention and take into account interface changes to improve user experience and boost patient acceptance of the system.
5. **Aljabr et al.** concluded that In order to manage pandemic circumstances, the article advises using an end-to-end Internet of Medical Things (IoMT) enabled architecture This architecture may accommodate pandemic control requirements in a variety of indoor and outdoor settings. The proposed paradigm enhances patient participation in real-time medical observation and judgment, facilitating real-time treatment in emergencies. It also encourages interaction between people and the IoMT system. By lowering follow-up visits, the architecture can lower morbidity and the associated financial burden. The response time will be accelerated in the event of a medical emergency. The recommended design can provide end-to-end social distancing while delivering necessary supplies and assist citizens, the government, and medical experts in better-managing pandemics.
6. **Selvaraj, S et al.** concluded that the Internet of Things (IoT) can effectively provide emergency services and monitor patients from remote locations, especially cardiac patients. The paper's goal is to examine several research initiatives connected to the Internet of Things-based healthcare system. The majority of current research is effective at tracking patients and sending information to the monitoring center. The ECG monitoring system is discussed in the study, which can quickly detect illness signs using machine learning techniques. The IoT-based healthcare system's performance is also examined in the report, along with its benefits and drawbacks High power consumption, a lack of resources, and security concerns brought on by the use of several devices are the main drawbacks of the current systems.
7. **Aljabr et al.** said that to manage pandemic circumstances, the report recommends using an end-to-end Internet of Medical Things (IoMT) enabled architecture. This architecture may accommodate pandemic control requirements in a variety of indoor and outdoor settings. The proposed paradigm

enhances patient participation in real-time medical observation and decision-making, facilitating real-time medical care in emergencies. It also encourages communication between people and the IoMT system. By lowering follow-up visits, the architecture can lower morbidity and the associated financial burden. The response time will be accelerated in the event of a medical emergency. The recommended design can provide end-to-end social distancing while delivering necessary supplies and assist citizens, the government, and medical experts in better-managing pandemics.

8. **Ghubaish et al.** The article covers the value of protecting Internet of Medical Things (IoMT) systems, which enable remote patient monitoring for those with chronic conditions. The authors offer cutting-edge methods for protecting data in IoMT systems throughout collection, transmission, and storage. Additionally, they provide a thorough review of all potential assaults on IoMT systems, including physical and network attacks. To satisfy all security needs and neutralize the majority of assaults, the authors suggest a security architecture that integrates several security measures. The authors suggest a security framework that integrates several security methods to satisfy all security demands and neutralize the majority of assaults.

3. CHALLENGES IN IMPLEMENTING IOT FRAMEWORK

The interconnected network of medical systems and devices that gather, transmit, and analyze patient health data is known as the Internet of Medical Things (IoMT) (Selvaraj & Sundaravaradhan, 2019). IoMT has the potential to transform healthcare by enabling real-time diagnostics, remote monitoring, and customized therapies, but it also has several drawbacks:

Privacy and Security Issues: Devices connected to the IoMT are susceptible to security lapses and unwanted access. As sensitive and highly personal information, medical data is a target for cyberattacks. It is a big issue to guarantee the confidentiality and privacy of patient information while it is being sent, stored, and processed.

Data Interoperability: IoMT devices are manufactured by different vendors and may use diverse communication protocols and data formats. Ensuring seamless interoperability among these devices and systems is essential for the meaningful exchange of data across the healthcare ecosystem.

Regulatory Compliance: IoMT devices often fall under medical device regulations, which vary by region. Complying with these regulations and obtaining necessary certifications can be complex and time-consuming, especially when devices are developed by different manufacturers and used in various healthcare settings.

Data interoperability: IoMT devices can use a variety of communication protocols and data formats because they are produced by many suppliers. The meaningful sharing of data across the healthcare ecosystem depends on these devices and systems having seamless interoperability.

Regulatory Compliance: Medical device rules, which differ by area, frequently apply to IoMT devices. It can be difficult and time-consuming to comply with these regulations and acquire the required certifications, particularly when devices are created by different manufacturers and used in various healthcare settings.

Battery Life and Power Efficiency: Many IoMT devices are battery-powered and need to operate for extended periods without frequent battery replacements. Designing energy-efficient devices that can capture and transmit data without depleting their power source is a technical challenge.

Ethical and Legal Considerations: As IoMT devices generate massive amounts of patient data, questions arise about data ownership, consent, and how data should be used. Ensuring that patients' rights and autonomy are respected while deriving meaningful insights from their data can be ethically and legally complex.

Healthcare Professional Training: Healthcare providers need to be trained to effectively use and interpret data from IoMT devices. This requires ongoing education to keep up with rapidly evolving technology and new diagnostic paradigms.

Data Overload and Integration: The vast amount of data generated by IoMT devices can overwhelm healthcare systems. Integrating this data into electronic health records and clinical workflows in a way that enhances patient care without burdening healthcare professionals is a challenge.

Cost and ROI: The initial investment, maintenance, and integration costs of IoMT devices can be significant. Healthcare organizations need to weigh these costs against the potential benefits in terms of improved patient outcomes, operational efficiency, and reduced healthcare expenses.

Addressing these challenges requires collaboration among technology developers, healthcare providers, regulatory bodies, and other stakeholders to create a secure, interoperable, and patient-centric IoMT ecosystem. In this chapter, important challenges that are focused more are mentioned in Fig-1. The major challenges mentioned above can be addressed and solved using fog computing (Alam et al., 2022; Villegas-Ch et al., 2023).

Below mentioned Table-1, illustrates the solution for important challenges, suggested technological solutions, and how challenges can be addressed. It may be identified from Table 2 that fog computing can be suggested to reduce the number of challenges as a recent advancement (Alam et al., 2022; Al-suhibany et al., 2021).

Figure 1. Challenges in implementing the IOMT framework

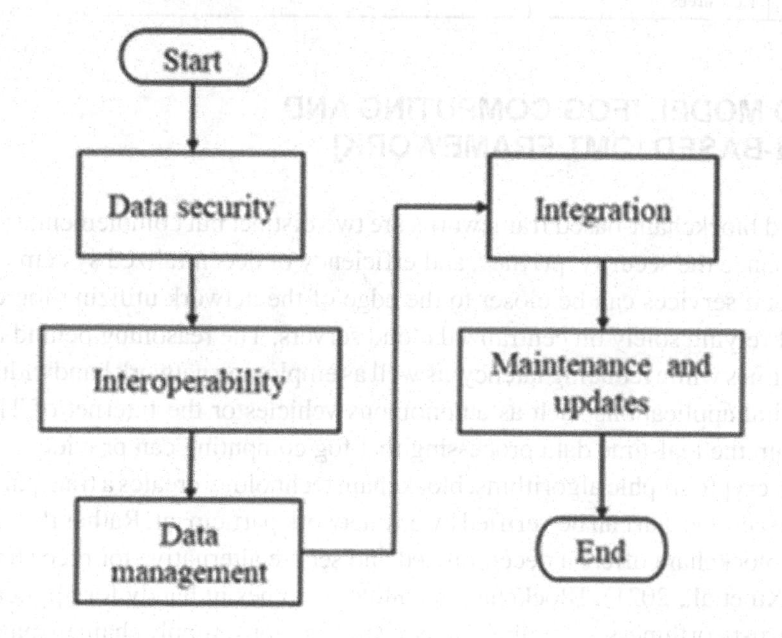

Table 1. Challenges and technological solution

Challenge	Technology Solution	How Technology Addresses the Challenge
Security and Privacy	Blockchain	Provides secure, immutable, and transparent data storage and sharing.
	Encryption	Protects data during transmission and storage, ensuring privacy.
	Access Control	Ensures only authorized personnel can access sensitive medical data.
Data Interoperability	Standardized Protocols	Enables seamless communication and data exchange among IoMT devices.
	Edge Computing	Converts diverse data formats into a common format for interoperability.
Regulatory Compliance	Edge Computing	Keeps sensitive data within legal jurisdictions to comply with regulations.
Data Accuracy	Edge Data Validation	Performs data validation and filtering at the edge to enhance accuracy.
	Sensor Calibration	Adjusts and ensures the accuracy of sensor readings for reliable data.
Network Reliability	Fog Computing	Reduces dependence on cloud connectivity, ensuring real-time processing.
	Redundancy and Failover Mechanisms	Provides backup resources and maintains system availability.
Battery Life	Edge Processing and Offloading	Offloads tasks to edge devices to save energy and extend battery life.
Ethical and Legal	Consent Management	Manages patient consent for data usage and ensures ethical practices.
	Localized Data Control	Allows data control and sharing decisions to be made at the local level.
Data Overload	Edge Preprocessing	Filters and aggregates data at the edge to reduce cloud data load.
	Cloud Bursting	Offloads intense data processing tasks to the cloud during peak times.
Real-Time Analytics	Fog Computing	Enables immediate data analysis at the edge for timely decision-making.
	Predictive Analytics	Uses historical data to anticipate medical trends and optimize care.
Cost and ROI	Fog Computing	Reduces cloud service costs by minimizing data transmission to the cloud.
	Reusable Edge Resources	Maximizes resource utilization, enhancing return on investment.

4. PROPOSED MODEL [FOG COMPUTING AND BLOCKCHAIN-BASED IOMT FRAMEWORK]

Fog computing and blockchain-based frameworks are two distinct but complementary technologies that can be used to enhance the security, privacy, and efficiency of decentralized systems. Distributed computing resources and services can be closer to the edge of the network utilizing fog computing, which is the antithesis of relying solely on centralized cloud servers. The reasoning behind this endeavor is to shorten response times while reducing latency, as well as employing network bandwidth more effectively and efficiently. Vital applications such as autonomous vehicles or the Internet of Things (IoT) would greatly benefit from the real-time data processing that fog computing can provide.

Using complex cryptographic algorithms, blockchain technology creates a transparent and unchangeable record of transactions that can be verified by any network participant. Rather than relying on a single central authority, blockchain offers a decentralized and secure alternative for recording and confirming transactions (Da Xu et al., 2021). Blockchain technology comes in handy for applications that require transparency and trustworthiness, including financial transactions, supply chain management, and voting systems. The combination of blockchain-based frameworks and fog computing results in sophisticated and secure decentralized systems. A trusted and decentralized infrastructure for applications like IoT and smart cities can be created thanks to blockchain technology's ability to record and authenticate transactions across the fog network transparently and securely (Aslam et al., 2021; Singh et al., 2020). To boost security, efficiency, and privacy across multiple healthcare applications, you can take advantage of fog computing and blockchain-driven algorithms. For instance, a blueprint of the fog and blockchain-based IOMT systems can be seen in Figure 2.

Figure 2. IoMT framework using blockchain and fog computing

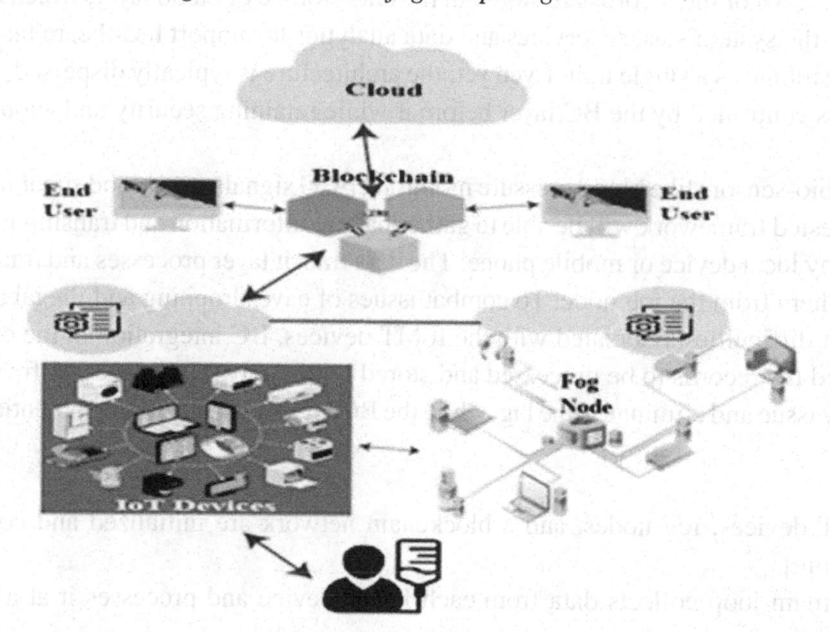

The use of a fog node between the IoMT device layer and cloud storage layer has several obvious benefits, such as reduced latency, low energy consumption, support for heterogeneity, and interoperability (Yaacoub et al., 2020). Its structure also supports flexibility and scalability, making it easier to add new apps without disrupting the entire healthcare system. The patient's mobility is further enhanced by this type of arrangement. The BC layer offers a distributed architecture that is safe and protects privacy for communications and medical records (Singh et al., 2020).

Below is an explanation of the layered architecture and the functions carried out at each layer:

- Sensing mechanism or layer: The fog layer receives the information from the perception layer and transmits it to the physical devices, sensors, and other monitoring equipment that gather data from patients and, in some situations, the environment.
- Fog layer: As opposed to what is typically feasible in a centralized or cloud-based design, transmission latency can frequently be fatal and lead to subpar medical care and support. In addition to promoting quick replies, the fog layer seeks to lessen the load of encryption on IoMT sensors, which have limited computational power.

- Data Transportation Layer: To aggregate the data obtained from the fog layer and transmit it to the cloud storage layer, the data transportation layer functions as a network layer. As it handles all data flows from the fog layer to the storage layer, this layer is the most exposed.
- BC layer: The BC layer is in charge of confirming the end users before granting access to the storage layer for a high level of data security with less latency and less of a load on resource-constrained physical devices. This is done with the assistance of the fog layer. Prohibiting any record modification without sufficient authorization and authentication also promotes the immutability of records.
- Cloud Layer; All of the records are stored in the data storage or cloud layer, which is also in charge of offering the system's users services and data analytics to support healthcare facilities. One perceives the storage as a single unit. Even yet, the architecture is typically dispersed, with many storage devices controlled by the BC layer before it while retaining security and anonymity features.

By utilizing bio-sensors like blood pressure monitors, ECG signals, and blood sugar monitors, among others, the suggested framework will be able to gather patient information and transmit it to the fog node, which may be any local device or mobile phone. The data transit layer processes and transfers the details after receiving them from the fog node. To combat issues of eavesdropping and illegal alteration and to address the trust difficulties associated with the IoMT devices, BC integration in the cloud computing layer has allowed the records to be processed and stored immutably. The suggested framework will address the latency issue and eliminate time lag, while the BC layer will address any potential security risks.

Steps:

1. IoMT devices, fog nodes, and a blockchain network are initialized and configured. [Data Sensing]
2. The main loop collects data from each IoMT device and processes it at a fog node [Data Collection].
3. Processed data is encrypted and hashed for security.
4. A blockchain transaction is created with the hashed data and added to the blockchain.
5. The blockchain's validation process is used to verify the integrity of transactions.
6. Device status is updated based on the validation results.

5. EXPERIMENTATION

Simulation of the model suggested in the proposed work section started with 40 nodes of simple IOT sensor node initialization with the values of the parameter given in Table 2. The first experimentation was to initialize all 40 nodes as a simple IOT node (which can be considered as an IOMT node) without FOG computing and Blockchain method to secure data (Aslam et al., 2021). Figure 3 shows a visualization of the IOT node in network simulator-3.

```
# Fog Computing and Blockchain code for IOMT
# Initialize IoMT devices, fog nodes, and blockchain network
iot_devices = initialize_iot_devices()
fog_nodes = initialize_fog_nodes()
```

```
blockchain = initialize_blockchain()
# Main loop for data processing
while True:
    for device in iot_devices:
        data = device.collect_data() # Collect data from IoMT device

        # Perform data processing at the fog node
        selected_fog_node = select_fog_node(device.location, fog_nodes)
        processed_data = selected_fog_node.process_data(data)

        # Encrypt and hash processed data
        encrypted_data = encrypt_data(processed_data)
        hashed_data = calculate_hash(encrypted_data)

        # Create blockchain transaction
        transaction = create_transaction(device.id, hashed_data)

        # Add transaction to the blockchain and validate
        blockchain.add_transaction(transaction)
        is_valid = blockchain.validate_transactions()

        # Update device status based on validation result
        device.update_status(is_valid)
# Helper functions
def initialize_iot_devices():
    # Initialize and configure IoMT devices
    # Return a list of IoMT devices
    pass
def initialize_fog_nodes():
    # Initialize and configure fog nodes
    # Return a list of fog nodes
    pass
def initialize_blockchain():
    # Initialize and configure the blockchain network
    # Return a blockchain instance
    pass
def select_fog_node(device_location, fog_nodes):
    # Select the nearest fog node based on the device's location
    # Return the selected fog node
    pass
def encrypt_data(data):
    # Encrypt data using encryption algorithms
    # Return encrypted data
    pass
```

```
def calculate_hash(data):
    # Calculate the cryptographic hash of data
    # Return hash value
    pass
def create_transaction(device_id, hashed_data):
    # Create a blockchain transaction
    # Return transaction object
    pass
```

Table 2. Node initialization parameter

Parameter	Description	Value
Node ID	Unique identifier for each sensor node.	1, 2, 3, ...
Location (x, y)	Spatial coordinates of the sensor node in the simulation.	(10, 15)
Heart Rate (bpm)	Simulated heart rate value.	75
Blood Pressure (mmHg)	Simulated blood pressure value (systolic/diastolic).	120/80
Temperature (°C)	Simulated temperature value.	98.6
Latency (ms)	Time taken for data transmission and processing.	40
Data Usage (MB/s)	The rate at which data is transmitted.	0.3
Battery Level (%)	Initial battery charge level.	100

6. RESULT

The proposed design can greatly lessen network traffic congestion, resource distribution, and communication time between IoMT devices. Simulation results of a simple 40-node sensor communication results compared to traditional fog computing have been presented in the given Table 3. Improvement was seen in terms of standard metrics and parameters. Table 4 shows the result of the commutating sensor node on blockchain security on the transfer of healthcare data. 20 healthcare equipment node data was securely transferred and at the destination node, it was validated.

Overall, Table 5 shows comparative results over standard metrics and improvements in percentage. A comparison of two simulations, the IOT simple model and the second IOT with FOG computing concept and blockchain security was made in the above table-5. The fog computing cluster had 5 nodes per cluster of fog connected with a high data transfer capability hub. Sometimes the data risk may be increased in choosing a computing node as a fog node. So, node identification as a FOG node is the interest of research work in this field.

Figure 3. Visualization of nodes ready for simulation

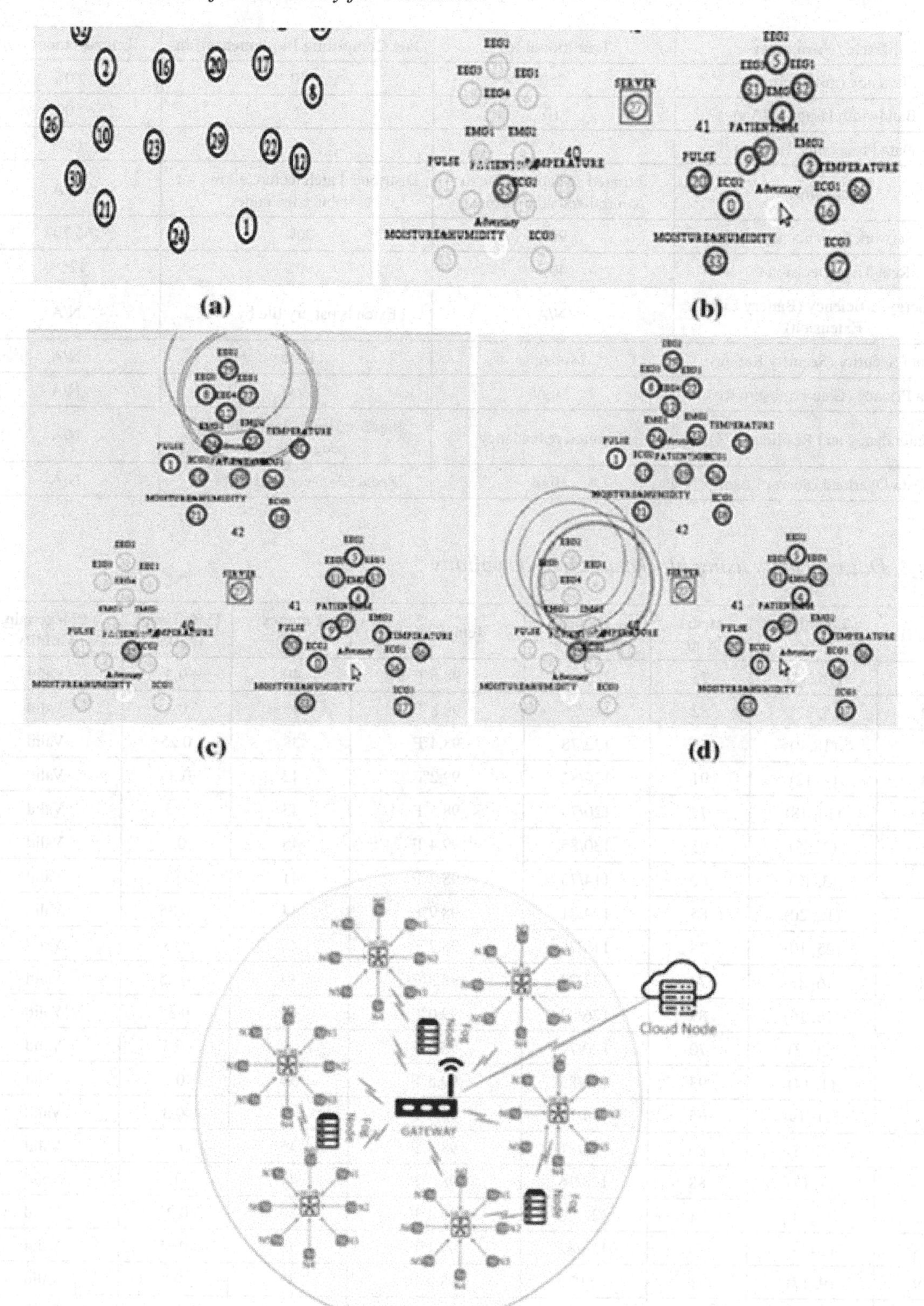

Table 3. Improvement in results after inclusion of fog computing

Metric / Parameter	Traditional IoT	Fog Computing Implementation	Improvement (%)
Latency (milliseconds)	250	50	80%
Bandwidth Usage (MB/s)	10	2	80%
Data Processing Time (s)	5	2	60%
Scalability	Limited scalability due to centralized architecture.	Distributed architecture allows for scalable edge nodes.	N/A
Network Dependency (%)	90%	30%	66.70%
Real-Time Decision (%)	40%	90%	125%
Energy Efficiency (Battery Life Extension)	N/A	Extends battery life by 40%.	N/A
Data Security (Security Rating)	Moderate	High	N/A
Data Privacy (Data Exposure Risk)	High	Low	N/A
Redundancy and Resilience (%)	Limited redundancy	Improved redundancy through edge nodes.	N/A
Data Overload (Server Load)	High	Reduced server load by 60%.	N/A

Table 4. Data security using blockchain and its validity

Node ID	Location (x, y)	Heart Rate	Blood Pressure	Temperature	Latency (ms)	Data Usage (MB/s)	Blockchain Validity
1	(10, 15)	75	120/80	98.6°F	40	0.3	Valid
2	(5, 22)	82	118/76	98.8°F	45	0.4	Valid
3	(18, 7)	68	122/78	98.4°F	38	0.25	Valid
4	(8, 12)	91	126/82	99.2°F	42	0.35	Valid
5	(14, 18)	77	120/79	98.5°F	43	0.3	Valid
6	(22, 5)	95	130/85	99.4°F	48	0.4	Valid
7	(3, 17)	62	114/75	98.2°F	41	0.3	Valid
8	(12, 20)	85	124/81	98.9°F	44	0.35	Valid
9	(25, 10)	78	118/76	98.7°F	46	0.3	Valid
10	(6, 8)	73	122/78	98.3°F	39	0.25	Valid
11	(16, 16)	89	126/82	99.0°F	47	0.35	Valid
12	(20, 3)	70	120/79	98.6°F	42	0.3	Valid
13	(1, 14)	93	130/85	99.5°F	50	0.4	Valid
14	(11, 19)	65	114/75	98.4°F	43	0.3	Valid
15	(23, 8)	80	124/81	98.8°F	45	0.35	Valid
16	(4, 12)	88	118/76	98.6°F	44	0.3	Valid
17	(15, 18)	71	122/78	98.4°F	39	0.25	Valid
18	(24, 6)	94	126/82	99.1°F	48	0.35	Valid
19	(9, 17)	79	120/79	98.9°F	42	0.3	Valid
20	(19, 4)	72	130/85	99.3°F	47	0.4	Valid

Table 5. Overall summarised comparative results of IOMT with and without foG computing as an advancement using blockchain

Metric / Parameter	Traditional IoMT	Fog Computing Implementation	Improvement (%)
Latency (milliseconds)	300	50	83%
Bandwidth Usage (MB/s)	12	3	75%
Data Processing Time (s)	8	3	62.50%
Interoperability	Limited integration due to diverse data formats.	Seamless data exchange with standardized protocols.	N/A
Regulatory Compliance (%)	Compliance challenges due to data jurisdiction.	Improved compliance with local data regulations.	N/A
Data Accuracy (%)	85%	92%	8.20%
Network Reliability (%)	Dependence on consistent cloud connectivity.	Reduced dependency through edge processing.	N/A
Energy Efficiency (%)	N/A	Increases battery life by 30%.	N/A
Data Security (Security Rating)	Moderate	High	N/A
Data Privacy (Data Exposure Risk)	High	Low	N/A
Real-Time Analytics (%)	Limited real-time insights due to cloud delays.	Improved real-time analytics at the edge.	N/A
Cost Efficiency (%)	N/A	Reduces cloud service costs by 40%.	N/A

CONCLUSION AND FUTURE WORK

The IoMT, FC, BC, and CC are examples of developing technologies that are assisting the transition of the globe into the era of digital communication. The interchange of information and data between healthcare facilities is facilitated by BFCM for IoMT. Networks that are energy-aware, scalable, and low-latency are provided by IoMT applications, smart sensors, actuators, and controllers in smart healthcare (Srivastava et al., 2022). To ensure the highest level of security and privacy, we started with IoMT technology in smart healthcare infrastructure, which creates enormous amounts of data that FC nodes should analyze at the network's edge.

IoMT devices are susceptible to a variety of assaults due to a lack of hardware and software security features. This study looks into potential security and privacy issues with fog-enabled IoMT. New security and privacy options for the IoMT made possible by the fog may also covered in the future. Decentralization can improve the security, authenticity, and integrity of data produced by IoMT devices (Dwivedi et al., 2019). It also outlines the bulk of these issues that a BC can resolve. It may also need to make sure in the future that IoT devices are private and personalized data and secure on the node. In this study, a distributed BC cloud strategy is suggested for effectively managing large IoMT data streams. The suggested architecture for the future is SDN for improvements of referenced work.

IoMT, a subdomain of the IoT that is employed in the medical domain and is also being heavily deployed, is being applied to every domain at a mass scale. This is crucial to the ability of healthcare facilities to deliver high-quality care and cost-effective too. We have suggested a BC and FC integration here as a framework to address the problems and difficulties associated with the IoMT. However, certain elements need to be thoroughly researched in subsequent research like BC and FC integration in IOMT aimed towards optimization of available domain work, design of a new scheduling method for optimized energy consumption and ultra-low latency, and Specific securities issues and their resolvent.

REFERENCES

Alam, S., Shuaib, M., Ahmad, S., Jayakody, D. N. K., Muthanna, A., Bharany, S., & Elgendy, I. A. (2022). Ghubaish -Based Solutions Supporting Reliable Healthcare for Fog Computing and Internet of Medical Things (IoMT) Integration. *Sustainability (Basel)*, *14*(22), 15312. doi:10.3390u142215312

Aljabr, A. A., & Kumar, K. (2022, December). Design and implementation of Internet of Medical Things (IoMT) using artificial intelligent for mobile-healthcare. Measurement. *Sensors (Basel)*, *24*, 100499. doi:10.1016/j.measen.2022.100499

Alsuhibany, S. A., Abdel-Khalek, S., Algarni, A., Fayomi, A., Gupta, D., Kumar, V., & Mansour, R. F. (2021, December 27). *Ensemble of Deep Learning Based Clinical Decision Support System for Chronic Kidney Disease Diagnosis in Medical Internet of Things Environment*.. Hindawi. doi:10.1155/2021/4931450

Aslam, T., Maqbool, A., Akhtar, M., Mirza, A., Khan, M. A., Khan, W. Z., & Alam, S. (2021). Blockchain based enhanced ERP transaction integrity architecture and PoET consensus. *Computers, Materials & Continua*, *70*(1), 1089–1108. doi:10.32604/cmc.2022.019416

Awaisi, K. S., Hussain, S., Ahmed, M., Khan, A. A., & Ahmed, G. (2020). Leveraging IoT and fog computing in healthcare systems. *IEEE Internet Things Mag.*, *3*(2), 52–56. doi:10.1109/IOTM.0001.1900096

Da Xu, L., Lu, Y., & Li, L. (2021). Embedding blockchain technology into IoT for security: A survey. *IEEE Internet of Things Journal*, *8*(13), 10452–10473. doi:10.1109/JIOT.2021.3060508

Dwivedi, A., Srivastava, G., Dhar, S., & Singh, R. (2019). A Decentralized Privacy-Preserving Healthcare Blockchain for IoT. *Sensors (Basel)*, *19*(2), 326. doi:10.339019020326 PMID:30650612

Dwivedi, R., Mehrotra, D., & Chandra, S. (2021). Potential of Internet of Medical Things (IoMT) applications in building a smart healthcare system: A systematic review. *Journal of Oral Biology and Craniofacial Research*, *12*(2), 302–318. doi:10.1016/j.jobcr.2021.11.010 PMID:34926140

Ghubaish, A., Salman, T., Zolanvari, M., Unal, D., Al-Ali, A., & Jain, R. (2021, June 1). Recent Advances in the Internet-of-Medical-Things (IoMT) Systems Security. *IEEE Internet of Things Journal*, *8*(11), 8707–8718. doi:10.1109/JIOT.2020.3045653

Kadhim, K. T., Alsahlany, A. M., Wadi, S. M., & Kadhum, H. T. (2020). An overview of patient's health status monitoring system based on internet of things (IoT). *Wireless Personal Communications*, *114*(3), 1–28. doi:10.100711277-020-07474-0

Kamarajugadda, K. K., Movva, P., Raju, M. N., Kant, S. A., & Thatavarti, S. (2021, February 2). *IoMT with Cloud-Based Disease Diagnosis Healthcare Framework for Heart Disease Prediction Using Simulated Annealing with SVM*. Springer. doi:10.1007/978-3-030-52624-5_8

Khan, I. A., Moustafa, N., Razzak, I., Tanveer, M., Pi, D., Pan, Y., & Ali, B. S. (2022). XSRU-IoMT: Explainable simple recurrent units for threat detection in Internet of Medical Things networks. *Future Generation Computer Systems*, *127*, 181–193. doi:10.1016/j.future.2021.09.010

Meola, A. (n.d.). IoT Healthcare in 2023: Companies, medical devices, and use cases. *Insider Intelligence*. https://www.insiderintelligence.com/insights/iot-healthcare/

Pradhan, B., Bhattacharyya, S., & Pal, K. (2021, March 19). *IoT-Based Applications in Healthcare Devices. IoT-Based Applications in Healthcare Devices*. Hindawi. doi:10.1155/2021/6632599

Selvaraj, S., & Sundaravaradhan, S. (2019, December 30). Challenges and opportunities in IoT healthcare systems: A systematic review. *SN Applied Sciences*, *2*(1), 139. doi:10.100742452-019-1925-y

Sharma, S. R. (2019, June 30). Internet of Things IoT: IoT in Healthcare. *International Journal of Trend in Scientific Research and Development, 3*(Issue-4), 980–982. https://doi.org/ doi:10.31142/ijtsrd23971

Singh, S. K., Rathore, S., & Park, J. H. (2020). BlockIoTIntelligence: A Blockchain-enabled Intelligent IoT Architecture with Artificial Intelligence. *Future Generation Computer Systems*, *110*, 721–743. doi:10.1016/j.future.2019.09.002

Srivastava, J., Routray, S., Ahmad, S., & Waris, M. M. (2022). Internet of medical things (IoMT)-Based Smart Healthcare System: Trends and Progress. *Computational Intelligence and Neuroscience*, *2022*, 7218113. doi:10.1155/2022/7218113 PMID:35880061

Tai, Y., Gao, B., Li, Q., Yu, Z., Zhu, C., & Chang, V. (2021, February 1). *Trustworthy and Intelligent COVID-19 Diagnostic IoMT Through XR and Deep-Learning-Based Clinic Data Access*. PubMed Central (PMC). doi:10.1109/JIOT.2021.3055804

Villegas-Ch, W., García-Ortiz, J., & Urbina-Camacho, I. (2023, May 30). *Framework for a Secure and Sustainable Internet of Medical Things, Requirements, Design Challenges, and Future Trends*. MDPI. doi:10.3390/app13116634

Yaacoub, J. P. A., Noura, M., Noura, H. N., Salman, O., Yaacoub, E., Couturier, R., & Chehab, A. (2020). Securing internet of medical things systems: Limitations, issues and recommendations. *Future Generation Computer Systems*, *105*, 581–606. doi:10.1016/j.future.2019.12.028

Chapter 10
Mobile Text Misinformation Identification Using Machine Learning

Sanjaikanth E. Vadakkethil Somanathan Pillai
https://orcid.org/0000-0003-3264-9923
University of North Dakota, USA

Wen-Chen Hu
University of North Dakota, USA

ABSTRACT

More than eighty percent of U.S. adults receive news from digital devices like smartphones, computers, or tablets. Unlike the traditional news dominated by organizations, this new kind of news could be created by anyone. It is quick and engaging. At the same time, misinformation may be easily generated or spread intentionally or unintentionally. Misinformation is a serious problem for the general public, and there is no method to solve the problem satisfactorily so far. Instead of covering general misinformation, this research tries to identify mobile health text misinformation by proposing a self-reconfigurable system. The system includes the preprocessing functions (involving lexical analysis, stopword removal, stemming, and synonym discovery), a dataflow graph from TensorFlow, and a reconfiguration method for self-improvement. Experiment results show the proposed method significantly improves the accuracy of the mobile health text misinformation detection compared to the one without using self-reconfiguration.

INTRODUCTION

More than six million people died because of the COVID-19 as of June 2023 (World Health Organization, 2023). These high casualties put everyone on the alert. People try to find any information that helps them fight the virus. Much information they receive is from their smartphones without doubt in these days because smartphones have become an indispensable device for everyone. One popular function for smartphone users is sending and receiving text messages. Instead of reading newspapers or watching

DOI: 10.4018/979-8-3693-2081-5.ch010

TV news, many mobile users especially younger generations receive their daily news or information via text messages. Other than useful and unbiased information, many of the messages are incorrect or may even be distorted on purpose (van der Linden, 2022). During the pandemic, the problem has become even more serious because the health text misinformation not only gives wrong information, but may also cause fatal results such as advocacy of the ineffectiveness of vaccine. This research tries to mitigate the problem by identifying mobile health text misinformation, so the mobile users can use the findings to better judge the messages they receive and take actions accordingly.

This research proposes a self-reconfigurable system for identifying mobile health text misinformation, which is briefly described as follows. This is a supervised learning system, so before the system is put into use, it needs training by using a set of text messages with known results. The initial parameters of the system are set by heuristics because the keywords of text messages are unknown in advance and have to be speculated. After the training phase, the system starts its testing phase by receiving text messages. Each message will go through a series of steps: preprocessing (including lexical analysis, stopword removal, and stemming), indexing and storage, and testing (classification) by using a dataflow graph. Instead of applying the results immediately, the first round of testing is used to reconfigure the system in order to generate better results later. It is because the initial configuration is usually not desirable as system parameters are unknown in the very beginning. After the first round of testing, better parameters could be found from the test results. The complete steps are repeated with better parameter and more accurate identifications are expected. Experiment results show the accuracy of the proposed method meets the expectation, but still has room for improvement. An explanation for this may be because the short messages do not provide much information and small deviation may cause a great impact on the results. Further refinements are needed before it is put into use.

The rest of this paper is organized as follows. Section 2 shows the background information about this research and related works on misinformation detection. The structure and components of the proposed system are given in Section 3. Section 4 proposes our major method, a self-reconfigurable dataflow graph, for detecting health text misinformation. The experiment results and evaluations are given in Section 5, followed by a conclusion and references.

BACKGROUND AND RELATED LITERATURE

This section gives the background information of this research and related research in case readers are interested in finding more relevant publications. Misinformation identification is critical and popular in these days because information could be created and sent by everyone, not just news agencies, and some may distribute misinformation unintentionally or intentionally. Many methods are used to detect all kinds of misinformation like politics, businesses, text messages, emails, or news. This research places the focus on mobile health text misinformation identification. If the results are favorable, the method may be extended to other kinds of information. Yu, Liu, Wu, Wang, & Tan (2019) propose an attention-based convolutional approach for misinformation identification model. An *Event2vec* module and the co-attention contribute to learning a good representation of an event. A convolutional neural network then extracts key features scattered among an input sequence and shapes high-level interactions among significant features, which help effectively identify misinformation and achieve practical early detection. An attention-based approach for identification of misinformation (AIM) is proposed by Liu, Yu, Wu, & Wang (2018). Based on the attention mechanism, AIM can select microblogs with the largest attention values for misinformation identification. The attention mechanism in AIM contains two parts: content attention and dynamic attention. Content attention is the calculated-based textual features of each microblog. Dynamic attention is related to the time interval between the posting time of a microblog and the beginning of the event. More generic misinformation detection can be found from the articles (Sharma, Qian, Jiang, Ruchansky, Zhang, & Liu, 2019; Zhou & Zafarani, 2020; Khan, Michalas, & Akhunzada, 2021; Savage, 2021; Mridha, 2021; Hakak, et al., 2021; Kaliyar, Goswami, & Narang, 2019; Mridha, et al., 2021).

This research focuses on conoravirus misinformation detection. Brennen, Simon, & Nielsen (2021) analyze visual content in misinformation concerning COVID-19. It shows the value in both attending to visual content in misinformation and unnecessarity of a concern with only the representational aspects and functions of misinformation. Another study by Gupta, Gasparyan, Misra, Agarwal, Zimba, and Yessirkepov (2020) identifies social media as a potential source of misinformation on COVID-19 and a perceived high risk of plagiarism. More stringent peer review and skilled post-publication promotion are advisable. They recommend editors should play a more active role in streamlining publication and promoting trustworthy information on COVID-19. Related research about coronavirus misinformation identification can be found from the articles (Ball & Maxmen, 2020; Fleming, 2020; Mian & Khan, 2020).

The media targeted by this research is short text messages. Sinha, Sakshi, and Sharma (2021) classify a tweet as real or fake. The complexity of natural language constructs along with variegated languages makes this task very challenging. In this work, a deep learning model to learn semantic word embeddings is proposed to handle this complexity. The evaluations on the benchmark dataset show that the proposed methods are superior to traditional natural language processing algorithms. Ahmed, Ali, Hussain, Baseer, and Ahmed (2021) analyze the performance of a fake news detection model based on neural networks using three feature extractors: TD-IDF vectorizer, Glove embeddings, and BERT embeddings. It was found that BERT embeddings for text transformation delivered the best performance. TD-IDF has been performed far better than Glove and competed the BERT as well at some stages. Other misinformation from social media can be found from the articles (Aldwairi & Alwahedi, 2018; Collins, Hoang, Nguyen, & Hwang, 2021; Guo, et al., 2020; Sitaula, et al., 2020).

This research uses the artificial intelligence methods to identify misinformation. Kula, Choraś, Kozik, Ksieniewicz, and Woźniak (2020) present an innovative solution for fake news detection that utilizes deep learning methods. Their experiments prove that the proposed approach is effective. Isha Priyavamtha, Vishnu Vardhan Reddy, Devisri, and Manek (2021) propose a model to detect fake news that includes three main phases: preprocessing, feature extraction, and classification. Input is first preprocessed to extract features using clustering algorithms. Subsequently, a model is developed to detect fake news. The proposed neural networks and linear support vector clustering algorithms resulted in 99.90% and 97.5% accuracy respectively. Another research using deep learning to identify misinformation can be found from the article (Islam, Liu, Wang, & Xu, 2020).

Misinformation detection is not an easy topic to tackle because the detection is usually subjective. In addition, a variety of misinformation exists which requires a great amount of data to be stored. Research of misinformation detection has been studied extensively, and this research does not intend to solve all the misinformation problems at once. Instead, it focuses on two themes: short text messages and health-related misinformation, especially the COVID-19. Interested readers can refer to other misinformation identification methods from the articles (Visser, Lawrence, & Reed, 2020; Reddy, Raj, Gala, & Basava, 2020; Schuster, Schuster, Shah, & Barzilay, 2020; Sethi, Rangaraju, & Shurts, 2019).

THE PROPOSED SYSTEM

This research is to identify mobile health text misinformation by using a self-reconfigurable system. This section introduces the proposed system, and details of the reconfiguration method will be given in the next section.

Five Classes of Short Text Messages

It is too simple to classify a mobile health text message as either true or fake because some other classes exist. This research categorizes a message into one of the following five classes:

- *True*, which is true information and is without a doubt. For example, it is true that the COVID-19 vaccine is effective because it has been authorized by the U.S. Food and Drug Administration (FDA) and vaccine programs have begun across the country.
- *Fake*, which is incorrect indisputably. For example, it is an obviously fake news that the COVID-19 vaccine contains microchips for government tracking because the current technology has not been this advanced yet.
- *Misinformative*, which is false or out-of-context information that is intentionally or unintentionally presented as fact to deceive.
- *Disinformative*, which is a type of misinformation that is intentionally delivered the false or misleading information to deceive or mislead readers.
- *Neutral*, which cannot be decided by the proposed method.

The differences between misinformation and disinformation are not distinct. This research treats the former as a mistake. If the information is intentionally to deceive, it is classified as disinformation. Otherwise, it is misinformation. That is misinformation actively demonstrates the information that is communicated to mislead, whereas disinformation can be recognized as malicious tricks and computational publicity.

System Structure of the Dataflow Graph

Construction of the proposed system is rather complicated. Keras (n.d.) and TensorFlow (n.d.) are used to facilitate the system construction. Keras is a high-level, open-source library for the neural network and TensorFlow is a software library for machine learning and artificial intelligence. A dataflow graph of TensorFlow consists of an operation and a tensor, where the operation is to find the outgoing tensor (class) of the ingoing tensor (text message). There are three phases before the system is ready for use in the final phase:

- *Training phase*: Train the dataflow graph by using a set of known test messages.
- *Initial testing phase*: Start testing the trained dataflow graph by using a set of unknown messages and receive the suggested results (classes).
- *Self-reconfiguration phase*: The system will automatically reconfigure itself based on the previous phases and their messages and results.

- *Final testing phase*: The system is ready for use. A mobile text message is submitted to the system, and one of the five class (true, fake, misinformation, disinformation, and neutral) will be recommended.

Figure 1 shows the dataflow graph, which is with 10 input buckets and 5 output Boolean nodes. Each input bucket includes a set of keywords and the bucket turns on the Boolean input node if the message includes the keyword in the bucket. The five output nodes of the output layer are the final classes. Only one of the five output nodes will be turned on for each message.

Figure 1. A sample dataflow graph from the TensorFlow

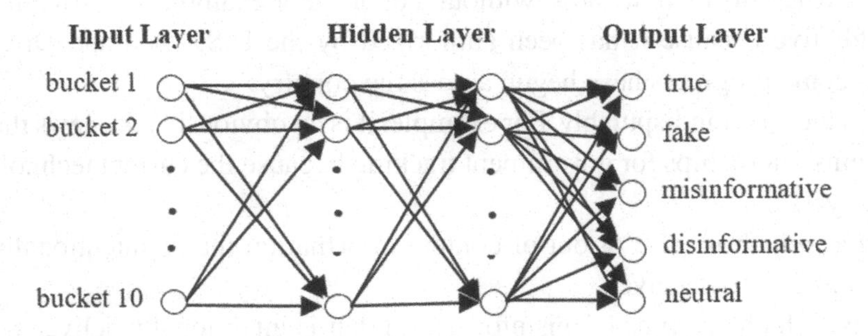

Training Phase

Initially, we randomly pick related words or phrases for the buckets of the input layer. Of course, the chosen ones are not ideal because we have no idea what the ideal input nodes are. The self-reconfiguration phase will try to find better input nodes based on the input messages and their found results/classes. Figure 2 shows the training phase of this system, which includes lexical analysis, stopword removal, stemming, synonym discovery, database, and a dataflow graph, and they will be described in this section.

Figure 2. The training phase

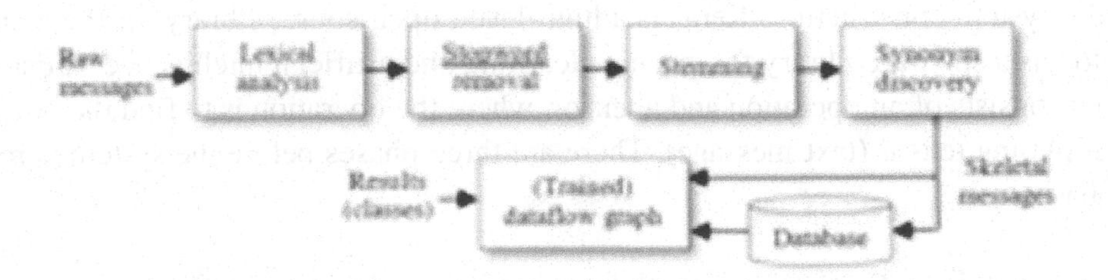

Lexical Analysis

Lexical analysis is the process of converting an input stream of characters into a stream of words or tokens, which are groups of characters with collective significance. It is the first stage of automatic indexing which is the process of algorithmically examining information items to generate lists of index terms. The lexical analysis phase produces candidate index terms that may be further processed, and eventually added to indexes. It also helps split the longer sentences into smaller chunks of the dataset to perform algorithms with better accuracy.

Removal of Stopwords

English stopwords such as is, has, an, the, etc. do not signify any importance as index terms when analyzing the dataset for information. It is crucial to remove the stopwords from the dataset as they do not help us find the true meaning of a sentence and can be removed without any negative consequences. Also, eliminating such words from consideration early in automatic indexing speeds processing, saves huge amounts of space in indexes. It has been recognized since the earliest days of information retrieval that many of the most frequently occurring words in English (like "the," "of," "and," "to," etc.) are worthless as index terms.

Stemming

It is a technique for improving retrieval effectiveness and reducing the size of indexing files is to provide searchers with ways of finding morphological variants of search terms. The stem need not be identical to the morphological root of the word; it is usually sufficient that related words map to the same stem, even if this stem is not in itself a valid root. It is a method for casting words into their original form which aims to the removal of inflectional endings from words. It performs morphological analysis on the words by returning the words into its dictionary meaning. For example, the stemming converts caring into care, troubled into trouble, geese into goose, etc.

Synonym Discovery

Many times, common terms like coronavirus, COVID-19, Omicron, and Delta virus could be treated the same while measuring the message similarity. Instead of building a thesaurus, which is not a trivial task, this research stores synonyms of a set of popular words such as COVID-19, vaccine, and message in a database. The database is checked whenever a similarity measurement runs. However, this approach is a temporary fix because it misses many words. Future research will consider taking advantage of online services like https://www.synonym.com/, which provides a list of synonyms of a word, but it slows down the execution tremendously. On the other hand, saving all synonyms in a database is not feasible since it would take much space from a database. More investigation needs to be conducted for this matter.

Database

In addition, the skeletal messages and a set of keywords (e.g., the initial 10 words or phrases for the input layer) have to be saved in a database for reconfiguration later. The database includes three tables:

(a) keyword table, (b) message table, and (c) message-keyword table. Table 1 shows sample values of database, of which kid, mid, and mkid are the primary keys of the tables keyword, message, and message-keyword-result, respectively. The mkid is the foreign key of the table message, and mid and kid are the foreign keys of the table message-keyword-result. The count is the number of the occurrences of the keyword in the messages. The next points to the next keyword in the message, and it is not needed at this moment, but is saved in case.

Table 1. Database tables used: (a) keyword table, (b) message table, and (c) message-keyword-result table

(a)	(b)	(c)
KID keyword Count 1 covid-19 116 2 cdc 28 3 vaccine 41 4 credit card 11 … … … K sign up 9	MID MKID (start) result (class) 1 103 misinformative 2 26 true 3 52 misinformative 4 1 disinformative … … … m 94 fake	MKID MID KID next 1 4 3 2 2 4 21 28 3 4 122 – 4 10 30 6 5 46 32 49 6 10 8 7 7 10 21 118 8 122 30 – 9 55 8 72 10 41 3 61 … … … … n 87 138 9

SELF-RECONFIGURABLE DATAFLOW GRAPH

There are four phases to build the proposed system mentioned in Section III, where the Phase III is to reconfigure the dataflow graph used by the system automatically. A discussion of the reconfiguration algorithm is given in this section.

Self-Reconfiguration Phase

The initial input words or phrases of the dataflow graph are found by heuristic. Therefore, the results of the first round of testing are usually not satisfactory because the selected words are usually too subjective or some critical words are missed. The self-reconfiguration phase tries to solve the problem partially at least. Figure 3 shows the control/data flow diagram of the self-reconfiguration phase. The skeletal messages are the messages after being preprocessed by the system including lexical analysis, stopword removal, stemming, etc. After one round of training and testing, the database saves the skeletal messages and their discovered results/classes, which are fed to the reconfiguration algorithm described in the next sub-section. The algorithm is to produce better input words for the dataflow graph based on the results of the first round of training and testing. The graph is retrained by the same set of training data, but with different input words. It is expected the reconfigured dataflow graph will generate more accurate testing results because better input words or phrases are used.

Figure 3. The data/control flow of the self-reconfiguration phase

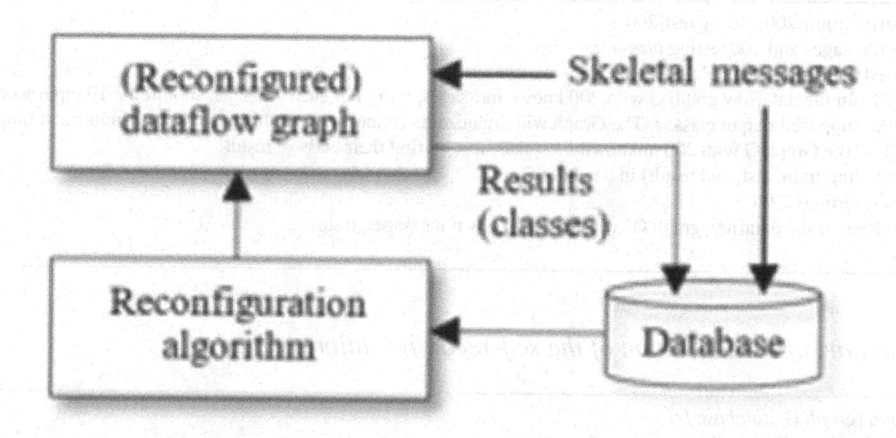

The Self-Reconfiguration Method

The self-reconfiguration algorithm is to replace the initial input words or phrases of the dataflow graph by better ones for testing after the first round of training and testing. The better input words are based on the first-round results because the system will have a better idea what the good input words are supposed to be after training and testing. Tables 2 and 3 give the proposed reconfiguration algorithm, which is to replace the input words based on the highly-occurred keywords and the LCSs (longest common subsequences) of the testing results and messages. The LCS is well known, but let's briefly review it here. Assume the two strings are given as follows:

S1 = disease control prevent announce covid-19 omicron vaccine
S2 = vaccine control prevent disease illness omicron sickness symptom

Their LCS *L* is as follows according to its name, longest common subsequence:

L = *LCS(S1, S2)* = *control prevent omicron*

Table 2 shows the first part of algorithm including the following steps: training, testing, calling the second part of algorithm described in Figure 6, which is to find the revised 10 new input words by using the LCS method and highly-occurred keywords. The dataflow graph is then retrained with the new input words. Afterward, the system is ready for use and better results are expected with the revised input words.

Table 3 shows the second part of the self-reconfiguration algorithm which takes the keyword occurrences and the LCSs of the testing results into consideration. Each of the five result sets (true, fake, misinformative, disinformative, and neutral) has a set of messages. The algorithm collects the top 20 keywords and retrieves the LCS from each set. Subsequently, collect the top 10 words after merging the keywords, LCSs, and the initial input words. The final 10 words will be new input words of the dataflow graph.

Table 2. First part of the algorithm of the self-reconfiguration method.

```
Dataflow-Graph (string train[200], string test[200])
Input: 200 training messages and 200 testing messages
Output: Reconfigured dataflow graph G'
1. (Training phase) Train the dataflow graph G with 200 known messages, train. For each message, submit the 10 input words and notify the Graph G what the supposed output class is. The Graph will organize its connection weights based on the inputs and outputs.
2. (Testing phase) Test the Graph G with 200 unknown messages, test, to find their classes, result.
3. Save all data (including train, test, and result) in database D.
4. G' ← Self-Reconfiguring(G, D)
5. (Training phase) Retrain the dataflow graph G' with the 200 known messages, train.
6. return(G')
```

Table 3. Second part of the algorithm of the self-reconfiguration method

```
SELF-RECONFIGURING (graph G, database D)
Input: graph G and database D including messages & results
Output: reconfigured dataflow graph G'
1. There is a set of messages for each of the 5 result
classes set[5] from the result[200] of database D.
2. final ← ϕ
3. for each set[i] in set do
4. j[20] ← FIND-TOP-WORDS(set[i])
5. k[10] ← FIND-TOP-WORDS(LCS(set[i]))
// m is a message in set[i] and k[10] ⊆ m
6. l[10] ← FIND-TOP-WORDS(m ∪ j[20])
7. final ← final ∪ l[10]
8. end for
// initial is the initial 10 input words or phrases
9. final ← FIND-TOP-WORDS( final ∪ initial)
10. G' ← G revised with the 10 new input words final
11. return(G')
```

EXPERIMENT RESULTS

In order to prove the method is effective, experiment results are provided in this section to validate the claim.

System Setup

A prototype system is built to prove the proposed method works. The following major software and tools are used to help the system construction:

- *Keras* (n.d.), which is an open-source software library that provides a Python interface for artificial neural networks. It acts as an interface for the TensorFlow library.
- *TensorFlow* (n.d.), which is a free and open-source software library for machine learning and artificial intelligence.
- *Xamarin* (n.d.), which is a cross-platform app development platform that helps to build a single app for all the device systems.

The prototype system can be found at GitHub (Vadakkethil Somanathan Pilla, 2023) including the following three files:

- *Round robin*, which is the strategy used for TensorFlow. In this approach, the model gets the input parameters in a Round-robin fashion from each of the target labels. This is a combination of LCS or repeated words for each label.
- *Classification bucket*, which is the classification model used for TensorFlow. In this model, we assign two buckets for each classifier. Each bucket receives the words from a combination of LCS or repeated words. If the input message contains the words in the bucket, it will set the input value to 1. Otherwise, it is 0.
- *Source data*, which contains more than 556 short text messages for training and testing.

Experiments

Figure 3 shows the experiment setup for evaluating the proposed system. The system actually could be located at either client or server, but the construction is convenient if the system is held at the server.

Figure 4. Another view of the proposed system for experiments

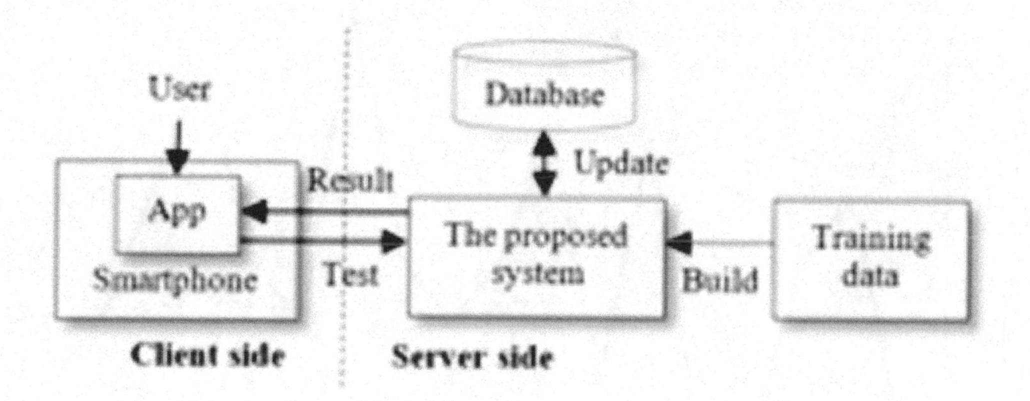

Figure 4 shows three screen shots from the experiment, where Figure 4.a gives a list of text messages to check, a disinformative message is found in Figure 4.b, and a true message is shown in Figure 4.c.

Evaluations and Discussions

Many messages are saved for training and testing. To better explain and show the evaluations, only 121 short text messages are used, and the results are shown in Figure 5, which displays the accuracy before and after self-reconfiguration. It shows the accuracy improves significantly after the reconfiguration. However, the consistency swerves greatly before and after reconfiguration and still has room for improvement.

Figure 5. The screen shots from the experiments: (a) selecting which message to check, (b) showing the message and its class, and (c) showing another message

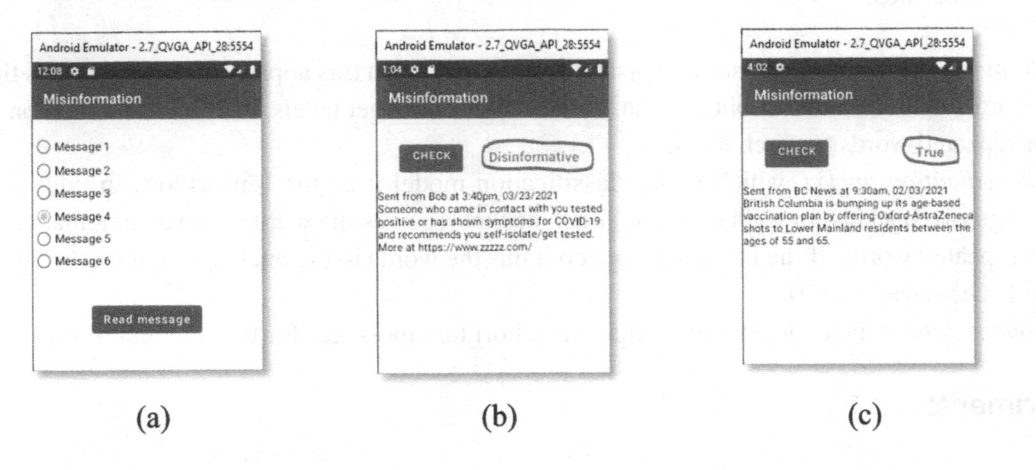

Figure 6. The accuracy before and after the self-reconfiguration

Figure 5 shows an example of the evaluation data of the proposed system, which is within expectations because it is obvious that the one with self-reconfiguration should outperform the one without. In addition, Table 4 gives another set of data by comparing the proposed method to various string matching methods (E Vadakkethil Somanathan Pillai & Hu, 2022) including

- *Keyword matching*, which gives the number of common keywords between two strings and is the simplest string matching method,
- *Phrase matching*, which considers the numbers and lengths of common phrases between two strings instead of individual keywords and expects to raise the accuracy,
- *LCS matching*, which uses the method of the longest common subsequence, and
- *LACS matching*, which is the longest approximate common subsequences and gives more .

For example, two strings are

S1 = disease control prevent announce covid-19 omicron vaccine
S2 = vaccine control prevent disease illness omicron sickness symptom

and some results from using the above four string matching methods are given next:

keyword-matching(S1, S2) = disease control prevent omicron vaccine
phrase-matching(S1, S2) = control prevent
LCS-matching(S1, S2) = control prevent omicron
LACS-matching(S1, S2) = disease control prevent omicron vaccine

Table 4 shows the simple string-matching methods outperform the proposed methods, which are more advanced and innovative. Though the tests show the results are not optimal, it is much better than the one without any help. For example, users can make a better judgement of whether the message is misinformation after consulting the recommendation from our method.

Table 4. Accuracy data from testing 121 short text messages by using the five methods, where mis. is misinformative and dis. is disinformative

		True	Fake	Mis.	Dis.	Neutral	Overall accuracy
Number of messages (121 total)		38	35	4	4	40	
The Proposed Method	Without reconfiguration	1/38=3%	31/35=89%	0/4=0%	2/4=50%	5/40=12%	39/121=32%
	With reconfiguration	11/38=29%	28/35=80%	3/4=75%	2/4=50%	13/40=32%	57/121=47%
Keyword matching		18/38=47%	33/35=94%	3/4=75%	3/4=75%	24/40=60%	81/121=67%
Phrase matching		16/38=42%	31/35=89%	2/4=50%	3/4=75%	23/40=58%	75/121=62%
LCS matching		15/38=40%	29/35=83%	2/4=50%	2/4=50%	26/40=65%	74/121=61%
LACS matching		16/38=42%	34/35=97%	3/4=75%	3/4=75%	28/40=70%	84/121=69%

Identifying misinformation is intrinsically difficult. People are not able to tell whether the information is correct easily, let alone computers. The following observations are noticed:

- Table 4 shows the proposed method is no better than other simple methods. Nevertheless, this research is not without merit. It reveals advanced and innovative methods may not always beat simple methods, but the former may have their advantages like finding hidden misinformation. A better approach (such as using data fusion) may be to integrate advantages from various methods and hope to come up with better results.
- The accuracy is satisfactory, but not optimal. It may be because the information provided by short messages is limited. To fix the problem, more information needs to be discovered from the messages.
- This self-reconfiguration applies to the input words of the dataflow graph and one time only. Better results may be achieved if the reconfiguration can be applied to other layers and more than once.

CONCLUSION

Smartphones are indispensable devices for people in these days, and tens or even hundreds of messages are sent to each device every day. All kinds of information can be found from the delivered messages such as news, greetings from family members or friends, advertisements, promotions, weather reports, etc. People are overwhelmed by the sheer amount of information and they spend much time trying to find a way to sort out the messages. Even worse is some messages give false or fake information and mislead the viewers consequently. The problem becomes more serious especially during the pandemic. This research proposes a self-reconfigurable system for identifying health text misinformation, so mobile users will take appropriate actions based on the findings. When an incoming message is received by the system, it is processed as follows. The message is converted into a skeletal message by the preprocessor of the system including lexical analyzer, stopword remover, stemmer, and synonym discovery. A dataflow graph is used to find the class (true, fake, misinformative, disinformative, or neutral) of the skeletal message. In addition, after the first round of testing, the system will use the results to reconfigure itself and expect to receive better results.

Future Research

So far, no methods can successfully identify all misinformation, but each method has its own advantages. Data fusion may be used to combine all advantages and expect to receive better results. Using RNN (recurrent neural network) to handle the sequential data will be considered next. The ANN is considered because this problem has no definite answers. For example, a message may be considered true for some people, but others may think it is disinformative, especially if it is related to politics, and ANN is competent for this kind of ambivalence. In addition, other than using artificial neural networks to detect misinformation, statistical means will be considered too. The statistical means includes the methods of Bayesian classifiers and hidden Markov models. It is less innovative, but may be more effective. On the other end, DL (deep learning) may be more innovative. It has been applied to NLP (natural language processing) for some time, and has received great success. This problem, mobile health misinformation identification, could be classified as one of the NLP problems. We will consider a variety of DL methods and adapt them to our problem, and see whether the problems are mitigated. Besides, there has been a rising interest in proactive intervention strategies to counter the spread of misinformation and its impact on society. Methods to mitigate the ill effects caused by misinformation will be investigated too.

REFERENCES

Ahmed, A., Ali, G., Hussain, A., Baseer, A., & Ahmed, J. (2021). Analysis of text feature extractors using deep learning on fake news. *Engineering, Technology, &. Applied Scientific Research, 11*(2), 7001–7005.

Aldwairi, M., & Alwahedi, A. (2018, November 5). Detecting fake news in social media networks. *Procedia Computer Science, 141*, 215–222. doi:10.1016/j.procs.2018.10.171

Ball, P., & Maxmen, A. (2020). The epic battle against coronavirus misinformation and conspiracy theories. *Nature, 581*(7809), 371–374. doi:10.1038/d41586-020-01452-z PMID:32461658

Bozuyla, M. (2021). AdaBoost ensemble learning on top of naive Bayes algorithm to discriminate fake and genuine news from social media. *European Journal of Science and Technology*, *5*(4), 499–513. doi:10.31590/ejosat.1005577

Brennen, J. S., Simon, F. M., & Nielsen, R. K. (2021). Beyond (mis) representation: Visuals in COVID-19 misinformation. *The International Journal of Press/Politics*, *26*(1), 277–299. doi:10.1177/1940161220964780

Collins, B., Hoang, D. T., Nguyen, N. T., & Hwang, D. (2021). Trends in combating fake news on social media – a survey. *Journal of Information and Telecommunication*, *5*(2), 247–266. doi:10.1080/24751839.2020.1847379

Fleming, N. (2020, June 17). Coronavirus misinformation, and how scientists can help to fight it. *Nature*, *583*(7814), 155–156. doi:10.1038/d41586-020-01834-3 PMID:32601491

Guo, B., Ding, Y., Yao, L., Liang, Y., & Yu, Z. (2020, September 4). The future of false information detection on social media: new perspectives and trends. *ACM Computing Surveys, 53*(4), 68, 1-36.

Gupta, L., Gasparyan, A. Y., Misra, D. P., Agarwal, V., Zimba, O., & Yessirkepov, M. (2020, July 13). Information and misinformation on COVID-19: A cross-sectional survey study. *Journal of Korean Medical Science*, *35*(27), e257. doi:10.3346/jkms.2020.35.e256 PMID:32657090

Hakak, S., Alazab, M., Khan, S., Gadekallu, T., Maddikunta, P., & Khan, W. (2021). An ensemble machine learning approach through effective feature extraction to classify fake news. *Future Generation Computer Systems*, *117*, 47–58. doi:10.1016/j.future.2020.11.022

Isha Priyavamtha, U. J., Vishnu Vardhan Reddy, G., Devisri, P., & Manek, A. S. (2021). Fake news detection using artificial neural network algorithm. In K. R. Venugopal, P. D. Shenoy, R. Buyya, L. M. Patnaik, & S. S. Iyengar (Eds.), *Data Science and Computational Intelligence. ICInPro 2021. Communications in Computer and Information Science* (Vol. 1483). Springer. doi:10.1007/978-3-030-91244-4_26

Islam, M. R., Liu, S., Wang, X., & Xu, G. (2020). Deep learning for misinformation detection on online social networks: A survey and new perspectives. *Social Network Analysis and Mining*, *10*(1), 82. doi:10.100713278-020-00696-x PMID:33014173

Kaliyar, R. K., Goswami, A., & Narang, P. (2019). Multiclass fake news detection using ensemble machine learning. In *Proceedings of 2019 IEEE 9th International Conference on Advanced Computing (IACC)*, (pp. 103-107). IEEE. 10.1109/IACC48062.2019.8971579

Keras. (n.d.). *Keras: the Python deep learning API*. Keras. https://keras.io

Khan, T., Michalas, A., & Akhunzada, A. (2021, September 15). Fake news outbreak 2021: Can we stop the viral spread? *Journal of Network and Computer Applications*, *190*, 103112. doi:10.1016/j.jnca.2021.103112

Kula, S., Choraś, M., Kozik, R., Ksieniewicz, P., & Woźniak, M. (2020). Sentiment analysis for fake news detection by means of neural networks. In V. V. Krzhizhanovskaya, (Eds), *Computational Science – ICCS 2020* (p. 12140). Lecture Notes in Computer Science. Springer. doi:10.1007/978-3-030-50423-6_49

Liu, Q., Yu, F., Wu, S., & Wang, L. (2018). Mining significant microblogs for misinformation identification: An attention-based approach. [TIST]. *ACM Transactions on Intelligent Systems and Technology*, *9*(5), 1–20. doi:10.1145/3173458

Mian, A. & Khan, S. (2020). Coronavirus: the spread of misinformation. *BMC Medinine, 18*(89).

Mridha, M. F., Keya, A. J., Hamid, M. A., Monowar, M. M., & Rahman, M. S. (2021). A comprehensive review on fake news detection with deep learning. *IEEE Access : Practical Innovations, Open Solutions*, *9*, 156151–156170. doi:10.1109/ACCESS.2021.3129329

Reddy, H., Raj, N., Gala, M., & Basava, A. (2020, February 18). Text-mining-based fake news detection using ensemble methods. *International Journal of Automation and Computing*, *17*(2), 210–221. doi:10.100711633-019-1216-5

Savage, N. (2021, March 12). Fact-finding mission. *Communications of the ACM*, *64*(3), 18–19. doi:10.1145/3446879

Schuster, T., Schuster, R., Shah, D. J., & Barzilay, R. (2020). The limitations of stylometry for detecting machine-generated fake news. *Computational Linguistics*, *46*(2), 499–510. doi:10.1162/coli_a_00380

Sethi, R. J., Rangaraju, R., & Shurts, B. (2019, May 30). Fact checking misinformation using recommendations from emotional pedagogical agents. In A. Coy, Y. Hayashi, & M. Chang (Eds.), *Intelligent Tutoring Systems* (pp. 99–104). doi:10.1007/978-3-030-22244-4_13

Sharma, K., Qian, F., Jiang, H., Ruchansky, N., Zhang, M., & Liu, Y. (2019, May). Combating fake news: a survey on identification and mitigation techniques. *ACM Transactions on Intelligent Systems and Technology, 10*(3), 1-42.

Sinha, H. & Sharma, Y. (2021). Text-convolutional neural networks for fake news detection in Tweets. In V. Bhateja, S. L. Peng, S.C. Satapathy, and Y. D. Zhang (eds), Evolution in Computational Intelligence. Advances in Intelligent Systems and Computing. Springer, Singapore.

Sitaula, N., Mohan, C. K., Grygiel, J., Zhou, X., & Zafarani, R. (2020). Credibility-based fake news detection. In K. Shu, S. Wang, D. Lee, & H. Liu (Eds.), *Disinformation, misinformation, and fake news in social media, Lecture Notes in Social Networks* (pp. 163–182). Springer. doi:10.1007/978-3-030-42699-6_9

TensorFlow. (n.d.). *TensorFlow: an end-to-end open source machine learning platform*. TensorFlow. https://www.tensorflow.org

Vadakkethil Somanathan Pilla, E. S. (2023). *A self-reconfigurable ANN*. https://github.com/sanjaikanth/ANNSelfConfigure

Vadakkethil Somanathan Pillai, E., S. & Hu, W.-C. (2022). *Effective information retrieval for mobile misinformation identification*. In 2022 International Conference on Engineering, Science and Technology (IConEST 2022), Austin, Texas.

van der Linden, S. (2022). Misinformation: Susceptibility, spread, and interventions to immunize the public. *Nature Medicine*, *28*(3), 460–467. doi:10.103841591-022-01713-6 PMID:35273402

Visser, J., Lawrence, J., & Reed, C. (2020). Reason-checking fake news. *Communications of the ACM*, *63*(11), 38–40. doi:10.1145/3397189

World Health Organization. (2023, June 28). *WHO Coronavirus (COVID-19) Dashboard: Overview*. WHO. https://covid19.who.int/

Xamarin. (n.d.). *Cross-platform with Xamarin*. Microsoft. https://dotnet.microsoft.com/en-us/apps/xamarin/cross-platform

Yu, F., Liu, Q., Wu, S., Wang, L., & Tan, T. (2019). Attention-based convolutional approach for misinformation identification from massive and noisy microblog posts. *computers & security, 83*, 106-121.

Zhou, X. & Zafarani, R. (2020, October). A survey of fake news: fundamental theories, detection methods, and opportunities. *ACM Computing Surveys, 53*(5), 109, 1-40.

Chapter 11
Navigating Cloud Security Risks, Threats, and Solutions for Seamless Business Logistics

Shalbani Das
Amity University, Kolkata, India

Shreyashi Mukherjee
Amity University, Kolkata, India

ABSTRACT

This chapter explores cloud security challenges faced by businesses adopting cloud technologies for logistics operations. It provides a roadmap to strengthen cloud security, safeguard digital assets, and foster solid business-CSP relationships. The chapter covers hazards, solutions (e.g., threat intelligence platforms, MFA, intrusion detection, encryption), shared responsibility with CSPs, and selecting reliable providers. Practical guidelines for a comprehensive cloud security strategy are offered, including risk assessments, access controls, incident response, and employee training. Understanding these aspects helps companies proactively secure their data and ensure seamless logistics in the cloud. By gaining a deep understanding of the risks, threats, and solutions associated with cloud security in business logistics, companies can proactively safeguard their critical data and ensure the seamless and secure operation of their logistical processes in the cloud.

1. INTRODUCTION TO CLOUD SECURITY RISKS AND THREATS

Although cloud computing has completely changed how businesses manage their data, it also comes with it some security dangers and threats that need to be understood and countered. The difficulties in safeguarding cloud-based data and applications are discussed in this introduction. Potential dangers include data breaches, unsafe interfaces and APIs, data loss and leakage, a lack of due diligence, risks associated with multi-tenancy, denial-of-service attacks, and compliance and legal difficulties. Organizations must

DOI: 10.4018/979-8-3693-2081-5.ch011

be proactive in implementing strong security measures such as robust authentication, access controls, encryption, and monitoring mechanisms to mitigate these risks (Butt et al., 2023). By understanding and addressing these challenges, businesses can protect their data and maintain trust in the cloud.

1.1 Understanding Cloud Computing and its Importance in Business Logistics

The utilization of computing resources like servers, storage, databases, software, and networking through the internet is a capability of cloud computing. Businesses can rent or subscribe to these services from cloud service providers instead of purchasing and maintaining physical hardware and software infrastructure (Bayarçelik et al., 2020). Applications and data are processed and stored remotely in data centers run by cloud service providers.

Importance in Business Logistics

1. ***Scalability:*** Businesses may scale their resources up or down based on demand thanks to cloud computing. It is essential to be able to quickly alter computing resources in the logistics industry since demand can fluctuate dramatically owing to seasonality or shifting market conditions.
2. ***Cost Savings:*** Traditional IT infrastructure necessitates hefty initial hardware and software license expenditures as well as continuous maintenance costs. In the pay-as-you-go approach of cloud computing, companies only pay for the resources they really utilise. Logistics businesses can avoid overprovisioning and cut operational costs by using this economic strategy.
3. ***Accessibility and Mobility:*** Remote access to data and applications is made possible by cloud-based logistics solutions from any location with an internet connection. For logistics managers and staff who must access real-time data, work with team members, and make quick decisions while on the go or working remotely, this accessibility is essential.
4. ***Data Management and Analytics:*** Large amounts of data, such as shipping information, inventory levels, transportation routes, and customer data, must be handled in logistics. Powerful data processing and storage capabilities provided by cloud computing enable effective data management, analysis, and insight generation for the improvement of logistical operations.
5. ***Integration and Collaboration:*** Enterprise resource planning (ERP) software, customer relationship management (CRM) systems, and third-party logistics partners are just a few of the numerous apps and systems that cloud-based logistics platforms can interact with. The supply chain is more efficient overall thanks to this integration, which also promotes collaboration and information flow.
6. ***Disaster Recovery and Security:*** Cloud providers implement robust security measures and data backup procedures. This helps protect logistics data from cyber threats and provides reliable disaster recovery options in case of hardware failures or natural disasters. For logistics businesses, data security and business continuity are paramount, making cloud computing an asset.
7. ***Innovation and Agility:*** Logistics businesses may experiment with cutting-edge technology and services thanks to cloud computing without having to make substantial upfront investments. Logistics companies may quickly adopt and implement new solutions to maintain their competitiveness in a market that is changing quickly thanks to access to a wide range of cloud-based tools and services.

In terms of corporate logistics, cloud computing is significant due to its capacity to increase effectiveness, lower costs, offer real-time access to and analysis of crucial data and promote innovation. Adopting cloud technologies is becoming necessary to stay ahead in the cutthroat global market as logistical operations get more sophisticated.

1.2 Overview of Cloud Security Risks and Threats

The administration of data and apps for businesses has significantly improved thanks to cloud computing. But technology also offers particular security concerns and dangers that businesses must comprehend and counteract (Kumar et al., 2019). To safeguard sensitive data and preserve operational integrity, organizations should be aware of the major cloud security risks and threats that will be covered in this review.

1. ***Data Loss:*** Data loss can occur due to human errors, technological errors, or other unforeseen causes, even though cloud services often feature reliable data backup mechanisms. Businesses must have data backup and recovery policies in place to mitigate the effects of data loss.
2. ***Misconfiguration:*** Cloud resources that are incorrectly configured can lead to security flaws. For instance, exposing data might result from leaving databases or storage containers out to the public without the proper access controls.
3. ***Data Breaches:*** The increased probability of data breaches is one of the main concerns with the cloud. If the stored data on the cloud is not protected properly, it may be exposed to threats and unauthorized access by any outsider. This can lead to major consequences for the business and its customers.
4. ***Insecure APIs:*** Application Programming Interfaces are abbreviated as APIs. They are necessary for applications and cloud services to communicate with one another. But if these APIs are not well protected, they might serve as a gateway for hackers to access sensitive data and cloud resources without authorization.
5. Insider Threats: Security concerns from staff members, independent contractors, or anybody else with access to the company's cloud infrastructure are referred to as insider threats. Insiders who are careless or malicious could accidentally or purposefully breach critical data or cloud resources.
6. ***Advanced persistent threats (APTs):*** Well-organized and well-funded threat actors conduct APTs, which are sophisticated and targeted cyberattacks. These attackers may employ a variety of methods to get unrestricted access to cloud systems over an extended period and remain unnoticed while stealing sensitive data.
7. ***Technology Vulnerabilities that Affect several Customers:*** Cloud providers service several clients on the same infrastructure, therefore a vulnerability affecting one client may potentially affect others. Vulnerabilities in shared technology underscore how crucial it is for cloud providers to establish strong isolation and security measures.
8. ***Issues with Compliance and Regulatory Compliance:*** Issues and compliance with industry norms and data protection legislation may provide difficulties when data is stored in the cloud. These conditions must be followed to avoid any reputational harm or legal repercussions.
9. ***Denial of Service (DoS) Attacks:*** An overwhelming amount of bandwidth or resource requests are used to overwhelm a cloud service during a DoS attack, making it unavailable to authorized users. Such assaults may result in operational disruptions and monetary losses.

10. ***Risks to Cloud Service Providers:*** Cloud providers could experience their own security problems, which might affect the security of the data of their clients. Businesses must carefully evaluate the security precautions and reputation of the cloud service providers they select.

Businesses must put in place a strong cloud security strategy that includes encryption, access controls, strong authentication mechanisms, regular audits and assessments, employee security training, and continuous monitoring of cloud environments for suspicious activity to reduce these risks and threats. Furthermore, enhancing cloud security and safeguarding priceless data and resources can be accomplished by following industry best practices and abiding by pertinent compliance standards. Organizations can profit from cloud computing while safeguarding their sensitive data and upholding operational integrity by comprehending and successfully managing these cloud security risks and threats.

Figure 1. Need for navigating cloud security risks in business logistics

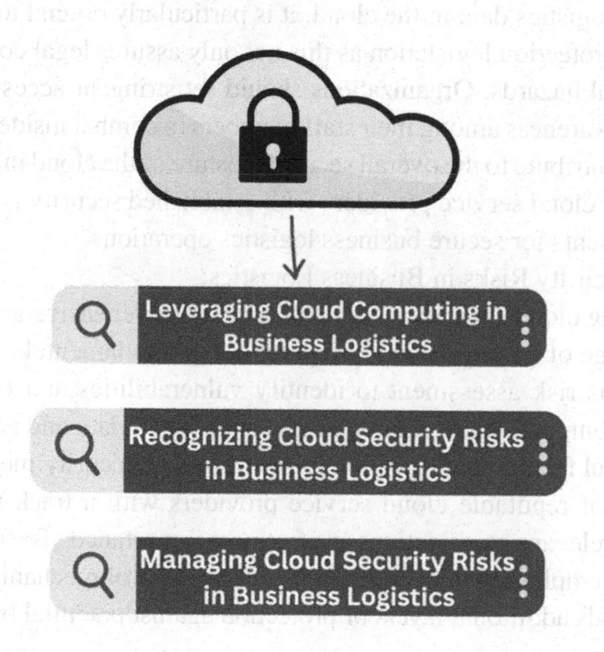

1.3 The Need for Navigating Cloud Security Risks in Business Logistics

The integration of cloud computing in business logistics has revolutionized the industry, offering unmatched flexibility, scalability, and efficiency. However, alongside these benefits, organizations must prioritize the management of cloud security risks to safeguard sensitive data, ensure operational integrity, and facilitate seamless logistics operations. This article emphasizes the significance of effectively addressing these risks within the context of business logistics.

1. Leveraging Cloud Computing in Business Logistics:
   Cloud computing serves as a powerful catalyst for optimizing logistics processes, enabling real-time collaboration, enhanced visibility, and streamlined resource management across the supply chain. By embracing cloud-based logistics solutions, organizations can efficiently manage inventory, transportation planning, warehouse operations, and overall supply chain visibility. However, to harness these benefits, a proactive approach is required to mitigate the associated security risks (Attaran et al., 2017).
2. Recognizing Cloud Security Risks in Business Logistics:
   Protecting against data breaches must be a top priority for cloud service providers handling sensitive logistics data. Sensitive data is protected by robust security methods, such as multi-factor authentication and encryption, which are essential in preventing unauthorized access. When storing and processing logistics data in the cloud, it is particularly crucial to follow industry-specific standards and data protection legislation as this not only assures legal compliance but also lowers potential reputational hazards. Organizations should set stringent access controls and promote a culture of security awareness among their staff members to combat insider threats. Additionally, as they significantly contribute to the overall security posture of the cloud infrastructure, it is essential to select trustworthy cloud service providers with established security procedures and transparent service level agreements for secure business logistics operations.
3. Managing Cloud Security Risks in Business Logistics:
   Effectively managing cloud security risks demands a comprehensive and multifaceted approach, encompassing a range of strategies and best practices. A fundamental step in this process is conducting a meticulous risk assessment to identify vulnerabilities and threats that pertain to the specific cloud environment. Understanding the sensitivity of data and complying with regulatory requirements are vital factors that drive the prioritization of security measures.
   - The selection of reputable cloud service providers with a track record of robust security practices and relevant certifications is of utmost importance. To further fortify the security infrastructure, employing data encryption, access control mechanisms, and multi-factor authentication adds additional layers of protection against potential breaches and unauthorized access.
   - Continual vigilance is crucial, and regular security audits and continuous monitoring must be in place to swiftly detect and respond to any suspicious activities or potential security breaches in real-time. Additionally, ensuring that critical data is regularly backed up and that employees are well-trained in cloud security best practices contributes significantly to maintaining a secure cloud environment.

- To effectively deal with security incidents, an incident response plan must be developed and regularly tested to guarantee a swift and organized response. Compliance management is equally imperative to avoid any legal ramifications related to industry-specific regulations and data protection laws.
- Regularly patching software and utilizing cloud-native security tools further bolsters the overall security posture. Clear and well-defined cloud governance policies are essential to maintain consistency and adherence to security standards throughout the organization.

By synergistically integrating these measures and staying agile in adapting to emerging threats, businesses can confidently safeguard their cloud operations and protect their valuable data from potential breaches and cyber threats. Proactive and thoughtful management of cloud security risks is a continuous endeavor that ensures the safety and resilience of cloud-based infrastructure and applications (Damenu et al., 2015).

2. COMMON CLOUD SECURITY RISKS AND THREATS

A paradigm shift in company operations has been sparked by the exponential use of cloud computing, which provides unmatched scalability, flexibility, and cost-effectiveness. Nevertheless, new challenges and weaknesses have appeared alongside this breakthrough technology. The need for protecting data, apps, and infrastructure stored in the cloud has made cloud security a top issue. In this post, we examine common cloud security dangers and vulnerabilities that enterprises face in the modern corporate environment.

2.1 Data Breaches and Unauthorized Access

Data breaches and unauthorized access are two prominent security risks that organizations must address in today's digital landscape. Due to the advanced methods, hackers use to find flaws in security systems, these threats have become more widespread. When unauthorized individuals access sensitive or confidential data kept in an organization's systems, a data breach occurs. These breaches may be made possible via employee account compromise, lax security procedures, or hacking techniques. Data Breaches may cause an extensive range of problems, including reputational harm, monetary losses, a decline in customer trust as well as legal implications. Unauthorized access, on the contrary, refers to individuals using computers, networks, or applications without the necessary authorization. Weak or stolen credentials, poor access safeguards, and bugs in software or hardware could all lead to unauthorized access. Once inside, hostile actors have the ability to influence, abuse, or extract sensitive information, seriously hurting businesses and customers. Mitigating these risks requires a comprehensive approach, encompassing robust authentication mechanisms, encryption of data, regular security audits, employee training, and vigilant monitoring of system activities. By prioritizing these measures, organizations can strengthen their defense against data breaches and unauthorized access, safeguard their critical assets, and maintain the trust of their stakeholders.

2.2 Insider Threats and Privilege Misuse

- ***Insider Threats:*** In terms of cloud security, insider threats refer to the dangers posed by employees who, purposefully or accidentally, exploit their authorized access to cloud infrastructure, apps, or data for nefarious objectives. Since insiders already have authorized access, it is difficult to identify these hazards. There can be numerous consequences. Some of them are unauthorized access to sensitive applications or information, destruction of important systems or data, theft of confidential business or intellectual property, interruption of business operations, and harm to the company's trust and reputation. Role-Based Access Control (RBAC) policies, routine user activity monitoring, awareness programs, and employee training. The use of Data Loss Prevention (DLP) solutions is all instruments that organizations can take to reduce these risks. These solutions protect sensitive data from unauthorized exposure or leakage.
- ***Privilege Misuse:*** Misuse of privileges poses a serious threat to cloud security and can interfere with smooth business logistics in a cloud computing environment. Security breaches and operational disruptions can result from authorized users abusing their access permissions beyond their allocated privileges. Unauthorized access to crucial data or applications, data loss or corruption as a result of file alteration or deletion, an increase in insider threats, and a compromised cloud infrastructure that affects business continuity are just a few possible effects. Organizations can use a number of strategies to reduce this risk, such as enforcing the least privilege principle, putting privileged access management (PAM) solutions in place, conducting routine audits and monitoring, enabling multi-factor authentication (MFA), utilizing user behavior analytics (UBA), educating staff members about security issues, creating incident response plans, and constantly enhancing cloud security measures. These tactics guarantee safe business operations and safeguard private information and cloud-based assets.

2.3 Insecure Interfaces and APIs

Application programming interfaces (APIs) are frequently offered by cloud services to facilitate easy integration and communication within the cloud ecosystem. These APIs serve as "bridges" that enable communication across various cloud components, simplifying the use of cloud resources by developers and applications. A poorly designed or poorly secured interface, however, might turn into a point of entry for malicious activity, posing serious hazards to the cloud infrastructure's overall security.

Attackers may access sensitive data or vital programs without authorization by taking advantage of API flaws, which could result in data breaches and information theft. Additionally, they have the ability to alter data, jeopardize the security of cloud services, or even launch assaults on other associated cloud environment components. Serious repercussions, including service interruptions, monetary losses, and reputational harm to the afflicted organization, may result from these scenarios.

Organizations must assess and strengthen their APIs on the front end in order to protect themselves against these risks. This procedure entails a thorough evaluation of the security controls, implementation, and design of APIs. Effective security testing, the use of appropriate systems for authentication and authorization, and the implementation of stringent access controls are all examples of best practices. The regular monitoring and tracking of API activity should be given top priority by organizations in order to quickly spot any suspicious or aberrant behavior. This minimizes the total impact on business operations and data integrity by allowing for the quick identification and remediation of potential security breaches.

Additionally, as trustworthy cloud service providers regularly update and improve their API offerings to stay ahead of new dangers, working with them can add extra layers of protection. Organizations can better safeguard their cloud ecosystem from potential API-related vulnerabilities and guarantee the secure and uninterrupted operation of their cloud-based services by implementing a layered and dynamic security approach.

2.4 Malware and Ransomware Attacks

The proliferation of malware and ransomware attacks in the constantly changing digital ecosystem has put a shadow over people, companies, and governments. These hostile attacks destroy data integrity, privacy, and economic stability by taking advantage of flaws in computer systems and networks. This article explores the subtleties of malware and ransomware assaults, illuminating their disastrous effects and emphasizing the critical requirement for proactive defense tactics.

- ***Malware Attacks:*** Malware, a condensed form of "malicious software," constitutes a diverse category of malevolent programs crafted with the intent to infiltrate computer systems and execute harmful actions. Among the most encountered malware are viruses, worms, Trojan horses, and spyware. Operating stealth, these nefarious entities can penetrate both indiscriminate and specifically targeted computer systems, employing a myriad of tactics, including deceptive downloads, subverted websites, and corrupted email attachments. Once inside a system, malware can wreak havoc by disrupting its performance, stealing sensitive data, or granting unauthorized access to hackers. Strong antivirus software, frequent system upgrades, and user education to prevent clicking on dubious links or downloading dubious files are all necessary for combating malware.
- ***Ransomware Attacks:*** Ransomware attacks have increased in frequency over the past few years, posing a major threat to both individuals and enterprises. Ransomware is a specific form of malicious software designed with harmful intent. It operates by either actively disrupting the normal functioning of a victim's computer system or encrypting vital data, making it inaccessible to its rightful owner. The attackers responsible for unleashing the ransomware then demand a ransom payment from the victim, using it as leverage to offer a potential solution: the restoration of access to the compromised system or the decryption of the locked data. Cybercriminals typically utilize software weaknesses or social engineering techniques to distribute ransomware payloads. Serious consequences, including monetary losses, reputational harm, and operational interruption, may result from a successful ransomware attack. To lessen the risk of ransomware attacks, businesses must implement network segmentation, create reliable backup strategies, and place a high focus on employee training.

2.5 Denial of Service (DoS) Attacks

Denial of Service (DoS) assaults have grown to be a major problem for people, companies, and organizations in today's linked world. These malicious attacks intend to disable targeted systems or networks, disrupt operations, and seriously harm the organization's finances and reputation.

I. Denial of Service (DoS) Attacks Defined:
Denial of service attacks, commonly referred to as DoS attacks, represent malevolent efforts to overwhelm a specific target system or network with an enormous influx of traffic or requests. The primary goal is to render the system or network unavailable to legitimate users, disrupting its regular operations and causing potential chaos or financial harm (Gu et al., 2007).

II. Types of DoS Attacks:
DoS assaults can take many different forms, including:
   a. **Flood Attacks:** These attacks flood the target system or network with an excessive amount of data packets, overwhelming its capacity to handle legitimate traffic.
   b. **SYN Flood Attacks:** This kind of attack sends numerous SYN requests but fails to complete the connection, using up server resources. It makes use of flaws in the TCP handshake process.
   c. **Distributed Denial of Service (DDoS) Attacks:** DDoS assaults employ a botnet made up of numerous hacked systems that concurrently fire attack packets against the target, making mitigation more difficult.

III. Consequences of DoS Attacks:
DoS assaults can have serious effects on organizations. They may interfere with how businesses operate, resulting in losses of money and damaged reputations. In other instances, the attack might be used as a smokescreen to hide other bad deeds, such as data theft or network infiltration.

IV. Defense Strategies:
To defend against DoS attacks, organizations should consider implementing the following strategies:
   a. **Traffic Filtering:** Deploying firewalls and intrusion prevention systems to filter and block suspicious traffic can help mitigate the impact of DoS attacks.
   b. **Bandwidth Management:** Employing traffic shaping and rate limiting techniques can prioritize legitimate traffic and help absorb the impact of an attack.
   c. **Load Balancing:** By sharing the load, traffic distribution among several servers or resources might reduce the severity of a DoS assault.
   d. **Incident Response Planning:** Organizations can respond quickly and successfully to a DoS assault by establishing an incident response strategy.

2.6 Loss of Data and Data Integrity Issues

In the modern digital era, data has evolved into a vital lifeline for organizations, underscoring the crucial need for its protection and integrity. Nevertheless, the looming specter of data loss and data integrity issues presents considerable challenges, affecting both businesses and individuals. This article delves deeply into the intricacies of these two concerns, shedding light on the potential consequences they may bring (Sivathanu et al., 2005). Additionally, the article explores a range of effective strategies to proactively mitigate these risks, thereby safeguarding the security and reliability of valuable data resources.

- ***Data Loss:*** In the digital landscape, data loss is a concerning phenomenon characterized by the irreversible destruction or unavailability of valuable information stored in digital formats. Data loss can be an unfortunate occurrence triggered by various factors, such as hardware malfunctions, human errors, natural disasters, or intentional malicious actions. The repercussions of data loss extend to significant outcomes, including financial losses, disruptions in business operations, potential violations of regulatory compliance, and harm to an organization's reputation. Safeguarding against data loss is crucial to mitigate these wide-ranging consequences and preserve the integrity of valuable information.

To proactively mitigate the risk of data loss, organizations must adopt robust measures. Implementing effective backup and recovery mechanisms becomes essential to fortify data protection strategies. Regularly backing up data and ensuring secure offsite storage provide a safety net, enhancing resilience in the face of potential data loss incidents. By diligently adhering to these practices, organizations can strengthen their ability to recover from setbacks, ensuring the continuity and integrity of their valuable digital assets.

- ***Data Integrity Issues:*** Data management involves handling and safeguarding data throughout its lifecycle. Data integrity issues come to the forefront when the accuracy, consistency, or security of data faces compromise during its storage, processing, or transmission phases. These concerns can stem from a variety of factors, including software errors, unauthorized alterations, data corruption, or intentional tampering. The outcomes of data integrity problems can be broad and impactful, potentially resulting in undesirable consequences like making erroneous decisions, encountering operational inefficiencies, breaching compliance standards, and experiencing a loss of trust from customers or stakeholders. Addressing data integrity proactively becomes essential to mitigate risks and maintain the reliability of data used for critical decision-making processes and interactions with stakeholders.

To ensure the reliability and credibility of their data, organizations must proactively address data integrity concerns. By implementing robust data management practices, such as regular data validation and access controls, organizations can foster trust among their clients and maintain the integrity of their data. These measures are crucial in building strong relationships with stakeholders and upholding the quality of data used for critical decision-making processes.

- ***Causes and Impact:*** The occurrence of data loss and data integrity issues can be attributed to a confluence of technical and human factors. Technical elements entail hardware failures, software glitches, power outages, and cyberattacks, each capable of disrupting data storage and accessibility. Conversely, human errors, like accidental deletions, mishandling of data, or inadequate security practices, also hold considerable responsibility for precipitating data loss and jeopardizing the integrity of stored information.

Addressing the intricate interplay between technical vulnerabilities and human fallibility is crucial in devising effective data protection strategies. By implementing comprehensive measures such as robust security protocols, regular data backups, and continuous training for employees, organizations can bolster their defense against data loss and uphold the integrity of valuable information. These proactive efforts not only mitigate the immediate financial losses but also safeguard against operational disruptions, foster strong customer relationships, avert legal and regulatory consequences, and preserve the organization's brand reputation.

The impact of these issues stretches beyond immediate financial losses, extending to disruptions in operations, compromised customer relationships, legal and regulatory consequences, and a diminished brand reputation. Recognizing the interplay between technical vulnerabilities and human fallibility is vital in formulating effective data protection strategies. By implementing comprehensive measures such as robust security protocols, regular backups, and continuous employee training, organizations can bolster their defense against data loss and uphold the integrity of valuable information. These efforts are essential for maintaining a secure data environment and safeguarding the trust and confidence of stakeholders.

3. CLOUD SECURITY SOLUTIONS FOR BUSINESS LOGISTICS

In today's logistics industry, businesses increasingly rely on cloud computing for their operations, making robust cloud security a critical priority. Customized cloud security solutions enable organizations to safeguard sensitive data, streamline logistics processes, and maintain a secure ecosystem. The foundation of cloud security lies in building a strong infrastructure with robust access controls, encryption, and network segmentation. Identity and Access Management (IAM) solutions provide precise control over user access to logistics systems. Data encryption ensures the confidentiality and integrity of logistics data (Sergi et al., 2021). Proactive threat intelligence and monitoring systems identify and mitigate potential security threats. Secure file-sharing and collaboration tools promote productivity while maintaining data security. Regular security audits, updates, and employee training enhance cloud security awareness. By prioritizing cloud security solutions, businesses can strengthen their logistics operations, build customer trust, and achieve sustainable success in the dynamic logistics landscape.

3.1 Cloud Service Providers (CSPs) and Their Security Offerings

Today's businesses rely heavily on cloud service providers (CSPs) as they offer a diverse array of cloud-based solutions that effectively enhance and simplify operations. The assurance of security is paramount for these providers who prioritize the protection of sensitive client data and the smooth execution of logistical tasks. In the context of business logistics, CSPs typically offer the following security services:

1. ***Data Encryption:*** CSPs often offer encryption services to protect data during transit and while it is stored, ensuring the safety of logistics information from unauthorized access.
2. ***Identity and Access Management (IAM):*** IAM solutions assist in controlling user identities and access to a range of resources and applications for logistics. It enables businesses to put in place stringent access controls that grant access to only authorized individuals.
3. ***Network Security:*** In the realm of cloud services, the security of logistical systems is of paramount importance to cloud service providers (CSPs). They employ a diverse array of network security measures to uphold this security. These measures include the strategic implementation of firewalls, intrusion detection/prevention systems, and virtual private networks (VPNs). By leveraging these robust security protocols, CSPs ensure the protection of communication channels and prevent unauthorized access to logistical systems. This proactive approach plays a pivotal role in safeguarding the integrity and confidentiality of the data involved in logistical operations.

4. ***DDoS Protection:*** The smooth operation of logistics operations can face challenges from Distributed Denial of Service (DDoS) attacks. To guarantee uninterrupted and dependable services, Cloud Service Providers (CSPs) provide specialized DDoS protection services. By implementing tailored measures, CSPs swiftly identify and mitigate DDoS attacks, safeguarding the accessibility and integrity of essential logistics applications and services. This proactive approach by CSPs is crucial in maintaining seamless logistics operations and creating a secure environment for businesses relying on cloud-based logistical solutions.
5. ***Security Compliance:*** To show their dedication to upholding strict security practices, CSPs comply with industry-standard security compliance frameworks like ISO 27001, SOC 2, and GDPR.
6. ***Regular Security Audits:*** CSPs regularly undertake security audits and assessments to find and fix any potential flaws in their services and infrastructure.
7. ***Incident Response and Monitoring:*** CSPs use incident response teams and 24/7 monitoring to identify and quickly address any potential security incidents.
8. ***Secure APIs and Integrations:*** CSPs make sure that their APIs are secure and adhere to best practices for organizations using cloud-based logistics applications and integrations to prevent unauthorized access and data breaches.
9. ***Data Backups and Disaster Recovery:*** CSPs frequently provide data backup and disaster recovery services, assisting organizations in maintaining continuity in the event of data loss or system malfunctions.
10. ***Security Consulting:*** Some CSPs offer security consulting services to help firms create and implement strong security plans that are suited to their logistical requirements.

Businesses may embrace cloud technologies with confidence in their logistical operations by utilizing these security services from respected CSPs, knowing that their vital data and procedures are safeguarded from any risks and disruptions (Kirubakaran et al., 2020).

3.2 Shared Responsibility Model

The Shared Responsibility model is a fundamental and collaborative approach to cloud security, wherein both the cloud service provider (CSP) and the business logistics organization jointly shoulder the responsibility of maintaining a secure cloud environment. While the CSP takes on the role of securing the underlying infrastructure and the services they offer, the business logistics organization is entrusted with the task of securing its applications, data, and user access within the cloud ecosystem (Migliano et al., 2014).

Within the framework of the Shared Responsibility model, numerous cloud security solutions can be implemented by business logistics organizations to ensure the protection of their critical assets:

1. ***Data Encryption:*** Implementing robust encryption methods becomes crucial to safeguard sensitive data during transmission and while at rest in the cloud. The organization must diligently encrypt its data before storing it in the cloud, while the CSP takes charge of encrypting data during its transfer and on its servers.

Figure 2. Shared responsibility model: Customer-cloud service provider

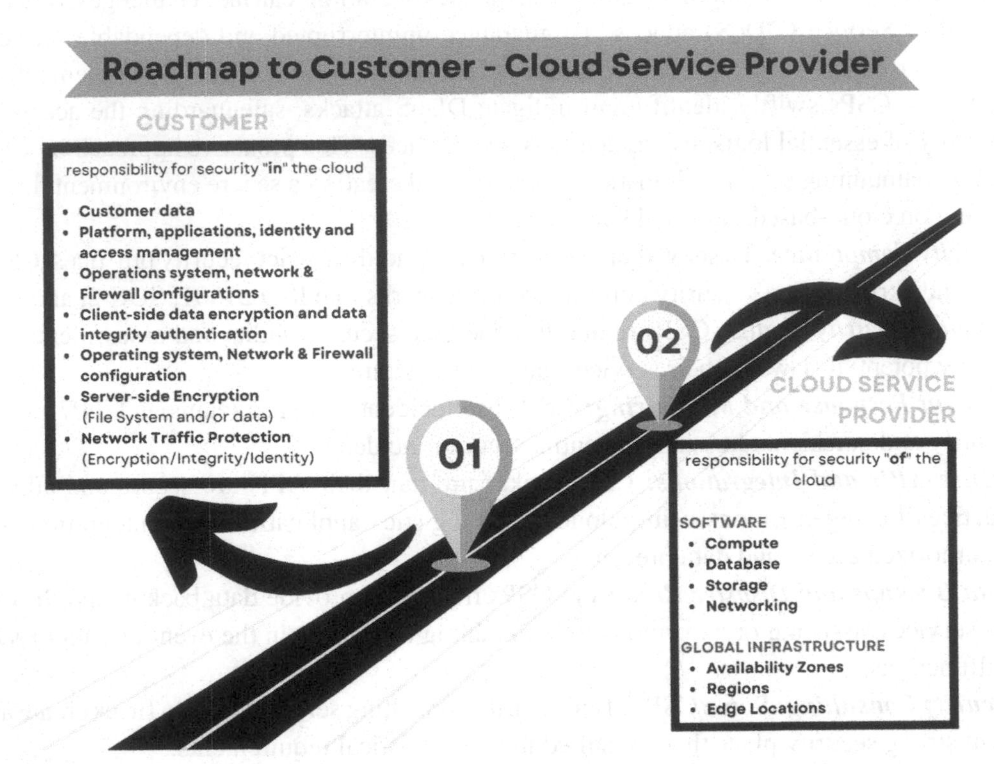

2. ***Identity and Access Management (IAM):*** Deploying IAM solutions helps efficiently manage user access to logistics applications and resources. The business logistics organization should establish strict access controls and enforce multi-factor authentication to bolster security, while the CSP assumes the responsibility of ensuring the security of IAM infrastructure.
3. ***Regular Security Audits:*** Conducting periodic security audits becomes instrumental in identifying and mitigating potential vulnerabilities in the cloud infrastructure and applications. The organization takes charge of performing internal audits, while the CSP may engage in conducting independent third-party audits to provide additional assurance.
4. ***Incident Response and Monitoring:*** Establishing 24/7 monitoring and incident response capabilities is essential to detect and respond promptly to any security incidents that may occur. Both the business logistics organization and the CSP collaborate in monitoring the cloud environment and jointly managing incident responses.
5. ***Compliance Management:*** Adhering to relevant industry and regulatory standards is vital to maintain the highest level of security and data privacy. The business logistics organization must ensure compliance for their applications and data, while the CSP assumes responsibility for maintaining compliance for their cloud services.
6. ***Secure Development Practices:*** Adopting secure coding practices becomes paramount when developing cloud-based applications to mitigate the risk of security vulnerabilities. The business logistics organization is responsible for ensuring the security of their applications, while the CSP focuses on enhancing the overall security of the cloud platform.

7. ***Disaster Recovery and Backup:*** Implementing robust disaster recovery and data backup plans is critical to ensure business continuity in the event of unforeseen disruptions. The organization is accountable for developing application-specific recovery plans, while the CSP ensures the overall resilience of the cloud infrastructure.
8. ***Employee Training and Awareness:*** Cultivating a security-aware culture among employees is essential to foster a proactive approach to cloud security. Educating employees about cloud security best practices and the shared responsibility model is a joint effort undertaken by both the organization and the CSP.

By embracing the Shared Responsibility Model and implementing these comprehensive cloud security solutions, business logistics organizations can significantly enhance their overall cloud security posture. As a result, they can effectively safeguard their valuable data and applications, fortify their logistics operations, and establish a robust security foundation within the dynamic cloud environment.

3.3 Selecting Reputable and Trustworthy CSPs

Selecting reputable and trustworthy Cloud Service Providers (CSPs) is of utmost importance when considering cloud security solutions for business logistics. Entrusting sensitive data and critical operations to a reliable CSP can significantly enhance the overall security posture of a logistics organization. When evaluating potential CSPs, businesses should prioritize providers with a proven track record in cloud security, robust compliance with industry standards and regulations, and transparent security practices. Additionally, assessing the CSP's data encryption methods, identity and access management features, incident response capabilities, and disaster recovery plans is essential. Reputable CSPs should offer comprehensive security audits, ongoing monitoring, and 24/7 support to promptly address any security incidents. By carefully choosing a trustworthy CSP that aligns with the organization's security requirements and goals, businesses can confidently leverage cloud technologies to optimize logistics operations while ensuring the confidentiality, integrity, and availability of their data and services.

3.4 Service Level Agreements (SLAs)

An organization and its cloud service provider (CSP) will agree to certain conditions and expectations in a formal contract known as a service level agreement (SLA). It outlines the performance standards and service standards that the CSP must satisfy, including criteria for uptime, response time, data accessibility, and customer assistance.

3.4.1 The Significance of Robust SLAs

Strong SLAs are essential for building a solid relationship between businesses and their CSPs. These contracts offer transparency and clarity, ensuring that all parties are aware of their respective duties and responsibilities. A well-structured SLA aids in establishing reasonable expectations and benchmarks, ensuring that the CSP provides services in line with the needs of the organization. Organizations are able to evaluate the CSP's performance objectively and hold them responsible for maintaining the agreed-upon service standards by defining performance indicators. Strong SLAs promote confidence and trust by assuring the organization that its vital activities and data are being handled with competence and dependability (Marquezan et al., 2014).

Figure 3. Service level agreements (SLAs)

3.4.2 Incident Response Plans for Strengthening Partnerships

SLAs include incident response plans, which specify the steps to take and who is responsible in the event of a security incident or data breach. The organization and the CSP will be ready to react quickly and successfully to any possible threats or interruptions if they have a well-defined incident response plan in place. A sense of readiness and assurance is created by this proactive approach to security, further solidifying the relationship between the two parties. Better communication and collaboration are made possible through incident response plans, ensuring a coordinated effort to reduce risks and any potential damage. Organizations and their CSPs show their dedication to proactive security measures and efficient risk management through these detailed plans, which are crucial components of a fruitful and reliable cloud service collaboration.

4. MANAGING CLOUD SECURITY RISKS IN BUSINESS LOGISTICS

Managing cloud security risks in business logistics is of paramount importance as organizations increasingly rely on cloud computing for their operations. To ensure a secure cloud environment, businesses must adopt a proactive approach that includes robust access controls, data encryption, regular security audits, and employee training on best security practices. Implementing multi-factor authentication and identity and access management (IAM) solutions helps safeguard against unauthorized access. Encryption of sensitive data both in transit and at rest ensures its confidentiality and integrity (Aviles et al., 2012). Regular security audits help identify and address vulnerabilities, while employee training fosters a culture of security awareness. By addressing cloud security risks effectively, organizations can protect their valuable data and maintain the seamless flow of logistics operations in the dynamic cloud environment.

4.1 Risk Assessment and Management Frameworks

In the dynamic field of business logistics, effectively managing cloud security risks requires the implementation of a robust risk assessment and management framework. Risk assessment and management frameworks are essential tools for effectively managing cloud security risks in business logistics. These frameworks provide a structured approach to identifying, analyzing, and mitigating potential risks associated with cloud computing. By conducting a thorough risk assessment, organizations can identify vulnerabilities, threats, and potential impact areas specific to their logistics operations in the cloud. Once risks are identified, appropriate risk management strategies can be implemented, such as adopting security best practices, selecting reputable cloud service providers (CSPs), and establishing robust Service Level Agreements (SLAs). Security measures should be regularly monitored and audited to assist in ensuring continuing compliance with security standards and laws. The organization's defense against possible threats is further strengthened by emphasizing a risk-aware culture and offering personnel training on cloud security. Businesses should proactively protect their logistical data and operations in the cloud by putting in place thorough risk assessment and management frameworks. This will allow them to make full use of cloud computing while maintaining a high level of security.

4.2 Incident Response Planning and Execution

An efficient incident response strategy is essential for handling security issues in the world of commercial logistics. A strategy that is precisely matched to the demands and difficulties of the logistics environment is necessary. Effectively managing cloud security risks in business logistics requires careful preparation and execution of incident responses. A well-defined incident response plan is an essential component of effectively managing cloud security risks in business logistics. The procedures, responsibilities, and actions to be done in the case of a security incident or data breach within the cloud environment are outlined in this comprehensive strategy, which acts as a thorough roadmap. Organizations may respond quickly and effectively, minimizing the impact of the incident on their logistics operations and data integrity, by having a clear and structured plan in place. Rapid incident detection and prompt communication are essential components of the incident response plan because they allow the response team to mobilize quickly to assess the situation and take the necessary action. The plan also emphasizes the importance of containment measures to prevent further spread of the incident, eradication of the threat, and recovery strategies to restore normalcy to the cloud environment. Additionally, a critical aspect of the incident response plan is the "lessons learned" phase, where the organization evaluates the incident's handling, identify areas for improvement, and applies these insights to strengthen its future incident response capabilities. Regular testing and simulations of the incident response plan are crucial to assess its effectiveness and validate the preparedness of the response team in handling various scenarios. These simulations provide an opportunity to identify any potential gaps or weaknesses in the plan, allowing organizations to refine and enhance their incident response strategies. By proactively investing in a well-structured incident response plan and regularly testing its execution, businesses can effectively safeguard their logistics operations, maintain the integrity of their data, foster a resilient and secure cloud environment, and can reduce the impact of security breaches, protect their sensitive logistics data, and maintain the trust of their customers and stakeholders.

4.3 Employee Training and Awareness Programs

It is impossible to exaggerate the value of personnel training and awareness programs when it comes to keeping a good security posture in the fast-paced world of commercial logistics. To foster a culture of security awareness, staff must be informed on cloud security threats and best practices.

Employee training and awareness programs are integral components of effectively managing cloud security risks in business logistics. As employees are key stakeholders in the cloud security landscape, educating them about best practices and potential threats is essential. These training initiatives provide employees with a comprehensive understanding of the organization's cloud security policies, procedures, and protocols. Employees are made aware of their role in safeguarding sensitive logistics data and the importance of adhering to security guidelines while accessing cloud resources. The training also addresses potential security breaches, phishing scams, and identifying and reporting unusual activity. An essential component of successfully managing cloud security risks in business logistics is fostering a security-conscious culture among personnel. Organizations can greatly lower the risk of human error and potential insider threats by developing a strong feeling of responsibility for data protection and cybersecurity. Training programs are essential to accomplishing this goal. These programs give staff members comprehensive information about the company's cloud security policies, practices, and best practices. Through interactive training and instructional sessions, staff members gain knowledge of the most recent cybersecurity trends, new threats, and best practices for safeguarding sensitive logistics data in the cloud environment. Through frequent updates and refresher training, staff members stay current with evolving industry standards and the state of cloud security. Employees may interact with cloud services in an educated manner by having access to the most recent information, ensuring they follow security procedures and comply with organizational policies. Furthermore, training programs include practical simulations and mock exercises to test employees' responses to potential security incidents, preparing them for real-world challenges. As a result of these comprehensive training and awareness efforts, organizations can elevate their overall cloud security posture and create a workforce that is proactive and vigilant in protecting the organization's valuable data and logistics operations in the cloud. Such a security-conscious workforce becomes a priceless asset in creating a secure and resilient cloud environment, protecting against potential cyber threats, and guaranteeing the continuity of logistics operations in a business climate that is becoming more and more dynamic and digitally driven.

4.4 Continuous Monitoring and Auditing

Effectively addressing cloud security threats in business logistics requires ongoing monitoring and auditing. Because cloud systems are dynamic, continual monitoring is necessary to identify and quickly address any possible security threats or breaches. Organizations can gain visibility into their cloud infrastructure and apps by installing real-time monitoring tools and solutions, which enables them to spot any unusual activity or departure from the norm. Continuous monitoring makes it possible to identify security incidents early, allowing for quick responses to reduce risks and stop additional harm. Regular security audits are also essential for determining the efficacy of current security procedures and locating possible weaknesses. Organizations can assess their compliance with security policies, industry standards, and legal obligations by periodically auditing the cloud environment. The overall posture of cloud security can be strengthened by swiftly addressing any holes or flaws found during audits. Continuous monitoring and auditing work hand in hand to create a proactive approach to cloud security, ensuring that potential risks are promptly identified, assessed, and mitigated. Organizations can preserve the integrity of their logistics operations, safeguard sensitive data, and uphold the confidence of their clients and stakeholders in the constantly changing cloud environment by implementing these practices into their cloud security plans.

4.5 Building a Resilient Cloud Security Strategy

Building a robust cloud security plan is crucial in the world of business logistics to safeguard critical data and guarantee business continuity. To build a strong security posture, organizations should use a defense-in-depth strategy that incorporates many levels of security measures. For business logistics to manage cloud security threats effectively, developing a robust cloud security plan is essential. A comprehensive cloud security plan consists of a multi-layered strategy that involves proactive, investigative, and reactive measures. It starts with thorough risk assessments and a clear understanding of the organization's specific security requirements and regulatory obligations. By selecting reputable and trustworthy Cloud Service Providers (CSPs) with proven security track records and robust Service Level Agreements (SLAs), businesses can establish a solid foundation for their cloud security. Implementing strong access controls, data encryption, and identity and access management (IAM) solutions further fortifies the cloud environment against potential threats. Continuous monitoring, real-time threat intelligence, and incident response planning are essential components of a resilient cloud security strategy for managing cloud security risks in business logistics. The implementation of continuous monitoring tools and solutions allows organizations to maintain constant vigilance over their cloud infrastructure and applications, enabling the prompt detection of potential security incidents. Businesses may take proactive steps to address potential hazards before they become more serious thanks to real-time threat intelligence, which gives them access to the most recent information on new threats and vulnerabilities. On the other hand, incident response planning makes sure that organizations have a clearly defined and tested procedure in place to deal with security problems quickly and effectively. Organizations may minimize any disruption to logistics operations, lower the potential impact on data integrity, and preserve seamless business continuity by responding quickly to security issues. Additionally, routine security audits are crucial for assessing the efficacy of current security controls, spotting possible vulnerabilities, and verifying compliance with security guidelines and legal requirements (Goldman et al., 2010). In addition, employee training initiatives promote a security-conscious culture within the company by giving staff members the information and abilities to identify and respond to security threats. By having a staff that actively contributes to cloud security, businesses may strengthen their first line of defense against potential vulnerabilities. Businesses may successfully navigate the cloud ecosystem by combining these diverse components into a thorough cloud security strategy. They can safeguard private logistics data, win over stakeholders and consumers, and uphold the resilience needed to succeed in the always-changing cloud environment. A strong and flexible cloud security plan is essential for staying ahead of new threats and protecting business logistics in an increasingly dynamic digital world as cloud technologies continue to develop.

5. FUTURE TRENDS IN CLOUD SECURITY

The future of cloud security is poised to be dynamic and multifaceted, driven by the emergence of cutting-edge technologies and an ever-evolving threat landscape. Organizations will need to embrace multi-cloud security strategies to maintain consistency across diverse cloud platforms. Zero Trust Architecture will evolve to encompass granular access controls, while data-centric security will take center stage, emphasizing encryption and access controls to protect sensitive data wherever it resides. AI and automation will play crucial roles in real-time threat detection and response, bolstering security operations. Additionally, quantum-resistant encryption, privacy-preserving technologies, and increased focus on IoT security will shape the cloud security landscape of tomorrow (Radwan et al., 2017).

5.1 Emerging Technologies and Their Impact on Cloud Security

In the area of business logistics, emerging technologies have a significant impact on cloud security, bringing both benefits and concerns. The rapid emergence of the Internet of Things (IoT) has transformed various industries, including logistics. With IoT devices becoming prevalent in logistics operations, data generation and cloud storage have surged, enabling real-time tracking and productivity gains. As businesses leverage these innovations, ensuring strong cybersecurity measures becomes essential for safeguarding sensitive data and optimizing logistics efficiency.

These cutting-edge innovations have a profound impact on cloud security. As AI and ML algorithms find increasing integration in logistics, they are revolutionizing data analytics, predictive modeling, and decision-making processes. These advanced technologies play a crucial role in streamlining supply chain management, optimizing routing, and enhancing overall logistics efficiency.

Nonetheless, the adoption of AI and ML technologies in logistics also introduces new security risks. With AI-driven attacks and the potential exploitation of ML models for malicious purposes, businesses must be vigilant in strengthening their security measures. Striking a balance between harnessing the benefits of these technologies and safeguarding against emerging threats becomes paramount for ensuring robust cloud security within the domain of business logistics.

Blockchain is another emerging technology with implications for cloud security in logistics. Blockchain's decentralized and immutable nature enhances data integrity and transparency in supply chains, reducing the risk of data tampering and fraud. However, implementing blockchain in the cloud requires careful consideration of security measures to protect against potential attacks on blockchain networks and smart contracts.

Additionally, edge computing is becoming more popular in corporate logistics since it allows for data processing and analysis closer to the location where the data is generated. Edge computing presents the problem of securing a distributed network of edge devices and preserving data privacy, even while it can improve real-time decision-making and decrease data transfer to the cloud.

Organizations must take a proactive, multi-layered approach to solve these rising technology-related cloud security challenges. This includes implementing robust access controls, data encryption, and identity and access management solutions. Regular security audits, continuous monitoring, and threat intelligence are essential to detect and respond to potential security incidents promptly. Employee training and awareness programs play a crucial role in promoting a security-conscious culture within the organization.

As businesses in the logistics sector continue to leverage emerging technologies to streamline operations, embracing these technologies while prioritizing cloud security becomes critical. Organizations can successfully navigate the dynamic landscape and protect their priceless logistical data and operations in the cloud by understanding the possible dangers and opportunities of emerging technologies and adopting proactive security measures.

5.2 The Role of Artificial Intelligence (AI) and Machine Learning (ML)

AI and ML are set to transform cloud computing in business logistics, revolutionizing operations with increased efficiency, cost savings, and improved decision-making. Predictive analytics, enabled by AI and ML, empowers businesses to anticipate demand, optimize inventory, and enhance supply chain efficiency by analyzing vast datasets from various sources. AI-driven automation, like robots and autonomous vehicles, streamlines warehouse and transportation, leading to faster order fulfillment and reduced costs. Moreover, AI and ML improve route optimization by analyzing real-time traffic and weather data, minimizing fuel consumption and carbon footprint. These technologies also detect patterns and anomalies, proactively addressing potential risks and safeguarding sensitive data. With the integration of AI and ML into cloud platforms, organizations can access scalable, cost-effective AI services tailored to their logistics needs. Embracing these technologies ensures a competitive edge, optimized operations, and a secure future in logistics (Zhang et al., *2023*).

5.3 Evolving Threat Landscape and Countermeasures

The threat landscape for cloud security is ever-evolving, with cybercriminals becoming more sophisticated in their tactics. To combat these evolving threats, various countermeasures are being employed are listed below.

Evolving Threat Landscape:

1. ***Targeted Cyberattacks:*** Ransomware, advanced persistent threats (APTs), and other sophisticated attacks can disrupt logistics operations and compromise sensitive data.
2. ***Insider Threats:*** Malicious insiders or negligent employees with access to cloud resources can pose significant risks to data security.
3. ***Emerging Technology Risks:*** The adoption of IoT devices and edge computing introduces new attack vectors that require careful consideration.

4. ***Data Breaches:*** Cloud-stored logistics data is a prime target for cybercriminals, leading to potential data breaches and privacy violations.
5. ***Cloud Misconfigurations:*** Improperly configured cloud services can expose sensitive data and leave organizations vulnerable to attacks.

Countermeasures:

1. ***Advanced Threat Detection:*** Implementing AI, ML, and behavioral analytics for real-time identification and response to suspicious activities.
2. ***Identity and Access Management (IAM):*** Strengthening access controls to prevent unauthorized access and insider threats.
3. ***Encryption:*** Protecting data with strong encryption both in transit and at rest to thwart unauthorized access.
4. ***Network Segmentation:*** Isolating critical systems and data from the rest of the network to limit the impact of potential breaches.
5. ***Security Awareness Training:*** Educating employees about the latest cyber threats and best security practices.
6. ***Collaboration with Reputable CSPs:*** Engaging with reliable Cloud Service Providers offering advanced security features.
7. ***Incident Response Planning:*** Creating a well-structured incident response plan tailored to the organization's unique security needs, outlining clear and efficient steps to address security incidents promptly.
8. ***Regular Security Evaluations:*** Performing scheduled and comprehensive security assessments to proactively detect any potential vulnerabilities and guarantee adherence to established security protocols and industry best practices.
9. ***Enhanced Security through Multi-Factor Authentication (MFA):*** Bolstering security protocols by integrating multi-factor authentication into various systems and applications, thus minimizing the risk of unauthorized access and potential breaches.
10. ***Thorough Cloud Service Provider Assessment:*** Exercising meticulous scrutiny when selecting Cloud Service Providers (CSPs), ensuring thorough examination of their security provisions, and confirming their compliance with industry standards and relevant regulations before engaging in any collaborative partnership.

By integrating these evolving threat landscape countermeasures into their cloud security strategy, businesses in the logistics industry can enhance their resilience against emerging cyber threats and safeguard their valuable data and operations.

5.4 Advancements in Cloud Security Tools and Solutions

Future trends in cloud computing for the area of corporate logistics include improvements in cloud security tools and solutions. Strong security measures become increasingly important as cloud-based services are used in logistics operations more and more. To meet the issues encountered by logistics organizations and stay up with the constantly shifting threat landscape, cloud security technology is always evolving.

One of the most significant developments is the incorporation of AI and ML into cloud security technologies. AI-driven algorithms enable real-time analysis of vast data, quick identification of potential threats, and proactive threat mitigation. ML models learn from historical data, enhancing security predictions and assisting in staying ahead of cyber threats, fortifying logistics operations against data breaches and insider threats.

Modern encryption technology is essential for protecting critical logistics data that is stored on the cloud. Techniques like homomorphic encryption and zero-knowledge proofs permit calculations on encrypted data without requiring data to be decrypted, maintaining data privacy and security, which is essential for safeguarding trade secrets and confidential customer information.

Cloud Access Security Brokers (CASBs) have evolved to provide enhanced visibility and control over cloud applications and data. In order to ensure uniform security measures across cloud services and to facilitate compliance with industry laws, CASBs offer complete security rules, including data loss prevention and access controls.

Advancements in container security and serverless computing security are critical in the cloud environment. Containers allow efficient deployment, but specialized tools manage vulnerabilities and secure container images. Serverless computing requires application-level security controls to protect data and prevent code injection attacks.

Cloud-native security solutions cater specifically to cloud-based applications and services, integrating seamlessly with cloud platforms and providing automated security measures. By embracing these advancements, logistics organizations can fortify their cloud infrastructure, protect sensitive data, and foster a secure and resilient cloud environment. Data security becomes fundamental to operational success and customer trust as business logistics embrace cloud computing.

6. THE IMPORTANCE OF NAVIGATING CLOUD SECURITY RISKS FOR SEAMLESS BUSINESS LOGISTICS

In today's digital environment, it is crucial to manage cloud security threats for flawless business logistics. Cloud computing is being used by logistics operations more and more to improve collaboration, share data, and expedite processes, which increases the risk of security flaws and cyberattacks. In the logistics sector, sensitive data, consumer information, and vital logistics systems stored in the cloud are prime targets for cybercriminals. For uninterrupted operations, companies must prioritize effective cloud security solutions, especially as logistics operations increasingly rely on cloud computing, leading to heightened security risks. Implementing cutting-edge security technologies is essential to strengthen the cloud infrastructure and safeguard valuable assets. Adhering to cloud security best practices, such as strict access controls, MFA, and encryption, helps protect sensitive data. Regular security audits and vulnerability assessments proactively address cloud environment gaps. Staying updated with security patches guards against known vulnerabilities. Dynamic threat monitoring with advanced threat intelligence tools and AI-driven security analytics is crucial to combat emerging threats. Navigating cloud security risks is critical for seamless business logistics in the evolving digital landscape. Embracing proactive cloud security ensures operational continuity and builds trust among customers and partners. Demonstrating a commitment to robust cloud security practices enhances an organization's reputation and credibility in the competitive logistics industry. Prioritizing the protection of sensitive data and maintaining a resilient cloud environment reduces potential financial and reputational losses from security breaches, including legal liabilities, data loss, service disruptions, and damage to the brand's reputation (Weintrit et al., 2013).

7. CONCLUSION

As we look to the future, the role of cloud security will continue to evolve. Organizations must remain vigilant and proactive in addressing emerging threats and technological advancements. A secure cloud environment will require the use of quantum-resistant encryption, privacy-preserving technology, and AI-driven security operations. Moreover, security measures must be expanded to include the entire ecosystem due to the growth of IoT devices and the advent of multi-cloud solutions.

Organizations should give priority to continual employee training, strict access controls, frequent security audits, and compliance with changing requirements to guarantee a secure and resilient cloud environment. Close collaboration with cloud service providers will continue to be necessary to maintain a strong security posture. Businesses can embrace the possibilities of the cloud, spur innovation, and protect their most valuable assets by adopting a proactive and all-encompassing strategy to cloud security. A solid cloud security plan will be a vital enabler for businesses looking to flourish in the digital era as cloud technology continues to develop.

In conclusion, navigating cloud security risks effectively is a critical aspect of ensuring seamless business logistics in the digital age. By implementing advanced security tools, adhering to best practices, and staying vigilant against emerging threats, organizations can create a secure and resilient cloud environment that protects sensitive data, mitigates risks, and inspires confidence among customers and partners. Prioritizing cloud security not only guarantees operational continuity but also positions businesses as trusted and reliable partners in the dynamic and competitive logistics landscape.

8. REFERENCES

Attaran, M. (2017). Cloud computing technology: Leveraging the power of the internet to improve business performance. *Journal of International Technology and Information Management*, *26*(1), 112–137. doi:10.58729/1941-6679.1283

Bayarçelik, E. B., & Bumin Doyduk, H. B. (2020). Digitalization of business logistics activities and future directions. *Digital Business Strategies in Blockchain Ecosystems: Transformational Design and Future of Global Business*, 201-238.

Butt, U. A., Amin, R., Mehmood, M., Aldabbas, H., Alharbi, M. T., & Albaqami, N. (2023). Cloud security threats and solutions: A survey. *Wireless Personal Communications*, *128*(1), 387–413. doi:10.100711277-022-09960-z

Damenu, T. K., & Balakrishna, C. (2015, September). Cloud security risk management: A critical review. In *2015 9th International Conference on Next Generation Mobile Applications, Services and Technologies* (pp. 370-375). IEEE. 10.1109/NGMAST.2015.25

Gu, Q., & Liu, P. (2007). Denial of service attacks. Handbook of Computer Networks: Distributed Networks, Network Planning, Control, Management, and New Trends and Applications, 3, 454-468.

Kirubakaran, S. S. (2020). Study of security mechanisms to create a secure cloud in a virtual environment with the support of cloud service providers. *Journal of trends in Computer Science and Smart technology (TCSST)*, *2*(03), 148-154.

Kumar, R., & Goyal, R. (2019). On cloud security requirements, threats, vulnerabilities and countermeasures: A survey. *Computer Science Review*, *33*, 1–48. doi:10.1016/j.cosrev.2019.05.002

Marquezan, C. C., Metzger, A., Franklin, R., & Pohl, K. (2014). Runtime management of multi-level SLAs for transport and logistics services. In *Service-Oriented Computing: 12th International Conference, ICSOC 2014, Paris, France, November 3-6, 2014. Proceedings 12* (pp. 560-574). Springer. 10.1007/978-3-662-45391-9_49

Migliano, J. E. B., Demajorovic, J., & Xavier, L. H. (2014). Shared responsibility and reverse logistics systems for e-waste in Brazil. [JOSCM]. *Journal of Operations and Supply Chain Management*, *7*(2), 91–109. doi:10.12660/joscmv7n2p91-109

Radwan, T., Azer, M. A., & Abdelbaki, N. (2017). Cloud computing security: Challenges and future trends. *International Journal of Computer Applications in Technology*, *55*(2), 158–172. doi:10.1504/IJCAT.2017.082865

Sergi, I., Montanaro, T., Benvenuto, F. L., & Patrono, L. (2021). A smart and secure logistics system based on IoT and cloud technologies. *Sensors (Basel)*, *21*(6), 2231. doi:10.339021062231 PMID:33806770

Sivathanu, G., Wright, C. P., & Zadok, E. (2005, November). Ensuring data integrity in storage: Techniques and applications. In *Proceedings of the 2005 ACM workshop on Storage security and survivability* (pp. 26-36). ACM. 10.1145/1103780.1103784

Weintrit, A. (2013). Technical infrastructure to support seamless information exchange in e-Navigation. In *Activities of Transport Telematics: 13th International Conference on Transport Systems Telematics, TST 2013,* (pp. 188-199). Springer Berlin Heidelberg. 10.1007/978-3-642-41647-7_24

Zhang, Z., & Bowes, B. (2023). The future of artificial intelligence (AI) and machine learning (ML) in landscape design: A case study in Coastal Virginia, USA. *arXiv preprint arXiv:2305.02327*.

Chapter 12
Revisiting Fully Homomorphic Encryption Schemes for Privacy-Preserving Computing

Nimish Jain
https://orcid.org/0000-0001-9607-0764
Vellore Institute of Technology, India

Aswani Kumar Aswani Cherukuri
https://orcid.org/0000-0001-8455-9108
Vellore Institute of Technology, India

Firuz Kamalov
Canadian University, Dubai, UAE

ABSTRACT

Homomorphic encryption (HME) is a sophisticated encryption technique that allows computations on encrypted data to be done without the requirement for decryption. This trait makes HME, appropriate for safe computation in scenarios involving sensitive data and also in cloud computing. The data is encrypted using a public key and the calculation is conducted on the encrypted data. The computed result is then decrypted with a private key to acquire the final output. It protects data while allowing complicated computations to be done on the encrypted data, resulting in a secure and efficient approach to analyse sensitive information. The ability of HME to do computations on encrypted data without decryption makes it a valuable tool for achieving privacy. This chapter is intended to give a clear idea about the various fully HME schemes present in the literature, as well as analysing and comparing the results of each of these schemes. The authors also provide applications and open-source tools of HME schemes, along with how HME can be used to establish and preserve privacy in various forms.

DOI: 10.4018/979-8-3693-2081-5.ch012

1. INTRODUCTION

The term "homomorphic" is derived from two Greek roots: "homo," which means "same," and "morph," which means "shape." The term homomorphism in mathematics refers to a structure-preserving map between two algebraic systems whose operations are the same or similar. The phrase "homomorphic encryption" refers to how this encryption approach allows computations to be conducted on encrypted data while preserving the data's structure, allowing the same computations to be performed on encrypted data as on unencrypted data. Homomorphic Encryption (HE) is a kind of encryption scheme that allows a third party (e.g., cloud, service provider) to perform certain computable functions on the encrypted data while preserving the features of the function and format of the encrypted data.

Encryption methods like RSA, AES, and DES are not homomorphic, meaning that they require the data to be decrypted before any computation can be performed. This makes it challenging to use these encryption methods in situations where data privacy is a critical concern, such as cloud computing and data analytics. In contrast, homomorphic encryption enables computations to be performed directly on encrypted data, without the need for decryption. This has significant implications for privacy-preserving technologies, as it allows for secure outsourcing of computation to untrusted servers, while maintaining the confidentiality of the data. Moreover, RSA, AES, and DES can be used for other aspects of security, such as key management and message authentication.

Privacy is a fundamental human right and refers to a person's ability to govern their own information, decisions, and activities, as well as defend themselves against unauthorised access or observation. Privacy can take different forms. Informational privacy means protecting personal information and having the right to decide how it is collected, used, and shared. Physical privacy is a person's right to be alone and not have other people touch them. Communication privacy has to do with keeping private talks and electronic messages private. In a variety of situations, including healthcare, banking, technology, and government, privacy plays a critical role in developing trust and creating a sense of security.

People often confuse the terms privacy and confidentiality (Folkman, 2000). Privacy is a broader notion that includes the control and protection of personal information as well as autonomy, whereas confidentiality focuses on the protection of specific sensitive information as well as the need to keep it confidential. While the former is a fundamental right that applies to many elements of a person's life, the latter is a principle or agreement that is implemented in certain settings to ensure the protection of sensitive data or information.

Data privacy, computing privacy, and communication privacy are all interconnected and necessary for securing personal information, preserving individual rights, and establishing trust in the digital domain. The ability of FHE to do computations on encrypted data without decryption makes it a valuable tool for achieving privacy. It protects data security, enables secure outsourcing, maintains privacy during computing, limits data exposure, conforms with rules, and promotes trust in third-party services. FHE creates new opportunities for privacy-preserving technologies and applications across multiple domains, contributing to a more privacy-conscious and secure digital ecosystem.

Unlike other review papers (Acar et al., 2018) in the literature, which typically provide a high-level overview of different FHE schemes, this paper goes a step further by providing a simple and step-by-step algorithm for each of the FHE schemes discussed. This makes the FHE schemes more accessible to a wider audience, including those who may not have a deep background in cryptography or computer science. By breaking down the algorithms into simple steps, readers can follow along and understand how the scheme works at a more fundamental level.

In addition to providing a simple and step-by-step algorithm for each FHE scheme, this paper also presents a comprehensive comparison of different FHE schemes and open-source libraries in a tabular form in Table 1 and Table 2 respectively. The table includes important features and characteristics of each FHE scheme, such as security assumptions, key sizes, supported operations, computational complexity, and limitations. For example, if a user needs an FHE scheme that can perform addition and multiplication operations, they can easily filter the table to identify which schemes meet these criteria. Additionally, if a user is concerned about the computational complexity of the FHE scheme, they can compare the performance metrics of different schemes side-by-side.

The rest of the article is structured in the following way. Section 2. explains the mathematical concept behind Homomorphism, followed by its classification and applications. Section 3 analyses the various FHE Schemes. Section 4 presents five open-source libraries implemented both in Python and C++.

2. BACKGROUND

This section provides mathematical concepts and background of homomorphic encryption.

2.1. Homomorphism

Let us take an example to understand this better. Let us take two messages m_1 and m_2 and their encrypted cipher texts $c_1=E(m_1)$ and $c_2=E(m_2)$. If function E is homomorphic, then one can obtain the value of $E(m_1+m_2)$ by using c_1 and c_2 without knowing the values of m_1 and m_2.

$$E(m_1+m_2) = c_1+c_2 = E(m_1) + E(m_2)$$

Imagine the above scenario with any operation "å", then we can define an Encryption Scheme (E) as homomorphic if it supports the following equation:

$$E(m_1 \star m_2) = E(m_1) \star E(m_2),\ \forall m_1,\ m_2 \in M$$

where M is the set of all possible messages.

In abstract algebra, a structure-preserving map between two algebraic structures or groups is homomorphism. Let us take a set S and an operation "å", that combines any two elements a and b to form another element, denoted a å b and $a,b \in S$. The qualifications for a set and operation (S,å) to be a group are as follows:

- Closure property:

  For all $a,b \in S$, the result of aå$b \in S$.

- Associativity property:

  For all $a,b,c \in S$, $(a \star b) \star c = a \star (b \star c)$.

- Identity element:

For an element $e \in S$, the equality $e \star a = a \star e = a$ hold. Here e is the identity element of set S.

- Inverse element:

For an identity element $e \in S$ and elements $a, b \in S$, $a \star b = b \star a = e$ holds.
Note:

- The identity element $e \in S$ is often taken as 1.
- The result of operation may differ if the order of operand is changed.

For example, $a \star b \neq b \star a, \ \forall a,\ b \in S$.
A group homomorphism from group (G,å) to group (H,å) is defined as $f: G \rightarrow H$ and holds if

$$f(g \star g`) = f(g) \star f(g`), \ \forall g,\ g` \in G$$

Group homomorphism comes into play when testing if an encryption scheme is homomorphic or not. Assume an encryption scheme (P,C,D,E,D) where

- P = Plain text
- C = Cipher text
- K = Key
- E = Encryption algorithm
- D = Decryption algorithm

and (P,å) and (C,å) are groups of plain texts and cipher texts, respectively. The encryption algorithm maps from plain text group (P) to cipher text group (C) using k from Key (K) is homomorphic for any operation "å" if

$$E_k(a) \star E_k(b) = E_k(a \star b), \ \forall a,\ b \in P \ \& \ k \in K$$

Here, k can be a symmetric key or a public key, depending on the encryption algorithm used.
Using the above equation, let us prove that RSA is homomorphic for "•" i.e. Modular multiplication. The plain text group and cipher text group, respectively, are (P,•) and (C,•). For any two plain texts $p_1, p_2 \in P$, and public key $k=(n,e)$,

$$E(p_1, k) = p_1^e (mod\ n)$$

$$E(p_2, k) = p_2^e (mod\ n)$$

$$E(p_1,k)"E(p_2,k) = p_1^e " p_2^e (mod\ n) = (p_1 " p_2)^e (mod\ n) = E(p_1 " p_2,k)$$

Therefore, RSA is homomorphic for modular multiplication operation (•).

2.2. Classification of Homomorphic Algorithms

There are limitations to homomorphic algorithms. The existing encryption schemes may not satisfy homomorphism for all kinds of operations and any number of operations. Some encryption algorithms are homomorphic for addition and multiplication operations only; some are homomorphic for an infinite number of subsequent operations and for just one multiplication operation, etc. Hence, they are classified into three homomorphic encryption schemes:

2.2.1. Partially Homomorphic Encryption (PHE)

PHE provides for encrypted data calculations, but only for a limited number of operations, often addition and multiplication. PHE schemes are valuable in scenarios where specific computations need to be performed on encrypted data while maintaining privacy. They provide a balance between computation capabilities and efficiency compared to FHE, which supports arbitrary computations but may have higher computational overhead.

PHE's applications include safe computing protocols, privacy-preserving data analysis, secure computation outsourcing, and secure multiparty computation. PHE methods can enable private computations in a variety of applications, such as financial analysis, healthcare data analysis, and secure collaborative machine learning. However, careful thought and study are required to ensure that the desired computations may be accomplished using a certain PHE scheme.

Overall, PHE is less computationally costly than other types of homomorphic encryption, but its utility is limited. Some examples include RSA (Ronald, 1978), Goldwasser-Micali (1982), El-Gamal (1985), Benaloh (1994), Paillier (1999), Okamoto-Uchiyama (1998), etc.

2.2.2. Somewhat Homomorphic Encryption (SWHE)

SWHE is an encryption scheme that falls between Partially Homomorphic Encryption (PHE) and Fully Homomorphic Encryption (FHE). SWHE enables more complicated operations on encrypted data, such as exponentiation and polynomial evaluation. This means that for the supported operation, computations can be conducted on encrypted data, however other operations may require extra procedures or computations in the plaintext domain.

SHE finds applications in cases where computations on encrypted data must be done, such as secure computation outsourcing or privacy-preserving data analysis. It enables operations such as summing and multiplication on encrypted variables while retaining data security. SHE has restrictions in the sorts of operations it supports as well as the number of operations that may be conducted before noise accumulation impairs the precision of the outputs.

SWHE is more computationally demanding than PHE and offers more capabilities. Some examples include BGN (2005), Polly Cracker scheme (1994), etc.

2.2.3. Fully Homomorphic Encryption (FHE)

FHE supports arbitrary calculations on encrypted data, such as conditional operations, branching, and looping. FHE is the most computationally costly type of homomorphic encryption, but it also offers the most functionality (Preethi, 2018). In terms of data privacy, FHE is a game changer since it enables secure computations on sensitive data, eliminating the need to reveal the data in its unencrypted form. This has far-reaching consequences in domains as diverse as cloud computing, machine learning, data analysis, and secure multi-party processing.

These algorithms mostly make use of techniques like bootstrapping to maintain homomorphism. Some examples include Ideal Lattice-Based (Gentry, 2009), FHE Schemes over Integers (Van Dijk et al., 2010), LWE-Based (Regev, 2009), NTRU-Like (López-Alt, Tromer, & Vaikuntanathan, 2012), etc.

2.3. Applications

All three schemes of homomorphic encryption i.e. PHE, SWHE and FHE has made themselves useful in any field which deals with data processing. It can be utilized in outsourcing storage and computations sector where the custom can share data with the outsourcing corporation without disclosing its sensitive data to the company, while also allowing the companies to perform operations on the data.

Drozdowski et al. (2019) offers a system architecture capable of performing biometric identification in the encrypted domain, as well as gives and analyses an implementation based on two current homomorphic encryption techniques. It also examines the technological aspects and challenges in this environment.

FHE enables computations on encrypted data, allowing for data analysis while maintaining privacy. It finds use in situations where sensitive data, such as medical records or financial data, must be analysed while maintaining privacy (Mohassel & Zhang, 2017). In the financial sector (López-Alt, Tromer, & Vaikuntanathan, 2012), FHE has secure financial computation applications, such as secure auctions, privacy-preserving payment systems, and secure financial analysis. It offers secure computing on encrypted financial data while protecting privacy.

Let's a sample client-server interaction scenario, the client needs to send some sensitive data to the server, and the server returns the data after performing some operations on the data. This can be achieved with or without using HE. Both the methods are demonstrated below:

2.3.1. Without Homomorphic Encryption

Client (C) has an asymmetric key pair (pu_C, pr_C) and message M that must be sent to server. Similarly, server (S) has its asymmetric key pair (pu_S, pr_S) and function f which will be applied on client message. To maintain confidentiality, client encrypts M using server's public key to form $E(M, pu_S)$ which is then sent to the server. The server decrypts $E(M, pu_S)$ using its private key pr_S to get M and performs the function f on M to get $f(M)$. $f(M)$ is encrypted using client's public key pu_C before being sent to the client. The client receives $E(f(M), pu_C)$ and decrypts it using its private key to get $f(M)$.

In this scenario, since the server can see the message, it may pose a huge security threat to the client. When dealing with sensitive data, there should be way to prevent the server from viewing the raw sensitive data.

2.3.2. With Homomorphic Encryption

Client (C) has a homomorphic encryption function *He*, it's corresponding decryption function *Hd* and a message *M* that must be processed by the server. The server (S) has the function *f* to be applied on client's data. Client encrypts the message *M* using homomorphic encryption to get *He*(*M*) and sends it to the server for computation. The server performs the operation *f* homomorphically to get *He*(*f*(*M*)) and sends it back to the client. The client decrypts the data using *Hd*(*He*(*f*(*M*))) to get *f*(*M*).

Unlike 2.3.1., here the server performs its operation blindfolded since it cannot see the original message. The confidentiality of the client's message is intact, for both the public and server.

Figure 1. A client-server scenario without HE

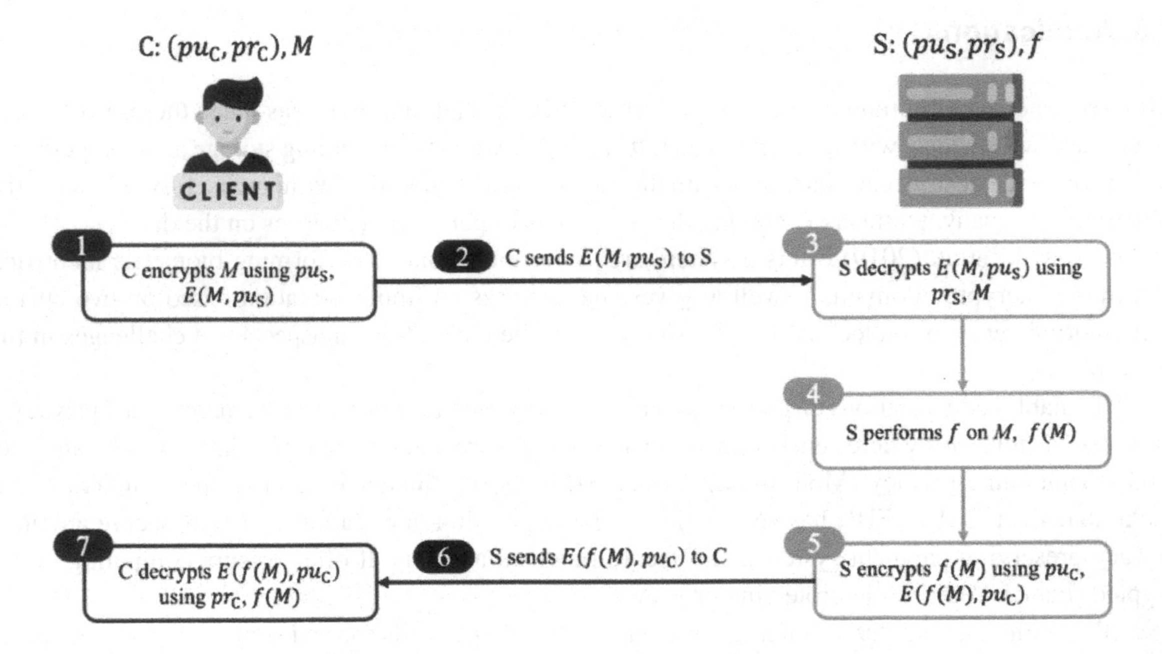

Figure 2. A client-server scenario with HE

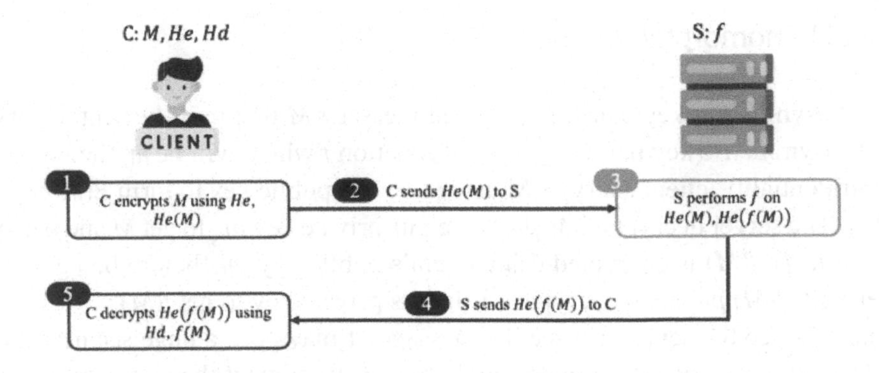

3. FULLY HOMOMORPHIC ENCRYPTION

To qualify as a FHE Scheme, an encryption algorithm should allow unlimited number of operations on the data while keeping the corresponding original data intact. The feasible concept of FHE was first published in 2009 by Gentry called Ideal lattice-based FHE scheme (Gentry, 2009). His work is promising, but computationally intensive. Ideal lattice-based FHE scheme was impractical for real-world scenario since the cost of operation was very high and was complex to implement.

Many new schemes and optimizations based on Gentry's work followed. They all had lattice-based approach in common which was hard to implement. Although this scheme was very promising, it was difficult to implement in real-world application due to high computational cost and difficult implementation dur to complex mathematics. Several optimizations and new schemes based on Gentry's work followed. To name a few FHE Schemes over Integers (Van Dijk et al., 2010), LWE-Based (Regev, 2009), NTRU-Like (López-Alt, Tromer, & Vaikuntanathan, 2012), etc. We will discuss these schemes in detail below.

3.1. Ideal Lattice-Based FHE Scheme

The first ever FHE Scheme was proposed in Gentry's thesis in 2009 and was based on GGH-type of encryption system (Goldreich et al., 1997). Goldreich–Goldwasser–Halevi (GGH) lattice-based cryptosystem is an asymmetric cryptosystem based on lattices. The Goldreich-Goldwasser-Halevi (GGH) cryptosystem takes advantage of the fact that the nearest vector problem might be difficult.

A lattice L with its basis $b_1, b_2, b_3, \ldots, b_n$ is formulated as follows:

$$L = \sum_{i=1}^{n} \vec{b_i} * v_i, \; v_i \in \mathbb{Z}$$

The basis of a lattice is not unique. There are infinitely many bases for a given lattice. A basis is called "good" if the basis vectors are almost orthogonal; otherwise, it is called "bad" basis of the lattice (Micciancio & Regev, 2009). We know that the amount of noise in a cipher text shouldn't cross a threshold beyond which the plain text cannot be recovered. Therefore, from time-to-time the noisy cipher text must be processed to either eliminate or decrease the noise level. Ideal Lattice-based approach uses methods like squashing and bootstrapping, to reduce noise. This enables us to perform infinite number of operations on cipher text without losing the integrity of plain text.

Before understanding Ideal Lattice-based FHE Scheme by Gentry, you should understand the meaning of Ideal of Ring Theory. An ideal of a ring is a special subset of its elements. For example, even numbers for a set of Integers. Addition and subtraction of even numbers preserves evenness and multiplying an even number by any integer (even or odd) results in an even number; these closure and absorption properties are the defining properties of an ideal.

Gentry's SWHE scheme using ideals and rings is described below:

Key Generation Algorithm:

1. Choose two prime numbers p and q such that q divides p–1.
2. Choose a generator g of the subgroup of F_p* of order q.

3. Choose two elements a,b uniformly at random from F_q and compute $f=g^a*f^b$, where f is a randomly chosen element of F_p.
4. The secret key is (a,b) and the public key is (h,p,q,g).

Encryption:

1. Let m be the plaintext message.
2. Choose a small integer t and a random element e in F_p.
3. Compute the ciphertext as $c=m*h^t*g^e \; mod \; p$.

Decryption:

1. Compute $s=at+be \; mod \; q$.
2. Compute $m' = c*g^{-s} mod \; p$.
3. Round m' to the nearest integer to obtain the decrypted plaintext message.

Homomorphic Addition:

To add two ciphertexts c1 and c2, compute c1*c2 mod p.

Homomorphic Multiplication:

To multiply two ciphertexts c_1 and c_2, first compute $c' = c_1 * c_2 mod \; p$. Then, given a plaintext message m with a small integer representation, compute $(c')^m \; mod \; p$ to obtain the ciphertext of the product.

The security of the SWHE scheme is based on the hardness of the learning with errors (LWE) problem, which involves the estimation of a random linear function of a noisy sample. The scheme provides limited homomorphic computations, such as addition and multiplication of encrypted messages, without revealing the underlying plaintext.

Gentry's FHE (Fully Homomorphic Encryption) approach employs a "squashing" strategy to deal with the noise that builds in ciphertexts after many homomorphic operations. The approach also contains a "bootstrapping" technique for refreshing the noise in ciphertexts, allowing for limitless homomorphic computations. Gentry's FHE system has the following procedure for squashing and bootstrapping.

Squashing:

1. Choose a small positive integer L.
2. Compute the function $f(x)=x^L-1$.
3. Evaluate the function on the ciphertext c to obtain a new ciphertext $c' = f(c) mod \; p$.
4. The squashing step reduces the noise in the ciphertext c by a factor of L, at the cost of losing information about the plaintext message. However, the information can be recovered using bootstrapping.

Bootstrapping:

1. Choose a fresh key pair (a', s') using the same key generation algorithm as before.
2. Evaluate the decryption circuit on the squashed ciphertext c' to obtain a new ciphertext c'' that encrypts the same plaintext message as c, but with noise reduced to a negligible level.
3. Compute a new public key $h' = (g, h_1', ..., h_n')$ using the same method as before, where $h_i' = g^{a'i} * f^{s'i}$ for a randomly chosen f in F_p.

4. Compute a new ciphertext c''' that encrypts the same plaintext message as c, but with the new public key h' and a much smaller level of noise.
5. The ciphertext c''' can now be used as input for further homomorphic computations.

The bootstrapping step involves two decryption and encryption operations, and a new public key is needed for each bootstrapping operation. Therefore, bootstrapping is computationally expensive and limits the practicality of the FHE scheme for large-scale computations. However, it allows for unlimited homomorphic computations on encrypted data, making it a powerful tool for privacy-preserving data analysis and machine learning.

3.2. FHE Schemes Over Integers

A new fully homomorphic encryption scheme was proposed in Van Dijk et al. (2010) that was based on the Approximate-Greatest Common Divisor (AGCD) problems. AGCD problems try to recover p from the given set of $x_i = pq_i + r_i$. The primary motivation behind the scheme is its conceptual simplicity. A symmetric version of the scheme is probably one of the simplest schemes.

The proposed symmetric SWHE scheme is described as follows:

Key Generation Algorithm:

1. Given a security parameter λ.
2. A random odd integer p of bit length η is generated. This will be treated as a private key.
3. Choose a random large number q.
4. Choose a small number r such that $r \ll p$.

Encryption Algorithm

The message m Î {0, 1} is encrypted by using the following:

$c = E(m) = m+2r+pq$

Decryption Algorithm

The following formula can be used for decryption:

$m = D(c) = (c \bmod p) \bmod$ 2

Homomorphism over Addition

$$E(m_1) + E(m_2) = m_1 + 2r_1 + pq_1 + m_2 + 2r_2 + pq_2 = (m_1 + m_2) + 2(r_1 + r_2) + (q_1 + q_2)q$$

The output clearly falls within the ciphertext space and can be decrypted if the noise $|(m_1+m_2) + 2(r_1+r_2)| < p/2$. Since $r_1, r_2 \ll p$, a various number of additions can still be performed on ciphertext before noise exceeds $p/2$.

Homomorphism over Multiplication

$$E(m_1)E(m_2) = (m_1 + 2r_1 + pq_1)(m_2 + 2r_2 + pq_2) = m_1m_2 + 2(m_1r_2 + m_2r_1 + 2r_1r_2) + kp$$

$$N = m_1m_2 + 2(m_1r_2 + m_2r_1 + 2r_1r_2)$$

The encrypted data can be decrypted if the noise is smaller than half of the private key. $N < p/2$. *N* grows exponentially with the multiplication operation. This puts more restriction over the homomorphic multiplication operation than addition.

3.3. LWE-Based FHE Scheme

Brakerski and Vaikuntanathan's LWE-based fully homomorphic encryption (FHE) scheme (Regev, 2009) is a lattice-based cryptosystem that builds upon the Learning with Errors (LWE) problem. Here is a high-level description of the scheme:

Key Generation

1. Choose a prime number p and an integer q such that $q>p^2$.
2. Let n be a positive integer and choose a random matrix $A \in Zq^{(nxm)}$ and random vectors s, e, and $u \in Zq^n$.
3. Compute $b=(A,As+e)$ and the matrix $B=(b|u)$.
4. The public key is (A,B), and the private key is kept secret.

Encryption Algorithm

To encrypt a binary message $m \in \{0,1\}$, generate a random vector $r \in Zq^n$ and a small noise vector $e' \in Zq^n$.

Then, compute the ciphertext c as follows:

$$c = Ar + m{*}p + e'$$

The ciphertext c is then sent to the recipient.

Homomorphic Operations

The scheme allows for homomorphic addition and multiplication of ciphertexts. Given two ciphertexts c_1 and c_2, the following operations can be performed:

- **Addition:** $c_1+c_2=c_1+c_2$
- **Multiplication:** $c_1{*}c_2 = (A{*}B')r + m_1m_2p + e_1{*}B'r + e_2Ar + e_1e_2$

Here, B' is the transpose of B, m_1 and m_2 are the plaintexts corresponding to c_1 and c_2, and e_1 and e_2 are the corresponding noise vectors.

Decryption

To decrypt a ciphertext c, compute the inner product of c with the private key vector s modulo p, and then round to the nearest integer modulo 2:

$m = round((c*s)/p) \ mod \ 2$

This recovers the original message m.

Brakerski and Vaikuntanathan's FHE scheme improves upon Regev's scheme by allowing for more homomorphic operations before the noise in the ciphertexts grows too large. However, the scheme is still limited by the size of the noise in the ciphertexts, which ultimately limits the number of homomorphic operations that can be performed.

3.4. NTRU-Like FHE Scheme

NTRU (N-th degree TRUncated polynomial) is a public key cryptosystem based on the shortest vector problem (SVP) in a lattice. In recent years, NTRU has been used as a basis for constructing fully homomorphic encryption (FHE) schemes. The basic idea behind NTRU-Like FHE schemes is to use a variant of the NTRU public key cryptosystem as the underlying encryption scheme. The encryption process involves encoding the message into a polynomial and then adding noise to it. The decryption process involves recovering the message by finding the closest polynomial to the ciphertext polynomial in a certain norm.

Key Generation:

1. Choose integers N, p, and q, where p and q are large primes congruent to 1 modulo $2N$, and p divides $q–1$.
2. Generate a random polynomial $f(x)$ of degree $N–1$ with coefficients in $\{-1,0,1\}$.
3. Compute the inverse polynomial $f^{-1}(x) \ mod \ q$.
4. Choose a small integer e and compute $g(x) = (1+f(x))^e \ mod \ p$.
5. Public key is $(p,q,g(x))$ and private key is $(f(x), f^{-1}(x))$.

Encryption:

1. Encode the message m into a polynomial $m(x)$ of degree $N–1$ with coefficients in $\{-1,0,1\}$.
2. Choose a small integer r and compute $h(x) = rg(x)+m(x) \ mod \ q$.
3. Send the ciphertext $(h(x))$.

Decryption:

1. Compute $c(x) = h(x)*f^{-1}(x) \ mod \ q$.
2. Compute $m(x) = round(c(x) \ mod \ p) \ mod \ 2$, where $round()$is the function that rounds to the nearest integer.
3. The decrypted message is the polynomial $m(x)$.

Homomorphic Addition:

1. Given two ciphertexts $h_1(x)$ and $h_2(x)$, compute $h_3(x) = h_1(x)+h_2(x) \ mod \ q$.
2. Send the ciphertext $(h_3(x))$.

Bootstrapping (Homomorphic Multiplication):

1. Decrypt the ciphertext $h(x)$ to obtain $c(x) = h(x)*f^{-1}(x) \ mod \ q$.

2. Choose a random element a from Z_p.
3. Compute $c'(x) = (c(x) + a*f(x)) mod\ q$.
4. Compute $m'(x) = round(c'(x) mod\ p) mod\ 2$.
5. Compute $h'(x) = 2r*(g(x)^a) mod\ q$.
6. Compute $h''(x) = h(x) - h'(x) mod\ q$.
7. Compute $h_3(x) = h''(x) + h'(x)*m'(x) mod\ q$.
8. The encrypted result is the ciphertext ($h_3(x)$).

The above bootstrapping step can be repeated multiple times to enable deeper homomorphic circuits. The fully homomorphic aspect of these schemes comes from the fact that the NTRU cryptosystem is somewhat homomorphic. This means that the addition of two ciphertexts results in a ciphertext that can be decrypted to the sum of the corresponding plaintexts. Multiplication of ciphertexts, however, is not directly possible in the NTRU cryptosystem. Therefore, NTRU-Like FHE schemes use a technique called "bootstrapping" to perform homomorphic multiplication.

3.5. TFHE Scheme

TFHE is an open-source library for fully homomorphic encryption, distributed under the terms of the Apache 2.0 license (Chillotti, 2016). The TFHE algorithm is a homomorphic encryption scheme that supports both addition and multiplication operations. It was proposed in 2018 and is designed to be more efficient than other FHE schemes, such as the BGV and FV schemes.

It also implements a dedicated Fast Fourier Transformation for the anticyclic ring $\mathbb{R}[X]/(X^N + 1)$, and uses AVX assembly vectorization instructions. The default parameter set achieves a 110-bit cryptographic security, based on ideal lattice assumptions. From the user point of view, the library can evaluate a net-list of binary gates homomorphically at a rate of about 50 gates per second per core, without decrypting its input. It suffices to provide the sequence of gates, as well as ciphertexts of the input bits. And the library computes ciphertexts of the output bits.

The key features of the TFHE algorithm include:

1. **Encryption:** The plaintext message is first encrypted using a symmetric key encryption scheme such as AES (Advanced Encryption Standard). This produces a ciphertext that is a stream of bits.
2. **Encoding:** The bits of the ciphertext are then encoded into a Torus, which is a mathematical structure that allows for efficient manipulation of the ciphertext using homomorphic operations.
3. **Homomorphic operations:** The TFHE algorithm supports both addition and multiplication operations on the encrypted data. These operations are performed using the encoded Torus values.
4. **Decryption:** The homomorphic result is then decoded back into a stream of bits and decrypted using the same symmetric key encryption scheme used in the encryption step.

The TFHE algorithm is designed to be efficient in terms of computational cost, memory usage, and ciphertext size. It achieves this by using a combination of symmetric key encryption and bitwise operations. Additionally, it supports rotation operations, which allows for efficient evaluation of circuits with loops or variable-length operations.

Table 1. FHE schemes

Scheme	Year	Security Level	Key Size	Homomorphic Operations	Implementation	Limitations
Gentry's FHE	2009	IND-CPA	2^80	Addition, Multiplication	Software	Slow evaluation speed
Brakerski-Gentry-Vaikuntanathan (BGV)	2011	IND-CPA	2^80	Addition, Multiplication, Rotation	Software, Hardware	Slow evaluation speed, large ciphertext expansion
Fan-Vercauteren (FV)	2012	IND-CPA	2^40	Addition, Multiplication, Rotation	Software, Hardware	Smaller ciphertext expansion, but slower evaluation speed
Homomorphic Hashing	2013	IND-CPA	N/A	Hashing	Software	Limited to hash functions
Brakerski-Gentry 2 (BGV2)	2014	IND-CPA	2^80	Addition, Multiplication, Rotation	Software, Hardware	Smaller ciphertext expansion, but slower evaluation speed
Approximate Number Homomorphism (ANH)	2015	IND-CPA	N/A	Approximate addition, multiplication	Software	Limited accuracy
Gentry-Sahai-Waters (GSW)	2016	IND-CPA	2^64	Addition, Multiplication, Rotation	Software, Hardware	Smaller ciphertext expansion, but slower evaluation speed
TFHE	2018	IND-CPA	N/A	Addition, Multiplication, Rotation	Software, Hardware	Fast evaluation speed, but requires high computational power
Brakerski-Gentry-Levin (BGL)	2018	IND-CPA	2^64	Addition, Multiplication, Rotation	Software, Hardware	Smaller ciphertext expansion, but slower evaluation speed

4. OPEN-SOURCE LIBRARIES

To make FHE more accessible and easier to use, several open-source libraries for FHE have been developed. These libraries provide a set of pre-built functions and APIs that allow developers to easily implement FHE in their applications without needing to understand the underlying mathematics and algorithms. Some of the popular open-source FHE libraries include HElib, SEAL, OpenFHE, TFHE, and HEAAN. These libraries support different FHE schemes and have varying levels of complexity and efficiency. Developers can choose the library that best suits their needs based on factors such as performance, ease of use, and compatibility with their existing systems.

Open-source FHE libraries are especially valuable for researchers and developers who are working on FHE-based applications but may not have the resources or expertise to develop their own implementation from scratch. By leveraging the work of others, they can quickly and easily incorporate FHE into their applications and advance the state of the art in secure computation.

4.1. HElib

HElib (homenc, 2022) is a C++ library for homomorphic encryption, supporting both the BGV and GSW schemes, focusing on effective use of the Smart-Vercauteren ciphertext packing techniques and the Gentry-Halevi-Smart optimizations. It provides a simple and efficient API for performing homomorphic operations on encrypted data. HElib has been used in several real-world applications, including secure machine learning and privacy-preserving data analysis.

4.2. SEAL

SEAL (Simple Encrypted Arithmetic Library) (Microsoft, 2023) is a C++ library for homomorphic encryption, supporting the CKKS and BFV schemes. It provides a simple and user-friendly API for performing homomorphic operations on encrypted data. SEAL has been used in several real-world applications, including secure machine learning, privacy-preserving data analysis, and secure cloud computing.

4.3. OpenFHE

OpenFHE (Badawi, 2022) is a C++ library for homomorphic encryption, supporting several schemes including BGV, BFV, CKKS, DM, and CGGI. It provides a flexible and modular API for performing homomorphic operations on encrypted data. Palisade has been used in several real-world applications, including secure machine learning, privacy-preserving data analysis, and secure cloud computing.

4.4. TFHE

TFHE (Fully Homomorphic Encryption over the Torus) (Chillotti, 2016) is a C++ library for homomorphic encryption, supporting the TFHE scheme. It is designed to be more efficient than other FHE schemes, such as the BGV and FV schemes. TFHE has been used in several real-world applications, including secure machine learning and privacy-preserving data analysis.

4.5. HEAAN

HEAAN (Homomorphic Encryption for Arithmetic of Approximate Numbers) (Cheon et al., 2016) is a C++ library for homomorphic encryption, supporting the HEAAN scheme. It is designed for efficient computation on encrypted data using approximate numbers. HEAAN has been used in several real-world applications, including secure machine learning and privacy-preserving data analysis.

Table 2. Open-source libraries for fully homomorphic encryption (FHE)

Library	Supported Schemes	Programming Language	API	License
HElib (homenc, 2022)	BGV, GSW	C++	Simple and efficient	BSD 3-Clause
SEAL (Microsoft, 2023)	CKKS, BFV	C++	Simple and user-friendly	MIT
OpenFHE (Badawi, 2022)	BGV, BFV, CKKS, DM, CGGI	C++	Flexible and modular	Apache 2.0
TFHE (Chillotti, 2016)	TFHE	C++	Efficient	LGPLv3
HEAAN (Cheon et al., 2016)	HEAAN	C++	Efficient computation on approximate numbers	MIT

5. FHE FOR PRESERVING PRIVACY

As we know, privacy must be protected in order to defend individuals' fundamental rights, autonomy, and personal security. It assures that people have control over their personal information, choices, and behaviors, allowing them to preserve their identities and lives without undue interference. It exhibits respect for personal boundaries and confidentiality, privacy creates confidence in relationships and institutions. Fully Homomorphic Encryption (FHE) plays a significant role in establishing privacy since it allows calculations on encrypted data without the need for decryption. The basic concept of FHE is sufficient to demonstrate how privacy can be maintained in systems that use FHE Schemes.

With FHE, data owners can engage in collaborative data sharing, secure cloud computing, and other privacy-conscious activities with confidence, eventually protecting privacy in an increasingly data-driven and linked society. This allows for private data analysis and computing, allowing anyone to perform operations on sensitive data without revealing its underlying information. This also allows for secure outsourcing of computations to untrusted servers (as demonstrated in Fig. 2.), enabling individuals and organizations to leverage external computing resources while maintaining control over their data. Let's discuss on how privacy can be achieved through FHE.

5.1. Privacy of Data

FHE protects data privacy by allowing computations to be done on encrypted data without requiring decryption. FHE algorithms can be used to encrypt data, assuring its confidentiality and protection. The encrypted data can then be stored, shared, and processed securely, reducing the danger of unauthorised access or disclosure. FHE enables secure data analysis, machine learning, and other computations on sensitive data while maintaining privacy by encrypting the data during the process.

Individuals can use this to protect their identities, financial information, health records, and other sensitive data. Data privacy is critical for complying with privacy legislation, establishing trust with persons whose data is collected, and reducing the dangers of identity theft, fraud, or discrimination. It also enables individuals to make informed decisions about sharing their data and adds to a responsible and ethical data management approach.

5.2. Privacy of Computing

FHE adds to computing privacy by ensuring that sensitive data is encrypted throughout computational operations. FHE allows computations to be done directly on encrypted data while protecting the underlying information's confidentiality. This permits secure compute outsourcing to untrusted servers or cloud providers, while the data remains encrypted and secure. FHE enables privacy-preserving calculations, allowing individuals and organisations to leverage processing capacity while protecting the privacy of the data being processed.

It ensures that sensitive data is safeguarded when calculations are outsourced to untrustworthy servers or third-party companies. Privacy of computing offers secure computation on encrypted data allowing organizations and individuals to use external computing resources without jeopardizing data privacy. This is especially useful when data owners wish to retain control over their data while using the power of computation. This enabled privacy-at-source instead of relying on third-party organization's data handling policy to protect their data.

5.3. Privacy of Communication

FHE contributes to communication privacy by maintaining the confidentiality of personal discussions and electronic communications. End-to-end encryption can be provided through encrypted communication protocols and secure messaging systems based on FHE principles, ensuring that only authorised parties can access the content of the communication. This protects against eavesdropping, interception, and spying, allowing individuals and organisations to interact with confidence while maintaining their privacy.

It protects sensitive conversations, personal information given across numerous channels, and sensitive business interactions. Communication privacy is critical for establishing trust in interpersonal relationships, executing secure economic transactions, and protecting people's freedom of speech. In addition to content secrecy, communication privacy concerns metadata protection. Metadata offers details about the communication, such as sender and recipient identities, timestamps, geographical data, and message routing information. Metadata protection is critical because it might disclose trends, relationships, and behavioural information that may jeopardise an individual's privacy.

5.4. Compliance With Privacy Regulations

By maintaining the confidentiality and security of personal information, FHE complies with privacy rules and data protection standards. It is important to note that compliance is a multifaceted process that requires consideration of legal and organizational factors. Organizations can use FHE to apply privacy-preserving practises and comply with legislation such as the General Data Protection Regulation (GDPR) (Spindler & Schmechel, 2016), California Consumer Privacy Act (CCPA) (Pardau, 2018), and other regional privacy laws.

6. CONCLUSION

In conclusion, Fully Homomorphic Encryption (FHE) schemes allow computation to be performed directly on encrypted data, without requiring decryption. This is a powerful tool for preserving data privacy, as it enables secure outsourcing of computation to untrusted servers, while maintaining the confidentiality of the data. FHE schemes are based on a variety of mathematical problems, including lattice-based problems, AGCD problems, and NTRU-like problems. Each scheme has its own strengths and weaknesses, and the choice of scheme depends on the specific application and security requirements. Python libraries like Pyfhel and C++ libraries like OpenFHE provide an easy-to-use interface for implementing FHE schemes, enabling developers to experiment and prototype new applications. As FHE continues to advance, it has the potential to enable new privacy-preserving technologies and applications in fields such as healthcare, finance, and data analytics.

REFERENCES

Acar, A., Aksu, H., Uluagac, A. S., & Conti, M. (2018). A survey on homomorphic encryption schemes: Theory and implementation. *ACM Computing Surveys*, *51*(4), 1–35. doi:10.1145/3214303

Al Badawi, A., Bates, J., Bergamaschi, F., Cousins, D. B., Erabelli, S., Genise, N., & Zucca, V. (2022, November). OpenFHE: Open-source fully homomorphic encryption library. In *Proceedings of the 10th Workshop on Encrypted Computing & Applied Homomorphic Cryptography* (pp. 53-63). 10.1145/3560827.3563379

Badawi, A. A. (2022). *OpenFHE: Open-Source Fully Homomorphic Encryption Library*. ePrint. https://eprint.iacr.org/2022/915

Benaloh, J. (1994, May). Dense probabilistic encryption. In *Proceedings of the workshop on selected areas of cryptography* (pp. 120-128). IEEE.

Boneh, D., Goh, E. J., & Nissim, K. (2005, February). Evaluating 2-DNF Formulas on Ciphertexts. In TCC (Vol. 3378, pp. 325-341).

Cheon, J. H., Kim, A., Kim, M., & Song, Y. (2016). *Implementation of HEA-AN*. Github. https://github.com/kimandrik/HEAAN

Chillotti, I. (2016). *TFHE: Fast Fully Homomorphic Encryption Library*.

Drozdowski, P., Buchmann, N., Rathgeb, C., Margraf, M., & Busch, C. (2019). On the Application of Homomorphic Encryption to Face Identification. *2019 International Conference of the Biometrics Special Interest Group (BIOSIG)*, Darmstadt, Germany.

ElGamal, T. (1985). A public key cryptosystem and a signature scheme based on discrete logarithms. *IEEE Transactions on Information Theory*, *31*(4), 469–472. doi:10.1109/TIT.1985.1057074

Fellows, M., & Koblitz, N. (1994). Combinatorial cryptosystems galore! *Contemporary Mathematics*, *168*, 51–51. doi:10.1090/conm/168/01688

Folkman, S. (2000). *Privacy and confidentiality*. APA.

Gentry, C. (2009, May). Fully homomorphic encryption using ideal lattices. In *Proceedings of the forty-first annual ACM symposium on Theory of computing* (pp. 169-178). IEEE. 10.1145/1536414.1536440

Goldreich, O., Goldwasser, S., & Halevi, S. (1997). Public-key cryptosystems from lattice reduction problems. In *Advances in Cryptology (CRYPTO'97)* (pp. 112–131). Springer. doi:10.1007/BFb0052231

Goldwasser, S., Micali, S., & Tong, P. (1982, November). Why and how to establish a private code on a public network. In *23rd Annual Symposium on Foundations of Computer Science (sfcs 1982)* (pp. 134-144). IEEE. 10.1109/SFCS.1982.100

Homenc. (2022). *Homenc/HElib: HElib Is an Open-source Software Library That Implements Homomorphic Encryption*. GitHub. https://github.com/homenc/HElib

López-Alt, A., Tromer, E., & Vaikuntanathan, V. (2012, May). On-the-fly multiparty computation on the cloud via multikey fully homomorphic encryption. In *Proceedings of the forty-fourth annual ACM symposium on Theory of computing* (pp. 1219-1234). ACM. 10.1145/2213977.2214086

Micciancio, D. & Regev, O. (2009). Lattice-based cryptography. *Post-quantum cryptography*, 147-191.

Microsoft. (2023). *SEAL*(Release 4.1). Github. https://github.com/Microsoft/SEAL

Mohassel, P., & Zhang, Y. (2017). Secureml: A system for scalable privacy-preserving machine learning. 2017 IEEE symposium on security and privacy. IEEE.

Okamoto, T., & Uchiyama, S. (1998). A new public-key cryptosystem as secure as factoring. In *Advances in Cryptology—EUROCRYPT'98: International Conference on the Theory and Application of Cryptographic Techniques Espoo* (pp. 308-318). Springer Berlin Heidelberg. 10.1007/BFb0054135

Paillier, P. (1999). Public-key cryptosystems based on composite degree residuosity classes. In *Advances in Cryptology—EUROCRYPT'99: International Conference on the Theory and Application of Cryptographic Techniques Prague*, (pp. 223-238). Springer Berlin Heidelberg. 10.1007/3-540-48910-X_16

Pardau, S. L. (2018). The california consumer privacy act: Towards a european-style privacy regime in the united states. *J. Tech. L. & Pol'y*, *23*, 68.

Preethi, G. & Cherukuri, A. (2018). Privacy preserving Hu's moments in encrypted domain. *Intelligent Systems Design and Applications: 17th International Conference on Intelligent Systems Design and Applications (ISDA 2017)*. Springer International Publishing.

Regev, O. (2009). On lattices, learning with errors, random linear codes, and cryptography. *Journal of the Association for Computing Machinery*, *56*(6), 1–40. doi:10.1145/1568318.1568324

Ronald, L. (1978). Rivest, Len Adleman, and Michael L. Dertouzos. 1978a. On data banks and privacy homomorphisms. *Foundations of Secure Computation*, *4*(11), 169–180.

Spindler, G., & Schmechel, P. (2016). Personal data and encryption in the European general data protection regulation. *J. Intell. Prop. Info. Tech. & Elec. Com. L.*, *7*, 163.

Van Dijk, M., Gentry, C., Halevi, S., & Vaikuntanathan, V. (2010). Fully homomorphic encryption over the integers. In *Advances in Cryptology–EUROCRYPT 2010: 29th Annual International Conference on the Theory and Applications of Cryptographic Techniques*. Springer Berlin Heidelberg.

Chapter 13
Safeguarding Privacy Through Federated Machine Learning Techniques

Sayani Chattopadhyay
Burdwan University, India

Shalbani Das
Amity University, Kolkata, India

ABSTRACT

The chapter thoroughly addresses ML privacy threats like risks, attacks, and leaks. It explores the methods of differential privacy, homomorphic encryption, and SMPC. Federated learning is detailed, covering concepts, benefits, techniques (averaging, aggregation). Advancements include transfer learning, differential privacy, edge device use. Real cases show privacy's value in healthcare, finance, IoT. The conclusion touches on trends, regulations, privacy-utility balance. The chapter aims to overview privacy-preserving and federated ML, stressing their role in data security with insights for researchers, practitioners, policymakers for privacy-conscious ML. Valuable insights are provided for researchers, practitioners, and policymakers aiming for a privacy-conscious future in machine learning.

1. INTRODUCTION TO PRIVACY PRESERVING AND FEDERATED MACHINE LEARNING

1.1 Overview of Machine Learning and Data Privacy Concerns

Machine learning is a subset of artificial intelligence that involves the use of algorithms to enable computer systems to learn from and make predictions or decisions based on data. It encompasses various techniques such as neural networks, decision trees, and clustering, and has found applications in diverse fields (Sharifani et al., 2023). However, the rapid growth of machine learning has raised significant data privacy concerns. As these algorithms require large amounts of data to function effectively, there is a

DOI: 10.4018/979-8-3693-2081-5.ch013

risk of sensitive information being mishandled or misused. Striking a balance between the benefits of machine learning and safeguarding individual privacy has become a pivotal challenge, prompting the need for robust privacy-preserving techniques and ethical guidelines in the development and deployment of machine learning systems.

1.2 The Need for Privacy-Preserving Techniques in Machine Learning

The proliferation of machine learning has amplified the need for privacy-preserving techniques to address growing concerns surrounding data security and individual privacy. As machine learning models thrive on large datasets, there's an inherent risk of exposing sensitive information during the training and inference processes. Traditional anonymization methods like data aggregation and masking are no longer sufficient to counter advanced privacy threats. Enterprising techniques like differential privacy, federated learning, and homomorphic encryption are emerging as effective solutions. Differential privacy adds controlled noise to the data, maintaining accuracy while safeguarding individual details. Federated learning decentralizes model training, allowing devices to learn locally and share only encrypted updates, minimizing data exposure. Homomorphic encryption enables computations on encrypted data, keeping the raw data hidden even during processing. These privacy-preserving techniques offer a path forward, ensuring the continued advancement of machine learning while respecting individuals' rights to data privacy (Guan et al., 2018).

1.3 Understanding Federated Machine Learning

Federated Machine Learning (FL) is a decentralized approach to training machine learning models across a network of devices or servers while keeping data localized and private. Unlike traditional centralization, where all data is collected in a single location for training, federated learning enables model training on individual devices or nodes without directly accessing their raw data. This is particularly valuable in scenarios where data cannot be easily shared due to privacy, security, or regulatory concerns (Lo et al., 2021).

In federated learning, the process typically involves the following steps:

1. ***Initialization:*** A global machine learning model is created and distributed to participating devices or nodes.
2. ***Local Training:*** Each device or node trains the global model using its own local data. These local models capture insights specific to the data on each device.
3. ***Aggregation:*** The locally trained models are sent back to a central server, where their updates are aggregated to refine the global model. This aggregation is often done using techniques that balance out the contributions of different devices while maintaining data privacy.
4. ***Model Update:*** The updated global model is then distributed back to the devices, and the cycle repeats.

Federated learning also offers several advantages:

1. ***Data Privacy:*** Raw data remains on local devices, reducing the risk of data breaches and privacy violations.

2. ***Efficiency:*** Fewer data needs to be transmitted, reducing bandwidth and communication costs.
3. ***Decentralization:*** FL works well in edge computing scenarios, where devices have limited connectivity or computational resources.
4. ***Real-time Personalization:*** Models can be adapted to individual devices, allowing for personalized predictions while maintaining privacy.
5. ***Regulatory Compliance:*** FL can help organizations comply with data protection regulations by minimizing data movement.

However, federated learning also comes with challenges. Ensuring consistent model performance across diverse local datasets can be complex. Dealing with device heterogeneity and handling communication delays requires careful consideration. Moreover, security measures must be implemented to safeguard the aggregation process and prevent malicious attacks.

2. PRIVACY THREATS IN MACHINE LEARNING

2.1 Data Privacy Risks and Challenges

Privacy threats in machine learning pose significant risks and challenges in the realm of data privacy, demanding comprehensive strategies to safeguard sensitive information. As machine learning algorithms increasingly rely on vast datasets, concerns arise regarding the potential exposure of personal and confidential data during various stages of the machine learning lifecycle.

1. ***Data Leakage:*** Machine learning models can inadvertently memorize training data, potentially revealing sensitive details about individuals. Attackers can exploit this vulnerability to extract private information, leading to breaches of privacy.
2. ***Membership Inference:*** Through trained models, attackers can determine whether a specific data point was part of the training dataset. This breach can compromise the privacy of individuals contributing data, even if the actual data isn't revealed.
3. ***Model Inversion:*** Attackers can reverse-engineer models to recreate inputs that led to specific outputs. This can disclose private information present in the model's decision-making process.
4. ***Adversarial Attacks:*** Malicious actors can manipulate inputs to trick machine learning models into making incorrect decisions. Such attacks can exploit vulnerabilities and disclose sensitive information.
5. ***Unintended Bias:*** Inaccurate or biased training data can lead to models that discriminate against certain groups or reinforce unfair biases, which may compromise privacy and fairness.
6. ***Differential Privacy Violations:*** Differential privacy techniques, aimed at adding noise to data to protect individual privacy, can be vulnerable to sophisticated attacks that reconstruct sensitive information.
7. ***Data Re-identification:*** Even when anonymized, aggregated data can sometimes be re-identified through cross-referencing with other datasets, jeopardizing individual privacy.
8. ***Transfer Learning Risks:*** Pre-trained models used in transfer learning might retain information from previous tasks, potentially revealing sensitive attributes of the training data (Al-Rubaie et al., 2019).

Addressing these challenges requires a multi-faceted approach. Some of them are stated below.

1. ***Privacy-Preserving Techniques:*** Differential privacy, federated learning, and secure multi-party computation can help protect data during training and inference without compromising accuracy.
2. ***Data Minimization:*** Collect and store only the necessary data, reducing the risk associated with holding excessive private information.
3. ***Robust Data Sharing Protocols:*** Implementing secure sharing protocols ensures that data is exchanged safely between parties without exposing raw information.
4. ***Bias Mitigation:*** Rigorous data preprocessing and algorithmic measures can mitigate bias in training data, reducing privacy vulnerabilities.
5. ***Transparency and Accountability:*** Developers and organizations must be transparent about data usage and model behavior, allowing users to make informed choices.
6. ***Regulatory Compliance***: Adhering to data protection regulations, such as GDPR, CCPA, and HIPAA, is crucial in maintaining data privacy standards.

As machine learning continues to evolve, addressing privacy threats is imperative to build trust and ensure responsible deployment of these technologies, striking a balance between innovation and the protection of individual privacy.

2.2 Adversarial Attacks on Machine Learning Models

Adversarial attacks on machine learning models represent a prominent privacy threat that exploits vulnerabilities in the way models make predictions. These attacks involve introducing carefully crafted inputs or perturbations into the model's input data to cause it to produce incorrect or unexpected outputs. Adversarial attacks can have profound consequences, including compromising data privacy, security, and the integrity of model predictions (Zhang et al, 2020). Here are some common types of adversarial attacks:

1. ***Adversarial Perturbations:*** Adversarial perturbations are small changes introduced into the input data that are imperceptible to humans but can lead to drastically different model predictions. These perturbations can be crafted to manipulate models' decisions, potentially leading to unauthorized access or incorrect outputs.
2. ***Black-Box Attacks:*** Attackers might not have direct access to the model's architecture or parameters but can still manipulate the model's behavior through trial and error, observing the model's responses to inputs.
3. ***White-Box Attacks:*** Attackers have complete knowledge of the model's architecture, parameters, and training data. This allows them to craft highly effective adversarial examples that exploit specific vulnerabilities.
4. ***Transfer Attacks:*** Adversarial examples generated for one model can often be effective against other models, even if they have different architectures or training data. This highlights the generalizability of adversarial attacks.
5. ***Targeted Attacks:*** In targeted attacks, adversaries aim to manipulate the model to produce a specific incorrect output, which could have severe consequences in applications like medical diagnosis or autonomous vehicles.

6. ***Non-Targeted Attacks:*** In non-targeted attacks, the attacker's goal is to cause the model to make any incorrect prediction, regardless of the specific output.
7. ***Physical Attacks:*** These attacks involve applying real-world modifications to input data, like stickers or noises, to fool machine learning models. Such attacks can have serious implications in security-sensitive applications.
8. ***Defensive Evasion:*** Adversaries might attempt to bypass security measures like intrusion detection systems by manipulating inputs to appear benign while still causing malicious effects.

   Addressing adversarial attacks requires a multi-pronged approach:

    1. ***Robust Model Design:*** Developing models with inherent resistance to adversarial attacks is essential. Techniques like adversarial training involve training models on a combination of clean and adversarial examples to increase their robustness.
    2. ***Adversarial Detection:*** Implementing mechanisms to detect and flag potential adversarial inputs during inference can help mitigate the impact of attacks.
    3. Input Preprocessing: Applying input preprocessing techniques can make models less sensitive to small perturbations, reducing their vulnerability to adversarial attacks.
    4. ***Ensemble Methods:*** Combining the predictions of multiple models or using diverse architectures can make it more challenging for attackers to craft effective adversarial examples.
    5. ***Regularization:*** Techniques like dropout and weight regularization can make models more robust to slight input variations.
    6. ***Ongoing Research:*** Continual research is necessary to develop improved adversarial attack and defense techniques, as the field is rapidly evolving.

As adversarial attacks continue to evolve, it's crucial for machine learning practitioners to be aware of these threats and to implement appropriate countermeasures to ensure the privacy, security, and reliability of their models in real-world applications.

2.3 Privacy Leakage in Model Training and Inference

Privacy leakage in model training and inference refers to the unintentional disclosure of sensitive or private information contained within data during the process of building and using machine learning models (Jegorova et al., 2022). This phenomenon poses significant risks, as machine learning algorithms can inadvertently learn patterns, details, or characteristics from the training data that should have remained confidential. Privacy leakage can occur through various mechanisms:

1. ***Memorization:*** Models might inadvertently memorize specific data points or relationships from the training data, potentially exposing private information during inference.
2. ***Overfitting:*** Overfitting occurs when a model becomes overly tailored to the training data, capturing noise rather than general patterns. This can lead to the inclusion of sensitive attributes in the model.
3. ***Data Leakage:*** When sensitive data is inadvertently included in the training dataset, it can lead to direct privacy breaches, as models learn from this sensitive information.
4. ***Feature Engineering:*** Constructing features based on sensitive attributes can indirectly expose private information to the model.

5. ***Reconstruction Attacks:*** Attackers might reverse-engineer models to reconstruct training data or inputs, potentially revealing private attributes.
6. ***Unintended Inference:*** During inference, models might make predictions in a way that reveals sensitive information about the input data.

Addressing privacy leakage requires a proactive and holistic approach:

1. ***Data Preprocessing:*** Scrutinize and preprocess training data to ensure sensitive attributes are properly anonymized or removed, reducing the risk of exposure.
2. ***Anonymization Techniques:*** Implement techniques like differential privacy, which adds noise to training data to protect individual privacy while maintaining model accuracy.
3. ***Model Regularization:*** Use techniques like weight regularization and dropout to prevent models from overfitting to sensitive data.
4. ***Feature Engineering:*** Avoid using features derived from sensitive attributes or carefully sanitize them to minimize the risk of exposing private information.
5. ***Data Augmentation:*** Augment training data with synthetic examples that maintain the statistical properties of the data while reducing the risk of sensitive information leakage.
6. ***Adversarial Attacks and Defense:*** Employ adversarial attack techniques to test models for privacy vulnerabilities and then develop defense mechanisms to counteract potential leakage.
7. ***Auditability and Transparency:*** Implement mechanisms to monitor and analyze model behavior, allowing for the detection of unexpected privacy leaks during training or inference.
8. ***Regulatory Compliance:*** Ensure compliance with relevant data protection regulations such as GDPR or HIPAA to safeguard data privacy and mitigate legal risks.

As the machine learning field advances, it's imperative to prioritize the development and adoption of techniques that mitigate privacy leakage, thereby maintaining the trust of users and stakeholders while deploying machine learning models responsibly.

3. PRIVACY PRESERVING TECHNIQUES

3.1. Differential Privacy

Differential Privacy is a rigorous framework that aims to provide privacy guarantees for individuals contributing data to statistical analyses or machine learning algorithms. It ensures that the inclusion or exclusion of a specific individual's data does not significantly alter the outcome of the analysis, thus safeguarding individual privacy. Differential Privacy consists of several key components, including mathematical foundations, noise addition mechanisms, and practical implementation strategies (Dwork et al., 2006).

Figure 1. Understanding differential privacy

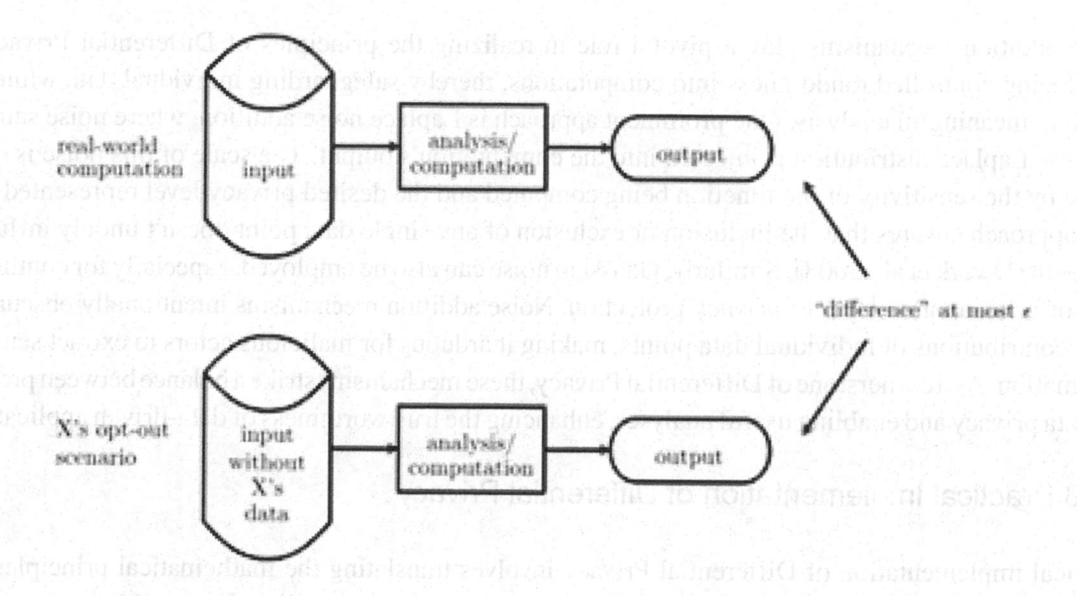

3.1.1 Mathematical Foundations of Differential Privacy

Differential Privacy is founded on mathematical principles that quantify the extent to which the presence or absence of an individual's data affects the outcome of a computation. This is expressed using the concept of privacy loss, which is defined by a parameter called ε (epsilon). The ε value reflects the maximum allowable change in the likelihood of observing an output due to a single individual's data inclusion or exclusion.

The mathematical definition of ε-differential privacy is given below.

$$\Pr[M(D) \in S] \leq e^{\varepsilon} . \Pr[M(D') \in S] + \delta$$

Where:

M represents a randomized algorithm (such as a data analysis or machine learning model).
D is the dataset with the specific individual's data included.
D' is the dataset with the specific individual's data excluded.
S is a set of possible outcomes or results of M.
δ is a parameter representing an upper bound on the probability that the privacy guarantee is violated.

In simpler terms, the equation states that the probability of observing an outcome S when analyzing dataset D is not significantly different from the probability of observing the same outcome S when analyzing dataset D', except by a factor of e^{ε}, which captures the privacy loss due to the individual's data. A smaller ε value implies stronger privacy guarantees, as it limits the extent to which an individual's presence affects the output. The δ parameter ensures that the privacy guarantee holds with a certain probability. Lower values of δ correspond to higher assurance of privacy.

3.1.2 Noise Addition Mechanisms for Differential Privacy

Noise addition mechanisms play a pivotal role in realizing the principles of Differential Privacy by introducing controlled randomness into computations, thereby safeguarding individual data while still enabling meaningful analysis. One prominent approach is Laplace noise addition, where noise sampled from the Laplace distribution is injected into the computation's output. The scale of this noise is determined by the sensitivity of the function being computed and the desired privacy level represented by ε. This approach ensures that the inclusion or exclusion of any single data point doesn't unduly influence the result (Dwork et al., 2008). Similarly, Gaussian noise can also be employed, especially for continuous data, offering another layer of privacy protection. Noise addition mechanisms intentionally obscure the exact contributions of individual data points, making it arduous for malicious actors to extract sensitive information. As a cornerstone of Differential Privacy, these mechanisms strike a balance between preserving data privacy and enabling useful analyses, enhancing the trustworthiness of data-driven applications.

3.1.3 Practical Implementation of Differential Privacy

Practical implementation of Differential Privacy involves translating the mathematical principles into real-world applications while balancing privacy protection and data utility. One well-known example is Google's use of Differential Privacy in its Chrome browser. Google collects aggregate data from users' browsing habits to improve features like auto-complete and suggest relevant search terms. To ensure user privacy, they add carefully calibrated noise to the collected data before analysis. This noise addition mechanism prevents individual users' browsing behaviors from being precisely inferred while still enabling valuable insights to be drawn from the aggregated data. Google determines the level of noise based on the desired privacy parameter ε, allowing them to strike a balance between maintaining user privacy and enhancing the browser's functionality. This practical implementation showcases how Differential Privacy can be integrated into data-driven applications, assuring users that their sensitive information remains protected while contributing to the improvement of services.

3.2 Homomorphic Encryption for Secure Machine Learning

Homomorphic encryption stands as a revolutionary solution at the crossroads of cryptography and machine learning, addressing the critical challenge of preserving data privacy while enabling sophisticated analysis. In the era of vast data availability and advanced analytics, traditional methods fall short in safeguarding sensitive information, often necessitating a trade-off between utility and confidentiality. Homomorphic encryption offers a groundbreaking alternative, allowing computations to be performed directly on encrypted data, without the need for decryption. This paradigm shift ensures that even the data owner remains oblivious to the content being processed, making it an ideal approach for secure machine learning. Researchers and practitioners are actively exploring various homomorphic encryption schemes, such as partial and full homomorphic encryption, to strike a balance between computational efficiency and versatility. By enabling operations like addition and multiplication on encrypted data, homomorphic encryption empowers the development of privacy-preserving algorithms, safeguarding individual data points while still allowing for meaningful insights and predictions. As industries and institutions grapple with the growing demand for data-driven decision-making and compliance with stringent privacy regulations, homomorphic encryption emerges as a beacon of hope, illuminating a path toward the harmonization of machine learning's potential with the imperative of data security.

Figure 2. Homomorphic encryption for machine learning

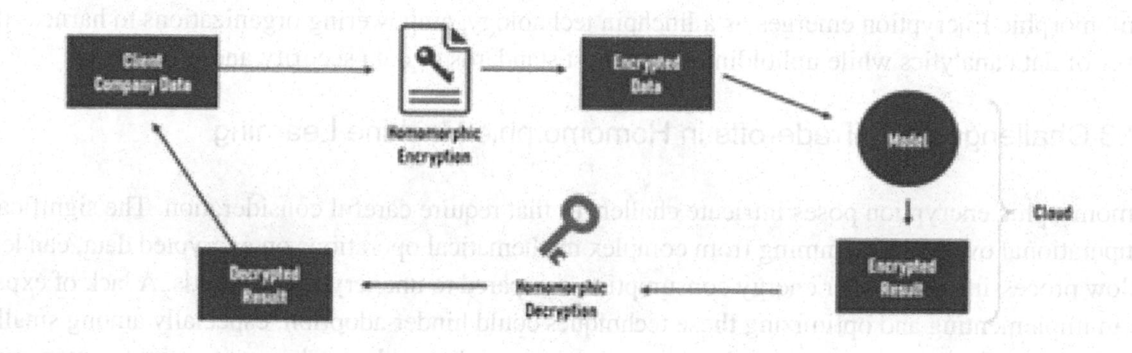

3.2.1 Homomorphic Encryption Fundamentals

Homomorphic encryption is a groundbreaking cryptographic technique that enables computations to be performed on encrypted data, preserving its confidentiality while allowing meaningful operations to be carried out. Unlike traditional encryption methods that require decryption before any processing can occur, homomorphic encryption empowers data to remain encrypted throughout its lifecycle, even during computation. This concept addresses the fundamental tension between data privacy and utility in the age of advanced analytics and machine learning. There are different types of homomorphic encryption, including partially homomorphic encryption, which supports only one type of operation (either addition or multiplication) on encrypted data, and fully homomorphic encryption, which supports both addition and multiplication. While homomorphic encryption comes with computational overhead due to its intricate mathematical operations, ongoing research focuses on optimizing its performance. The potential impact of homomorphic encryption is far-reaching, as it offers a secure pathway for outsourcing data analysis, enabling collaborative machine learning across organizations without exposing sensitive information. This technology finds applications in domains like healthcare, finance, and cloud computing, where data privacy is paramount, and the ability to derive insights without compromising confidentiality is invaluable.

3.2.2 Secure Data Processing With Homomorphic Encryption

Secure Data Processing with Homomorphic Encryption revolutionizes the way sensitive information is handled and analyzed, presenting a breakthrough solution at the intersection of cryptography and data analytics. Homomorphic encryption empowers organizations to perform computations on encrypted data without the need for decryption, effectively shielding the underlying information from exposure while enabling valuable insights to be extracted. This approach fundamentally redefines data privacy and security by ensuring that even during processing, data remains in its encrypted state, impervious to unauthorized access or breaches. Homomorphic encryption offers a range of applications, including secure outsourcing of computations to third parties, collaborative data analysis among multiple entities, and privacy-preserving machine learning. By preserving confidentiality without sacrificing functionality, homomorphic encryption addresses the pervasive challenge of balancing the demand for data-driven insights with the imperative to protect individual privacy. As industries navigate an era of stringent data protection regulations and increasing threats to sensitive information, Secure Data Processing with Homomorphic Encryption emerges as a linchpin technology, empowering organizations to harness the power of data analytics while upholding the highest standards of data security and privacy.

3.2.3 Challenges and Trade-offs in Homomorphic Machine Learning

Homomorphic encryption poses intricate challenges that require careful consideration. The significant computational overhead, stemming from complex mathematical operations on encrypted data, can lead to slow processing and higher energy consumption compared to unencrypted methods. A lack of expertise in implementing and optimizing these techniques could hinder adoption, especially among smaller organizations. Balancing security and performance is crucial, as enhanced security might compromise processing speed, particularly in resource-limited settings. Vulnerabilities like side-channel attacks persist despite encryption, potentially necessitating additional protective measures. The interplay between privacy and utility raises concerns about reduced accuracy in machine learning models due to encrypted data. Certain algorithms might struggle with encrypted data, requiring modifications for compatibility. Regulatory compliance adds complexity, as organizations must align encryption with stringent data protection rules. Effective key management is pivotal for security. Scaling up homomorphic encryption for large datasets and complex computations is challenging. Ongoing research reflects the evolving nature of this field, introducing uncertainties about best practices and strategies (Wood et al., 2020).

In navigating these challenges and trade-offs, organizations must carefully evaluate their specific use cases, security needs, and performance requirements. As the fields of homomorphic encryption and machine learning continue to mature, addressing these obstacles is pivotal to realizing the full potential of secure and privacy-preserving machine learning applications.

3.3 Secure Multi-Party Computation (SMPC)

Secure Multi-Party Computation (SMPC) stands as a formidable privacy-preserving technique that addresses the critical challenge of enabling collaborative computations while safeguarding the confidentiality of individual inputs. By employing cryptographic protocols, SMPC allows multiple parties to collectively perform computations on their encrypted data without the need to reveal their sensitive information. This ensures that each participant's input remains hidden throughout the process, making SMPC an invaluable tool for domains where data privacy is paramount. SMPC's ability to facilitate secure collaboration while keeping data confidential has far-reaching implications for industries such as finance, healthcare, and research, where data analysis requires a delicate balance between sharing insights and protecting personal or proprietary information.

Figure 3. Strengthening privacy using secure multi-party computation

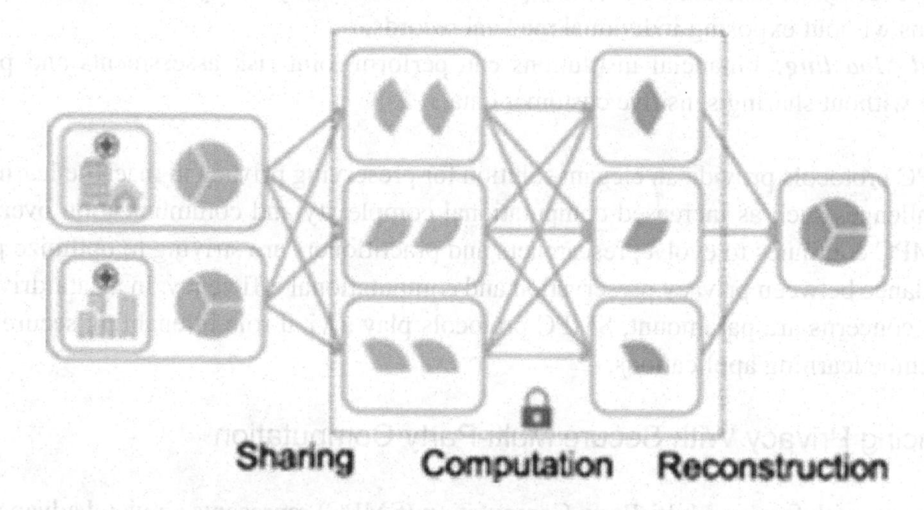

3.3.1 SMPC Protocols and Applications in Machine Learning

SMPC Protocols, often referred to as Secure Multi-Party Computation protocols, have emerged as a cornerstone of privacy-preserving solutions in the realm of machine learning. These protocols enable multiple parties to collaboratively compute complex functions on their private inputs while maintaining data confidentiality (Zhao et al., 2019). With their cryptographic foundations, SMPC protocols provide a robust framework for secure data analysis. In the context of machine learning, SMPC finds application in various scenarios:

1. ***Privacy-Preserving Training:*** SMPC protocols allow multiple parties to jointly train machine learning models on their respective datasets without sharing the raw data. This is especially useful in scenarios where data cannot be centralized due to privacy concerns or regulatory constraints.
2. ***Cross-Institutional Collaboration:*** Organizations can collaborate on machine learning projects without exposing sensitive data. SMPC facilitates model training across institutions, ensuring that individual data remains encrypted during computations.
3. ***Ensemble Learning:*** SMPC enables the construction of ensemble models without sharing raw data. Multiple parties can collaboratively build and combine models to achieve improved predictive accuracy.
4. ***Collaborative Predictive Analysis:*** SMPC allows parties to make predictions collectively while keeping their individual data private. This is particularly relevant in situations where parties seek to gain insights without revealing proprietary or sensitive information.
5. ***Data Aggregation:*** In cases where data needs to be aggregated for analysis, SMPC ensures that the aggregation process occurs without any party disclosing their individual data points.
6. ***Privacy-Preserving Data Mining:*** SMPC protocols can be applied to extract meaningful patterns and insights from encrypted data while keeping the underlying data confidential.
7. ***Fraud Detection and Anomaly Detection:*** Parties can collaboratively identify fraudulent activities or anomalies in a distributed dataset without revealing the specific instances being flagged.

8. ***Healthcare Analysis:*** In healthcare, SMPC protocols enable analysis of patient data across multiple institutions without exposing individual medical records.
9. ***Financial Modeling:*** Financial institutions can perform joint risk assessments and predictive modeling without sharing sensitive customer data.

While SMPC protocols provide an elegant solution for preserving privacy in machine learning, they come with challenges such as increased computational complexity and communication overhead. As the field of SMPC continues to evolve, researchers and practitioners are striving to optimize protocols and strike a balance between privacy preservation and computational efficiency. In a data-driven world where privacy concerns are paramount, SMPC protocols play a vital role in enabling secure and collaborative machine learning applications.

3.3.2 Enhancing Privacy With Secure Multi-Party Computation

Enhancing Privacy with Secure Multi-Party Computation (SMPC) represents a pivotal advancement in the realm of data security and collaborative computing. SMPC offers a robust framework that empowers multiple parties to collectively analyze and compute their private data without the need to reveal individual inputs. This revolutionary approach transforms the dynamics of data collaboration by ensuring that sensitive information remains encrypted throughout the process, eliminating the risks associated with data exposure. By harnessing cryptographic protocols, SMPC enables organizations to achieve a delicate balance between data-driven insights and individual privacy preservation. SMPC finds a profound application in various domains where data confidentiality is paramount (Zhou et al., 2021). Industries ranging from healthcare to finance, research, and beyond benefit from collaborative analyses that respect data privacy. Healthcare institutions can pool medical insights without compromising patient confidentiality, while financial entities can conduct risk assessments collectively without disclosing proprietary data. Moreover, SMPC transcends geographical boundaries, facilitating global collaborations that honor diverse privacy regulations.

However, the path to privacy enhancement through SMPC is not without challenges. The computational overhead and communication complexities introduced by cryptographic operations require careful optimization. Yet, as technology advances, solutions are being devised to strike a harmonious balance between secure computation and operational efficiency. In the evolving landscape of data privacy, SMPC stands as a beacon of innovation, fostering a new era of collaborative data analysis where confidentiality remains inviolate. By allowing organizations to extract valuable insights while safeguarding individual contributions, SMPC contributes to building trust, empowering innovation, and reshaping the boundaries of secure data collaboration.

3.4 Federated Learning Protocols

The landscape of machine learning is undergoing a transformative shift through the implementation of Federated Learning Protocols. These protocols facilitate a revolutionary approach wherein collaborative model training takes place across an array of geographically distributed devices or servers. A remarkable feature of this paradigm is its ability to ensure the utmost privacy of sensitive data, setting it apart from traditional methods that concentrate data in a centralized manner. By embracing this innovative approach, Federated Learning Protocols introduce a higher standard of security and confidentiality, proving particularly beneficial in scenarios where data privacy holds paramount importance. Unlike conventional methods that concentrate data, federated learning empowers individual devices to participate in model improvement without disclosing raw information. This progressive framework introduces an advanced standard of security and secrecy, rendering it particularly suitable for situations where data privacy is of utmost importance (Aledhari et al., 2020). By amalgamating machine learning and decentralized systems, federated learning protocols forge a path for collaborative intelligence without undermining the integrity of individual data.

3.4.1 Difference Between Centralized and Decentralized Federated Learning

Table 1 provides a comprehensive comparison between Centralized and Decentralized Federated Learning methodologies, highlighting the key distinctions and advantages of each approach.

Table 1. Comparison between centralized and decentralized federated learning

Aspect	Centralized Federated Learning	Decentralized Federated Learning
Data Location	Centralized server or cloud	Distributed across multiple devices or nodes
Data Sharing	Data remains on client devices	Data shared among participants
Data Privacy	Potential privacy concerns	Enhanced privacy through local data storage
Communication	Server-client communication	Peer-to-peer or peer-to-server communication
Model Training	Centralized model training	Local model training with periodic aggregation
Network Bandwidth	High requirements	Lower bandwidth requirements
Scalability	Limited by server capacity	Highly scalable across devices/nodes
Fault Tolerance	Single point of failure	Distributed, more fault-tolerant
Data Security	Vulnerable to attacks	Reduced attack surface
Implementation Complexity	Lower complexity	Higher complexity
Customization	Limited customization	More customization options
Collaboration	Server-centric collaboration	Collaborative learning approach

3.4.2 Federated Averaging Algorithm

Federated Averaging is a popular algorithm used in Federated Learning to train a global model while keeping data decentralized on individual devices or nodes. Here's an overview of the Federated Averaging algorithm:

1. ***Initialization:*** The process begins with initializing a global model on a central server.
2. ***Client Selection:*** A subset of client devices or nodes is selected from the network to participate in the training process. This selection can be random or based on certain criteria.
3. ***Model Distribution:*** The current global model is sent to the selected clients. Each client trains the model using its local data without sharing the raw data with the central server or other clients.

4. ***Local Training:*** On each client, the model is trained using the local data. This training can involve multiple iterations of gradient descent or other optimization techniques to minimize a chosen loss function.
5. ***Model Aggregation:*** After local training, the updated models from all clients are aggregated to create a new global model. This aggregation typically involves averaging the model parameters across the clients.
6. ***Model Update:*** The central server updates the global model with the aggregated model obtained from the clients.
7. ***Iteration:*** Steps 3-6 are repeated for a certain number of iterations or until convergence criteria are met.

Key features and benefits of the Federated Averaging algorithm include:

1. ***Privacy:*** Raw data remains on the clients, enhancing data privacy and reducing the risk of exposing sensitive information.
2. ***Decentralization:*** The algorithm allows for distributed learning across devices or nodes, making it suitable for scenarios where data cannot be centralized.
3. ***Reduced Communication:*** Communication overhead is minimized as only model updates are exchanged, not raw data.
4. ***Scalability:*** Federated Averaging can scale to many devices, enabling training on massive, decentralized datasets.
5. ***Customization:*** Each client can perform local training based on its unique data distribution, allowing for customized learning.
6. ***Federated Learning Challenges:*** Challenges such as non-IID (non-identically distributed) data, stragglers (slow nodes), and communication heterogeneity need to be addressed.

Federated Averaging has been used in various domains, including healthcare, finance, and IoT, where data privacy and decentralized learning are paramount. However, it's important to note that while Federated Averaging addresses privacy concerns, it introduces challenges related to system architecture, algorithm design, and convergence analysis (Nilsson et al., 2018).

3.4.3 Secure Aggregation Techniques in Federated Learning

Secure aggregation techniques play a crucial role in enhancing the privacy and security of Federated Learning by allowing participants to collaboratively aggregate model updates without exposing individual updates or raw data. Here are some key secure aggregation techniques used in Federated Learning:

1. ***Federated Averaging with Differential Privacy (DP)***: Differential Privacy is a framework that adds noise to the model updates before aggregation, ensuring that individual contributions remain private. This prevents malicious users from inferring specific data points from the updates. Noise is added to gradients or model parameters during aggregation, and careful tuning of noise parameters is necessary to balance privacy and utility.

2. ***Homomorphic Encryption:*** Homomorphic encryption enables computations on encrypted data without the need for decryption. Participants encrypt their model updates before sending them to the server. The server performs aggregation on the encrypted updates and returns the encrypted result. The result is decrypted to obtain the aggregated update. Fully Homomorphic Encryption (FHE) and Partially Homomorphic Encryption (PHE) are used depending on the specific scenario.
3. ***Multi-Party Computation (MPC):*** MPC allows participants to collaboratively compute functions on their inputs without revealing those inputs to each other. In Federated Learning, participants compute an aggregate update without sharing the individual updates. Secure function evaluation protocols, such as garbled circuits or secret sharing, are used to achieve this.
4. ***Zero-Knowledge Proofs (ZKPs):*** Zero-Knowledge Proofs allow a participant to prove the correctness of their update or computation without revealing the actual data or computation. This can be used to verify the validity of updates during aggregation without exposing sensitive information (Li et al., 2014).
5. ***Secure Aggregation Schemes:*** These schemes combine cryptographic techniques, such as homomorphic encryption, secret sharing, and secure multi-party computation, to securely aggregate model updates. Examples include Secure Aggregation via Secret Sharing (SecAgg) and Secure Federated Averaging (SecFedAvg).
6. ***Trusted Execution Environments (TEEs)***: TEEs provide isolated environments for executing code securely. Participants' updates are processed within TEEs to prevent leakage of sensitive information. Intel SGX and ARM TrustZone are examples of TEE technologies.
7. ***Private Set Intersection (PSI):*** PSI protocols enable two parties to find the intersection of their datasets without revealing the non-intersecting elements. This can be used to match relevant data between clients and servers without sharing the actual data.

It's important to note that these techniques have their own strengths, limitations, and computational costs. The choice of technique depends on factors such as the level of security required, computation overhead, communication efficiency, and specific use case requirements.

4. ADVANCEMENTS IN FEDERATED LEARNING

Federated Learning is a groundbreaking advancement in machine learning that addresses data privacy concerns by enabling model training on decentralized devices while keeping data localized. This approach preserves privacy, enhances security, and leverages diverse data sources for improved model generalization. By allowing collaborative training without sharing raw data, Federated Learning offers a privacy-conscious solution that is efficient, scalable, and adaptable across various domains, although it comes with challenges like communication overhead and aggregation methods that researchers are actively refining.

4.1 Federated Transfer Learning

Federated Transfer Learning merges with Federated Learning and Transfer Learning to train machine learning models across decentralized data sources while incorporating knowledge from related tasks. It starts with a globally pre-trained model and refines it on local devices, benefiting from both broad initial knowledge and personalized fine-tuning. This approach accelerates convergence, enhances model performance, and maintains data privacy. Challenges include communication overhead and biased updates, but the technique has broad applications such as medical research, edge computing, and industrial IoT. As the field advances, addressing aggregation issues and biases will be key to maximizing Federated Transfer Learning's potential.

Let's consider the example of personalized keyboard prediction on smartphones using Federated Transfer Learning.

In this scenario, smartphone users often rely on keyboard prediction to enhance typing speed and accuracy. However, language preferences, slang, and commonly used phrases can vary widely among users. Federated Transfer Learning can be employed to improve the keyboard prediction system while respecting user privacy.

Initially, a global model is pre-trained on a vast dataset containing diverse text from various sources. This pre-trained model learns general language patterns, grammar, and common phrases. Then, this model is distributed to individual smartphones (Liu et al., 2020).

On each smartphone, the global model is fine-tuned using the user's personal typing history and local language nuances. For instance, a user who frequently communicates in a specific dialect, slang, or technical jargon can fine-tune the model to better predict their unique typing patterns.

Here's how Federated Transfer Learning benefits this scenario:

1. ***Knowledge Sharing***: The pre-trained global model has a grasp of general language patterns, benefiting each user's personalized model.
2. ***Data Privacy***: Personal typing history and language preferences remain on the device, ensuring user privacy as raw data is not shared.
3. ***User-Specific Prediction***: Fine-tuning allows the model to adapt to each user's specific typing habits, resulting in more accurate and contextually relevant predictions.
4. ***Efficient Model Improvement***: The global model's pretraining reduces the effort needed for each device to learn language basics, speeding up the adaptation process.
5. ***Localized Variations***: Federated Transfer Learning allows the model to capture localized language variations, improving its accuracy for regional slang and dialects.
6. ***User Autonomy***: Users have control over enhancing their keyboard prediction experience without relinquishing their private typing history.

In this example, Federated Transfer Learning enables smartphones to collaboratively improve keyboard prediction while keeping user data private. The technique harnesses the collective knowledge of a trained global model and fine-tunes it individually on each device, leading to more accurate and personalized predictions without compromising privacy.

4.2 Differential Privacy in Federated Learning

Differential Privacy in Federated Learning is a crucial technique that addresses the challenge of data privacy in collaborative machine-learning settings. In Federated Learning, participants contribute their local data to train a shared model without centralizing the data. However, the aggregated model updates can inadvertently reveal individual data points, posing a privacy risk. Differential Privacy counters this risk by injecting carefully calibrated noise into the aggregated updates before applying them to the model.

This noise ensures that the impact of any individual data point on the updates remains obscured. The level of noise is controlled to strike a balance between privacy protection and model accuracy. By adding noise, Differential Privacy guarantees that no single participant's data is identifiable in the aggregated updates. Even if an adversary tries to reverse-engineer the original data from the noisy updates, they would only encounter statistical randomness rather than specific data points.

Imagine a ride-sharing company using Federated Learning to improve its fare prediction model while preserving user privacy. Each user's app refines the model using their ride history and location data. By adding Differential Privacy, the company guarantees that even if a user's data is used to update the model, their personal details cannot be discerned. This shields sensitive information while collectively enhancing the model for all users, illustrating how Differential Privacy safeguards privacy in collaborative learning scenarios.

4.3 Federated Learning for Edge Devices

Federated Learning for Edge Devices is a transformative approach that enables machine learning models to be trained directly on decentralized edge devices, such as smartphones, IoT devices, and sensors. This paradigm shifts traditional model training from centralized servers to the edge, allowing devices to learn and improve while minimizing the need for constant data transmission to a central location (Lim et al., 2020). In Federated Learning for Edge Devices, each edge device maintains its data locally, addressing concerns about privacy, security, and bandwidth limitations. Model updates are computed locally on these devices and then shared with a central server or aggregator, which combines the updates to refine the global model. This way, the central server only receives aggregated insights rather than raw data, ensuring data privacy is upheld.

Thus, Federated Learning for Edge Devices empowers localized learning while preserving privacy and optimizing resource utilization. This innovation paves the way for smarter edge devices that collaboratively learn and adapt, leading to more efficient, personalized, and responsive AI-driven applications.

This approach offers several benefits:

1. ***Privacy Preservation:*** Data stays on the edge device, reducing the risk of sensitive information exposure during transmission.
2. ***Bandwidth Efficiency:*** Federated Learning minimizes the need to transfer large volumes of data to a central server, conserving bandwidth.
3. ***Real-time Learning:*** Edge devices can adapt and learn from their local environments in real-time, enabling quick responses to changing conditions.
4. ***Latency Reduction:*** Decentralized learning reduces the delay caused by sending data to a central server and waiting for model updates.
5. ***Scalability:*** Federated Learning supports collaborative training across a vast network of edge devices, making it suitable for large-scale applications.
6. ***Personalization:*** Devices can tailor models to user preferences and local contexts, enhancing user experiences.
7. ***Robustness:*** Training on diverse edge data helps models generalize better and become more robust.

Real-world applications of Federated Learning for Edge Devices are numerous. For instance, smartphones can learn users' behaviors for personalized services, IoT devices can collectively improve predictive maintenance models, and edge sensors can contribute to environmental monitoring networks.

5. APPLICATIONS OF PRIVACY-PRESERVING AND FEDERATED MACHINE LEARNING IN DIFFERENT SECTORS

5.1 Healthcare and Medical Data Privacy

Privacy-preserving and federated machine learning have emerged as invaluable tools in safeguarding healthcare and medical data privacy while enabling advanced data analysis. In the realm of healthcare, these techniques address the delicate balance between extracting insights from sensitive patient information and maintaining confidentiality. Privacy-preserving techniques like homomorphic encryption and secure multi-party computation allow healthcare institutions to collaborate and perform analyses on encrypted data without compromising individual patient privacy. This is especially crucial for scenarios involving rare diseases or conditions where data sharing is essential but compliance with privacy regulations is paramount. Federated machine learning extends the concept by enabling multiple institutions to collaboratively train machine learning models without sharing raw data. Instead, models are trained locally, and only aggregated model updates are shared, minimizing the risk of data exposure. Such approaches are pivotal in accelerating medical research, drug discovery, and treatment personalization while ensuring that sensitive patient data remains under strict control and protection.

5.2 Financial Data Privacy and Fraud Detection

In the domain of financial data privacy and fraud detection, the implementation of privacy-preserving and federated machine learning techniques holds immense promise. These methods allow financial institutions to collaborate on fraud detection models without compromising the confidentiality of customer information. Privacy-preserving techniques, such as differential privacy, enable the aggregation of insights from multiple sources while adding noise to the data to protect individual details. This empowers institutions to collectively analyze patterns of fraudulent activities without directly accessing each other's sensitive data. Federated machine learning takes this a step further by enabling banks and financial organizations to collaboratively build robust fraud detection models. Each participant trains the model on their local data, and only aggregated model updates are exchanged, preventing the exposure of raw transaction details. This approach strengthens fraud detection capabilities across the industry, as the models learn from diverse data sources while adhering to stringent data privacy regulations and maintaining the trust of customers in safeguarding their financial information.

5.3 Internet of Things (IoT) and Privacy Challenges

In the realm of the Internet of Things (IoT), where devices collect vast amounts of sensitive data, privacy-preserving, and federated machine learning techniques play a pivotal role in addressing privacy challenges. These approaches enable IoT devices to share insights and collaborate on data analysis without compromising the privacy of individuals. Privacy-preserving methods, such as secure aggregation and homomorphic encryption, allow IoT devices to transmit encrypted data, ensuring that raw information remains confidential while still contributing to collective analysis. Federated machine learning extends this concept by enabling IoT devices to collaboratively train models without sending raw data to a central server. Instead, model updates are shared, allowing devices to collectively learn and improve while maintaining data locally. This is crucial in applications like healthcare monitoring, smart cities, and industrial automation, where privacy concerns are paramount. By implementing privacy-preserving and federated machine learning, the IoT ecosystem can harness the potential of data-driven insights while preserving the privacy and security of individuals' personal information in an increasingly connected world.

6. IMPLEMENTATION OF PRIVACY-PRESERVING FEDERATED MACHINE LEARNING SCENARIO

An implementation of a simple privacy-preserving federated machine learning scenario using a Jupyter Notebook is given below. We have used a dummy diabetes dataset and demonstrated how two healthcare providers, represented by virtual workers, can collaborate to train a model while keeping patient data private. The user has to make sure to have Jupyter Notebook installed and then use the "!pip install torch torchvision" command to install the required packages.

However, the code demonstrates how healthcare providers can collaboratively train a machine learning model to predict diabetes while keeping their patient data private. This privacy-preserving federated learning approach ensures that sensitive patient information is not shared while still enabling model training for better medical predictions. Note that this is a simplified example for demonstration purposes, and in practice, real-world considerations for data privacy, security, and model aggregation would be more complex.

6.1 Python Code

```
!pip install torch torchvision
import torch
# Generate dummy diabetes dataset
data = torch.randn(400, 8)  # 400 samples, 8 features
target = torch.randint(0, 2, (400, 1))  # Binary labels (0 or 1)
# Split the data between two healthcare providers
data_provider_a = data[:200]
target_provider_a = target[:200]
data_provider_b = data[200:]
target_provider_b = target[200:]
# Define a simple neural network model
class Model(torch.nn.Module):
    def __init__(self):
        super(Model, self).__init__()
        self.fc = torch.nn.Linear(8, 1)

    def forward(self, x):
```

```
        return torch.sigmoid(self.fc(x))
model = Model()
# Define a loss function
criterion = torch.nn.BCELoss()
# Federated learning process
for epoch in range(10):
    # Train on healthcare provider A's data
    preds_provider_a = model(data_provider_a)
    loss_provider_a = criterion(preds_provider_a, target_provider_a.float())
    model.zero_grad()
    loss_provider_a.backward()

    with torch.no_grad():
        for param in model.parameters():
            param -= 0.1 * param.grad

    # Train on healthcare provider B's data
    preds_provider_b = model(data_provider_b)
    loss_provider_b = criterion(preds_provider_b, target_provider_b.float())
    model.zero_grad()
    loss_provider_b.backward()

    with torch.no_grad():
        for param in model.parameters():
            param -= 0.1 * param.grad

    print(f"Epoch {epoch+1}: Provider A's Loss {loss_provider_a.item()}, Pro-
vider B's Loss {loss_provider_b.item()}")
# Test the federated model
test_data = torch.randn(1, 8)  # New test data point
with torch.no_grad():
    prediction = model(test_data)
    probability = prediction.item()
    print("Test Data:")
    print(test_data)
    print(f"Prediction for the test data: {probability} (Probability of diabe-
tes)")
```

6.2 Output

Figure 4. Output of the Python code demonstrating a machine-learning model to predict diabetes while keeping patient data private

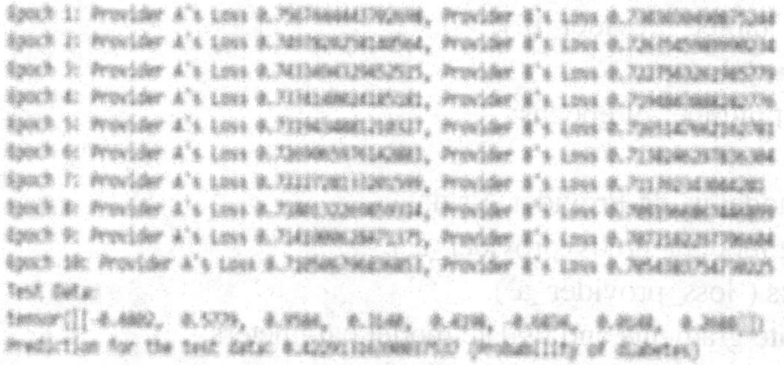

6.3 Methodology

i. We start by importing the required libraries, primarily torch.
ii. We generate dummy diabetes data consisting of features (e.g., glucose levels, BMI, etc.) and binary labels (0 or 1) representing the presence or absence of diabetes. In reality, you'd have real patient data.
iii. We split the data and labels between two healthcare providers, data_provider_a and data_provider_b, simulating the separation of data across providers.
iv. We define a simple neural network model named Model with a single fully connected layer (torch.nn.Linear) followed by a sigmoid activation. This is a basic architecture for binary classification tasks like diabetes prediction.
v. We define a loss function criterion using binary cross-entropy loss (BCELoss) since it's suitable for binary classification tasks.
vi. The federated learning loop runs for a few epochs, with each provider training the model on their respective data. The process includes computing predictions, calculating losses, backpropagation, and updating the model's parameters using gradient descent.
vii. The with torch.no_grad(): block ensures that no gradients are computed during the model evaluation step to save memory and computational resources.
viii. After the federated learning process, we test the federated model using a new test data point. The model predicts the probability of the test patient having diabetes.

6.4 Explanation

Here's a summarized version of the explanation for the key steps in the code:

1. **Initialization:**
   - Import required libraries (`torch`).
   - Define the neural network model (`Model`) and the loss function (`criterion`).
2. **Data Generation:**
   - Generate synthetic diabetes dataset (`data` and `target`).
   - Split data between two healthcare providers (`data_provider_a`, `target_provider_a`, `data_provider_b`, `target_provider_b`).
3. **Federated Learning Loop:**
   Loop through a set number of epochs:
   For each epoch:
      - Train model using Provider A's data:
   - Predict using model (`preds_provider_a`).
   - Calculate loss (`loss_provider_a`).
   - Backpropagate gradients and update model parameters.

- Train model using Provider B's data:
   - Predict using model (`preds_provider_b`).
   - Calculate loss (`loss_provider_b`).
   - Backpropagate gradients and update model parameters.

4. **Testing Federated Model:**
   - Generate new test data (`test_data`).
   - Use `torch.no_grad()` to evaluate model without gradients.
   - Compute prediction for test data (`prediction`).
5. **Output:**
   - Display final prediction probability for test data (diabetes probability).

7. FUTURE TRENDS AND OPEN CHALLENGES

Looking ahead, several future trends and open challenges are poised to shape the landscape of privacy-preserving machine learning. The evolving privacy regulations and standards, such as GDPR and CCPA, will continue to influence how organizations handle sensitive data, necessitating the development of adaptable privacy-preserving techniques that align with these legal frameworks. Ensuring the scalability and efficiency of privacy-preserving methods remains a challenge, as the increasing volume of data and complexity of computations can strain existing techniques. Moreover, striking a balance between privacy and utility is a central concern, requiring innovative approaches that maintain data privacy while extracting meaningful insights. As the field advances, researchers and practitioners must collaborate to devise solutions that maximize the benefits of machine learning while safeguarding individual privacy. This calls for continuous research into more efficient algorithms, improved encryption methods, and the integration of advanced technologies like federated learning to address these challenges and steer privacy-preserving machine learning toward a more secure and productive future (Xu et al., 2021).

8. CONCLUSION

In conclusion, privacy-preserving and federated machine learning have emerged as vital tools for maintaining data privacy in various domains. These techniques, such as homomorphic encryption and secure multi-party computation, enable collaboration and analysis while upholding individual privacy rights. Their applications span healthcare, finance, IoT, and beyond, fostering innovation without compromising confidentiality. As privacy regulations evolve and data volumes increase, challenges of scalability, efficiency, and achieving the right balance between privacy and utility persist. The future holds promise as researchers strive to develop more robust methods and integrate cutting-edge technologies like federated learning. These efforts will shape a landscape where data-driven insights coexist harmoniously with stringent privacy protection. As we forge ahead, the marriage of privacy and machine learning will drive progress and empower industries while respecting the individual's right to data privacy. The rapid advancements in machine learning have led to transformative applications across various domains. However, the unprecedented growth in data-driven technologies has also raised concerns about data privacy and security. As data becomes the lifeblood of machine learning models, protecting sensitive information while ensuring accurate model performance becomes imperative. This chapter delves into the realm of "Privacy-Preserving and Federated Machine Learning Techniques" that aim to safeguard data privacy in the age of data-driven insights.

REFERENCES

Al-Rubaie, M., & Chang, J. M. (2019). Privacy-preserving machine learning: Threats and solutions. *IEEE Security and Privacy*, *17*(2), 49–58. doi:10.1109/MSEC.2018.2888775

Aledhari, M., Razzak, R., Parizi, R. M., & Saeed, F. (2020). Federated learning: A survey on enabling technologies, protocols, and applications. *IEEE Access : Practical Innovations, Open Solutions*, *8*, 140699–140725. doi:10.1109/ACCESS.2020.3013541 PMID:32999795

Dwork, C. (2006, July). Differential privacy. In *International colloquium on automata, languages, and programming* (pp. 1-12). Berlin, Heidelberg: Springer Berlin Heidelberg. 10.1007/11787006_1

Dwork, C. (2008, April). Differential privacy: A survey of results. In *International conference on theory and applications of models of computation* (pp. 1-19). Berlin, Heidelberg: Springer Berlin Heidelberg.

Guan, Z., Bian, L., Shang, T., & Liu, J. (2018, August). When machine learning meets security issues: A survey. In 2018 IEEE international conference on intelligence and safety for robotics (ISR) (pp. 158-165). IEEE. doi:10.1109/IISR.2018.8535799

Jegorova, M., Kaul, C., Mayor, C., O'Neil, A. Q., Weir, A., Murray-Smith, R., & Tsaftaris, S. A. (2022). Survey: Leakage and privacy at inference time. *IEEE Transactions on Pattern Analysis and Machine Intelligence*, 1–20. doi:10.1109/TPAMI.2022.3229593 PMID:37015684

Li, F., & McMillin, B. (2014). A survey on zero-knowledge proofs. [). Elsevier.]. *Advances in Computers*, *94*, 25–69. doi:10.1016/B978-0-12-800161-5.00002-5

Lim, W. Y. B., Luong, N. C., Hoang, D. T., Jiao, Y., Liang, Y. C., Yang, Q., Niyato, D., & Miao, C. (2020). Federated learning in mobile edge networks: A comprehensive survey. *IEEE Communications Surveys and Tutorials*, *22*(3), 2031–2063. doi:10.1109/COMST.2020.2986024

Liu, Y., Kang, Y., Xing, C., Chen, T., & Yang, Q. (2020). A secure federated transfer learning framework. *IEEE Intelligent Systems*, *35*(4), 70–82. doi:10.1109/MIS.2020.2988525

Lo, S. K., Lu, Q., Wang, C., Paik, H. Y., & Zhu, L. (2021). A systematic literature review on federated machine learning: From a software engineering perspective. *ACM Computing Surveys*, *54*(5), 1–39. doi:10.1145/3450288

Nilsson, A., Smith, S., Ulm, G., Gustavsson, E., & Jirstrand, M. (2018, December). A performance evaluation of federated learning algorithms. In *Proceedings of the second workshop on distributed infrastructures for deep learning* (pp. 1-8). IEEE. 10.1145/3286490.3286559

Sharifani, K., & Amini, M. (2023). Machine Learning and Deep Learning: A Review of Methods and Applications. *World Information Technology and Engineering Journal*, *10*(07), 3897–3904.

Wood, A., Najarian, K., & Kahrobaei, D. (2020). Homomorphic encryption for machine learning in medicine and bioinformatics. *ACM Computing Surveys*, *53*(4), 1–35. doi:10.1145/3394658

Xu, R., Baracaldo, N., & Joshi, J. (2021). Privacy-preserving machine learning: Methods, challenges and directions. *arXiv preprint arXiv:2108.04417*.

Zhang, J., Li, C., Ye, J., & Qu, G. (2020, September). Privacy threats and protection in machine learning. In *Proceedings of the 2020 on Great Lakes Symposium on VLSI* (pp. 531-536). 10.1145/3386263.3407599

Zhao, C., Zhao, S., Zhao, M., Chen, Z., Gao, C. Z., Li, H., & Tan, Y. A. (2019). Secure multi-party computation: Theory, practice and applications. *Information Sciences*, *476*, 357–372. doi:10.1016/j.ins.2018.10.024

Zhou, J., Feng, Y., Wang, Z., & Guo, D. (2021). Using secure multi-party computation to protect privacy on a permissioned blockchain. *Sensors (Basel)*, *21*(4), 1540. doi:10.339021041540 PMID:33672175

Chapter 14
Security, Privacy, and Technical Challenges in a Blockchain-Internet of Things-Based Environment

Amit Kumar Tyagi
https://orcid.org/0000-0003-2657-8700
National Institute of Fashion Technology, New Delhi, India

Meghna Manoj Nair
Tandon School of Engineering, New York University, USA

Khushboo Tripathi
Amity University, Gurugram, India

ABSTRACT

Blockchain and internet of things (IoT) is a combination that has massive potential to bring about revolutionary changes in various useful applications/ industries by enabling secure and transparent data exchange, decentralized control, and improved efficiency. However, this convergence also requires significant security, privacy, and technical challenges that must be addressed for successful implementation and widespread adoption. This chapter explains the security, privacy, and technical challenges that arise in a blockchain-IoT-based environment. Firstly, it examines the security issues related to the distributed nature of blockchain networks and the vulnerabilities that can be exploited in IoT devices and communication channels. Further, the authors discuss the importance of cryptographic techniques, secure key management, and access control mechanisms to protect data integrity and prevent unauthorized access.

DOI: 10.4018/979-8-3693-2081-5.ch014

1. INTRODUCTION

In recent years, the convergence of blockchain technology and the Internet of Things (IoT) has emerged as a promising paradigm for various industries. The combination of blockchain and IoT brings new opportunities and possibilities for decentralized and secure applications, enabling devices to communicate and transact autonomously without the need for intermediaries. However, along with these opportunities, the integration of blockchain and IoT also presents significant security, privacy, and technical challenges that need to be addressed. Applications that utilize both blockchain and IoT technology face unique security challenges in today's digital landscape. One major issue is the vulnerability of IoT devices themselves, as they often have limited computational power and security measures. These devices can be exploited by malicious actors to compromise the integrity of the blockchain network. Moreover, the decentralized nature of blockchain poses challenges in terms of securing data privacy and ensuring proper authentication and authorization mechanisms for IoT devices (Mohanta et al., 2020). Additionally, the immutability of blockchain data presents a challenge when it comes to removing or updating sensitive information that may have been inadvertently recorded. As blockchain and IoT continue to evolve, addressing these security challenges becomes important to build robust and trustworthy applications in this domain. Some of the key security challenges are listed and explained below:

- Device Vulnerabilities: IoT devices are often resource-constrained and may lack robust security measures. They can be vulnerable to various attacks such as malware infections, physical tampering, or unauthorized access. Compromised devices within a blockchain-IoT environment can lead to a breakdown of trust and compromise the integrity of the entire network.
- Distributed Denial-of-Service (DDoS) Attacks: The decentralized nature of blockchain-IoT systems can make them targets for DDoS attacks. Attackers can flood the network with a large volume of malicious requests, overwhelming the devices and disrupting normal operations. These attacks can hinder the availability and reliability of IoT devices and compromise the overall system performance.
- Smart Contract Vulnerabilities: The are contracts which are capable of self-executing through the agreement terms that are directly converted to codes and form an essential part of numerous blockchain-IoT use cases. However, coding errors or vulnerabilities in smart contracts can be exploited by attackers to manipulate transactions, steal sensitive information, or disrupt the execution of the contract.

Privacy challenges are another significant technology, faced by several applications utilizing blockchain and IoT. One of the main issues is the potential exposure of sensitive data collected by IoT devices. Since blockchain is designed to be transparent and immutable, any data stored on the blockchain is visible to all participants, raising issues about privacy and confidentiality. This becomes particularly problematic when dealing with personal information or sensitive business data. Another challenge lies in managing user identities and ensuring their privacy in a decentralized environment (Choo et al., 2020). Blockchain-based authentication mechanisms need to strike a delicate balance between providing sufficient privacy while maintaining the necessary level of trust and accountability. Addressing these privacy challenges is important to foster trust and widespread adoption of blockchain and IoT applications while safeguarding individuals' sensitive information. Two important aspects of this are elaborated below:

- Data Privacy: IoT devices generate vast amounts of sensitive data, including personal information and behavioral patterns. Storing and processing this data on a blockchain raises issues about data privacy. While blockchain offers transparency and immutability, it also poses challenges in terms of ensuring the confidentiality of sensitive information. It is important to implement robust privacy-preserving mechanisms to protect user data while maintaining the benefits of a decentralized blockchain system.
- Identity Management: In a blockchain-IoT environment, establishing and managing identities for devices and users is critical. Ensuring the privacy of identities and preventing unauthorized access or identity theft is a significant challenge. Traditional identity management systems may not be suitable for the decentralized nature of blockchain-IoT, requiring innovative approaches that balance privacy and security.

Here, one of the other challenges faced is that of technical issues and problems. Both blockchain and IoT generate enormous amounts of data, and integrating them requires addressing the issue of handling high transaction volumes in a timely and efficient manner. Additionally, the latency and bandwidth limitations of IoT devices can hinder real-time data processing and blockchain consensus mechanisms. Another technical challenge is interoperability. IoT devices often operate on different protocols and standards, making it challenging to establish seamless integration with blockchain networks. Ensuring compatibility and effective communication between diverse devices and blockchain platforms requires careful consideration. Moreover, the security of IoT devices and blockchain networks is a constant issue. Protecting against unauthorized access, data tampering, and ensuring secure communication channels are critical to maintaining the integrity of the system. Overcoming these technical challenges is essential to fully use the potential of blockchain and IoT applications and achieve their desired outcomes (Ferrag et al., 2020). The two main aspects of this challenge are discussed below:

- Scalability: Both blockchain and IoT face scalability challenges individually, and their combination exacerbates the problem. Blockchain systems, such as Bitcoin or Ethereum, often suffer from limited transaction processing capacity, leading to delays and increased costs. In an IoT-based environment, where numerous devices generate a high volume of transactions, scalability becomes a critical issue that must be addressed to enable efficient and timely processing.
- Interoperability: IoT devices typically operate on different platforms, protocols, and communication standards. Integrating these diverse devices into a blockchain-IoT ecosystem requires seamless interoperability. Ensuring compatibility and smooth communication between devices and different blockchain networks poses a significant technical challenge.

Hence, the integration of blockchain and IoT holds immense potential for revolutionizing industries and enabling autonomous and secure transactions. However, to fully realize this potential, it is important to address the security, privacy, and technical challenges inherent in such an environment. Robust security measures, privacy-preserving mechanisms, scalable solutions, and interoperability standards must be developed to ensure the successful deployment and operation of blockchain-IoT systems. Only by effectively addressing these challenges can we unlock the transformative power of blockchain and IoT integration. Figure 1 given below explains about the interaction and use of blockchain and IoT based frameworks.

Figure 1. Blockchain and IoT based framework

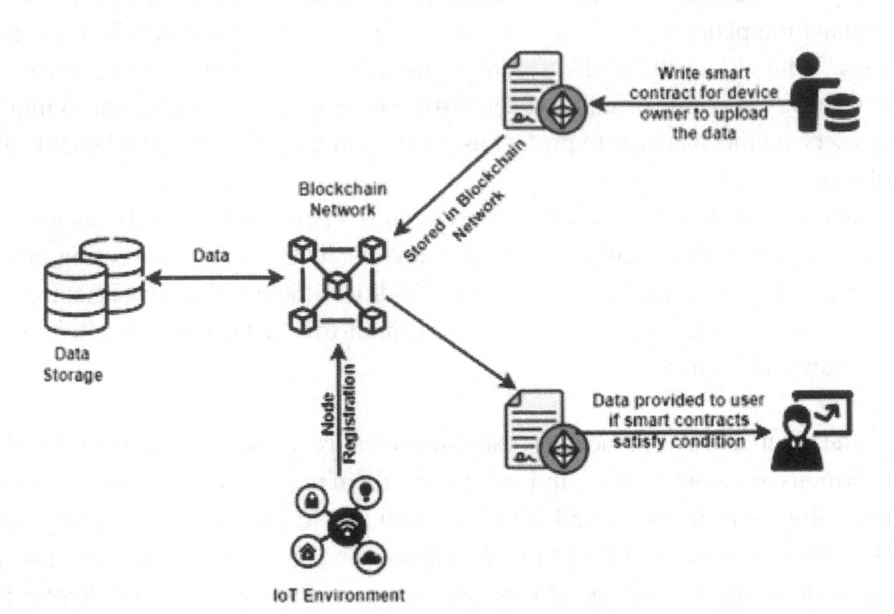

2. BACKGROUND WORK

Applications that use the combined power of blockchain and the Internet of Things (IoT) have the potential to revolutionize various industries. One prominent application is supply-chain management, where blockchain ensures transparency, immutability, and traceability of goods as they move through the supply chain, while IoT devices provide real-time tracking and monitoring of assets (Dorri et al., 2017). This enables stakeholders to verify the authenticity and quality of products, streamline logistics, and mitigate fraud. In the energy sector, blockchain and IoT can be employed to create decentralized energy grids, where IoT devices monitor energy production and consumption, and blockchain facilitates peer-to-peer energy trading and ensures transparent and secure transactions. Additionally, in healthcare, blockchain + IoT applications can enhance patient data security, enable secure sharing of medical records, and automate the monitoring of patients' vital signs. These applications demonstrate the potential for blockchain and IoT to revolutionize various sectors, promoting efficiency, transparency, and trust in our increasingly connected world. Researchers have focused on addressing security challenges in blockchain + IoT environments by proposing various solutions (Mohanta, Satapathy, Panda et al, 2019). These include the development of secure authentication mechanisms for IoT devices, such as lightweight cryptographic protocols, to prevent unauthorized access. Additionally, the use of secure identity management systems, such as decentralized identity (DID), has been explored to establish tamper-proof identities for IoT devices. Smart contract security has also received significant attention, with efforts to detect and mitigate vulnerabilities in smart contract code through static and dynamic analysis techniques. Privacy preservation in blockchain + IoT environments has been a major area of research. Techniques such as off-chain data storage, where sensitive data is stored outside the blockchain, have been proposed to protect privacy. Zero-knowledge proofs have been investigated as a means to validate data without revealing its contents. Selective disclosure mechanisms have also been explored to allow users to control the level of information they disclose while maintaining transaction integrity. Privacy-enhancing technologies, such as secure multiparty computation and homomorphic encryption, have been examined for their potential applications in preserving privacy in blockchain + IoT settings. Research efforts have been dedicated to addressing technical challenges in blockchain + IoT environments, particularly scalability (Waheed et al., 2020).

Proposed solutions include sharding, where the blockchain is partitioned into smaller shards to improve throughput. Sidechains and off-chain transactions have also been explored to alleviate the burden on the main blockchain. Interoperability challenges have been tackled through the development of standardized communication frameworks and protocols that facilitate seamless integration between blockchain and IoT devices. Additionally, efforts have been made to optimize IoT device architectures to overcome limitations in computational power, energy efficiency, and communication bandwidth. Researchers have proposed integration frameworks and architectures that combine blockchain and IoT technologies effectively (Goyal, et al., 2020). These frameworks aim to provide secure and privacy-preserving communication, efficient data handling, and seamless interoperability between IoT devices and blockchain networks. Proposed architectures consider edge computing, where data processing and storage occur closer to the IoT devices, reducing latency and enhancing security. Several research works have presented case studies and real-world applications that demonstrate the potential benefits and challenges of integrating blockchain and IoT. These include supply chain management, healthcare systems, energy grids, and smart cities. These studies shed light on the practical implications, feasibility, and effectiveness of using blockchain and IoT together, highlighting the security, privacy, and technical considerations specific to each use case. Many of the existing research works have provided important information into the security, privacy, and technical challenges in the integration of blockchain and IoT (Ferrag & Shu, 2021). These studies have proposed various solutions, frameworks, and architectures to address these challenges and have explored real-world applications to evaluate the practicality and effectiveness of blockchain and IoT environments. Continued research in this area is essential to drive innovation, enhance security, protect privacy, and overcome technical hurdles for the successful adoption of blockchain and IoT technologies (Raghuvanshi, et al., 2022).

3. APPLICATIONS USING BLOCKCHAIN-IOT BASED ENVIRONMENT

The combination of blockchain and the Internet of Things (IoT) opens up a wide range of applications across various industries. Here are some examples of how blockchain can be utilized in an IoT-based environment:

- Supply Chain Management: Blockchain can enhance transparency and traceability in supply chain management. By integrating IoT devices such as sensors and RFID tags with blockchain, stakeholders can track and verify the movement of goods in real-time. This ensures the authenticity of products, prevents counterfeit items, and improves efficiency by automating processes such as inventory management and product recalls.

- Smart Energy Grids: Blockchain can play a vital role in decentralized energy systems. IoT devices, such as smart meters and sensors, can collect data on energy production, consumption, and distribution. This data can be recorded on a blockchain, allowing for secure and transparent peer-to-peer energy transactions. Blockchain-enabled microgrids can optimize energy usage, enable efficient peer-to-peer energy trading, and facilitate renewable energy integration.
- Autonomous Vehicles: Blockchain and IoT can enable secure and autonomous vehicle-to-vehicle (V2V) and vehicle-to-infrastructure (V2I) communication. IoT devices installed in vehicles can gather and share data about traffic conditions, accidents, and road infrastructure. This data can be stored on a blockchain, ensuring its integrity and enabling decentralized decision-making for autonomous vehicles. Blockchain can also facilitate secure payments and data sharing between different stakeholders in the transportation ecosystem.
- Healthcare and Medical Data Management: IoT devices, such as wearables and medical sensors, can collect patient health data in real-time. By considering blockchain, this sensitive data can be stored securely, and patients can have control over their own medical records. Blockchain technology enables secure data sharing and interoperability between healthcare providers, ensuring accurate and up-to-date medical information for improved patient care.
- Smart Home Systems: Blockchain and IoT integration can enhance the security and privacy of smart home devices. IoT devices, such as smart locks, cameras, and appliances, can be connected to a blockchain-based network. This enables secure and tamper-proof control over the devices, protects against unauthorized access, and allows for automated and transparent execution of smart contracts, such as energy management or sharing economy applications.
- Agriculture and Food Supply: Blockchain can enhance trust and transparency in the agriculture and food industry. IoT devices, such as soil sensors and drones, can collect data on crop growth conditions, pesticide usage, and transportation logistics. This data can be recorded on a blockchain, providing immutable records of the entire supply chain. Consumers can verify the origin and quality of food products, while producers can ensure fair payments and optimize their processes based on real-time data.

Note that these examples illustrate how the combination of blockchain and IoT can revolutionize various sectors by improving security, transparency, and efficiency. The integration of these technologies opens up new opportunities for decentralized and autonomous systems, enabling innovative applications and transforming traditional industries.

4. SIMULATION TOOLS TO IMPLEMENT BLOCKCHAIN-IOT BASED ENVIRONMENT

Implementing a blockchain-IoT environment can be complex, but there are simulation tools available that can help in the development, testing, and evaluation of such systems. These simulation tools provide a virtual environment to model and simulate the behavior of blockchain and IoT components (Mohanty et al., 2020). Here are a few simulation tools commonly used to implement a blockchain-IoT based environment:

- Ethereum Simulator (Ganache): One of the infamous Ethereum based blockchain simulator is Ganache which provides a platform for developers to curate a localized Ethereum network for testing and other purposes. It provides a user-friendly interface and enables developers to simulate the behavior of smart contracts, transactions, and interactions with IoT devices. Another advantage of it is the various tools it offers for debugging and testing these smart contracts before it gets deployed into the original Ethereum network base.
- Hyperledger Composer: Hyperledger Composer is a development toolset provided by the Hyperledger project for building and testing blockchain applications. It includes a modeling language to define the structure and behavior of blockchain networks. With Hyperledger Composer, developers can create a simulated blockchain network and define IoT device interactions using transaction processors. It supports the simulation of multiple IoT devices and their interactions with the blockchain network.
- Contiki-NG: Contiki-NG is an open-source operating system specifically designed for resource-constrained IoT devices. It provides a simulation environment for modeling and testing IoT devices in a blockchain-IoT environment. Contiki-NG supports various IoT protocols and can be used to simulate the behavior of IoT devices and their communication with blockchain networks. It offers features like energy modeling, network simulation, and support for real-time constraints.
- OMNeT++: OMNeT++ is a modular, component-based simulation framework primarily used for network simulations. It provides an extensive library of network protocols and models, making it suitable for simulating the interactions between IoT devices and blockchain networks. OMNeT++ supports the implementation of custom models and allows developers to simulate IoT devices, communication protocols, and blockchain transactions.
- NetSim: NetSim is a commercial network simulation tool that offers a set of features for simulating and analyzing various network applications. It supports the simulation of IoT devices, network protocols, and blockchain networks. NetSim provides a drag-and-drop interface for designing the network topology and supports customization through programming interfaces. It enables developers to simulate the behavior of IoT devices and their interactions with blockchain-based systems.

Hence, these simulation tools provide a way to experiment and evaluate the performance and behavior of blockchain-IoT systems without the need for physical devices and infrastructure. They allow developers to validate their designs, test different configurations, and identify potential issues or bottlenecks before deploying the system in a real-world environment.

5. OPEN ISSUES IN BLOCKCHAIN-IOT BASED ENVIRONMENT

While blockchain and IoT integration offers exciting possibilities, there are several open issues and challenges that need to be addressed in a blockchain-IoT based environment. Here are some of the key open issues (Yu et al., 2018):

- Scalability: Blockchain systems like Bitcoin and Ethereum face scalability challenges, and when combined with the massive scale of IoT devices, scalability becomes an even more important issue. Scaling the blockchain-IoT network to handle a large number of transactions and device interactions while maintaining low latency and high throughput remains a challenge.
- Energy Efficiency: IoT devices are often resource-constrained, running on limited power sources. Integrating blockchain technology requires additional computational power and energy consumption, which can be a significant burden for IoT devices. Finding energy-efficient mechanisms and protocols for blockchain-IoT integration is essential to ensure the long-term sustainability of the ecosystem.
- Interoperability: IoT devices operate on various platforms, protocols, and standards. Achieving seamless interoperability and communication between different devices and blockchain networks is a complex task. Developing standardized protocols and frameworks that allow IoT devices to interact with multiple blockchain platforms is important for widespread adoption and integration.
- Privacy and Security: IoT devices generate massive amounts of sensitive data, raising issue about privacy and security. While blockchain offers transparency and immutability, ensuring the privacy of IoT data and protecting against unauthorized access or manipulation is a challenge. Developing robust privacy-preserving mechanisms and secure identity management solutions is necessary to address these issues.
- Governance and Consensus: Blockchain networks require consensus mechanisms to validate transactions and maintain the integrity of the system. In a blockchain-IoT environment, determining the appropriate consensus algorithm and governance model becomes more complex due to the large number of devices and stakeholders involved. Designing scalable and efficient consensus mechanisms that can accommodate the dynamics of IoT devices is an ongoing research area.
- Legal and Regulatory Challenges: The integration of blockchain and IoT raises legal and regulatory challenges. Issues related to data ownership, liability, intellectual property rights, and compliance with existing regulations need to be addressed. Establishing a legal framework that governs blockchain-IoT systems and aligns with existing laws is important for their widespread adoption.
- Standardization: The lack of standardized frameworks, protocols, and interfaces for blockchain-IoT integration hinders interoperability and slows down development and deployment. Developing industry-wide standards that ensure compatibility, security, and interoperability between different blockchain systems and IoT devices is essential for the growth and maturity of the ecosystem.

Hence, these open issues require collaborative efforts from researchers, industry experts, and policymakers. Through ongoing research, innovation, and the development of practical solutions, the potential of blockchain-IoT integration can be fully realized, leading to transformative applications and benefits across various sectors.

5.1 Security Issues in Blockchain-IoT Based Environment

The integration of blockchain and the Internet of Things (IoT) brings about unique security challenges in a blockchain-IoT based environment. Here are some key security issues that need to be addressed (Ch, et al., 2020).

- Device Vulnerabilities: IoT devices are often resource-constrained and may lack robust security measures. They can be vulnerable to various attacks such as malware infections, physical tampering, or unauthorized access. Compromised devices within a blockchain-IoT environment can lead to a breakdown of trust and compromise the integrity of the entire network.
- Distributed Denial-of-Service (DDoS) Attacks: The decentralized nature of blockchain-IoT systems can make them attractive targets for DDoS attacks. Attackers can flood the network with a large volume of malicious requests, overwhelming the devices and disrupting normal operations. These attacks can hinder the availability and reliability of IoT devices and compromise the overall system performance.
- Data Privacy: IoT devices generate vast amounts of sensitive data, including personal information and behavioral patterns. Storing and processing this data on a blockchain raises issues about data privacy. While blockchain offers transparency and immutability, it also poses challenges in terms of ensuring the confidentiality of sensitive information. It is important to implement robust privacy-preserving mechanisms to protect user data while maintaining the benefits of a decentralized blockchain system.
- Smart Contract Vulnerabilities: These self executing contracts which include agreement terms directly written into codes are a significant component of numerous blockchain-IoT use cases. However, coding errors or vulnerabilities in smart contracts can be exploited by attackers to manipulate transactions, steal sensitive information, or disrupt the execution of the contract. Thorough security auditing and testing of smart contracts are essential to mitigate these risks.
- Identity Management: In a blockchain-IoT environment, establishing and managing identities for devices and users is critical. Ensuring the privacy of identities and preventing unauthorized access or identity theft is a significant challenge. Traditional identity management systems may not be suitable for the decentralized nature of blockchain-IoT, requiring innovative approaches that balance privacy and security.
- Insider Threats: The decentralized and autonomous nature of blockchain-IoT systems can introduce new insider threats. Malicious actors with authorized access to the network or devices can exploit their privileges to manipulate transactions, tamper with data, or disrupt the network's operation. Implementing strong access controls, monitoring mechanisms, and conducting regular audits can help mitigate insider threats.
- Supply Chain Attacks: Blockchain-based supply chain systems can be vulnerable to attacks at various stages of the supply chain, including the production, distribution, and verification processes. Attackers can introduce counterfeit components, tamper with data, or manipulate smart contracts, leading to supply chain disruptions, counterfeit products, or financial losses. Implementing secure verification mechanisms, traceability, and trusted supplier relationships are important to prevent supply chain attacks.

In summary, these security challenges require a multi-layered approach that combines robust device security, secure communication protocols, encryption mechanisms, access control, and regular security audits. Additionally, collaboration between blockchain developers, IoT device manufacturers, and security experts is vital to ensure the development and deployment of secure blockchain-IoT systems.

5.2 Privacy Issues in Blockchain-IoT Based Environment

Integrating blockchain and the Internet of Things (IoT) in a combined environment raises important privacy considerations. Here are some key privacy issues that need to be addressed in a blockchain-IoT based environment (Picone et al., 2021):

- Data Privacy: IoT devices generate vast amounts of data, including personal and sensitive information. Storing this data on a blockchain raises issues about privacy, as blockchain is designed to be transparent and immutable. Ensuring the confidentiality of user data while considering the benefits of blockchain's transparency is a challenge. Techniques such as data encryption, differential privacy, and zero-knowledge proofs can be employed to protect sensitive information.
- User Identity and Anonymity: In a blockchain-IoT environment, user identities can be linked to their IoT devices and recorded on the blockchain. This creates potential privacy risks, as the recorded transactions and interactions can be used to identify individuals and track their activities. Preserving user anonymity and developing privacy-enhancing identity management mechanisms is important to protect user privacy.
- Consent and Control: IoT devices continuously collect data from their surroundings, including personal data from individuals. In a blockchain-IoT environment, it is essential to obtain user consent and provide individuals with control over their data. Clear consent mechanisms, data ownership frameworks, and user-centric data management solutions should be implemented to empower users and respect their privacy preferences.
- Cross-Chain Privacy: Interoperability between different blockchain networks in a blockchain-IoT environment can present privacy challenges. When data flows across multiple blockchain platforms, there is a risk of exposing sensitive information to unintended parties. Developing privacy-preserving techniques, such as zero-knowledge proofs or secure multi-party computation, can help protect data privacy in cross-chain interactions.
- Data Pseudonymization: Pseudonymization techniques can be employed to replace personally identifiable information (PII) with pseudonyms, allowing data to be used for analysis and processing while preserving privacy. By unlinking data from specific individuals, the privacy risks associated with data storage on the blockchain can be mitigated.
- Regulatory Compliance: Blockchain-IoT systems must adhere to applicable privacy regulations, such as the General Data Protection Regulation (GDPR). Ensuring compliance with these regulations can be challenging due to the decentralized and immutable nature of blockchain. Organizations deploying blockchain-IoT solutions need to implement privacy-by-design principles and develop mechanisms to accommodate regulatory requirements.

Addressing these privacy issues requires a holistic approach that combines technical measures, policy frameworks, and user empowerment. Implementing privacy-enhancing technologies, incorporating privacy considerations into the design and development of blockchain-IoT systems, and fostering transparency and user control over data are essential for creating a privacy-respecting blockchain-IoT environment. Collaboration between stakeholders, including technologists, policymakers, and privacy experts, is important to strike the right balance between the benefits of blockchain and the protection of individual privacy.

5.3 Trust Issues in Blockchain-IoT Based Environment

Integrating blockchain and the Internet of Things (IoT) brings about various trust issues that need to be addressed in a blockchain-IoT based environment. Here are some key trust issues that arise (Bhushan et al., 2021):

- Device Trustworthiness: In an IoT environment, devices interact and share data with each other. However, not all IoT devices can be trusted. Malfunctioning or compromised devices can produce inaccurate or malicious data, leading to unreliable information and potential system vulnerabilities. Ensuring the trustworthiness of IoT devices through secure bootstrapping, device attestation, and continuous monitoring is essential to maintain the integrity of the system.
- Data Integrity: Data integrity is important in a blockchain-IoT environment to ensure that the data generated by IoT devices is accurate and has not been tampered with. Blockchain provides a tamper-proof and immutable ledger, but ensuring the integrity of data at the source is equally important. Implementing robust data validation mechanisms, cryptographic techniques, and secure communication protocols can help ensure data integrity within the system.
- Consensus and Validation: Blockchain relies on consensus mechanisms to validate transactions and maintain the integrity of the network. In a blockchain-IoT environment, achieving consensus among a large number of IoT devices with varying computational capabilities and trust levels can be challenging. Designing efficient and secure consensus mechanisms that can handle the dynamic nature of IoT devices is important for establishing trust in the system.
- Trust in Smart Contracts: Smart contracts play a vital role in automating transactions and agreements in a blockchain-IoT environment. However, trust issues can arise if smart contracts have coding errors, vulnerabilities, or malicious intent. Conducting thorough security audits, code reviews, and testing of smart contracts is essential to build trust in their functionality and ensure that they operate as intended.
- Transparency and Accountability: Blockchain's transparency is a double-edged sword when it comes to trust. While it provides transparency by allowing participants to verify transactions and data, it also raises issues about privacy and the exposure of sensitive information. Striking a balance between transparency and privacy is important to maintain trust in a blockchain-IoT environment. Additionally, establishing mechanisms for accountability, such as auditing and attribution of actions, can help address trust issues and provide recourse in case of malicious activities.
- Trust in Decentralization: Blockchain's decentralized nature is a key aspect of its trust model. However, ensuring the trustworthiness and resilience of a decentralized blockchain-IoT network is a challenge. Establishing trust in the governance, operation, and maintenance of the network requires consensus among participants, robust security measures, and mechanisms to address malicious behavior.

Hence, these trust issues require a combination of technical, operational, and governance measures. Implementing secure device provisioning, robust data validation mechanisms, rigorous security practices, and transparent governance structures can help build trust in a blockchain-IoT environment. Collaboration among stakeholders, including IoT device manufacturers, blockchain developers, and industry standards bodies, is essential to address these trust issues effectively.

5.4 Legal Issues in Blockchain Based IoT Based Environment

Integrating blockchain and the Internet of Things (IoT) in a combined environment raises several legal issues that need to be addressed. Here are some key legal issues in a blockchain-based IoT environment (Joshi et al., 2018):

- Data Privacy and Protection: IoT devices generate and collect vast amounts of data, including personal and sensitive information. Storing and processing this data on a blockchain can raiseissues regarding data privacy and protection. Compliance with relevant data protection regulations, such as the General Data Protection Regulation (GDPR), is essential. Organizations must ensure that appropriate consent mechanisms, data anonymization techniques, and privacy-enhancing technologies are implemented to protect user privacy and comply with applicable laws.
- Data Ownership and Control: Determining data ownership and control in a blockchain-IoT environment can be complex. Smart contracts and blockchain technology introduce decentralized and autonomous data management. Clear legal frameworks should be established to define data ownership rights, consent mechanisms, and the ability for individuals to control their data. Smart contracts should align with existing legal principles to ensure enforceability and compliance with contractual obligations.
- Liability and Accountability: The decentralized and distributed nature of blockchain can raise challenges in assigning liability and accountability. When a transaction or interaction occurs within a blockchain-IoT system, determining responsibility for any damages or breaches can be difficult. Establishing clear liability frameworks and contractual agreements that define the roles and responsibilities of different stakeholders is important to address potential legal disputes.
- Intellectual Property Rights: In a blockchain-based IoT environment, the creation and exchange of intellectual property (IP) assets can occur. Smart contracts and blockchain records can represent IP rights, such as patents, copyrights, or trademarks. Ensuring that IP rights are protected and enforced within the blockchain ecosystem requires clear legal frameworks and mechanisms for registering, transferring, and enforcing IP assets on the blockchain.
- Regulatory Compliance: Blockchain-based IoT systems must comply with existing regulations and legal frameworks in the jurisdictions where they operate. These regulations may cover various aspects, such as consumer protection, data protection, financial transactions, cybersecurity, and intellectual property. Organizations deploying blockchain-IoT solutions should stay updated with applicable laws and ensure compliance with regulatory requirements.
- Jurisdictional Challenges: Blockchain operates across borders, which can create jurisdictional challenges in legal matters. Determining the applicable laws, jurisdiction, and dispute resolution mechanisms can be complex in a decentralized and global blockchain-IoT environment. Addressing jurisdictional challenges requires international cooperation, harmonization of laws, and the development of legal frameworks that can adapt to the unique characteristics of blockchain technology.

In summary, these legal issues in a blockchain-based IoT environment requires collaboration among legal experts, policymakers, industry stakeholders, and technologists. Establishing clear legal frameworks, ensuring compliance with existing regulations, and developing new legal solutions that align with the decentralized and distributed nature of blockchain are essential for the widespread adoption and successful integration of blockchain and IoT technologies.

6. FUTURE RESEARCH OPPORTUNITIES TOWARDS BLOCKCHAIN-IOT BASED ENVIRONMENT

The integration of blockchain and the Internet of Things (IoT) presents numerous research opportunities for further advancements. Here are some future research opportunities in the field of blockchain-IoT based environments (Ejaz et al., 2019):

- Scalable and Efficient Consensus Mechanisms: Developing consensus mechanisms that are specifically designed for IoT environments can address scalability and efficiency challenges. Exploring lightweight consensus algorithms, such as proof-of-stake or directed acyclic graph (DAG) structures, that can accommodate the resource constraints of IoT devices while ensuring secure and efficient transaction validation is an area for further research.
- Interoperability and Standardization: Enhancing interoperability between different blockchain platforms and IoT devices is a critical research area. Developing standardized protocols, data formats, and communication frameworks that enable seamless data exchange and interoperability among heterogeneous devices and blockchain networks can unlock the full potential of blockchain-IoT integration.
- Privacy-Preserving Techniques: Advancing privacy-enhancing technologies in the context of blockchain-IoT environments is important. Research techniques such as zero-knowledge proofs, homomorphic encryption, and differential privacy can help protect sensitive data generated by IoT devices while ensuring the transparency and accountability of blockchain systems.
- Energy Efficiency and Sustainability: Investigating energy-efficient blockchain protocols and mechanisms to reduce the energy consumption of IoT devices and blockchain networks is an important area of research. Developing energy-aware consensus algorithms, optimizing data storage and verification processes, and exploring off-chain solutions can contribute to the sustainability of blockchain-IoT environments.
- Security and Trust: Enhancing the security and trustworthiness of blockchain-IoT systems is a key research area. Investigating robust authentication mechanisms, secure device bootstrapping, decentralized identity management, and threat detection and mitigation techniques can help protect IoT devices and blockchain networks from malicious activities and ensure the integrity of data and transactions.
- Data Management and Analytics: Exploring efficient and scalable data management techniques for IoT-generated data in a blockchain environment is an important research opportunity. Developing data aggregation and compression mechanisms, data analytics algorithms, and data lifecycle management strategies can facilitate effective utilization of IoT data while ensuring its integrity and confidentiality on the blockchain.

- Governance and Legal Frameworks: Researching governance models and legal frameworks that address the unique challenges of blockchain-IoT environments is necessary. Exploring mechanisms for decentralized decision-making, dispute resolution, and compliance with regulatory requirements can provide the necessary guidelines for the responsible deployment and operation of blockchain-IoT systems.
- Real-World Use Cases and Applications: Investigating and evaluating the practical implementation of blockchain-IoT solutions in various industries and sectors is an important area of research. Conducting case studies, assessing the economic and social impact, and identifying the challenges and opportunities of real-world deployments can help refine and optimize the integration of blockchain and IoT technologies.

Note that these research opportunities hold the potential to overcome current limitations, address emerging challenges, and drive innovation in the field of blockchain-IoT based environments. Continued research and collaboration among academia, industry, and policymakers will contribute to the development of scalable, secure, and privacy-preserving solutions that add the synergies between blockchain and IoT.

7. RESEARCH STATEMENTS TOWARDS BLOCKCHAIN-IOT BASED ENVIRONMENT

Here are a few research statements that focus on the integration of blockchain and the Internet of Things (IoT) in a combined environment (Mohanta, Jena, Panda et al, 2019; Simaiya et al., 2020):

- Investigating the Scalability and Performance of Blockchain-IoT Systems: A Comparative Study of Consensus Mechanisms and Data Management Approaches. This research statement aims to evaluate and compare different consensus algorithms and data management strategies in blockchain-IoT environments to identify scalable and high-performance solutions that can handle the massive influx of data generated by IoT devices.
- Enhancing Privacy and Data Protection in Blockchain-IoT Systems: Novel Techniques for Secure and Privacy-Preserving Data Sharing and Management. This research statement focuses on developing innovative privacy-enhancing technologies, such as zero-knowledge proofs, secure data sharing protocols, and selective disclosure mechanisms, to protect sensitive IoT-generated data while ensuring the transparency and accountability of blockchain systems.
- Energy Efficiency in Blockchain-IoT Networks: Designing Energy-Aware Protocols and Resource Optimization Strategies for Sustainable IoT Environments. This research statement aims to explore energy-efficient blockchain protocols, lightweight consensus algorithms, and resource optimization techniques to minimize the energy consumption of IoT devices and blockchain networks, thereby promoting sustainability and prolonging the battery life of IoT devices (Shabandri & Maheshwari, 2019).
- Security and Trust in Blockchain-IoT Systems: Threat Detection, Authentication, and Secure Device Management. This research statement focuses on developing robust security mechanisms for blockchain-IoT systems, including secure device bootstrapping, decentralized identity management, threat detection algorithms, and authentication protocols, to protect IoT devices and ensure the integrity of transactions and data.

- Interoperability and Standardization in Blockchain-IoT Networks: Enabling Seamless Data Exchange and Communication Among Heterogeneous Devices and Blockchain Platforms. This research statement aims to develop standardized protocols, data formats, and communication frameworks that facilitate interoperability and seamless data exchange between diverse IoT devices and different blockchain networks, promoting the integration and collaboration of various ecosystems.
- Governance and Legal Frameworks for Blockchain-IoT Deployments: Assessing Regulatory Compliance, Data Ownership, and Decentralized Decision-Making Models. This research statement focuses on exploring governance models, legal frameworks, and regulatory compliance mechanisms specific to blockchain-IoT environments. It investigates issues such as data ownership, decentralized decision-making, and compliance with privacy and security regulations to establish responsible and legally compliant blockchain-IoT deployments.

Hence, these research statements provide a starting point for exploring various aspects of blockchain-IoT integration. Researchers can delve deeper into these areas to propose innovative solutions, algorithms, and frameworks that advance the field and contribute to the successful implementation of blockchain in IoT-based environments.

8. RECOMMENDED SOLUTIONS FOR RAISED ISSUES IN BLOCKCHAIN-IOT BASED ENVIRONMENT

Overcoming challenges in blockchain and IoT-based applications requires a multi-faceted approach that combines technological advancements, standardization efforts, and robust security and privacy measures. Firstly, addressing scalability issues necessitates the exploration of innovative solutions such as sharding, off-chain transactions, and optimized data processing techniques. Interoperability challenges can be tackled through the development and adoption of standardized communication protocols and frameworks that enable seamless integration between diverse IoT devices and blockchain networks (Abdelmaboud et al., 2022). Moreover, improving security requires implementing strong authentication mechanisms, encryption techniques, and continuous monitoring to detect and mitigate potential vulnerabilities. Additionally, preserving privacy in blockchain + IoT environments can be achieved through the use of privacy-enhancing technologies and carefully designed data sharing and disclosure mechanisms (Shi et al., 2020). Collaboration among researchers, industry experts, and policymakers is important to drive advancements in these areas and establish best practices for the successful deployment and widespread adoption of blockchain and IoT applications. Here are some recommended solutions for the key issues raised in a blockchain-IoT based environment (Azbeg et al., 2018):

Security Issues:

- Implement robust device security measures, including secure bootstrapping, firmware integrity checks, and regular security updates.
- Utilize secure communication protocols, encryption mechanisms, and intrusion detection systems to safeguard the network infrastructure.
- Conduct thorough security audits, adopt secure coding practices, and implement code verification mechanisms to mitigate smart contract vulnerabilities.

- Employ privacy-enhancing techniques, such as data encryption, zero-knowledge proofs, and differential privacy, to protect sensitive information.

Privacy Issues:

- Use data encryption, data minimization, and selective disclosure mechanisms to protect sensitive data while using blockchain's transparency.
- Implement privacy-enhancing technologies like zero-knowledge proofs, homomorphic encryption, and decentralized identity management to preserve user anonymity and enhance privacy.
- Provide explicit consent mechanisms and user control over data collection, storage, and processing.
- Comply with privacy regulations, such as GDPR, by implementing privacy-by-design principles and ensuring individuals' rights are respected.

Trust Issues:

- Establish a decentralized and tamper-resistant infrastructure by using blockchain technology.
- Implement robust authentication mechanisms, secure device bootstrapping, and decentralized identity management to enhance trust among IoT devices.
- Ensure transparency and auditability of transactions through blockchain's immutable and transparent nature.
- Foster trust through trusted supplier relationships, traceability mechanisms, and supply chain security measures.

Legal Issues:

- Address legal challenges by complying with relevant regulations and data protection laws, such as GDPR.
- Conduct privacy impact assessments and implement technical and organizational measures to meet regulatory obligations.
- Explore smart contract legality and enforceability, ensuring compliance with existing legal frameworks.
- Collaborate with legal experts and policymakers to develop legal frameworks and governance models specific to blockchain-IoT environments.

Critical Implementation Challenges:

- Develop scalable blockchain solutions that can handle the large volume of data generated by IoT devices.
- Focus on interoperability and standardization by developing protocols, data formats, and frameworks that enable seamless data exchange among different devices and blockchain networks.
- Optimize resource utilization and energy efficiency through lightweight consensus algorithms, off-chain solutions, and energy-aware protocols.
- Strengthen security measures by implementing authentication mechanisms, intrusion detection systems, and secure data management practices.
- Foster collaboration between academia, industry, and standards bodies to develop best practices, frameworks, and standards for secure and efficient blockchain-IoT implementations.

Hence, these recommended solutions provide a starting point for addressing the issues in a blockchain-IoT based environment. However, it is important to note that the specific implementation and adoption of these solutions may vary depending on the unique requirements and constraints of each use case or application.

9. CONCLUSION

As discussed above, the integration of blockchain and IoT brings numerous benefits, issues, and challenges related to security, privacy, etc. We have addressed these issues and challenges in this chapter. From a security perspective, robust device security measures, secure communication protocols, regular security updates, and smart contract auditing are essential to protect against attacks and vulnerabilities. Privacy issues was addressed through techniques like data encryption, selective disclosure, decentralized identity management, and explicit user consent mechanisms. Also, maintaining trust in a blockchain-IoT environment was discussed with a decentralized and tamper-resistant infrastructure, for providing a better transparency in transactions, authentication mechanisms, and supply chain security measures. We also discussed few scalable consensus mechanisms, standardized protocols, energy-efficient solutions, and optimized data management techniques that are important to handle the large volume of data and ensure efficient operations (including legal and regulatory compliance). Hence, collaboration, and the adoption of best practices towards this technology integration will contribute to the advancement and successful integration of blockchain and IoT technologies, unlocking new possibilities and transforming industries across various sectors.

REFERENCES

Abdelmaboud, A., Ahmed, A. I., Abaker, M., Eisa, T. A., Albasheer, H., Ghorashi, S. A., & Karim, F. K. (2022, February 18). Blockchain for IoT applications: Taxonomy, platforms, recent advances, challenges and future research directions. *Electronics (Basel), 11*(4), 630. doi:10.3390/electronics11040630

Azbeg, K., Ouchetto, O., Andaloussi, S. J., Fetjah, L., & Sekkaki, A. (2018). Blockchain and IoT for security and privacy: a platform for diabetes self-management. In *2018 4th international conference on cloud computing technologies and applications (Cloudtech)*, (pp. 1-5). IEEE. 10.1109/CloudTech.2018.8713343

Bhushan, B., Sinha, P., Sagayam, K. M., & Andrew, J. (2021, March 1). Untangling blockchain technology: A survey on state of the art, security threats, privacy services, applications and future research directions. *Computers & Electrical Engineering, 90*, 106897. doi:10.1016/j.compeleceng.2020.106897

Ch, R., Srivastava, G., Gadekallu, T.R., Maddikunta, P.K., & Bhattacharya, S. (2020). Security and privacy of UAV data using blockchain technology. *Journal of Information security and Applications*.

Choo, K. K., Yan, Z., & Meng, W. (2020, June). Blockchain in industrial IoT applications: Security and privacy advances, challenges, and opportunities. *IEEE Transactions on Industrial Informatics, 16*(6), 4119–4121. doi:10.1109/TII.2020.2966068

Deshmukh, A., Sreenath, N., Tyagi, A. K., & Eswara Abhichandan, U. V. (2022). Blockchain Enabled Cyber Security: A Comprehensive Survey. *2022 International Conference on Computer Communication and Informatics (ICCCI)*, (pp. 1-6). IEEE. 10.1109/ICCCI54379.2022.9740843

Dorri, A., Kanhere, S. S., & Jurdak, R. (2017). Towards an optimized blockchain for IoT. In *Proceedings of the second international conference on Internet-of-Things design and implementation* (pp. 173-178). ACM. 10.1145/3054977.3055003

Ejaz, W., Anpalagan, A., Ejaz, W., & Anpalagan, A. (2019). *Blockchain technology for security and privacy in internet of things. Internet of Things for Smart Cities: Technologies*. Big Data and Security.

Ferrag, M. A., & Shu, L. (2021, May 6). The performance evaluation of blockchain-based security and privacy systems for the Internet of Things: A tutorial. *IEEE Internet of Things Journal*, *8*(24), 17236–17260. doi:10.1109/JIOT.2021.3078072

Ferrag, M. A., Shu, L., Yang, X., Derhab, A., & Maglaras, L. (2020, February 11). Security and privacy for green IoT-based agriculture: Review, blockchain solutions, and challenges. *IEEE Access : Practical Innovations, Open Solutions*, *8*, 32031–32053. doi:10.1109/ACCESS.2020.2973178

Goyal, S., Sharma, N., Kaushik, I., Bhushan, B., & Kumar, A. (2020). Blockchain as a Lifesaver of IoT: Applications, Security, and Privacy Services and Challenges. In *Security and Trust Issues in Internet of Things* (pp. 209-237). CRC Press.

Jayaprakash, V., & Tyagi, A. K. (2022). Security Optimization of Resource-Constrained Internet of Healthcare Things (IoHT) Devices Using Asymmetric Cryptography for Blockchain Network. In: Giri, D., Mandal, J.K., Sakurai, K., De, D. (eds) *Proceedings of International Conference on Network Security and Blockchain Technology*. Springer, Singapore. 10.1007/978-981-19-3182-6_18

Joshi, A. P., Han, M., & Wang, Y. (2018, May 1). A survey on security and privacy issues of blockchain technology. *Mathematical Foundations of Computing*, *1*(2).

Mohanta, B. K., Jena, D., Panda, S. S., & Sobhanayak, S. (2019, December 1). Blockchain technology: A survey on applications and security privacy challenges. *Internet of Things.*, *8*, 100107. doi:10.1016/j.iot.2019.100107

Mohanta, B. K., Jena, D., Ramasubbareddy, S., Daneshmand, M., & Gandomi, A. H. (2020, July 13). Addressing security and privacy issues of IoT using blockchain technology. *IEEE Internet of Things Journal*, *8*(2), 881–888. doi:10.1109/JIOT.2020.3008906

Mohanta, B. K., Satapathy, U., Panda, S. S., & Jena, D. (2019). A novel approach to solve security and privacy issues for iot applications using blockchain. In *2019 International Conference on Information Technology (ICIT)*, (pp. 394-399). IEEE. 10.1109/ICIT48102.2019.00076

Mohanty, S. N., Ramya, K. C., Rani, S. S., Gupta, D., Shankar, K., Lakshmanaprabu, S. K., & Khanna, A. (2020, January 1). An efficient Lightweight integrated Blockchain (ELIB) model for IoT security and privacy. *Future Generation Computer Systems*, *102*, 1027–1037. doi:10.1016/j.future.2019.09.050

Nair, M. & Tyagi, A. K. (2023). Blockchain technology for next-generation society: current trends and future opportunities for smart era. *Blockchain Technology for Secure Social Media Computing*. IET Digital Library. . doi:10.1049/PBSE019E_ch11

Nair, M. M., & Tyagi, A. K. (2021). Privacy: History, Statistics, Policy, Laws, Preservation and Threat Analysis. Journal of Information Assurance & Security, 16(1), 24-34.

Pandey, A. A., Fernandez, T. F., Bansal, R., & Tyagi, A. K. (2022). Maintaining Scalability in Blockchain. In A. Abraham, N. Gandhi, T. Hanne, T. P. Hong, T. Nogueira Rios, & W. Ding (Eds.), *Intelligent Systems Design and Applications. ISDA 2021. Lecture Notes in Networks and Systems* (Vol. 418). Springer. doi:10.1007/978-3-030-96308-8_4

Picone, M., Cirani, S., & Veltri, L. (2021). Blockchain Security and Privacy for the Internet of Things. *Sensors (Basel)*, *21*(3), 892. doi:10.339021030892 PMID:33525636

Raghuvanshi, A., Singh, U.K., & Joshi, C. (2022). A review of various security and privacy innovations for IoT applications in healthcare. *Advanced Healthcare Systems: Empowering Physicians with IoT-Enabled Technologies*. IEEE.

Shabandri, B., & Maheshwari, P. (2019). Enhancing IoT security and privacy using distributed ledgers with IOTA and the tangle. In *2019 6th International conference on signal processing and integrated networks (SPIN)*, (pp. 1069-1075). IEEE. 10.1109/SPIN.2019.8711591

Sheth, H. S. K. (2022). Deep Learning, Blockchain based Multi-layered Authentication and Security Architectures. *2022 International Conference on Applied Artificial Intelligence and Computing (ICAAIC)*, (pp. 476-485). IEEE. 10.1109/ICAAIC53929.2022.9793179

Shi, S., He, D., Li, L., Kumar, N., Khan, M. K., & Choo, K. K. (2020, October 1). Applications of blockchain in ensuring the security and privacy of electronic health record systems: A survey. *Computers & Security*, *97*, 101966. doi:10.1016/j.cose.2020.101966 PMID:32834254

Simaiya, S., Lilhore, U. K., Sharma, S. K., Gupta, K., & Baggan, V. (2020, June 1). Blockchain: A new technology to enhance data security and privacy in Internet of things. *Journal of Computational and Theoretical Nanoscience*, *17*(6), 2552–2556. doi:10.1166/jctn.2020.8929

Srivastava, S. Anshu, B., R., S., G., Tyagi, A.K. (2023). Blockchain Enabled Internet of Things: Current Scenario and Open Challenges for Future. In: Abraham, A., Bajaj, A., Gandhi, N., Madureira, A.M., Kahraman, C. (eds) Innovations in Bio-Inspired Computing and Applications. IBICA 2022. Lecture Notes in Networks and Systems, vol 649. Springer, Cham. doi:10.1007/978-3-031-27499-2_59

Tyagi, A. K. (2023). Decentralized everything: Practical use of blockchain technology in future applications. In R. Pandey, S. Goundar, & S. Fatima (eds.), Distributed Computing to Blockchain. Academic Press. doi:10.1016/B978-0-323-96146-2.00010-3

Tyagi, A. K. (2022). SecVT: Securing the Vehicles of Tomorrow Using Blockchain Technology. In A. A. Sk, T. Turki, T. K. Ghosh, S. Joardar, & S. Barman (Eds.), *Artificial Intelligence. ISAI 2022. Communications in Computer and Information Science* (Vol. 1695). Springer. doi:10.1109/ICCCI54379.2022.9740965

Tyagi, A. K., Chandrasekaran, S., & Sreenath, N. (2022). Blockchain Technology:– A New Technology for Creating Distributed and Trusted Computing Environment. *2022 International Conference on Applied Artificial Intelligence and Computing (ICAAIC).* (pp. 1348-1354). IEEE. 10.1109/ICAAIC53929.2022.9792702

Tyagi, A. K., Dananjayan, S., Agarwal, D., & Thariq Ahmed, H. F. (2023). Blockchain—Internet of Things Applications: Opportunities and Challenges for Industry 4.0 and Society 5.0. *Sensors (Basel), 23*(2), 947. doi:10.339023020947 PMID:36679743

Tyagi, A. K. (2021). Analysis of Security and Privacy Aspects of Blockchain Technologies from Smart Era' Perspective: The Challenges and a Way Forward. In Recent Trends in Blockchain for Information Systems Security and Privacy. CRC Press.

Tyagi, A. K. (2021, October). AARIN: Affordable, Accurate, Reliable and INnovative Mechanism to Protect a Medical Cyber-Physical System using Blockchain Technology. *IJIN, 2*, 175–183.

Varsha, R. (2020, January 1). Deep Learning Based Blockchain Solution for Preserving Privacy in Future Vehicles. *International Journal of Hybrid Intelligent Systems, 16*(4), 223–236.

Waheed, N., He, X., Ikram, M., Usman, M., Hashmi, S. S., & Usman, M. (2020, December 6). Security and privacy in IoT using machine learning and blockchain: Threats and countermeasures. *ACM Computing Surveys, 53*(6), 1–37. doi:10.1145/3417987

Yu, Y., Li, Y., Tian, J., & Liu, J. (2018, December). Blockchain-based solutions to security and privacy issues in the internet of things. *IEEE Wireless Communications, 25*(6), 12–18. doi:10.1109/MWC.2017.1800116

Chapter 15
Audio Steganalysis Using Fractal Dimension and Convolutional Neural Network (CNN) Model

Alaba Joy Lawal
Federal University of Technology, Akure, Nigeria

Otasowie Owolafe
https://orcid.org/0000-0002-6659-8100
Federal University of Technology, Akure, Nigeria

Aderonke F. Thompson
Federal University of Technology, Akure, Nigeria

ABSTRACT

The rate at which secret messages are being transmitted through various digital signal media is alarming; these operations are done in an unsuspicious manner and users transmit these messages without knowledge of the embedded secret messages. Audio steganalysis deals with detecting the presence of secret messages in audio messages. Some of the existing steganalysis methods are laden with having prior knowledge of the steganography methods adopted in embedding the secret message in an audio signal, which reduces the detection efficiency. Consequently, this research developed a Higuchi-based audio steganalysis method that detects secret messages without having prior knowledge of the embedding techniques used. The algorithm reduces the fractal dimension of the audio signal to extract relevant features, while convolutional neural network was used as classifier. The research records high accuracy (96%) when compared with previous research. The accuracy of the developed system shows its effectiveness in detecting embedded messages without prior knowledge of the deployed steganography method.

DOI: 10.4018/979-8-3693-2081-5.ch015

1. INTRODUCTION

Before cryptographic systems were created, steganography techniques have been utilized extensively for millennia. In order to ensure that their secrets stayed hidden, ancient Greek couriers tattooed messages on their shaved heads before letting their hair grow (Rabah, 2004).

Apart from the first known case, wax tables were also used as a cover source. The text was written on the underlying wood, and the message was covered with a new wax layer, which made the tablets appear blank. During World War 2, invisible ink was used to write information on pieces of paper so that the paper appeared to the average person as blank pieces of paper. Liquids such as urine, milk, vinegar, and fruit juices were used because when each of these substances is heated, they darken and become visible to the human eye.

Another clever invention in steganography was the "Ave Maria" cipher. The book contains a series of tables, each of which has a list of words, one per letter. To code a message, each letter of the message is replaced by the corresponding words. If the tables are used in order, one table per letter, then the coded message appears as an innocent prayer (Doshi et al., 2012).

All of these approaches to steganography have one thing in common, which is, hiding the secret message in the physical object that is sent. The cover media is merely a distraction and could be anything.

The ability to transport, replicate, reproduce, and exchange information over the Internet has been made possible by the quick advancement of information technology in the form of smart devices, communications, and digital content. The online distribution of digital media and the transformation in the digital world also suggest that negative information can be concealed and spread via these channels. Governmental institutions and the forensic divisions of various military organizations are among the most severely impacted groups as they struggle to identify terrorist-prone covert and damaging information.

Addressing the above issue, hidden information detection techniques such as steganalysis have shown some promising solutions. However, there are some rising concerns when using this approach. For instance, the study presented by Chen et al., (2017) as well as Mohtasham-zadeh and Mosleh, (2019) suffer the limitations of low prediction accuracy, inability to give significant differences between covers and stegos.

Ghasemzadeh and Arjmandi, (2017) were able to show that calibrated features based on re-embedding technique improves the performance of audio steganalysis, but still suffers a low detection ratio.

This research is therefore motivated by the need to solve the limitations in the reviewed literature through the use of a Convolutional Neural Network.

2. LITERATURE REVIEW

2.1. Steganography

Steganography methods have been used for centuries. In ancient Greek times, messengers tattooed messages on their shaved heads and the messages remain invisible when their hair grows.(Rabah, 2004) The message to be hidden was written on the wood and was covered with a new wax layer. During Second World War, milk, fruit juices, vinegar were used for writing secret messages. Invisible inks were used to hide information in the 20th century. During 1999'secret messages are hidden into some digital files. Government, industries and terrorist organization use steganography for hiding secret data.

2.1.1 Types of Steganography

(i) Text Steganography: It consists of hiding information inside the text files. In this method, the secret data is hidden behind every nth letter of every word of a text message. Numbers of methods are available for hiding data in a text file. These methods are (i) Format Based Method; (ii) Random and Statistical Method; (iii) Linguistics Method.

(ii) Image Steganography: Hiding the data by taking the cover object as the image is referred to as image steganography. In image steganography, pixel intensities are used to hide the data. In digital steganography, images are a widely used cover source because there are many bits present in the digital representation of an image.

(iii). Audio Steganography: It involves hiding data in audio files. This method hides the data in Windows Audio-Visual (WAV), AU (AUdio file) and MP3 sound files. There are different methods of audio steganography. These methods are i) Low Bit Encoding ii) Phase Coding iii) Spread Spectrum.

(iv). Video Steganography: It is a technique of hiding any kind of files or data into digital video format. In this case video (combination of pictures) is used as a carrier for hiding the data. Generally, Discrete Cosine Transform (DCT) alter the values (for example from 8.667 to 9) which are used to hide the data in each of the images in the video, which is unnoticeable by the human eye. H.264, Mp4, MPEG, AVI are the formats used by video steganography.

(v). Network or Protocol Steganography: It involves hiding the information by taking the network protocol such as TCP (Transmission Control Protocol), UDP (User Datagram Protocol), ICMP (Internet Control Message Protocol), IP (Internet protocol) etc, as the cover object. In the OSI layer network model there exist covert channels where steganography can be used.

2.2 Cryptography

Cryptography (the science of secret writing) is an ancient art; the first documented use of cryptography in writing dates back to circa 1900 B.C. when an Egyptian scribe used non-standard hieroglyphs in an inscription. Some experts argue that cryptography appeared spontaneously sometime after writing was invented, with applications ranging from diplomatic missives to war-time battle plans. It is no surprise, then, that new forms of cryptography came soon after the widespread development of computer communications. In data and telecommunications, cryptography is necessary when communicating over any untrusted medium, which includes just about any network, particularly the Internet. (Kessler, 2007)

There are five primary functions of cryptography today:

i. *Privacy/confidentiality:* Ensuring that no one can read the message except the intended receiver.
ii. *Authentication:* The process of proving one's identity.
iii. *Integrity:* Assuring the receiver that the received message has not been altered in any way from the original.
iv. *Non-repudiation:* A mechanism to prove that the sender sent this message.
v. *Key exchange:* The method by which crypto keys are shared between sender and receiver.

In cryptography, we start with the unencrypted data, referred to as *plaintext*. The plaintext is *encrypted* into *ciphertext*, which will in turn (usually) be *decrypted* back into usable plaintext. The encryption and decryption are based upon the type of cryptography scheme being employed and some form of a key. This process is sometimes written as:

$$C = E_K(P) \tag{2.1}$$

$$P = D_K(C) \tag{2.2}$$

where **P** is plaintext, **C** is ciphertext, **E** is the encryption method, **D** is the decryption method, and **k** is the key.

In many of the descriptions below, two communicating parties will be referred to as Alice and Bob; this is the common nomenclature in the crypto field and literature to make it easier to identify the communicating parties. If there is a third and fourth party to the communication, they will be referred to as Carol and Dave, respectively. A malicious party is referred to as Mallory, an eavesdropper as Eve, and a trusted third party as Trent.

Cryptography is most closely associated with the development and creation of the mathematical algorithms used to encrypt and decrypt messages, whereas cryptanalysis is the science of analyzing and breaking encryption schemes. Cryptology is the term referring to the broad study of secret writing and encompasses both cryptography and cryptanalysis.

2.3 Differences Between Steganography and Cryptography

In contrast to steganography, cryptography changes the secret message from one form to another, where the message is scrambled, unreadable, and the existence of a message is often unknown. Encrypted messages can be located and intercepted but cannot be decoded easily. This nature hiding information in cipher protects the message, but the interception of the message can just be as damaging because it gives clue to an opponent or enemy that someone is communicating with someone else. Steganography brings out the opposite approach and tries to hide all evidence during communication.

The differences between steganography and cryptography are:

- Steganography hides a message within another message normally called a cover and looks like a normal graphic, video, or sound file. In cryptography, encrypted message looks like a meaningless jumble of characters.
- In steganography, a collection of graphic images, video files, or sound files in a storage medium may not leave a suspicion. In cryptography, the collection of random characters on a disk will always leave suspicion.
- In steganography, a smart eavesdropper can detect something suspicious from a sudden change of a message format. In cryptography, a smart eavesdropper can detect a secret communication from a message that has been cryptographically encoded.
- Steganography requires caution when reusing pictures or sound files. In cryptography, caution is required when reusing keys.

2.4 Steganographic Tools

Some of the steganographic tools are:

- OutGuess.
- StegHide.
- JPHS.
- JSteg.
- wbStego4open.
- Invisible Secrets.

These tools are available across the platforms such as LINUX, WINDOWS, MAC-OS, and UNIX. They also used various embedding algorithm as well as different types of cover image such as JPEG, BMP.

OutGuess: It inserts the hidden information into the redundant bits of data source. It is a universal steganographic tool. The program extracts the redundant bits and writes them back after modification. It uses JPEG images or PNM (Portable Any Map) files as cover images. The images will be used as a concrete example of data objects, though OutGuess can use any kind of data, as long as a handler is provided.

StegHide: It is a steganographic tool that hides bits of a data file in some of the least significant bits of cover file. The existence of the data file is invisible and cannot be guessed. It hides data in .BMP, .WAV and .AU files, blowfish encryption, MD5 hashing of passphrases to blowfish keys, and pseudo-random distribution of hidden bits in the container data.

JPHS: It refers to Jpeg Hide and Seek. It uses lossy compression algorithm. It is available in both Windows and Linux versions. JPHS includes two programs JPHIDE and JPSEEK. JPHIDE.EXE hides a data file in Jpeg file. JPSEEK.EXE is used to recover the hidden file from Jpeg file. Since the hidden file is distributed to the Jpeg image the visual and statistical effects are very less. JPHS uses LSB methods for hiding information. It is designed in such a way that it is impossible to prove that the host file contains a hidden file. When the insertion rate is very less (under 5%), it is very difficult to know about the hidden data. As the insertion percentage increases the statistical nature of the jpeg coefficients differs from "normal" to the extent that it raises suspicion.

JSteg: It is a more effective tool to hide data file into image file. It is being used as the best choice of hacker's community. It is the first software used for embedding the data into JPEG image. Later, the JStegShell was designed.

WbStego4open: It does not require registration. It is an open-source application which works in Windows and Linux platform. Bitmaps, Text files, PDF files, and HTML files can be considered as carrier files. It is an effective tool for embedding copyright information without modifying carrier file.

Invisible Secrets: This tool is used to hide data in image or sound files. It provides extra protection by using AES encryption algorithm. During the creation of stego files, a password is created and stored.

Other steganography tools: Some of the other tools used for image steganography comprises Crypto123, Hermetic stego, IBM DLS, Invisible Secrets, Info stego, Syscop, StegMark, Cloak, Contraband Hell, Contraband, Dound, Gif it Up, S-Tools, JSteg_Shell, Blindside, CameraShy, dc-Steganograph, F5, Gif Shuffle, Hide4PGP, JstegJpeg, Mandelste, PGMStealth, Steghide.

2.5 Audio Steganography

The word steganography comes from the Greek Steganos, which means covered or secret and - graphy means writing or drawing. Therefore, steganography means, literally, covered writing. Steganography is the art and science of hiding secret information in a cover file such that only sender and receiver can detect the existence of the secret information (Warkentin et al., 2007)

Secret information is encoded in a manner such that the very existence of the information is concealed. The main goal of steganography is to communicate securely in a completely undetectable manner and to avoid drawing suspicion to the transmission of hidden data (Shirali-Shahreza and Manzuri-Shalmani, 2008). It will not only prevent others from knowing the hidden information, but it also prevents others from thinking that the information even exists. The model of steganography method must be such that no one will be able to suspect the presence of any hidden message.

The basic model of Audio steganography consists of CMP (Carrier which is the Audio file, Message and Password). Carrier is also known as a cover file, which conceals secret information. The model for steganography is shown in Figure 1. Message is the data that the sender wishes to remain it confidential. Message can be plain text, image, audio or any type of file. Password is known as a stego-key, which ensures that only the recipient who knows the corresponding decoding key will be able to extract the message from a cover file. The cover file with the secret information is known as a stego-file.

Figure 1. Basic audio steganographic model

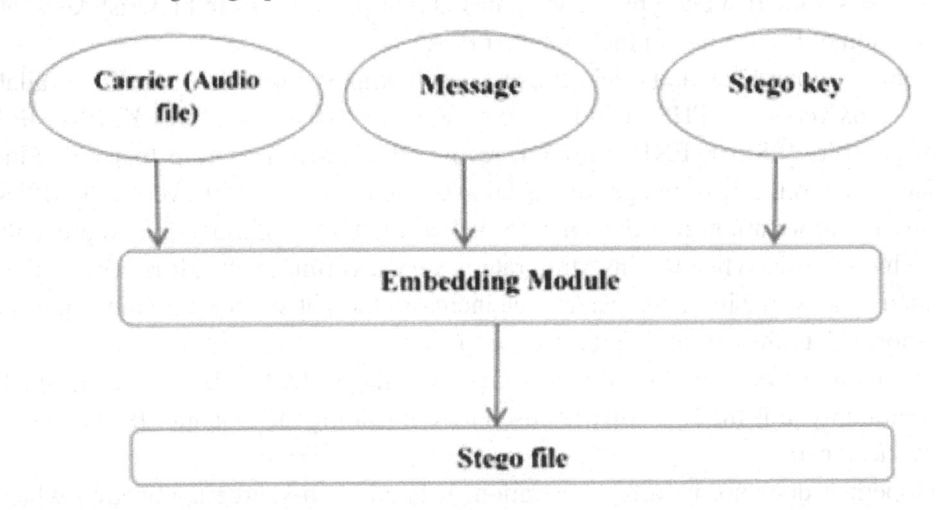

The information hiding process consists of the following two steps (Pooyan and Delforouzi, 2007).

(a) Identification of redundant bits in a cover file. Redundant bits are those bits that can be modified without corrupting the quality or destroying the integrity of the cover file. Message Stego key Embedding Module Stego file Carrier (Audio file) (Jayaram et al., 2011)
(b) To embed the secret information in the cover file, the redundant bits in the cover file is replaced by the bits of the secret information

2.6 Methods of Audio Steganography

a. **Least Significant Bit (LSB) Coding:** This is the simplest method to embed secrete data behind a digital audio media. In this method least significant bit of sample word is replaced by the least significant bit of secrete data. This method can embed large size of data.

b. **Parity coding:** In parity coding, audio signal is broken down into separate areas of samples and hide the secret message in the parity bit of each sample area. If the parity bit of a sample area does not match the secret message bit to be embedded, the LSB of one of the samples in the area is inverted. Therefore, this will give a wider range of choices on where to hide the secret bit and will keep the change in the signal more unobservable. (Gibson, 2002)

c. **Phase coding:** Phase coding is based on the reality that, unlike noises, audio phase components are imperceptible to the human ear. Rather than adding noises, this technique encodes the secret data bits to phase shifts in the phase spectrum of the audio signal, attaining inaudible encodings in terms of signal-to-noise ratio. In phase coding, the phase of an initial audio segment is substituted with a reference phase that represents the data. The following segments phase is modified back to maintain the relative phase between segments. Phase coding, when applicable, is one of the most efficient audio steganographic methods in terms of the Signal to Noise Ratio (SNR). When the phase relation between each frequency component is dramatically changed, noticeable phase dispersion will occur. On the other hand, on the condition that the alteration of the phase is small enough, inaudible steganography can be accomplished.

d. **Spread spectrum coding:** This is equivalent to implementing LSB coding by spreading the secret data bits over the entire audio signal. However, different from LSB coding, the SS techniques spread the secret bits over the frequency spectrum of the audio media by using a code that is independent of the genuine signal. Subsequently, the resultant signal will utilize a bandwidth wider than what is essentially needed for communication.

   Two types of spread spectrum are used in SS audio steganography:

   i. Direct spread spectrum: the secret data is distributed using a constant named the chip rate then adapted with a pseudorandom signal and then interleave with the cover signal.

   ii. Frequency-hopping spread spectrum: the frequency spectrum of the audio medium is changed so that it hops quickly among frequencies.

e. **Echo hiding:** In echo hiding techniques, secret data is inserted into an audio medium by introducing an echo into the discrete signal. It allows high data communication rates and offers greater robustness. To hide secret message effectively, three echo related factors are involved and changed: Amplitude, decay rate, and offset (delay time) from the genuine audio signal. All of those factors should be set lower than the human hearing threshold to keep the echo imperceptible. Additionally, offset values are changed corresponding to the binary secret data targeted. A specific offset value represents a binary one, and another offset value represents a binary zero (Rafiee, 2019).

Steganography, in general, relies on the imperfection of the human auditory and visual systems. Audio steganography takes advantage of the psychoacoustical masking phenomenon of the Human Auditory System (HAS).

Psychoacoustical or auditory masking property renders a weak tone imperceptible in the presence of a strong tone in its temporal or spectral neighbourhood. This property arises because of the low differential range of the HAS even though the dynamic range covers 80dB below ambient level. Frequency masking occurs when the human ear cannot perceive frequencies at a lower power level if these frequencies are present in the vicinity of tone or noise-like frequencies at a higher level. Additionally, a weak pure tone is masked by wide-band noise if the tone occurs within a critical band.

This property of inaudibility of weaker sounds is used in different ways for embedding information. Embedding of data by inserting inaudible tones in cover audio signal has been presented recently (Warkentin et al., 2007). In audio steganography, a secret message is embedded into a digitized audio signal which results in the slight altering of a binary sequence of the corresponding audio file.

3. REVIEW OF RELATED WORKS

Chen et al., (2017) developed a CNN based model for digital audio steganalysis and the research showed that a well-designed CNN architecture can significantly improve the detection performances for audio stegangraphy in the time domain when compared to the conventional steganalytic methods. The research used a total of 40,000 cover-stego pairs and half of the pairs were used for training, and the rest were used for testing. The networks were trained with 50,000 iterations, and in each iteration, a mini-batch of 64 audio clips (32 cover/stego pairs) were used as input. The research recorded good result, however it can only detect steganography in the time domain and not the frequency domain.

Han, et al., (2018) proposed a linear prediction based audio steganalysis method, which suffices to bring a significant difference between the cover and the stego. By incorporating a linear prediction method technique from signal coding and speaker identification files into audio steganalysis, the researchers created a new method for the analysis of audio after observing that existing methods can only achieve good detection accuracies when the hidden ratio is high. It was discovered that the developed system cannot work on other audio file formats such as AU, AMR, and AAC.

Lin et al., (2019) developed an audio steganalysis method based on Convolutional Neural Network. A high pass filter (HPF) layer, whose weights are initialized with derivative-based filters, is placed at the beginning of the network. At the end of the network, the extracted features are fed into a binary classifier, which consists of a fully connected layer and a softmax layer. It was observed that the developed CNN cannot solve the problem of audio steganalysis with mismatched covers.

Wang, et al., (2019) proposed a fully designed CNN architecture for MP3 steganalysis based on rich high-pass filtering (HPF). The authors made use of a dataset containing 33038 stereo WAV audio clips with a sampling rate of 44.1 kHz and a duration of 10s were constructed. The WAV audios were encoded into MP3 files with two common bitrates of 128 kbps and 320 kbps. Experiments were carried out using RHFCN to detect two typical MP3 steganographic algorithms which are Huffman Codes Mapping (HCM) and Equal Length Entropy Codes Substitution (EECS). The developed system was only evaluated on various MP3 steganographic algorithms, bitrates and relative payloads.

Ren, et al., (2019) presented a research titled: Spec-Resnet: A general Audio Steganalysis scheme based on a deep residual network for spectrograms for detecting steganography schemes in different embedding domains for AAC and MP3. The architecture consists of three main components vis-a-viz- the spectrogram preprocess module (SPM), the Deep Residual Steganalysis Network (S-ResNet) and the Classification Module (CM). The developed system is only limited to AAC and MP3 audio formats.

Paulin, et al., (2016) developed an improved audio steganalysis model using deep belief networks for the classification of audio files. The research stem from the fact that there is a need to develop a DBN-based steganalyzer to automatically identify the type of steganographic technique applied to the original speech signals. The research experiment was carried out on the Noizeus database. The authors used the mel-frequency cepstrum to extract features from the resulting speech signals. The signals are framed into 16 ms and the hamming window is also applied. Several MFCC coefficients ranging from 10 to 25 were tested and the optimal number of MFCC coefficients for the DBN, the SVM and the GMM based steganalyzers were found. The retained MFCC coefficients are the inputs for each classifier. These frames are classified into two groups, marked and unmarked. The developed system was only evaluated by two classifiers namely support vector machines (SVMs) and Gaussian mixture models (GMMs).

Mohtasham-zadeh and Mosleh, (2019) propose a new approach to audio steganalysis that uses fractal dimensions as features and convolutional neural network (CNN) as a classifier. Various steganalysis methods have been introduced so far. Some of them can detect hidden message by extracting features from the input and reference signals and comparing them with each other. In such methods, the reference signal extraction is very important.

The dataset was divided into two phases, which are the training and the testing phase. 70% was allocated for training and 30% for testing. The wavelet features in the research work showed the lowest level of accuracy.

Zeng et al., (2011) presented an Audio Steganalysis of Spread Spectrum Hiding Based on Statistical Moment. The research utilizes two algorithms for steganalysis spread spectrum hiding based on machine learning theory and Discrete Wavelet Transform (DWT). In algorithm 1, Gaussian Mixture Model (GMM) and Generalized Gaussian Distribution (GGD) were introduced to characterize the probability distribution of wavelet sub-band thereafter, the absolute Probability Distribution Function (PDF) moment is extracted as feature vectors. In algorithm II, the distance metric between GMM and GGD of wavelet sub-band to distinguish cover and stego audio was proposed. Four distances (Kullback-Leibler Distance, Bhattacharyya Distance, Earth Mover's Distance, L2 Distance) were calculated as feature vectors and Support Vector Machine (SVM) classifier was utilized for classification. It was observed that the research work has low detecting rate with various embedding ratio and high complexity.

4. MODEL DESIGN

The proposed system comprises of the following components:

i. Audio files acquisition
ii. Feature extraction
iii. Classification
iv. Prediction

4.1 Audio Acquisition

The two types of audio needed in this research are the cover audios and stego audios. The cover audios are plain audios with nothing embedded in them, while stego audios are the ones that have secret messages embedded in them. The dataset called Audio Steganalysis Dataset, IIE

(ASDIIE) was downloaded from: https://github.com/Charleswyt/tf_audio_steganalysis/tree/master/papers. Of the total dataset downloaded the audio stego dataset was 85 audio clips with duration of 10sec each and a total of 49.0MB, while the audio cover dataset consists of 96 audio clips with duration of 10sec each and total of 66.0MB. This was the dataset used to train the convolutional neural network and the dataset used for evaluation and prediction of the model was 20 audio clips with MP3, wav and MP4A file formats.

4.2 Feature Extraction

For reasons of efficiency and effectiveness, rather than operating on the audio data obtained, classification methods operate on an abstraction of the audio data expressed as a small feature set. The size of this feature set is known as its dimensionality. The objective in selecting these features is to capture properties of the underlying audio data that have statistical or psychological saliency.

Steganography algorithms cause irregularities and intangible changes when applied to audio signals. Applying features that can accurately reflect the differences between clean and stego audio signals are an important step in steganalysis process. The use of many common features in audio steganalysis systems cannot properly distinguish clean signals from stego signals. The fractal dimension as features was used because these features can capture sufficiently the irregularities in the audio signals. Since the fractal dimension of an audio frame depends greatly on sample values, the smallest change of samples will change the value of the respective fractal dimensions. As a result, such an attribute can have a great effect on the steganalysis problem. Higuchi's algorithms were employed to extract fractal dimensions.

The algorithm was based on a finite set of time series observations $X_{(1)}, X_{(2)}, X_{(3)}, \ldots, X_{(N)}$ taken at a regular interval. Based on this series, a new time series x_k^m is constructed as presented in the expression;

$$x_k^m ; x(m), x(m+k), x(m+2k) \ldots, x\left(m + \left[\frac{N-m}{k}\right].k\right)(m = 1, 2, \ldots, k)$$

where k and m are integers, m and k indicate the initial time and the interval time, respectively. For a time interval equal to k, k sets of new time series is obtained. x_k^m, which is the length of the curve, is expressed in equation 1:

$$L_m(k) = \frac{\left[\sum_{i=1}^{\frac{N-m}{k}} \left(X(m+ik) - X(m+(i-1)k)\right)\right] p}{k} \tag{1}$$

N is the total length of the data sequence x and the normalization factor for the curve length of subset time series is defined in equation (2):

$$p = \left(\frac{N-1}{\left[\frac{N-m}{k} \right] k} \right) \tag{2}$$

The length of the curve for the time interval k, (L(k)), is the average value over k sets of $L_m(k)$. If (L(k)) $\propto f^{-D}$ then the curve is fractal with the dimension D.

An average length is computed for all-time series having the same delay (or scale) k, as the mean of the k lengths $L_m(k)$ for m = 1, …, k. This procedure was repeated for each k ranging from 1 to k_{max}, which yields the sum of average time series lengths $L(k)$ for each k as indicated in equation (3):

$$FD_{Higuchi} = \sum_{m=1}^{k} L_m(k) \tag{3}$$

Fractal dimension helps to reduce the dimensionality of audio. The fractal dimension is used as features because these features can capture well the irregularities in the audio signals. Since the fractal dimension of an audio frame depends greatly on sample values, the smallest change of samples will change the value of the respective fractal dimensions. As a result, such an attribute can have a great effect on the steganalysis problem.

4.3 Classification

The architecture of the CNN has six layers: Input Layer, convolution Layer, ReLU Layer, Fully Connected Layer, softmax Layer and classification Layer. The input layer gets the audio into the model, a layer was created to 2D convolution with height 50, width 1 and a filter followed by a ReLU (Rectified Linear Unit) layer. The extracted features are fed into the binary classifier, which consists of a fully connected layer and a softmax layer followed by a classification output layer. However, all the weights in the CNN architecture can be automatically determined from the training data, without the interference of human. 182 cover and stego files were used altogether, about 128 used for training which is 70% for training.

The analytical expression of the convolution within the CNN architecture is given in equation (4):

$$h_j^{(n)} = \sum_{k=1}^{k} h_k^{(n-1)} * w_{kj}^{(n)} + b_j^n \tag{4}$$

where $*$ denotes a 2-D convolution operation, $h_j^{(n)}$ is the jth feature map output in the nth hidden layer, $h_k^{(n-1)}$ is the kth channel in the (n−1)th hidden layer, $w_{kj}^{(n)}$ is the kth channel in the jth filter in the nth layer and b_j^n is its corresponding bias term.

4.4 Prediction

Different audios were predicted based on the training model from the training phase. If the audio has any secret message embedded it will assign 1 to it and return STEGO as the output, and likewise, if the message is clean it will assign 0 and return COVER as the output.

4.4.1 Ratio Selection

The ratios are 30/70, 70/30 and 80/20, 30/70 implies taking the first 30% audios of the dataset for testing and the remaining 70% for training, 70/30 employs taking the first 70% audio of the dataset for training and the remaining 30% for testing and 80/20 means taking the first 80% audio of the dataset for training and remaining 20% for testing.

4.4.2 Training Model

To generate a training dataset, it is necessary to label every fractal dimension vector to determine the audio frame type. A zero label is allocated to clean frames, and a one label is allocated to stego frames.

4.4.3 Testing

During this testing, it returns the label 0 or 1 based on the knowledge from the trained model. Performance metrics (prediction accuracy, precision and recall) was also calculated in the testing phase.

5. SYSTEM IMPLEMENTATION RESULT AND EVALUATION

This section presents the implementation of the developed audio steganography system; interface design, implementation technique and experimental setup. Higuchi's, algorithm was employed to extract fractal dimensions from audio frames and Convolutional Neural Network for classification.

The performance of the developed system was evaluated based on its computational time, prediction accuracy, precision and recall

5.1 Interface Design

The interface design is a very important session, for any system the interface must be very simple and must be very easy to use by all users both the experienced and the less experienced users. The interface design of this dissertation is user friendly and it allows users to enjoy easy interaction with the system. Figure 2 illustrates the main interface design for the audio steganalysis design.

5.1.1 Function of Each Button on the Initial Page of Interface Design

Select Cover Folder: this button will help the user of this system to select the desired folder that contains the cover audio clips.

Figure 2. Interface showing the initial page of audio steganalysis software

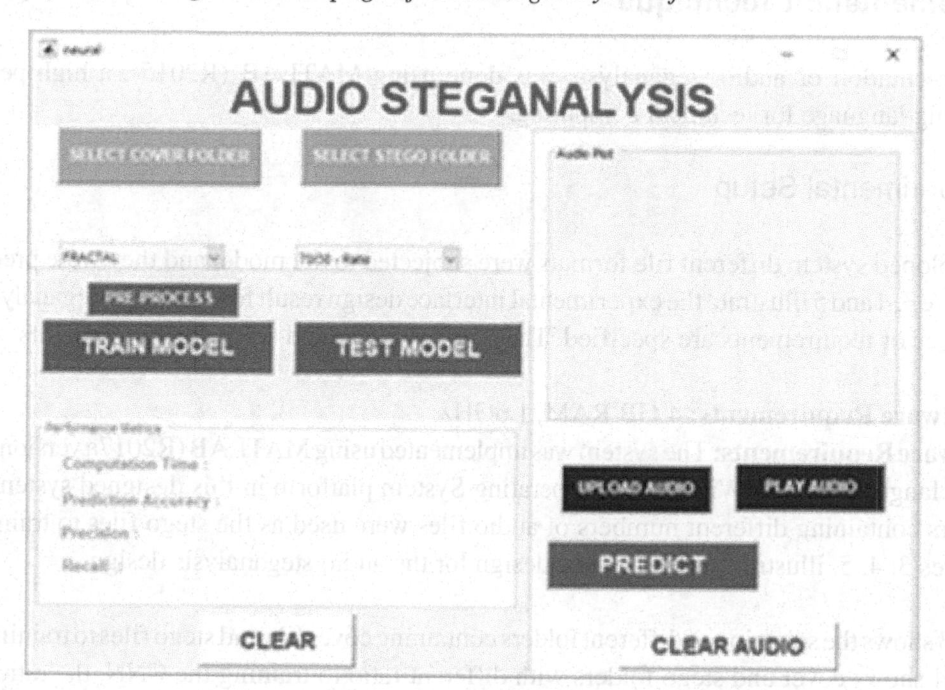

Select Stego Folder: this button is meant for the user to add the desired folder containing the stego audio clips.

Ratio list button: it enables the user to make a choice of the ratio options to use, there are three options, 70/30, 30/70, 80/20

Pre-Process: this is where the feature extraction takes place to reduce the data's dimensionality and reduce its size.

Train model: CNN was used as the classifier; it gets the number of data to use to test from the ratio list button

Test model: it uses the remaining percentage to test the model to know how effective the system works. This is where the computational time, prediction accuracy, precision and recall were calculated.

Performance metric: it is a frame where the values of computational time, prediction accuracy, precision and recall were displayed.

Clear button: it removes the values of the performance metrics, so as not to confuse it with another test result.

Upload audio: this is where the desired audio will be subjected to test to know if it is a cover audio or stego.

Play audio: the audio uploaded can also be played here

Predict: with the knowledge the CNN has gotten from the training stage the desired audio uploaded will be predicted as stego or cover.

Clear audio: it allows the user to clear the details of the earlier uploaded audio and upload another one.

5.2 Implementation Technique

The implementation of audio steganalysis was done using MATLAB (R2015), a high-performance programming language for technical computing.

5.2.1 Experimental Setup

In this developed system different file formats were subjected to the model and they were predicted correctly, Figure 3, 4 and 5 illustrate the experimental interface design result for the audio steganalysis system.

Two types of requirements are specified. They are hardware and software requirements.

a. **Hardware Requirements:** 4 GB RAM, 1.6GHz
b. **Software Requirements:** The system was implemented using MATLAB (R2017a version) programming language on the Windows 10 Operating System platform in this designed system, different folders containing different numbers of audio files were used as the stego files to train the CNN. Figures 3, 4, 5, illustrates the interface design for the audio steganalysis design

Figure 3 shows the selection of different folders containing cover file and stego files to training the CNN

Figure 4 shows cover and stego folders with different ratio to training the CNN, the ratio is used to compare the differences in selecting the first 70 for training and the last 30 for testing and using the first 30 for testing and the last 70 for training.

Figure 3. Different cover and stego audio files

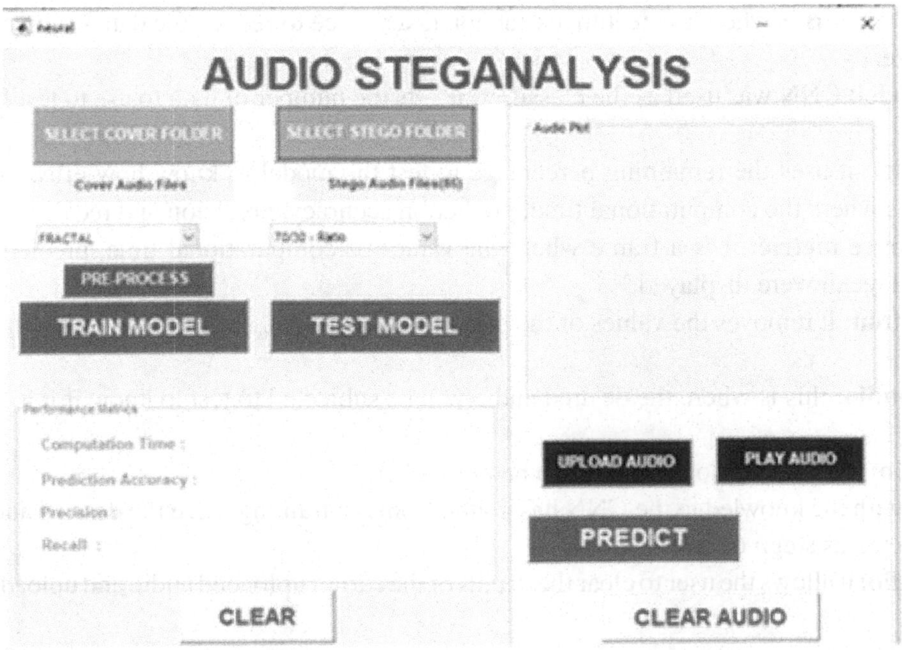

Figure 4. Different stego audio folder with 30/70 ratio

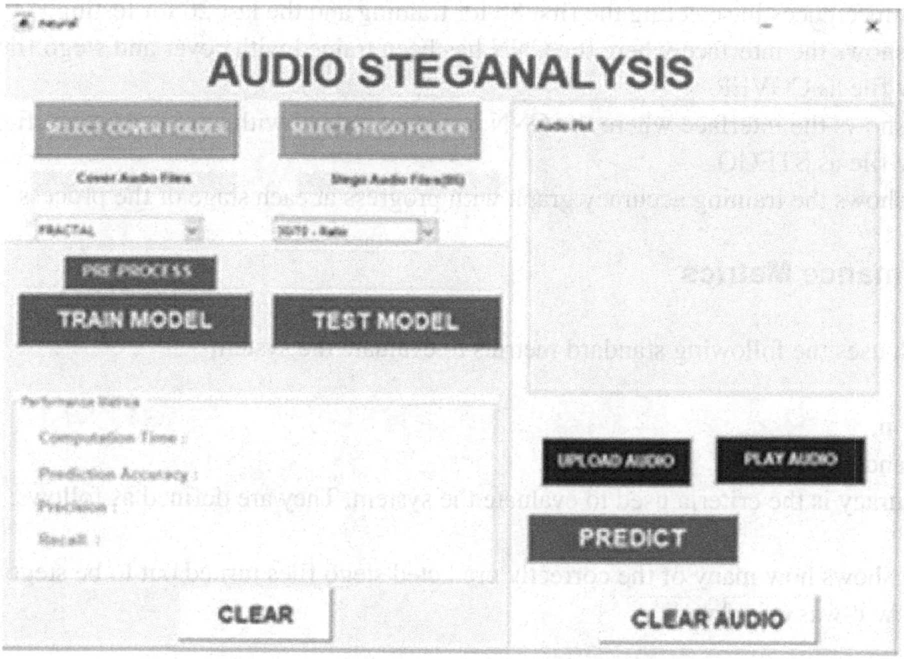

Figure 5. Different stego audio folder with 80/20 ratio

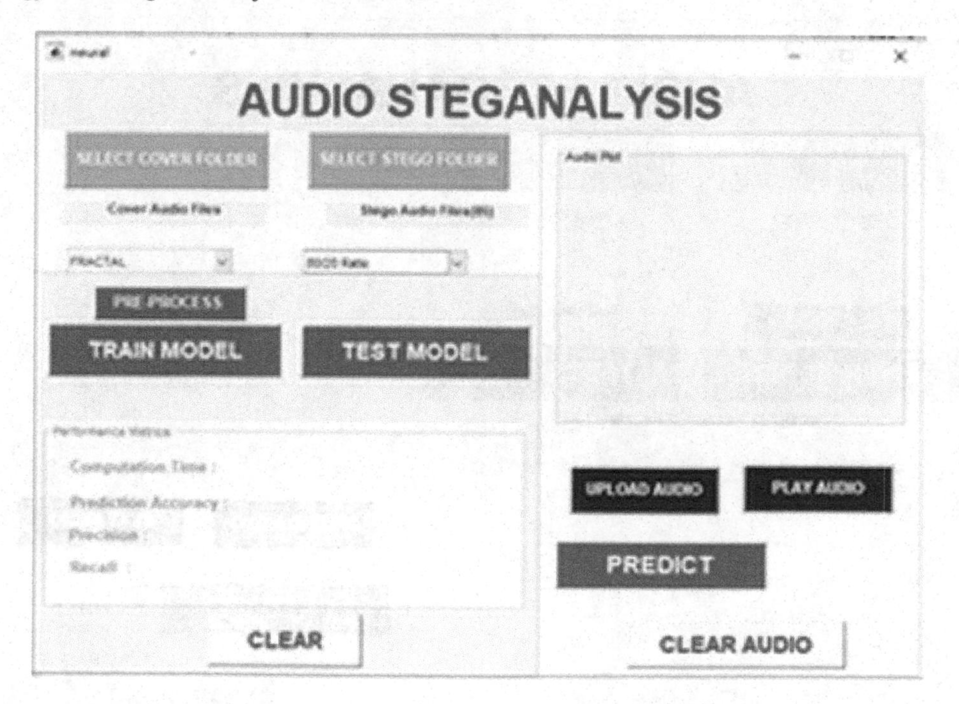

Figure 5 shows cover and stego folders with different ratio to training the CNN, the ratio is used to compare the differences in selecting the first 80 for training and the last 20 for testing.

Figure 6 shows the interface where the CNN has been trained with cover and stego files and it predicts the new file as COVER

Figure 7 shows the interface where the CNN has been trained with cover and stego files and it predicts the new file as STEGO

Figure 8 shows the training accuracy graph with progress at each stage of the process

5.5 Performance Metrics

This research uses the following standard metrics to evaluate the system

i. precision,
ii. recall, and
iii. the accuracy is the criteria used to evaluate the system. They are defined as follows:

Precision shows how many of the correctly predicted stego files turned out to be stego files. This is how it was calculated:

Figure 6. COVER prediction file

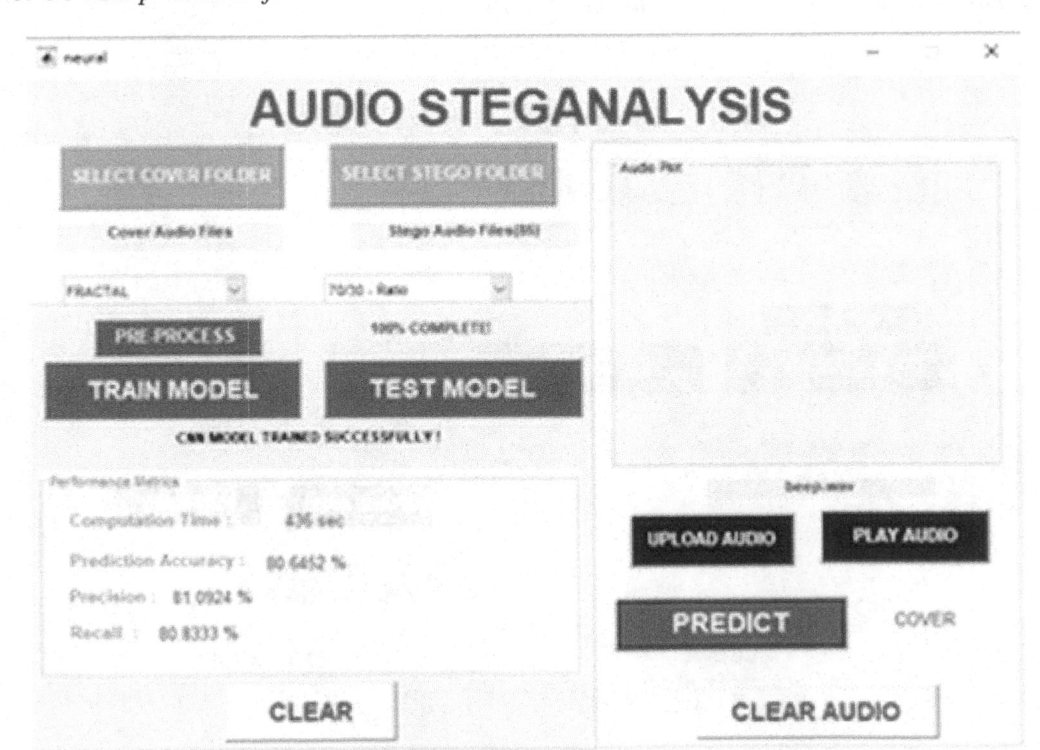

Figure 7. STEGO prediction file

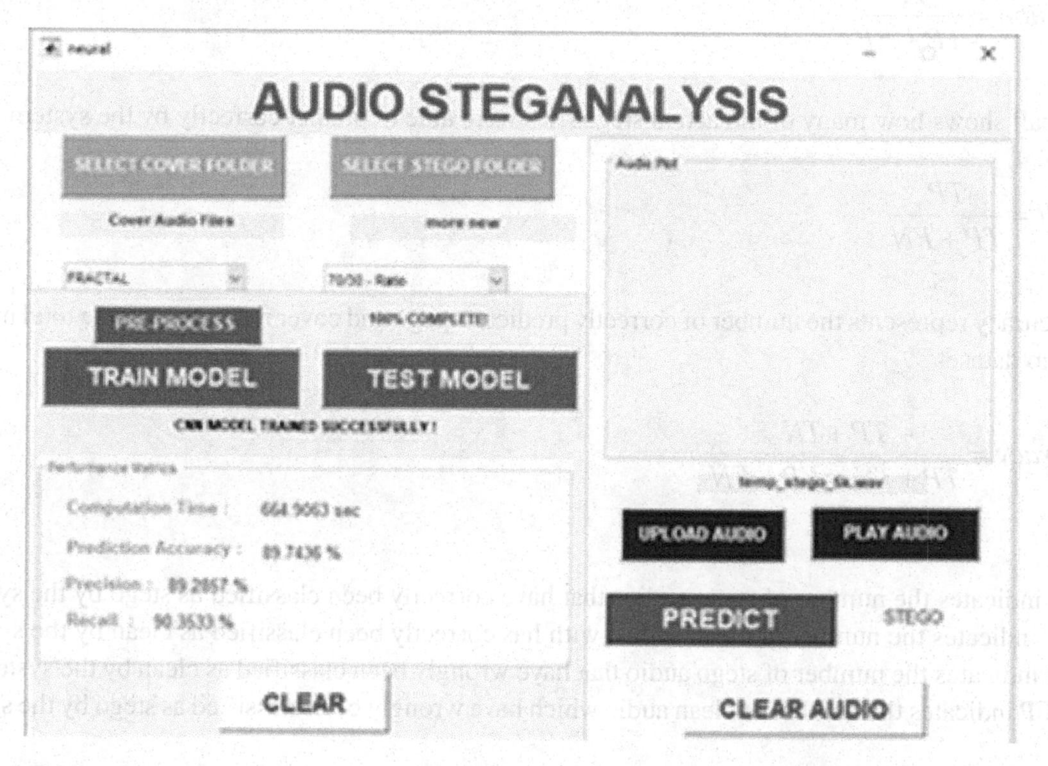

Figure 8. Training accuracy plot

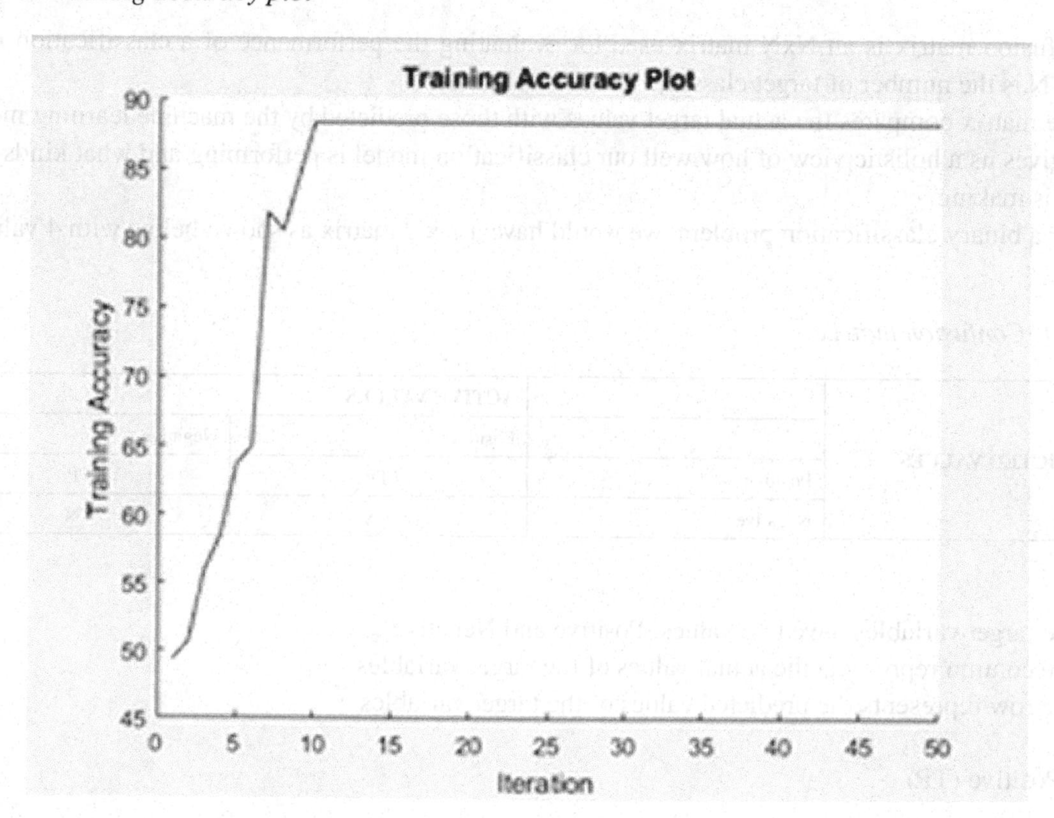

$$Precision = \frac{TP}{TP + FP} \tag{5}$$

Recall shows how many of the actual stego files were able to predict correctly by the system

$$Recall = \frac{TP}{TP + FN} \tag{6}$$

Accuracy represents the number of correctly predicted stego and cover medium over the total number of audio dataset

$$Accuracy = \frac{TP + TN}{TP + TN + FP + FN} \tag{7}$$

where

TP indicates the number of stego audios that have correctly been classified as stego by the system,

TN indicates the number of clean audios with has correctly been classified as clean by the system,

FN indicates the number of stego audio that have wrongly been classified as clean by the system, Finally, FP indicates the number of clean audio which have wrongly been classified as stego by the system.

5.5.1 Confusion Matrix

A confusion matrix is an NxN matrix used for evaluating the performance of a classification model where N is the number of target classes.

The matrix compares the actual target values with those predicted by the machine learning model.

It gives us a holistic view of how well our classification model is performing and what kinds of errors it is making.

For a binary classification problem, we would have a 2 x 2 matrix as shown below with 4 values:

Table 1. Confusion matrix

		ACTIVE VALUES	
PREDICTED VALUES		Positive	Negative
	Positive	TP	FP
	Negative	FN	TN

The target variables have two values: Positive and Negative

The column represents the actual values of the target variables

The row represents the predicted values of the target variables

True Positive (TP)

The predicted values match the actual values
The actual audio was stego and model predicted stego
True Negative (TN)
The predicted values match the actual value
The actual signal was cover and the model predicted the cover signal
False Positive (FP) Type 1 error
The predicted values were falsely predicted
The actual signal was cover but the model predicted stego signal
Also known as type 1 error
False Negative (FN) Type 2 error
The predicted values were falsely predicted
The actual signal was stego but the model predicted cover value
Also known as type 2 error

The confusion matrix of one of the process is as given below.

Table 2. Confusion matrix of stego/cover audio prediction

		ACTIVE VALUES	
PREDICTED VALUES		Stego	Cover
	Stego	12	4
	Cover	2	13

Table 3. Variations between the three ratios 80/20, 70/30, 30/70

	%		
	80/20	**70/30**	**30/70**
Computational time	654.6719	460.0469	443.1406
Prediction accuracy	78.022	80.6452	80.6452
Precision	78.9286	81.0924	81.0924
Recall	77.4709	80.8333	80.8333

Figure 9 shows the graphical representation of the differences in the ratios in the three performance metric methods with 181 audio clips. Ratio 80/20 shows 78.02% prediction accuracy, 78.92% precision, 77.47% recall; ratio 70/30 shows 80.64% prediction accuracy, 81.09% precision, 80.83% recall and ratio 30/70 shows 80.64% prediction accuracy, 81.09% precision, 80.83% recall.

Figure 10 shows the variation in the performance metrics in the three different ratios using 135 audio clips. Ratio 80/20 shows 81.89% prediction accuracy, 81.39% precision, 81.18% recall; ratio 70/30 shows 84.61% prediction accuracy, 84.12% precision, 85.05% recall and ratio 30/70 shows 87.17% prediction accuracy, 88.09% precision, 89.13% recall.

Figure 9. Chart showing variations between the three ratios 80/20, 70/30, 30/70 using 181 audio clips

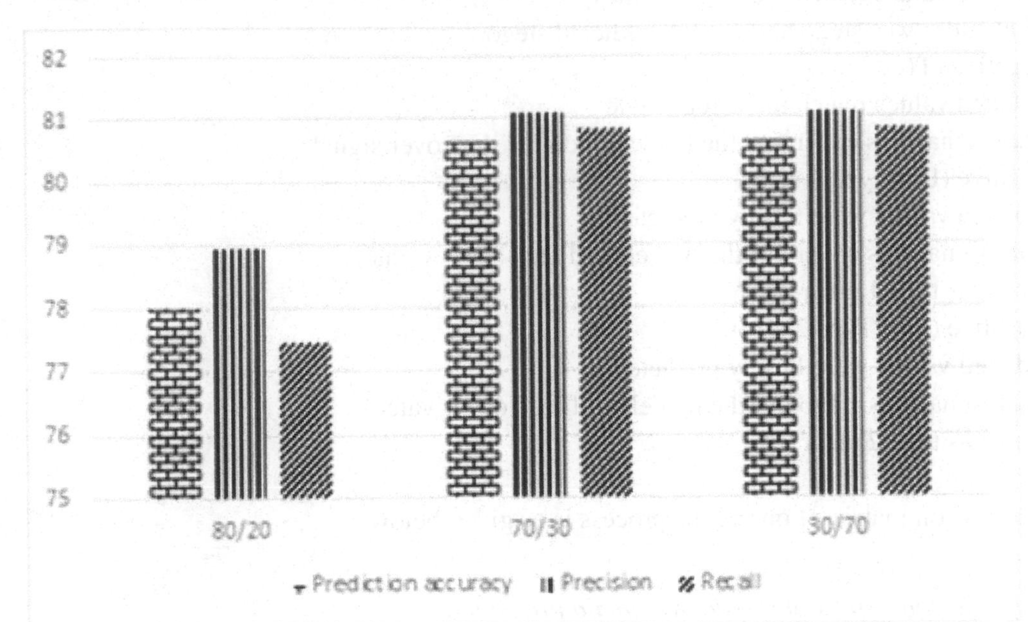

Figure 10. Chart showing variations between the three ratios 80/20, 70/30, 30/70 using 135 audio clips

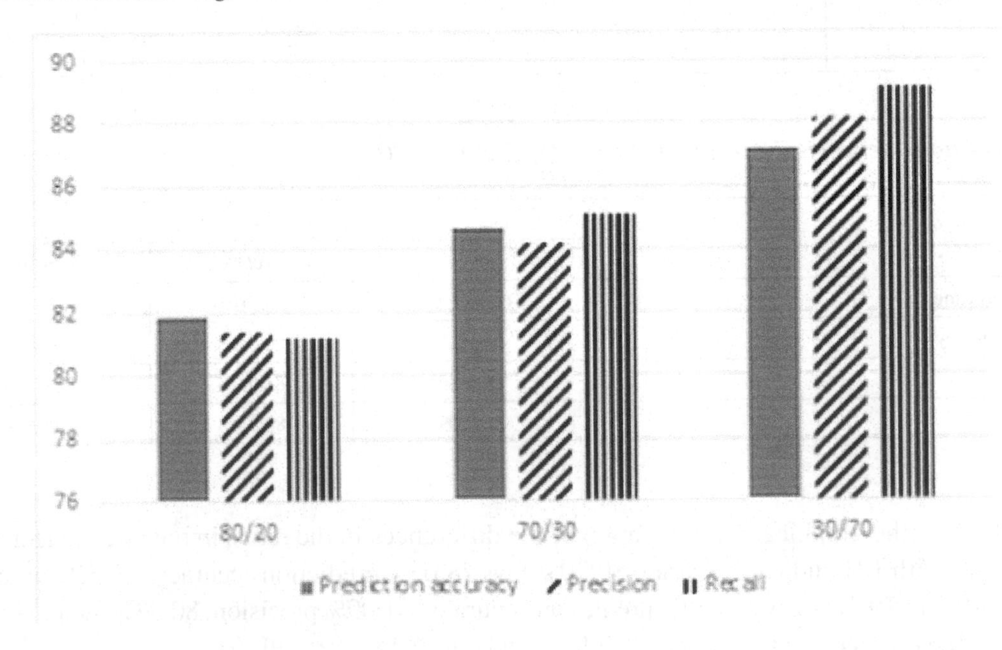

Figure 11 shows the differences in the three ratios when subjected to 146 audio clips. Ratio 80/20 shows 94.51% prediction accuracy, 94.56% precision, 94.43% recall; ratio 70/30 shows 96.77% prediction accuracy, 97.06% precision, 96.67% recall and ratio 30/70 shows 96.77% prediction accuracy, 96.88% precision, 96.88% recall.

Table 4. Variations between the three ratios 80/20, 70/30, 30/70 using a folder that has 135 audio clips

	%		
	80/20	70/30	30/70
Computational time	879.8438	570.2969	575.7656
Prediction accuracy	81.8966	84.6154	87.1795
Precision	81.3907	84.127	88.0952
Recall	81.1887	85.0543	89.1304

Table 5. Chart showing variations between the three ratios 80/20, 70/30, 30/70 using a folder that has 146 stego audio clips

	%		
	80/20	70/30	30/70
Computational time	721.92	469.45	468.03
Prediction accuracy	94.51	96.77	96.77
Precision	94.56	97.06	96.88
Recall	94.43	96.67	96.88

Figure 11. Chart showing variations between the three ratios 80/20, 70/30, 30/70 using a folder that has 146 audio clips

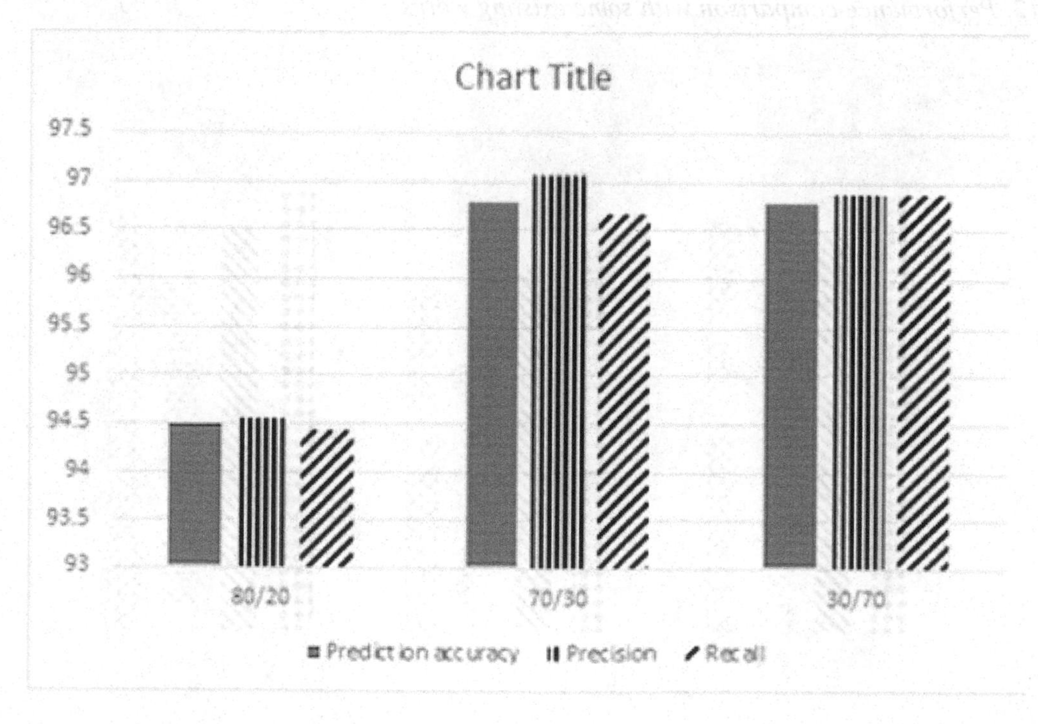

4.5 Performance Evaluation With Some Existing Works

Table 6 describes the performance comparison of this research work with some existing works.

Table 6. General performance comparison with some existing works

Name and year of Researchers	Accuracy (%)	Computational Time	Recall	Precision
Developed work	96.02	553.1	85.1	96.2
Chen et al., 2017	88.3	786.2	80.3	88.4
Wang et al., 2019	80.44	707.4	79.3	90.2
Lin et al., 2019	90.50	723.5	81.2	91.2

Figure 11 shows the comparison of the developed model with some existing works in accuracy, the developed model has 96.02%, Chen et al., (2017) 88.3%; Wang et al (2019) 80.44% and Ling et al., (2019) 90.50%; the recall of the developed model is 85.1%; Chen et al., (2017), 80.3% Wang et al., (2019), 79.3%; and Ling et al., (2019) 81.2% and precision of the developed model is 96.2%; Chen et al., (2017), 88.4% Wang et al., (2019), 90.2%; and Ling et al., (2019), 91.2%. From table 6 the accuracy of the developed work is higher compared to other existing work, i.e the new model predicts correctly compare to the existing models.

Figure 12. Performance comparison with some existing works

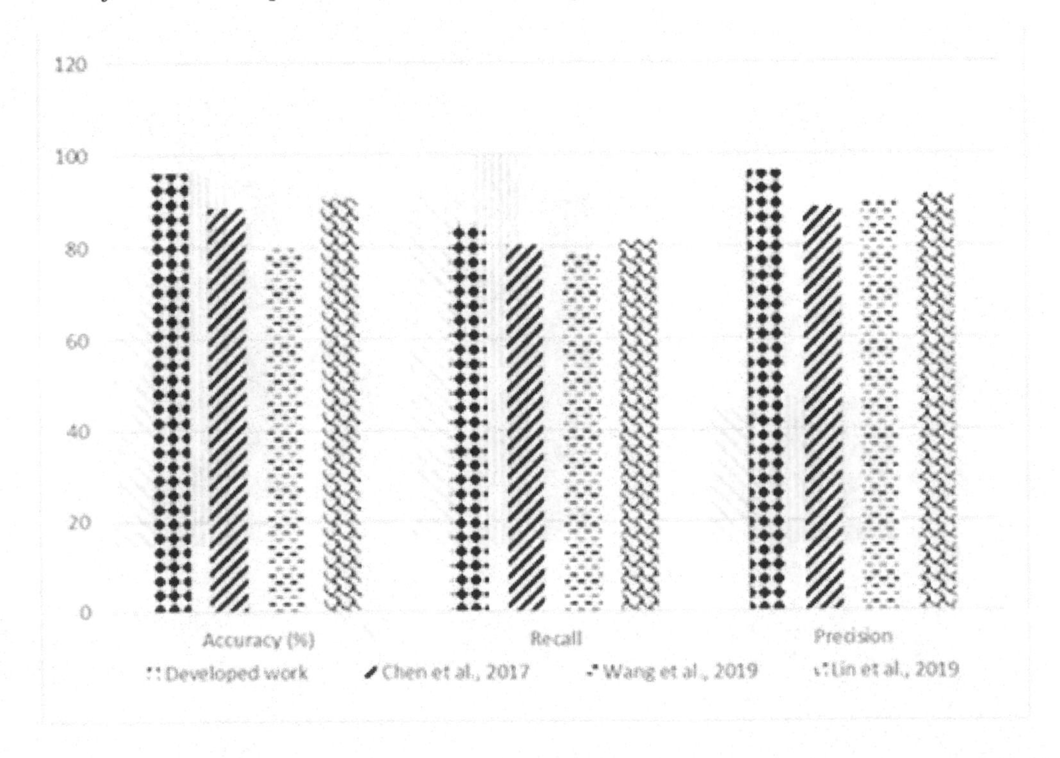

6. CONCLUSION

There are a lot of existing methods used to hide messages into an audio file and there are also many for predicting if an audio contains a secret message or not. The primary focus of this research work is the development of an audio steganalysis system to detect the presence of hidden messages in an audio file of any file format without prior knowledge of the steganography method used.

The classifier (Convolutional Neural Network) uses an audio clip of 10 seconds duration and 392kb size to train the model.

Data transmission has been made very simple, fast and accurate using the internet, one of the main problems that remain with the transmission of data over the internet is that it may pose a security threat.

It becomes very important to consider data security, as it is one of the essential factors that need attention during the process of data distribution.

REFERENCES

Chen, B., Luo, W., & Li, H. (2017). Audio steganalysis with convolutional neural network. *IH and MMSec 2017 - Proceedings of the 2017 ACM Workshop on Information Hiding and Multimedia Security*, (pp. 85–90). ACM. 10.1145/3082031.3083234

Chen, B., Luo, W., & Luo, D. (2018). Identification of audio processing operations based on convolutional neural network. *IH and MMSec 2018 - Proceedings of the 6th ACM Workshop on Information Hiding and Multimedia Security*, (pp. 73–77). IEEE. 10.1145/3206004.3206005

Doshi, R., Jain, P., & Gupta, L. (2012). Steganography and its Applications in Security. [IJMER]. *International Journal of Modern Engineering Research*, 2(6), 4634–4638.

Ghasemzadeh, H., & Arjmandi, M. K. (2017). Universal audio steganalysis based on calibration and reversed frequency resolution of human auditory system. *IET Signal Processing*, *11*(8), 916–922. doi:10.1049/iet-spr.2016.0690

Gibson, T. (2002). *Methods of Audio Steganography*, (3), 154–156. http://www.snotmonkey.com/work/school/405/methods.html

Han, C., Xue, R., Zhang, R., & Wang, X. (2018). A new audio steganalysis method based on linear prediction. *Multimedia Tools and Applications*, *77*(12), 15431–15455. doi:10.1007/s11042-017-5123-x

Jayaram, R., Ranganatha, & Anupama. (2011). Information Hiding Using Audio Steganography - A Survey. *The International Journal of Multimedia & Its Applications*, *3*(3), 86–96. doi:10.5121/ijma.2011.3308

Kessler, G. C. (2007). *An Overview of Cryptography. 1998*(November 2006), 1–23.

Lin, Y., Wang, R., Yan, D., Dong, L., & Zhang, X. (2019). *Audio Steganalysis with Improved Convolutional Neural Network*, (August), 210–215. doi:10.1145/3335203.3335736

Lin, Z., Huang, Y., & Wang, J. (2018). RNN-SM: Fast Steganalysis of VoIP Streams Using Recurrent Neural Network. *IEEE Transactions on Information Forensics and Security*, *13*(7), 1854–1868. doi:10.1109/TIFS.2018.2806741

Mohtasham-zadeh, V., & Mosleh, M. (2019). Audio Steganalysis based on collaboration of fractal dimensions and convolutional neural networks. *Multimedia Tools and Applications*, *78*(9), 11369–11386. doi:10.1007/s11042-018-6702-1

Paulin, C., Selouani, S. A., & Hervet, É. (2016). Audio steganalysis using deep belief networks. *International Journal of Speech Technology*, *19*(3), 585–591. doi:10.1007/s10772-016-9352-6

Pooyan, M., & Delforouzi, A. (2007). LSB-based audio steganography method based on lifting wavelet transform. *ISSPIT 2007 - 2007 IEEE International Symposium on Signal Processing and Information Technology*, (pp. 600–603). IEEE. 10.1109/ISSPIT.2007.4458198

Rabah, K. (2004). Steganography-The Art of Hiding Data. *Information Technology Journal*, *3*(3), 245–269. doi:10.3923/itj.2004.245.269

Rafiee, H. (2019)... *Presenting a Method for Improving Echo Hiding.*, *2*(1). doi:10.22067/cke.v2i1.74388

RenY.LiuD.XiongQ.FuJ.WangL. (2019). *Spec-ResNet: A General Audio Steganalysis scheme based on Deep Residual Network of Spectrogram.* 1–12. https://arxiv.org/abs/1901.06838

Shirali-Shahreza, S., & Manzuri-Shalmani, M. T. (2008). High Capacity Error Free Wavelet Domain Speech Steganography. Computer Engineering Department Sharif University of Technology, Tehran, IRAN Computer Engineering Department Sharif University of Technology.

Wang, Y., Yi, X., Zhao, X., & Su, A. (2019). RHFCN: Fully CNN-based Steganalysis of MP3 with Rich High-pass Filtering. *ICASSP, IEEE International Conference on Acoustics, Speech and Signal Processing*, (pp. 2627–2631). IEEE. 10.1109/ICASSP.2019.8683626

Warkentin, M., Schmidt, M. B., & Bekkering, E. (2007). Steganography and steganalysis. *Intellectual Property Protection for Multimedia Information Technology*, (January), 374–380. doi:10.4018/978-1-59904-762-1.ch019

Zeng, W., Hu, R., & Ai, H. (2011). Audio steganalysis of spread spectrum information hiding based on statistical moment and distance metric. *Multimedia Tools and Applications*, *55*(3), 525–556. doi:10.1007/s11042-010-0564-5

Chapter 16
6G Enabled Internet of Things–Artificial Intelligence–Based Digital Twins:
Cybersecurity and Resilience

Shabnam Kumari
SRM Institute of Science and Technology, Chennai, India

Aderonke Thompson
Federal University of Technology, Akure, Nigeria

Shrikant Tiwari
https://orcid.org/0000-0001-6947-2362
Galgotias University, Greater Noida, India

ABSTRACT

The convergence of sixth-generation (6G) wireless networks, internet of things (IoT), and artificial intelligence (AI) has changed the way for the development of 6G-enabled IoT-AI based digital twins. These digital twins, virtual representations of physical objects or systems, offer enhanced capabilities for real-time monitoring, optimization, and control. However, as these systems become more interconnected and critical to various domains, cybersecurity and resilience become important issues. This work explores the cyber-security challenges and resilience requirements associated with 6G-enabled IoT-AI based digital twins. It examines potential vulnerabilities, threats, and attacks that could compromise the integrity, confidentiality, and availability of digital twin ecosystems. Moreover, it discusses the measures and strategies that can be employed to ensure cybersecurity and resilience, including secure design principles, authentication and access control mechanisms, anomaly detection, data encryption, and secure communication protocols.

DOI: 10.4018/979-8-3693-2081-5.ch016

1. INTRODUCTION ABOUT 6G-ENABLED, IOT-AI-BASED DIGITAL TWINS

6G-enabled IoT-AI based digital twins are an emerging concept that combines the capabilities of sixth-generation (6G) wireless networks, the Internet of Things (IoT), and artificial intelligence (AI) to create virtual representations of physical objects, processes, or systems (Mahmood & Hu, 2020; Yao et al., 2020). A digital twin is a virtual model that mirrors the real-world counterpart, capturing its characteristics, behavior, and interactions. In the context of 6G-enabled IoT-AI based digital twins, these virtual representations are enhanced with advanced AI algorithms, considering the massive amount of data generated by IoT devices and the ultra-low latency and high bandwidth provided by 6G networks. This convergence enables real-time data analysis, predictive modeling, and decision-making capabilities, leading to enhanced performance, efficiency, and innovation across various domains.

By considering the power of 6G networks, which are expected to provide unprecedented connectivity speeds, ultra-low latency, large device density, and high reliability, IoT devices can transmit large volumes of data to the cloud or edge computing platforms for processing (Wu et al., 2016). AI algorithms, including machine learning and deep learning techniques, can then analyze this data to derive meaningful information, patterns, and predictions.

This information are used to build and refine digital twins, which serve as virtual replicas of physical objects or systems. Digital twins can be applied to a wide range of applications/ scenarios, such as smart cities, industrial automation, healthcare, transportation, and more. They enable real-time monitoring, optimization, and control of physical assets, allowing for proactive maintenance, efficient resource allocation, and improved decision-making. The integration of AI with digital twins enhances their capabilities by enabling intelligent automation, anomaly detection, optimization, and autonomous decision-making. AI algorithms can learn from historical data and continuously adapt to changing conditions, allowing digital twins to provide more accurate predictions and recommendations. Note that 6G-enabled IoT-AI based digital twins hold great potential for transforming industries and enabling innovative applications. They can enable autonomous systems, optimize resource usage, enhance sustainability, improve safety, and create new business models. However, the development and deployment of these technologies also raise important issues regarding data privacy, security, ethics, and the responsible use of AI. Hence, as research and development in 6G networks, IoT, and AI continue to progress, we can expect to see further advancements in the capabilities and applications of IoT-AI based digital twins, unlocking new opportunities for industries and society as a whole. Now figure 1 provides a detail description/ difference between 5G and 6G.

1.1 Background

The integration of blockchain technology with 6G-enabled IoT-AI based digital twins can offer several benefits and address key challenges related to data integrity, security, trust, and privacy (Mishra & Sharma, 2019; Zhao & Yao, 2018). Blockchain is a decentralized and distributed ledger that provides immutability, transparency, and tamper resistance to transactions and data records. Here's how blockchain can enhance the functionality of 6G-enabled IoT-AI based digital twins:

Figure 1. Difference between 5G vs. 6G

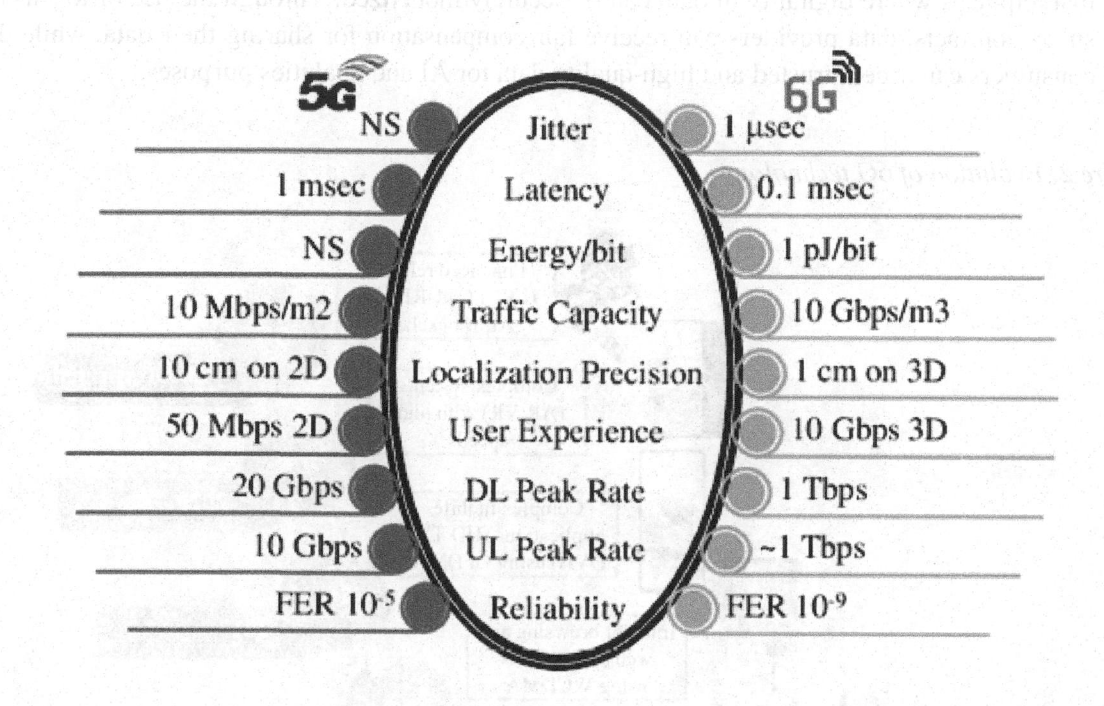

- Data Integrity and Immutability: Blockchain can ensure the integrity and immutability of the data collected and stored by IoT devices. Each transaction or data update can be recorded as a block on the blockchain, creating an auditable and tamper-proof record. This ensures that the digital twin's data is reliable and trustworthy.
- Secure Data Sharing and Access Control: Blockchain allows for secure and controlled data sharing among multiple stakeholders. Access control mechanisms can be implemented using smart contracts, enabling fine-grained permissions and data sharing policies. This ensures that only authorized entities can access and interact with the digital twin's data.
- Trusted Interactions and Smart Contracts: Blockchain can facilitate trusted interactions between different entities involved in the lifecycle of digital twins. Smart contracts, which are self-executing contracts with predefined rules, can automate and enforce agreements between parties. For example, smart contracts can define the terms of data sharing, ownership, and usage, ensuring transparency and trust.
- Provenance and Traceability: Blockchain can enable the tracking and tracing of data and events within the digital twin ecosystem. Each data update or interaction can be recorded on the blockchain, providing an immutable audit trail. This helps in establishing the provenance of data, verifying its origin, and ensuring data reliability and accountability.
- Data Privacy and Consent Management: Blockchain-based solutions can empower individuals to have more control over their data (Zhou et al., 2020). Through the use of decentralized identity management and attribute-based access control, individuals can maintain ownership of their data and grant consent for its usage. This enhances privacy and gives individuals the ability to revoke access to their data when desired.

- Incentivization and Data Marketplaces: Blockchain can enable the creation of decentralized data marketplaces where digital twin data can be securely monetized. Through the use of tokens and smart contracts, data providers can receive fair compensation for sharing their data, while data consumers can access trusted and high-quality data for AI and analytics purposes.

Figure 2. Evolution of 6G technology

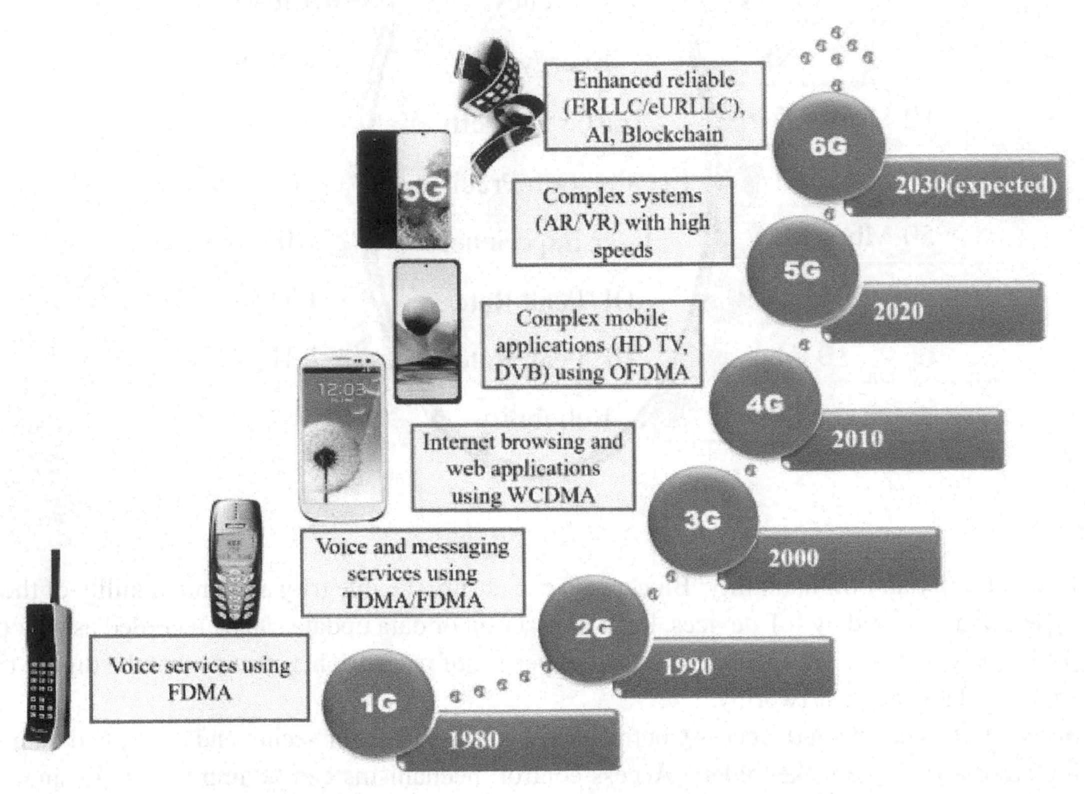

Figure 2 discusses the evolution of 6G technology in detail. In summary, by combining the features of blockchain technology with 6G-enabled IoT-AI based digital twins, we can create a robust and trusted ecosystem for managing, sharing, and utilizing data. This enhances the reliability, security, and transparency of digital twin operations, enabling new business models and fostering innovation in various industries. However, it's essential to consider the scalability, interoperability, and energy efficiency aspects when implementing blockchain in the context of 6G-enabled IoT-AI based digital twins.

1.2 Organization of the work

This work is summarized into 8 sections.

2. CYBER-SECURITY CHALLENGES IN 6G-ENABLED IOT

While 6G-enabled IoT brings numerous benefits and advancements, it also introduces various cyber security challenges that need to be addressed. Here are some key cyber security challenges in 6G-enabled IoT:

- Increased Attack Surface: With a massive number of connected devices and expanded network infrastructure, the attack surface for potential cyber threats expands significantly. Each IoT device becomes a potential entry point for attackers to exploit vulnerabilities and gain unauthorized access to networks or systems.
- Device Vulnerabilities: IoT devices often have limited computational resources and may prioritize functionality over security. This can result in inadequate security measures, outdated firmware, or lack of security patches, making devices more susceptible to exploitation and compromise.
- Data Privacy and Protection: 6G-enabled IoT generates large amount of sensitive data, including personal information, business data, and operational details. Ensuring the privacy and protection of this data throughout its lifecycle, from collection to storage and transmission, is a critical challenge. Unauthorized access, data breaches, or mishandling of data can have severe consequences.
- Authentication and Access Control: Proper authentication and access control mechanisms are important in 6G-enabled IoT to prevent unauthorized access to devices, networks, and services. Weak or compromised authentication mechanisms can allow malicious actors to gain unauthorized control over devices or inject malicious code into the network.
- Network Infrastructure Security: The underlying network infrastructure supporting 6G-enabled IoT must be adequately secured. This includes securing routers, gateways, base stations, and communication links to prevent network-level attacks, such as Distributed Denial of Service (DDoS) attacks, eavesdropping, or man-in-the-middle attacks.
- Supply Chain Risks: The complex supply chain involved in developing and deploying IoT devices introduces potential risks. Compromised components or tampering at any stage of the supply chain can lead to the distribution of insecure devices or the insertion of malicious software or hardware.
- Lack of Standardization: With the rapid evolution of IoT technologies, there is often a lack of standardized security protocols and practices. Inconsistent implementations across different devices and platforms can create vulnerabilities and interoperability challenges, making it difficult to establish a cohesive and secure ecosystem.
- Security Updates and Patch Management: IoT devices may have limited or no mechanisms for receiving security updates or patches. This makes it challenging to address vulnerabilities or apply necessary security fixes in a timely manner, leaving devices and networks exposed to known security threats.
- Human Factors: Human error and negligence can introduce significant cyber security risks in 6G-enabled IoT. Weak passwords, improper configuration, or failure to follow security best practices can undermine the security of devices and networks.

Note that these cyber security challenges require a multi-faceted approach, involving industry collaboration, standards development, and best practices adoption (Zhou et al., 2020). Key strategies include implementing robust authentication mechanisms, encryption protocols, secure firmware updates, network segmentation, intrusion detection systems, and comprehensive security audits. Additionally, user awareness and education programs can help promote responsible IoT device usage and ensure that individuals understand the importance of cyber security in the 6G-enabled IoT landscape.

3. 6G-ENABLED IOT TECHNOLOGY AND APPLICATIONS

3.1 Integration of IoT in 6G Networks

The integration of IoT in 6G networks plays an important role in enabling advanced connectivity, data exchange, and intelligent decision-making (Alaba et al., 2017; Lu et al., 2017; Nan et al., 2018). Here are some key aspects of IoT integration in 6G networks:

- Enhanced Device Connectivity: 6G networks aim to support massive device connectivity, and IoT devices play a significant role in achieving this goal. IoT devices, including sensors, actuators, wearables, and smart objects, can seamlessly connect to 6G networks, creating a large network of interconnected devices.
- Ultra-Reliable Low-Latency Communication (URLLC): 6G networks will provide ultra-reliable and low-latency communication, which is critical for real-time IoT applications. This enables time-sensitive IoT use cases such as autonomous vehicles, industrial automation, remote surgery, and smart grid systems that require near-instantaneous response times.
- Edge Computing and Distributed Intelligence: 6G networks use edge computing capabilities, bringing data processing and intelligence closer to the network edge. This enables IoT devices to perform local data processing, reducing latency and network congestion. Edge computing also enables faster decision-making, efficient resource allocation, and real-time analytics for IoT applications.
- Contextual Awareness: 6G networks integrate contextual awareness, enabling IoT devices to understand and adapt to their surroundings. This includes location-based services, environmental sensing, and context-aware analytics. Contextual information enhances the functionality of IoT devices and enables personalized services, efficient resource utilization, and adaptive decision-making.
- Network Slicing: Network slicing in 6G networks allows the creation of customized virtual networks tailored to the specific requirements of IoT applications. IoT applications with distinct needs, such as low-power sensors, high-bandwidth devices, or critical communications, can have dedicated network slices optimized for their unique characteristics.
- Quality of Service (QoS) Optimization: 6G networks prioritize QoS optimization for IoT devices, considering factors such as latency, reliability, and energy efficiency. IoT devices with diverse requirements can benefit from QoS-aware resource allocation and dynamic network optimization techniques, ensuring that each device receives the necessary resources for optimal performance.
- Security and Privacy: 6G networks emphasize robust security and privacy measures for IoT integration. Advanced authentication, encryption, and access control mechanisms protect IoT devices and the data they generate. Additionally, privacy-preserving techniques, such as secure data aggregation and anonymization, are employed to address privacy issue in IoT deployments.
- Hybrid Network Architecture: 6G networks may incorporate hybrid network architectures, combining different communication technologies to cater to diverse IoT requirements. This includes integrating cellular networks, low-power wide-area networks (LPWANs), satellite communica-

tion, and short-range wireless technologies like Bluetooth and Wi-Fi to provide seamless connectivity for a wide range of IoT devices.
- Data Analytics and AI: 6G networks use data analytics and artificial intelligence (AI) techniques to extract information from the massive amounts of data generated by IoT devices. AI algorithms can analyze IoT data in real-time, identify patterns, detect anomalies, and enable predictive modeling for efficient decision-making and optimization of IoT applications.
- Vertical Industry Applications: 6G networks integrate IoT across various industry sectors, including smart cities, healthcare, manufacturing, transportation, agriculture, and more. IoT integration enables the deployment of innovative applications and services that enhance efficiency, productivity, and quality of life across different domains.

In summary, by integrating IoT into 6G networks, a highly interconnected and intelligent ecosystem is created, allowing for seamless communication, intelligent data processing, and transformative applications. The integration of IoT in 6G networks paves the way for advanced use cases and services that use the power of connected devices, real-time analytics, and intelligent decision-making.

3.2 Applications and Use Cases of 6G-Enabled IoT

6G-enabled IoT opens up a wide range of applications and use cases across various industries. Here are some examples of applications and use cases that can be realized through the integration of 6G and IoT:

- Smart Cities: 6G-enabled IoT can enhance the efficiency and sustainability of cities. Smart city applications include smart transportation systems, intelligent traffic management, optimized energy consumption, environmental monitoring, smart waste management, and real-time monitoring of urban infrastructure.
- Industrial Automation: IoT integration in industrial settings enables the implementation of smart factories and Industry 4.0 concepts. 6G-enabled IoT can support real-time monitoring and control of industrial processes, predictive maintenance of machinery, asset tracking, and optimization of supply chain management.
- Healthcare: In the healthcare sector, 6G-enabled IoT can revolutionize patient care. It enables remote patient monitoring, real-time health tracking, telemedicine services, wearable health devices, and smart healthcare systems for efficient healthcare delivery and personalized treatment (George & Tyagi, 2022; Rekha, Tyagi, & Anuradha, 2020).
- Agriculture: IoT integration in agriculture, often referred to as smart farming or precision agriculture, enables optimized crop management, efficient water and resource utilization, livestock monitoring, soil monitoring, and real-time data-driven decision-making for improved agricultural productivity and sustainability.
- Environmental Monitoring: 6G-enabled IoT can facilitate comprehensive environmental monitoring. It allows real-time monitoring of air quality, water quality, noise levels, weather conditions, and natural resource management. This data can be used for early detection of environmental issues, disaster management, and sustainable resource planning.
- Autonomous Vehicles: 6G networks and IoT can support the development and deployment of autonomous vehicles. IoT sensors and connectivity enable real-time vehicle-to-vehicle (V2V) and

vehicle-to-infrastructure (V2I) communication, enhancing road safety, traffic management, and transportation efficiency.

- Smart Energy Management: IoT integration with 6G networks enables smart energy management systems. It facilitates real-time monitoring and control of energy consumption, load balancing, demand response, and integration of renewable energy sources. This leads to optimized energy usage, reduced costs, and enhanced grid stability.
- Retail and Supply Chain Optimization: 6G-enabled IoT enhances retail and supply chain operations. It enables inventory tracking, smart shelves, automated stock management, demand forecasting, and seamless integration of online and offline shopping experiences.
- Public Safety and Emergency Management: IoT integration in 6G networks enhances public safety and emergency response capabilities. It enables real-time surveillance, early warning systems, disaster management, emergency services coordination, and effective communication during crisis situations.
- Personalized and Immersive Experiences: 6G-enabled IoT can provide personalized and immersive experiences in areas such as entertainment, gaming, tourism, and augmented reality (AR)/ virtual reality (VR). It enables interactive and context-aware content delivery, immersive simulations, and virtual experiences.

Figure 3 explains several possibilities in different disciplines. These are few examples and the possibilities of 6G-enabled IoT applications are extensive (refer figure 4). As 6G networks and IoT technologies continue to evolve, new and innovative use cases will emerge, driving advancements in various industries and transforming the way we live, work, and interact with the world around us.

Figure 3. 6G system in smart era

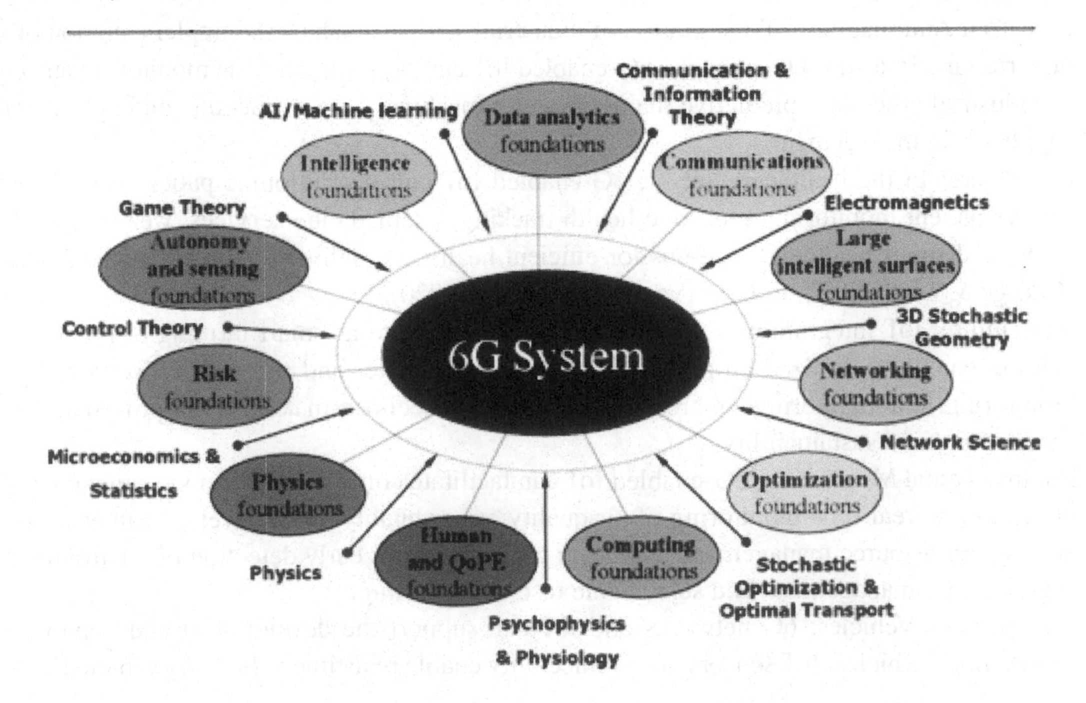

Figure 4. Use case of 6G network

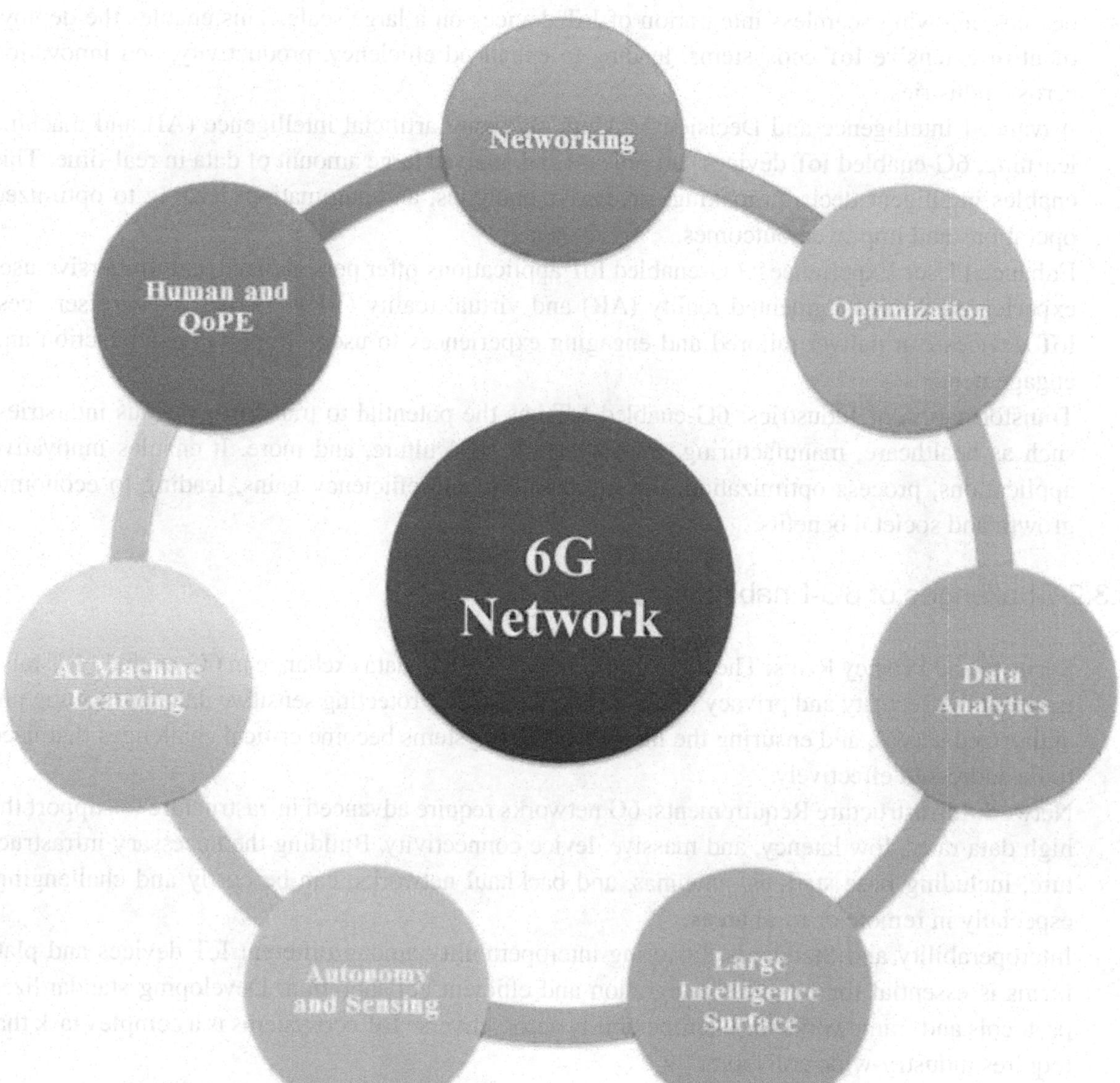

3.3 Benefits and Challenges of 6G-Enabled IoT

6G-enabled IoT offers a multitude of benefits, but it also comes with certain challenges (Nair, 2023). Here's an overview of the benefits and challenges associated with 6G-enabled IoT:

3.3.1 Benefits of 6G-Enabled IoT

- Ultra-Fast and Reliable Connectivity: 6G networks provide extremely high data rates and low latency, ensuring fast and reliable connectivity for IoT devices. This enables real-time communication, supports mission-critical applications, and enhances user experiences.

- Massive Device Connectivity: 6G networks can accommodate a massive number of connected devices, allowing seamless integration of IoT devices on a large scale. This enables the deployment of extensive IoT ecosystems, leading to enhanced efficiency, productivity, and innovation across industries.
- Advanced Intelligence and Decision-Making: By using artificial intelligence (AI) and machine learning, 6G-enabled IoT devices can process and analyze large amount of data in real-time. This enables intelligent decision-making, predictive analytics, and automation, leading to optimized operations and improved outcomes.
- Enhanced User Experiences: 6G-enabled IoT applications offer personalized and immersive user experiences. From augmented reality (AR) and virtual reality (VR) to context-aware services, IoT devices can deliver tailored and engaging experiences to users, improving satisfaction and engagement.
- Transformation of Industries: 6G-enabled IoT has the potential to transform various industries, such as healthcare, manufacturing, transportation, agriculture, and more. It enables innovative applications, process optimization, improved safety, and efficiency gains, leading to economic growth and societal benefits.

3.3.2 Challenges of 6G-Enabled IoT

- Security and Privacy Risks: The increased connectivity and data exchange in 6G-enabled IoT raise issues about security and privacy (Abraham et al., 2022). Protecting sensitive data, preventing unauthorized access, and ensuring the integrity of IoT systems become critical challenges that need to be addressed effectively.
- Network Infrastructure Requirements: 6G networks require advanced infrastructure to support the high data rates, low latency, and massive device connectivity. Building the necessary infrastructure, including base stations, antennas, and backhaul networks, can be costly and challenging, especially in remote or rural areas.
- Interoperability and Standards: Ensuring interoperability among different IoT devices and platforms is essential for seamless integration and efficient collaboration. Developing standardized protocols and frameworks for interoperability across diverse IoT ecosystems is a complex task that requires industry-wide collaboration.
- Energy Efficiency and Sustainability: With the increasing number of connected devices, energy consumption becomes a significant issue. 6G-enabled IoT must address the challenge of energy efficiency, implementing power-saving mechanisms and sustainable practices to minimize the environmental impact.
- Data Management and Analytics: The massive volume of data generated by IoT devices poses challenges in terms of data storage, processing, and analysis. Effective data management strategies, including data governance, data privacy, and scalable analytics solutions, are necessary to extract meaningful information and derive value from IoT data.
- Regulatory and Ethical issues: As IoT applications become more pervasive, there is a need for robust regulatory frameworks and ethical guidelines. Balancing innovation with privacy protection, data ownership, and ethical use of IoT technologies is important to ensure responsible deployment and usage.

- Skillsets and Workforce Readiness: The successful implementation of 6G-enabled IoT requires skilled professionals with expertise in areas such as IoT development, data analytics, cybersecurity, and AI. Bridging the skills gap and ensuring a workforce prepared for the demands of 6G-enabled IoT is a challenge that needs attention.

Hence, addressing these challenges will be key to realizing the full potential of 6G-enabled IoT and unlocking its benefits across various sectors. Collaborative efforts from industry stakeholders, policymakers, researchers, and technology providers are essential to overcome these challenges and build a robust and sustainable 6G-enabled IoT ecosystem.

4. AI AND DIGITAL TWINS IN 6G-ENABLED IOT TECHNOLOGY AND APPLICATIONS

4.1 Role of AI in 6G-Enabled IoT

Artificial Intelligence (AI) plays an important role in 6G-enabled IoT by enabling intelligent decision-making, data analytics, and automation (Tyagi et al., 2022; Tyagi et al., 2023). Here are some key roles of AI in 6G-enabled IoT:

- Data Analytics and Information: AI algorithms and techniques are used to analyze large amount of data generated by IoT devices in real-time. AI-powered analytics enable the extraction of meaningful information, patterns, and correlations from the data, facilitating informed decision-making and predictive modeling.
- Intelligent Automation: AI in 6G-enabled IoT enables intelligent automation of processes and workflows. By using AI technologies such as machine learning and natural language processing, IoT devices can learn from data patterns and make automated decisions, reducing manual intervention and improving operational efficiency.
- Context-Awareness and Personalization: AI enables IoT devices to understand their environment and adapt accordingly. Context-awareness techniques, such as sensor fusion and machine learning, allow IoT devices to perceive their surroundings and tailor their behavior or services based on the context. This leads to personalized and enhanced user experiences.
- Anomaly Detection and Security: AI algorithms can detect anomalies and patterns that indicate potential security breaches or abnormal behavior in IoT networks. By continuously monitoring IoT data, AI can identify and respond to security threats in real-time, enhancing the security posture of 6G-enabled IoT systems.
- Energy Efficiency and Optimization: AI techniques can optimize energy consumption in 6G-enabled IoT devices and networks. By analyzing energy usage patterns, AI algorithms can identify opportunities for energy savings, optimize resource allocation, and implement energy-efficient strategies, leading to improved sustainability and reduced operational costs.
- Intelligent Resource Management: AI enables intelligent resource management in 6G-enabled IoT networks. By analyzing network conditions, device capabilities, and user requirements, AI algorithms can optimize resource allocation, bandwidth utilization, and network performance, ensuring efficient use of network resources.

- Predictive Maintenance: AI-powered predictive maintenance is a critical application in 6G-enabled IoT. By analyzing data from IoT sensors and applying machine learning algorithms, AI can predict equipment failures or maintenance needs in advance. This allows for proactive maintenance, minimizing downtime and optimizing asset utilization.
- Edge Intelligence: AI at the edge is an important aspect of 6G-enabled IoT. By deploying AI algorithms directly on IoT devices or at the network edge, real-time data processing and decision-making can occur closer to the data source. This reduces latency, conserves network bandwidth, and enables faster response times for time-sensitive applications.
- Autonomous Decision-Making: AI enables autonomous decision-making in 6G-enabled IoT systems. By combining sensor data, machine learning, and decision algorithms, AI can automate decision-making processes, allowing IoT devices to take actions and make intelligent choices based on predefined rules or learned patterns.
- Natural Language Processing and Human-Machine Interaction: AI techniques, including natural language processing (NLP) and speech recognition, enable seamless human-machine interaction in 6G-enabled IoT systems. Voice commands, chatbots, and virtual assistants allow users to interact with IoT devices and services in a more intuitive and natural way.

Hence, the integration of AI in 6G-enabled IoT enhances the capabilities of IoT devices, improves operational efficiency, enables intelligent decision-making, and enhances user experiences. AI-driven analytics and automation are essential for unlocking the full potential of IoT data and realizing the transformative benefits of 6G-enabled IoT applications.

4.2 Integration of AI and Digital Twins in 6G-Enabled IoT

The integration of AI and digital twins in 6G-enabled IoT systems brings numerous benefits and advancements. Here's how AI and digital twins can be integrated in the context of 6G-enabled IoT:

- Enhanced Analytics and Predictive Capabilities: AI algorithms can analyze the data collected from IoT devices and sensors, and provide advanced analytics and predictive information. By combining AI with digital twins, organizations can use the virtual models and real-time data to train AI models and make accurate predictions about the behavior, performance, and maintenance needs of physical assets.
- Real-time Monitoring and Control: AI-powered analytics can continuously monitor the data from IoT devices and compare it with the digital twin models. This enables real-time monitoring and control of physical assets or processes. AI algorithms can detect anomalies, identify performance issues, and trigger automated actions or alerts based on predefined thresholds, ensuring optimal operations and proactive maintenance.
- Simulation and Optimization: Digital twins provide a virtual environment to simulate and optimize various applications. By incorporating AI techniques, organizations can run simulations and use machine learning algorithms to identify optimal settings, configurations, or strategies. This helps in optimizing resource allocation, improving efficiency, and predicting the impact of changes before implementing them in the real world.
- Autonomous Decision-making: AI algorithms can use the real-time data from IoT devices and digital twins to make autonomous decisions. By continuously analyzing the data, AI systems can

take actions, adjust parameters, or optimize operations in real-time, based on predefined rules or learned patterns. This enables autonomous decision-making, reducing human intervention and improving overall efficiency.

- Predictive Maintenance and Asset Management: AI algorithms integrated with digital twins can predict equipment failures or maintenance needs. By analyzing historical data, sensor readings, and contextual information, AI systems can identify patterns and predict when maintenance should be performed, allowing for proactive maintenance and minimizing downtime. This leads to improved asset management and cost savings.
- Context-aware Services and Personalization: AI algorithms combined with digital twins enable context-aware services and personalization. By analyzing real-time data from IoT devices and considering the virtual models, AI systems can provide tailored recommendations, personalized experiences, and adaptive services based on the specific context and preferences of users.
- Continuous Learning and Optimization: AI algorithms can continuously learn from the data collected from IoT devices and digital twins, improving their performance over time. By using machine learning and reinforcement learning techniques, AI systems can adapt, optimize their models, and refine their decision-making processes, leading to continuous improvement and enhanced efficiency.

Note that the integration of AI and digital twins in 6G-enabled IoT systems enhances the capabilities of IoT devices, enables real-time decision-making, improves operational efficiency, and drives innovation across industries (Goyal & Tyagi, 2020; Nair, Tyagi, & Sreenath, 2021; Tyagi & Bansal, 2023; Abraham et al., 2021; Tyagi, A. K, 2022). It brings together the power of AI algorithms for data analysis, prediction, and automation, and the virtual modeling capabilities of digital twins, resulting in more intelligent and adaptive IoT systems.

5. CYBERSECURITY IN 6G-ENABLED IOT TECHNOLOGY

5.1 Security Challenges in 6G-Enabled IoT Technology

Based on the general trends and challenges observed in the security of IoT technology, we can anticipate some potential security challenges that may arise with the integration of 6G and IoT. Here are a few examples:

- Massive Scale: 6G-enabled IoT is expected to support a significantly larger number of connected devices compared to previous generations. Managing the security of a massive IoT ecosystem poses challenges in terms of authentication, encryption, and secure communication between billions of devices and the network.
- Device Vulnerabilities: The large number of IoT devices, including sensors, actuators, and edge devices, may have inherent security vulnerabilities due to limitations in resources, lack of proper security controls, or inadequate software development practices. These vulnerabilities could be exploited by attackers to gain unauthorized access, manipulate data, or disrupt services.
- Data Privacy and Integrity: IoT devices collect and transmit large amount of sensitive data. Ensuring the privacy and integrity of this data becomes critical in 6G-enabled IoT (Rekha, Malik,

Tyagi et al, 2020; Tyagi, 2016). Any compromise in data privacy could lead to unauthorized access, data breaches, or misuse of personal information.

- Firmware and Software Security: IoT devices often have limited computing resources and may rely on firmware or software that is not frequently updated or patched. This can result in outdated or unpatched software, making devices more susceptible to attacks targeting known vulnerabilities.
- Network Security: The integration of 6G networks with IoT devices introduces new security challenges at the network level. Issues such as secure network access, secure data transmission, network segmentation, and isolation of critical services from non-critical ones become important to prevent unauthorized access and protect the network from potential attacks.
- Supply Chain Security: The complex supply chain involved in manufacturing IoT devices can introduce security risks. Tampering with devices, unauthorized modifications, or the inclusion of malicious components during the manufacturing process could lead to compromised devices that pose security threats to the entire IoT ecosystem.
- Interoperability and Standards: Interoperability between different IoT devices, platforms, and protocols is essential for seamless communication and functionality. However, differences in security implementations and standards across devices and platforms can introduce vulnerabilities and create challenges in ensuring consistent security measures throughout the IoT ecosystem.
- Distributed Denial of Service (DDoS) Attacks: IoT devices can be hijacked and used as part of a botnet to launch DDoS attacks, overwhelming network resources and causing service disruptions. With the increased number of connected devices in 6G-enabled IoT (Pal et al., 2022), the potential impact of DDoS attacks could be even more significant.
- Trust and Identity Management: Establishing trust and managing identities of IoT devices, applications, and users is important for secure communication and access control. Ensuring secure authentication, authorization, and proper identity management mechanisms becomes essential to prevent unauthorized access and malicious activities.
- Resilience and Continuity: 6G-enabled IoT systems may be used in critical applications such as healthcare, transportation, or industrial control systems. Ensuring the resilience and continuity of these systems in the face of cyber-attacks, natural disasters, or other disruptions becomes a significant security challenge.

Note that the security challenges in 6G-enabled IoT technology will likely evolve as the technology develops and standards mature. Researchers, industry experts, and policymakers will need to work collaboratively to address these challenges and develop robust security measures to protect the integrity, privacy, and reliability of 6G-enabled IoT systems.

5.2 Authentication and Access Control in 6G-Enabled IoT Technology

Authentication and access control are critical aspects of ensuring the security of 6G-enabled IoT technology. With the integration of billions of IoT devices in 6G networks, establishing the identity of devices and individuals, and managing access to resources becomes essential to prevent unauthorized access and protect sensitive data. Here are some considerations for authentication and access control in 6G-enabled IoT:

- Strong Device Authentication: IoT devices should undergo a secure and robust authentication process to verify their identity before accessing the network or interacting with other devices. This can involve using cryptographic keys, certificates, or unique identifiers to ensure that only authorized and trusted devices can connect to the network.
- Secure Communication Protocols: Implementing secure communication protocols, such as Transport Layer Security (TLS), is important for ensuring confidentiality, integrity, and authenticity of data exchanged between IoT devices and the network. Encryption and digital signatures can be employed to protect data during transit.
- Mutual Authentication: In addition to device authentication, mutual authentication can be implemented to verify the identity of both the device and the network or application it is connecting to. This two-way authentication helps prevent unauthorized devices or networks from gaining access to each other.
- Access Control Policies: Implementing access control policies based on the principle of least privilege is essential to limit the actions and resources that IoT devices can access. Access control mechanisms can include role-based access control (RBAC), attribute-based access control (ABAC), or other access control models depending on the specific requirements of the IoT ecosystem.
- Fine-Grained Access Control: IoT devices may require access to different resources or services based on their specific capabilities and responsibilities. Fine-grained access control enables granular control over which resources or services a device can access, helping to prevent unauthorized access and potential misuse.
- Secure Identity and Credential Management: Establishing and managing identities, authentication credentials, and access control policies for IoT devices is critical. Robust identity and credential management systems can include secure storage and distribution of cryptographic keys, certificate management, and revocation mechanisms to ensure the integrity of the IoT ecosystem.
- Multi-Factor Authentication: Employing multi-factor authentication (MFA) can enhance the security of IoT devices. MFA combines multiple authentication factors, such as something the device knows (e.g., password), something the device has (e.g., a physical token), or something the device is (e.g., biometrics), to strengthen the authentication process and reduce the risk of unauthorized access (Dutta et al., 2023; Ranchhodbhai & Tripathi, 2019).
- Continuous Monitoring and Auditing: Implementing continuous monitoring and auditing mechanisms helps detect and respond to potential security breaches or anomalous behavior in real-time. Monitoring can include device behavior analysis, anomaly detection, and intrusion detection systems to identify potential threats or unauthorized activities.
- Secure Over-the-Air (OTA) Updates: Implementing secure OTA update mechanisms ensures that IoT devices receive patches, security updates, or firmware upgrades in a secure and trusted manner. This helps address vulnerabilities and ensures that devices have the latest security measures in place.
- User Access Control: In addition to device-level access control, managing access and permissions for users interacting with IoT devices or accessing IoT services is important. Implementing strong authentication mechanisms, user roles, and access control policies for user interactions with IoT systems enhances overall security.

Hence, to consider these authentication and access control measures during the design and implementation of 6G-enabled IoT systems to build a secure and trusted IoT ecosystem. Additionally, continuous monitoring, vulnerability assessments, and regular security updates are essential to adapt to emerging threats and maintain the security of 6G-enabled IoT technology.

5.3 Data Privacy and Confidentiality in 6G-Enabled IoT Technology

Data privacy and confidentiality are important aspects of ensuring the security and trustworthiness of 6G-enabled IoT technology (Agarwal & Tripathi, 2022; Midha et al., 2017). As 6G networks and IoT devices continue to evolve, it becomes increasingly important to protect the privacy of sensitive data generated by IoT devices and ensure that the data remains confidential. Here are some considerations for data privacy and confidentiality in 6G-enabled IoT:

- Data Minimization: Adopt a data minimization approach by collecting and storing only the necessary data required for the intended purpose. Minimizing the collection and retention of personal or sensitive data reduces the potential risks associated with data breaches or unauthorized access.
- Data Encryption: Apply strong encryption mechanisms to protect data at rest and in transit. Encryption algorithms and protocols, such as Advanced Encryption Standard (AES) or Transport Layer Security (TLS), can be employed to ensure that data remains confidential and is accessible only to authorized parties.
- Secure Data Storage: Implement secure storage mechanisms for IoT data to prevent unauthorized access or data leakage. This can include secure databases, encrypted file systems, or hardware-based security modules to safeguard sensitive data stored on IoT devices or in cloud-based environments.
- Secure Data Transfer: Employ secure communication protocols and encryption mechanisms to protect data as it is transmitted between IoT devices, gateways, and the network infrastructure. This ensures that data remains confidential and cannot be intercepted or tampered with during transmission.
- User Consent and Transparency: Obtain explicit user consent for collecting and processing their personal data, and provide clear and transparent information about how their data will be used. Users should have the ability to understand and control the data collected by IoT devices and the option to revoke consent if desired.
- Anonymization and Pseudonymization: Anonymize or pseudonymize data whenever possible to protect the privacy of individuals. This can involve removing or obfuscating personally identifiable information (PII) or using pseudonyms to ensure that data cannot be directly linked to specific individuals.
- Access Controls and Authentication: Implement strong access controls and authentication mechanisms to ensure that only authorized individuals or systems can access and process sensitive IoT data. This includes role-based access control (RBAC), multi-factor authentication (MFA), and user-specific access privileges.
- Secure Identity and Credential Management: Establish secure identity and credential management systems to ensure that only authorized devices or users can access and process IoT data. This includes secure storage and distribution of cryptographic keys, certificates, and robust identity verification processes.

- Data Breach Response and Incident Management: Develop and implement robust incident response plans and procedures to address potential data breaches or security incidents. This includes timely detection, containment, and mitigation of breaches, as well as notification and communication with affected parties.
- Compliance with Privacy Regulations: Adhere to applicable privacy regulations and standards, such as the General Data Protection Regulation (GDPR), to ensure that data privacy and confidentiality requirements are met. Understand and comply with the specific legal and regulatory frameworks that govern data protection in the relevant jurisdictions.

Hence, by implementing these measures, stakeholders involved in 6G-enabled IoT technology can enhance data privacy and confidentiality, building trust among users and ensuring that sensitive data is protected throughout the IoT ecosystem. Continuous monitoring, regular security assessments, and staying updated with evolving privacy regulations are essential to maintain data privacy in a rapidly evolving technological landscape.

5.4 Threat Detection and Incident Response in 6G-Enabled IoT Technology

Threat detection and incident response are important components of ensuring the security and resilience of 6G-enabled IoT technology. As the complexity and scale of IoT ecosystems increase with the integration of 6G networks, it becomes essential to have effective mechanisms in place to detect and respond to potential threats and security incidents. Here are some considerations for threat detection and incident response in 6G-enabled IoT:

- Threat Intelligence: Establish mechanisms to gather and analyze threat intelligence specific to the 6G-enabled IoT landscape. Stay updated on emerging threats, vulnerabilities, and attack techniques targeting IoT devices and networks. Collaborate with industry forums, security vendors, and research organizations to collect informationf of the latest threats.
- Anomaly Detection: Implement anomaly detection techniques to identify abnormal behavior patterns in IoT devices and networks. Deviations from normal behavior can indicate potential security incidents or the presence of malicious activities. Machine learning algorithms and behavioral analytics can help in identifying anomalies and raising alerts.
- Intrusion Detection and Prevention: Deploy intrusion detection and prevention systems (IDPS) to monitor network traffic and detect potential intrusions or unauthorized access attempts. IDPS solutions can analyze network packets, signatures, and behavior patterns to identify malicious activities and trigger appropriate response measures.
- Endpoint Security: Implement robust security measures on IoT endpoints to detect and prevent malicious activities at the device level. This can include endpoint protection platforms (EPP), antivirus software, integrity monitoring, and vulnerability management solutions to ensure the security of individual devices.
- Security Information and Event Management (SIEM): Implement a SIEM system to aggregate and analyze security event logs and data from various IoT devices and network components. SIEM can provide real-time visibility into security incidents, facilitate correlation of events, and enable faster incident response.

- Incident Response Planning: Develop and document a comprehensive incident response plan specific to 6G-enabled IoT technology. The plan should outline roles and responsibilities, communication procedures, containment measures, forensics processes, and recovery strategies in the event of a security incident.
- Incident Response Team: Establish a dedicated incident response team comprising individuals with expertise in IoT security, network security, forensics, and incident management. The team should be trained and equipped to handle security incidents promptly and effectively.
- Incident Mitigation and Containment: In the event of a security incident, take immediate measures to contain the impact and prevent further propagation of the incident. This may involve isolating affected devices or segments of the network, disabling compromised accounts, or temporarily suspending affected services.
- Forensics and Investigation: Conduct thorough forensic analysis to understand the root cause of security incidents, determine the extent of compromise, and gather evidence for potential legal action. Preserve relevant logs, data, and artifacts to support the investigation and aid in remediation efforts.
- Lessons Learned and Continuous Improvement: After each security incident, conduct a post-incident review to identify lessons learned and areas for improvement in threat detection, incident response processes, and security controls. Use this feedback to enhance security measures and update incident response plans accordingly.

Note that by incorporating these practices, organizations can enhance their ability to detect and respond to security threats in 6G-enabled IoT technology. Continuous monitoring, threat intelligence sharing, and regular training and awareness programs are essential to stay ahead of emerging threats and ensure the resilience of IoT ecosystems.

6. CYBERSECURITY AND RESILIENCE IN 6G-ENABLED IOT TECHNOLOGY

6.1 Security and Resilience Integration in 6G Networks

Integrating security and resilience is of paramount importance in 6G networks to ensure the protection of critical assets, maintain service continuity, and effectively respond to security threats and disruptions. Here are some key considerations for integrating security and resilience in 6G networks:

- Threat Intelligence and Risk Assessment: Conducting comprehensive threat intelligence and risk assessments helps identify potential security threats, vulnerabilities, and risks to the network infrastructure and services. This enables proactive security measures and resilience strategies to be implemented based on the identified risks.
- Secure Network Architecture: Designing a secure network architecture is fundamental to integrating security and resilience. This includes incorporating security mechanisms, such as firewalls, intrusion detection and prevention systems (IDPS), secure gateways, and encryption, at various layers of the network to protect against unauthorized access, data breaches, and other security threats
- Resilience in Authentication and Access Control: Implementing robust authentication and access control mechanisms is essential to ensure that only authorized entities can access network

resources. Integration of resilient authentication mechanisms, such as multi-factor authentication and biometrics, enhances security and reduces the risk of unauthorized access.
- Threat Detection and Incident Response: Deploying advanced threat detection systems, including behavior analytics, anomaly detection, and machine learning-based algorithms, helps identify security incidents and potential breaches in real-time. Integration of incident response processes enables prompt mitigation of security threats and rapid restoration of services.
- Data Privacy and Confidentiality: Implementing strong data privacy and confidentiality measures, such as encryption, access controls, and data anonymization techniques, safeguards sensitive information transmitted and stored within the network. Resilience in data privacy ensures compliance with privacy regulations and protects user data from unauthorized access or disclosure.
- Secure-by-Design Approach: Adopting a secure-by-design approach in the development and deployment of 6G networks ensures that security issues are incorporated from the outset. This includes designing secure protocols, APIs, and interfaces, conducting security testing and code reviews, and integrating secure software development practices throughout the development lifecycle.
- Continuous Monitoring and Analysis: Implementing real-time monitoring and analysis of network traffic, logs, and security events helps detect and respond to security incidents promptly. This includes monitoring for abnormal behavior, conducting network forensics, and using Security Information and Event Management (SIEM) solutions to aggregate and correlate security events.
- Resilient Encryption and Cryptography: Deploying resilient encryption and cryptography mechanisms safeguards sensitive data transmitted over the network. Integration of secure encryption algorithms, key management systems, and secure cryptographic protocols ensures the confidentiality and integrity of data, even in the face of sophisticated attacks.
- Security Awareness and Training: Promoting security awareness and providing regular training to network administrators, operators, and end-users is important. Educating stakeholders about security best practices, potential threats, and incident response procedures enhances the overall security posture and resilience of the network.
- Collaboration and Information Sharing: Establishing collaborative relationships with cybersecurity organizations, industry peers, and governmental agencies promotes information sharing and cooperation. This allows for the exchange of threat intelligence, best practices, and lessons learned, strengthening the collective security and resilience capabilities.

In summary, by integrating security and resilience throughout the design, implementation, and operation of 6G networks, stakeholders can establish strong security basics, mitigate risks, and ensure the uninterrupted delivery of secure services. This holistic approach enhances the overall security posture and resilience, making 6G networks more robust and capable of withstanding evolving security threats and disruptions.

6.2 Threat Intelligence and Predictive Analytics for 6G-Enabled IoT Technology

Threat intelligence and predictive analytics play important roles in ensuring the security and reliability of 6G-enabled IoT technology (Sai et al., 2023; Subasree & Sakthivel, 2022). By using these capabilities, organizations can proactively identify potential threats, mitigate risks, and enhance the overall security posture of their IoT deployments. Here's an overview of threat intelligence and predictive analytics in the context of 6G-enabled IoT:

6.2.1 Threat Intelligence

- Threat Monitoring: Continuous monitoring of IoT devices, networks, and systems to collect real-time data and identify potential security incidents or anomalies.
- Vulnerability Assessment: Regular assessment of IoT devices and infrastructure to identify vulnerabilities that could be exploited by malicious actors.
- Information Sharing: Collaboration with industry peers, security vendors, and cybersecurity organizations to share threat intelligence and stay informed about emerging threats and attack trends.
- Threat Hunting: Proactive searching for signs of malicious activity within the IoT environment, using techniques such as log analysis, behavior analytics, and anomaly detection.
- Dark Web Monitoring: Monitoring underground forums, marketplaces, and other illicit platforms to gather intelligence on potential IoT-related threats and attacks.

6.2.2 Predictive Analytics

- Data Analysis: Analyzing large volumes of IoT data, including device telemetry, network traffic, and user behavior, to identify patterns and indicators of potential security threats.
- Machine Learning and AI: Applying machine learning algorithms and AI techniques to detect anomalies, predict potential security incidents, and automate threat detection and response.
- Behavioral Analytics: Analyzing the behavior of IoT devices and users to establish baselines and identify deviations that may indicate suspicious or malicious activity.
- Predictive Maintenance: Using predictive analytics to identify potential failures or vulnerabilities in IoT devices or infrastructure, allowing proactive maintenance or security patching to prevent or mitigate risks.
- Risk Scoring: Assigning risk scores to IoT devices or network entities based on historical data, contextual information, and threat intelligence, enabling prioritization of security measures and resource allocation.

6.2.3 Threat Detection and Response

- Real-time Alerting: Generating real-time alerts or notifications based on predefined security policies, abnormal behavior, or indicators of compromise, allowing for prompt incident response.
- Automated Incident Response: Integrating predictive analytics with automated incident response mechanisms to enable swift and automated actions in response to identified threats or attacks.
- Threat Intelligence Feeds: Integrating threat intelligence feeds and APIs to enrich security analytics with up-to-date information on known threats, malware signatures, or malicious IP addresses.
- Threat Visualization: Presenting threat intelligence and predictive analytics results in visual formats, such as dashboards or heat maps, to provide intuitive information and facilitate decision-making.

- Forensic Analysis: Conducting post-incident forensic analysis by correlating IoT data, network logs, and security events to determine the root cause of a security breach and prevent future incidents.

Note that by considering threat intelligence and predictive analytics, organizations can gain actionable information, which improve incident response times, and better anticipate and prevent security breaches in 6G-enabled IoT technology. These capabilities contribute to the overall security and resilience of IoT ecosystems, protecting critical assets, data, and services from emerging threats and vulnerabilities.

6.3 Blockchain for Secure Transactions and Auditing for 6G-Enabled IoT Technology

Blockchain technology offers a promising solution for secure transactions and auditing in 6G-enabled IoT technology (Gomathi et al., 2023; Midha & Tripathi, 2020; Hura et al., 2021; Midha & Triptahi, 2019; . A. K. et al., 2023; Tyagi, 2022; Tyagi, 2023; Tyagi, A. K, 2022). By considering/ using the inherent properties of blockchain, such as decentralization, immutability, and transparency, organizations can enhance the security and accountability of IoT transactions and data management. Here's how blockchain can be applied for these purposes (refer figure 5):

6.3.1 Secure Transactions

- Decentralized Architecture: Blockchain operates on a decentralized network of nodes, eliminating the need for a central authority. This ensures that no single entity has control over the entire network, reducing the risk of single points of failure or malicious attacks.
- Smart Contracts: Smart contracts are self-executing contracts with predefined conditions and rules. In the context of IoT, smart contracts can automate and secure transactions between IoT devices, ensuring that predefined conditions are met before the transaction is executed.
- Trustless Environment: Blockchain's consensus mechanisms, such as Proof-of-Work (PoW) or Proof-of-Stake (PoS), create a trustless environment where transactions are verified and recorded without the need for trust in a central authority.
- Data Integrity: Transactions recorded on the blockchain are immutable, meaning they cannot be altered or deleted once validated. This ensures the integrity and authenticity of IoT transactions, reducing the risk of fraud or data tampering.

6.3.2 Auditing and Transparency

- Immutability: As mentioned earlier, data stored on the blockchain cannot be altered or deleted. This feature ensures that audit trails and transaction histories remain transparent and verifiable over time.
- Real-time Data Access: Blockchain enables real-time access to transaction data, allowing stakeholders to monitor and audit IoT transactions and events as they occur.
- Permissioned Blockchains: In some use cases, a permissioned blockchain can be used to restrict access to authorized parties only, ensuring that auditing activities are conducted by trusted entities.

Figure 5. Blockchain and 6G: Applications, benefits, and challenges

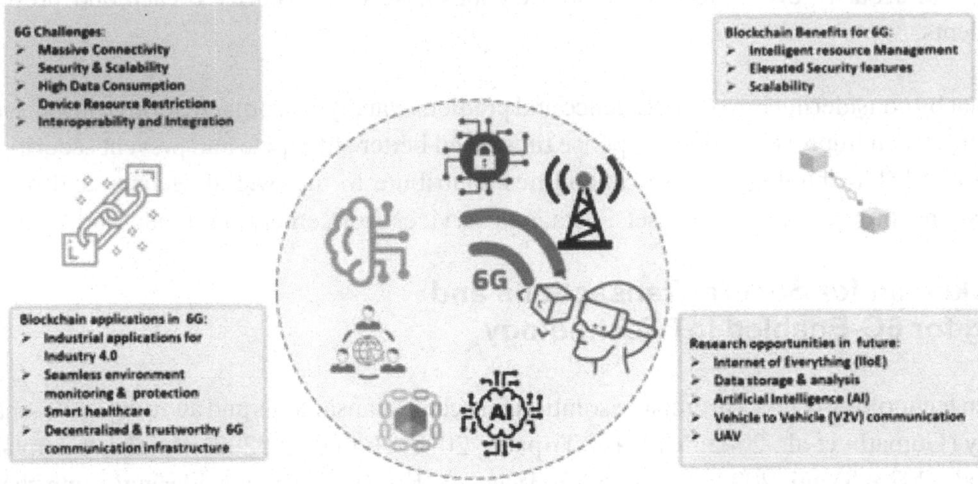

- Event Logging: IoT devices can log events and transactions directly onto the blockchain, creating an auditable trail of data interactions and ensuring transparency in the entire data lifecycle.

6.3.3 Data Security and Privacy

- Encryption: Blockchain can be used in conjunction with encryption techniques to protect sensitive data transmitted between IoT devices and recorded on the blockchain.
- Identity Management: Blockchain-based identity management solutions enable secure authentication and authorization of IoT devices and users, ensuring that only legitimate entities participate in transactions.
- Data Access Control: Through smart contracts and permissioned blockchains, organizations can control data access, specifying who can read or write data to the blockchain, enhancing data privacy.

6.3.4 Scalability and Efficiency

- Layer 2 Solutions: To address scalability challenges associated with the high transaction volume in IoT, layer 2 solutions like sidechains or state channels can be employed to process off-chain transactions while still benefiting from the security of the main blockchain.
- Consensus Mechanism Optimization: Selecting appropriate consensus mechanisms, such as delegated PoS (DPoS) or sharding, can improve the efficiency and transaction throughput of the blockchain network.

Note that implementing blockchain for secure transactions and auditing in 6G-enabled IoT technology introduces a robust and transparent framework for managing IoT interactions (Gomathi et al., 2023; . A. K. et al., 2023; Tyagi, 2022; Tyagi, 2023). By using the decentralized and immutable nature of blockchain, organizations can enhance security, data integrity, and overall trust in IoT transactions, making the technology more reliable and suitable for critical applications in the 6G era.

6.4 Trust Management and Distributed Consensus for 6G-Enabled IoT Technology

Trust management and distributed consensus are important aspects of 6G-enabled IoT technology, ensuring secure and reliable communication, coordination, and decision-making among interconnected IoT devices. Here's an overview of how trust management and distributed consensus can be applied in the context of 6G-enabled IoT:

6.4.1 Trust Management

- Identity and Authentication: Establishing the trustworthiness of IoT devices and entities through robust identity management and authentication mechanisms. This involves verifying the identity of devices, ensuring secure communication channels, and validating the integrity and authenticity of exchanged data.
- Reputation Systems: Employing reputation systems to assess the trustworthiness of IoT devices based on their past behavior, performance, and interactions within the network. Reputation scores can help determine the level of trust placed in a device and influence decision-making processes.
- Trust Models: Implementing trust models, such as direct trust or indirect trust models, to evaluate the trustworthiness of devices based on factors such as historical interactions, recommendations from trusted entities, or observed behavior patterns.
- Trust Establishment and Update: Establishing trust relationships between devices or entities through secure protocols and mechanisms. Regularly updating trust information based on ongoing interactions and feedback from the network enhances trust management capabilities.

6.4.2 Distributed Consensus

- Consensus Algorithms: Deploying distributed consensus algorithms, such as Proof-of-Work (PoW), Proof-of-Stake (PoS), or Practical Byzantine Fault Tolerance (PBFT), to achieve agreement and coordination among IoT devices. Consensus algorithms ensure that devices reach a common understanding despite the presence of faulty or malicious nodes.
- Fault Tolerance: Designing fault-tolerant consensus mechanisms that can withstand node failures, network partitions, or malicious attacks. This enables the IoT network to continue functioning reliably even in the presence of disruptions or compromised devices.
- Scalability and Efficiency: Employing consensus mechanisms that can scale to accommodate the increasing number of IoT devices and their communication requirements. Optimizing consensus algorithms for efficiency helps reduce computational and communication overhead in resource-constrained IoT environments.
- Privacy-Preserving Consensus: Exploring privacy-preserving consensus mechanisms that allow devices to reach consensus while protecting sensitive data or maintaining the privacy of participants. Techniques like zero-knowledge proofs, homomorphic encryption, or secure multi-party computation can be employed to achieve privacy in consensus protocols.

6.4.3 Trust and Consensus Integration

Trust-Based Consensus: Integrating trust management mechanisms into the consensus process to influence decision-making and agreement among devices. Trust scores or reputation information can be considered in the consensus algorithm to prioritize or weight the opinions of more trusted devices.

- Trust-Enhanced Security: Considering trust information to enhance security measures within the IoT network. For example, devices with higher trust levels may have greater access privileges, while devices with lower trust scores may undergo additional security checks or validations.
- Dynamic Trust and Consensus: Adapting trust and consensus mechanisms dynamically based on the evolving network conditions, device behavior, and changing trustworthiness of entities. This enables the network to adjust its decision-making processes in response to fluctuating trust levels or emerging threats.

In summary, by integrating trust management and distributed consensus mechanisms, 6G-enabled IoT technology can establish secure and reliable communication channels, facilitate coordinated decision-making, and ensure the integrity and trustworthiness of IoT interactions. These mechanisms are essential for building resilient, trustworthy, and scalable IoT ecosystems in the 6G era.

6.5 Regulatory and Policy Issues for 6G-Enabled IoT Technology

The deployment and operation of 6G-enabled IoT technology require careful consideration of regulatory and policy frameworks to address various challenges and ensure the responsible and ethical use of these technologies. Here are some key regulatory and policy issues for 6G-enabled IoT:

- Data Protection and Privacy: Establishing robust data protection regulations and privacy frameworks to safeguard the personal and sensitive data collected and processed by IoT devices. This includes defining clear guidelines on data ownership, consent requirements, data minimization, and ensuring compliance with relevant data protection laws, such as the General Data Protection Regulation (GDPR).
- Security and Cybersecurity: Developing regulatory frameworks that enforce minimum security standards for IoT devices and networks. This includes guidelines for secure device authentication, data encryption, access controls, vulnerability management, and incident response. Policies should also encourage industry collaboration, information sharing, and adherence to cybersecurity best practices.
- Spectrum Allocation: Allocating appropriate spectrum resources for 6G networks to support the massive connectivity and bandwidth requirements of IoT devices. Regulatory bodies need to establish frameworks for spectrum management, avoiding interference and ensuring efficient use of available frequencies.
- Interoperability and Standards: Encouraging the adoption of open standards and promoting interoperability among IoT devices and systems. Regulatory policies can play a role in mandating compliance with specific protocols, promoting seamless integration, and fostering innovation through open APIs and interfaces.

- Liability and Accountability: Defining liability frameworks to address potential damages or harms caused by IoT devices or system failures. Clear guidelines on liability allocation among stakeholders, including device manufacturers, IoT service providers, and network operators, can ensure accountability and protect end-users.
- Consumer Protection: Implementing consumer protection policies to safeguard the interests and rights of end-users in IoT transactions and services. This includes regulations on fair pricing, transparency in service provision, clear product labeling, and mechanisms for dispute resolution.
- Environmental Impact: Considering the environmental impact of 6G-enabled IoT deployments and encouraging sustainable practices. Regulatory frameworks can promote energy-efficient IoT devices, e-waste management, and adherence to environmental standards during the manufacturing, use, and disposal of IoT products.
- Governance and Oversight: Establishing regulatory bodies or mechanisms to oversee and enforce compliance with IoT regulations and policies. These bodies can monitor the implementation of security measures, privacy practices, and ethical guidelines, as well as enforce penalties for non-compliance.
- International Collaboration: Promoting international cooperation and harmonization of regulations to facilitate cross-border IoT deployments. Encouraging collaboration among regulatory bodies, standardization organizations, and industry stakeholders can foster interoperability, knowledge exchange, and consistency in regulatory approaches.

Note that regulatory and policy issues for 6G-enabled IoT technology will vary across jurisdictions and may evolve as the technology landscape advances. Flexibility, adaptability, and ongoing dialogue between policymakers, industry players, and other stakeholders are key to developing effective regulatory frameworks that balance innovation, security, privacy, and societal benefits in the 6G era.

7. FUTURE DIRECTIONS AND RESEARCH OPPORTUNITIES OF 6G-ENABLED IOT TECHNOLOGY

7.1 Advanced Threat Detection and Mitigation Techniques of 6G-Enabled IoT Technology

6G technology is still in the research and development phase, and its specific characteristics and features are not yet fully defined. However, we discussed here few advanced threat detection and mitigation techniques that are commonly employed in IoT security. These techniques can be expected to be relevant for 6G-enabled IoT technology as well.

- Device Authentication: Ensuring the authenticity of IoT devices is important. Techniques like digital certificates, secure boot, and two-factor authentication can be used to verify the identity of devices before granting access to the network.
- Encryption: Strong encryption protocols, such as Transport Layer Security (TLS) and Advanced Encryption Standard (AES), can be used to secure the communication between IoT devices and the network. This ensures that data transmitted between devices is protected from unauthorized access.

- Intrusion Detection Systems (IDS): IDS can monitor network traffic and identify suspicious activities or anomalies. Advanced IDS systems use machine learning algorithms to detect and respond to emerging threats in real-time.
- Behavior Analytics: Analyzing the behavior of IoT devices can help identify abnormal patterns that may indicate a security breach. Machine learning algorithms can be used to establish baseline behavior and detect deviations, enabling early detection of potential threats.
- Secure Firmware Updates: Regular firmware updates can address security vulnerabilities. Implementing secure over-the-air (OTA) firmware update mechanisms ensures that updates are authenticated, tamper-proof, and free from malware.
- Containerization: Containerization involves isolating IoT applications and services in separate containers to limit the impact of a security breach. If one container is compromised, the attack is contained and does not spread to other parts of the system.
- Blockchain Technology: Blockchain can enhance the security of IoT networks by providing a decentralized and tamper-resistant ledger. It can be used for secure device identity management, secure data exchange, and ensuring data integrity.
- Threat Intelligence: Considering threat intelligence sources and sharing information about emerging threats among different organizations can improve the overall security posture of IoT networks. This can help identify new attack vectors and develop proactive security measures.
- Physical Security: Physical security measures, such as tamper-resistant hardware, secure storage, and access controls, play an important role in protecting IoT devices from physical attacks.

Note that the threat landscape is constantly evolving, and new vulnerabilities and attack vectors may emerge as technologies like 6G and advanced IoT systems develop. Therefore, it is essential to regularly update security measures and stay informed about the latest security practices to address emerging threats effectively.

7.2 Adaptive and Self-Healing Networks of 6G-Enabled IoT Technology

6G technology is still in the early stages of development, and specific details about its features and capabilities are not yet fully defined. So some information for 6G-enabled IoT technology is discussed as:

7.2.1 Adaptive Networks

- Dynamic Spectrum Access: Adaptive networks can use dynamic spectrum access techniques to efficiently utilize the available frequency spectrum. This allows IoT devices to dynamically access different frequency bands based on real-time demand and interference conditions.
- Network Slicing: Network slicing enables the creation of multiple virtual networks on a shared physical infrastructure. This allows different IoT applications to have dedicated network slices tailored to their specific requirements, such as latency, bandwidth, and security, ensuring efficient resource utilization and optimal performance.
- Intelligent Resource Management: Adaptive networks can employ intelligent algorithms to manage network resources effectively. These algorithms can dynamically allocate resources based on traffic patterns, device capabilities, and quality-of-service requirements, ensuring optimal network performance and responsiveness.

- Machine Learning and Artificial Intelligence: By using machine learning and artificial intelligence techniques, adaptive networks can continuously analyze network data, predict future demand, and optimize network configurations to meet changing IoT application requirements (refer figure 6).

Figure 6. 6G and its expansion with other technologies

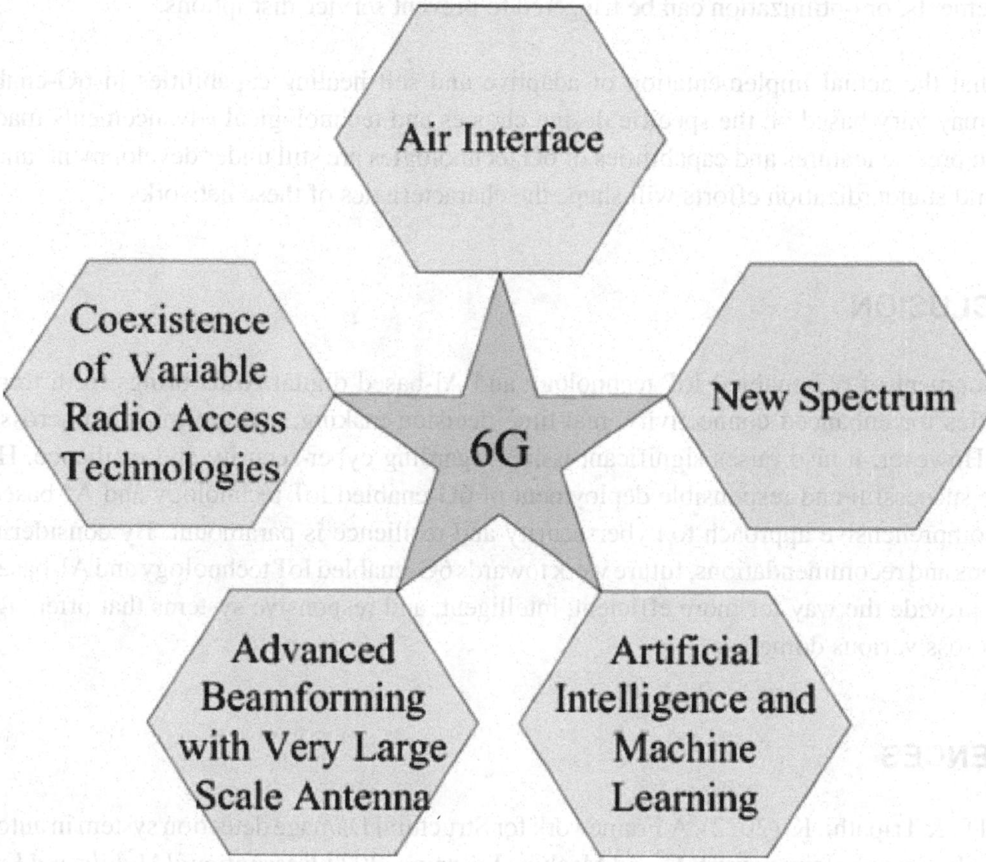

7.2.2 Self-Healing Networks

- Fault Detection and Localization: Self-healing networks can incorporate mechanisms to detect faults or anomalies in real-time. These mechanisms can employ techniques like monitoring network performance metrics, analyzing device health data, and using machine learning algorithms to identify and locate network failures or abnormal behavior.
- Fault Isolation and Reconfiguration: Once a fault is detected, self-healing networks can automatically isolate the affected components or devices to prevent the fault from propagating further. They can then reconfigure the network by dynamically rerouting traffic or activating backup resources to maintain uninterrupted service.

- Redundancy and Resilience: Self-healing networks can incorporate redundant components or paths to ensure high availability and resilience. If a device or link fails, alternative routes or redundant devices can be activated automatically to maintain connectivity and service continuity.
- Proactive Maintenance: Self-healing networks can employ predictive analytics and monitoring to anticipate potential failures or performance degradation. By identifying issues before they cause significant problems, proactive maintenance actions such as firmware updates, component replacements, or optimization can be triggered to prevent service disruptions.

Note that the actual implementation of adaptive and self-healing capabilities in 6G-enabled IoT networks may vary based on the specific design choices and technological advancements made in the future. The precise features and capabilities of 6G technologies are still under development, and further research and standardization efforts will shape the characteristics of these networks.

8. CONCLUSION

The development of 6G-enabled IoT technology and AI-based digital twins brings forth tremendous opportunities for enhanced connectivity, real-time decision-making, and optimization across various domains. However, it also raises significant issues regarding cyber-security and resilience. Hence, to ensure the successful and responsible deployment of 6G-enabled IoT technology and AI-based digital twins, a comprehensive approach to cybersecurity and resilience is paramount. By considering these implications and recommendations, future work towards 6G-enabled IoT technology and AI-based digital twins can provide the way for more efficient, intelligent, and responsive systems that offer significant benefits across various domains.

REFERENCES

Agarwal, D., & Tripathi, K. (2022). A Framework for Structural Damage detection system in automobiles for flexible Insurance claim using IOT and Machine Learning. *2022 International Mobile and Embedded Technology Conference (MECON),* (pp. 5-8). IEEE. 10.1109/MECON53876.2022.9751889

Alaba, F. A., Othman, M., Hashem, I. A., & Alotaibi, F. (2017). Internet of Things security: A survey. *Journal of Network and Computer Applications*, *88*, 10–28. doi:10.1016/j.jnca.2017.04.002

Alam, F., Malik, H., & Yim, D. K. (2019). Towards Digital Twins for Internet of Things. In *2019 IEEE International Conference on Pervasive Computing and Communications Workshops (PerCom Workshops)* (pp. 38-43). IEEE.

George, T. T., & Tyagi, A. K. (2022). Reliable Edge Computing Architectures for Crowdsensing Applications. *2022 International Conference on Computer Communication and Informatics (ICCCI)*, (pp. 1-6). IEEE. 10.1109/ICCCI54379.2022.9740791

Gomathi, L., Mishra, A. K., & Tyagi, A. K. (2023). *Industry 5.0 for Healthcare 5.0: Opportunities, Challenges and Future Research Possibilities.* 2023 7th International Conference on Trends in Electronics and Informatics (ICOEI), Tirunelveli, India. 10.1109/ICOEI56765.2023.10125660

Goyal, D. & Tyagi, A. (2020). *A Look at Top 35 Problems in the Computer Science Field for the Next Decade*. Taylor and Francis. . doi:10.1201/9781003052098-40

Hussain, S., Ali, T., Tabassum, H., Kim, D. S., & Hussain, R. (2018). Digital Twin for Smart Manufacturing: A Review. *IEEE Access : Practical Innovations, Open Solutions*, *6*, 3948–3960.

Jajula, S. K., Tripathi, K., & Bajaj, S. B. (2023). Review of Detection of Packets Inspection and Attacks in Network Security. In P. Dutta, S. Chakrabarti, A. Bhattacharya, S. Dutta, & V. Piuri (Eds.), *Emerging Technologies in Data Mining and Information Security. Lecture Notes in Networks and Systems* (Vol. 491). Springer. doi:10.1007/978-981-19-4193-1_58

Lu, Y., Zhang, Y., Zhang, Y., & Zhang, D. (2017). AI-Driven Smart Digital Twins for Internet of Things: A Survey. In *2017 IEEE International Congress on Big Data (BigData Congress)* (pp. 154-161). IEEE.

Mahmood, A. N., & Hu, J. (2020). Digital Twins and Artificial Intelligence Models for Internet of Things: A Survey. *IEEE Access : Practical Innovations, Open Solutions*, *8*, 23022–23042.

Midha, S., Kaur, G., & Tripathi, K. "Cloud deep down — SWOT analysis," 2017 2nd International Conference on Telecommunication and Networks (TEL-NET), 2017, pp. 1-5, 10.1109/TEL-NET.2017.8343560

Midha, S., & Tripathi, K. (2020). Remotely Triggered Blackhole Routing in SDN for Handling DoS. In: Dutta, M., Krishna, C., Kumar, R., Kalra, M. (eds) *Proceedings of International Conference on IoT Inclusive Life (ICIIL 2019)*. Springer, Singapore. 10.1007/978-981-15-3020-3_1

Midha, S., & Tripathi, K. (2021). Extended Security in Heterogeneous Distributed SDN Architecture. In G. Hura, A. Singh, & L. Siong Hoe (Eds.), *Advances in Communication and Computational Technology. Lecture Notes in Electrical Engineering* (Vol. 668). Springer. doi:10.1007/978-981-15-5341-7_75

Midha, S., Tripathi, K., & Sharma, M. K. (2021, April). Practical Implications of Using Dockers on Virtualized SDN. *Webology.*, *18*(Special Issue 01), 312–330. doi:10.14704/WEB/V18SI01/WEB18062

Midha, S., & Triptahi, K. (2019). Extended TLS security and Defensive Algorithm in OpenFlow SDN. *2019 9th International Conference on Cloud Computing, Data Science & Engineering (Confluence)*, (pp. 141-146). IEEE. 10.1109/CONFLUENCE.2019.8776607

Mishra, A., & Sharma, S. K. (2019). Digital Twins: A Comprehensive Survey. *Journal of King Saud University-Computer and Information Sciences*.

Mishra, S., & Tyagi, A. K. (2022). The Role of Machine Learning Techniques in Internet of Things-Based Cloud Applications. In S. Pal, D. De, & R. Buyya (Eds.), *Artificial Intelligence-based Internet of Things Systems. Internet of Things (Technology, Communications and Computing)*. Springer. doi:10.1007/978-3-030-87059-1_4

Nair, M. N. (2023). 6G: Technology, Advancement, Barriers, and the Future. 6G-Enabled IoT and AI for Smart Healthcare. CRC Press.

Nair, M M. & Tyagi. A. K. (2023). "Blockchain technology for next-generation society: current trends and future opportunities for smart era", in the book: Blockchain Technology for Secure Social Media Computing,. DOI: . doi:10.1049/PBSE019E_ch11

Nair, M. M., Kumari, S., & Tyagi, A. K. (2021) Internet of Things, Cyber Physical System, and Data Analytics: Open Questions, Future Perspectives, and Research Areas. In: Goyal D., Gupta A.K., Piuri V., Ganzha M., Paprzycki M. (eds) *Proceedings of the Second International Conference on Information Management and Machine Intelligence*. Springer, Singapore. 10.1007/978-981-15-9689-6_36

Nair, M. M., & Tyagi, A. K. (2021). Privacy: History, Statistics, Policy, Laws, Preservation and Threat Analysis. Journal of Information Assurance & Security, 16(1), 24-34.

Nair, M. M., Tyagi, A. K., & Sreenath, N. (2021). The Future with Industry 4.0 at the Core of Society 5.0: Open Issues, Future Opportunities and Challenges. *2021 International Conference on Computer Communication and Informatics (ICCCI)*, (pp. 1-7). IEEE. 10.1109/ICCCI50826.2021.9402498

Nan, L., Wu, D., Zhu, J., Fan, Y., & Fan, S. (2018). Manufacturing in the age of artificial intelligence: An evolving perspective. *Journal of Manufacturing Science and Engineering*, *140*(4), 040801.

Ranchhodbhai P.N, & Tripathi K. (2019). Identifying and Improving the Malicious Behavior of Rushing and Blackhole Attacks using Proposed IDSAODV Protocol. *International Journal of Recent Technology and Engineering*, *8*(3), 6554-6562.

Rekha, G., Malik, S., Tyagi, A. K., & Nair, M. M. (2020). Intrusion Detection in Cyber Security: Role of Machine Learning and Data Mining in Cyber Security. *Advances in Science, Technology and Engineering Systems Journal*, *5*(3), 72–81. doi:10.25046/aj050310

Rekha, G., Tyagi, A. K., & Anuradha, N. (2020) Integration of Fog Computing and Internet of Things: An Useful Overview. In: Singh P., Kar A., Singh Y., Kolekar M., Tanwar S. (eds) *Proceedings of ICRIC 2019. Lecture Notes in Electrical Engineering*. Springer, Cham. 10.1007/978-3-030-29407-6_8

Rong, C., Zhang, D., & Yang, A. (2014). Edge computing in the Internet of Things. *IEEE Transactions on Industrial Informatics*, *10*(2), 1568–1576.

Sai, G. H., Tripathi, K., & Tyagi, A. K. (2023). Internet of Things-Based e-Health Care: Key Challenges and Recommended Solutions for Future. In: Singh, P.K., Wierzchoń, S.T., Tanwar, S., Rodrigues, J.J.P.C., Ganzha, M. (eds) *Proceedings of Third International Conference on Computing, Communications, and Cyber-Security*. Springer, Singapore. 10.1007/978-981-19-1142-2_37

Sheth, H. S. K., & Tyagi, A. K. (2022). Mobile Cloud Computing: Issues, Applications and Scope in COVID-19. In A. Abraham, N. Gandhi, T. Hanne, T. P. Hong, T. Nogueira Rios, & W. Ding (Eds.), *Intelligent Systems Design and Applications. ISDA 2021. Lecture Notes in Networks and Systems* (Vol. 418). Springer. doi:10.1007/978-3-030-96308-8_55

Somisetti, K. T., & Verma, J. K. (2020). Design, Implementation, and Controlling of a Humanoid Robot. *2020 International Conference on Computational Performance Evaluation (ComPE)*. (pp. 831-836). IEEE. 10.1109/ComPE49325.2020.9200020

Subasree, S., & Sakthivel, N. K. (2022). Combining the advantages of radiomic features based feature extraction and hyper parameters tuned RERNN using LOA for breast cancer classification. *Biomedical Signal Processing and Control, 72*. doi:10.1016/j.bspc.2021.103354

Tripathi, K., Pandey, M., & Verma, S. (2011). Comparison of reactive and proactive routing protocols for different mobility conditions in WSN. In *Proceedings of the 2011 International Conference on Communication, Computing & Security (ICCCS '11)*. Association for Computing Machinery, New York, NY, USA. 10.1145/1947940.1947974

Tyagi, A. K. (2022). *Using Multimedia Systems, Tools, and Technologies for Smart Healthcare Services*. IGI Global. doi:10.4018/978-1-6684-5741-2

Tyagi, A. K. (2023). Decentralized everything: Practical use of blockchain technology in future applications. In R. Pandey, S. Goundar, & S. Fatima (eds.), Distributed Computing to Blockchain. Academic Press. doi:10.1016/B978-0-323-96146-2.00010-3

Tyagi, A., Kukreja, S., Nair, M. M., & Tyagi, A. K. (2022). Machine Learning: Past, Present and Future. *NeuroQuantology : An Interdisciplinary Journal of Neuroscience and Quantum Physics, 20*(8). doi:10.14704/nq.2022.20.8.NQ44468

Tyagi, A. K. (2016, March). Article: Cyber Physical Systems (CPSs) – Opportunities and Challenges for Improving Cyber Security. [Published by Foundation of Computer Science] [FCS] [, NY, USA.]. *International Journal of Computer Applications, 137*(14), 19–27. doi:10.5120/ijca2016908877

Tyagi, A. K., & Bansal, R. (2023). A Step-To-Step Guide to Write a Quality Research Article. In: Abraham, A., Pllana, S., Casalino, G., Ma, K., Bajaj, A. (eds) Intelligent Systems Design and Applications. ISDA 2022. Lecture Notes in Networks and Systems. Springer, Cham. doi:10.1007/978-3-031-35510-3_36

Tyagi, A. K., Dananjayan, S., Agarwal, D., & Thariq Ahmed, H. F. (2023). Blockchain—Internet of Things Applications: Opportunities and Challenges for Industry 4.0 and Society 5.0. *Sensors (Basel), 23*(2), 947. doi:10.339023020947 PMID:36679743

Tyagi, A. K., Fernandez, T. F., Mishra, S., & Kumari, S. (2021). Intelligent Automation Systems at the Core of Industry 4.0. In A. Abraham, V. Piuri, N. Gandhi, P. Siarry, A. Kaklauskas, & A. Madureira (Eds.), *Intelligent Systems Design and Applications. ISDA 2020. Advances in Intelligent Systems and Computing* (Vol. 1351). Springer. doi:10.1007/978-3-030-71187-0_1

Tyagi, A. K., & Sreenath, N. (2023). Fog and Edge Computing in Navigation of Intelligent Transportation System. In *Intelligent Transportation Systems: Theory and Practice. Disruptive Technologies and Digital Transformations for Society 5.0*. Springer. doi:10.1007/978-981-19-7622-3_7

Tyagi, A. K. (2022). *Handbook of Research on Technical, Privacy, and Security Challenges in a Modern World*. IGI Global. doi:10.4018/978-1-6684-5250-9

Wu, D., Rosen, D. W., Wang, L., & Schaefer, D. (2016). Cloud-Based Design and Manufacturing: A New Paradigm in Digital Manufacturing and Design Innovation. *Computer Aided Design, 59*, 1–14. doi:10.1016/j.cad.2014.07.006

Yao, Y., Lin, X., Huang, K., Liu, Z., & Lu, X. (2020). Digital Twins for IoT-Enabled Smart Cities: A Survey. *IEEE Communications Surveys and Tutorials*, *22*(2), 1511–1555.

Zhao, F., & Yao, J. (2018). Digital Twin Driven Prognostics and Health Management for Complex Equipment. *Journal of Manufacturing Science and Engineering*, *140*(3), 030801.

Zhou, J., Chen, X., & Chen, C. (2020). Digital twin-driven decision-making method for production and maintenance planning in smart manufacturing. *Journal of Manufacturing Systems*, *56*, 238–253.

Chapter 17
Industry 4.0: Linking With Different Technologies – IoT, Big Data, AR and VR, and Blockchain

K. Vijay
Rajalakshmi Engineering College, India

S. Gnanavel
https://orcid.org/0000-0003-2344-0482
SRM Institute of Science and Technology, India

K. R Sowmia
Rajalakshmi Engineering College, India

R. Vijayakumar
https://orcid.org/0000-0002-6874-9275
Rajalakshmi Engineering College, India

Mahmoud Elsisi
National Kaohsiung University of Science and Technology, Taiwan

ABSTRACT

As the present, fourth generation of production, "Industry 4.0" describes the state of the art. Under this general term, you'll find a number of manufacturing, data-sharing, and automation technologies. Industry 4.0 is driving significant transformation across many different business sectors by focusing on improving process, resource utilisation, and efficiency. The internet revolution has had a dramatic impact on several B2C industries, including media, retail, and finance. The industrial sector, which includes manufacturing, energy, agriculture, transportation, and others, accounts for over two-thirds of global GDP. These sectors will be profoundly impacted by digital transformation initiatives during the next decade. The World Economic Forum predicts that the digital revolution, often known as the fourth industrial revolution, will have far-reaching consequences for our personal lives, professional life, and social connections.

DOI: 10.4018/979-8-3693-2081-5.ch017

1. INTRODUCTION

Four sorts of foundational disruptive technologies enable Industry 4.0 to bring these innovations to fruition all along the value chain: big data and machine learning; blockchain technology; artificial intelligence; virtual reality and augmented reality; and the Internet of Things. Within a few years of full implementation, the fourth industrial revolution will increase industrial productivity by at least 30 percent. Machine failure, quality control, productivity, and product costs have all seen significant reductions as industries have begun to implement AI (Rosati et al., 2023). Both businesses and individuals can benefit from AI. One benefit is that it increases the likelihood that customers will become paying subscribers to new offerings. However, it also opened up new possibilities for the manufacturing sector, including enhanced customer service, simplified maintenance, improved logistical monitoring, and an overall higher level of complexity. This allows businesses to better connect with their customers through digital channels like smart customer service, smart dealerships, and smart experience centres. Leveraging AI in industries also makes it simple to track and manage production and other services in real time. With the help of cutting-edge robotics and 3D printing technologies, AI-based automation in industries may also guarantee top-notch service. To sum up, AI is essential in many areas of Industry 4.0.

The five technologies that are the primary emphasis of this chapter are big data and machine learning, blockchain technology, artificial intelligence (AI), VR/AR, and the internet of things (IoT). The benefits and drawbacks of various data-related, communication-related, and security-related applications and procedures in Industry 4.0 are discussed in this chapter. Within the context of Industry 4.0, we introduce and extensively examine the applications of a wide range of Big Data and machine learning (ML), blockchain technology (Blockchain), artificial intelligence (AI), virtual reality (VR), and internet of things (IoT) techniques. This chapter identifies and analyses the most pressing technological, data-related, and security issues that must be resolved before Big Data and ML, Blockchain Technology, AI, VR/AR, and the Internet of Things (IoT) can be used successfully in Industry 4.0. In this chapter, we address the challenges of Industry 4.0 and offer directions for future study (Harini et al., 2018).

Devices and machines with intelligence Device (i), Edge (ii), Cyber (iii), Data Analytics (iv), and Application (v) are the five levels into which the functions of the Industry 4.0 ecosystem can be divided. All types of hardware, including computers, robotics, PLCs, controllers, and even smart watches, are included in the devices layer. Information transmitted from connected industrial machines via the ZigBee, wifi, and Bluetooth protocols of the physical layer is stored in the edge layer. The cyber layer's responsibilities include web service data processing and supply chain management. It also facilitates the use of secure services and products by connected devices. Certain machine learning techniques and cloud analytics are applied to IIoT data in the data analytics layer. Fig 1 shows the framework layers of Industry 4.0 as well its operations as explained earlier.

Big Data and ML

The IT industry has come a long way in its ability to process large data sets, including extraction, loading, and conversion. However, the value lies not in the quantity but in the insights that can be gained from it. Predictive analysis and machine learning can use this data to help businesses make better decisions..

Together, data and ML can look into the future and determine the likelihood of specific outcomes, such as future customer behaviour.

Figure 1. The Industry 4.0 framework's layers of smart industry operations

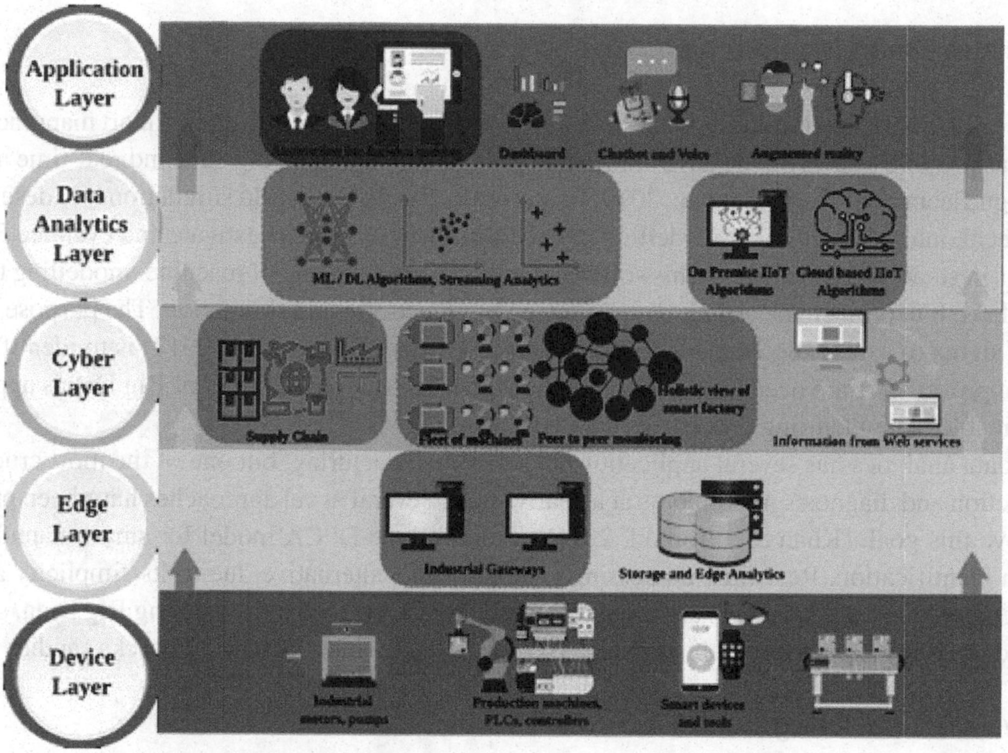

It is possible to foretell the chance that:

- a person who makes a purchase of some kind;
- a patient developing a certain illness,
- being impacted by current events in the economy, etc.

SEO experts can also benefit greatly from big data and AI because:

- Discover what the future holds for SEO,
- have a firm grasp on the fundamentals of digital marketing campaign design,
- You will be able to foresee conversion rates and adjust tactics for maximum results.

Website analytics, click-through rates, bounce rates, visitor demographics, etc., need to be regularly collected, so businesses must set up mechanisms to do so.

Big Data Applications in Industry 4.0

Big Data in Smart Manufacturing:

The ability of industrial machinery and robotic systems to learn from data enables "smart manufacturing," which has positive effects on the environment. In pervasive production, big data and real-time analytics play a significant role (Kerin & Pham, 2019; Ryalat et al., 2023). The hybrid simulation tool described by Nagadi et al. integrates different modelling methodologies in order to investigate and evaluate Big Data solutions in smart manufacturing. This software facilitates the mapping of machine, modelling tool, and accumulated blueprint characteristic data, followed by object-oriented simulation. The purpose of using lean six sigma to assess Big Data's effect on smart industries (Davies et al., 2017) is to identify places where improvements are needed and new directions to investigate in the field of Big Data's application to sustainable manufacturing processes.

Big data analytics has several applications in smart manufacturing, but one of the most crucial is in the detection and diagnosis of problems at an early stage. Several novel approaches have been presented to achieve this goal. (Khan & Turowski, 2016) introduced the DPCA model for smart manufacturing problem identification. Real-time processing is an attractive alternative due to its simplicity and ease of implementation, both of which are crucial in many Industry 4.0 use cases. Using Big Data, semantic data, and ontology expertise, (Trappey et al., 2017) describes a smart factory that packs candies to order.

Additive Manufacturing

By using additive manufacturing, businesses may quickly and cheaply create one-of-a-kind, sophisticated machine components or consumer goods on demand, with minimal waste and energy use. Predicting how much a finished product (a machine or machine part) will set you back is a difficult but crucial step in additive manufacturing. Smart enterprises can now accurately predict product prices using machine learning and Big Data techniques. However, the manufacturing knowledge/information required for precise predictions may be gleaned from the raw data created during the production and supply chain process.

Product/machine Design

Product and machine designs benefit from Big Data, AI, and ML methods (Eswaran & Raju Bahubalendruni, 2022). The function of human designers in modern enterprises may be reduced to merely providing directions and monitoring as AI and Big Data increasingly take over the design process. AI, aided by Big Data approaches for gleaning useful insights from existing data, will handle most design-related tasks. AI algorithms, for instance, can aid human designers in areas such as alternative discovery, risk assessment, sensor data incorporation, prototype generation, and supply chain process optimisation (Eswaran & Raju Bahubalendruni, 2022). There have already been several attempts along these lines. Data-driven product design is advocated, for instance, by (Priya, 2021). The writers also consider how Big Data might aid in product development and how data relates to the design process.

Big Data Methods in Industry 4.0

Manufacturing's Addiction to Real-Time Big Data Programmes can be executed locally, remotely, or on demand with version 4.0. Speed, bandwidth, access mechanisms, and storage of industrial Big Data all play a role in determining the necessary computing resources. Information may be gleaned from massive databases with the use of data analysis and visualisation technologies. Some of the most common approaches of analysis used with industrial Big Data are as follows:

Descriptive Analytics

Analysing historical company data, or "descriptive analytics," allows businesses to recognise trends and understand their causes.Analyses like these are extremely useful in decision-making since they reveal the advantages and disadvantages of a firm or a strategy after it has been put into practise for some time. Data for descriptive analysis can be gathered using one of two methods: (i) data aggregation or (ii) data mining (Lacko, 2022). Industry-specific data requires collection, aggregation, and analysis before it can be put to practical use (Lacko, 2022).

Predictive Analytics

Predictive analytics, allows firms to anticipate potential problems and take preventative measures by analysing past data. In a number of Industry 4.0 use cases, the ability to foresee and respond to future events in an industrial setting is of paramount importance. Predictive upkeep, product price, lifespan, and failure forecasting are just a few examples of where this technology has been useful. Companies could make accurate predictions about future machine patterns and behaviours with the help of statistical modelling, machine learning, and other advanced predictive analytic technologies. In addition, it aids the industrial control group in determining how best to plan out shipments, set up distribution centres, and arrange retail outlets to maximise output and revenue.

Prescriptive Analytics

Prescriptive analytics, allows corporations to improve decision-making by looking back at past data. It's worth noting that prescriptive analysis relies on predictive analysis to define a strategy for moving forward in light of the results of the latter. The modern business world is shifting from using predictive analytics to using prescriptive analytics (Kumar et al., 2022) with the help of big data. It not only foretells what will happen, but also specifies what might be done to take advantage of these connections. Prescriptive analytics can help industries avoid difficulties by allowing them to explain the impact of each choice and choose the best one. Using prescriptive analytics, businesses can make more informed, data-driven decisions and better leverage automation to get more done in less time. Prescriptive analytics of time-dependent parameters, as stated by (Faheem & Butt, 2022), simplifies decision-making by delivering credible and plausible results.

2. BLOCKCHAIN TECHNOLOGY

Blockchain is a decentralised database that may be used to record and disseminate data without the intervention of any third parties. Its original intent was to facilitate the electronic transmission of funds only. However, in recent years, it has developed into a powerful tool (Nilaiswariya et al., 2021).

Many people think that blockchain will drastically alter business as usual across many sectors, from banking and insurance to healthcare and retail sales. Due to its decentralised nature, it is safe and transparent for many uses, including but not limited to:

- Record-keeping: great for keeping tabs on your health, your fitness, your schooling, etc.
- Safely facilitating financial transactions for fintech companies.
- Distributed, open-source, wiki-based knowledge sharing.
- Reduce or do away with the possibility of fraud or identity theft.

Advertising platforms across the globe can now conduct secure, transparent transactions using blockchain technology. By centralising the purchasing and selling of advertisements on blockchain platforms, businesses can provide a solid, market-driven economic basis.

Because of this, everyone involved in a transaction can feel safe, and ad fraud can be drastically reduced.

Blockchain is important to our industrial 4.0 Strategy because it provides a platform for developing and deploying technological capabilities that has the potential to serve as a backbone for all industrial applications. This includes the industrial, agricultural, medical, creative, and commercial sectors (Ratsel, 2023). Reliable, interconnected networks that eliminate the need for middlemen will serve as the backbone of the fourth industrial revolution. Blockchain will drive whole new manufacturing business models by "distributing trust" between all parties. In the financial sector, where blockchain's disruptive qualities have already been tested, broker activity is being challenged by technologies that can validate information swiftly and securely without human involvement. Blockchain is a foundation for technological capabilities that could one day serve as the backbone for applications in virtually every business, not just finance, banking, and related sectors like real estate and law.

Healthcare:

Blockchain technology allows hospitals and other medical facilities to record patients' entire medical histories. Permissioned Blockchains, where confidentiality is agreed upon, make it possible to safeguard personal information. Essential transactions can be viewed and requested by parties as needed to protect the privacy of doctors and patients.

Education:

Blockchain is being explored by educational institutions as a solution to reduce the burden of maintaining student and alumnus records and the risk of fake certifications. With an increasingly mobile and digital population, it is essential to have a centralised database of credentials and achievements to replace the current paper-based certification systems, which are vulnerable to loss and fraud.

Government:

Blockchain is attracting the attention of governments as a method to enhance public service and streamline administrative procedures. Transactions recorded on distributed ledgers provide governments with new ways to boost openness, combat fraud, and build trust.

Logistics/Transportation:

The logistics, transportation, and supply chain industries stand to benefit greatly from blockchain technology. As such, it represents a novel approach to monitoring the flow of goods and services while also promoting ethical and sustainable purchasing practises.

3. ARTIFICIAL INTELLIGENCE (AI)

When we talk about robots having artificial intelligence (AI), we're referring to their ability to learn and respond in ways that imitate human intelligence. In doing so, it paves the way for people to plan ahead and make decisions. One area where AI is sure to have a major impact is customer service.

The way in which customers communicate with companies is evolving as a result of the widespread use of AI-based, human-assisted chatbots. The goal of AI is to continuously find methods to improve the quality of the service it provides. It's in everything we do, from online shopping (with Google and Amazon) to entertainment (with Netflix and Spotify) to even the music we listen to.

Many other developments in technology can be traced back to AI as well:

- Recognisable faces
- The rise of Alexa-style voice assistants
- 24/7 online chat and email assistance

It's essential in boosting satisfaction and loyalty among existing patrons. Incorporating human-assisted AI in customer service improves productivity and response times while freeing up human agents to focus on other complicated challenges.

There has been an increase in the widespread adoption of AI in a variety of settings in recent years. As part of the effort to meet these challenges and make the shift to Industry 4.0, artificial intelligence (AI) technology is being used to reduce the likelihood of machine failure, enhance quality control, boost industrial efficiency, drastically cut product costs, and significantly increase the pool of potential purchasers. Smart businesses that follow Industry 4.0 standards will reap future benefits from AI provisioning, in no small part due to the flexibility of learning frameworks. We go over when progressive businesses would be best served by introducing AI frameworks. The sections that follow are the core of our reply to your inquiry. Elements of the Fourth Industrial Revolution include artificial intelligence (AI) use cases in Industry 4.0, AI integration in applications, and data sets for training and testing AI models in the context of smart industries. In this article, we will go through some of the most crucial applications of AI in the coming Fourth Industrial Revolution.

Applications of AI in Industry 4.0

Some of AI's most important roles in the 4.0 industrial revolution are described here.

- **Predictive Quality and Yield:**

Artificial intelligence (AI) frameworks help boost yields in smart industries by making accurate predictions about product quality throughout the course of their entire life cycles. Improved forecasting methods on already-existing products can be analysed with predictive analytics to better understand product quality, which is what customers want. Industry 4.0 relies on Quality 4.0, a quality management subsystem, to guarantee high-quality end results (Alhayani et al., 2023). Quality data collected in large quantities by various smart industrial devices makes the use of sophisticated analytics for predicting product quality and yield a realistic possibility in smart industries. Production yield, quality management, and customer value can all be boosted with the use of real-time monitoring and quality predictions made at various phases of a product's lifecycle.

In smart industries, the quality control loop includes iterative estimates of product yield. Predictive quality analysis facilitates the establishment of performance baselines, the monitoring of smart machines' actual performance, the comparison and analysis of performance with benchmark criteria, and the adoption of corrective measures. They're great for looking into the future and predicting what sorts of quality issues will develop once the product hits the shelves.

- **Predictive Maintenance:**

Predictive maintenance systems are extremely useful for executives, managers, and employees in today's modern businesses. It is used in high-tech equipment to foresee potential issues and plan maintenance accordingly. Industry 4.0 compliant small and medium-sized businesses perceive greater economic and life cycle improvements of products, according to research analysing the value and cost aspects faced in CNC machines and their predictive positive implications (Tyagi et al., 2023).

The literature demonstrates the importance of cyber-physical systems and IIoT in supporting real-time management of intelligent industrial machines in the context of Industry 4.0. In (Rosati et al., 2023), a decentralised method is created for run-time analysis of machine maintenance plans, which is consistent with the aforementioned paradigm. Using a job shop enabled environment, the provided framework (Tyagi et al., 2023) schedules maintenance based on intelligence for identically parallel multi-component machines. This framework incorporates an intelligent algorithm that scales its execution time based on the number of machines in use, and it does so within the context of a CPS-IIoT paradigm. Memetic Algorithm and Particle Swarm Optimisation, two common centralised heuristics, were pitted against this approach, and the results showed that the latter were inferior.

We evaluate the strengths and weaknesses of fog computing in comparison to traditional cloud computing for keeping tabs on machines in real time. This study examines the latency and success rates of ML-based apps in the context of Industry 4.0. The widespread use of artificial intelligence (AI) has increased in recent years. As part of the effort to meet the challenges and make the shift to Industry 4.0, artificial intelligence technology is being deployed to reduce the likelihood of machine failure, enhance quality control, boost industrial efficiency, drastically lower product costs, and significantly increase the pool of potential purchasers. Because learning frameworks can be tailored to suit any need, intelligent businesses that implement Industry 4.0 standards stand to gain significantly from AI provisioning in the future. We talk about when innovative businesses should introduce AI systems. What follows are the meat and potatoes of our reply to your inquiry. Artificial intelligence (AI) in Industry 4.0 includes use cases, AI integration in applications, and data sets for training and testing AI models in the context of smart industries. We'll talk about some of the most consequential ways that AI will be used during the Fourth Industrial Revolution.

- **Smart Manufacturing:**

The modern manufacturing industry has successfully blended operational and information technologies with the help of IIoT, AI, data analytics, Industry 4.0, and smart manufacturing processes.Monitoring the physical processes occurring on the production floor, smart manufacturing machines use data received from Industrial Internet of Things (IIoT) devices to make effective changes to planning, production, and maintenance. Industry 4.0 defines smart manufacturing as an ecosystem of interdependent, cooperative production facilities that can respond instantly to changes in demand, supply, and other factors related to the manufacturing process and the consumer market.

Various strategies for smart production can be found in the scholarly literature. Intelligent agents and cloud services are two examples of agent-based architectures that can be used in smart production (Ahmad et al., 2022). Agents in the architecture maintain simplicity, fortifying the framework to withstand the demands of supervising the growth of several objects at once. Similar standardisation of procedures and readily changeable open-source software are at the heart of the digital twin-driven (Radanliev et al., 2022; Alhayani et al., 2023) strategy for speeding up production. Using additive manufacturing, products can be assembled by adding raw materials in consecutive layers.When applied properly, additive manufacturing provides a superior means of producing fast, low-cost models for use in intelligent production. Industry 4.0's foundation was laid in Germany, but other nations have already created their own sets of standards for ICT-enabled smart production.

- **AI in Robotics for Industries:**

The combination of AI and robots has matured into a potent resource for today's enterprises. Kipper et al. argue that incorporating robotic systems into smart businesses can facilitate future advancements in Industry 4.0 and beyond. According to the existing body of literature, it is preferable to develop robotics that are customised to meet individual industrial requirements. For instance, the value and function of robots in intelligent production are extensively examined in (M. & Parisa, 2023). In addition, robots play a crucial part in smart industry production (Ryalat et al., 2023).

Several robotics applications in Industry 4.0 use AI to improve robot performance across a wide range of tasks. Below, we will go through some of the most crucial applications of AI in robotics within Industry 4.0:

- **Assembling and Manufacturing:**

Robots in factories and assembly lines are significantly more productive thanks to AI. Combining AI with other cutting-edge enabling technologies like vision systems allows robots to define, learn, and improve processes in exceedingly complex production domains like aerospace. Cognitive robotic systems leverage AI and ML tools like improved data management and Natural Language Processing (NLP) to monitor this form of robot automation (Tyagi et al., 2023).

- **Packaging:**

Robots are utilised in the packaging process in smart industries. Artificial intelligence (AI) can also be used to improve robots' abilities in packaging activities, which may lead to a more efficient, accurate, and cost-effective solution.

- **Production Task Scheduling by Robots:**

Robotic workers and stationary factories are common components of conventional manufacturing lines. Tools that can be reconfigured, as well as mobile robots with complex control units and inherent job scheduling systems, are invaluable in today's workplaces. We recently conducted a poll (He et al., 2023) in which we discussed the difficulties encountered by Industry 4.0 in its pursuit of more unified scheduling across sectors, as well as potential solutions including the cooperation of humans and robots in order to make better decisions. In order for robots to intelligently schedule their tasks, numerous novel AI-based strategies have been presented in the literature. In (Ahmad et al., 2022), for instance, robotic system resources in an Industry 4.0 context are divided up using a slicing concept and artificial intelligence (AI) according on the requirements of the manufacturing process. Scheduling many operations with a workshop that allows for a fluid transfer of materials in the industrial business for mobile robotic systems offers above-average performance as a benchmark (Radanliev et al., 2022). Retail and other high-tech industries are increasingly using robots with artificial intelligence for customer service. Computer vision (CV) and natural language processing (NLP) are two examples of enabling technologies that help artificial intelligence-based robots communicate with humans more naturally.

- **Generative Design:**

Generative design, aided by AI and other pertinent technologies like vision and VR, provides us with product designs we could never have dreamed up on our own. In the design process of smart industries, having multiple possibilities for a given drawing is a big benefit. Each and every one of the AI-generated designs may accomplish the designer-specified tasks. From those alternatives, we can pick one that lives up to the designers' hopes and standards. Generative design technique takes advantage of high-powered computers to generate structures that use only as much material as is strictly necessary to get optimal results. By scanning and sensor-enabling prototypes, generative designers may track their performance in real time and incorporate that information into future iterations of their work.

They (Alhayani et al., 2023) looked on the capabilities of DL models based on Generative Adversarial Networks (GANs) for attributeaware generative design, which generates designs with the required visual features. Furthermore, the authors evaluated how GANs may help companies appeal to a more diverse customer base.

- **Market Adaption/Supply Chain:**

Industrial AI is crucial for effective supply chain integration in the planning, design, and execution of today's businesses (He et al., 2023). From an Industry 4.0 point of view, most supply chain paradigms can be classified as either "green," "resilient," "agile," or "lean" (He et al., 2023). Several attempts have been made in this direction. Small businesses, for example, have focused urban production to boost productivity (M. & Parisa, 2023) and have chosen a greener production strategy by integrating Industry 4.0 into their manufacturing supply chain. Industry 4.0 maturity is assessed by interviews and focus groups using IIoT, automation, and predictive analytics (He et al., 2023). In addition, the organization's progress towards sustainability and the outlook for Industry 4.0's eventual maturity are both presented.

Additionally, by examining inventory management from a number of customer and business model perspectives, a comprehensive framework for modern industries is built (Tyagi et al., 2023). Low-power wireless personal area networks, which are common among IIoT edge devices, benefit greatly from a rescheduling recommendation system (Qahtan et al., 2023). Here, the use of interference graphs in scheduling improves performance in contrast to random rescheduling. Production line task scheduling calls for teamwork and the effective administration of a group of resources.

AI Techniques in Industry 4.0

There have been several examples of how AI has proved helpful in Industry 4.0 environments. Predictive quality helps to ensure high-quality goods and also improves the efficiency of various manufacturing processes. Several novel methods have been proposed to assist businesses maximise the benefits of AI and ML, including supervised learning, unsupervised learning, semi-supervised learning, and reinforcement learning. In this article, we take a close look at the many ways in which AI and ML are being used to usher in the Fourth Industrial Revolution. For simplicity's sake, let's classify them as either Statistical/ conventional methods (i) and DL strategies (ii)

Statistical/Traditional AI/ML

When looking for AI-based solutions, Industry 4.0 often resorts to statistical/traditional methods (He et al., 2023). In order to enable autonomous material differentiation over a wide range of substrates, including aluminium, copper, MDF, mild steel, and more, Penumuru et al. have incorporated Computer Vision (CV) and traditional ML algorithms into industrial machines and robots. Many different types of categorization methods are used to accomplish this goal. K-nearest neighbours, logistic regression, random forests, and support vector machines are all types of machine learning algorithms. The experimental outcomes verify the classifiers' efficacy. In (Radanliev et al., 2022), we observe the application of Logistic Regression and RF classifiers to the autonomous monitoring and analysis of HVAC system performance.

Unfortunately, unexpected breakdowns of machinery used in continuous operations in industry are common, and the time it takes to repair the unit and get it back online can be considerable. Some smart manufacturing defect detection work uses statistical ML techniques. A survey on failure detection in industry 4.0 applications using accurate prediction with ML algorithms and providing related countermeasures was undertaken by Angelopoulos et al. The authors didn't stop there, though; they also developed a framework for human involvement in in-the-loop, error-reducing strategies employed during the production process that are grounded in machine learning.

Predictive maintenance in smart industries is recommended because of its potential to forewarn of machine failure and ensure that machines are available to perform following industrial operations. In order to train ML models, we make use of data collected by IIoT gadgets performing event-based monitoring of factory machinery (Ahmad et al., 2022). The same holds true for production planning and control; with the correct resources, information, and approach, ML approaches can be used to great effect. For instance, the methods now utilised by IIoT devices to gather data and analyse it with ML approaches, such as conventional ML and DL algorithms, employed for a wide range of jobs in intelligent industrial processes are thoroughly outlined in Cadavid et al. By generalising ML algorithms like SVM, KNN, and neural networks, Bajic et al. investigated their usefulness in smart manufacturing for addressing industry-wide decision making problems. 4.0 Illustrations of Use.

In smart industries, sensors built into manufacturing lines track each worker's output and productivity. Work scheduling and improvement of the scheduling process are two areas where classical ML has made significant contributions, both of which have boosted productivity in industrial machines. Industrial prognosis, which aims to foretell how long machines will last in factories despite their advanced age and tremendous usage, also makes use of traditional ML methods. Data fusion methods and prognostic models of varying types for usage in industry 4.0 contexts are explored in (Ryalat et al., 2023).

Deep Learning

Similar to other fields, the potential of deep learning (DL) algorithms in a variety of Industry 4.0 situations has been the topic of substantial investigation. Several innovative DL-based strategies have been presented to deal with issues in the Industry 4.0 sphere. Data analytics solutions, such as machine failure prediction and recommendation systems, were developed by Miskuf et al. using a DL-based technique for application in Industry 4.0 contexts. The DL model is built on the open-source H2O ML framework, and it is evaluated using the UCI repository's text recognition data set. The authors compare their DL method to conventional ML techniques like logistic regression. See (Alhayani et al., 2023) for a DL-based system that uses a geometric DL architecture for effective CP network administration.

To investigate lean management practises, (Alhayani et al., 2023) integrates DL frameworks with EEG sensors. Soft sensors analyse the collected data to determine the observable patterns of behaviour. But real smart industry leaders employ this framework effectively to develop enduring organisational goals and provide dependable smart manufacturing systems. Monitoring brain electrical activity with EEG sensors is one use of DL-based soft sensors in lean shop floor management (Radanliev et al., 2022). Industry can benefit from the use of smart technologies by analysing brain activity data. 4.0.0 Assess in-house operations and give better suggestions to upper management.

Rapid expansion is occurring in the integration of DL methods into Industry 4.0 software. Subakti et al. introduced a DL-based framework for autonomous identification of machines and their parts, which is a crucial feature of an augmented reality system for visualising and analysing equipment and interacting with it indoors. To achieve this, machine images have been used to fine-tune a preexisting deep model called MobileNet (M. & Parisa, 2023). MobileNet was chosen because its architecture is well-suited to low-powered computing devices. To develop multi-path communication in an industry 4.0 ecosystem, however, Pokhrel et al. presented a Deep Q-Network based framework. Using proofs of concept and information and operational technology convergence, the authors also analysed the resulting difficulties and made recommendations for how to best overcome them. In the context of industry 4.0, the multi-agent deep reinforcement learning approach utilised in (Tyagi et al., 2023) is used to offload activities and permit multi-channel access to mobile edge computing processes. The new solution drastically improves the channel success rate thanks to the collaborative nature of the edge devices, while simultaneously decreasing the calculation delay.

With the help of DL methods, the construction industry is undergoing a digital transformation that has enabled improved management of complex environments thanks to collaboration between the public, private, and governmental sectors (Qahtan et al., 2023).

Datasets for Industry 4.0

Data analytics is becoming increasingly important in AI-based industrial applications. The availability of enough training data is another factor that can limit an ML algorithm's usefulness. We provide an overview of the benchmark datasets used to train and evaluate AI frameworks for Industry 4.0 applications.

Production Datasets

Artificial intelligence algorithms educated on appropriate production datasets must be used to make accurate decisions for sustainable and reliable production operations. Depending on the classification of the industry and the items it produces, these databases can help predict the future of that industry. Honti et al. employed natural language processing (NLP) and data mining tools to assess the I4.0+ economic and innovation index assessment. In addition, the writers in (Alhayani et al., 2023) learned from two hundred or more examples of supply chain innovation through use cases and adapted the on-demand standard services to the specific requirements of their clients. Romeo et al. employ two real-world datasets to evaluate multiple DL and standard ML algorithms for usage in industrial design support system validation. In order to address problems in additive manufacturing, Elhoone et al. apply ANN frameworks to a parametric design dataset. This allows for the use of cyber additive manufacturing techniques. Type-2 fuzzy sets have been used for uncertainty assessment in the oil and gas industry for applications involving the processing of massive seismic data sets.

Cyber-Physical Systems Datasets

With the use of CPS, artificial intelligence systems could improve the ecosystem's core security-centric operations by keeping an eye on the operational features of Industry 4.0. The information gathered by CPS could be very useful for teaching AI frameworks to provide novel safety features. For instance, Moustafa et al. address manufacturing system security concerns by combining a mixture-hidden Markov model with CPS datasets. It also provides the devices with a clever level of protection against unnatural activity. Pan et al. gathered and generated the CPS dataset to help with the development and assessment of intrusion detection algorithms for power systems. There are 37 distinct events and scenarios that were extracted from the original dataset. These include eight natural disasters, twenty-eight attacks, and one non-event. The data can be applied with equal effectiveness to investigations of both two- and three-category classification schemes. Both (Alhayani et al., 2023) and (Das, 2023) describe similar cyberattacks on industrial control systems like a gas pipeline or a water storage tank and use the same datasets. In order to train and test algorithms that can identify harmful from benign network activities, this dataset was compiled. The authors of (Das, 2023) suggest and present a dataset for use in simulating and recording intrusion detection in industrial control systems. The modbus dataset includes a wide variety of information types, including frame, label, attack type, attacker, victim, and date/time stamp data (Eswaran & Raju Bahubalendruni, 2022).

Image Datasets

The academic literature also has a number of picture datasets that can be used to train and evaluate AI models for a wide range of Industry 4.0 use cases. To train and assess AI models for material recognition and classification in the context of industry 4.0, for instance, Penumuru et al. compiled an image dataset. Aluminium, copper, medium-density fiberboard (MDF), and mild steel appear often in the images included with the dataset. A standardised image dataset of manufacturing machinery was created in (Lacko, 2022). Experts painstakingly sorted 11,000 images of 24 different types of industrial devices into eight distinct categories. The Kinect 2.0 sensor was used to take all of these pictures, which have a combined frame size of 102,457,575 and a depth frame size of 51,24,524, from a distance of 1 to 5 metres. Severstal: Steel Defect identification is a collection of images presented in (Kumar et al., 2022) for the goal of testing and enhancing image-based flaw identification methods. The dataset consists of 18,106 photos in total, with 12,600 used for training and 5,506 for testing. Images can be labelled as (i) perfect, (ii) containing a single defect, or (iii) containing multiple defects.

Automation in product inspection is a cornerstone of smart industries and a key use of artificial intelligence in the context of Industry 4.0. Automating solder joint inspection during PCB construction is described by Schwebig et al. The dataset contains a collection of images captured by numerous kinds of optical examination tools. The collection also features both colour and black-and-white images. However, Ntavelis et al. developed a GANs-based strategy to generate/enhance industrial images from a reduced sample of natural photographs. The artificial datasets can be used to train DL models. A dataset of three-channel pictures of pump components is used to evaluate the approach. In addition, every photo was taken under a unique set of lighting conditions.

Text Datasets

Today, companies use artificial intelligence (AI) systems to automatically analyse and collect customer feedback about a product, company, or service (Manavalan & Jayakrishna, 2019). By assessing customers' reactions to a product, sentiment analysis can help businesses in the smart economy make better ones. Efforts have already been made in this direction. In (Mittal et al., 2018), for instance, researchers analysed customers' negative reactions to various items using sentiment analysis to learn more about their problems and how to fix them. As a result, the effectiveness of the proposed sentiment analysis system was assessed using a dataset consisting of customer reviews submitted on Amazon regarding a certain product. Another similar dataset is constructed in (Das, 2023), this time using sentiment-analyzed Amazon customer reviews. In addition, (Evangelista et al., 2023) compiles a database of 26,993 positive and 13,203 negative consumer comments from reviews. NLP techniques are then applied to the collected feedback on the product in order to extract common threads and organise the feedback into relevant categories. However, (Eswaran & Raju Bahubalendruni, 2022) uses a Twitter crawl to examine how the public feels about Industry 4.0. We do this by amassing a dataset of tweets about Industry 4.0 and analysing them to ascertain the sentiments expressed therein. Text mining was used to rank the significance of phrases linked to Industry 4.0.

In Industry 4.0, text-based datasets are utilised for a variety of purposes beyond just sentiment analysis. For instance, in (Lacko, 2022), a text mining dataset has been suggested and gathered consisting of Industry 4.0 employment adverts. The dataset is compiled by crawling numerous websites for job postings. The dataset's primary goal is to gather data on the skills and knowledge that various sectors need to thrive.

Survey Datasets

In order to extract actionable intelligence from data, it is crucial to solicit feedback and conduct surveys from knowledgeable industry workgroups. Many cases of Industry 4.0 have already made use of comparable datasets. To examine the diffusion of intelligent businesses, Frank et al. used cluster analysis on data collected from 92 distinct sectors. The dataset is used to assess the methodical uptake of foundational supporting technologies in contemporary industry. Using a European industrial survey dataset, Medic' et al. evaluated the feasibility of using Fuzzy-based analytics to make strategic decisions.

4. VIRTUAL REALITY AND AUGMENTED REALITY

The adoption of AR/VR tools is essential for the development of Industry 4.0. Both create or utilise a physical setting to convey content. A virtual reality (VR) headset creates an immersive environment that feels very real to the user. However, augmented reality merges the digital and physical realms into a single experience.

The success of AR/VR apps like Pokemon Go, L'Oréal's beauty app, Google Lens, etc. demonstrates the industry's response to these technologies. Moreover, many websites these days incorporate VR/AR technology to deliver unique, immersive experiences for their visitors (Saini, Mummoorthy, Chandrika, Gowri Ganesh, Samuel, Jayashree et al, 2023).

If used properly, augmented and virtual reality may bring several advantages to organisations. For instance:

- Engaging and dynamic content can increase traffic and sales.
- Customers are more likely to remember and associate a brand with an AR or VR experience.
- It gives people the ability to virtually examine and try out a product.
- It helps consumers shop with assurance.

Industry 4.0 and AR/VR Technology on the US Market

The success of Industry 4.0 can be accurately evaluated with the use of augmented reality technology and devices, which can be used by enterprises to observe their position at various phases of development. Many different types of businesses have started purchasing technological equipment in the augmented reality and virtual reality industry as it has grown rapidly in recent years.

The market for AR and VR in the US is expected to grow to $35 billion by 2025, according to forecasts from Goldman Sachs Global Investment Research. At now, this technology is being heavily utilised by the gaming industry to create simulations that either fully immerse players in virtual reality or make the game world a palpable reality. It is important to note, however, that augmented and virtual reality technologies are being utilised more frequently in the medical field to aid in the education of medical professionals, the performance of complex tests, and the visualisation of the human body. With the use of augmented and virtual reality technology, life-changing medical procedures can be planned in advance.

One-third of US business owners say they have no plans to implement augmented reality or virtual reality solutions. The shortage of investment capital is to blame for the negative outlook of entrepreneurs.

Creating an in-house technological infrastructure is also part of the implementation cost, in addition to hardware, software, and the time and money spent training staff.

More than a third of business owners said they had not yet accepted proposals from specialised companies to help them implement AR/VR technology solutions. According to the findings, about one-fifth of business owners are already using such solutions. The time it takes for a corporation to complete each step of the implementation process ranges from three to twelve months.

The number of accidents in factories can be reduced by as much as 70% if workers' individual production processes are connected and the possible hazards of risky manoeuvres are identified. In the United States, the market potential of augmented and virtual reality technologies is largely underappreciated, in part because traditional production methods are still widely accepted despite the fact that they do not necessitate sophisticated information technology infrastructures. With the help of augmented and virtual reality technologies, American business owners are progressively modernising their operations without making any hasty choices or making significant investments.

Almost 40% of businesses plan to implement AR/VR in some capacity within the next year. This means that the technology is phased in over time, but not every precaution can be taken at once. This is because the organisation has specific requirements that not every hardware and software developer can meet. Only about 2.5% of businesses can afford to fully implement AR/VR technologies. These businesses, often known as the "smart factories of the future," are cutting-edge and relatively new, having launched when augmented and virtual reality technology were already commonplace.

The Role of VR/AR in the Fourth Industrial Revolution

- Design optimization
- Plant maintenance and control
- Operations instruction and personnel training
- Incident assistance and resolution

We highlight a number of advantages that industrial organisations can gain from implementing VR and AR as part of Industry 4.0.

The Value of Virtual and Augmented Reality in the Fourth Industrial Revolution:

- Process improvement
- Minimized downtime
- Increased safety
- Cost savings

Design Optimization With Virtual Reality and Augmented Reality

- **Industrial prototyping with Virtual Reality**

Prototyping products can be expensive in some industries since it's required to build actual versions of them so that their qualities can be evaluated and their designs can be scrutinised.

The automotive business is one that needs these expensive procedures. In the past, in order to evaluate the product's actual utility, it was necessary to construct a version of the product that would eventually be sold, although one of inferior quality.

And we say up till now since VR is the ideal tool for cutting down on expenses connected to prototyping projects. With the use of this technology, we can develop a simulation of a product that looks and functions almost exactly like the actual thing. With this digital model, you may also try out various coatings before committing to a physical prototype.

When it comes to pre-production visualisation of vehicle interiors and exteriors, BMW was an early adopter of virtual reality (VR). The dashboard and controls, for instance, can undergo a virtual check to ensure they are legible from the driver's vantage point. The German firm can now make decisions without resorting to the costly practise of using simulation tunnels in prototyping, all thanks to this cutting-edge method.

- **Assembly and installation design with Augmented Reality**

Throughout the building and planning phases of a project, mixed reality, or Augmented Reality, could be of great assistance. The technician needs the extra data offered by these hands-free devices to ensure that the final product will fit in the available area in the plant.

For this reason, we have teamed up with Dicoma Pack, a leading producer of bottling lines for Spanish wineries, to create AR industrial apps for businesses whose primary focus is the installation of such machinery.

In order to guarantee that building sites are ready for assembly, we have built a programme for Microsoft Hololens, the company's Mixed Reality glasses. The device employs augmented reality to ensure that the installation can take place inside the client's factory's existing infrastructure and space restrictions.

Plant Maintenance and Control With Augmented Reality

Augmented reality is also being put to use in the realm of equipment upkeep and repair. The operator usually doesn't have the relevant documentation for the equipment on hand when a breakdown happens, making it difficult to get it back up and running. He has to waste time searching for them or consulting a specialist in order to get the apparatus back up and running.

The answer to these problems lies in augmented reality. Augmented reality glasses allow the user to view virtual instruction manuals that are displayed onto the lens in the event of an issue. The glasses flag certain issues and give the wearer upkeep tips.

The industry already makes use of glasses like Epson's Moverio, and a similar project has been completed with the previously mentioned company Dicoma Pack. Caterpillar and Bosch, two other multinational corporations, have also used this technology, albeit on tablets, to provide assistance with repairs.

Controlling installations can also benefit from the use of Augmented Reality technologies. Silver-level supervisors can monitor every step of the manufacturing process in real time with the use of a tablet computer or wearable computer. The device would only need a photograph of the machine to identify it and then display data on how productive and efficient it is. Crucial information for the technician to make choices that will improve plant-wide efficiency.

Operations Training and Operator Training With Virtual Reality

Virtual reality is also useful for training technicians to operate complex industrial gear. To help fix problems or occurrences, we can create environments where people can engage with machines in the same way they can see them working in real life.

Wearing VR goggles transports a worker to a virtual factory where a stalled machine is displayed, allowing him to inspect it and fix the problem just as if he were in the physical plant.

As a result, VR is rapidly approaching the training sector, providing manufacturing firms with a more effective and cost-efficient method of educating their staff. It saves money by reducing the need for a technician to train each employee, it speeds up the training process, and it keeps production running while employees learn to use the machines.

This makes it an even better tool for teaching in potentially dangerous settings. 3M is one company that has already implemented this technology; they utilise a computer simulation to demonstrate to construction workers the potential dangers of not taking these precautions. The benefit of not needlessly endangering employees should be considered here, in addition to the financial savings noted above.

Assistance and Incident Resolution

When used to machine upkeep and repair, Augmented Reality telecare solutions take things to the next level, with the experienced technician guiding the factory operator through the troubleshooting procedure in real time.

Thanks to a built-in camera in the worker's glasses, the machinery manufacturer's technical support team can see exactly what the worker sees at any given time. This live view is crucial to fixing the problem since it lets them direct the operator precisely through each procedure. Directly optimising production times, this solution prevents lengthy downtime while waiting for technical support to arrive. Suppliers of industrial machinery can save money thanks to its utilisation since they no longer need to pay for the time and resources of technicians to travel to and from servicing calls.

5. INTERNET OF THINGS: IOT

The Internet of Things (IoT) seeks to unite the digital and physical spheres. The Internet of Things has applications in anything from package tracking to home automation systems. It has changed several sectors and enabled the linking of countless gadgets. It has a unique identifier and can connect to the internet (Babu & Jayashree, 2015). Furthermore, it allows companies to gather information about their customers and measure how those customers feel about the items and services they offer. This allows companies to better target their customers with their marketing efforts (Priya, 2021). It can also use for monitoring the crop details with the help of the different IOT components (Babu & Jayashree, 2015).

Smart devices that can sense the industrial environment, collect relevant data, process it, and establish reliable connection are the backbone of the IIoT and the key to automating industrial activities. It is predicted in (Babu & Jayashree, 2015) that IIoT will soon be used for industrial automation. Industry 4.0 will rely heavily on it as well. The main purpose of the Industrial Internet of Things (IIoT) is to link intelligent manufacturing equipment and devices to the web, to one another, and to the people who oversee them. Typical IIoT solutions for smart industries include hardware, networking, communication infrastructure, data, cloud/edge installations, data analytics, and intelligent processing of data to take appropriate actions. Many uses for IIoTs can be identified within the framework of Industry 4.0. In order to make informed judgements about the amount and quality of products for sale, manufacturers rely extensively on real-time monitoring of manufacturing lines. IIoT data from production lines is becoming increasingly heterogeneous, and technologies like RFID and wireless sensor networks are used to analyse and make decisions based on this data (Sowmia et al., 2023). The potential of IIoT-based systems for monitoring and assessing production processes is demonstrated by these use cases and applications. Introducing collaborative scheduling amongst many clusters of jobs is another way to improve task scheduling for delay-insensitive applications (Harini et al., 2018). Improving job scheduling tactics for IIoT applications can lead to this method. IIoTs belong in the realm of Industry 4.0, where they can be put to many interesting uses. Figure 4 is a summary of the manufacturing sector's utilisation of IIoTs in the 4.0 version of the industry.

Figure 2. The most important uses of IIoT in the framework of Industry 4.0

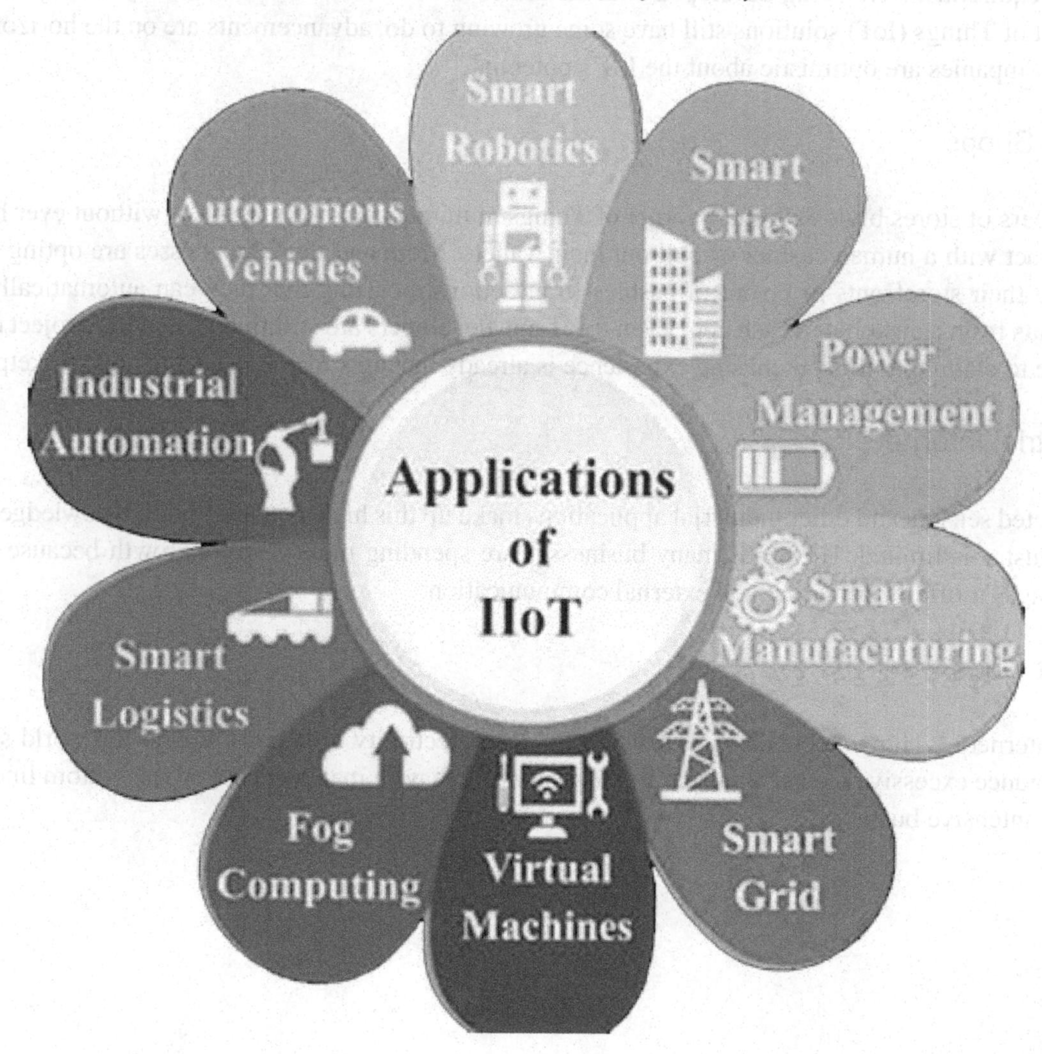

Usages of IoT for Acceptance of Industry 4.0

Adopting industry 4.0 is a welcomed challenge due to specialised IoT applications. Here is a list of them:

Smart Homes

Thanks to the Internet of Things, architects and builders of tomorrow's homes can ensure the safety of their occupants. Many Internet of Things app development firms brag about offering their customers automatic lighting systems and locking protocols, both of which are made possible by the application's technological features.

Self-Driven Cars

Self-driving cars that guarantee a significant decrease in road accidents and conform to the established safety requirements are being developed with the aid of sensors with embedded IoT systems. Although Internet of Things (IoT) solutions still have some growing to do, advancements are on the horizon, and many companies are optimistic about the IoT's potential.

Retail Shops

Customers of stores built with the Internet of Things in mind can make purchases without ever having to interact with a human cashier or pull out their wallets. More and more businesses are opting out of staffing their storefronts in favour of cashless transactions, boasting that they can automatically take payments from a customer's cash app. Even if IoT app developers are still fine-tuning the project codes, it's safe to claim that this purchasing experience is already having a major impact on the marketplaces.

Industrial Internet

Connected sensors and other industrial applications make up this high-potential field. Knowledge about the industry is limited. However, many businesses are spending money on its growth because of the advantages it offers in internal and external communication.

Smart Grids

This Internet of Things technology is crucial for clean electricity initiatives around the world since it helps reduce excessive electricity use. Similar factors can have a major impact on the bottom line of an energy-intensive business.

A Major Evolution of IoT and Industry 4.0

The Internet of Things is to thank for the rapid development of industry 4.0, in which all devices are interconnected over a single network and most tasks are performed automatically. Decisions may be made with more precision thanks to real-time data monitoring, and the likelihood of future dangers in the industry can be mitigated through careful asset management. The major transitional periods between IoT and industrial 4.0 include:

- Getting things connected
- Generating insights
- Optimizing operations and processes
- Innovation

The primary goal of the Internet of Things is to "smarten" every environment. Industry 4.0, on the other hand, is made up of things like cyber security, AR, robots that can work independently, digital twins, cloud storage, Big Data, linked gadgets, and heavy machinery. Heavy machinery, smart factory grids, and connected gadgets are where industry 4.0 and IoT meet. To achieve manufacturing excellence, IoT must play a central role in all factory processes and significantly enhance them. Because it combines IT with OT for processes and produces significant results, IoT is the ideal solution for businesses.

Benefits of Using IoT in Industries

- **Increased efficiency**

One of the biggest advantages of the Internet of Things is that it helps increase productivity. By streamlining manufacturing procedures, it can raise productivity levels. It may also be automated, which is great for increasing output and decreasing waste in production facilities. The performance of the production assets is monitored using the integrated sensors, which allows for adjustments and improvements to be made as needed.

- **Predictive maintenance**

The efficiency and effectiveness of assets have a significant role in determining industrial output. With the support of IoT-enabled predictive maintenance, process managers can foresee and react to a failing asset's operability, preventing long-term damage to productivity and operations. The factory's assets are equipped with Internet of Things sensors that track their status and performance in real time, notifying management of any problems immediately. These problems are fixed as soon as possible, saving the company a tonne of money.

- **Real-time data monitoring**

Assets can be monitored in real time to see how they're doing and have adjustments made to the process as needed to boost output and product quality. Furthermore, data monitoring in real-time aids in making decisions and boosts manufacturing productivity.

- **Reduces cost**

With IoT's predictive maintenance and real-time data monitoring capabilities, machines can be made smart enough to operate autonomously with little to no human intervention, drastically cutting costs. Since fewer people are involved, fewer mistakes will be made, and the price will drop accordingly.

Challenges in Internet of Things

However, what needs to be emphasized here is the fact that, along with the comfort, it comes with the risk of a data breach. IoT is made possible by these crucial elements:

- **Low-cost and low-power sensor technology**

The main component of IoT is the collection, storage, and sharing of data. It is only possible because of the presence of effective sensors. The availability of low-cost sensors is making IoT more accessible to manufacturers.

- **Connectivity**

Data sharing essentially requires connectivity between the sender and the receiver. The internet provides IOT with this and makes it efficient and easier to use.

- **Platforms for cloud computing**

Cloud computing platforms provide us with access to infrastructure, making them beneficial for both businesses and consumers. There are multiple cloud computing platforms providing individuals with this facility. The internet of things comes out as the interaction between the physical world and connectivity. Being such an important aspect of human life, IoT is sure to face several challenges.

We are here to share with you the various challenges in the internet of things.

- **Security challenges**

The first and foremost on the list of challenges is security. As the backbone of IoT is data storage and sharing, the biggest question arises about the security of data. Enabling every small physical object with the feature of sharing information may attract multiple raised brows.

- **Lack of encryption**

Encryption sounds like the ultimate answer to security issues. But hackers may manipulate these algorithms and turn a protective system into the most serious loophole.

- **Lack of sufficient testing and updating**

With the increasing market of IoT, production has to be faster. To compete in the race of production, manufacturers lack tests and updates. The main focus of IoT manufacturers now seems to be production, not security. Thus products lack proper and regular testing and updates. This makes IOTs prone to being attacked by hackers.

- **Weak login details**

With every device asking for login details, it may at times turn difficult to produce tough credentials. This leads to easy hacking, wherein the user, out of leniency, fills in weak credentials and login details.

- **Design challenges**

Moving on to another challenge in the internet of things, we come to the design challenges IoT faces.

- **Battery sizes**

Providing users with extended battery life and smaller, handy product is a great challenge for the manufacturers of IoT products. Manufacturers continuously face the challenge of delivering the best in the smallest and lightest products.

- **System Security**

It is also essential to create a design that is robust and reliable. The strength of the product must be maintained from its modeling stage till its deployment.

- **Increment in cost**

With the deployment of sensors in ordinary daily objects, the price shoots up. Although attractive the IOTs are still considered a luxury thus the customers willing to pay large amounts for these products are small. Manufacturers have to keep this aspect in mind while designing a product. They have to manage to keep the pricing of the products under a certain limit to keep it open to a bigger market base.

- **Timing of launch**

It is also essential to solve design problems within the required time frame so that the manufacturer can launch its product onto the market at the right time. Timing plays a crucial role when you are competing in a niche filled with several other companies delivering similar assets and services.

- **Deployment challenges**

Moving ahead, we must talk about the deployment challenges that are a major part of the challenges in the internet of things.

- **Connectivity**

So far, we have learned correctly that connectivity is the backbone of IoT. Without good connectivity, the products are ordinary physical products that have no connection with the technology of IoT. Poor connectivity will lead to no data collection, no data storage, and no data sharing, making IOTs useless.

- **Cross-platform capability**

Technologies change and improve every day. These small improvements every day lead to major transformations. Keeping this in mind, the IoT products must be deployed in such a way that they can keep pace with the new technologies. For IoT products to be of use for a long period, they must be able to cooperate with the new and advanced technologies.

- **Data processing**

IoT products are enabled to collect, store, and share data. But what lies underneath is the very important aspect of data processing. The device may collect a very large amount of data, but the development teams must ensure that the collected data is processed well and stored properly to ensure the smooth sharing of only relevant data.

- **Need for skill set**

To handle these technical challenges in the internet of things (IoT), skilled manpower needs to be in place. Only those with skills and the ability to think critically will be able to solve the various challenges faced by this forever-changing technology.

However, this does not mean that due to the presence of challenges, we will stop manufacturing or using IoT devices.

CONCLUSION

Intelligent machines, Big Data, the Industrial Internet of Things (IIoT), robotics, high-speed communication networks, blockchain, and the broader economic change are all examples of how AI will drive future industries. However, considerable barriers prevent its widespread implementation in Industry 4.0 contexts. In this chapter, we'll compare and contrast AI with some of the other technologies that make up Industry 4.0. With an emphasis on security, adversarial assaults, communication, interpretability, and data-related difficulties, we have assessed and examined the core applications, enabling technologies, techniques, and related challenges of AI and Big Data in Industry 4.0. We have analysed the existing benchmark dataset in depth for use in training and evaluating AI-based solutions in Industry 4.0. Therefore, the technological answers provided by Industry 4.0 may appeal to many contemporary businesses. Managers and owners should think carefully before making any changes. Existing companies can find success in new domestic and international markets with the help of virtual reality and other forms of information technology.

REFERENCES

Ahmad, T., Zhu, H., Zhang, D., & Tariq, R. A. (2022). Energetics Systems and artificial intelligence: Applications of industry 4.0. *Energy Reports, 8*. doi:10.1016/j.egyr.2021.11.256

Alhayani, B., Kwekha-Rashid, A. S., Mahajan, H. B., Ilhan, H., Uke, N., Alkhayyat, A., & Mohammed, H. J. (2023). 5G standards for the Industry 4.0 enabled communication systems using artificial intelligence: Perspective of smart healthcare system. *Applied Nanoscience, 13*(3), 1807–1817. doi:10.100713204-021-02152-4 PMID:35096498

Alladi, T., Chamola, V., Parizi, R., & Choo, K. (2019). Blockchain applications for industry 4.0 and industrial iot: A review. *IEEE Access, 7*.

Babu, R. & Jayashree, K. (2015). A Survey on the Role of IoT and Cloud in Health Care. *International Journal of Scientific, Engineering and Technology Research (IJSETR), 4*(12).

DasS. (2023). An Article On: Augmented Reality Contrast to Ergonomic Design. SSRN. https://ssrn.com/abstract=4320316 doi:10.2139/ssrn.4320316

Davies, R., Coole, T., & Smith, A. (2017). Review of socio-technical considerations to ensure successful implementation of industry 4.0. *Procedia Manufacturing, 11*, 1288–1295. doi:10.1016/j.promfg.2017.07.256

Eswaran, M., & Raju Bahubalendruni, M. V. A. (2022). Challenges and opportunities on AR/VR technologies for manufacturing systems in the context of industry 4.0: A state of the art review. *Journal of Manufacturing Systems, 65*.

Evangelista, A., Manghisi, V. M., Romano, S., De Giglio, V., & Cipriani, L. (2023). Advanced visualization of ergonomic assessment data through industrial Augmented Reality. *Procedia Computer Science, 217*.

Faheem, M., & Butt, R. A. (2022). Big datasets of optical-wireless cyber-physical systems for optimizing manufacturing services in the internet of things-enabled industry 4.0. *Data in Brief, 42*, 108026. doi:10.1016/j.dib.2022.108026 PMID:35330737

Harini, S., Jothika, K., & Jayashree, K. (2018). A review of big data computing and cloud. *International Journal of Pure and Applied Mathematics, 118*(18), 1847–1855.

He, C., Zhang, C., Bian, T., Jiao, K., Su, W., Wu, K.-J., & Su, A. (2023). A Review on Artificial Intelligence Enabled Design, Synthesis, and Process Optimization of Chemical Products for Industry 4.0. *Processes (Basel, Switzerland), 11*(2), 330. doi:10.3390/pr11020330

Kerin, M., & Pham, D. T. (2019). A review of emerging industry 4.0 technologies in remanufacturing. *Journal of Cleaner Production, 237*, 117805. doi:10.1016/j.jclepro.2019.117805

Khan, A., & Turowski, K. (2016). A survey of current challenges in manufacturing industry and preparation for industry 4.0. *Proceedings of the First International Scientific Conference Intelligent Information Technologies for Industry (IITI'16)*. Springer.

Kim, J. H. (2017). A review of cyber-physical system research relevant to the emerging it trends: industry 4.0, iot, big data, and cloud computing. *Journal of industrial integration and management, 2*(3), 1750011.

Kumar, R., Rani, S., & Al Awadh, M. (2022). Exploring the Application Sphere of the Internet of Things in Industry 4.0: A Review, Bibliometric and Content Analysis. *Sensors (Basel), 22*(11), 4276. doi:10.339022114276 PMID:35684897

Lacko, J. (2022, April 1). Camera Modes in Multi-user Virtual Reality Applications in Industry 4.0. *Acta Montanistica Slovaca, 27*(2).

Manavalan, E., & Jayakrishna, K. (2019). A review of Internet of Things (IoT) embedded sustainable supply chain for industry 4.0 requirements. *Computers & Industrial Engineering, 127*, 925–953. doi:10.1016/j.cie.2018.11.030

Mittal, S., Khan, M. A., Romero, D., & Wuest, T. (2018). A critical review of smart manufacturing & industry 4.0 maturity models: Implications for small and medium-sized enterprises (smes). *Journal of Manufacturing Systems, 49*, 194–214. doi:10.1016/j.jmsy.2018.10.005

Nilaiswariya, R., Manikandan, J., & Hemalatha, P. (2021). Improving Scalability And Security Medical Dataset Using Recurrent Neural Network And Blockchain Technology. In *2021 International Conference on System, Computation, Automation and Networking (ICSCAN),* (pp. 1-6). IEEE.

Osterrieder, P., Budde, L., & Friedli, T. (2020). The smart factory as a key construct of industry 4.0: A systematic literature review. *International Journal of Production Economics, 221*, 107476. doi:10.1016/j.ijpe.2019.08.011

Parisa, M. (2023). Determinants of big data analytics adoption in small and medium-sized enterprises (SMEs). *Industrial Management & Data Systems, 123*(1).

Priya, V. & Vijay, P. (2021). The Healthy Skin Framework-Iot Based. *Psychology and Education Journal, 58*(2), 7731-7734.

Qahtan, S., Yatim, K., Zulzalil, H., Osman, M. H., Zaidan, A. A., & Alsattar, H. A. (2023). Review of healthcare industry 4.0 application-based blockchain in terms of security and privacy development attributes: Comprehensive taxonomy, open issues and challenges and recommended solution. *Journal of Network and Computer Applications, 209*, 103529. doi:10.1016/j.jnca.2022.103529

Radanliev, P., De Roure, D., Nicolescu, R., Huth, M., & Santos, O. (2022). Digital twins: Artificial intelligence and the IoT cyber-physical systems in Industry 4.0. *International Journal of Intelligent Robotics and Applications, 6*(1), 171–185. doi:10.100741315-021-00180-5

Radanliev, P., De Roure, D., Page, K., & Jason, R. C. (2020). Cyber risk at the edge: Current and future trends on cyber risk analytics and artificial intelligence in the industrial internet of things and industry 4.0 supply chains. *Cybersecurity, 3*(1), 1–21. doi:10.118642400-020-00052-8

Ratsel. (2023). *A Game-Based Evaluating Tool for the Dyslexic Using Augmented Reality Gamification.* Information and Communication Technology for Competitive Strategies. LNNS.

Rosati, R., Romeo, L., Cecchini, G., Tonetto, F., Viti, P., Mancini, A., & Frontoni, E. (2023). From knowledge-based to big data analytic model: A novel IoT and machine learning based decision support system for predictive maintenance in Industry 4.0. *Journal of Intelligent Manufacturing, 34*(1), 107–121. doi:10.100710845-022-01960-x

Ryalat, M., ElMoaqet, H., & AlFaouri, M. (2023). Design of a Smart Factory Based on Cyber-Physical Systems and Internet of Things towards Industry 4.0. *Applied Sciences (Basel, Switzerland)*, *13*(4), 2156. doi:10.3390/app13042156

Samuel, P., Jayashree, K., Babu, R., & Vijay, K. (2023). Artificial Intelligence, Machine Learning, and IoT Architecture to Support Smart Governance. In K. Saini, A. Mummoorthy, R. Chandrika, & N. Gowri Ganesh (Eds.), *AI, IoT, and Blockchain Breakthroughs in E-Governance* (pp. 95–113). IGI Global. doi:10.4018/978-1-6684-7697-0.ch007

Samuel, P., Reshmy, A. K., Rajesh, S., Kanipriya, M., & Karthika, R. A. (2023). AI-Based Big Data Algorithms and Machine Learning Techniques for Managing Data in E-Governance. In K. Saini, A. Mummoorthy, R. Chandrika, & N. Gowri Ganesh (Eds.), *AI, IoT, and Blockchain Breakthroughs in E-Governance* (pp. 19–35). IGI Global. doi:10.4018/978-1-6684-7697-0.ch002

Sanchez, M., Exposito, E., & Aguilar, J. (2020). Industry 4.0: Survey from a system integration perspective. *International Journal of Computer Integrated Manufacturing*, *33*(10-11), 1–25. doi:10.1080/0951192X.2020.1775295

Sivaranjani, P. (2020, May). Employee Tracking System using Blockchain. *Test Engineering and Management*, *83*, 5154–5156.

Sowmia, K. R., Prithi, S., Vijay, K., Eugene Berna, I., & Bhuvaneswaran, B. (2023). *Crop Monitoring System with Water Moisture Level using Arduino.* 2023 5th International Conference on Smart Systems and Inventive Technology (ICSSIT), Tirunelveli, India. 10.1109/ICSSIT55814.2023.10060913

Trappey, A. J., Trappey, C. V., Govindarajan, U. H., Chuang, A. C., & Sun, J. J. (2017). A review of essential standards and patent landscapes for the internet of things: A key enabler for industry 4.0. *Advanced Engineering Informatics*, *33*, 208–229. doi:10.1016/j.aei.2016.11.007

Tyagi, A. K., Dananjayan, S., Agarwal, D., & Thariq Ahmed, H. F. (2023). Blockchain—Internet of Things Applications: Opportunities and Challenges for Industry 4.0 and Society 5.0. *Sensors (Basel)*, *23*(2), 947. doi:10.339023020947 PMID:36679743

Yli-Ojanpera, M., Sierla, S., Papakonstantinou, N., & Vyatkin, V. (2019). Adapting an agile manufacturing concept to the reference architecture model industry 4.0: A survey and case study. *Journal of Industrial Information Integration*, *15*, 147–160. doi:10.1016/j.jii.2018.12.002

Chapter 18
Industry 4.0 in Manufacturing, Communication, Transportation, Healthcare

R. Felista Sugirtha Lizy
https://orcid.org/0000-0003-3648-0205
A.P.C. Mahalaxmi College for Women, India

Ibrahim M. H.
Sathakathullah Appa College, India

Chinnadurai Manthiramoorthy
Boston University, USA

ABSTRACT

This chapter gives a summary of the effects of Industry 4.0 (I 4.0) on various sectors, including manufacture, communication, transportation, and healthcare. A new wave of technical improvements called "Industry 4.0" focuses on automation, connectivity, and data exchange in manufacturing processes. The chapter highlights how I 4.0 is transforming manufacturing processes by improving productivity, efficiency, and reducing operational costs. Additionally, the chapter discusses I 4.0 adoption in the communications and transportation sectors, leading to better connectivity, safety, and improved customer experience. The healthcare sector is also benefiting from I 4.0 by enhancing patient care through personalized medicine, remote monitoring, and data analytics. The chapter concludes by addressing the possible advantages and difficulties of implementing I 4.0 in various industries, offering insightful information for academics, professionals, and decision-makers.

DOI: 10.4018/979-8-3693-2081-5.ch018

1. INTRODUCTION

An AI system is a machine-based setup with the ability to make forecasts, recommendations, or assessments (Silva M. C. & da Costa C. A., 2018) that influence real-world or virtual scenarios, all within a predefined set of human-defined goals.

Incorporating cutting-edge digital technologies (Marco Ardolino et al., 2022) into the manufacturing, communication, transportation, and healthcare sectors is known as industry 4.0. It involves utilising AI systems to forecast, suggest, and make choices that affect actual or virtual environments. The goal of this effort is to promote partnerships between people and technology that combine human ingenuity and innovation (Yang F., & Gu S., 2021) with the accuracy and speed of Web 4.0 tools. Employers are liberated from menial activities and given more time to collaborate with intelligent machines thanks to the use of these technologies in manufacturing operations. Various intelligent digital technologies, including industrial IoT networks, AI, Big Data, robots, and automation, are covered by the word "Industry 4.0". It facilitates the advancement of smart industrial and intellectual factories, which boosts output, effectiveness, and adaptability. I 4.0 is also a part of the "Fourth Industrial Revolution" (FIR), that started in the 1800s and has subsequently changed corporate practises and industrial processes.

Figure 1. Industry technological pillars

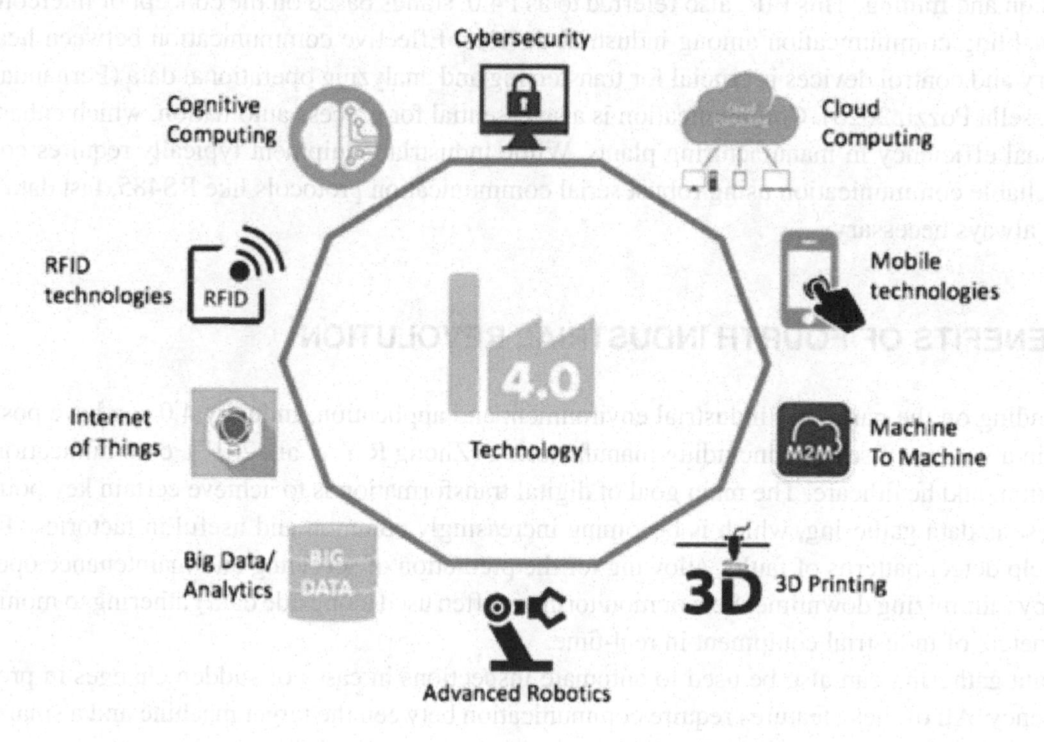

The FIR, known as I 4.0, is causing significant transformations in various areas for example engineering, communication, carriage also health care. Businesses are incorporating innovative technologies like the use of cloud computing, analytics, AI, machine learning, and the IoT in their production procedures and overall business operations.

These advanced plants, also known as "smart factories," (Wang S., 2016) are outfitted by robotics, implanted package, then sensors that ruck and examine the information to support managerial. By integrating information since industrial processes with information from corporate systems like ERP, supply chain, and customer service, previously isolated insights are now connected, leading to improved visibility.

Implementing digital technologies in manufacturing brings several benefits, including improved mechanization, protective conservation, enhancement of processes through self optimization, improved proficiency, then enhanced shopper awareness. The industrial subdivision consumes tremendous latent to squeeze this insurgency through establishing keen plants. Through the study of immense amounts of information (Duan L. et al., 2019) composed since instruments on the plant base, present perceptibility of industrial resources becomes possible. Additionally, predictive maintenance tools are utilized to minimize equipment downtime.

Shrewd plants introduce radical IoT campaigns, which contribute to increased productivity and quality. By employing AI-powered visual insights in place of human inspection models, production errors are reduced, resulting in time and cost savings. By connecting a Smartphone to the cloud, quality control staff can remotely monitor manufacturing operations for very little money. Instant fault detection is made possible by machine learning algorithms, avoiding the need for more costly repairs down the road.

The principles and technology of Industry 4.0 (Böhmann T. et al., 2016) offer advantages to various sectors, with detached then progression engineering, in addition to industries such as lubricant then emission and mining. This FIR, also referred to as I 4.0, stands based on the concept of interconnecting too enabling communication among industrial devices. Effective communication between heavy machinery and control devices is crucial for transferring and analyzing operational data (Fernanda Strozzi & Rossella Pozzi, 2023). Communication is also essential for process automation, which enhances operational efficiency in manufacturing plants. While industrial equipment typically requires consistent and reliable communication using robust serial communication protocols like RS485, fast data transfer is not always necessary.

2. BENEFITS OF FOURTH INDUSTRIAL REVOLUTION

Depending on the particular industrial environment and application, Industry 4.0 can have positive effects in a variety of sectors, including manufacturing (Zhong R.Y. et al., 2017), communication, transportation, and healthcare. The main goal of digital transformation is to achieve certain key points. One of these is data gathering, which is becoming increasingly common and useful in factories. This data can help detect patterns of faults, allowing for the prediction of servicing and maintenance operations, thereby minimizing downtime. Sensor monitoring is often used alongside data gathering to monitor vital parameters of industrial equipment in real-time.

Data gathering can also be used to automate inspections in cases of sudden changes in production efficiency. All of these features require communication between the target machine and a smart device, such as a computer or rugged PLC, which is more suitable for industrial settings.

Using a powerful device can centralize the management of different machines and enable telemetry acquisition and load balancing. Programmable devices like PCs and PLCs are cost-effective and highly customizable, as they can be added onto existing industrial equipment. Machine-to-Machine (M2M) communication is another way to achieve Industry 4.0 goals, although it typically requires machines to have these features built-in.

Equipment management and monitoring are also adopted to reduce energy consumption by accurately determining when machines are in use. Energy savings are crucial in modern factories for two main reasons: reducing the carbon footprint and managing increased energy costs.

Coined by Germany, the term "Industry 4.0" represents the modification of conventional engineering into intelligent systems. This transition involves the utilization of sensors, intelligent robotics, cloud computing, big data, the internet of things (IoT), cyber-physical systems (CPS) (Ashima R. et al., 2021), and immersive technologies. These elements facilitate both horizontal in addition vertical combination of businesses, enabling seamless M2M message, information sharing, and real-time updates.

Supply chains for production, manufacturing, and logistics could become smarter (Christopher Münch, 0223), more adaptable, swifter, easier, and more effective with the implementation of Industry 4.0. It makes it easier to connect the real world and the virtual one (Bai C. et al., 2020), which improves comprehension of difficult activities.

By implementing horizontal and vertical integration, Industry 4.0 brings forth several benefits, including interoperability, digitization, visualization, and automation. These advantages facilitate collaboration and enhance the utilization of resources. The probable of I 4.0 also the IoT is vast when it comes to automation, real-time tracking, route optimization, risk management, and integration. However, their impact on the logistics supply chain has been relatively overlooked. Research on Industry 4.0, however, has less of an emphasis on its effects on the logistics supply chain and is more concerned with making factories smart.

Businesses that operate online must completely embrace the idea of Industry 4.0 and investigate its numerous directions in order to gain market share. Efficient route optimization, parcel consolidation, and resource sharing through horizontal and vertical integration (Stock T. & Seliger G., 2016) can enhance mobility in congested metropolitan areas. Additionally, the usage of Information and Communication Technology (ICT) also e-commerce has the potential to reduce the necessity for travel in various aspects, such as shopping, leisure trips, and business travel.

3. CONCEPT AND ELEMENTS OF INDUSTRY 4.0

ICT improvements across numerous industries, having as a part of manufacturing, communication, transportation, and healthcare, have given rise to the idea of Industry 4.0. A network system that is flexible, responsive, automated, digitised, and streamlined is what defines I 4.0. It serves as a bridge connecting the physical (Tao F., 2018) and digital realms, facilitating seamless interactions not only between machines and humans but also between machines themselves. The foundational elements of Industry 4.0 include the following components or building blocks.

4. THE I 4.0 OF SMART MANUFACTURING

According toward experts in the research community, the pivotal component of I 4.0 remains the establishment of a shrewd plant. They believe that the revolution brought about by I 4.0 revolves around the concept of a keen plant. However, creating a smart factory requires several essential machineries for instance Cyber-Physical Systems (CPS) (Lee J. et al., 2015), Internet of Things (IoT), Big Data (BD), Cloud Computing (CC), Augmented Reality (AR), Virtual Reality (VR), Simulation, Autonomous robots (Chuqiao Xu et al., 2023), as well as Horizontal and Vertical Integration. These elements could combined or integrated in many ways to create a decentralised smart factory that communicates over a cloud-based network.

Figure 2. Components and concepts of I 4.0

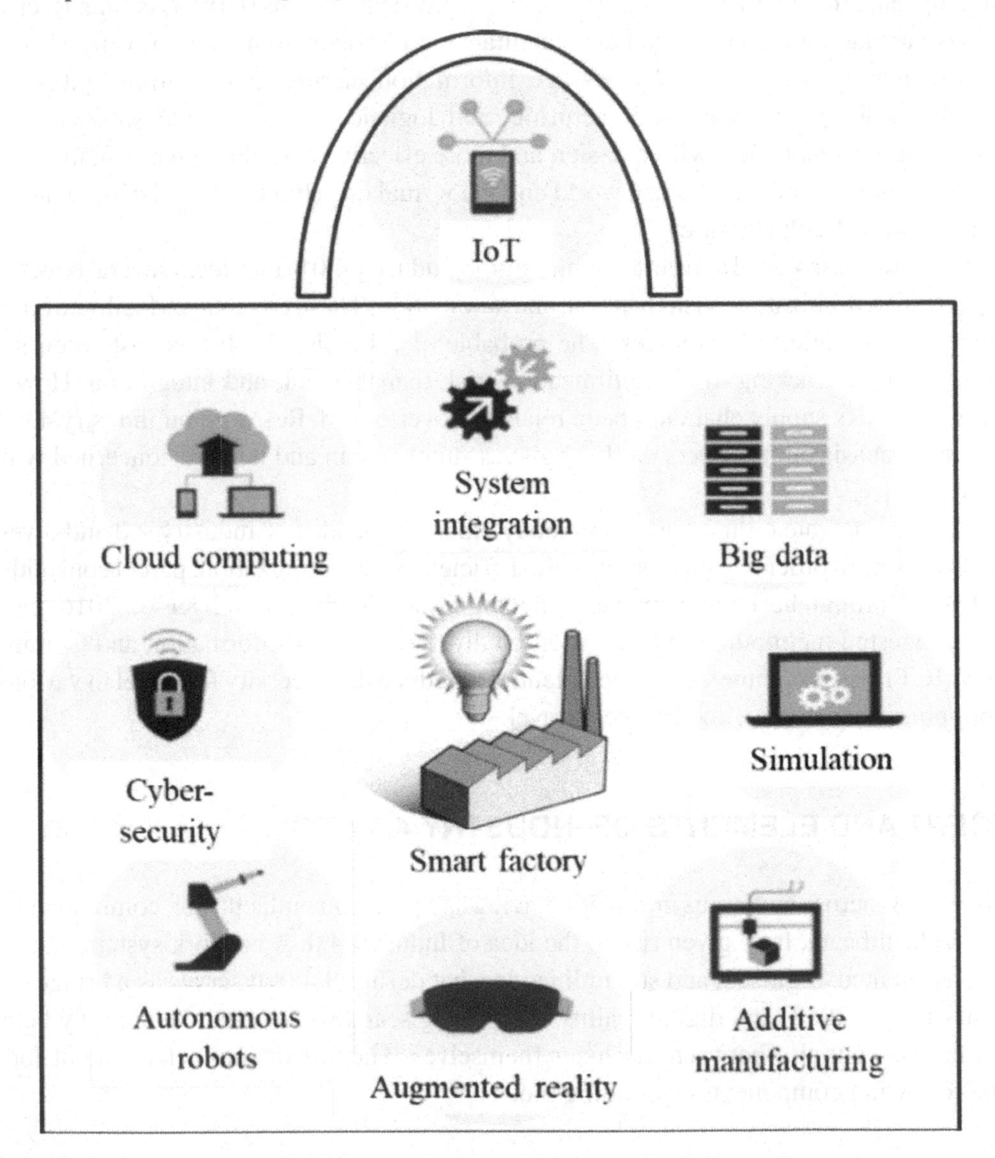

Machines are able to communicate with one another, with things, with people, and with sensors in this smart manufacturing setting. By combining these elements, a smart factory can gather, store, process, analyse, interpret, and share data to effectively manage both the factory's physical and digital components. The illustration below demonstrates how to establish a smart factory.

Figure 3. The smart factory of I 4.0's

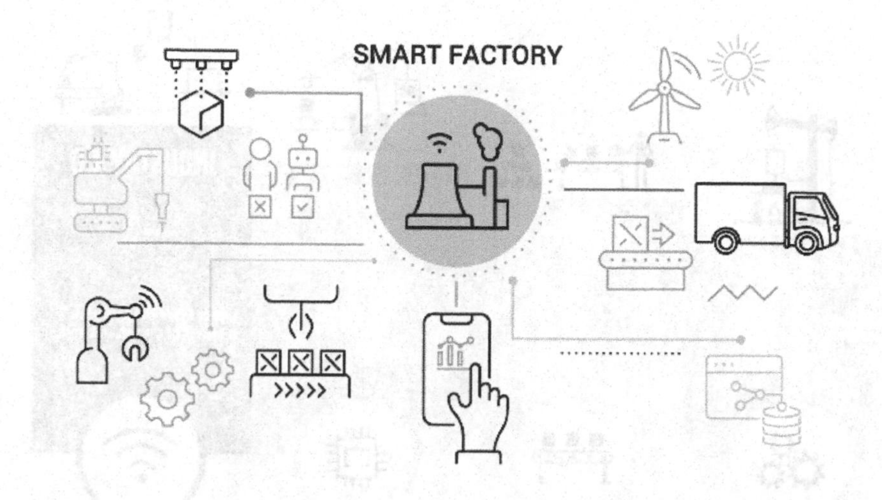

I 4.0 denotes to the cardinal conversion of the engineering sector also includes production, communication, transportation, and healthcare. By adding abilities in analytics and business intelligence, cutting-edge involving people and machines techniques like advancements in the transmission of digital instructions, touch interfaces, augmented reality systems, like 3D printing in the actual world, this revolutionises the sector. It entails using intelligent robots in smart factories to produce intelligent goods and services. Rapid technical breakthroughs are the hallmark of Industry 4.0, which is regarded as the most recent and important technological shift and transition in the sector. Electronic information network systems (Internet) are at the heart of Industry 4.0, which is what is powering this revolution. In addition to extending this technology to business models, supply networks for products, and the industry as a whole, it strives to digitalize and automate every process within an organisation. This is accomplished by fusing cutting-edge embedded system technology with intelligent product manufacturing processes.

With Industry 4.0, you can achieve:

- Low-cost manufacturing;
- Increased productivity (Döring T. et al., 2016);
- Higher-quality goods and services;
- manufacturing with fewer mistakes;
- Minimum production time;
- Flexible production systems that can respond to customer needs more quickly.

5. TECHNOLOGIES BASED ON I 4.0

I 4.0 is built on 9 essential technological elements. The creation of intelligent and self-governing systems is made possible by these technological developments that link the physical and digital worlds. Even if businesses and supply chains are currently utilising some cutting-edge technologies, I 4.0 is only fully realised when these technologies are coupled.

Figure 4. Industrial revolutions

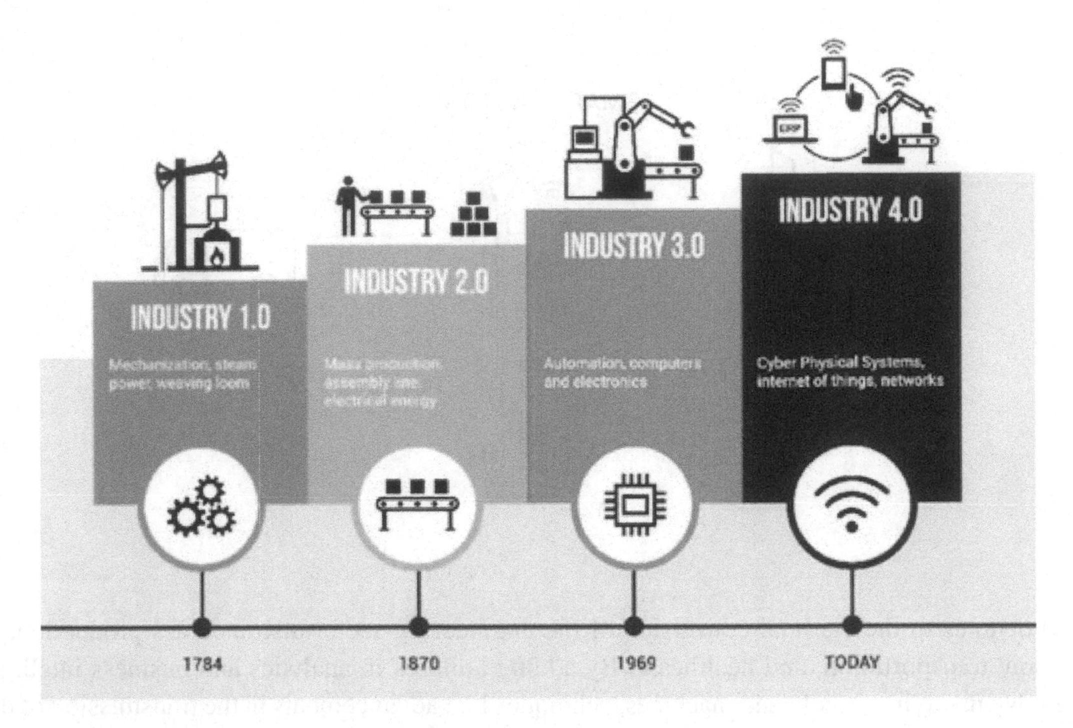

Figure 5. Technologies used in Industry 4.0

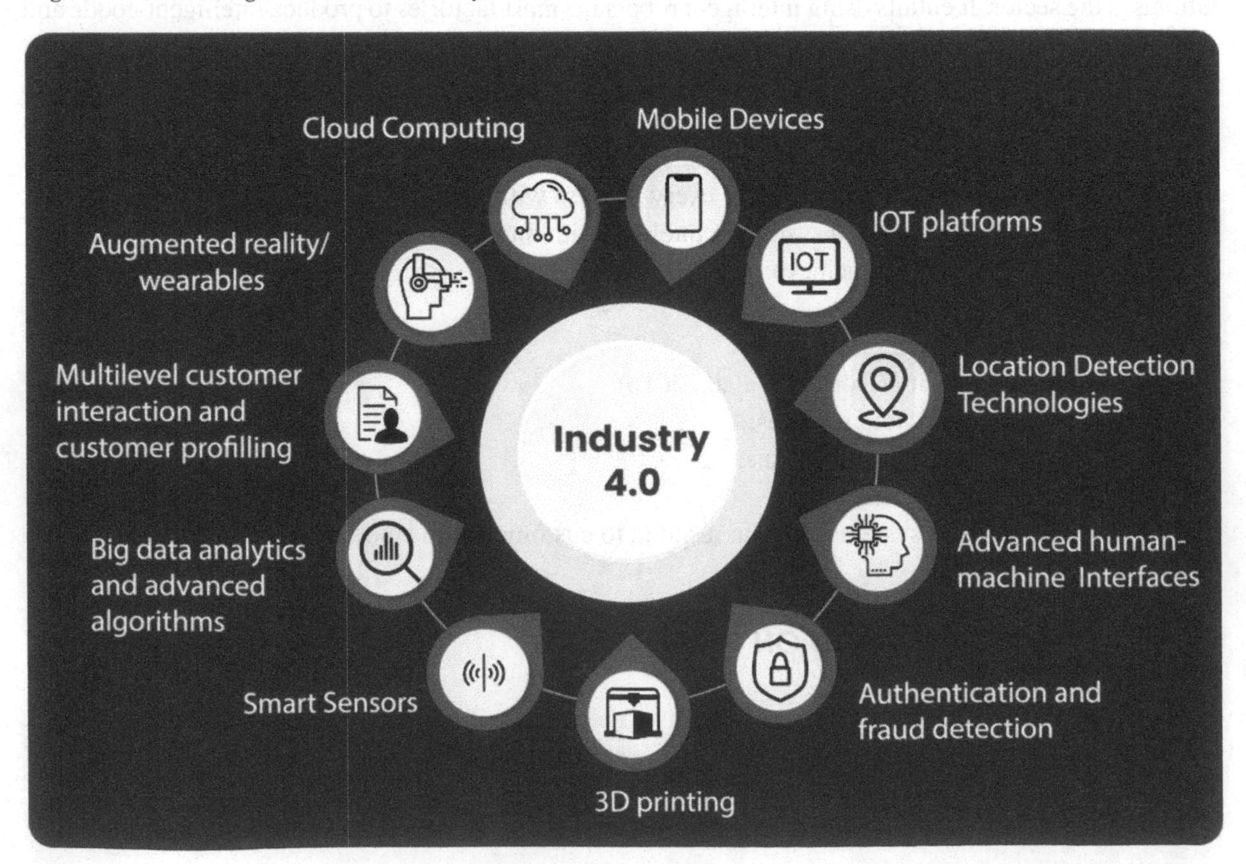

Before contemplating investing in Industry 4.0 solutions for your company (Romero D., & Vernadat F., 2016), familiarise yourself with the following 12 terminology and expressions:

- Enterprise Resource Planning (ERP): A traditional of apparatuses for information management across all business operations inside an organisation (Narain Gupta, 2022).
- The concept of linking physical objects like machinery or sensors to the Internet is stated to by way of the "Internet of Things" (IoT) (Wang Y., & Kung L., 2018).
- Specifically in the industrial framework, the IIoT refers to the connections established between individuals, information, and machines within the industry.
- Large collections of designed or formless information that can stay examined to identify patterns and trends are known as big data.
- Artificial intelligence (AI) (Bag S et al., 2021) denotes to the skill of computer systems to accomplish responsibilities and make judgments that previously relied on humanoid aptitude.
- Machine-to-machine (M2M) communication entails the exchange of information between different machines using wired or wireless networks.
- Digitization is the transformation of various types of information into a digital format.
- Cloud computing involves the storing (Mourtzis D. et al., 2017), managing, and dealing out of information on a web of interconnected remote servers accessed via the Internet.
- Real-time data processing involves continuously and automatically processing data to get results that are immediate or nearly immediate.
- Ecosystem: The interconnectivity of multiple production processes, including supply chain management, inventories (Satie L. Takeda-Berger, & Enzo M. Frazzon, 2023), finance, and customer relations.

Additionally, two more terms are worth noting:

- CPS are a manufacturing environment supported by I 4.0 that offers actual information gathering, examination, also transparency diagonally wholly characteristics of a industrial operation.
- Revolutionise: The impact of smart manufacturing on how companies are managed and expanded.

By familiarizing yourself with these core concepts, you can explore how smart manufacturing can revolutionize your business operations and growth strategies.

5.1. AI and BD Analytics

In the framework of I 4.0, big data (BD) is obtained from several sources. This includes collecting data from the factory floor's assets, machinery, and IoT-enabled gadgets. Additionally, data is also obtained from external sources such as customer reviews, market trends, weather, and traffic apps. These diverse data sources play a vital role in informing research and development, design, and logistics processes. Real-time insights are produced through the use of analytics powered by artificial intelligence and machine learning. Following that, these insights are put to use to improve automation and decision-making in all facets of manufacturing and SCM is the coordination in addition oversight of wholly events involved in the stream of things and amenities since the sourcing of raw resources to the delivery of the final product to the end customer. It encompasses various interconnected processes, including procurement, production, inventory management, transportation, and distribution.

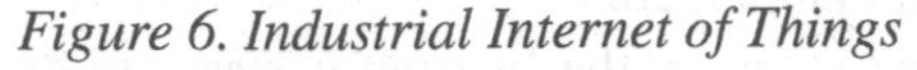

Figure 6. Industrial Internet of Things

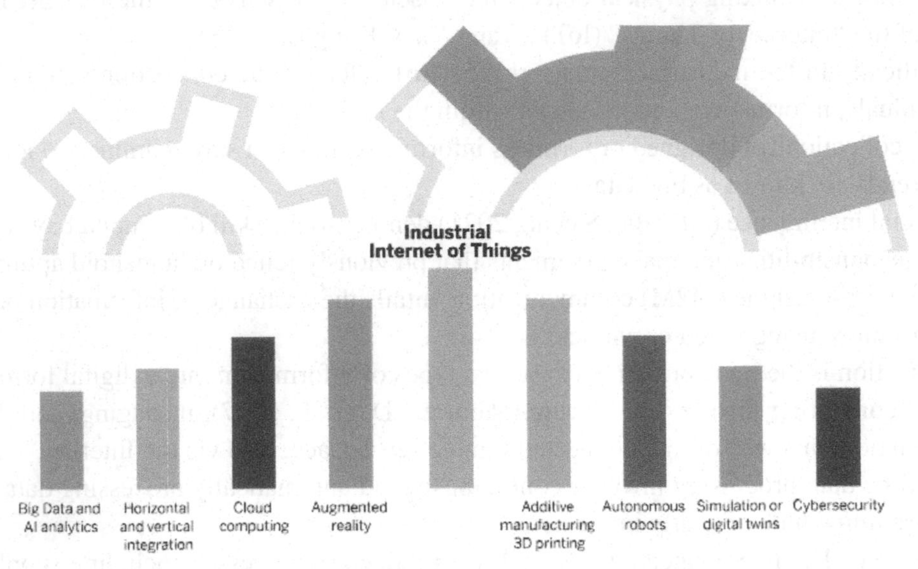

The aims of effective SCM are to improve the flow of goods, info, and assets throughout the whole stock chain network, ensuring that products are delivered to customers in a timely manner although lessening expenses and make the most of client fulfilment. It contains premeditated scheduling, synchronization, and association between suppliers, manufacturers, distributors, retailers, and customers (Schumacher A., Erol S., & Sihn W., 2016) to streamline operations, improve efficiency, and respond to market demands.

Key aspects of supply chain management include demand forecasting, supplier management, production planning, inventory control, logistics management, and performance measurement. With the advent of technologies such as automation, data analytics, and real-time tracking, supply chain management has evolved to leverage digital solutions and innovative strategies to enhance visibility, agility, and responsiveness in a dynamic business environment.

5.2. Integration of the Horizontal and Vertical

Horizontal and vertical integration are essential concepts in many industries, including manufacturing, communication, transportation, and healthcare. When it comes to horizontal integration, there is a strong relationship between processes at the "field level" that extends from the manufacturing the factory floor to numerous production facilities and the whole supply chain. On the other hand, integration of vertical involves the unification of all organisational levels, permitting the smooth transfer of information travelling both ways, from the shop level to the top level. This eliminates the need for separate data and knowledge repositories and optimises overall operations by bringing production activities into tight alignment with other company processes (i.e., R and D, quality control, sales, and marketing).

Figure 7. AI and BD analytics

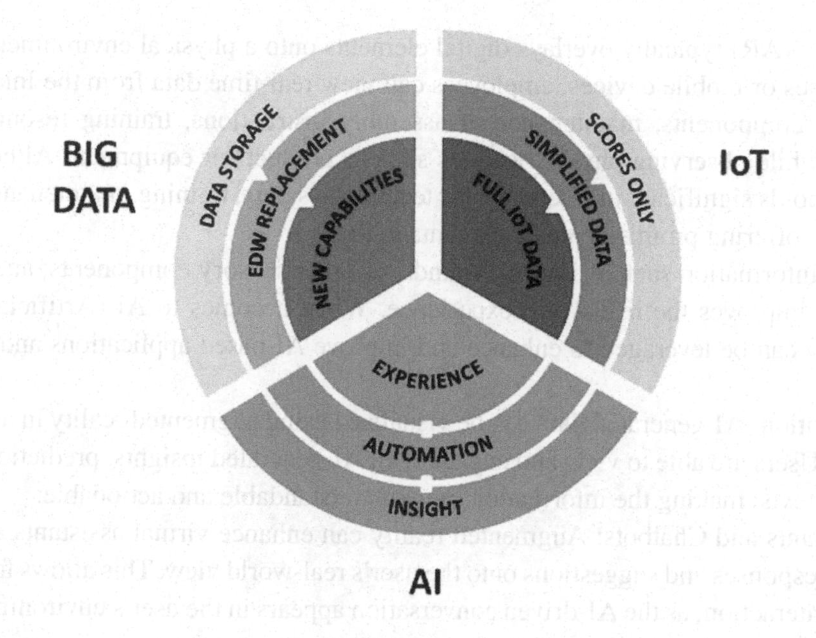

5.3. Using the Cloud

Cloud computing serves as the fundamental catalyst for I 4.0 and digital transformation, acting as the "great enabler." Today's cloud technology forms the basis for advanced technologies like artificial intelligence, machine learning, and seamless integration of the IoT. It empowers organizations (Lu Y., & Yao Y., 2017) to foster innovation and development. Within I 4.0, the cloud plays a central role in facilitating real time communication and coordination among cyber-physical systems. Furthermore, the data that fuels I 4.0 advancements is securely stored in the cloud, ensuring accessibility and enabling efficient operation of the interconnected systems that make up I 4.0.

Figure 8. Utilising the cloud in Industry 4.0

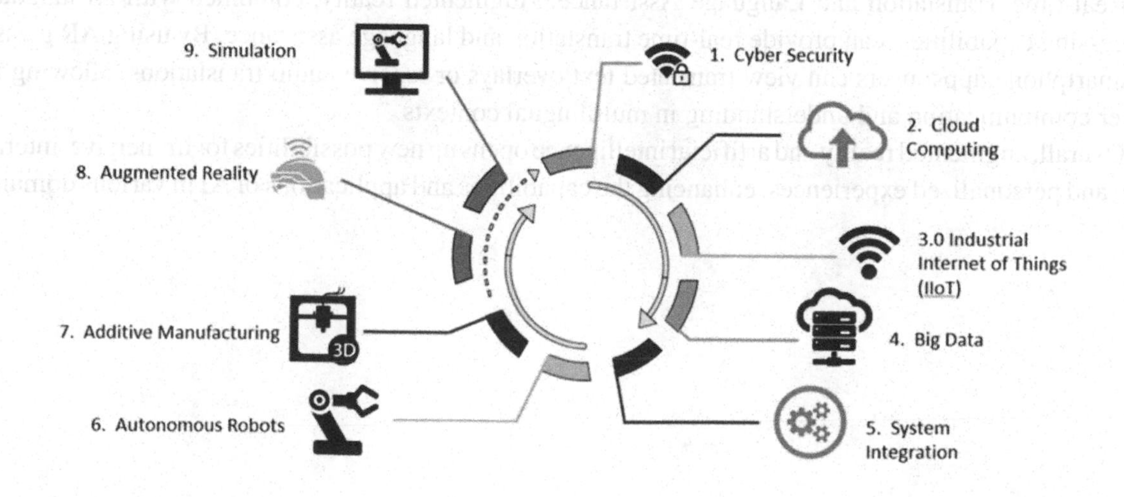

5.4. AR: Augmented Reality

Augmented reality (AR) typically overlays digital elements onto a physical environment. Through the use of smart glasses or mobile devices, employees can view real-time data from the Internet of Things (IoT), digitalized components, maintenance or assembly instructions, training resources, and other relevant content while observing physical objects such as products or equipment. Although still in its early stages, AR holds significant implications for technician safety, training, maintenance, service, and quality assurance, offering promising advancements in these areas.

Using digital information such as images, sounds, or other sensory components, augmented reality (AR) technology improves the real-world experience. When it comes to AI (Artificial Intelligence), augmented reality can be leveraged to enhance and improve AI-based applications and experiences in various ways:

Data Visualization: AI-generated data can be visualised using augmented reality in a more engaging and natural way. Users are able to view and engage with AI-generated insights, predictions, or analytics in real-world contexts, making the information more understandable and actionable.

Virtual Assistants and Chatbots: Augmented reality can enhance virtual assistants and chatbots by overlaying their responses and suggestions onto the user's real-world view. This allows for a more seamless and natural interaction, as the AI-driven conversation appears in the user's environment, rather than being confined to a screen or text-based interface.

Object Recognition and Information: AI-powered object recognition algorithms can be integrated into augmented reality applications, enabling real-time identification and information display about objects in the user's surroundings. For example, pointing a smartphone's camera at a product can trigger AI-powered recognition that displays relevant information, reviews, or pricing details.

Enhanced Training and Education: Augmented reality can be combined with AI to create immersive training and educational experiences. AI algorithms can analyze user actions and provide real-time feedback and guidance, while augmented reality overlays interactive visual elements to simulate scenarios and enhance learning outcomes.

Personalized Experiences: By leveraging AI algorithms, augmented reality can deliver personalized experiences based on user preferences, behaviors, or contextual data. AI can analyze user data to provide customized content, recommendations, or real-time information overlays in augmented reality applications, tailoring the experience to individual needs.

Real-time Translation and Language Assistance: Augmented reality, combined with AI language processing capabilities, can provide real-time translation and language assistance. By using AR glasses or smartphone apps, users can view translated text overlays or receive audio translations, allowing for better communication and understanding in multilingual contexts.

Overall, augmented reality and artificial intelligence opens up new possibilities for immersive, interactive, and personalized experiences, enhancing the capabilities and applications of AI in various domains.

Figure 9. I 4.0's uses of augmented reality

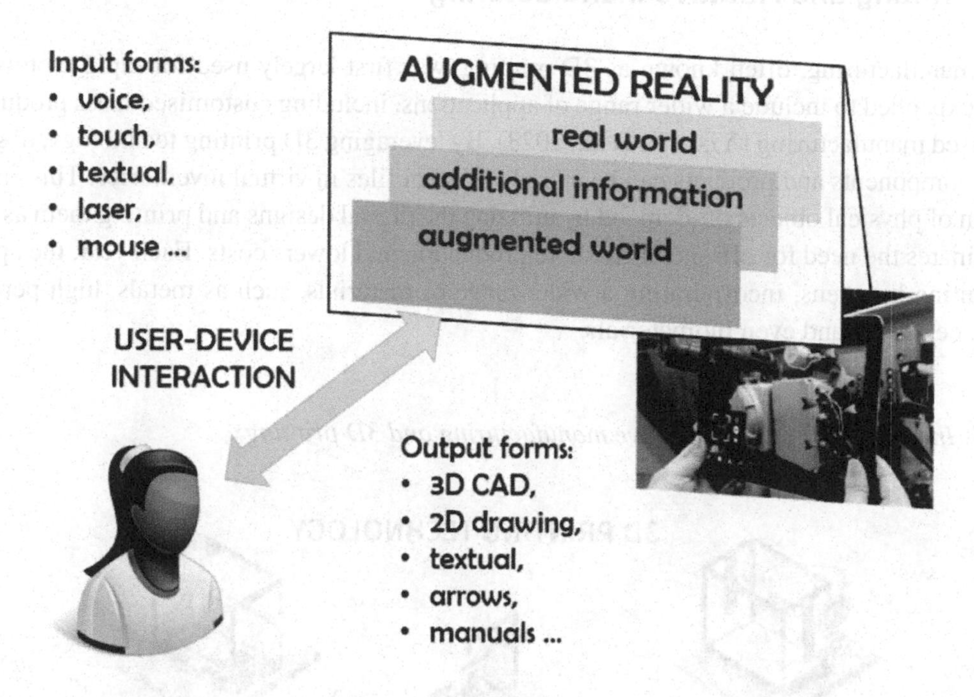

5.5. Internet of Things for Industry (IIoT)

In the context of I 4.0, the IIoT holds such significance that the terms are often used interchangeably. Within I 4.0, a diverse range of physical objects utilize sensors and RFID tags to gather real-time data regarding their condition, performance, and whereabouts. These physical items include gadgets, robots, machinery, equipment, and products. This technological advancement enables businesses to enhance their supply chains, swiftly create and adapt products, avoid equipment disruptions, stay updated on consumer preferences, monitor product and inventory movement, and achieve numerous other benefits.

Figure 10. I 4.0's IIoT

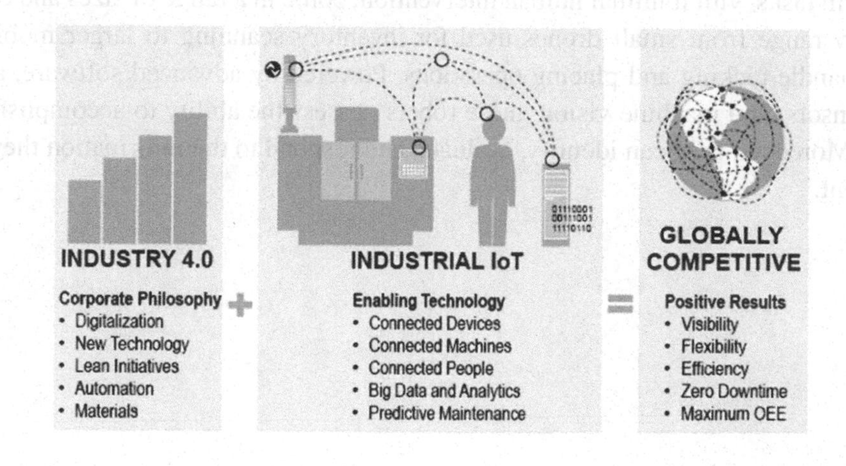

5.6. 3D Printing and Additive Manufacturing

Additive manufacturing, often known as 3D printing, was first largely used for rapid prototyping but has since expanded to include a wider range of applications, including customised mass production and decentralised manufacturing (Yixin Li et al., 2023). By leveraging 3D printing technology, design blueprints for components and products can be stored as digital files in virtual inventories. This enables the production of physical objects on-demand by utilizing the digital designs and printing them as required. This eliminates the need for off-site or offshore production and lowers costs. Each year, the application of 3D printing broadens, incorporating a wider range of materials, such as metals, high-performance polymers, ceramics, and even biomaterials.

Figure 11. Industry 4.0's use of additive manufacturing and 3D printing

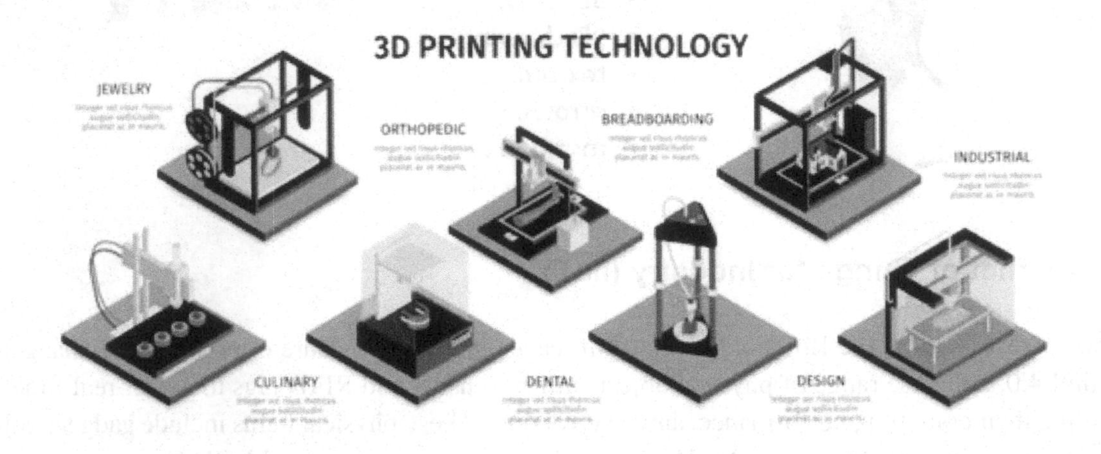

5.7. Autonomous Robots

The advent of I 4.0 takes accompanied in a innovative time of autonomous robots. These robots, engineered to perform tasks with minimal human intervention, come in a range of sizes and cater to diverse objectives. They range from small drones used for inventory scanning to larger mobile robots that autonomously handle picking and placing operations. Powered by advanced software, artificial intelligence (AI), sensors, and machine vision, these robots possess the ability to accomplish complex and intricate tasks. Moreover, they can identify, evaluate, and respond to the information they receive from their environment.

Figure 12. Autonomous robots in Industry 4.0

Autonomous Robots
Simulation
Big Data
Augmented Reality
INDUSTRY 4.0
System Integration
Additive Manufacturing
Internet of Things
Cloud Computing
Cybersecurity

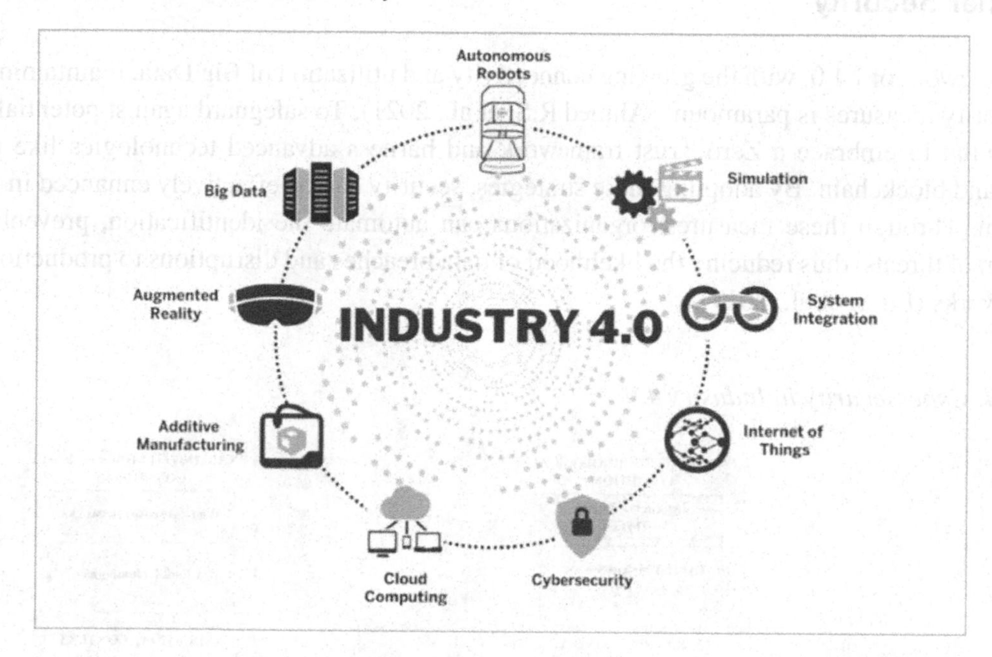

5.8. Digital Twins (DT) or Simulations

A DT refers to a computer-generated depiction of a everyday physical apparatus, item, progression, or scheme. It was produced with the use of sensor data from the IoT. The digital twin stands essential to I 4.0 since it helps with better understanding, evaluation, and improvement of industrial systems and goods. By utilizing a digital twin, businesses gain the ability to pinpoint faulty components, forecast potential problems, and enhance the operational efficiency of their assets (Liu Y. et al., 2017). A digital twin, for instance, can be used by an operator to identify a specific problematic component, anticipate issues, and extend the life of the asset.

Figure 13. Simulation/digital twins in Industry 4.0

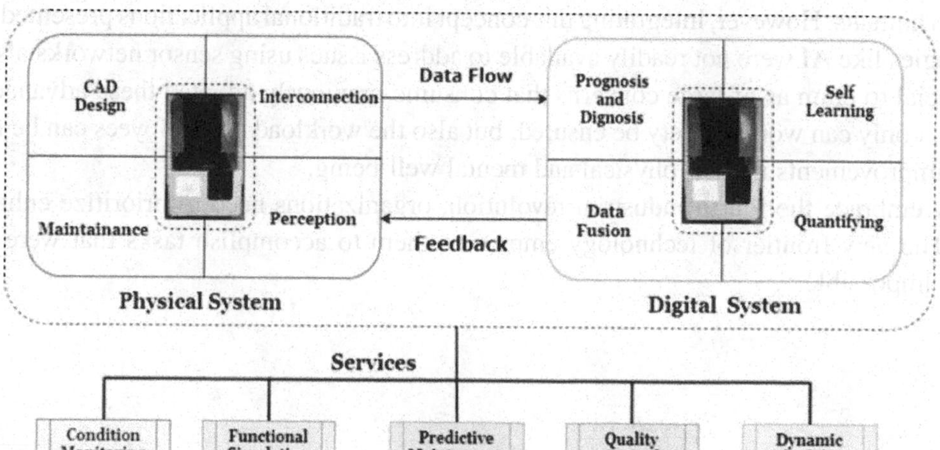

CAD Design
Interconnection
Maintainance
Perception
Physical System
Data Flow
Feedback
Prognosis and Dignosis
Self Learning
Data Fusion
Quantifying
Digital System
Services
Condition Monitoring
Functional Simulation
Predictive Maintenance
Quality Control
Dynamic Scheduling

5.9. Cyber Security

In the framework of I 4.0, with the growing connectivity and utilization of Big Data, maintaining robust cybersecurity measures is paramount (Ahmed R.S. et al., 2021). To safeguard against potential threats, it is essential to embrace a Zero Trust framework and harness advanced technologies like machine learning and blockchain. By adopting these strategies, security can be effectively enhanced in the I 4.0 ecosystem. Through these measures, organizations can automate the identification, prevention, and mitigation of threats, thus reducing the likelihood of data breaches and disruptions to production within their networks (Lu Y. et al., 2017).

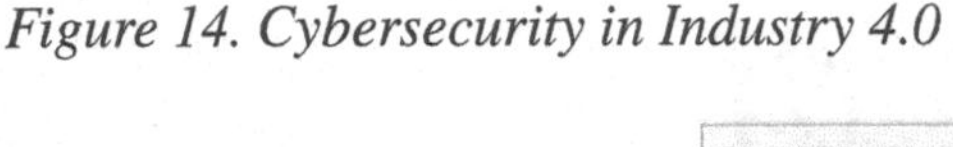
Figure 14. Cybersecurity in Industry 4.0

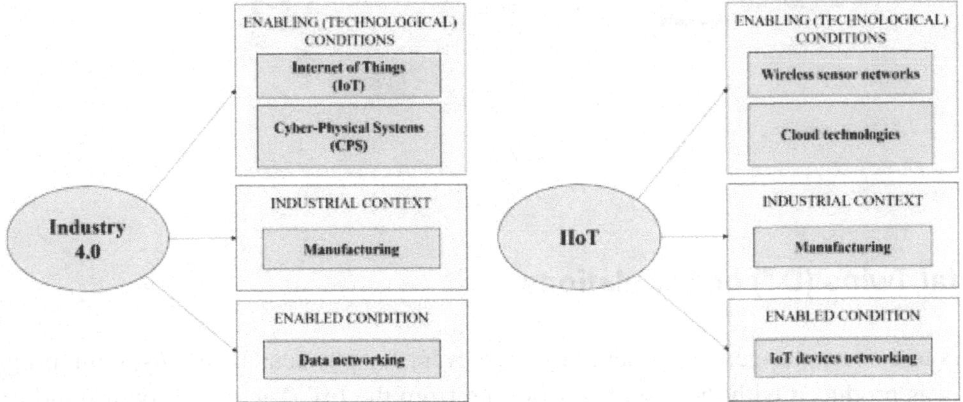

6. I 4.0 DESIGNING A FACTORY

Artificial Intelligence and Machine Learning are now crucial tools that drive outside humble computerization also the usage of manufacturing robots (Hermann M. et al., 2016). These technologies not only help reduce costs but also enhance the quality of products in the market.

One example of advanced automation is collaborative robotics, where industrial robots can work side by side with humans. However, integrating this concept into traditional applications presented challenges as technologies like AI were not readily available to address issues using sensor networks also package.

It is crucial to cram as of large concerns that consume previously adopted these advancements. By doing so, not only can worker safety be ensured, but also the workload of employees can be minimized, leading to improvements in their physical and mental well-being.

To fully embrace the fourth industrial revolution, organizations need to prioritize enhancing productivity. The new frontier of technology empowers them to accomplish tasks that were previously considered impossible.

Figure 15. The Industry 4.0 plant layout

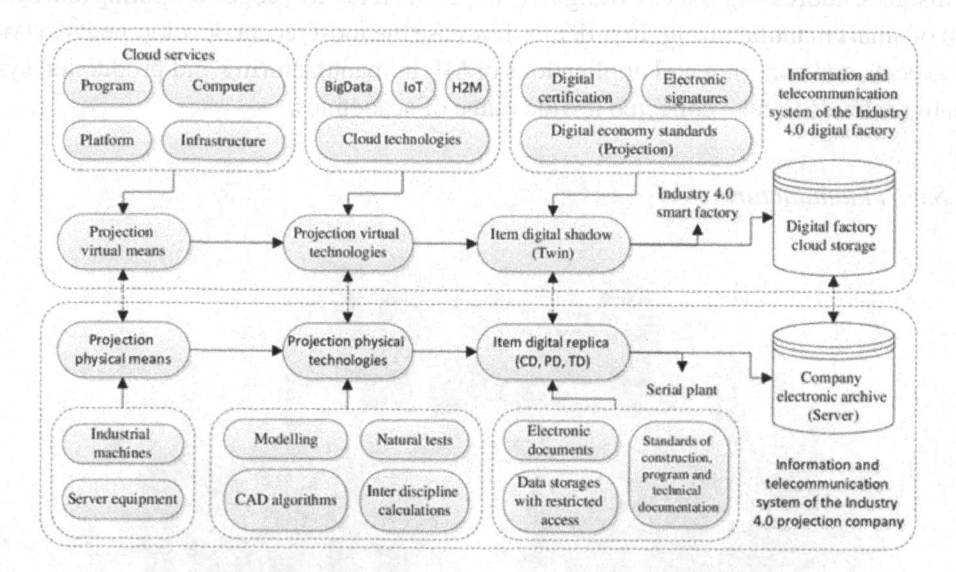

Smart Manufacturing has emerged as a novel domain within the manufacturing industry, aligning with the advent of I 4.0. As depicted in Figure 15, it encompasses various components. Driven by technology, this approach leverages the IoT and internet-connected strategies to monitor and streamline manufacturing processes. The primary objective is to utilize vast amounts of data for automating production, enhancing efficiency, promoting sustainability, optimizing the supply chain, and proactively identifying potential system challenges. By employing advanced analytics, including artificial intelligence and machine learning, manufacturers gain valuable perceptions towards optimize the performance of separate resources and the overall industrial operations.

6.1. Segmentation of Global Smart Manufacturing

The manufacturing industry has experienced significant advancements through the widespread adoption of AI and machine learning, particularly within the framework of I 4.0. Machine learning techniques have made a profound impact on the manufacturing sector. The emphasis on I 4.0 has led to the establishment of smart factories that leverage intelligent sensors, devices, and machinery to continually gather production data. This data-driven approach enables enhanced decision-making and optimization within the manufacturing processes. Processing this gathered data allows ML approaches to produce insightful data that improves industrial productivity without significantly altering resource needs. Furthermore, machine learning techniques have the capability to predict intricate manufacturing patterns, paving the way for intelligent decision support systems across multiple manufacturing tasks. These tasks encompass nonstop scrutiny, analytical conservation, eminence enhancement, progression optimization, supply chain administration, and job arrangement. While various machine learning approaches have been employed in diverse manufacturing applications, there remain challenges and concerns that require resolution. These include managing and processing big data, comprehending and utilizing data effectively in real-time for actionable insights, addressing issues (Wang X. et al., 2017) related to edge computing and cybersecurity in the realm of smart manufacturing. In order to showcase the most recent developments in both the core theoretical aspects and experimental applications of ML in manufacturing and production systems, this singular matter intends to take collected a wide range of academics.

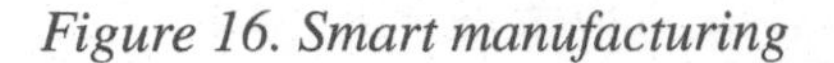

Figure 16. Smart manufacturing

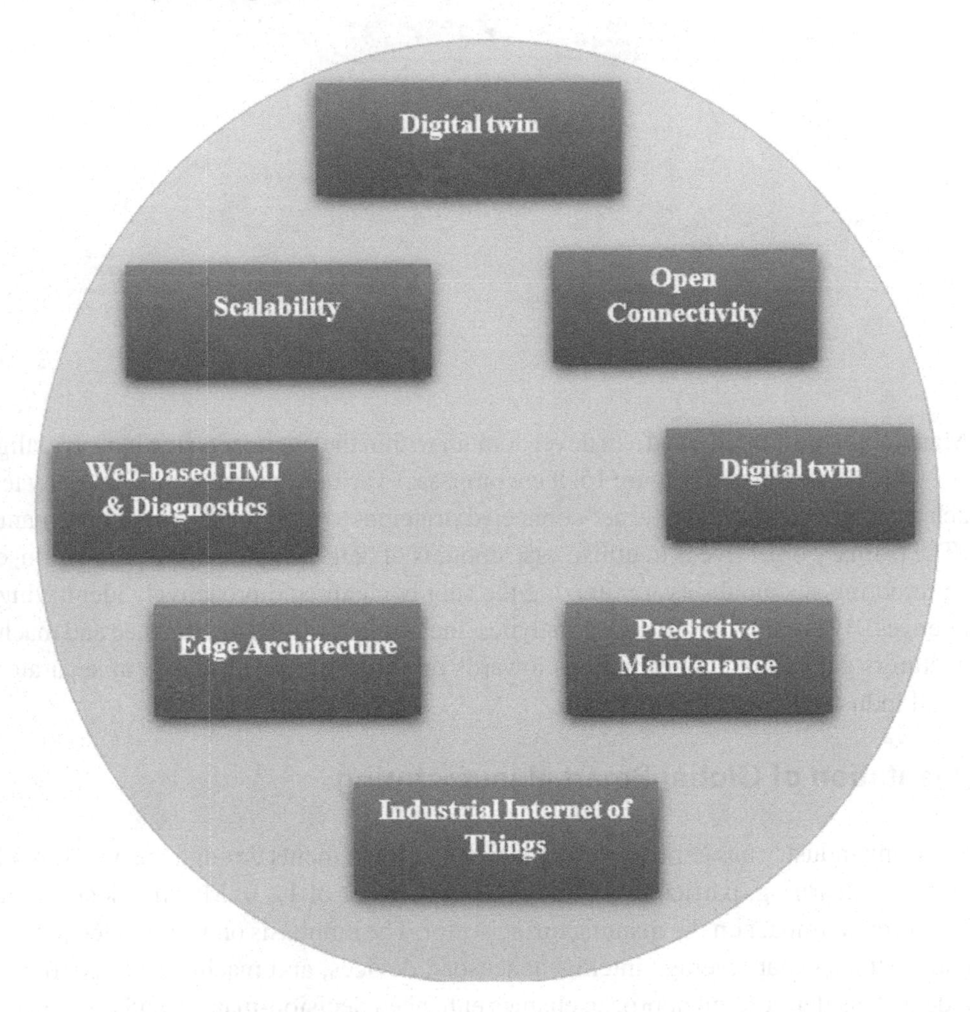

6.2. The Components of I 4.0

I 4.0 creates a CPS environment rich in modern technologies and digital solutions by fusing IT and operational technology. New opportunities are being opened up by this transformation in a variety of industries, including manufacturing, communication, transportation, and healthcare. With the use of sensors, RFID tags, software, and electronics, the IIoT connects physical objects to enable actual-time data collection and internet-based communication.

The widespread adoption of smart sensors and IoT technologies enables the collection and storage of a vast amount of industrial data, providing valuable insights into various aspects of production. Leveraging data from the IIoT, businesses can employ online simulations to create digital twins, virtual replicas of real-world products or systems. This concept enhances process understanding and enables optimization.

Cloud computing plays a crucial role in facilitating the digital twin paradigm by utilizing internet connectivity for data storage, processing, and accessibility. Alongside IIoT and digital twins, other advanced technologies like augmented reality, additive manufacturing, robotics, and virtual reality contribute to the present cohort of manufacturing practices.

Machine learning, a sub-field of artificial intelligence, holds significant latent in identifying complex production patterns and supporting decision-making across areas such as prognostic care, course optimization, job arrangement, eminence upgrading, supply chain management, and also sustainability.

Notably, major corporations are investing substantial resources in advancing AI and machine learning, driving the integration of technology and AI in the manufacturing sector. According to McKinsey, machine learning alone contributes an annual value between $3.5 trillion and $5.8 trillion, with AI and machine learning approaches accounting for 40% of the potential value generated through analytics. Deep learning, computer vision, and reinforcement learning are three AI techniques that have already found use in manufacturing contexts, including structural health monitoring, research on brain-computer interfaces, real-time monitoring and control, defect minimization in additive manufacturing, and augmented reality-based maintenance applications.

The introduction of machine learning in production processes enables intelligent comprehension and enhancement of these processes by evaluating the data collected during production. Autonomous vehicles and machines are clear examples of AI and machine learning applications in the industry, as they can replace operators in monotonous or physically risky tasks. Through the use of sensors and machine learning, continuous evaluation of product quality can occur at each phase of production, departing from the traditional end-of-process evaluation.

The use of predictive maintenance (Wei J et al., 2017) is more accessible and effective with the use of miniaturized and cost-effective sensors, providing real-time information about machine health and enabling the prediction of incorrect operation or failures in individual components. Machine learning also contributes to demand prediction, particularly in industries where production is time-sensitive and cannot be stored for periods of high demand, such as electricity generation. By analyzing historical patterns of energy consumption and meteorological data, machine learning algorithms can optimize energy demand and estimate renewable energy production.

AI plays a critical role in processing and making real-time judgments on Big Data. Key AI approaches such as deep learning, computer visualization, and strengthening knowledge have by now found practical applications within the manufacturing domain. For instance, computer visualization consumes employed in mechanical well-being monitoring, enabling high altitudinal resolution even with cost-effective devices. AI can also explore the potential of brain-computer interfaces for production operators, enhancing industrial safety and ergonomics. Ontology, on the other hand, can be utilized to store and organize knowledge about manufacturing systems.

Actual monitoring, switch, and fault mitigation can be achieved through the analysis of information made by work procedures alike preservative engineering. Machine learning techniques enable the diagnosis and prediction of performance for manufacturing equipment. Additionally, augmented reality tools have been implemented in maintenance tasks, allowing for immediate adaptability in maintenance methods.

Figure 17. Components of I 4.0

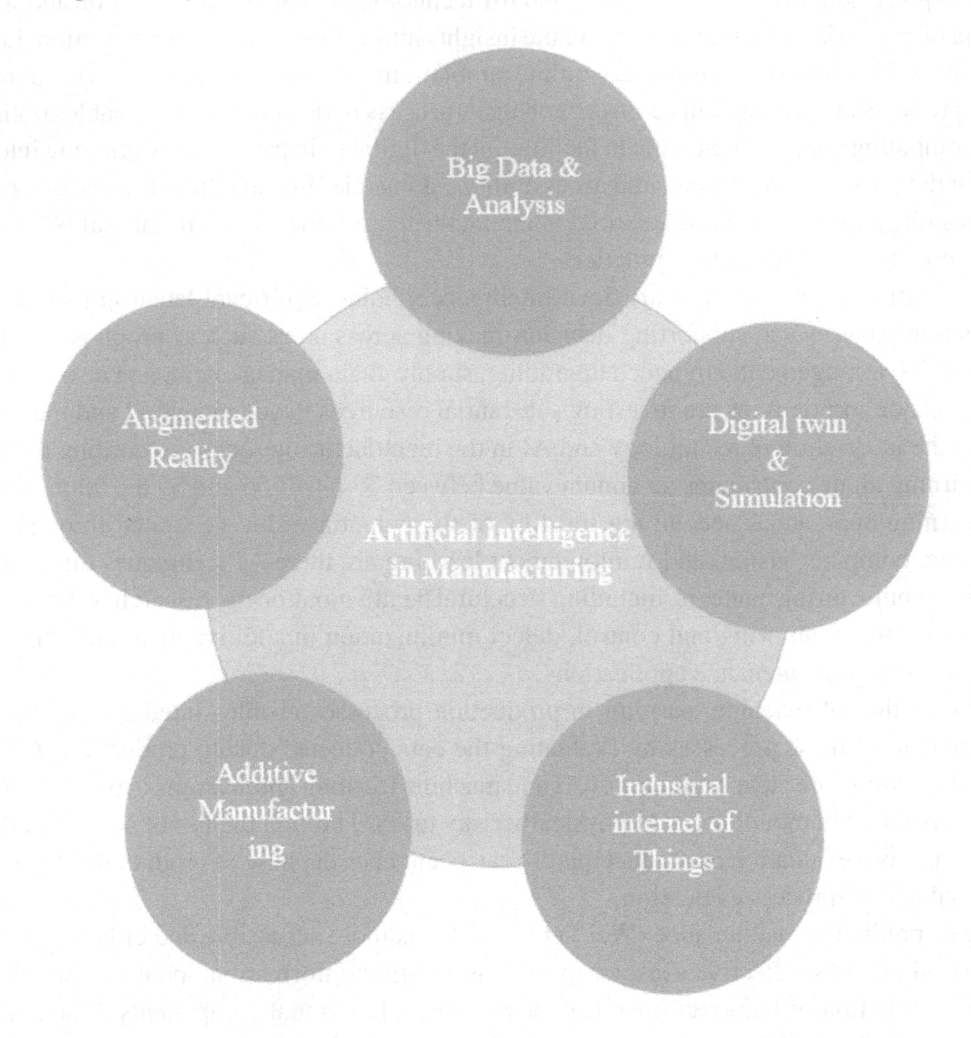

The production process undergoes a transformation known as "Smart Manufacturing" through the integration of machine learning methods. By analyzing data collected during production, these methods enable intelligent understanding and improvement of the processes. This continuous evaluation of data results in the creation of new, flexible methods to changes in production. As a result, individual processes become better connected and optimized. The automatic and real-time implementation of these optimizations is what defines "Smart Manufacturing."

Artificial intelligence and machine learning find practical applications in autonomous vehicles and machines. These technologies allow for the replacement of operators in monotonous tasks or tasks that pose physical risks.

In terms of quality control, the traditional approach involved evaluating product quality until after production is complete. However, with the usage of sensors and machine learning, continuous evaluation of quality can occur at each phase of production.

Predictive maintenance has been made possible by advancements in miniaturization and affordability of sensors. By incorporating numerous measuring points in machines, real-time insights into their overall health can be obtained. These algorithms for machine learning can be trained using datasets, enabling the prediction of incorrect operations or failures in individual components.

Demand prediction poses a common challenge in the industry, particularly when dealing with perishable goods or fluctuating production conditions, such as renewable energy sources. Machine learning can address this challenge by analyzing historical patterns of energy consumption to derive expected demand. It also becomes possible to predict the output of renewable energy using meteorological data.

Chatbots, computer systems capable of engaging in text or voice conversations, have multiple applications. They serve as information providers and perform tasks, reducing barriers to accessing technological solutions. Primarily used in customer service, chatbots accompany customers during the purchasing process or filter inquiries to direct them to specialized human advisors. By offering cost reduction and 24/7 service, chatbots also have the ability to learn from common problems.

7. APPLICATIONS OF AI IN I 4.0

7.1. Using AI in Manufacturing

- Industrial robots empowered by AI are deployed to handle routine tasks, minimizing human errors.
- Applications such as muster, fusing, painting, typical challenging, spontaneous and put-away, expire molding, sweltering, crystal manufacturing, and also crushing showcase the diverse usage of manufacturing robotics.
- With the aid of AI, industrial robots can monitor and enhance their accuracy and efficiency, continuously improving their performance.
- AI may be used to identify and get rid of organisational processing bottlenecks.

7.2. AI in Increasing Product Awareness

- AI enables businesses to experiment with increasing asset efficiency and contributes to increased product awareness.
- Manufacturers may collect data from virtual models and create data-driven goods thanks to digital twins.
- Producers can design different product variations to cater to market preferences for personalization.

7.3. AI in Monitoring and Safety

- In several businesses, artificial intelligence (AI) improves monitoring and safety. It can be used for personnel identification, thermal scanning, contact tracking, sanitation, and employee contact tracking.
- AI solutions aid in long-term security, less downtime, and superior final goods.
- AI-based analytical solutions are used by engineering organisations to improve productivity.

7.4. AI in Providing Appropriate Information

- ML and AI are able to detect small flaws in circuit boards that are invisible to the human eye.
- Collaborative robots may communicate with people and follow their instructions, increasing long-term safety.

7.5. AI in Manufacturing and Design

- AI is crucial for the creation of products employing generative architecture.
- It uses comprehensive design details and parameters to find the most appropriate output solutions.

7.6. AI in Defect Detection

- Real-time defect detection can be achieved through the utilization of AI technologies such as cameras, lasers, and scanning devices.
- By implementing this system (Kagermann H. et al., 2013), waste caused by defects can be minimized without the need for human intervention, resulting in time and resource savings.

7.7. AI in Enhancing Product Efficiency

- AI integration into manufacturing operations enhances production efficiency.
- It uses very accurate and potent robots in place of optical inspections.
- AI implementation requires collaboration between manufacturers and experts to find customized solutions.

7.8. AI in Quality Assurance

- AI improves quality assurance by enabling computer vision for the timely detection of product defects.
- It minimizes downtime, enhances product development, and warns manufacturing teams of failures.

7.9. AI in Optimizing Processes

- In Industry 4.0, AI optimises workflows and encourages high productivity.
- It enables human-robot collaboration and intelligent support systems.
- AI offers both possibilities and challenges in actual manufacturing facility.

7.10. AI in Supply Chain Monitoring

- AI technologies make supply chain management more intelligent.
- Predictive analytics can effectively predict product demand.
- Stock management and order records can be handled by AI apps.

Figure 18. AI's contributions to Industry 4.0

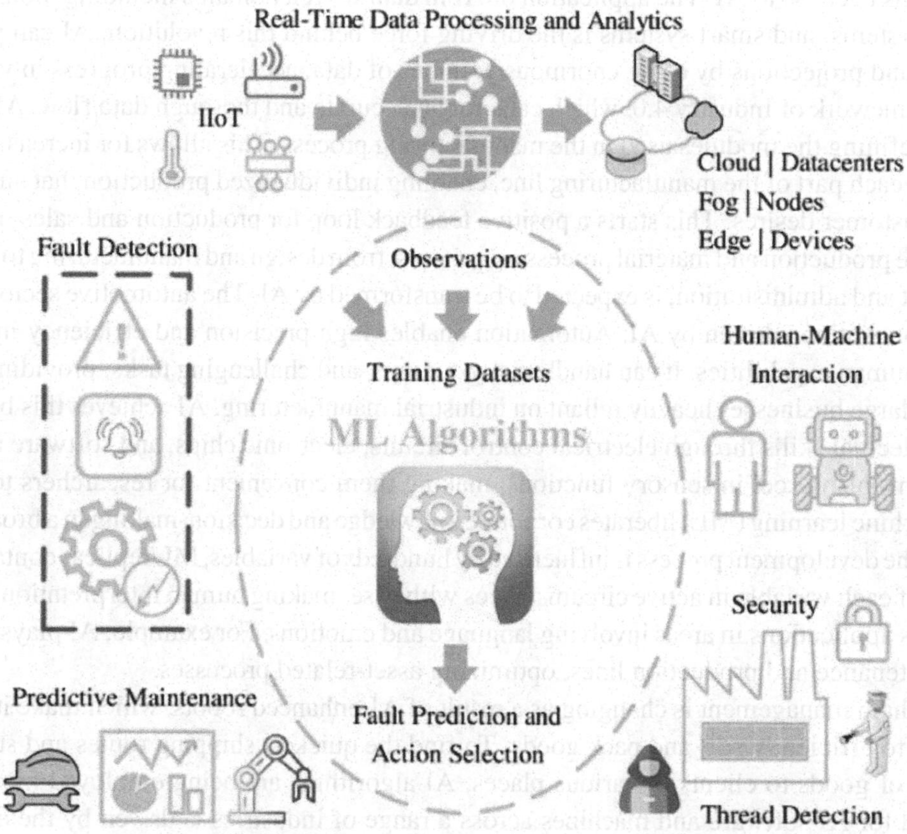

7.11. AI in Production Management

- Inventory management, market management, and production management all require AI.
- Robots with AI capabilities complete tasks swiftly and enhance sales, customer service, manufacturing, and quality.
- Process optimization, cost savings, quick decision-making, and improved customer experience are all benefits of AI systems.

7.12. Digitalization and Industry 4.0

- For the heavy usage of AI and ML frameworks, alphanumeric information must be well-matched then reusable.
- Industries want to be conscious of their level of making digital and preparation for I-4.0 implementation.
- A number of indicators have been created to gauge Industry 4.0 maturity.
- Improved quality control, coordination with human machines, risk analysis, and real-time monitoring can enhance productivity.

Healthcare, life sciences, real estate, education, manufacturing, and other fields have all seen revolutionary breakthroughs because to AI. The application of AI in data-driven domains including biology, robotics, connected systems, and smart systems is the driving force behind this revolution. AI can produce useful insights and projections by using enormous volumes of data, accelerating progress in various areas.

In the framework of Industry 4.0, which calls for an accurate and thorough data flow, AI plays a crucial role in refining the modules used in the manufacturing process. This allows for increased scalability and detail in each part of the manufacturing line, enabling individualized production that anticipates and embodies customer desires. This starts a positive feedback loop for production and sales input.

The entire production and material processing process, from design and manufacturing to supply chain management and administration, is expected to be transformed by AI. The automotive sector has already witnessed innovations driven by AI. Automation enables high precision and efficiency in production, surpassing human capabilities. It can handle risky, tedious, and challenging tasks, providing a competitive edge to large businesses heavily reliant on industrial manufacturing. AI achieves this by mimicking human intellectual skills through electrical control circuits, electronic chips, and software mechanisms.

AI systems also excel in sensory functions, making them convenient for researchers to connect on servers. Machine learning (ML) liberates corporate knowledge and decision-making in a broader domain. Even when the development process is influenced by hundreds of variables, ML replicas container forecast the impact of each variable in active circumstances with ease, making human interpretation challenging. AI also finds applications in areas involving language and emotions. For example, AI plays a significant role in maintenance and production lines, optimizing asset-related processes.

Supply chain management is changing as a result of AI-enhanced robots, which make it possible for warehouses to efficiently sort and pack goods. To find the quickest shipping routes and streamline the distribution of goods to clients in various places, AI algorithms are being employed more and more. The demand for AI software and machines across a range of industries is driven by the abundance of vast data on product assessments and performance. Manufacturers may proactively prevent equipment disruptions and anticipate maintenance needs using predictive system management, which is powered by AI-driven predictive analytics.

AI is driving transformative changes across industries by leveraging data and enabling advancements in arenas for instance robotics, engineering, supply chain management, and then predictive analytics. Its ability to mimic human intelligence and handle complex tasks beyond human capacity makes it a powerful tool for improving efficiency and decision-making in various domains.

8. HEALTHCARE I 4.0

The healthcare industry is embracing I 4.0 concepts to enhance its services. Ideas for instance interoperability, visibility, decentralization, present capabilities, provision direction, and modularity are being adopted. To integrate the fourth industrial revolution into healthcare, technologies like the IIoT, cloud-based design, and engineering are being utilized.

Incorporating I 4.0 into healthcare involves the utilization of various technologies, including information combination, artificial intelligence, big data, cybersecurity, the internet of things, robotics, 3D printing, and virtual reality. These elements are being integrated into the healthcare industry to drive advancements and improvements in patient care and overall healthcare services. Healthcare places a greater emphasis on human-to-human interaction than on human-machine interaction, in contrast to other industries.

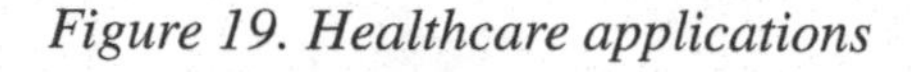

Figure 19. Healthcare applications

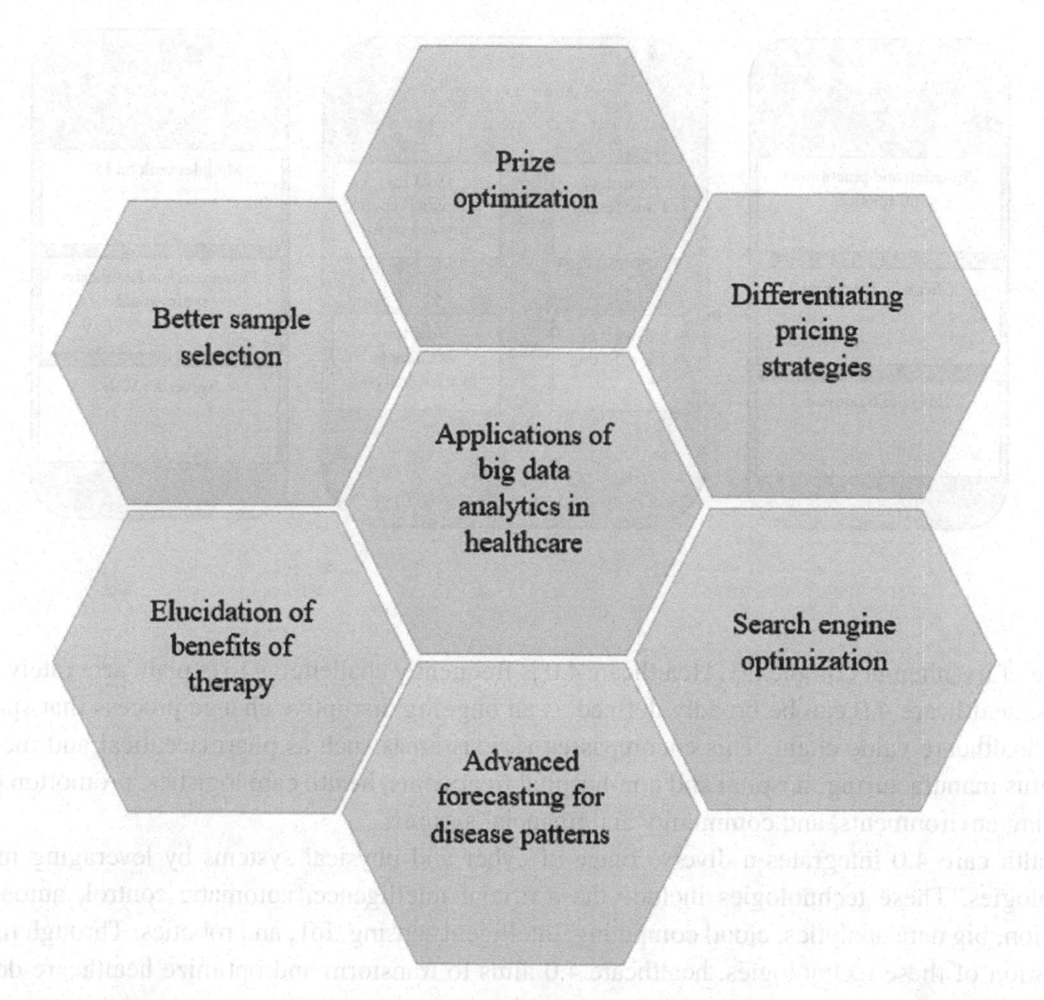

By using integrated healthcare platforms, healthcare is described as the delivery of virtualized, scattered, and present amenities to patients, experts, and carers. It seeks to facilitate the shift from empirical data to precision medicine through collaboration, coherence, and convergence. This is accomplished by establishing a smart health network made up of patients, gadgets, medical suppliers, and healthcare professionals.

Healthcare 4.0 is a human-centered approach, gathering information from both individual users and healthcare organisations to offer individualised guidance and care based on in-depth data analysis. It shifts away from the conventional hospital centric care model towards a extra computer-generated and scattered one by using technologies like artificial intelligence, data analytics, deep learning, genomics, home healthcare, robotics, and 3D printing of tissue and implants.

Healthcare 4.0 is a strategic concept based on the ideas of I 4.0 that intends to use technology to recover health care services and communication amongst health care participants. It consists of the three components of people, technology, and design.

Figure 20. Healthcare Industry 4.0

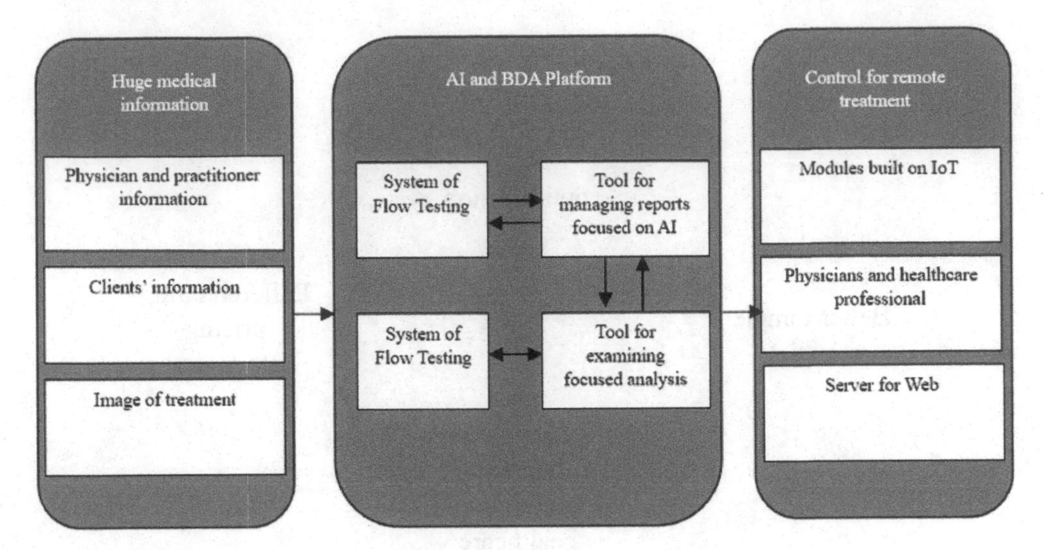

Due of its inherent complexity, Healthcare 4.0 is frequently challenging to explain accurately. Nonetheless, healthcare 4.0 can be broadly defined as an ongoing disruptive change process that spans the entire healthcare value chain. This encompasses various areas such as pharmaceutical and medicinal apparatus manufacturing, hospital and non-hospital treatments, health care logistics, promotion of well breathing environments, and community and financial systems.

Health care 4.0 integrates a diverse range of cyber and physical systems by leveraging multiple technologies. These technologies include the artificial intelligence, automatic control, autonomous execution, big data analytics, cloud computing, intelligent sensing, IoT, and robotics. Through the tight integration of these technologies, healthcare 4.0 aims to transform and optimize healthcare delivery. These technologies promote the digitization of healthcare services and businesses in addition to enabling the digitalization of healthcare products and technologies.

Healthcare 4.0 represents a transformative approach to healthcare that leverages technology to enhance service delivery, improve connectivity among stakeholders, and drive advancements across the entire healthcare value chain.

9. INDUSTRY 4.0'S USE OF AI

Business operations are about to undergo a transformation thanks to that adoption I 4.0 in a number of trades, including industrial, communication, transportation, and healthcare. Corporate executives will be able to create creative and reliable business models thanks to the important information that artificial intelligence (AI) will give them. Unlike humans, AI can detect patterns and phenomena that are not easily visible, thereby offering a deeper understanding of the data. This, in turn, will facilitate data-oriented decision-making, free from individual biases.

AI and Machine Learning (ML) tools will gather data from diverse sources, allowing businesses to identify growth opportunities, expand their reach, and even develop fresh goods and services. Additionally, new opportunities and applications will be made possible by the IoT interaction together with cutting-edge skills like blockchain and edge computing. As AI continues to advance, it will offer even more advantages, contributing to the creation of a wired, intelligent, and smart society.

Figure 21. Future of AI

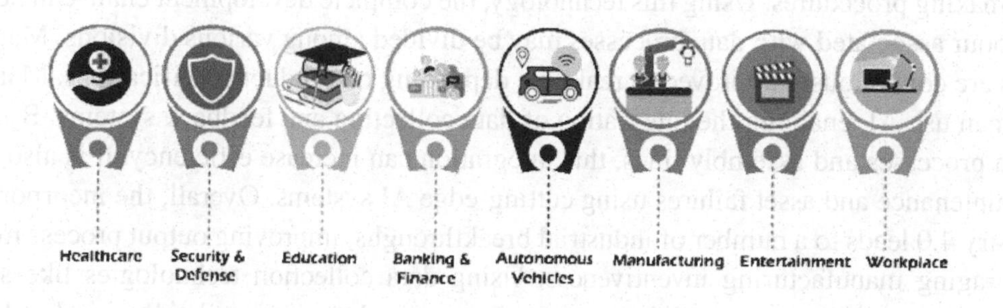

In the context of manufacturing, AI will help streamline operations by identifying and refining ineffective procedures. Future advancements in robotics as a service will enable machines to replicate human functions like image and speech recognition. Additionally, this system can monitor and assess production targets, which aids in the creation of prognostic conservation models.

The knowledge of an I 4.0 in various sectors such as manufacturing, communication, transportation, and healthcare involves the idea of smart factories operating continuously to maximize production efficiency. However, this continuous operation requires employees to work in shifts, which can disrupt their work-life balance. It means that employees will no longer have a fixed routine in their shift system, leading to non-standard employment, shift work, disturbance in daily rhythm, and social disconnection. Furthermore, the use of information systems in production blurs the line between employees' personal and professional lives, resulting in psychosocial risks. Kocaay's research highlights the importance of employers evaluating the I 4.0's effect on workplace health and safety, monitoring software changes popular equipment then apparatus, and providing necessary training to workers. Industry 4.0 also demands employees to possess a range of new and specialized skills, which can be challenging for those accustomed to traditional production practices. Therefore, employees must be motivated to adapt to new production systems, be open to learning, and embrace flexibility and continuing education. Employers will need to focus on training existing employees and recruiting individuals who are capable of learning and adapting effectively.

10. CONCLUSION

Making advantage of machine learning in numerous industries for instance manufacturing, communication, conveyance, formerly healthcare, known as Industry 4.0, is a developing trend with major implications for the near term. This transformation will not only affect large corporations nonetheless, minor and medium of sized one's dealings, as the price of hardware required for data collection and processing continues to decrease, making this technology more accessible. This article highlights six potential applications of Industry 4.0, showcasing just a small example of the potential changes it can bring. For instance, a manufacturing organisation can effectively manage and track their supply chain, perform quality assurance, and reduce their overall energy consumption by using IIoT.

I 4.0, through the assistance of artificial intelligence, permits automation of control across dissimilar phases of making procedures. Using this technology, the complete development chain can be integrated and the labour associated with data processes may be divided among various divisions. Manufacturing operations are continuously improved in real time depending on product specifications. Manufacturing processes can use AI, enabling the integration of data collecting and feedback systems. By combining production processes and assembly lines, this integration can increase efficiency. It is also possible to predict maintenance and asset failures using cutting-edge AI systems. Overall, the incorporation of AI with Industry 4.0 leads to a number of industrial breakthroughs, improving output process management and encouraging manufacturing inventiveness. Using data collection technologies like sensors and cameras, the corporal illustration of the construction atmosphere is completely visualised, and cloud technology is used to collect, store, and analyse the information made by intellectual mechanisms. This will eventually allow Industry 4.0 to operate seamlessly by gathering and utilising cloud data.

REFERENCES

Ahmed, R. S., Ahmed, E. S. A., & Saeed, R. A. (2021) Machine learning in cyber-physical systems in industry 4.0. In Artificial Intelligence Paradigms for Smart Cyber-Physical Systems, 20–41. IGI Global.

Ardolino, M., Bacchetti, A., Dolgui, A., Franchini, G., Ivanov, D., & Nair, A. (2022). The impacts of digital technologies on coping with the COVID-19 pandemic in the manufacturing industry: A systematic literature review. *International Journal of Production Research*, 1–24. doi:10.1080/00207543.2022.2127960

Ashima, R., Haleem, A., Bahl, S., Javaid, M., Mahla, S. K., & Singh, S. (2021). Automation and manufacturing of smart materials in additive manufacturing technologies using internet of things towards the adoption of industry 4.0. [Crossref, Google Scholar.]. *Materials Today: Proceedings*, *45*, 5081–5088. doi:10.1016/j.matpr.2021.01.583

Bag, S., Pretorius, J. H., Gupta, S., & Dwivedi, Y. K. (2021). Role of institutional pressures and resources in the adoption of big data analytics powered artificial intelligence, sustainable manufacturing practices and circular economy capabilities. [Crossref, Google Scholar.]. *Technological Forecasting and Social Change*, *163*, 120420. doi:10.1016/j.techfore.2020.120420

Bai, C., Dallasega, P., Orzes, G., & Sarkis, J. (2020). Industry 4.0 technologies assessment: A sustainability perspective. [Crossref, Google Scholar.]. *International Journal of Production Economics*, *229*, 107776. doi:10.1016/j.ijpe.2020.107776

Böhmann, T., Leimeister, J. M., & Riedl, C. (2016). Design principles for Industries 4.0 scenarios. In *Proceedings of the 49th Hawaii International Conference on System Sciences*. IEEE.

Döring, T., Schneider, U., Uhlmann, E., & Thoben, K. D. (2016). Dynamic production networks in the context of Industry 4.0: A literature review. *Journal of Intelligent Manufacturing*, *27*(1), 111–128.

Duan, L., Xu, L. D., Cai, H., & Zheng, L. R. (2019). Artificial intelligence with internet of things: A conceptual framework. *Journal of Industrial Information Integration*, *13*, 1–6.

Gupta, N., Dutta, G., Mitra, K., & Tiwari, M. K. (2022). Analytics with stochastic optimisation: Experimental results of demand uncertainty in process industries. *International Journal of Production Research*, 1–18.

Hermann, M., Pentek, T., & Otto, B. (2016). Design principles for Industry 4.0 scenarios: *A literature review*, 1-12.

Kagermann, H., Wahlster, W., & Helbig, J. (2013). Recommendations for implementing the strategic initiative INDUSTRIE 4.0. *Final report of the Industrie 4.0 working group*. DIN.

Lee, J., Bagheri, B., & Kao, H. A. (2015). A cyber-physical systems architecture for Industry 4.0-based manufacturing systems. *Manufacturing Letters*, *3*, 18–23. doi:10.1016/j.mfglet.2014.12.001

Li, Y., Hu, F., Liu, Y., Ryan, M., & Wang, R. (2023). A hybrid model compression approach via knowledge distillation for predicting energy consumption in additive manufacturing. *International Journal of Production Research*, *61*(13), 4525–4547. doi:10.1080/00207543.2022.2160501

Liu, Y., Gao, Q., He, Y., Wang, W., & Ren, X. (2017). Resource virtualization for cyber-physical systems in cloud manufacturing. *Journal of Intelligent Manufacturing*, *28*(5), 1117–1129.

Lu, Y., Xu, L. D., & Li, X. (2017). Internet of things (IoT) for smart precision agriculture and farming in rural areas. *Computer Networks*, *114*, 1–14.

Lu, Y., & Yao, Y. (2017). Artificial intelligence in service. *Science China. Information Sciences*, *60*(10), 100301.

Mourtzis, D., Vlachou, E., Milas, N., & Xanthopoulos, N. (2017). The paradigm shift towards cloud manufacturing and its impact on job design. *Journal of Manufacturing Systems*, *43*, 184–191.

Münch, C., Wehrle, M., Kuhn, T., & Hartmann, E. (2023). The research landscape around the physical internet – a bibliometric analysis. *International Journal of Production Research*, 1–19. doi:10.1080/00207543.2023.2205969

Romero, D., & Vernadat, F. (2016). Enterprise information systems state of the art: Past, present and future trends. *Computers in Industry*, *79*, 3–13. doi:10.1016/j.compind.2016.03.001

Schumacher, A., Erol, S., & Sihn, W. (2016). A maturity model for assessing Industry 4.0 readiness and maturity of manufacturing enterprises. *Procedia CIRP*, *52*, 161–166. doi:10.1016/j.procir.2016.07.040

Silva, M. C., & da Costa, C. A. (2018). Cyber-physical systems and Industry 4.0: A contemporary overview. *Procedia Manufacturing*, *25*, 268–275.

Stock, T., & Seliger, G. (2016). Opportunities of sustainable manufacturing in Industry 4.0. *Procedia CIRP*, *40*, 536–541. doi:10.1016/j.procir.2016.01.129

Strozzi, F., & Pozzi, R. (2023). Trend and seasonality features extraction with pre-trained CNN and recurrence plot. *International Journal of Production Research*, 1–12. doi:10.1080/00207543.2023.2227903

Takeda-Berger, S. L., & Frazzon, E. M. (2023). An inventory data-driven model for predictive-reactive production scheduling. *International Journal of Production Research*, 1–25. doi:10.1080/00207543.2023.2217297

Tao, F., Cheng, J., Qi, Q., Zhang, M., Zhang, H., & Sui, F. (2018). Digital twin-driven product design, manufacturing and service with big data. *International Journal of Advanced Manufacturing Technology*, *94*(9-12), 3563–3576. doi:10.1007/s00170-017-0233-1

Wang, S., Wan, J., Zhang, D., Li, D., & Zhang, C. (2016). Towards smart factory for Industry 4.0: A self-organized multi-agent system with big data-based feedback and coordination. *Computer Networks*, *101*, 158–168. doi:10.1016/j.comnet.2015.12.017

Wang, X., Wan, J., & Imran, M. (2017). Internet of things for industrial automation systems: A survey. *IEEE Transactions on Industrial Informatics*, *13*(5), 2233-2247.

Wang, Y., & Kung, L. (2018). A survey on industrial Internet of Things: A cyber-physical systems perspective. *Journal of Industrial Information Integration*, *10*, 28–40.

Wei, J., Yang, Y., & Xu, L. D. (2017). Industrial Internet of Things-based intelligent energy management system for sustainable machining in Industry 4.0. *Journal of Cleaner Production*, *142*, 476–489.

Xu, C., Wang, J., Tao, J., Zhang, J., & Zhong, R. Y. (2023). A knowledge augmented image deblurring method with deep learning for in-situ quality detection of yarn production. *International Journal of Production Research*, *61*(13), 4220–4236. doi:10.1080/00207543.2021.2010827

Yang, F., & Gu, S. (2021). Industry 4.0, a revolution that requires technology and national strategies. *Complex & Intelligent Systems*, *7*(3), 1311–1325. doi:10.1007/s40747-020-00267-9

Zhong, R. Y., Xu, X., Klotz, E., & Newman, S. T. (2017). Intelligent manufacturing in the context of industry 4.0: A review. *Engineering (Beijing)*, *3*(5), 616–630. doi:10.1016/J.ENG.2017.05.015

Chapter 19
Transformative Effects of Blockchain and IoT in Shaping Industry 5.0 Environments

Shabnam Kumari
SRM Institute of Science and Technology, Chennai, India

Mahmoud Ragab
https://orcid.org/0000-0002-4427-0016
King Abdulaziz University, Saudi Arabia

ABSTRACT

In the era of Industry 5.0, characterized by the convergence of physical and digital worlds, the integration of blockchain technology and the internet of things (IoT) has emerged as a pivotal paradigm shift. This chapter explores the perspectives, issues, and challenges associated with the amalgamation of Blockchain and IoT to foster a transformative environment for industries. This chapter begins by providing an overview of Industry 5.0 and its key principles, emphasizing the need for robust and secure data handling in this context. It then explains the application of blockchain as a distributed ledger technology to enhance the IoT ecosystem by enabling trust, security, and transparency in data transactions. Various use cases and real-world applications of this fusion (of IoTs and blockchain) are discussed, ranging from supply chain management to smart cities and healthcare. Despite its promising potential, the integration of blockchain and IoT also presents several critical issues and challenges.

1. INTRODUCTION

Industry 5.0 is the next evolution of the manufacturing industry, where smart factories use emerging technologies such as the Internet of Things (IoT), Artificial Intelligence (AI), and blockchain to create a more connected and efficient manufacturing process. The integration of blockchain technology and IoT devices in Industry 5.0 has the potential to create new opportunities for businesses and consumers. However, this integration also presents several security, privacy, and technical challenges that need to

DOI: 10.4018/979-8-3693-2081-5.ch019

be addressed to ensure the success of this emerging ecosystem. This work aims to explore these challenges in detail and proposes potential solutions. Security challenges include the vulnerability of IoT devices to attacks and the need for secure communication between devices. Privacy challenges arise from the large amount of data generated by IoT devices and the need to protect user data. Technical challenges include the scalability of blockchain technology, interoperability between different blockchain networks, and the energy consumption of blockchain mining. Addressing these challenges is important to ensure the successful integration of blockchain and IoT in Industry 5.0. This work will examine the potential solutions to these challenges, including the use of secure hardware modules for IoT devices and the development of consensus algorithms that reduce energy consumption. Ultimately, this work highlights the importance of understanding and mitigating these challenges to achieve the full potential of blockchain and IoT in Industry 5.0.

In the rapidly evolving digital landscape, the convergence of blockchain technology and IoT has opened up new possibilities and challenges in terms of security, privacy, and technical issues. This combination has the potential to revolutionize various industries, ranging from healthcare and supply chain management to energy and transportation. Now few of essential perspectives of blockchain can be discussed here as:

- Blockchain technology, often associated with cryptocurrencies like Bitcoin, is a decentralized and immutable ledger that enables secure and transparent transactions. It provides a tamper-proof record of all activities, ensuring trust and accountability in a network of participants. On the other hand, the IoT refers to the interconnection of physical devices, sensors, and systems that collect and exchange data over the internet, enabling intelligent decision-making and automation.
- When these two technologies converge, they create a powerful ecosystem where IoT devices can securely communicate and transact with each other through blockchain networks. This has the potential to address several challenges, such as data integrity, trust, and interoperability, which are inherent in IoT environments.
- From a security perspective, the integration of blockchain and IoT introduces several benefits. Blockchain's decentralized nature eliminates single points of failure, making it more resilient to cyber-attacks. Additionally, the use of cryptographic algorithms ensures secure authentication and authorization of IoT devices, protecting against unauthorized access and data manipulation. Blockchain also enables secure and auditable firmware updates, ensuring the integrity and authenticity of IoT device software.
- Privacy is another critical aspect in the blockchain-IoT environment. As IoT devices collect large amount of personal and sensitive data, preserving privacy becomes paramount. Blockchain's immutability and transparency can help address privacy issues by providing individuals with control over their data and enabling selective data sharing through smart contracts. Privacy-enhancing techniques, such as zero-knowledge proofs and homomorphic encryption, can be employed to further protect sensitive information.

From a technical perspective, integrating blockchain and IoT involves addressing scalability, latency, and energy efficiency challenges. Traditional blockchain networks may face scalability issues when dealing with the massive influx of IoT-generated data. However, advancements in blockchain technologies, such as sharding and off-chain solutions, are being explored to improve scalability without compromising security. Latency, or the delay in data transmission, is another consideration. IoT applications often require real-time or near-real-time data processing. Optimizing consensus mechanisms and network protocols can help reduce latency, ensuring timely decision-making in IoT environments. Furthermore, energy efficiency is important in IoT deployments, as many devices operate on limited power sources. Blockchain's energy-intensive consensus mechanisms, such as proof-of-work, may not be suitable for resource-constrained IoT devices. Therefore, alternative consensus algorithms like proof-of-stake or delegated proof-of-stake can be considered to reduce energy consumption. In summary, the convergence of blockchain and IoT holds immense potential for transforming various industries. However, it is important to address the associated security, privacy, and technical challenges. By adding blockchain's decentralized and transparent nature, combined with privacy-enhancing techniques and optimized technical solutions, a secure, private, and scalable blockchain-IoT ecosystem can be built, facilitating trust, interoperability, and innovation in the digital world.

2. LITERATURE REVIEW

A review in the area of blockchain is conducted by (Mohanta et al., 2019) and for the same they have conducted this survey, five databases—Sciencedirect, IEEE Xplore, Web of Science, ACM Digital Library, and Inderscience—were taken into consideration. 100+ research papers were taken into account in the final databases for the survey after the initial step of removal. The primary goal of the study is to give the academic research community a thorough overview of the numerous applications of Blockchain technology. The difficulties of implementing Blockchian and the related security and privacy issues have been highlighted in this work. For the first time, a survey of this kind has been conducted, reviewing Blockchain applications and the security and privacy issues that go along with them. On recently released linked publications, a thorough summary of the state of blockchain research has been constructed (Ma et al., 2020). More research has been done on the primary security, privacy, and trust technologies in crowdsourcing services and applications related to this sector in order to demonstrate its functional worth. Lastly, the benefits and difficulties of blockchains are covered. In order to aid future study on blockchain technology used in crowdsourcing services, it is intended that this document would serve as a useful reference.

The study conducted by (Bernabe et al., 2019) which provides a thorough analysis of the state-of-the-art privacy-preserving research techniques and solutions in blockchain, as well as the primary related privacy challenges in this exciting and disruptive technology. The survey includes privacy strategies in permissioned and private blockchains as well as privacy-preserving research proposals and solutions in public and permissionless blockchains, such as Bitcoin and Ethereum. The analysis of various blockchain use cases includes looking at areas including eGovernment, eHealth, cryptocurrency, Smart cities, and cooperative ITS. Identifying the blockchain quality attributes and analyzing the current implementation quality challenges are the goals of this research. A survey of the literature is done by (Koteska et al., 2017) to find out what standards of quality are currently needed for blockchain implementation. The research on the standards for using blockchain technology is still in its early stages, according to the findings. The findings of this study may be applied to further examination of the qualities necessary for Blockchain implementations and enhancement of the standard of Blockchain systems.

By addressing the structure of the blockchain technology, the various consensus algorithms, as well as the prospects and limitations from the perspective of the security and privacy of data in blockchains, an attempt has made by (Joshi et al., 2018) to do a thorough survey on the technology. We also explore upcoming patterns to which blockchain technology may be able to adapt. A thorough survey of the blockchain applications has been presented by (Gadekallu et al., 2022) for the metaverse in order to better understand the function of blockchain in the metaverse. We begin by giving a general overview of blockchain and the metaverse and highlighting the reasons for using blockchain for the metaverse. We then go into great detail about technical aspects of blockchain-based metaverse methods, including data collection, storage, sharing, interoperability, and privacy protection. We outline the technological difficulties of the metaverse for each perspective before highlighting how blockchain can be useful. Additionally, we look into how blockchain will affect important metaverse enablers including the IoT, digital twins, multisensory and immersive apps, artificial intelligence, and big data. A study presented by (Mohanta et al., 2020) examine and catalogue the IoT system's security and privacy problems. Second, we offer various security solutions based on blockchain technology. The brief study is explained, along with the inclusion of IoT technologies and enabling technology. Last but not least, a case study utilizing the Ethereum-based blockchain system in a smart IoT system is executed, and the outcomes are examined. An article presented by (Leng et al., 2022) focuses on enterprise Blockchains and offers a thorough study of its fundamental elements, supporting technology, and potential uses.

A systematic review paper is presented by (Xu et al., 2021) where they first examine Industry 5.0's evolutionary path and its three defining traits: human-centricity, sustainability, and resiliency. It is explained how Industry 5.0 is interpreted, and its varied essence is examined. Then, this study designs a tri-dimension system architecture for implementing Industry 5.0, namely, the technical dimension, reality dimension, and application dimension. The article goes on to explore important enablers, the next implementation path, prospective applications, and difficulties of realistic Industry 5.0 applications. Lastly, the current research's shortcomings are reviewed along with possible future research possibilities. It is anticipated that this review work would spark exciting discussions and debates and unite the talents of all living things to create a thorough Industry 5.0 system. The European Commission unveiled Industry 5.0 ten years after the launch of Industry 4.0. Although Industry 5.0 is thought to be value-driven, Industry 4.0 is thought to be technology-driven. The coexistence of two Industrial Revolutions raises issues, which calls for debates and explanations (Martynov et al., 2019).

In order to organize the digital industry in businesses and identify the necessary technologies to ensure the transition from the current state of the industry to Industry 4.0 and then to Industry 5.0, the article analyses current and potential technologies (Dutta et al., 2020) has presented the analysis. Additionally, it provides a formal explanation of industries 4.0 and 5.0, allowing for the presentation of the issue as a problem that can be solved mathematically. In the industry 5.0, a complex formal description of the organization based on its architectural methodology enables for increased business information support efficiency. In order to organize the digital industry in businesses and figure out how to secure the transition from the existing state of the industry to industry 5.0, this is essential. This transition's cost will be determined and its effectiveness will be made by using this method for industry 4.0 and then industry 5.0.

3. BLOCKCHAIN: INTERNET OF THINGS BASED ENVIRONMENT

Blockchain and the IoT are two rapidly growing technologies that have the potential to revolutionize various industries. The combination of blockchain and IoT creates a secure and decentralized network of devices that can communicate with each other without the need for a central authority. In a blockchain-IoT environment, devices are connected to a blockchain network, allowing them to securely share data and interact with each other. The blockchain provides a tamper-proof ledger that records all transactions and data exchanges between the devices, ensuring that data is not tampered with or manipulated. This makes the blockchain-IoT environment ideal for applications that require a high level of security and trust. One of the main benefits of a blockchain-IoT environment is increased transparency and accountability. Each device in the network has a unique identity and can be traced back to its owner, ensuring that all actions and transactions are recorded and auditable. This makes it easier to track and prevent fraud and other malicious activities. Another benefit of a blockchain-IoT environment is increased efficiency and cost savings. Devices can communicate with each other in real-time, eliminating the need for intermediaries and reducing the time and costs associated with manual processes. For example, in a supply chain environment, blockchain-IoT technology can be used to track and monitor the movement of goods, ensuring that they are delivered on time and in the right condition.

In conclusion, a blockchain-IoT environment has the potential to transform various industries, including supply chain management, healthcare, energy, and more. By creating a secure and decentralized network of devices, the technology can increase transparency, accountability, efficiency, and cost savings, making the way for a more connected and automated future.

Blockchain

Blockchain is a distributed digital ledger technology that allows for secure and transparent recording of transactions. In essence, it is a decentralized database that stores information across a network of computers, making it very difficult to tamper with or hack. Each block in the chain contains a unique cryptographic code, as well as a record of all transactions that have occurred on the network. Once a block is added to the chain, it cannot be modified without also modifying all subsequent blocks, making it virtually impossible to alter the history of transactions. One of the most well-known applications of blockchain technology is in cryptocurrency, such as Bitcoin and Ethereum, which use blockchain to record all transactions on their networks. However, blockchain has many other potential use cases, such as supply chain management, voting systems, and data security. In summary, blockchain offers a promising solution for creating secure, transparent, and decentralized systems that can be trusted by all parties involved (Dutta et al., 2020; Yli-Huumo et al., 2016; Zheng et al., 2017).

Internet of Things

Internet of Things refers to the network of physical devices, vehicles, home appliances, and other items that are embedded with sensors, software, and connectivity to enable them to exchange data and communicate with each other over the internet. In other words, IoT is a system of interconnected devices that can collect and share data with each other without requiring human intervention. These devices can range from simple sensors and actuators to complex machines and systems. IoT technology has the potential to revolutionize many industries by enabling real-time data analysis, automation, and remote monitoring. For example, in the healthcare industry, IoT devices can be used to monitor patients' important signs and provide real-time feedback to healthcare providers, improving patient outcomes and reducing costs. Similarly, in the transportation industry, IoT can be used to track vehicles in real-time, optimize routes, and reduce fuel consumption, making transportation more efficient and cost-effective. IoT technology also has applications in smart homes, agriculture, manufacturing, and many other industries. However, the widespread adoption of IoT also raises issues about data privacy and security, as well as the potential for cyber-attacks and unauthorized access to sensitive information. These challenges must be addressed in order to fully realize the potential of IoT (Li et al., 2015; Mukhopadhyay & Suryadevara, 2014; Rose et al., 2015; Yli-Huumo et al., 2016; Zheng et al., 2017). We can find components of IoT as discussed in figure 1.

Figure 1. Components of IoT

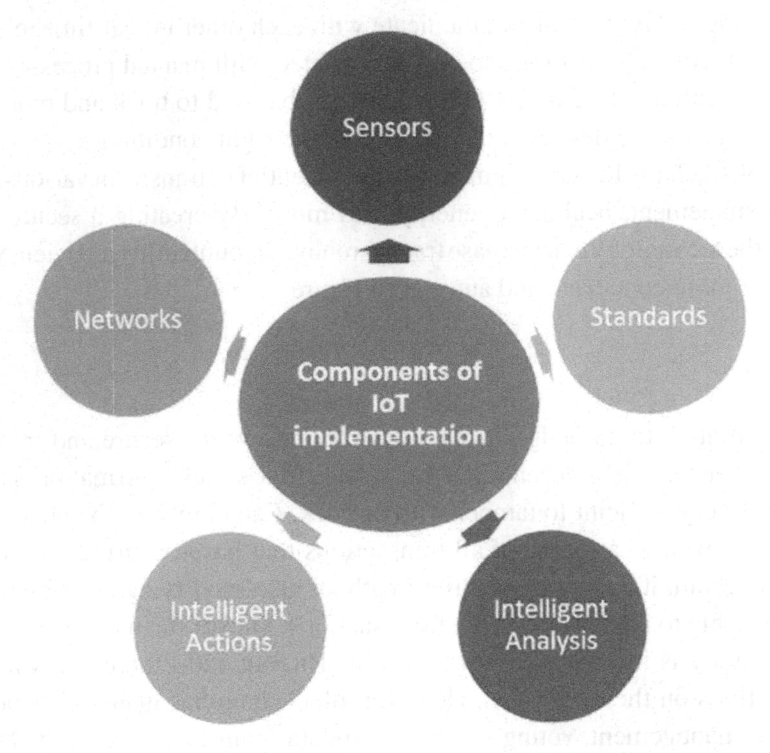

Industry 5.0

Industry 5.0 is a concept that is still in its early stages, but it is being discussed as the next phase in the evolution of industrialization. It is seen as a response to Industry 4.0, which focused on the integration of automation, data exchange, and advanced technologies such as the IoT and artificial intelligence (AI) in manufacturing processes. Industry 5.0 is characterized by a shift towards more human-centered manufacturing processes, where technology is used to enhance human capabilities and creativity, rather than replace them. The concept emphasizes the importance of human skills and creativity, such as problem-solving, critical thinking, and emotional intelligence, in the manufacturing process. One of the key features of Industry 5.0 is the integration of advanced technologies such as robotics, AI, and IoT with human workers, in what is known as a "collaborative workforce." This means that humans and machines work together in a way that maximizes the strengths of both, creating a more efficient and effective manufacturing process. Another feature of Industry 5.0 is the focus on sustainability and social responsibility. This means that manufacturing processes are designed to minimize environmental impact and promote social well-being, such as ensuring safe working conditions and fair labor practices. Industry 5.0 is still a relatively new concept, and it remains to be seen how it will be implemented and how effective it will be in addressing the challenges facing the manufacturing industry. However, the concept represents an important shift in thinking about the role of technology in manufacturing, emphasizing the importance of human skills and creativity in a more sustainable and socially responsible manufacturing process (Fazal et al., 2022; Maddikunta et al., 2022). Now the evolution of industry 5.0 can be found in figure 2.

Figure 2. Evolution of Industry 5.0

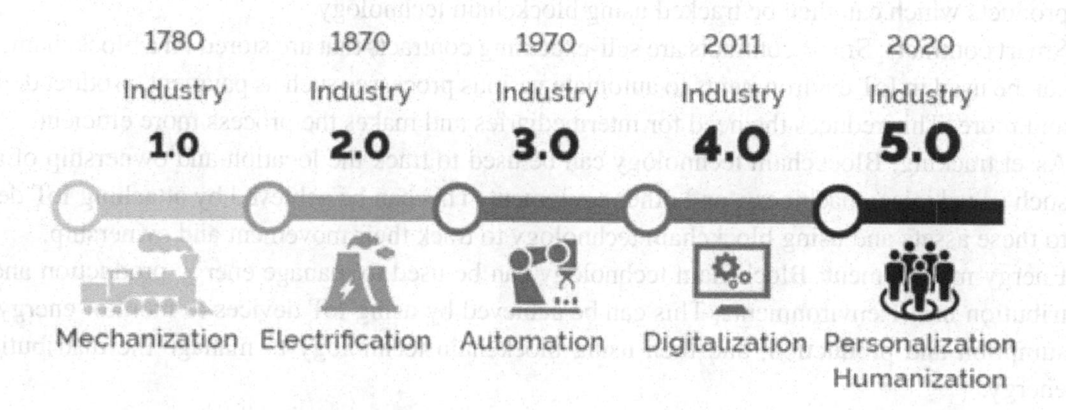

Blockchain: Internet of Things

Blockchain and IoT can be used together to create a secure and transparent system for managing IoT devices and data. Blockchain technology can provide a tamper-proof and decentralized ledger for storing data generated by IoT devices. This can improve data security and eliminate the need for a centralized authority to manage the system. In addition, blockchain can provide a mechanism for securing IoT devices by using smart contracts to enforce access control policies and automate security protocols. For example, a blockchain-based IoT system can be used to monitor and track the supply chain of goods from the manufacturer to the retailer. Each item in the supply chain can be equipped with a unique identifier that is recorded on the blockchain, and IoT devices can be used to track the item's location and condition in real-time. This can help prevent counterfeiting, reduce theft, and improve supply chain efficiency.

Another potential application of blockchain and IoT is in the energy industry. Smart grids can be built using IoT devices that monitor energy consumption and production in real-time. The data generated by these devices can be stored on a blockchain, providing a secure and transparent system for tracking energy usage and distribution. This can improve energy efficiency, reduce costs, and promote renewable energy production.

In summary, the combination of blockchain and IoT has the potential to create a more secure and efficient system for managing IoT devices and data. However, there are still challenges to be addressed, such as scalability and interoperability, before this technology can be widely adopted (Fernández-Caramés & Fraga-Lamas, 2018; Ferrag et al., 2018; Wang et al., 2019).

Applications of Blockchain: Internet of Things Based Environments

Blockchain technology has been found to have various applications in the IoT based environments. Some of these applications include:

- Supply chain management: Blockchain technology can be used to track the movement of goods and products through the supply chain. This helps to ensure that products are authentic and have not been tampered with or counterfeited. This can be achieved by embedding IoT devices into products which can then be tracked using blockchain technology.
- Smart contracts: Smart contracts are self-executing contracts that are stored on a blockchain. They can be used in IoT environments to automate various processes such as payment, product delivery, and more. This reduces the need for intermediaries and makes the process more efficient.
- Asset tracking: Blockchain technology can be used to track the location and ownership of assets such as vehicles, machinery, and other equipment. This can be achieved by attaching IoT devices to these assets and using blockchain technology to track their movement and ownership.
- Energy management: Blockchain technology can be used to manage energy production and distribution in IoT environments. This can be achieved by using IoT devices to monitor energy consumption and production, and then using blockchain technology to manage the distribution of energy.

In summary, the combination of IoT and blockchain technology has the potential to revolutionize various industries by enabling greater transparency, efficiency, and security.

4. INDUSTRY 5.0 AND ITS PERSPECTIVE FOR MODERN SOCIETY

Industry 5.0, also known as "human-centered industry", is the latest evolution of the industrial revolution that places the human being at the center of technological development. It is a fusion of the latest advances in artificial intelligence, robotics, automation, and the IoT with the creative and problem-solving skills of human beings. The goal of Industry 5.0 is to add the strengths of both humans and machines to create new forms of collaboration, productivity, and innovation (refer figure 3). Rather than replacing human workers with machines, Industry 5.0 seeks to empower humans with the latest technology to enhance their skills and capabilities, while at the same time improving the overall efficiency and sustainability of the production process.

From a societal perspective, Industry 5.0 offers several potential benefits. For one, it could help address the growing skills gap in many industries, by providing workers with the training and tools they need to adapt to new roles and responsibilities. It could also lead to the creation of new jobs and industries, as companies adopt new technologies and business models. Moreover, Industry 5.0 has the potential to improve the quality of life for workers, by reducing the physical and mental burden of repetitive or dangerous tasks, and enabling more flexible and remote work arrangements. It could also promote a more sustainable approach to production, by optimizing the use of resources and reducing waste and pollution. In summary, Industry 5.0 represents a shift towards a more human-centered, collaborative, and sustainable approach to industry and technology, with the potential to create new opportunities and benefits for society as a whole.

Figure 3. Relationship of Industry 5.0 for a sustainable future

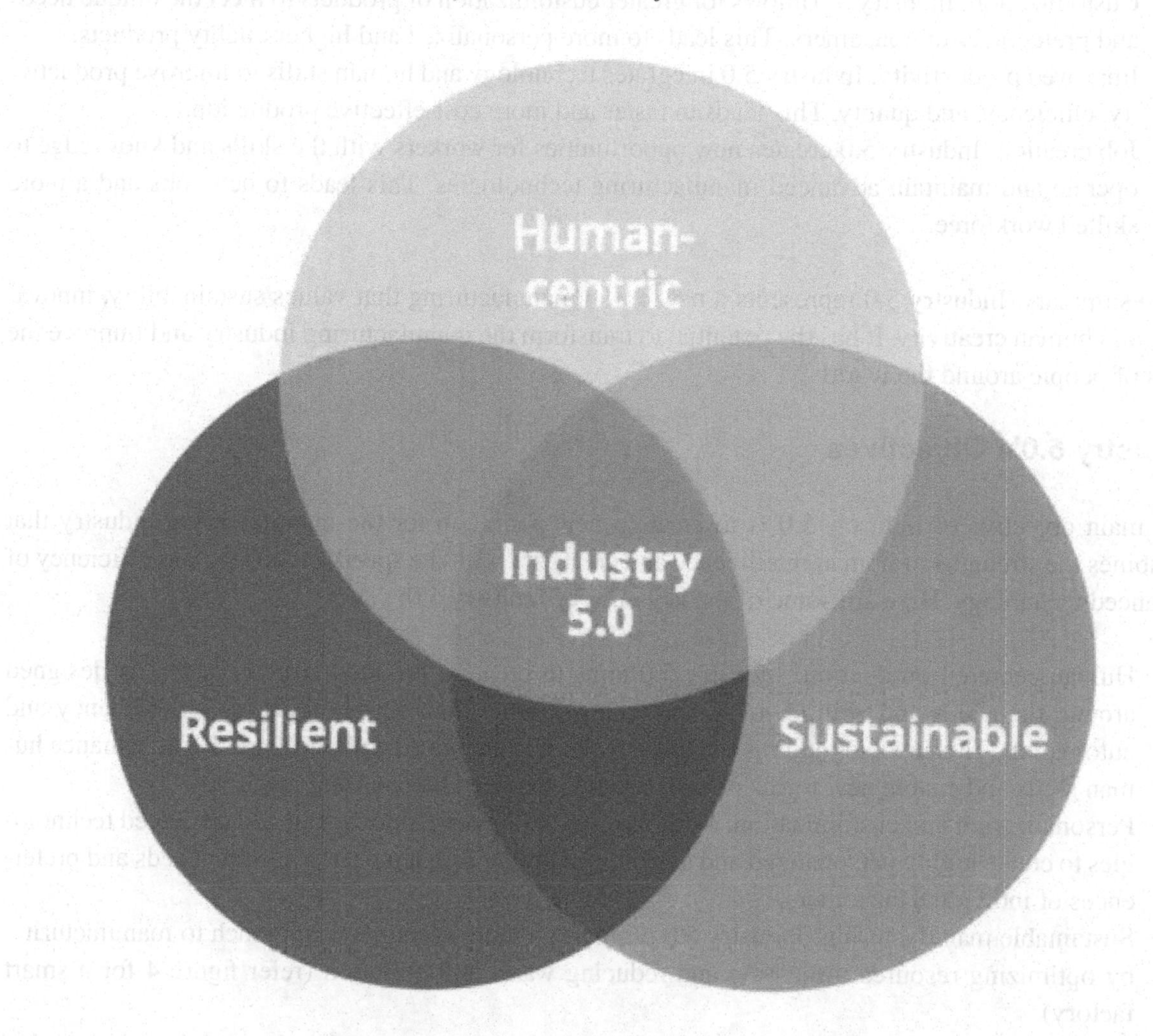

Importance of Industry 5.0 for Modern Society

Industry 5.0 is a new paradigm in manufacturing that focuses on the integration of technology and human skills to improve productivity, efficiency, and quality. It represents a shift from the traditional factory-based approach to manufacturing to a more human-centric approach that emphasizes creativity, innovation, and flexibility. Here are some reasons why Industry 5.0 is important for modern society:

- Sustainable production: Industry 5.0 emphasizes the use of sustainable materials, processes, and practices in manufacturing. This reduces the environmental impact of production and promotes sustainable development.
- Human-centric approach: Industry 5.0 values the role of humans in the manufacturing process and emphasizes the importance of their creativity and innovation. This leads to the development of new products, processes, and technologies that better meet the needs of society.

- Customization: Industry 5.0 allows for greater customization of products to meet the unique needs and preferences of consumers. This leads to more personalized and higher quality products.
- Improved productivity: Industry 5.0 integrates technology and human skills to improve productivity, efficiency, and quality. This leads to faster and more cost-effective production.
- Job creation: Industry 5.0 creates new opportunities for workers with the skills and knowledge to operate and maintain advanced manufacturing technologies. This leads to new jobs and a more skilled workforce.

In summary, Industry 5.0 represents a new era in manufacturing that values sustainability, innovation, and human creativity. It has the potential to transform the manufacturing industry and improve the lives of people around the world.

Industry 5.0's Objectives

The main objective of Industry 5.0 is to create a new paradigm for the manufacturing industry that combines the strengths of human intelligence and creativity with the speed, precision, and efficiency of advanced technology. Here are some of the key aims of Industry 5.0:

- Human-centered production: Industry 5.0 aims to create a production process that is designed around the needs and abilities of human beings, rather than simply focusing on efficiency and automation. This involves adding advanced technologies like AI, robotics, and IoT to enhance human skills and enable new forms of collaboration between humans and machines.
- Personalization and customization: With Industry 5.0, manufacturers can add advanced technologies to create highly personalized and customized products that meet the specific needs and preferences of individual customers.
- Sustainable manufacturing: Industry 5.0 promotes a more sustainable approach to manufacturing by optimizing resource utilization and reducing waste and pollution (refer figure 4 for a smart factory)
- Agility and flexibility: Industry 5.0 enables manufacturers to quickly adapt to changing market conditions, customer demands, and production requirements by adding advanced technologies like digital twins, simulation, and real-time data analytics.
- Human skill development: Industry 5.0 aims to empower workers with the skills and knowledge they need to thrive in a rapidly evolving industrial landscape. This involves providing training and development opportunities that enable workers to add the latest technologies and stay ahead of the curve.

In summary, the main aim of Industry 5.0 is to create a more collaborative, human-centered, and sustainable manufacturing ecosystem that adds the strengths of both humans and machines to create new opportunities and value for businesses and society.

Figure 4. Importance of Industry 5.0 for smart factory

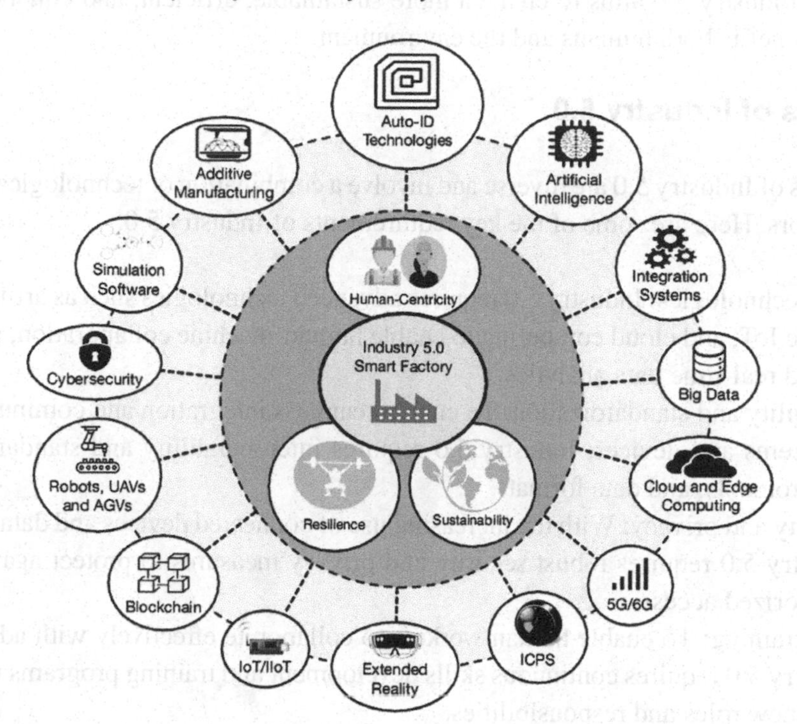

Industry 5.0's Characteristics

Industry 5.0 is a term used to describe the fifth industrial revolution that is currently underway. This new industrial revolution is characterized by several key features:

- Human-centric approach: Industry 5.0 focuses on putting human beings at the center of technological advancements. It emphasizes the importance of collaboration between humans and machines to achieve better results.
- Sustainable production: This industrial revolution emphasizes sustainable production, which means reducing waste, minimizing energy consumption, and using environmentally friendly materials.
- Customization: Industry 5.0 allows for customized production to meet the needs of individual consumers, rather than mass production of standardized products.
- Integration of digital and physical systems: Industry 5.0 integrates physical systems with digital technologies such as artificial intelligence, the IoT, and cloud computing.
- Augmentation of human capabilities: This industrial revolution aims to enhance human capabilities through the use of technology, rather than replacing human workers with machines.
- Interdisciplinary collaboration: Industry 5.0 requires collaboration between several fields, including engineering, computer science, social sciences, and humanities.
- Localized production: Industry 5.0 emphasizes the importance of localized production, which means producing goods and services in the same location where they will be consumed.

In summary, Industry 5.0 aims to create a more sustainable, efficient, and collaborative industrial ecosystem that benefits both humans and the environment.

Requirements of Industry 5.0

The requirements of Industry 5.0 are diverse and involve a combination of technological, organizational, and societal factors. Here are some of the key requirements of Industry 5.0:

- Advanced technologies: Industry 5.0 requires advanced technologies such as artificial intelligence, robotics, the IoT, and cloud computing to enable human-machine collaboration, personalized production, and real-time data analytics.
- Interoperability and standardization: To enable seamless integration and communication between several systems and devices, Industry 5.0 requires interoperability and standardization of technologies, protocols, and data formats.
- Data security and privacy: With the increasing use of connected devices and data-driven technologies, Industry 5.0 requires robust security and privacy measures to protect against cyber threats and unauthorized access.
- Skills and training: To enable human workers to collaborate effectively with advanced technologies, Industry 5.0 requires continuous skills development and training programs to enable workers to adapt to new roles and responsibilities.
- Cultural and organizational change: Industry 5.0 requires a cultural shift towards a more collaborative and innovative mindset, as well as organizational change to support new forms of collaboration and decision-making.
- Regulatory and ethical frameworks: Industry 5.0 requires appropriate regulatory and ethical frameworks to ensure that new technologies and business models are aligned with societal values and priorities, and to prevent potential harms such as job displacement or environmental damage.

In summary, the requirements of Industry 5.0 reflect the need for a detailed and integrated approach that involves not only technological innovation but also organizational and societal change, as well as appropriate governance and regulation to ensure that the benefits of Industry 5.0 are shared equitably and sustainably.

5. IMPORTANCE OF BLOCKCHAIN: INTERNET OF THINGS BASED ENVIRONMENT FOR INDUSTRY 5.0

Blockchain and IoT are two emerging technologies that have the potential to revolutionize the way we do business. When combined, they can create an efficient, secure, and transparent environment for Industry 5.0. Here are some of the reasons why the integration of blockchain and IoT is important:

- Improved Data Security: The use of blockchain in IoT ensures that data transmitted between devices is secure and tamper-proof. Blockchain's decentralized and distributed ledger technology ensures that data cannot be altered or deleted without consensus, making it an ideal solution for IoT devices.

- Transparency: Blockchain allows for complete transparency in transactions and interactions between devices, which can help to improve trust and accountability in Industry 5.0. With blockchain, all transactions are recorded and can be traced back to their source, creating a transparent and auditable record.
- Increased Efficiency: By using blockchain, IoT devices can interact with each other without the need for intermediaries. This means that transactions can be completed faster and with fewer errors, improving efficiency and reducing costs.
- Enhanced Customer Experience: With the use of blockchain and IoT, businesses can provide their customers with a seamless and secure experience. Customers can have complete control over their data, ensuring their privacy is protected, and they can trust that their data is being used in a secure and transparent manner.
- Cost Savings: By using blockchain and IoT, businesses can reduce costs associated with intermediaries and intermediation. This can help to lower transaction costs, reduce fraud and errors, and improve the In summary efficiency of the supply chain.

In summary, the integration of blockchain and IoT can help to create a more efficient, secure, and transparent environment for Industry 5.0. With the potential to reduce costs, improve customer experience, and enhance In summary, efficiency, businesses that adopt this technology will be well-positioned to succeed in the future.

6. POPULAR ISSUES IN BLOCKCHAIN: INTERNET OF THINGS BASED ENVIRONMENT FOR INDUSTRY 5.0

Due to its intrinsic capacity to provide immutability, chronology, and auditability in industrial systems, blockchain (BC) is a favored option as a security enabler for Industry 5.0 ecosystems. Only a few books are suggested that outline the applications for Industry 5.0 that are supported by BC. The essay offers a groundbreaking study on BC's role in Industry 5.0 as a security enabler. We highlighted the key drivers, possible applications, and proposed an architectural vision of BC-based Industry 5.0 across various application verticals based on a descriptive survey technique and research questions. In order to create innovative BC-assisted solutions in Industry 5.0 verticals, the survey aims to propose ideas that would help future researchers and scientific community (Verma et al., 2022).

Security Issues in Blockchain: Internet of Things Based Environment for Industry 5.0

The combination of blockchain and the IoT is a promising approach for enabling secure and transparent data sharing in Industry 5.0. However, there are several security issues that need to be addressed in order to ensure the safe and reliable operation of these systems. Here are some of the key security issues in a blockchain-IoT based environment for Industry 5.0:

- Device security: IoT devices are vulnerable to a variety of security threats, such as malware, ransomware, and denial-of-service attacks. It is important to ensure that these devices are properly secured and updated to prevent these threats.

- Data privacy: In a blockchain-IoT based environment, sensitive data such as personal information or business secrets may be shared among multiple parties. It is important to ensure that this data is protected from unauthorized access or disclosure.
- Smart contract vulnerabilities: Smart contracts are self-executing programs that run on the blockchain, and they are vulnerable to several security issues such as bugs, vulnerabilities, and hacking attacks. It is important to thoroughly test and audit smart contracts to ensure their security and reliability.
- Network security: Blockchain networks are vulnerable to a variety of attacks such as 51% attacks, sybil attacks, and DDoS attacks. It is important to implement strong security measures such as network segmentation, firewalls, and intrusion detection systems to, prevent these attacks.
- Governance and regulation: The lack of clear governance and regulation in blockchain-based systems can create security risks such as fraud, market manipulation, and money laundering. It is important to establish appropriate governance and regulatory frameworks to ensure the integrity and fairness of these systems.

In summary, addressing these security issues requires an useful approach that involves not only technological solutions but also organizational and regulatory measures. By implementing strong security measures and governance frameworks, blockchain-IoT based environments can enable secure and transparent data sharing in Industry 5.0 while minimizing the risks of security breaches and other security threats.

Privacy Issues in Blockchain: Internet of Things Based Environment for Industry 5.0

The combination of blockchain and IoT in Industry 5.0 has the potential to enhance data privacy by enabling secure and transparent data sharing among multiple parties. However, there are several privacy issues that need to be addressed in order to ensure the protection of personal information and other sensitive data. Here are some of the key privacy issues in a blockchain-IoT based environment for Industry 5.0:

- Data ownership: In a blockchain-IoT based environment, data may be collected from multiple sources and shared among multiple parties. It is important to establish clear rules and frameworks for data ownership and control to ensure that individuals have control over their personal data.
- Data aggregation and profiling: The collection and aggregation of data from multiple sources can create detailed profiles of individuals and their behaviors, raising issues about surveillance and privacy invasion. It is important to establish appropriate data protection measures such as anonymization and data minimization to protect the privacy of individuals.
- Transparency and consent: The transparency of blockchain-based systems can create challenges in obtaining informed consent from individuals for the collection and use of their personal data. It is important to establish clear and transparent processes for obtaining consent and providing individuals with information about how their data will be used.
- Regulatory compliance: Blockchain-based systems may be subject to different privacy regulations and requirements in different jurisdictions. It is important to ensure that these systems comply with relevant privacy laws and regulations to avoid legal risks and protect the privacy of individuals.

- Security breaches: Security breaches in blockchain-based systems can result in the disclosure of sensitive personal information, leading to privacy violations and other negative consequences. It is important to implement strong security measures to prevent security breaches and ensure the confidentiality of personal data.

In summary, addressing these privacy issues requires an useful approach that involves not only technological solutions but also organizational and regulatory measures. By implementing strong privacy protection measures and regulatory frameworks, blockchain-IoT based environments can enhance data privacy in Industry 5.0 while enabling secure and transparent data sharing among multiple parties.

Technical Issues in Blockchain: Internet of Things Based Environment for Industry 5.0

The combination of blockchain and IoT in Industry 5.0 presents several technical challenges that need to be addressed in order to ensure the reliability, scalability, and efficiency of these systems. Here are some of the key technical issues in a blockchain-IoT based environment for Industry 5.0:

- Scalability: Blockchain-based systems have limited scalability due to the processing and storage requirements of consensus mechanisms and the increasing size of the blockchain. This can create challenges in handling the large volumes of data generated by IoT devices in Industry 5.0.
- Interoperability: There are multiple blockchain platforms available, and each has its own technical specifications and protocols. It is important to ensure interoperability among different blockchain platforms and IoT devices to enable seamless data sharing and communication.
- Energy consumption: Blockchain-based systems are computationally intensive and require significant amounts of energy to maintain consensus and validate transactions. This can create environmental issues and limit the scalability of these systems.
- Latency: The latency in blockchain-based systems can create delays in processing and validating transactions, which can be particularly problematic in real-time applications such as IoT-based industrial control systems.
- Data quality and reliability: The quality and reliability of data generated by IoT devices can be variable due to factors such as sensor errors and data corruption. It is important to establish appropriate data validation and quality control mechanisms to ensure the accuracy and reliability of data in blockchain-based systems.

In summary, addressing these technical issues requires an useful approach that involves not only technological solutions but also organizational and regulatory measures. By implementing appropriate technical solutions and frameworks, blockchain-IoT based environments can enable reliable, scalable, and efficient data sharing and communication in Industry 5.0.

Trust Issues in Blockchain: Internet of Things Based Environment for Industry 5.0

Blockchain technology has gained significant attention in recent years due to its ability to provide a secure and transparent distributed ledger system. When combined with the IoT technology, it creates an environment where data can be shared, and devices can communicate with each other. Industry 5.0 is the integration of these technologies in the manufacturing and industrial sectors, where they can be used to improve productivity, efficiency, and transparency. However, one of the main challenges in implementing a blockchain-IoT environment for Industry 5.0 is trust issues. Trust is essential in any system, and the lack of trust can lead to significant problems, such as security breaches, data manipulation, and fraud. In a blockchain-IoT environment, trust is necessary for the following reasons:

- Device Authentication: Devices need to be authenticated before they can participate in the network. Without proper authentication, malicious actors can introduce fake devices that can disrupt the system.
- Data Integrity: Data must be reliable and trustworthy. The IoT generates massive amounts of data, and if the data is corrupted or tampered with, it can lead to significant problems.
- Smart Contracts: Smart contracts are automated contracts that are executed when certain conditions are met. These contracts are essential in a blockchain environment, and they need to be trustworthy.

To address these trust issues, several measures can be taken:

- Encryption: Data should be encrypted to protect it from unauthorized access. Encryption ensures that only authorized parties can access the data.
- Identity Management: Identity management ensures that devices and users are authenticated before they can access the network. This prevents unauthorized access and ensures that only legitimate users can access the network.
- Consensus Mechanisms: Consensus mechanisms are used to ensure that the network agrees on the state of the ledger. This prevents malicious actors from introducing fake transactions or manipulating the ledger.
- Auditing: Auditing is essential in a blockchain-IoT environment. It allows for the monitoring of the system and the detection of any anomalies or suspicious activities.

In conclusion, trust is critical in a blockchain-IoT environment for Industry 5.0. The lack of trust can lead to significant problems, and several measures need to be taken to ensure that the system is secure and trustworthy. Encryption, identity management, consensus mechanisms, and auditing are essential in ensuring that the system is reliable and trustworthy.

Scalability Issues in Blockchain: Internet of Things Based Environment for Industry 5.0

Blockchain technology has been identified as a promising solution to address several challenges in IoT industry. However, there are scalability issues that must be addressed in the context of an IoT-based environment for Industry 5.0. One of the major scalability issues is related to the processing power required to handle the large number of transactions in a blockchain-based IoT network. As more and more IoT devices are added to the network, the amount of data that needs to be processed increases significantly. This can result in slower transaction times and increased latency, which can negatively impact the overall performance of the network. Another scalability issue is related to the storage capacity required to store the blockchain data. As the number of transactions increases, so does the amount of data that needs to be stored. This can quickly become a challenge, especially when dealing with large-scale IoT networks with millions of devices generating data continuously. Finally, there is a challenge related to the energy consumption required to maintain a blockchain-based IoT network. As the number of devices in the network increases, so does the energy required to process and store the data. This can become a significant issue in environments where energy consumption is an issue, such as in remote locations or in environments with limited energy resources. To address these scalability issues, there are ongoing efforts to develop new blockchain technologies that are specifically designed for IoT environments. These technologies aim to optimize the processing and storage of data, while minimizing energy consumption. In addition, there are efforts to develop new consensus mechanisms that are better suited for IoT networks, such as Proof of Stake (PoS) and Delegated Proof of Stake (DPoS), which require less energy than traditional Proof of Work (PoW) mechanisms. For fining limitations in industry 5.0, please refer figure 5.

7. SECURITY, PRIVACY, LEGAL AND TECHNICAL CHALLENGES IN BLOCKCHAIN: INTERNET OF THINGS BASED ENVIRONMENT FOR INDUSTRY 5.0

IoT is changing Industry 5.0 to include blockchain-driven safe connectivity; yet, some of its core qualities face difficulties, including decentralization, security flaws, and lack of interoperability. The problems with IoT are solved by centralized technology based on blockchain. IoT and blockchain are coming together, as seen by Blockchain of Things (BCoT). In-depth analyses are done on the developments in heterogeneous multi-system information fusion for BCoT and multi-virtual sensor IoT. The difficulties that BCoT industrial applications may face in the future are thoroughly examined. Sustainable Cities and Society (SCS), a BCoT initiative, is dedicated to creating resilient cities that are socially, economically, and environmentally sustainable. Dew computing-based BCoT makes the smart city possible even in remote locations with erratic Internet connectivity (Debashis et al., 2022).

Security Challenges in Blockchain: Internet of Things Based Environment for Industry 5.0

The combination of blockchain and IoT technology in Industry 5.0 offers many benefits, including increased transparency, reduced costs, and improved security (Malik et al., 2022; Nair, 2023; Nair & Tyagi, 2023; Nair & Tyagi, 2023; Tyagi, 2021; Tyagi & Bansal, 2023). However, there are also several security challenges that need to be addressed to ensure the safe and secure operation of Industry 5.0 systems. One of the primary security challenges in a blockchain-IoT environment is the potential for distributed denial of service (DDoS) attacks. Since IoT devices are often less secure than traditional computers, they are susceptible to being hacked and used in DDoS attacks. This can result in the blockchain network being overwhelmed with traffic, leading to a disruption of service.

Another security challenge is the potential for malicious actors to gain control of a significant portion of the blockchain network's computing power, known as a 51% attack. This would allow the attacker to manipulate transactions and potentially double-spend cryptocurrencies. Additionally, since blockchain transactions are irreversible, it is essential to ensure that smart contracts are secure and free of vulnerabilities. If a smart contract is compromised, it can result in the loss of funds or sensitive information.

Furthermore, privacy is a critical issue in Industry 5.0 environments, where sensitive data is collected from a large number of IoT devices. The blockchain must be designed to protect the privacy of users and prevent the exposure of sensitive data. Finally, interoperability is another significant security challenge. Since Industry 5.0 systems will likely involve multiple blockchains and IoT devices, it is important to ensure that these systems can communicate and exchange data securely.

To address these challenges, it is important to implement robust security protocols and best practices, including regular security audits, multi-factor authentication, and encryption. Additionally, ongoing research and development of new security solutions are necessary to keep up with evolving threats and ensure the safety and security of Industry 5.0 systems.

Figure 5. Limitations, opportunities, and future research towards Industry 5.0

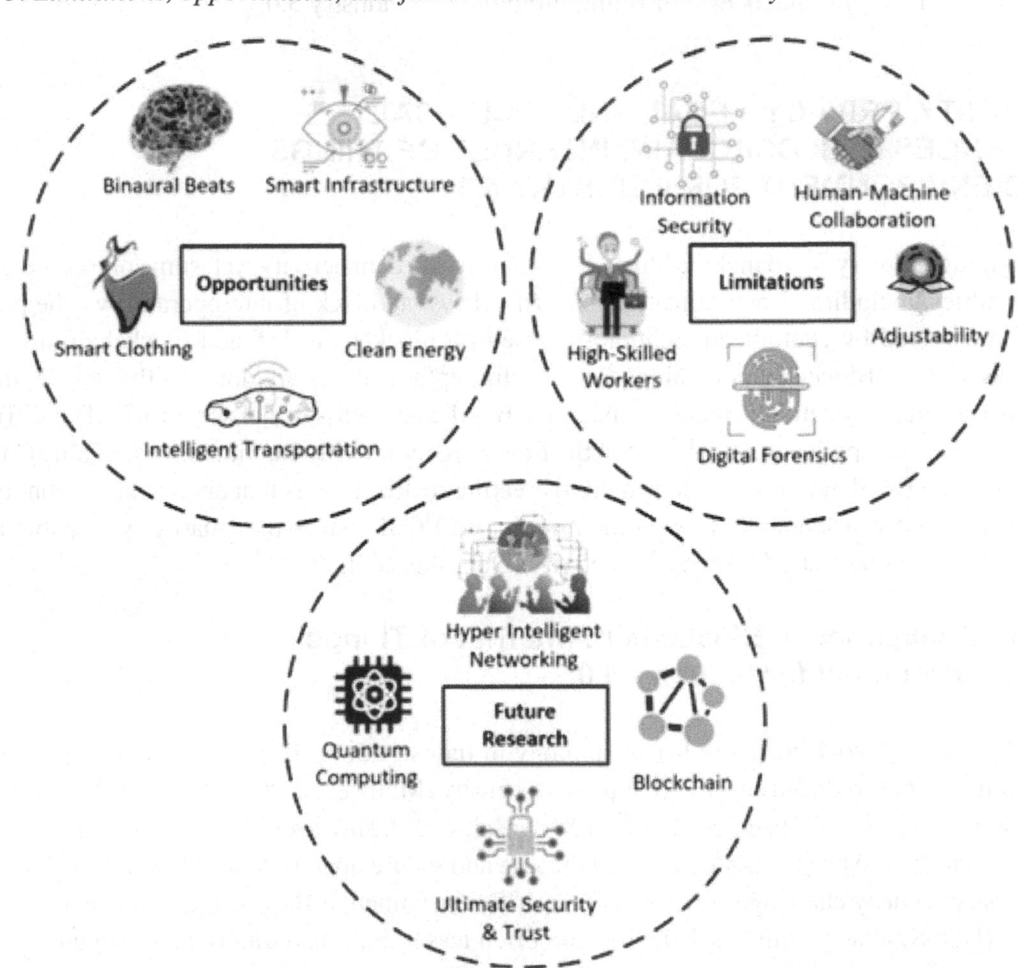

Privacy challenges in Blockchain: Internet of Things Based Environment for Industry 5.0

Blockchain and the IoT are two emerging technologies that are poised to transform the way we live and work (Nair et al., 2023; Tyagi & Bansal, 2023). Industry 5.0, the next wave of industrial revolution, is expected to be characterized by the integration of these technologies to create a more interconnected, intelligent and efficient industrial environment. However, this integration also poses a number of privacy challenges that need to be addressed to ensure the security and privacy of users' data. One of the main privacy challenges in a Blockchain-IoT-based environment is the collection and processing of large amounts of data. IoT devices generate large amount of data, which are stored on the blockchain. This creates a challenge for privacy as the data is stored on a public ledger that can be accessed by anyone with the necessary permissions. This means that sensitive data, such as personal and financial information, could potentially be accessed by unauthorized parties.

Another challenge is the issue of data ownership. In a Blockchain-IoT-based environment, multiple parties may have access to the same data, making it difficult to determine who owns the data and who has the right to access it. This creates privacy risks as data could be accessed by unauthorized parties, leading to potential misuse of personal information. In addition, there is the challenge of managing user consent. In a Blockchain-IoT-based environment, users may not be aware of what data is being collected and how it is being used. It is important to ensure that users are informed about the collection and use of their data and are given the option to opt-out if they do not wish to have their data collected or used in a certain way. Finally, there is the challenge of data security. The decentralized nature of blockchain technology can make it difficult to protect data from unauthorized access, especially in a world where cyber-attacks are becoming increasingly sophisticated. It is important to ensure that appropriate security measures are in place to protect the data stored on the blockchain. In conclusion, the integration of Blockchain and IoT in Industry 5.0 presents exciting opportunities for businesses and individuals. However, it is important to address the privacy challenges that arise to ensure the security and privacy of users' data. This can be achieved through the implementation of appropriate data protection measures, including data encryption, user consent management, and the use of decentralized identity management systems.

Legal Challenges in Blockchain: Internet of Things Based Environment for Industry 5.0

The convergence of blockchain and IoT have the potential to revolutionize Industry 5.0 by enabling secure and transparent tracking of goods, efficient supply chain management, and decentralized autonomous organizations (DAOs) (Nair et al., 2021; Tyagi et al., 2022; Tyagi et al., 2023). However, this new technological paradigm also presents a range of legal challenges that must be addressed to ensure its successful deployment.

- Data Privacy: With the growing volume of data generated by IoT devices and recorded on the blockchain, data privacy is a significant issue. It is necessary to ensure that personal data is collected and processed in accordance with relevant data protection laws and regulations.

- Smart Contracts: Smart contracts, which are self-executing agreements that run on the blockchain, are a central feature of Industry 5.0. However, their use raises various legal issues, including the legal validity of the contract, the role of intermediaries, and the enforceability of smart contract terms.
- Liability: With the rise of decentralized autonomous organizations (DAOs), where decision-making is governed by code rather than people, the question of liability arises. Who is responsible if something goes wrong in a DAO, and how can damages be recovered?
- Intellectual Property: The use of blockchain and IoT in Industry 5.0 raises various intellectual property issues, including patent infringement, copyright infringement, and trade secret protection.
- Jurisdiction: The decentralized nature of blockchain and IoT means that it is challenging to determine which jurisdiction applies in cases of legal disputes. This issue is compounded by the fact that blockchain and IoT operate across multiple jurisdictions and may involve multiple parties.

To address these challenges, legal frameworks must be developed that take into account the unique features of blockchain and IoT. These frameworks must ensure the protection of individual rights and interests while facilitating the development and deployment of innovative Industry 5.0 solutions. Additionally, industry stakeholders must collaborate with legal experts to identify and mitigate legal risks associated with blockchain and IoT.

Technical Challenges in Blockchain: Internet of Things Based Environment for Industry 5.0

The convergence of blockchain and IoT present a new paradigm for Industry 5.0 that has the potential to revolutionize the way we do business. However, this new technology also poses several technical challenges that must be addressed to ensure its successful deployment.

- Scalability: With the increasing number of IoT devices connected to the blockchain, the system's scalability becomes a critical issue. The blockchain's limited capacity to process transactions per second could slow down the network, causing delays and congestion.
- Interoperability: With different IoT devices and blockchain protocols operating in silos, achieving interoperability between them is a challenge. This means that different devices cannot communicate with each other or exchange data efficiently, making it difficult to achieve seamless integration of IoT and blockchain technologies.
- Security: While blockchain is considered a secure technology due to its decentralized nature, the increasing number of IoT devices connected to the network raises issues about security. These devices are often prone to hacking, and if compromised, they can lead to significant data breaches.
- Standardization: The absence of a standardized framework for IoT and blockchain technologies means that different platforms use different protocols, resulting in compatibility issues. The lack of a common language and standards makes it difficult for different devices and systems to work together, which could hinder Industry 5.0's development.
- Energy Consumption: The proof-of-work consensus mechanism used in some blockchain networks, such as Bitcoin, is highly energy-intensive. With the increasing number of IoT devices connected to the blockchain, this could become a significant challenge in terms of energy consumption and environmental impact.

To overcome these challenges, Industry 5.0 stakeholders must work collaboratively to develop scalable, interoperable, and secure blockchain and IoT-based solutions that are compatible with existing systems. This requires standardization of protocols, the adoption of energy-efficient consensus mechanisms, and the implementation of robust security measures to protect against cyber threats. Additionally, it is essential to invest in research and development to ensure that these technologies can keep pace with the growing demands of Industry 5.0.

8. FUTURE WORK TOWARDS BLOCKCHAIN AND IOT IN SHAPING INDUSTRY 5.0 ENVIRONMENT

The convergence of blockchain and the Internet of Things (IoT) has the potential to revolutionize various industries, including Industry 5.0, which represents the next phase of industrial development. Here are some potential future directions and applications for the transformational power of blockchain and IoT in Industry 5.0:

- Supply Chain Management: Blockchain can be used to create transparent and immutable supply chains. IoT devices can monitor the movement and condition of goods in real-time, and this data can be recorded on a blockchain for traceability and verification. This ensures the authenticity of products and enhances supply chain efficiency.
- Quality Assurance: IoT sensors can continuously monitor the quality of products during manufacturing. Data from these sensors can be securely stored on a blockchain, providing an immutable record of product quality. This can help identify and address quality issues in real-time.
- Smart Contracts: Blockchain-based smart contracts can automate and enforce agreements between various parties in Industry 5.0. For example, smart contracts can automatically trigger payments when certain conditions are met, reducing the need for intermediaries and streamlining business processes.
- Asset Tracking and Management: IoT devices can track the location and condition of industrial assets, such as machinery and equipment. This data can be recorded on a blockchain to ensure the integrity and provenance of assets, reducing the risk of theft or fraud.
- Energy Management: In Industry 5.0, energy efficiency is crucial. IoT sensors can monitor energy consumption in real-time, and blockchain can be used to create decentralized energy grids and optimize energy distribution.
- Data Security and Privacy: Blockchain provides a secure and decentralized platform for storing sensitive industrial data. IoT devices generate vast amounts of data, and blockchain can ensure that this data is tamper-proof and only accessible to authorized parties.
- Decentralized Autonomous Organizations (DAOs): Industry 5.0 may see the emergence of decentralized autonomous organizations governed by smart contracts and blockchain technology. These DAOs can manage and make decisions about industrial processes, investments, and resource allocation.
- Interoperability: Developing standards and protocols that enable different IoT devices and blockchain platforms to communicate and work together seamlessly is essential for the success of Industry 5.0.

- Data Monetization: Companies can explore new business models by monetizing the data generated by IoT devices through blockchain-based data marketplaces. This allows organizations to sell or share data securely and transparently.
- Regulatory Compliance: Blockchain can help in ensuring compliance with industry regulations and standards by providing an immutable audit trail of all transactions and data.
- Environmental Sustainability: Blockchain and IoT can be used to monitor and reduce the environmental impact of industrial processes by tracking resource consumption, emissions, and waste production.
- Collaborative Ecosystems: Industry 5.0 may foster collaborative ecosystems where different companies and stakeholders share data and resources on a blockchain to optimize production, logistics, and maintenance.

Note that the widespread adoption of blockchain and IoT in Industry 5.0 will require overcoming technical, regulatory, and security challenges. Additionally, issues regarding data privacy, scalability, and energy consumption must be addressed for these technologies to reach their full potential in transforming industrial processes. Figure 5 provides a detailed description about future work and opportunities towards industry 5.0.

9. LESSON LEARNED FOR INDUSTRY 5.0

Industry 5.0 is a relatively new concept, and its full potential and lessons are still being explored. However, based on its underlying principles, here are some lessons that can be learned for Industry 5.0:

- Importance of Human Collaboration: Industry 5.0 places a strong emphasis on the collaboration between humans and machines to achieve optimal results. This means that industries need to recognize the value of human input and the need for machines to augment human capabilities rather than replace them entirely.
- Focus on Social Responsibility: Industry 5.0 highlights the importance of social responsibility and sustainability in manufacturing processes. Industries need to ensure that their processes are environmentally friendly and that their products and services contribute positively to society.
- Adoption of Emerging Technologies: Industry 5.0 requires the adoption of emerging technologies such as AI, robotics, and IoT to improve efficiency, reduce waste, and optimize processes.
- Customization: Industry 5.0 recognizes the importance of customization and personalization in meeting the needs and preferences of consumers. This means that industries need to be agile and flexible in their manufacturing processes to accommodate customization.
- Education and Training: Industry 5.0 requires a highly skilled workforce that can work collaboratively with machines. Therefore, industries need to invest in education and training to equip their employees with the necessary skills to work in Industry 5.0.
- Data Privacy and Security: With the increasing use of data in Industry 5.0, industries need to prioritize data privacy and security to protect sensitive information and maintain the trust of their customers.

In summary, the lessons learned from Industry 5.0 emphasize the importance of human collaboration, social responsibility, adoption of emerging technologies, customization, education and training, and data privacy and security (Gomathi et al., 2023; Sai et al., 2023; Sharma et al., 2020; Tyagi & Nair, 2020; Satapathy et al., 2020; Varsha et al., 2021). These principles can help industries achieve greater efficiency, sustainability, and positive social impact.

10. CONCLUSION

The intersection of Blockchain and IoT in Industry 5.0 holds great potential for businesses and industries. However, this convergence also presents various challenges related to security, privacy, and technical aspects that we have discussed in this chapter. Also, this chapter has explained blockchain, IoT, Industry 5.0 and their importance, issues and challenges respectively. As discussed above (for security), blockchain provides a decentralized and immutable ledger that ensures the integrity and authenticity of IoT data. However, the distributed nature of blockchain also introduces new attack vectors that we discussed in this work. For privacy, the use of blockchain and IoT in Industry 5.0 raises several issues like data protection and privacy, which has been addressed by implementing privacy-preserving techniques such as zero-knowledge proofs, differential privacy, and homomorphic encryption in the previous decade, such information has been included in this work. Also, Industry 5.0 presents several technical challenges, such as scalability, interoperability, and standardization, which can be solved by developing efficient consensus mechanisms, building robust communication protocols, and promoting the standardization of blockchain and IoT technologies. Hence, the convergence of blockchain and IoT in Industry 5.0 offers tremendous opportunities for businesses and industries. To address the security, privacy, and technical challenges to realize the full potential of this technology. By employing secure protocols, privacy-preserving techniques, and promoting standardization, Industry 5.0 can achieve a more secure, efficient, and trustworthy ecosystem.

REFERENCES

Bernabe, J. B., Canovas, J. L., Hernandez-Ramos, J. L., Moreno, R. T., & Skarmeta, A. (2019). Privacy-preserving solutions for blockchain: Review and challenges. *IEEE Access : Practical Innovations, Open Solutions*, *7*, 164908–164940. doi:10.1109/ACCESS.2019.2950872

Debashis, AKarmakar, ABanerjee, PBhattacharyya, SRodrigues, J. BCoT: Introduction to Blockchain-Based Internet of Things for Industry 5.0. In (2022). *Blockchain based Internet of Things* (pp. 1–22). Springer Singapore.

Deshmukh, A., Patil, D. S., Pawar, P. D., Kumari, S., & P., M. (2023). Recent Trends for Smart Environments With AI and IoT-Based Technologies: A Comprehensive Review. In A. Tyagi (Ed.), *Handbook of Research on Quantum Computing for Smart Environments* (pp. 435-452). IGI Global. doi:10.4018/978-1-6684-6697-1.ch023

Dutta, P., Choi, T. -M. Somani, S., & Butala, R. (2020). Blockchain technology in supply chain operations: Applications, challenges and research opportunities. *Transportation research part e: Logistics and transportation review, 142*, 102067.

Fazal, N., Haleem, A., Bahl, S., Javaid, M., & Nandan, D. (2022). Digital management systems in manufacturing using industry 5.0 technologies. In *Advancement in Materials, Manufacturing and Energy Engineering, Vol. II: Select Proceedings of ICAMME 2021*, (pp. 221-234). Singapore: Springer Nature Singapore. 10.1007/978-981-16-8341-1_18

Fernández-Caramés, T. M., & Fraga-Lamas, P. (2018). A Review on the Use of Blockchain for the Internet of Things. *IEEE Access: Practical Innovations, Open Solutions, 6*, 32979–33001. doi:10.1109/ACCESS.2018.2842685

Ferrag, M. A., Derdour, M., Mukherjee, M., Derhab, A., Maglaras, L., & Janicke, H. (2018). Blockchain technologies for the internet of things: Research issues and challenges. *IEEE Internet of Things Journal, 6*(2), 2188–2204. doi:10.1109/JIOT.2018.2882794

Gadekallu, T. R., Huynh-The, T., Wang, W., Yenduri, G., Ranaweera, P., Pham, Q.-V., Benevides da Costa, D., & Liyanage, M. (2022). Blockchain for the metaverse: A review. *arXiv preprint arXiv:2203.09738.*

Gomathi, L., Mishra, A. K., & Tyagi, A. K. (2023). *Industry 5.0 for Healthcare 5.0: Opportunities, Challenges and Future Research Possibilities.* 2023 7th International Conference on Trends in Electronics and Informatics (ICOEI), Tirunelveli, India. 10.1109/ICOEI56765.2023.10125660

Goyal, D. & Tyagi, A. (2020). *A Look at Top 35 Problems in the Computer Science Field for the Next Decade*. Taylor and Francis. . doi:10.1201/9781003052098-40

Joshi, A. P., Han, M., & Wang, Y. (2018). A survey on security and privacy issues of blockchain technology. *Mathematical Foundations of Computing, 1*(2), 121–147. doi:10.3934/mfc.2018007

Koteska, B., Karafiloski, E., & Mishev, A. (2017). Blockchain implementation quality challenges: a literature. In *SQAMIA: 6th workshop of software quality, analysis, monitoring, improvement, and applications.* IEEE.

Leng, J., Sha, W., Wang, B., Zheng, P., Zhuang, C., Liu, Q., Wuest, T., Mourtzis, D., & Wang, L. (2022). Industry 5.0: Prospect and retrospect. *Journal of Manufacturing Systems, 65*, 279–295. doi:10.1016/j.jmsy.2022.09.017

Li, S., Da Xu, L., & Zhao, S. (2015). The internet of things: A survey. *Information Systems Frontiers, 17*(2), 243–259. doi:10.100710796-014-9492-7

Ma, Y., Sun, Y., Lei, Y., Qin, N., & Lu, J. (2020). A survey of blockchain technology on security, privacy, and trust in crowdsourcing services. *World Wide Web (Bussum), 23*(1), 393–419. doi:10.100711280-019-00735-4

Maddikunta, P. K. R., Pham, Q.-V., B, P., Deepa, N., Dev, K., Gadekallu, T. R., Ruby, R., & Liyanage, M. (2022). Industry 5.0: A survey on enabling technologies and potential applications. *Journal of Industrial Information Integration, 26*, 100257. doi:10.1016/j.jii.2021.100257

Malik, S., Bansal, R., & Tyagi, A. K. (Eds.). (2022). *Impact and Role of Digital Technologies in Adolescent Lives*. IGI Global., doi:10.4018/978-1-7998-8318-0

Martynov, V. V., Shavaleeva, D. N., & Zaytseva, A. A. (2019). Information technology as the basis for transformation into a digital society and industry 5.0. In *2019 International Conference" Quality Management, Transport and Information Security, Information Technologies"(IT&QM&IS)*, (pp. 539-543). IEEE. 10.1109/ITQMIS.2019.8928305

Mohanta, B. K., Jena, D., Panda, S. S., & Sobhanayak, S. (2019). Blockchain technology: A survey on applications and security privacy challenges. *Internet of Things*, *8*, 100107. doi:10.1016/j.iot.2019.100107

Mohanta, B. K., Jena, D., Ramasubbareddy, S., Daneshmand, M., & Gandomi, A. H. (2020). Addressing security and privacy issues of IoT using blockchain technology. *IEEE Internet of Things Journal*, *8*(2), 881–888. doi:10.1109/JIOT.2020.3008906

Mukhopadhyay, S. C., & Suryadevara, N. K. (2014). *Internet of things: Challenges and opportunities*. Springer International Publishing. doi:10.1007/978-3-319-04223-7

Nair, M. (2023). 6G: Technology, Advancement, Barriers, and the Future. In 6G-Enabled IoT and AI for Smart Healthcare. CRC Press.

Nair M. & Tyagi, A. K. (2023). Blockchain technology for next-generation society: current trends and future opportunities for smart era. In the book: *Blockchain Technology for Secure Social Media Computing*. IET Digital Library.. doi:10.1049/PBSE019E_ch11

Nair, M. M., Fernandez, T. F., & Tyagi, A. K. (2023). *Cyberbullying in Digital Era: History, Trends, Limitations, Recommended Solutions for Future*. *2023 International Conference on Computer Communication and Informatics (ICCCI)*, Coimbatore, India, 10.1109/ICCCI56745.2023.10128624

Nair, M. M., & Tyagi, A. K. (2023). AI, IoT, blockchain, and cloud computing: The necessity of the future. R. Pandey, Goundar, S., & Fatima, S. (eds). Distributed Computing to Blockchain. Academic Press. doi:10.1016/B978-0-323-96146-2.00001-2

Nair, M. M., Tyagi, A. K., & Sreenath, N. (2021). The Future with Industry 4.0 at the Core of Society 5.0: Open Issues, Future Opportunities and Challenges. *2021 International Conference on Computer Communication and Informatics (ICCCI)*, (pp. 1-7). IEEE. 10.1109/ICCCI50826.2021.9402498

Rajani, D., Menon, S. C., Kute, S., & Tyagi, A. K. (2022). Preserving Privacy of Social Media Data Using Artificial Intelligence Techniques. In A. Tyagi (Ed.), *Handbook of Research on Technical, Privacy, and Security Challenges in a Modern World* (pp. 186–204). IGI Global. doi:10.4018/978-1-6684-5250-9.ch010

Rose, K., Eldridge, S., & Chapin, L. (2015). The internet of things: An overview. *The internet society (ISOC)*, 80, 1-50.

Sai, G. H., Tyagi, A. K., & Sreenath, N. (2023). Biometric Security in Internet of Things Based System against Identity Theft Attacks. *2023 International Conference on Computer Communication and Informatics (ICCCI)*, Coimbatore, India. 10.1109/ICCCI56745.2023.10128186

Tyagi, A. K. (Ed.). (2021). *Multimedia and Sensory Input for Augmented, Mixed, and Virtual Reality*. IGI Global. doi:10.4018/978-1-7998-4703-8

Tyagi, A. K., Agarwal, K., Goyal, D., & Sreenath, N. (2020). A Review on Security and Privacy Issues in Internet of Things. In H. Sharma, K. Govindan, R. Poonia, S. Kumar, & W. El-Medany (Eds.), *Advances in Computing and Intelligent Systems. Algorithms for Intelligent Systems*. Springer. doi:10.1007/978-981-15-0222-4_46

Tyagi, A. K., & Bansal, R., & Anshu, D. S. (2023). A Step-To-Step Guide to Write a Quality Research Article. In: Abraham, A., Pllana, S., Casalino, G., Ma, K., Bajaj, A. (eds) Intelligent Systems Design and Applications, ISDA 2022. Lecture Notes in Networks and Systems. Springer, Cham. doi:10.1007/978-3-031-35510-3_36

Tyagi, A. K., Dananjayan, S., Agarwal, D., & Thariq Ahmed, H. F. (2023). Blockchain—Internet of Things Applications: Opportunities and Challenges for Industry 4.0 and Society 5.0. *Sensors (Basel)*, *23*(2), 947. doi:10.339023020947 PMID:36679743

Tyagi, A. K., Fernandez, T. F., Mishra, S., & Kumari, S. (2021). Intelligent Automation Systems at the Core of Industry 4.0. In A. Abraham, V. Piuri, N. Gandhi, P. Siarry, A. Kaklauskas, & A. Madureira (Eds.), *Intelligent Systems Design and Applications. ISDA 2020. Advances in Intelligent Systems and Computing* (Vol. 1351). Springer. doi:10.1007/978-3-030-71187-0_1

Tyagi, A. K., & Nair, M. M. (2020). Internet of Everything (IoE) and Internet of Things (IoTs): Threat Analyses, Possible Opportunities for Future [JIAS]. *Journal of Information Assurance & Security*, *15*(4).

Tyagi, A. K., Rekha, G., & Sreenath, N. (2020). Beyond the Hype: Internet of Things Concepts, Security and Privacy Concerns. In S. Satapathy, K. Raju, K. Shyamala, D. Krishna, & M. Favorskaya (Eds.), *Advances in Decision Sciences, Image Processing, Security and Computer Vision. ICETE 2019. Learning and Analytics in Intelligent Systems* (Vol. 3). Springer. doi:10.1007/978-3-030-24322-7_50

Varsha, R., Nair, S. M., Tyagi, A. K., Aswathy, S. U. & Krishnan, R. (2021). The Future with Advanced Analytics: A Sequential Analysis of the Disruptive Technology's Scope. In: Abraham A., Hanne T., Castillo O., Gandhi N., Nogueira Rios T., Hong TP. (eds) Hybrid Intelligent Systems. Springer, Cham. doi:10.1007/978-3-030-73050-5_56

Verma, A., Bhattacharya, P., Madhani, N., Trivedi, C., Bhushan, B., Tanwar, S., Sharma, G., Bokoro, P. N., & Sharma, R. (2022). Blockchain for Industry 5.0: Vision, Opportunities, Key Enablers, and Future Directions. *IEEE Access : Practical Innovations, Open Solutions*, *10*, 69160–69199. doi:10.1109/ACCESS.2022.3186892

Wang, X., Zha, X., Ni, W., Ren, P. L., Guo, Y. J., Niu, X., & Zheng, K. (2019). Survey on blockchain for Internet of Things. *Computer Communications*, *136*, 10–29. doi:10.1016/j.comcom.2019.01.006

Xu, X., Lu, Y., Vogel-Heuser, B., & Wang, L. (2021). Industry 4.0 and Industry 5.0—Inception, conception and perception. *Journal of Manufacturing Systems*, *61*, 530–535. doi:10.1016/j.jmsy.2021.10.006

Yli-Huumo, J., Ko, D., Choi, S., Park, S., & Smolander, K. (2016). Where is current research on blockchain technology?—A systematic review. *PLoS One*, *11*(10), e0163477. doi:10.1371/journal.pone.0163477 PMID:27695049

Zheng, Z., Xie, S., Dai, H., Chen, X., & Wang, H. (2017). An overview of blockchain technology: Architecture, consensus, and future trends. In *In 2017 IEEE international congress on big data (BigData congress)* (pp. 557–564). IEEE. doi:10.1109/BigDataCongress.2017.85

Chapter 20
The Rise of Industry 6.0:
Seizing the Opportunities of the Post-COVID-19 Era for Sustainable Manufacturing

Robertas Damaševičius
https://orcid.org/0000-0001-9990-1084
Vytautas Magnus University, Lithuania

Sanjay Misra
https://orcid.org/0000-0002-3556-9331
Institute for Energy Technology, Halden, Norway

ABSTRACT

The COVID-19 pandemic has led to significant disruptions to global economies, leading to the need for rapid transformation in the manufacturing sector. Industry 6.0, the next stage in the evolution of manufacturing, has emerged as a possible solution to these challenges. It builds on the previous industrial revolutions and incorporates advanced technologies such as artificial intelligence (AI), and the industrial internet of things (IIoT) to create a more efficient and sustainable manufacturing environment. This chapter aims to provide a comprehensive overview of Industry 6.0 and its potential in the post-COVID era. It examines the fundamental principles, objectives, and evolution of industrial revolutions, and outlines the role of Industry 6.0 in promoting sustainable manufacturing practices. Additionally, it explores the potential of Industry 6.0 to provide mass personalization of services and products, enhance production capacity, and improve the fault-free environment as illustrated by a real-world scenario.

1. INTRODUCTION

The idea of Industry 4.0 was introduced in 2011 to describe the 4th in-dustrial revolution, which involves the integration of advanced technologies such as artificial intelligence (AI), the Internet of Things (IoT), and big data analytics into manufacturing and other industries (Groumpos, 2021). Since then, there have

DOI: 10.4018/979-8-3693-2081-5.ch020

been discussions about potential future developments that could lead to In-dustry 5.0 and beyond, but these are still in the realm of speculation (Jamil et al., 2022; Jeyaraman et al., 2022). Industry 6.0 represents a significant leap forward from Industry 5.0, build-ing on the advancements made in previous industrial revolutions (Georgescu, 2019). One possible direction for Industry 6.0 could be the development of "cognitive factories" (Wurster et al., 2021) that are even more intelligent and autonomous than those of Industry 4.0 and 5.0. This could involve the use of advanced AI systems that are can learn and adapt to new situations, and that can make decisions and take actions in real-time based on data from a wide range of sources (Singh, 2023). Another possibility is the creation of fully integrated and interconnected supply chains that span multiple industries and regions (Hassan et al., 2023). This could in-volve the use of advanced blockchain and distributed ledger technologies to securely and transparently track and manage the flow of goods and services across borders, while also ensuring compliance with various regulations and standards.

Several papers discuss various aspects of Industry 6.0 and its potential impact on society and industries. Chourasia et al. (Chourasia et al., 2022) highlight how the COVID-19 pandemic has accelerated the need for advanced manufactur-ing industries to provide mass personalization of goods and services while enhancing their capability for fault-free, zero failure, and anti-fragile produc-tion. The chapter emphasizes the importance of Industry 6.0 to promote sustainability and living in harmony with nature, and its potential to de-liver wealth and prosperity across all planetary boundaries. Duggal et al.

Duggal et al. (2022) present a comprehensive overview of the technological developments and patent pathways throughout the previous industrial revolutions up to In-dustry 4.0. The chapter highlights the lack of human-machine workforce synergy in Industry 4.0 and the need for customized manufacturing. The chapter also proposes two expected phases of Industry 5.0 and highlights the subdomains that could be its focal areas. Finally, the chapter suggests a pathway to achieve the goals of Industry 6.0. Peng et al. (2020) discuss the integration of Industry 6.0, IoT, and 6G communication technology in the Industrial Internet of Everything (IIoE), enabling industrial optimiza-tion and automation. These papers show the potential of Industry 6.0 to transform industries and promote sustainable development while addressing the challenges and opportunities posed by technological advancements and global crises.

The scope of the chapter is to explore the emergence of Industry 6.0, its features, and how it advances beyond Industry 5.0. The chapter aims to analyze the opportunities and challenges presented by Industry 6.0 in the post-COVID era, and how it can lead to the creation of a fault-free environment, zero failure, anti-fragile, and improve production capacity (Chourasia et al., 2022). The chapter also aims to discuss the impact of Industry 6.0 on different sectors such as manufacturing, healthcare, transportation, and communica-tion. It will highlight how Industry 6.0 can improve the quality of life by providing mass personalization of goods and services and promoting living harmony with nature. The chapter will also discuss the role of advanced technologies such as the Industrial Internet of Everything (IIoE), the IoT, and 6G mobile communication technology in the development of Industry 6.0. The chapter will provide an in-depth analysis of the current research pools and patent pathways throughout the industrial revolutions and high-light significant products and services that have landmarked each revolution up to Industry 4.0. The chapter will conclude by discussing the challenges and future directions for Industry 6.0 and how it can lead to the creation of wealth, prosperity, and growth for nations across all planetary boundaries. The scope of the chapter will cover both theoretical and practical aspects of Industry 6.0 and present a comprehensive picture of this emerging technol-ogy.

2. OVERVIEW OF INDUSTRIAL REVOLUTIONS

The history of industrial revolutions (Yavari & Pilevari, 2020) dates back to the late 18th century when the world experienced its 1st industrial revolution, also known as Industry 1.0. This was a period of radical change as manual labor was replaced with machine-based manufacturing systems, leading to an increase in productivity and the emergence of the factory system. Industry 1.0 is often associated with the steam engine, which was developed by James Watt, and the spinning jenny, which was invented by James Hargreaves.

The second industrial revolution, or Industry 2.0, occurred in the late 19th and early 20th centuries. During this period, new technologies such as the telegraph, telephone, and electric power were developed, leading to the creation of mass production and assembly line manufacturing.

The third industrial revolution, or Industry 3.0, began in the mid-20th century with the development of electronics and computer technology. This period is characterized by the emergence of automated production processes and the use of computers for data processing and control. The development of the first programmable logic controller (PLC) in the 1960s paved the way for the automation of industrial processes.

Industry 4.0, the fourth industrial revolution, the concept spearheaded by Klaus Schwab (2017), is the current period of industrialization and began in the late 20th century with the widespread adoption of the internet and digital technologies. Industry 4.0 is characterized by the integration of cyber-physical systems, the IoT, big data analytics (Sathish Kumar et al., 2022), and cloud computing. It has enabled the development of smart factories that are highly automated and can respond to changing production demands in real-time.

Industry 5.0, also known as human-machine collaboration, is the latest industrial revolution that focuses on integrating humans and machines in a collaborative work environment (Alves et al., 2023). It emphasizes the importance of human creativity, problem-solving, and critical thinking in the production process. The goal is to create a more flexible and adaptive production system that can respond to changing market demands (Golovianko et al., 2023; Wang et al., 2023).

Industry 6.0 is the next stage of industrial evolution and is still in its early stages (Yadav et al., 2022). It is envisioned as a sustainable and environmentally conscious form of industry that focuses on global prosperity and wealth distribution. It aims to create a harmonious relationship between nature and technology while promoting sustainability. Industry 6.0 is expected to leverage emerging technologies such as AI, blockchain, and quantum computing to create a more intelligent and responsive manufacturing system (Duggal et al., 2021).

3. IMPACT OF COVID-19 ON ADVANCED MANUFACTURING INDUSTRIES

The COVID-19 pandemic has led to unique disruption to economies and societies worldwide (Girdhar et al., 2021). Advanced manufacturing industries have not been spared, with significant impacts felt across the sector. This section discusses the effects of the COVID-19 pandemic on advanced manufacturing industries and the opportunities it presents for Industry 6.0 and circular economy (Kumar et al., 2021).

Firstly, the pandemic has led to a shift in customer behavior, with consumers now more focused on their individual specific needs, and there is a growing demand for personalized goods and services. Advanced manufac-turing industries have responded by providing mass personalization of goods and services, leveraging advanced technologies such as AI and IoT (Yunana et al., 2021) to deliver customized products and services to meet individual customer needs.

Secondly, the COVID-19 pandemic has presented an opportunity for advanced manufacturing industries to enhance their capability for a fault-free environment, zero failure, anti-fragile, and improve production capac-ity. The pandemic has highlighted the need for robust and resilient supply chains that can withstand disruptions caused by global crises. Advanced manufacturing industries have responded to this by integrating advanced technologies such as predictive maintenance, smart manufacturing, and dig-ital twins into their production processes to ensure continuous production and supply chain resilience.

Thirdly, the COVID-19 pandemic has accelerated the adoption of remote work and digital technologies in advanced manufacturing industries. Many advanced manufacturing industries have implemented digital solutions to enable remote work, such as virtual collaboration tools, digital workflows, and remote monitoring technologies. This shift towards remote work has increased the demand for advanced technologies that can support remote work, such as 5G, edge computing, and cloud technologies (Agbaegbu et al., 2021).

Finally, the COVID-19 pandemic has created an opportunity for ad-vanced manufacturing industries to promote living in harmony with nature, support sustainability, and promote the human virtual digital twin. Industry 6.0 aims to leverage these opportunities by integrating advanced technolo-gies into manufacturing processes, promoting sustainability, and ensuring resilience in supply chains (Chourasia et al., 2022).

4. INDUSTRY 6.0: UNDERLYING CONCEPTS AND TECHNOLOGIES

4.1. Sustainability of Industry 6.0 in a Global Perspective

Industry 6.0 is not only about technological advancements, but also about sustainable growth. The key objectives of Industry 6.0 are to develop and implement technologies that promote sustainable development, while creating wealth and prosperity for nations across all planetary bound-aries. In this context, the sustainability of Industry 6.0 becomes a critical aspect that needs to be explored in depth.

Sustainability is defined as the ability to meet the needs of the present generation without compromising the ability of future generations to meet their own needs (Okewu et al., 2017). The United Nations' Sustainable Development Goals (SDGs) provide a roadmap for countries to achieve sustainable development across social, economic, and environmental dimensions (Emmanuel et al., 2020). Industry 6.0 can contribute significantly to achieving these goals through the deployment of advanced technologies that enhance resource efficiency, reduce waste, and promote environmental protection. Industry 6.0 can leverage technologies such as the IoT, AI, and blockchain to promote sustainable development. For instance, IoT-based solutions can optimize energy consumption in manufac-turing processes, reduce carbon emissions, and promote the use of renewable energy sources. AI can be used to improve resource efficiency by identifying and mitigating wasteful practices in manufacturing processes. Blockchain can enable transparent and secure tracking of supply chain activities, ensur-ing ethical sourcing and promoting responsible production practices.

In addition to environmental sustainability, Industry 6.0 can also pro-mote social sustainability by enhancing the well-being of workers, promoting equal opportunities, and fostering social inclusion. For instance, technologies such as Augmented Reality (AR) can support risk management (Abioye et al., 2021) and improve worker safety and reduce the risk of accidents in manufacturing processes. The deployment of robots and automation can reduce the need for human intervention in hazardous work environments, improving worker safety and health (Patalas-maliszewska et al., 2021). The use of AI-based recruitment solutions can eliminate bias in hiring practices, promoting equal opportunities for all.

Industry 6.0 can also foster economic sustainability by promoting eco-nomic growth, creating new job opportunities, and supporting local communities. The deployment of advanced technologies can enhance production efficiency, reduce costs, and improve product quality, enabling businesses to compete globally. The development of local technology ecosystems can support the growth of local businesses and create a more sustainable and resilient economy. The sustainability of Industry 6.0 is critical to ensure that the benefits of technological advancements are harnessed in a responsible and ethical manner. Industry 6.0 can contribute significantly to achieving sustainable development across social, economic, and environmental dimensions. By promoting resource efficiency, reducing waste, and enhancing worker well-being, Industry 6.0 can create a more sustainable future for all.

4.2. Deploying 6G in Industry 6.0

As the world continues to push the boundaries of technology, 6G mobile communication technology is emerging as the next-generation wireless communication system with the potential to provide better communication characteristics than 5G (You et al., 2021). This technology will enable more devices to be connected, faster data transfer, and new applications that require low latency and high reliability, such as autonomous vehicles, telemedicine, and industrial automation. Industry 6.0 is one of the sectors that can greatly benefit from the integration of 6G, as it enables real-time monitoring, data collection, and analysis, which are essential in optimizing and automating industrial processes (Alsharif et al., 2020). However, the deployment of 6G in Industry 6.0 comes with some challenges such as the development of hardware and software technologies that can support 6G networks. Unlike 5G, which can use existing infrastructure, 6G requires new technologies that can operate at higher frequencies and provide greater bandwidth, i.e. there is a need for new antennas, chips, and other equipment to support 6G networks (Jiang et al., 2021).

Another challenge is the development of new network architectures that can efficiently support the diverse requirements of Industry 6.0 applications. Industrial systems require reliable and low-latency connectivity to support real-time monitoring and control, as well as high bandwidth to handle large amounts of data. 6G networks must be designed to meet these requirements while also providing seamless connectivity across different devices and networks. Additionally, there is a need to address the security and privacy concerns associated with Industry 6.0 and 6G. As more devices and systems become connected, the risk of cyber-attacks and data breaches increases. It is essential to develop security and privacy measures that can protect critical infrastructure and sensitive data. Lastly, there is a need to address the issue of cost. Deploying 6G networks and upgrading existing infrastructure can be expensive, and the benefits may not be immediately realized. Therefore, there is a need for a cost-effective approach to deploying 6G in Industry 6.0.

While 6G has the potential to revolutionize Industry 6.0, there are several challenges that need to be addressed to make it a reality. These challenges include developing new hardware and software technologies, designing efficient network architectures, addressing security and privacy concerns, and finding cost-effective ways to deploy 6G networks.

4.3. Human-Machine Workforce Synergy in Industry 6.0

Industry 6.0 is characterized by an advanced level of automation and optimization, with machines and systems becoming increasingly intelligent and interconnected. This leads to the emergence of a new paradigm in the workforce, where humans and machines work together in a highly synergistic manner to achieve better results and drive innovation. One of the key features of Industry 6.0 is the increasing use of AI and ML algorithms to automate routine and repetitive tasks, allowing human workers to focus on more complex and creative activities (Chourasia et al., 2022). This also enables the development of more personalized and customized products and services, as AI algorithms can analyze vast amounts of data to identify patterns and insights that would be impossible for humans to discern. In addition, Industry 6.0 also involves the integration of physical and virtual workspaces, with workers able to access data and collaborate with colleagues from anywhere in the world (Lee & Kundu, 2022). This requires the development of new communication and collaboration tools, as well as the implementation of robust security protocols to protect sensitive data.

However, the rise of Industry 6.0 also raises concerns about the impact on the workforce. As automation and AI become increasingly prevalent, there is a risk of displacement for workers in certain sectors, and there is a need for re-skilling and up-skilling to prepare the workforce for the new jobs that will emerge in this new era (Li, 2022). To address these challenges, there is a need for a holistic approach to workforce development (Ozkan-Ozen & Kazancoglu, 2022), where education and training programs are aligned with the changing needs of the industry. This includes the development of new curricula that emphasize the development of soft skills such as creativity, critical thinking, and collaboration, as well as technical skills such as data analysis, coding, and robotics (Wogu et al., 2019). The human-machine workforce synergy in Industry 6.0 offers immense potential for innovation and growth, but it also requires a thoughtful and proactive approach to ensure that the benefits are shared widely and that the workforce is equipped to thrive in this new era.

4.4. Industrial Internet of Everything (IIoE) in Industry 6.0

The integration of Industry 6.0, the IoT, and 6G mobile communication technology is the cornerstone of the Industrial Internet of Everything (IIoE) (Snyder & Byrd, 2017), enabling intelligent industry, optimizing industrial processes and automation. Industry 6.0 technologies, such as AI, robotics, and 3D printing (Kalkal et al., 2021), can benefit from the real-time data generated by IoT devices and the high-speed, low-latency communication capabilities of 6G networks. The IoT is a network of interconnected devices that communicate and exchange data through the internet, making it possible to collect and analyze data from a wide range of sources. This data can be used to optimize industrial processes, improve efficiency, and reduce waste. For example, sensors placed on machinery can detect when it is about to fail, enabling predictive maintenance to prevent costly downtime.

The integration of Industry 6.0, IoT, and 6G mobile communication technology will enable real-time monitoring, analysis, and optimization of industrial processes, leading to improved efficiency, productivity, and cost savings. The IIoE will also enable the creation of new business models and revenue streams, as companies can offer value-added services based on real-time data insights. However, the integration of these technologies also poses new challenges, such as the need for high cybersecurity standards, the management of large amounts of data, and the integration of legacy systems. It is essential to address these challenges to realize the potential of Industry 6.0, IoT, and 6G mobile communication technology in the industrial sector.

4.4.1. Enabling Industrial Optimization and Automation

Industry 6.0 envisions the integration of various technologies for enabling industrial optimization and automation such as IoT, AI, robotics, additive manufacturing, AR and VR, and 6G mobile communication technology, to enable industrial optimization and automation.

IoT enables the seamless communication of data between machines, products, and people, leading to real-time decision-making and optimized production processes.

AI involves the use of computer algorithms to perform tasks that typically require human-level intelligence, such as visual recognition, speech recognition, decision-making, and language translation. In Industry 6.0, AI is used to streamline production processes, predict equipment failures, and improve product quality.

Robotics involves the design, construction, and operation of robots to perform tasks that are dangerous, difficult, or repetitive for humans (Devaraja et al., 2020). In Industry 6.0, robots are used to automate production processes, reducing costs, and improving efficiency.

Additive manufacturing (or 3D printing) involves the creation of three-dimensional objects by adding layers of material. In Industry 6.0, additive manufacturing enables the production of complex, customized parts and products on demand, reducing waste and improving efficiency.

AR and virtual reality (VR) technologies involve the creation of virtual environments that simulate the real world or enhance it with additional in-formation. In Industry 6.0, AR and VR are used to improve worker training, enhance product design, and enable remote maintenance and repairs.

6G technology promises to deliver ultra-high-speed wireless communication, low latency, and massive machine-type connectivity. In Industry 6.0, 6G technology enables the real-time exchange of data between machines, products, and people, leading to optimized production processes and improved product quality.

4.4.2. Challenges in Ensuring High Quality of Services (QoS) in IIoE The Industrial Internet of Everything (IIoE) is a Key Enabler of Industry

6.0, which is the next phase of the industrial revolution. The IIoE involves the deep integration of Industry 6.0, the IoT, and 6G mobile communication technology to enable industrial optimization and automation. However, ensuring the high quality of services (QoS) in IIoE is a major challenge (Kesavan & Prabhu, 2018).

One of the main challenges in ensuring QoS in IIoE is the sheer amount of real-time information that is generated by the pervasive smart devices that make up the IoT. This information needs to be aggregated and processed quickly and reliably in order to support industrial automation and optimization. However, the sheer volume of data can overload communication networks and compromise QoS. In addition, the reliability of the communication networks themselves can be a challenge in disaster scenarios (Damasevicius, Bacanin, & Misra, 2023). Large-scale disasters such as earthquakes, hurricanes, or terrorist attacks can damage entire communication networks and cut off data aggregation, making it difficult to maintain QoS. To address these challenges, new strategies and technologies are being developed. For example, intelligent networked information broker (NIB) based data aggregation strategies such as the Intelligent NIB based Data Aggregation Strategy (IDAS) pro-posed by Peng et al. (Peng et al., 2020) use predictive analytics and machine learning to optimize data collection and aggregation in disaster scenarios.

Other technologies such as edge computing and fog computing can also help address the challenges of QoS in IIoE by enabling more efficient and reliable data processing closer to the source of the data (Venckauskas et al., 2019). Furthermore, the development of more robust and reliable communication networks, including 6G mobile communication technology, can help ensure that data is transmitted quickly and reliably, even in disaster scenarios.

4.5. Transhumanism and Industry 6.0

Transhumanism is a movement that calls for the use of technology to enhance human abilities beyond current biological limitations (Guerreiro et al., 2022). In the context of Industry 6.0, transhumanism can play a significant role in advancing automation and optimization in the manufacturing industry. One application of transhumanism in Industry 6.0 is the use of wearable technology to augment human capabilities (Ray et al., 2019). For instance, workers in the manufacturing industry can wear exoskeletons to enhance their strength and endurance, allowing them to work for longer hours without experiencing fatigue or in-juries. Wearable technology can also improve worker safety by providing real-time monitoring and feedback on their posture and movements.

Another area where transhumanism can contribute to Industry 6.0 is in the development of human-machine interfaces (HMIs). HMIs are interfaces that enable humans to interact with machines and computer systems. Transhumanism can advance the development of more sophisticated HMIs that allow humans to communicate and collaborate with machines in real-time. This can lead to more efficient and effective industrial processes, as well as improved product quality. However, there are concerns around worker exploitation and the potential for further automation to displace human workers. There are also concerns around privacy and data security, as the use of wearable technology and HMIs may involve the collection and storage of sensitive personal data.

The role of transhumanism in Industry 6.0 is complex and multifaceted. While it has the potential to significantly enhance industrial processes and improve worker safety and productivity, there are also ethical considerations that need to be addressed. As such, a thoughtful and responsible approach is required to make sure that the benefits of transhumanism in Industry 6.0 are realized while minimizing any potential negative impacts.

4.6. Digital Twin and Metaverse

Digital twin technology and metaverse are two of the most important emerging technologies that have the potential to revolutionize the industrial landscape of Industry 6.0.

Digital twin technology is a virtual replica of a physical product, process, or system that uses real-time data to simulate the behavior of the physical entity (Bot'in-Sanabria et al., 2022). By creating a digital twin, companies can analyze data from sensors and other sources to optimize the performance of their physical as-sets. This technology is particularly useful in Industry 6.0, where the focus is on smart factories that use automation, machine learning, and AI to optimize production and reduce waste. The digital twin technology provides a way for companies to visualize, monitor, and optimize their operations in real-time, enabling them to quickly identify and respond to issues before they become major problems. By providing a virtual representation of the physical system, digital twins allow companies to test different scenarios and simulations, and experiment with changes to the system before implementing them in the real world.

Metaverse is a virtual space that is created by the convergence of the physical and digital worlds (Koohang et al., 2023). It is a fully immersive environment that enables users to interact with each other and with digital objects in a three-dimensional space. Metaverse is a new and emerging technology that has the potential to transform the way we live, work, and interact with each other. In Industry 6.0, metaverse technology can be used to create immersive and interactive training simulations, allowing workers to practice new skills and procedures in a safe and controlled environment (Fracaro et al., 2022). It can also be used to monitor and optimize production processes in real-time, providing operators with a virtual representation of the factory floor and enabling them to make quick decisions based on real-time data (Damasevicius, Maskeliunas, & Misra, 2023). Furthermore, metaverse can be used to enhance collaboration and communication between workers, enabling them to work together more effectively and efficiently. This technology can also be used to create virtual showrooms and product demonstrations, pro-viding customers with an immersive experience that allows them to interact with products in a way that was not possible before.

Digital twin technology and metaverse are two of the most promising emerging technologies that have the potential to revolutionize the industrial landscape of Industry 6.0. By leveraging these technologies, companies can create smarter, more efficient, and more productive factories that are better equipped to meet the challenges of the future.

4.7. Cognitive Factories

Industry 6.0 represents the next stage of the industrial revolution, which is expected to transform the way factories operate. One of the key features of Industry 6.0 is cognitive factories, which are factories that are capable of processing and analyzing large amounts of data in real-time, and then using this data to make informed decisions and optimize production processes (ElMaraghy & ElMaraghy, 2022). Cognitive factories use advanced technologies such as AI, machine learning, and the Industrial Internet of Things (IIoT) to achieve their goals. Cognitive factories bring several benefits to the industrial landscape. For instance, they enable factories to adapt to changing demands in real-time, reduce downtime, and improve overall efficiency. In addition, they provide manufacturers with a better understanding of their production processes, enabling them to optimize operations and reduce waste.

To create a cognitive factory, manufacturers must first develop a com-prehensive data strategy that outlines how data will be collected, analyzed, and used to improve operations. This involves deploying sensors and other IIoT devices throughout the factory floor to collect data on various aspects of production, such as equipment performance, energy usage, and product quality. The data collected is then fed into an AI-powered platform that can process and analyze the data in real-time. This platform can provide insights into production processes that were previously unknown, enabling manufacturers to make data-driven decisions that can improve overall efficiency. However, the deployment of cognitive factories also presents several challenges. For instance, manufacturers must ensure that their data is secure and protected from cyber threats. In addition, they must invest in the necessary infrastructure and personnel to support the deployment and maintenance of these technologies.

Cognitive factories are expected to play a critical role in the development and deployment of Industry 6.0. They represent a new era in manufacturing that is driven by data and analytics, and they have the potential to revolutionize the way that factories operate. As such, cognitive factories are an area of intense research and development in Industry 6.0, and they are expected to continue to gain traction in the coming years.

5. EXAMPLE OF INDUSTRIAL MANUFACTURING SCENARIO

In Industry 6.0, a manufacturing scenario could involve a cognitive factory that leverages advanced automation, AI, and data analytics to optimize production processes and increase efficiency. For example, imagine a factory that produces automotive components such as engines. In this scenario, advanced sensors are integrated into the machines and equipment, collecting real-time data on performance, energy consumption, and maintenance needs. The data is then analyzed using machine learning algorithms to predict potential issues before they occur, enabling proactive maintenance and reducing downtime. Additionally, robots and autonomous vehicles are used to transport materials and products between different stages of the manufacturing process, improving speed and reducing the risk of accidents. The use of AR and VR technology also allows workers to visualize and interact with digital representations of machines and equipment, enabling them to better understand complex processes and identify potential improvements (Paulauskas et al., 2023).

Here is an example of a manufacturing scenario in Industry 6.0 using a sequence of events:

1. A customer places an order for a customized product through an online platform, providing specific requirements and design specifications.
2. The order is received and processed by an automated system, which sends the specifications to a digital twin of the factory.
3. The digital twin analyzes the specifications and initiates the production process by communicating with the production line equipment.
4. The production line equipment, including robots, sensors, and ma-chines, is controlled by an intelligent system that utilizes real-time data and analytics to optimize the manufacturing process.
5. As the product is being manufactured, the intelligent system monitors and adjusts the process to ensure high quality and efficiency.
6. Once the product is complete, it is inspected by sensors and quality control systems to ensure it meets the customer's specifications.
7. The product is then packaged and shipped to the customer, with real-time tracking and monitoring provided through an IoT-enabled logistics system.

This scenario illustrates the seamless integration of digital and physical technologies in Industry 6.0, allowing for efficient and customizable manufacturing processes that meet the demands of modern consumers. The implementation of Industry 6.0 technologies in this manufacturing scenario leads to a more efficient and productive factory with reduced costs, increased quality, and improved worker safety.

Figure 1 depicts a manufacturing scenario in which a user places an order with a smart factory, which then retrieves the necessary raw materials from an automated storage and retrieval system (ASRS). The factory then uses a robot arm to assemble the product and a quality control (QC) system to check the product's quality. If the product meets the required standards, the arm retrieves packaging materials and packages the product. Once the product is packaged, the factory stores the finished goods in the ASRS and notifies the user that the order is complete.

Figure 1. Sequence diagram of a manufacturing scenario

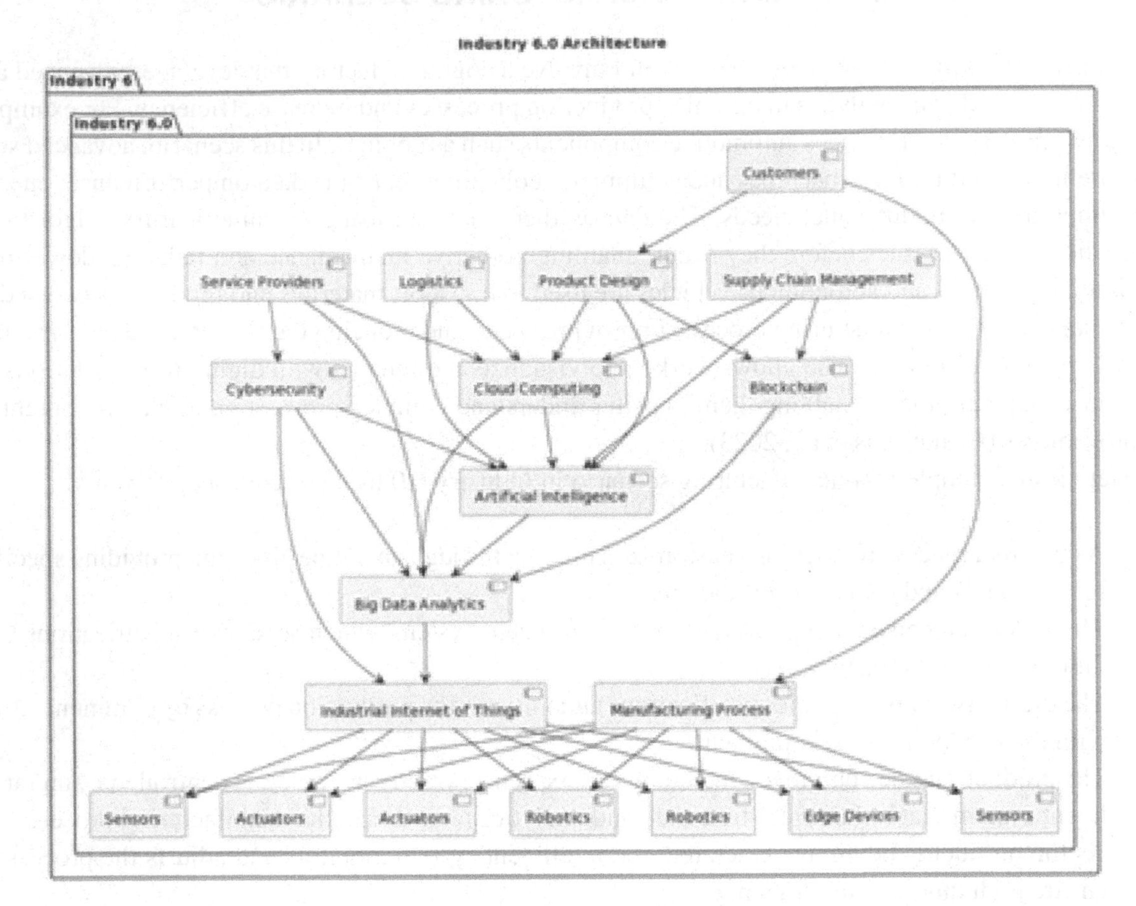

5.1. Architecture of Industry 6.0 System

A diagram in Figure 2 shows a high-level view of the various components and technologies that make up Industry 6.0. The main components are Industrial Internet of Things (IIoT), Big Data Analytics (BDA), Artificial Intelligence (AI), Cloud Computing (CC), Blockchain (BC), and Cybersecurity (CS). These components are interconnected and work together to enable various aspects of Industry 6.0, such as manufacturing process, The Component diagram represents the generic architecture of Industry 6.0. The central component of the architecture is the IIoT, which serves as the foundation for Industry 6.0. The IIoT is responsible for collecting data from various devices and sensors in the manufacturing process, such as robots, machines, and tools. The data is transmitted through communication networks and stored in the cloud or on-premises data center.

The IIoT is supported by several components, including edge computing, big data analytics, and machine learning. Edge computing refers to the processing of data at the edge of the network, closer to the devices that generate the data. This enables real-time processing and reduces the latency of the system. Big data analytics and machine learning are used to analyze the vast amounts of data collected by the IIoT to identify patterns, make predictions, and optimize the manufacturing process. The architecture also includes several components that are responsible for managing the manufacturing process, such as

Manufacturing Execution Systems (MES) and Enterprise Resource Planning (ERP) systems. MES is responsible for managing the production process, including scheduling, tracking, and re-porting. ERP systems are responsible for managing the business processes of the manufacturing company, including finance, accounting, and supply chain management. The architecture also includes several components that are responsible for ensuring the security and reliability of the system, such as cybersecurity and reliability engineering. Cybersecurity refers to the protection of the system from cyber threats, such as hacking and malware. Reliability engineering refers to the design and implementation of the system to ensure that it operates reliably and consistently.

Figure 2. Architecture of Industry 6.0

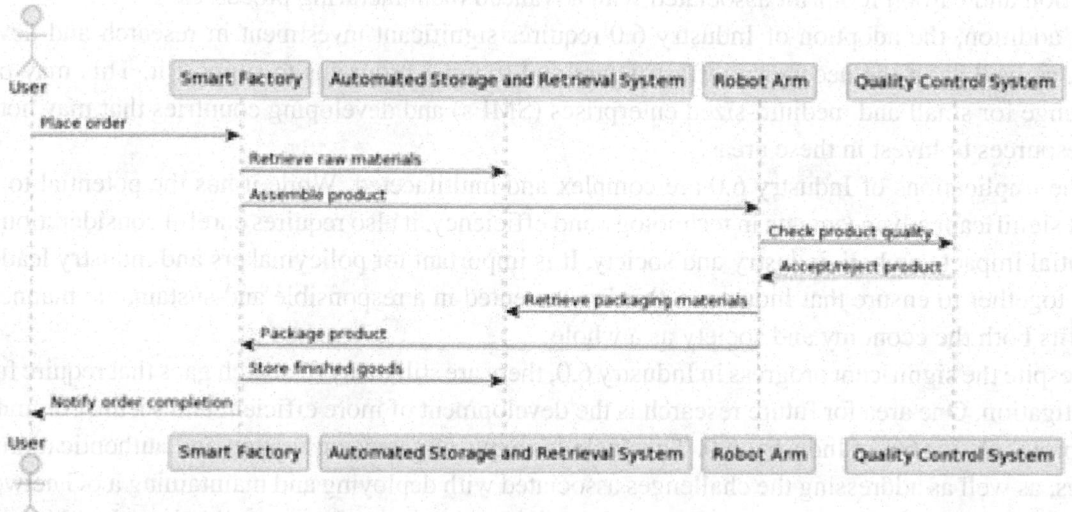

The architecture of Industry 6.0 is designed to support the digital trans-formation of the manufacturing industry by leveraging advanced technologies such as IIoT, big data analytics, and machine learning. It is a highly scalable and adaptable architecture that can be customized to meet the specific needs of individual manufacturing companies.

6. CONCLUSION AND FUTURE DIRECTIONS

The findings suggest that Industry 6.0 has the potential to revolutionize the manufacturing industry, enabling unprecedented levels of efficiency, automation, and optimization. However, there are significant challenges that must be addressed, including the need to ensure high quality of services, to overcome technological challenges, and to foster effective human-machine synergy. The successful deployment of Industry 6.0 will require a collaborative effort among stakeholders, including researchers, industry leaders, policymakers, and the workforce.

The implications of Industry 6.0 on both industry and society are vast and complex. On the one hand, Industry 6.0 has the potential to bring about significant advancements in technology and automation, leading to increased efficiency and productivity in manufacturing processes. This can translate to reduced costs for manufacturers, higher quality products for consumers, and increased job opportunities in advanced manufacturing industries. However, Industry 6.0 also brings about some challenges and potential negative impacts. The increasing reliance on automation and digital technologies may lead to job displacement for low-skilled workers. This may also result in increased economic inequality if new job opportunities created in advanced manufacturing industries require higher levels of education and skills such as practical knowledge and understanding of robotics and IoT (Plauska & Damasevicius, 2014).

The integration of Industry 6.0 with IoT and 6G communication technology raises concerns about data privacy and security. There are also environmental concerns related to the increasing energy consumption and carbon footprint associated with advanced manufacturing processes.

In addition, the adoption of Industry 6.0 requires significant investment in research and development, as well as in the necessary infrastructure and training programs to support it. This may pose a challenge for small and medium-sized enterprises (SMEs) and developing countries that may not have the resources to invest in these areas.

The implications of Industry 6.0 are complex and multifaceted. While it has the potential to bring about significant advancements in technology and efficiency, it also requires careful consideration of its potential impacts on both industry and society. It is important for policymakers and industry leaders to work together to ensure that Industry 6.0 is implemented in a responsible and sustainable manner that benefits both the economy and society as a whole.

Despite the significant progress in Industry 6.0, there are still many re-search gaps that require further investigation. One area for future research is the development of more efficient and secure communication protocols for 6G in Industry 6.0. This includes exploring new encryption and authentication techniques, as well as addressing the challenges associated with deploying and maintaining a 6G network in an industrial setting. Another area of research is the development of more sophisticated and intelligent AI systems that can operate autonomously and adapt to changing conditions in real-time. This includes exploring new techniques for training AI systems, as well as developing more effective methods for integrating AI with other industrial automation systems. Finally, there is a need to investigate the potential for Industry 6.0 to contribute to sustainable development. This includes exploring the potential for Industry 6.0 to reduce carbon emissions and improve energy efficiency, as well as investigating the potential for Industry 6.0 to contribute to the circular economy and support more sustainable forms of production and consumption.

REFERENCES

Abioye, T. E., Arogundade, O. T., Misra, S., Adesemowo, K., & Damasevicius, R. (2021). Cloud-based business process security risk manage-ment: A systematic review, taxonomy, and future directions. *Comput-ers*, *10*(12), 160. doi:10.3390/computers10120160

Agbaegbu, J., Arogundade, O. T., Misra, S., & Damasevicius, R. (2021). Ontolo-gies in cloud computing—Review and future directions. *Future Internet*, *13*(12), 302. doi:10.3390/fi13120302

Alsharif, M. H., Kelechi, A. H., Albreem, M. A., Chaudhry, S. A., Zia, M. S., & Kim, S. (2020). M. Sul-tan Zia, S. Kim, Sixth generation (6g)wireless networks: Vision, re-search activities, challenges and potential solutions. *Symmetry*, *12*(4), 676. doi:10.3390ym12040676

Alves, J., Lima, T. M., & Gaspar, P. D. (2023). Is industry 5.0 a human-centred approach? a systematic review. *Processes (Basel, Switzerland)*, *11*(1), 193. doi:10.3390/pr11010193

Bot'ın-Sanabria, D. M., Mihaita, S., Peimbert-Garc'ıa, R. E., Ram'ırez-Moreno, M. A., Ram'ırez-Mendoza, R. A., & Lozoya-Santos, J. J. (2022). Dig-ital twin technology challenges and applications: A comprehensive re-view. *Remote Sensing (Basel)*, *14*(6), 1335. doi:10.3390/rs14061335

Chourasia, A., Tyagi, A., Pandey, S., Walia, R., & Murtaza, Q. (2022). Sustain-ability of industry 6.0 in global perspective: Benefits and challenges, Mapan. *Journal ofMetrology Society of India 37*(2), 443–452.

Damasevicius, R., Bacanin, N., & Misra, S. (2023). From sensors to safety: Inter-net of emergency services (IOES) for emergency response and disaster management. *Journal of Sensor and Actuator Networks*, *12*(3), 41. doi:10.3390/jsan12030041

Damasevicius, R., Maskeliunas, R., & Misra, S. (2023). Supporting and shaping hu-man decisions through internet of behaviors (iob): Perspectives and im-plications. *Studies in Computational Intelligence*, *1105*, 115–144. doi:10.1007/978-3-031-37454-8 6

Devaraja, R. R., Maskeliunas, R., & Damasevicius, R. (2020). Aisra: Anthropo-morphic robotic hand for small-scale industrial applications. Lecture Notes in Computer Science. ACM. doi:10.1007/978-3-030-58799-4 54

Duggal, A. S., Malik, P. K., Gehlot, A., Singh, R., Gaba, G. S., Ma-sud, M., & Al-Amri, J. F. (2021). A sequential roadmap to industry 6.0: Exploring future manufacturing trends. *IET Communications*, *16*(5), 521–531. doi:10.1049/cmu2.12284

ElMaraghy, H., & ElMaraghy, W. (2022). Adaptive cognitive manufacturing sys-tem (acms)–a new paradigm. *International Journal of Production Research*, *60*(24), 7436–7449. doi:10.1080/00207543.2022.2078248

Emmanuel, M., Ananya, S., & Misra, M. (2020). A Deep Neural Network-Based Advisory Framework for Attainment of Sustainable Development Goals 1-6. *Sustainability*. doi:10.3390/su122410524

Fracaro, S. G., Glassey, J., Bernaerts, K., & Wilk, M. (2022). Immersive technolo-gies for the training of operators in the process industry: A system-atic literature review. *Computers & Chemical Engineering*, *160*, 107691. doi:10.1016/j.compchemeng.2022.107691

Georgescu, C. E. (2019). *Industry 6.0–new dimensions for industrial cooperation on the belt and road.* ICI.

Girdhar, A., Kapur, H., Kumar, V., Kaur, M., Singh, D., & Dama-sevicius, R. (2021). Effect of co-vid-19 outbreak on urban health and environ-ment. *Air Quality, Atmosphere & Health*, *14*(3), 389–397. doi:10.100711869-020-00944-1 PMID:33072226

Golovianko, M., Terziyan, V., Branytskyi, V., & Malyk, D. (2023). Industry 4.0 vs. industry 5.0: Co-exis-tence, transition, or a hybrid. *Procedia Computer Science*, *217*, 102–113. doi:10.1016/j.procs.2022.12.206

Groumpos, P. P. (2021). A critical historical and scientific overview of all in-dustrial revolutions. *IFAC-PapersOnLine*, *54*(13), 464–471. doi:10.1016/j.ifacol.2021.10.492

Guerreiro, J., Loureiro, S. M. C., Romero, J., Itani, O., & Eloy, S. (2022). Transhu-manism and engagement-facilitating technologies in society. *Journal of Promotion Management*, *28*(5), 537–558. doi:10.1080/10496491.2021.2009615

Hassan, N. M., Khan, S. A. R., Ashraf, M. U., & Sheikh, A. A. (2023). Interconnec-tion between the role of blockchain technologies, supply chain integra-tion, and circular economy: A case of small and medium-sized enter-prises in pakistan. *Science Progress*, *106*(3), 00368504231186527. doi:10.1177/00368504231186527 PMID:37437130

Jamil, S., Rahman, M., Abbas, M. S., & Fawad. (2022). Resource allocation using reconfigurable intelligent surface (ris)-assisted wireless networks in industry 5.0 scenario. *Telecom*, *3*(1), 163–173. doi:10.3390/telecom3010011

Jeyaraman, M., Nallakumarasamy, A., & Jeyaraman, N. (2022). Industry 5.0 in orthopaedics. *Indian Journal of Orthopaedics*, *56*(10), 1694–1702. doi:10.100743465-022-00712-6 PMID:36187596

Jiang, W., Han, B., Habibi, M. A., & Schotten, H. D. (2021). The road towards 6g: A comprehensive survey. *IEEE Open Journal of the Communications Society*, *2*, 334–366. doi:10.1109/OJCOMS.2021.3057679

Kalkal, A., Kumar, S., Kumar, P., Pradhan, R., Willander, M., Packirisamy, G., Kumar, S., & Malhotra, B. D. (2021). Recent advances in 3d printing technologies for wearable (bio)sensors. *Additive Manufacturing*, *46*, 102088. doi:10.1016/j.addma.2021.102088

Kesavan, M., & Prabhu, J. (2018). A survey, design and analysis of iot security and qos challenges. *International Journal of Information System Modeling and Design*, *9*(3), 48–66. doi:10.4018/IJISMD.2018070103

Koohang, A., Nord, J. H., Ooi, K.-B., Tan, G. W.-H., Al-Emran, M., Aw, E. C.-X., Baabdullah, A. M., Buhalis, D., Cham, T.-H., Dennis, C., Dutot, V., Dwivedi, Y. K., Hughes, L., Mogaji, E., Pandey, N., Phau, I., Raman, R., Sharma, A., Sigala, M., & Wong, L.-W. (2023). Shaping the metaverse into reality: A holistic multidisciplinary understand-ing of opportunities, challenges, and avenues for future investigation. *Journal of Computer Information Systems*, *63*(3), 735–765. doi:10.1080/08874417.2023.2165197

Kumar, N. M., Mohammed, M. A., Abdulkareem, K. H., Damasevi-cius, R., Mostafa, S. A., Maashi, M. S., & Chopra, S. S. (2021). Artificial intelligence-based solution for sorting covid related medical waste streams and supporting data-driven decisions for smart circular economy practice. *Process Safety and Environmental Protection*, *152*, 482–494. doi:10.1016/j.psep.2021.06.026

Lee, J., & Kundu, P. (2022). Integrated cyber-physical systems and industrial metaverse for remote manufacturing. *Manufacturing Letters*, *34*, 12–15. doi:10.1016/j.mfglet.2022.08.012

Li, L. (2022). Reskilling and upskilling the future-ready workforce for industry 4.0 and beyond. *Information Systems Frontiers*, 1–16. PMID:35855776

Okewu, E., Misra, S., Maskeliunas, R., Damasevicius, R., & Fernandez-Sanz, L. (2017). Optimizing green computing awareness for environmental sustainability and economic security as a stochastic optimization problem. *Sustainability (Basel)*, *9*(10), 1857. doi:10.3390u9101857

Ozkan-Ozen, Y. D., & Kazancoglu, Y. (2022). Analysing workforce development challenges in the industry 4.0. *International Journal of Manpower*, *43*(2), 310–333. doi:10.1108/IJM-03-2021-0167

Patalas-maliszewska, J., Halikowski, D., & Damasevicius, R. (2021). An automated recognition of work activity in industrial manufacturing using convolutional neural networks. *Electronics (Basel)*, *10*(23), 2946. doi:10.3390/electronics10232946

Paulauskas, L., Paulauskas, A., Blazauskas, T., Damasevicius, R., & Maskeliunas, R. (2023). Reconstruction of industrial and historical heritage for cultural enrichment using virtual and augmented reality. *Technologies*, *11*(2), 36. doi:10.3390/technologies11020036

Peng, M., Garg, S., Wang, X., Bradai, A., Lin, H., & Hossain, M. S. (2020). Learning-based iot data aggregation for disaster scenarios. *IEEE Access: Practical Innovations, Open Solutions*, *8*, 128490–128497. doi:10.1109/ACCESS.2020.3008289

Plauska, I., & Damasevicius, R. (2014). Educational robots for internet-of-things supported collaborative learning. *Communications in Computer and Information Science*, *465*, 346–358. doi:10.1007/978-3-319-11958-8_28

Ray, T. R., Choi, J., Bandodkar, A. J., Krishnan, S., Gutruf, P., Tian, L., Ghaffari, R., & Rogers, J. A. (2019). Bio-integrated wearable systems: A comprehensive review. *Chemical Reviews*, *119*(8), 5461–5533. doi:10.1021/acs.chemrev.8b00573 PMID:30689360

Sathish Kumar, K., Om Prakash, P., Alangudi Balaji, N., & Damasevicius, R. (2022). Internet of things and big data analytics for smart healthcare. Handbook of Intelligent Healthcare Analytics: Knowledge Engineering with Big Data Analytics. Wiley. doi:10.1002/9781119792550.ch7

Schwab, K. (2017). *The fourth industrial revolution*. Currency.

Singh, K. (2023). Evaluation planning for artificial intelligence-based industry 6.0 metaverse integration. *Intelligent Human Systems Integra-tion (IHSI 2023): Integrating People and Intelligent Systems 69*(69).

Snyder, T., & Byrd, G. (2017). The internet of everything. *Computer*, *50*(6), 8–9. doi:10.1109/MC.2017.179

Venckauskas, A., Morkevicius, N., Jukavicius, V., Damasevicius, R., Toldinas, J., & Grigaliūnas, Š. (2019). An edge-fog secure self-authenticable data transfer protocol. *Sensors (Basel)*, *19*(16), 3612. doi:10.339019163612 PMID:31431005

Wang, F. -Y., Yang, J., Wang, X., Li, J., Han, Q. (2023). Chat with chatgpt on industry 5.0: Learning and decision-making for intelligent industries. *IEEE/CAA Journal of Automatica Sinica, 10*(4).

Wogu, I. A., Misra, S., Assibong, P. A., Olu-Owolabi, E. F., Maskeliunas, R., & Damasevicius, R. (2019). Artificial intelligence, smart class-rooms and online education in the 21st century: Implications for hu-man development. *Journal of Cases on Information Technology*, *21*(3), 66–79. doi:10.4018/JCIT.2019070105

Wurster, M., Exner, Y., Kaiser, J.-P., Stricker, N., & Lanza, G. (2021). Towards planning and control in cognitive factories - a generic model including learning effects and knowledge transfer across system entities. Procedia CIRP, 103, 158 – 163. doi:10.1016/j.procir.2021.10.025

Yadav, R., Arora, S., & Dhull, S. (2022). A path way to industrial revolution 6.0. *Int. J. Mech. Eng*, *7*, 1452–1459.

Yavari, F., & Pilevari, N. (2020). Industry revolutions development from industry 1.0 to industry 5.0 in manufacturing. *Journal of Industrial Strategic Management*, *5*(2), 44–63.

You, X., Wang, C.-X., Huang, J., Gao, X., Zhang, Z., Wang, M., Huang, Y., Zhang, C., Jiang, Y., Wang, J., Zhu, M., Sheng, B., Wang, D., Pan, Z., Zhu, P., Yang, Y., Liu, Z., Zhang, P., Tao, X., & Liang, Y.-C. (2021). Towards 6g wireless communica-tion networks: Vision, enabling technologies, and new paradigm shifts. *Science China. Information Sciences*, *64*(1), 110301. doi:10.100711432-020-2955-6

Yunana, K., Alfa, A., Misra, S., Damasevicius, R., Maskeliunas, R., & Oluranti, J. (2021). Internet of things: Applications, adoptions and components - a conceptual overview, Advances in Intelligent Systems and Computing 1375 AIST 494 – 504. doi:. doi:10.1007/978-3-030-73050-550

Compilation of References

Abdelmaboud, A., Ahmed, A. I., Abaker, M., Eisa, T. A., Albasheer, H., Ghorashi, S. A., & Karim, F. K. (2022, February 18). Blockchain for IoT applications: Taxonomy, platforms, recent advances, challenges and future research directions. *Electronics (Basel), 11*(4), 630. doi:10.3390/electronics11040630

Abioye, T. E., Arogundade, O. T., Misra, S., Adesemowo, K., & Damasevicius, R. (2021). Cloud-based business process security risk manage-ment: A systematic review, taxonomy, and future directions. *Comput-ers, 10*(12), 160. doi:10.3390/computers10120160

Ab Rahman, N. H., & Choo, K. K. R. (2015). A survey of information security incident handling in the cloud. *computers & security, 49*, 45-69.

Acar, A., Aksu, H., Uluagac, A. S., & Conti, M. (2018). A survey on homomorphic encryption schemes: Theory and implementation. *ACM Computing Surveys, 51*(4), 1–35. doi:10.1145/3214303

Agarwal, D., & Tripathi, K. (2022). A Framework for Structural Damage detection system in automobiles for flexible Insurance claim using IOT and Machine Learning. *2022 International Mobile and Embedded Technology Conference (MECON),* (pp. 5-8). IEEE. 10.1109/MECON53876.2022.9751889

Agbaegbu, J., Arogundade, O. T., Misra, S., & Damasevicius, R. (2021). Ontolo-gies in cloud computing—Review and future directions. *Future Internet, 13*(12), 302. doi:10.3390/fi13120302

Ahmad, T., Zhu, H., Zhang, D., & Tariq, R. A. (2022). Energetics Systems and artificial intelligence: Applications of industry 4.0. *Energy Reports, 8*. doi:10.1016/j.egyr.2021.11.256

Ahmad, W., Rasool, A., Javed, A., Baker, T., & Jalil, Z. (2022). Cyber Security in IoT-Based Cloud Computing: A Comprehensive Survey. *Electronics (Basel), 11*(1), 16. doi:10.3390/electronics11010016

Ahmed, A., Ali, G., Hussain, A., Baseer, A., & Ahmed, J. (2021). Analysis of text feature extractors using deep learning on fake news. *Engineering, Technology, &. Applied Scientific Research, 11*(2), 7001–7005.

Al-Riyami, S., Al-Fedaghi, S., & Al-Turjman, F. (2022). A Blockchain-Based System for Securing IoT Services in Cloud Environments. *IEEE Transactions on Industrial Informatics, 18*(3), 1655–1662.

Al-Rubaie, M., & Chang, J. M. (2019). Privacy-preserving machine learning: Threats and solutions. *IEEE Security and Privacy, 17*(2), 49–58. doi:10.1109/MSEC.2018.2888775

Alaba, F. A., Othman, M., Hashem, I. A., & Alotaibi, F. (2017). Internet of Things security: A survey. *Journal of Network and Computer Applications, 88*, 10–28. doi:10.1016/j.jnca.2017.04.002

Alam, F., Malik, H., & Yim, D. K. (2019). Towards Digital Twins for Internet of Things. In *2019 IEEE International Conference on Pervasive Computing and Communications Workshops (PerCom Workshops)* (pp. 38-43). IEEE.

Alam, S., Shuaib, M., Ahmad, S., Jayakody, D. N. K., Muthanna, A., Bharany, S., & Elgendy, I. A. (2022). Ghubaish -Based Solutions Supporting Reliable Healthcare for Fog Computing and Internet of Medical Things (IoMT) Integration. *Sustainability (Basel), 14*(22), 15312. doi:10.3390u142215312

Alazab, M. R., Kabir, A. M. R., & Kumar, N. (2022). A Secure Blockchain-Based Model for the Internet of Things. *IEEE Internet of Things Journal, 9*(6), 4855–4862.

Al Badawi, A., Bates, J., Bergamaschi, F., Cousins, D. B., Erabelli, S., Genise, N., & Zucca, V. (2022, November). OpenFHE: Open-source fully homomorphic encryption library. In *Proceedings of the 10th Workshop on Encrypted Computing & Applied Homomorphic Cryptography* (pp. 53-63). 10.1145/3560827.3563379

Aldwairi, M., & Alwahedi, A. (2018, November 5). Detecting fake news in social media networks. *Procedia Computer Science, 141*, 215–222. doi:10.1016/j.procs.2018.10.171

Aledhari, M., Razzak, R., Parizi, R. M., & Saeed, F. (2020). Federated learning: A survey on enabling technologies, protocols, and applications. *IEEE Access : Practical Innovations, Open Solutions, 8*, 140699–140725. doi:10.1109/ACCESS.2020.3013541 PMID:32999795

Alhayani, B., Kwekha-Rashid, A. S., Mahajan, H. B., Ilhan, H., Uke, N., Alkhayyat, A., & Mohammed, H. J. (2023). 5G standards for the Industry 4.0 enabled communication systems using artificial intelligence: Perspective of smart healthcare system. *Applied Nanoscience, 13*(3), 1807–1817. doi:10.100713204-021-02152-4 PMID:35096498

Ali, M. D., & Kaur, D. S. (2020). Byod cyber forensic eco-system. [IJARET]. *International Journal of Advanced Research in Engineering and Technology, 11*(9).

Aljabr, A. A., & Kumar, K. (2022, December). Design and implementation of Internet of Medical Things (IoMT) using artificial intelligent for mobile-healthcare. Measurement. *Sensors (Basel), 24*, 100499. doi:10.1016/j.measen.2022.100499

Alladi, T., Chamola, V., Parizi, R., & Choo, K. (2019). Blockchain applications for industry 4.0 and industrial iot: A review. *IEEE Access, 7.*

Almadani, M. S., Alotaibi, S., Alsobhi, H., Hussain, O. K., & Hussain, F. K. (2023). *Blockchain-based multi-factor authentication: A systematic literature review*. Internet of Things. Research Gate.

Alnahari, W., & Quasim, M. T. (2021, July). Authentication of IoT device and IoT server using security key. In *2021 International Congress of Advanced Technology and Engineering (ICOTEN)* (pp. 1-9). IEEE. 10.1109/ICOTEN52080.2021.9493492

Alsharif, M. H., Kelechi, A. H., Albreem, M. A., Chaudhry, S. A., Zia, M. S., & Kim, S. (2020). M. Sul-tan Zia, S. Kim, Sixth generation (6g)wireless networks: Vision, re-search activities, challenges and potential solutions. *Symmetry, 12*(4), 676. doi:10.3390ym12040676

Alsuhibany, S. A., Abdel-Khalek, S., Algarni, A., Fayomi, A., Gupta, D., Kumar, V., & Mansour, R. F. (2021, December 27). *Ensemble of Deep Learning Based Clinical Decision Support System for Chronic Kidney Disease Diagnosis in Medical Internet of Things Environment.*. Hindawi. doi:10.1155/2021/4931450

Alves, J., Lima, T. M., & Gaspar, P. D. (2023). Is industry 5.0 a human-centred approach? a systematic review. *Processes (Basel, Switzerland), 11*(1), 193. doi:10.3390/pr11010193

Al-Qahtani, A. F., & Cresci, S. (2022). The COVID-19 scamdemic: A survey of phishing attacks and their countermeasures during COVID-19. *IET Information Security, 16*(5), 324–345. doi:10.1049/ise2.12073 PMID:35942004

Ambika, N. (2020). Improved Methodology to Detect Advanced Persistent Threat Attacks. In N. K. Chaubey & B. B. Prajapati (Eds.), *Quantum Cryptography and the Future of Cyber Security* (pp. 184–202). IGI Global. doi:10.4018/978-1-7998-2253-0.ch009

Ambika, N. (2021). A Reliable Blockchain-Based Image Encryption Scheme for IIoT Networks. In *Blockchain and AI Technology in the Industrial Internet of Things* (pp. 81–97). IGI Global.

Anant, V., Donchak, L., Kaplan, J., & Soller, H. (2020). *The consumer-data opportunity and the privacy imperative.* McKinsey. https://www. mckinsey. com/business-functions/risk-and-resilience/our-insights/the-consumer-data-opportunity-and-the-privacy-imperative

Anderson, J., & Keahey, K. (2022). Migrating towards Single Sign-On and Federated Identity. In Practice and Experience in Advanced Research Computing (pp. 1-8). Springer. doi:10.1145/3491418.3530770

Ardolino, M., Bacchetti, A., Dolgui, A., Franchini, G., Ivanov, D., & Nair, A. (2022). The impacts of digital technologies on coping with the COVID-19 pandemic in the manufacturing industry: A systematic literature review. *International Journal of Production Research*, 1–24. doi:10.1080/00207543.2022.2127960

Armbrust, M., Fox, A., Griffith, R., Joseph, A. D., Katz, R. H., Konwinski, A., Lee, G., Patterson, D. A., Rabkin, A., Stoica, I., & Zaharia, M. (2009). Above the clouds: A Berkeley view of cloud computing" in, EECS Department, University of California, Berkeley, Tech. Rep. UCB/EECS-2009-28.

Asadi, A. N., Azgomi, M. A., & Entezari-Maleki, R. (2019). Unified power and performance analysis of cloud computing infrastructure using stochastic reward nets. *Computer Communications*, *138*, 67–80. doi:10.1016/j.comcom.2019.03.004

Ashima, R., Haleem, A., Bahl, S., Javaid, M., Mahla, S. K., & Singh, S. (2021). Automation and manufacturing of smart materials in additive manufacturing technologies using internet of things towards the adoption of industry 4.0. [Crossref, Google Scholar.]. *Materials Today: Proceedings*, *45*, 5081–5088. doi:10.1016/j.matpr.2021.01.583

Ashraf, I., Park, Y., Hur, S., Kim, S. W., Alroobaea, R., Zikria, Y. B., & Nosheen, S. (2022). A survey on cyber security threats in iot-enabled maritime industry. *IEEE Transactions on Intelligent Transportation Systems*, *24*(2), 2677–2690. doi:10.1109/TITS.2022.3164678

Aslam, T., Maqbool, A., Akhtar, M., Mirza, A., Khan, M. A., Khan, W. Z., & Alam, S. (2021). Blockchain based enhanced ERP transaction integrity architecture and PoET consensus. *Computers, Materials & Continua*, *70*(1), 1089–1108. doi:10.32604/cmc.2022.019416

Attaran, M. (2017). Cloud computing technology: Leveraging the power of the internet to improve business performance. *Journal of International Technology and Information Management*, *26*(1), 112–137. doi:10.58729/1941-6679.1283

Awaisi, K. S., Hussain, S., Ahmed, M., Khan, A. A., & Ahmed, G. (2020). Leveraging IoT and fog computing in healthcare systems. *IEEE Internet Things Mag.*, *3*(2), 52–56. doi:10.1109/IOTM.0001.1900096

Azbeg, K., Ouchetto, O., Andaloussi, S. J., Fetjah, L., & Sekkaki, A. (2018). Blockchain and IoT for security and privacy: a platform for diabetes self-management. In *2018 4th international conference on cloud computing technologies and applications (Cloudtech)*, (pp. 1-5). IEEE. 10.1109/CloudTech.2018.8713343

Babu, R. & Jayashree, K. (2015). A Survey on the Role of IoT and Cloud in Health Care. *International Journal of Scientific, Engineering and Technology Research (IJSETR)*, *4*(12).

Badawi, A. A. (2022). *OpenFHE: Open-Source Fully Homomorphic Encryption Library*. ePrint. https://eprint.iacr.org/2022/915

Bag, S., Pretorius, J. H., Gupta, S., & Dwivedi, Y. K. (2021). Role of institutional pressures and resources in the adoption of big data analytics powered artificial intelligence, sustainable manufacturing practices and circular economy capabilities. [Crossref, Google Scholar.]. *Technological Forecasting and Social Change*, *163*, 120420. doi:10.1016/j.techfore.2020.120420

Bagga, J. (2023). SAP Cloud Integration: Security. In *A Practical Guide to SAP Integration Suite: SAP's Cloud Middleware and Integration Solution* (pp. 371–388). Apress. doi:10.1007/978-1-4842-9337-9_7

Bai, C., Dallasega, P., Orzes, G., & Sarkis, J. (2020). Industry 4.0 technologies assessment: A sustainability perspective. [Crossref, Google Scholar.]. *International Journal of Production Economics*, *229*, 107776. doi:10.1016/j.ijpe.2020.107776

Balas, V., Solanki, K., Kumar, R., & Khari, M. (2019). The History, Present and Future with IoT. Internet of Things and Big Data Analytics for Smart Generation. Springer.

Ball, P., & Maxmen, A. (2020). The epic battle against coronavirus misinformation and conspiracy theories. *Nature*, *581*(7809), 371–374. doi:10.1038/d41586-020-01452-z PMID:32461658

Bandari, V. (2023). Enterprise Data Security Measures: A Comparative Review of Effectiveness and Risks Across Different Industries and Organization Types. *International Journal of Business Intelligence and Big Data Analytics*, *6*(1), 1–11.

Bayarçelik, E. B., & Bumin Doyduk, H. B. (2020). Digitalization of business logistics activities and future directions. *Digital Business Strategies in Blockchain Ecosystems: Transformational Design and Future of Global Business*, 201-238.

Bello, S. A., Oyedele, L. O., Akinade, O. O., Bilal, M., Delgado, J. M. D., Akanbi, L. A., & Owolabi, H. A. (2021). Cloud computing in construction industry: Use cases, benefits and challenges. *Automation in Construction*, *122*, 103441. doi:10.1016/j.autcon.2020.103441

Benaloh, J. (1994, May). Dense probabilistic encryption. In *Proceedings of the workshop on selected areas of cryptography* (pp. 120-128). IEEE.

Bernabe, J. B., Canovas, J. L., Hernandez-Ramos, J. L., Moreno, R. T., & Skarmeta, A. (2019). Privacy-preserving solutions for blockchain: Review and challenges. *IEEE Access : Practical Innovations, Open Solutions*, *7*, 164908–164940. doi:10.1109/ACCESS.2019.2950872

Bhandary, M., Parmar, M., & Ambawade, D. (2020). Securing logs of a system-an iota tangle use case. *International Conference on Electronics and Sustainable Communication Systems (ICESC)* (pp. 697-702). Coimbatore, India: IEEE. 10.1109/ICESC48915.2020.9155563

Bhushan, B., Sinha, P., Sagayam, K. M., & Andrew, J. (2021, March 1). Untangling blockchain technology: A survey on state of the art, security threats, privacy services, applications and future research directions. *Computers & Electrical Engineering*, *90*, 106897. doi:10.1016/j.compeleceng.2020.106897

Bodkhe, U., Tanwar, S., Parekh, K., Khanpara, P., Tyagi, S., Kumar, N., & Alazab, M. (2020). Blockchain for industry 4.0: A comprehensive review. *IEEE Access : Practical Innovations, Open Solutions*, *8*, 79764–79800. doi:10.1109/ACCESS.2020.2988579

Boneh, D., Goh, E. J., & Nissim, K. (2005, February). Evaluating 2-DNF Formulas on Ciphertexts. In TCC (Vol. 3378, pp. 325-341).

Bot'ın-Sanabria, D. M., Mihaita, S., Peimbert-Garc'ıa, R. E., Ram'ırez-Moreno, M. A., Ram'ırez-Mendoza, R. A., & Lozoya-Santos, J. J. (2022). Dig-ital twin technology challenges and applications: A comprehensive re-view. *Remote Sensing (Basel)*, *14*(6), 1335. doi:10.3390/rs14061335

Bozuyla, M. (2021). AdaBoost ensemble learning on top of naive Bayes algorithm to discriminate fake and genuine news from social media. *European Journal of Science and Technology*, *5*(4), 499–513. doi:10.31590/ejosat.1005577

Brennen, J. S., Simon, F. M., & Nielsen, R. K. (2021). Beyond (mis) representation: Visuals in COVID-19 misinformation. *The International Journal of Press/Politics*, *26*(1), 277–299. doi:10.1177/1940161220964780

Butt, U. A., Amin, R., Mehmood, M., Aldabbas, H., Alharbi, M. T., & Albaqami, N. (2023). Cloud security threats and solutions: A survey. *Wireless Personal Communications*, *128*(1), 387–413. doi:10.100711277-022-09960-z

Böhmann, T., Leimeister, J. M., & Riedl, C. (2016). Design principles for Industries 4.0 scenarios. In *Proceedings of the 49th Hawaii International Conference on System Sciences*. IEEE.

Ch, R., Srivastava, G., Gadekallu, T.R., Maddikunta, P.K., & Bhattacharya, S. (2020). Security and privacy of UAV data using blockchain technology. *Journal of Information security and Applications*.

Chen, B., Luo, W., & Li, H. (2017). Audio steganalysis with convolutional neural network. *IH and MMSec 2017 - Proceedings of the 2017 ACM Workshop on Information Hiding and Multimedia Security*, (pp. 85–90). ACM. 10.1145/3082031.3083234

Chen, B., Luo, W., & Luo, D. (2018). Identification of audio processing operations based on convolutional neural network. *IH and MMSec 2018 - Proceedings of the 6th ACM Workshop on Information Hiding and Multimedia Security*, (pp. 73–77). IEEE. 10.1145/3206004.3206005

Chen, L., Wang, Z., & Li, X. (2019). Blockchain-driven Security Framework for Resource Management in Edge Computing. *IEEE Transactions on Cloud Computing*, *6*(5), 1903–1916.

Chen, Q., Wu, Y., & Lim, G. (2021). Scalable and Secure Blockchain-based Identity Management in Edge Computing. *Journal of Network and Computer Applications*, *95*, 105240.

Chen, Y., Paxson, V., & Katz, R. (2010). What's New About Cloud. *Computers & Security*.

Chen, Y.-C., Chou, Y.-P., & Chou, Y.-C. (2019). An Image Authentication Scheme Using Merkle Tree Mechanisms. *Future Internet*, *11*(7), 149. doi:10.3390/fi11070149

Chen, Z., Zhang, X., & Wang, C. (2022). A Blockchain-Based Efficient Data Sharing Scheme in the Industrial Internet of Things. *IEEE Transactions on Industrial Informatics*, *18*(5), 3456–3463.

Cheon, J. H., Kim, A., Kim, M., & Song, Y. (2016). *Implementation of HEA-AN.* Github. https://github.com/kimandrik/HEAAN

Chhabra, G. S., Singh, V., & Singh, M. (2018). Hadoop-based analytic framework for cyber forensics. *International Journal of Communication Systems*, *31*(15), e3772. doi:10.1002/dac.3772

Chillotti, I. (2016). *TFHE: Fast Fully Homomorphic Encryption Library*.

Choo, K. K., Yan, Z., & Meng, W. (2020, June). Blockchain in industrial IoT applications: Security and privacy advances, challenges, and opportunities. *IEEE Transactions on Industrial Informatics*, *16*(6), 4119–4121. doi:10.1109/TII.2020.2966068

Chourasia, A., Tyagi, A., Pandey, S., Walia, R., & Murtaza, Q. (2022). Sustain-ability of industry 6.0 in global perspective: Benefits and challenges, Mapan. *Journal of Metrology Society of India 37*(2), 443–452.

Christopher, M., Lowson, R., & Peck, H. (2004). Creating agile supply chains in the fashion industry. *International Journal of Retail & Distribution Management*, *32*(8), 367–376. doi:10.1108/09590550410546188

Collins, B., Hoang, D. T., Nguyen, N. T., & Hwang, D. (2021). Trends in combating fake news on social media – a survey. *Journal of Information and Telecommunication*, *5*(2), 247–266. doi:10.1080/24751839.2020.1847379

Damasevicius, R., Bacanin, N., & Misra, S. (2023). From sensors to safety: Inter-net of emergency services (IOES) for emergency response and disaster management. *Journal of Sensor and Actuator Networks*, *12*(3), 41. doi:10.3390/jsan12030041

Damasevicius, R., Maskeliunas, R., & Misra, S. (2023). Supporting and shaping hu-man decisions through internet of behaviors (iob): Perspectives and im-plications. *Studies in Computational Intelligence*, *1105*, 115–144. doi:10.1007/978-3-031-37454-8 6

Damenu, T. K., & Balakrishna, C. (2015, September). Cloud security risk management: A critical review. In *2015 9th International Conference on Next Generation Mobile Applications, Services and Technologies* (pp. 370-375). IEEE. 10.1109/NGMAST.2015.25

Darabkh, K., Odetallah, S., Al-qudah, Z., & Khalifeh, A. (2018). A New Density-Based Relaying Protocol for Wireless Sensor Networks. 14th International Wireless Communications & Mobile Computing Conference, IWCMC.

Darabkh, K., Zomot, J., & Al-qudah, Z. (2019). EDB-CHS-BOF: Energy and distance-based cluster head selection with balanced objective function protocol. *IET Communications*, *13*(19), 3168–3180. doi:10.1049/iet-com.2019.0092

Dargahi, S., Abolhassani, B. H., & Marjani, M. (2021). A Novel Blockchain-Based Access Control Model for Cloud-Edge Computing Systems. *IEEE Transactions on Industrial Informatics*, *17*(6), 4166–4173.

DasS. (2023). An Article On: Augmented Reality Contrast to Ergonomic Design. SSRN. https://ssrn.com/abstract=4320316 doi:10.2139/ssrn.4320316

Dastjerdi, A. V., Gupta, H., Calheiros, R. N., Ghosh, S. K., & Buyya, R. (2016). Fog computing: Principles, architectures, and applications. *Internet of Things Journal*, *3*(5), 516–553.

Davies, R., Coole, T., & Smith, A. (2017). Review of socio-technical considerations to ensure successful implementation of industry 4.0. *Procedia Manufacturing*, *11*, 1288–1295. doi:10.1016/j.promfg.2017.07.256

Da Xu, L., Lu, Y., & Li, L. (2021). Embedding blockchain technology into IoT for security: A survey. *IEEE Internet of Things Journal*, *8*(13), 10452–10473. doi:10.1109/JIOT.2021.3060508

Debashis, AKarmakar, ABanerjee, PBhattacharyya, SRodrigues, J. BCoT: Introduction to Blockchain-Based Internet of Things for Industry 5.0. In (2022). *Blockchain based Internet of Things* (pp. 1–22). Springer Singapore.

Deshmukh, A., Patil, D. S., Pawar, P. D., Kumari, S., & P., M. (2023). Recent Trends for Smart Environments With AI and IoT-Based Technologies: A Comprehensive Review. In A. Tyagi (Ed.), *Handbook of Research on Quantum Computing for Smart Environments* (pp. 435-452). IGI Global. doi:10.4018/978-1-6684-6697-1.ch023

Deshmukh, A., Sreenath, N., Tyagi, A. K., & Eswara Abhichandan, U. V. (2022). Blockchain Enabled Cyber Security: A Comprehensive Survey. *International Conference on Computer Communication and Informatics,* (pp. 1-6). IEEE. 10.1109/ICCCI54379.2022.9740843

Devaraja, R. R., Maskeliunas, R., & Damasevicius, R. (2020). Aisra: Anthropo-morphic robotic hand for small-scale industrial applications. Lecture Notes in Computer Science. ACM. doi:10.1007/978-3-030-58799-4 54

Devi, M. P., Choudhry, M. D., Raja, G. B., & Sathya, T. (2022). A roadmap towards robust IoT-enabled cyber-physical systems in cyber industrial 4.0. In *Handbook of research of internet of things and cyber-physical systems: An integrative approach to an interconnected future* (pp. 293–313). CRC Press. doi:10.1201/9781003277323-16

Devi, M. P., Choudhry, M. D., Sundarrajan, M., & Sivapriyanga, P. (2022). An efficient 24× 7 patient's vital parameter monitoring framework using machine learning based Internet of Biomedical Things: a comprehensive approach. In Advances in Image and Data Processing using VLSI Design, Volume 2: Biomedical applications (pp. 14-1). Bristol, UK: IOP Publishing.

Dorri, A., Kanhere, S. S., & Jurdak, R. (2017). Towards an optimized blockchain for IoT. In *Proceedings of the second international conference on Internet-of-Things design and implementation* (pp. 173-178). ACM. 10.1145/3054977.3055003

Doshi, R., Jain, P., & Gupta, L. (2012). Steganography and its Applications in Security. [IJMER]. *International Journal of Modern Engineering Research*, *2*(6), 4634–4638.

Drozdowski, P., Buchmann, N., Rathgeb, C., Margraf, M., & Busch, C. (2019). On the Application of Homomorphic Encryption to Face Identification. *2019 International Conference of the Biometrics Special Interest Group (BIOSIG)*, Darmstadt, Germany.

Duan, L., Xu, L. D., Cai, H., & Zheng, L. R. (2019). Artificial intelligence with internet of things: A conceptual framework. *Journal of Industrial Information Integration*, *13*, 1–6.

Duggal, A. S., Malik, P. K., Gehlot, A., Singh, R., Gaba, G. S., Ma-sud, M., & Al-Amri, J. F. (2021). A sequential roadmap to industry 6.0: Exploring future manufacturing trends. *IET Communications*, *16*(5), 521–531. doi:10.1049/cmu2.12284

Dutta, P., Choi, T. -M. Somani, S., & Butala, R. (2020). Blockchain technology in supply chain operations: Applications, challenges and research opportunities. *Transportation research part e: Logistics and transportation review*, *142*, 102067.

Dwivedi, A., Srivastava, G., Dhar, S., & Singh, R. (2019). A Decentralized Privacy-Preserving Healthcare Blockchain for IoT. *Sensors (Basel)*, *19*(2), 326. doi:10.339019020326 PMID:30650612

Dwivedi, R., Mehrotra, D., & Chandra, S. (2021). Potential of Internet of Medical Things (IoMT) applications in building a smart healthcare system: A systematic review. *Journal of Oral Biology and Craniofacial Research*, *12*(2), 302–318. doi:10.1016/j.jobcr.2021.11.010 PMID:34926140

Dwork, C. (2006, July). Differential privacy. In *International colloquium on automata, languages, and programming* (pp. 1-12). Berlin, Heidelberg: Springer Berlin Heidelberg. 10.1007/11787006_1

Dwork, C. (2008, April). Differential privacy: A survey of results. In *International conference on theory and applications of models of computation* (pp. 1-19). Berlin, Heidelberg: Springer Berlin Heidelberg.

Döring, T., Schneider, U., Uhlmann, E., & Thoben, K. D. (2016). Dynamic production networks in the context of Industry 4.0: A literature review. *Journal of Intelligent Manufacturing*, *27*(1), 111–128.

D'Silva, D., & Ambawade, D. D. (2021, April). Building a zero-trust architecture using kubernetes. In *2021 6th international conference for convergence in technology (i2ct)* (pp. 1-8). IEEE. 10.1109/I2CT51068.2021.9418203

Ejaz, W., Anpalagan, A., Ejaz, W., & Anpalagan, A. (2019). *Blockchain technology for security and privacy in internet of things. Internet of Things for Smart Cities: Technologies.* Big Data and Security.

ElGamal, T. (1985). A public key cryptosystem and a signature scheme based on discrete logarithms. *IEEE Transactions on Information Theory*, *31*(4), 469–472. doi:10.1109/TIT.1985.1057074

ElMaraghy, H., & ElMaraghy, W. (2022). Adaptive cognitive manufacturing sys-tem (acms)–a new paradigm. *International Journal of Production Research*, *60*(24), 7436–7449. doi:10.1080/00207543.2022.2078248

Emmanuel, M., Ananya, S., & Misra, M. (2020). A Deep Neural Network-Based Advisory Framework for Attainment of Sustainable Development Goals 1-6. *Sustainability*. doi:10.3390/su122410524

Eswaran, M., & Raju Bahubalendruni, M. V. A. (2022). Challenges and opportunities on AR/VR technologies for manufacturing systems in the context of industry 4.0: A state of the art review. *Journal of Manufacturing Systems, 65*.

Evangelista, A., Manghisi, V. M., Romano, S., De Giglio, V., & Cipriani, L. (2023). Advanced visualization of ergonomic assessment data through industrial Augmented Reality. *Procedia Computer Science, 217*.

Fachkha, C., & Debbabi, M. (2015). Darknet as a source of cyber intelligence: Survey, taxonomy, and characterization. *IEEE Communications Surveys and Tutorials*, *18*(2), 1197–1227. doi:10.1109/COMST.2015.2497690

Faheem, M., & Butt, R. A. (2022). Big datasets of optical-wireless cyber-physical systems for optimizing manufacturing services in the internet of things-enabled industry 4.0. *Data in Brief*, *42*, 108026. doi:10.1016/j.dib.2022.108026 PMID:35330737

Falahati, B., Fu, Y., & Wu, L. (2012). Reliability assessment of smart grid considering direct cyber-power interdependencies. *IEEE Transactions on Smart Grid*, *3*(3), 1515–1524. doi:10.1109/TSG.2012.2194520

Fazal, N., Haleem, A., Bahl, S., Javaid, M., & Nandan, D. (2022). Digital management systems in manufacturing using industry 5.0 technologies. In *Advancement in Materials, Manufacturing and Energy Engineering, Vol. II: Select Proceedings of ICAMME 2021*, (pp. 221-234). Singapore: Springer Nature Singapore. 10.1007/978-981-16-8341-1_18

Fellows, M., & Koblitz, N. (1994). Combinatorial cryptosystems galore! *Contemporary Mathematics*, *168*, 51–51. doi:10.1090/conm/168/01688

Fernandes, D. A., Soares, L. F., Gomes, J. V., Freire, M. M., & Inácio, P. R. (2014). Security issues in cloud environments: A survey. *International Journal of Information Security*, *13*(2), 113–170. doi:10.100710207-013-0208-7

Fernández-Caramés, T. M., & Fraga-Lamas, P. (2018). A review on the use of blockchain for the Internet of Things. *IEEE Access : Practical Innovations, Open Solutions*, *6*, 32979–33001. doi:10.1109/ACCESS.2018.2842685

Ferrag, M. A., & Shu, L. (2021, May 6). The performance evaluation of blockchain-based security and privacy systems for the Internet of Things: A tutorial. *IEEE Internet of Things Journal*, *8*(24), 17236–17260. doi:10.1109/JIOT.2021.3078072

Ferrag, M. A., Derdour, M., Mukherjee, M., Derhab, A., Maglaras, L., & Janicke, H. (2018). Blockchain technologies for the internet of things: Research issues and challenges. *IEEE Internet of Things Journal*, *6*(2), 2188–2204. doi:10.1109/JIOT.2018.2882794

Ferrag, M. A., Shu, L., Yang, X., Derhab, A., & Maglaras, L. (2020, February 11). Security and privacy for green IoT-based agriculture: Review, blockchain solutions, and challenges. *IEEE Access : Practical Innovations, Open Solutions*, *8*, 32031–32053. doi:10.1109/ACCESS.2020.2973178

Fleming, N. (2020, June 17). Coronavirus misinformation, and how scientists can help to fight it. *Nature*, *583*(7814), 155–156. doi:10.1038/d41586-020-01834-3 PMID:32601491

Folkman, S. (2000). *Privacy and confidentiality*. APA.

Fosso Wamba, S., Kala Kamdjoug, J. R., Epie Bawack, R., & Keogh, J. G. (2020). Bitcoin, Blockchain and Fintech: A systematic review and case studies in the supply chain. *Production Planning and Control*, *31*(2-3), 115–142. doi:10.1080/09537287.2019.1631460

Foster, I., Zhao, Y., Raicu, I., & Lu, S. Y. (2008). *Cloud computing and grid computing 360-degree compared. Proceedings of the Grid Computing Environments Workshop (GCE'08)*, Austin, TX. 10.1109/GCE.2008.4738445

Fracaro, S. G., Glassey, J., Bernaerts, K., & Wilk, M. (2022). Immersive technolo-gies for the training of operators in the process industry: A system-atic literature review. *Computers & Chemical Engineering*, *160*, 107691. doi:10.1016/j.compchemeng.2022.107691

Gadekallu, T. R., Huynh-The, T., Wang, W., Yenduri, G., Ranaweera, P., Pham, Q.-V., Benevides da Costa, D., & Liyanage, M. (2022). Blockchain for the metaverse: A review. *arXiv preprint arXiv:2203.09738*.

Garcia, M., Kim, D., & Park, H. (2021). A Hybrid Consensus Protocol for Enhanced Security in Edge Computing with Blockchain. *Journal of Parallel and Distributed Computing*, *125*, 109–120.

Garg, N., Bawa, S., & Kumar, N. (2020). An efficient data integrity auditing protocol for cloud computing. *Future Generation Computer Systems*, *109*, 306–316. doi:10.1016/j.future.2020.03.032

Gazzan, M., & Sheldon, F. T. (2023). Opportunities for Early Detection and Prediction of Ransomware Attacks against Industrial Control Systems. *Future Internet*, *15*(4), 144. doi:10.3390/fi15040144

Gentry, C. (2009, May). Fully homomorphic encryption using ideal lattices. In *Proceedings of the forty-first annual ACM symposium on Theory of computing* (pp. 169-178). IEEE. 10.1145/1536414.1536440

George, T. T., & Tyagi, A. K. (2022). Reliable Edge Computing Architectures for Crowdsensing Applications. *2022 International Conference on Computer Communication and Informatics (ICCCI),* (pp. 1-6). IEEE. 10.1109/ICCCI54379.2022.9740791

Georgescu, C. E. (2019). *Industry 6.0–new dimensions for industrial cooperation on the belt and road.* ICI.

Ghasemzadeh, H., & Arjmandi, M. K. (2017). Universal audio steganalysis based on calibration and reversed frequency resolution of human auditory system. *IET Signal Processing*, *11*(8), 916–922. doi:10.1049/iet-spr.2016.0690

Ghubaish, A., Salman, T., Zolanvari, M., Unal, D., Al-Ali, A., & Jain, R. (2021, June 1). Recent Advances in the Internet-of-Medical-Things (IoMT) Systems Security. *IEEE Internet of Things Journal*, *8*(11), 8707–8718. doi:10.1109/JIOT.2020.3045653

Gibson, T. (2002). *Methods of Audio Steganography*, (3), 154–156. http://www.snotmonkey.com/work/school/405/methods.html

Girdhar, A., Kapur, H., Kumar, V., Kaur, M., Singh, D., & Dama-sevicius, R. (2021). Effect of covid-19 outbreak on urban health and environ-ment. *Air Quality, Atmosphere & Health*, *14*(3), 389–397. doi:10.100711869-020-00944-1 PMID:33072226

Goldreich, O., Goldwasser, S., & Halevi, S. (1997). Public-key cryptosystems from lattice reduction problems. In *Advances in Cryptology (CRYPTO'97)* (pp. 112–131). Springer. doi:10.1007/BFb0052231

Goldwasser, S., Micali, S., & Tong, P. (1982, November). Why and how to establish a private code on a public network. In *23rd Annual Symposium on Foundations of Computer Science (sfcs 1982)* (pp. 134-144). IEEE. 10.1109/SFCS.1982.100

Golovianko, M., Terziyan, V., Branytskyi, V., & Malyk, D. (2023). Industry 4.0 vs. industry 5.0: Co-existence, transition, or a hybrid. *Procedia Computer Science*, *217*, 102–113. doi:10.1016/j.procs.2022.12.206

Gomathi, L., Mishra, A. K., & Tyagi, A. K. (2023). *Industry 5.0 for Healthcare 5.0: Opportunities, Challenges and Future Research Possibilities.* 2023 7th International Conference on Trends in Electronics and Informatics (ICOEI), Tirunelveli, India. 10.1109/ICOEI56765.2023.10125660

Goyal, D. & Tyagi, A. (2020). *A Look at Top 35 Problems in the Computer Science Field for the Next Decade.* Taylor & Francis. . doi:10.1201/9781003052098-40

Goyal, S., Sharma, N., Kaushik, I., Bhushan, B., & Kumar, A. (2020). Blockchain as a Lifesaver of IoT: Applications, Security, and Privacy Services and Challenges. In *Security and Trust Issues in Internet of Things* (pp. 209-237). CRC Press.

Greenberg, A., Lahiri, P., Maltz, D. A., Patel, P., & Sengupta, S. (August 2008). Towards a next generation data center architecture: Scalability and commoditization. *Proceedings of the ACM Workshop on Programmable Router and Extensible Services for Tomorrow (PRESTO)*, Seattle, WA, USA, 55–62. 10.1145/1397718.1397732

Groumpos, P. P. (2021). A critical historical and scientific overview of all in-dustrial revolutions. *IFAC-PapersOnLine*, *54*(13), 464–471. doi:10.1016/j.ifacol.2021.10.492

Gu, Q., & Liu, P. (2007). Denial of service attacks. Handbook of Computer Networks: Distributed Networks, Network Planning, Control, Management, and New Trends and Applications, 3, 454-468.

Guan, Z., Bian, L., Shang, T., & Liu, J. (2018, August). When machine learning meets security issues: A survey. In 2018 IEEE international conference on intelligence and safety for robotics (ISR) (pp. 158-165). IEEE. doi:10.1109/IISR.2018.8535799

Guazzelli, A., Stathatos, K., & Zeller, M. (2009). Efficient deployment of predictive analytics through open standards and cloud computing. *SIGKDD Explorations*, *11*(1), 32–38. doi:10.1145/1656274.1656281

Gubbi, J., Buyya, R., Marusic, S., & Palaniswami, M. (2013). Internet of Things (IoT): A vision, architectural elements, and future directions. *Future Generation Computer Systems*, *29*(7), 1645–1660. doi:10.1016/j.future.2013.01.010

Guerreiro, J., Loureiro, S. M. C., Romero, J., Itani, O., & Eloy, S. (2022). Transhu-manism and engagement-facilitating technologies in society. *Journal of Promotion Management*, *28*(5), 537–558. doi:10.1080/10496491.2021.2009615

Guo, B., Ding, Y., Yao, L., Liang, Y., & Yu, Z. (2020, September 4). The future of false information detection on social media: new perspectives and trends. *ACM Computing Surveys, 53*(4), 68, 1-36.

Gupta, L., Gasparyan, A. Y., Misra, D. P., Agarwal, V., Zimba, O., & Yessirkepov, M. (2020, July 13). Information and misinformation on COVID-19: A cross-sectional survey study. *Journal of Korean Medical Science*, *35*(27), e257. doi:10.3346/jkms.2020.35.e256 PMID:32657090

Gupta, N., Dutta, G., Mitra, K., & Tiwari, M. K. (2022). Analytics with stochastic optimisation: Experimental results of demand uncertainty in process industries. *International Journal of Production Research*, 1–18.

Hakak, S., Alazab, M., Khan, S., Gadekallu, T., Maddikunta, P., & Khan, W. (2021). An ensemble machine learning approach through effective feature extraction to classify fake news. *Future Generation Computer Systems*, *117*, 47–58. doi:10.1016/j.future.2020.11.022

Han, C., Xue, R., Zhang, R., & Wang, X. (2018). A new audio steganalysis method based on linear prediction. *Multimedia Tools and Applications*, *77*(12), 15431–15455. doi:10.100711042-017-5123-x

Han, Y., Wen, Y., Guo, C., & Huang, H. (2015). Incorporating Cyber Layer Failures in Composite Power System Reliability Evaluations. *Energies*, *8*(9), 9064–9086. doi:10.3390/en8099064

Harini, S., Jothika, K., & Jayashree, K. (2018). A review of big data computing and cloud. *International Journal of Pure and Applied Mathematics*, *118*(18), 1847–1855.

Hassan, N. M., Khan, S. A. R., Ashraf, M. U., & Sheikh, A. A. (2023). Interconnec-tion between the role of blockchain technologies, supply chain integra-tion, and circular economy: A case of small and medium-sized enter-prises in pakistan. *Science Progress*, *106*(3), 00368504231186527. doi:10.1177/00368504231186527 PMID:37437130

He, C., Zhang, C., Bian, T., Jiao, K., Su, W., Wu, K.-J., & Su, A. (2023). A Review on Artificial Intelligence Enabled Design, Synthesis, and Process Optimization of Chemical Products for Industry 4.0. *Processes (Basel, Switzerland)*, *11*(2), 330. doi:10.3390/pr11020330

Hermann, M., Pentek, T., & Otto, B. (2016). Design principles for Industry 4.0 scenarios: *A literature review*, 1-12.

Herrera-Cubides, J. F., Gaona-García, P. A., & Salcedo-Salgado, G. A. (2019). Towards the construction of a user unique authentication mechanism on LMS platforms through model-driven engineering (MDE). *Scientific Programming*, *2019*, 2019. doi:10.1155/2019/9313571

Homenc. (2022). *Homenc/HElib: HElib Is an Open-source Software Library That Implements Homomorphic Encryption*. GitHub. https://github.com/homenc/HElib

Hussain, S., Ali, T., Tabassum, H., Kim, D. S., & Hussain, R. (2018). Digital Twin for Smart Manufacturing: A Review. *IEEE Access : Practical Innovations, Open Solutions*, *6*, 3948–3960.

Isha Priyavamtha, U. J., Vishnu Vardhan Reddy, G., Devisri, P., & Manek, A. S. (2021). Fake news detection using artificial neural network algorithm. In K. R. Venugopal, P. D. Shenoy, R. Buyya, L. M. Patnaik, & S. S. Iyengar (Eds.), *Data Science and Computational Intelligence. ICInPro 2021. Communications in Computer and Information Science* (Vol. 1483). Springer. doi:10.1007/978-3-030-91244-4_26

Islam, M. R., Liu, S., Wang, X., & Xu, G. (2020). Deep learning for misinformation detection on online social networks: A survey and new perspectives. *Social Network Analysis and Mining*, *10*(1), 82. doi:10.100713278-020-00696-x PMID:33014173

Jajula, S. K., Tripathi, K., & Bajaj, S. B. (2023). Review of Detection of Packets Inspection and Attacks in Network Security. In P. Dutta, S. Chakrabarti, A. Bhattacharya, S. Dutta, & V. Piuri (Eds.), *Emerging Technologies in Data Mining and Information Security. Lecture Notes in Networks and Systems* (Vol. 491). Springer. doi:10.1007/978-981-19-4193-1_58

Jamil, S., Rahman, M., Abbas, M. S., & Fawad. (2022). Resource allocation using reconfigurable intelligent surface (ris)-assisted wireless networks in industry 5.0 scenario. *Telecom*, *3*(1), 163–173. doi:10.3390/telecom3010011

Javaid, M., Niyaz, Q., Sun, W., & Alhameed, A. R. (2021). Blockchain for Secure and Efficient Data Sharing in Cloud-Based Industrial IoT. *IEEE Transactions on Industrial Informatics*, *17*(3), 1837–1845.

Jayaprakash, V., & Tyagi, A. K. (2022). Security Optimization of Resource-Constrained Internet of Healthcare Things (IoHT) Devices Using Asymmetric Cryptography for Blockchain Network. In: Giri, D., Mandal, J.K., Sakurai, K., De, D. (eds) *Proceedings of International Conference on Network Security and Blockchain Technology*. Springer, Singapore. 10.1007/978-981-19-3182-6_18

Jayaram, R., Ranganatha, & Anupama. (2011). Information Hiding Using Audio Steganography - A Survey. *The International Journal of Multimedia & Its Applications*, *3*(3), 86–96. doi:10.5121/ijma.2011.3308

Jegorova, M., Kaul, C., Mayor, C., O'Neil, A. Q., Weir, A., Murray-Smith, R., & Tsaftaris, S. A. (2022). Survey: Leakage and privacy at inference time. *IEEE Transactions on Pattern Analysis and Machine Intelligence*, 1–20. doi:10.1109/TPAMI.2022.3229593 PMID:37015684

Jeyaraman, M., Nallakumarasamy, A., & Jeyaraman, N. (2022). Industry 5.0 in orthopaedics. *Indian Journal of Orthopaedics*, *56*(10), 1694–1702. doi:10.100743465-022-00712-6 PMID:36187596

Jiang, W., Han, B., Habibi, M. A., & Schotten, H. D. (2021). The road towards 6g: A comprehensive survey. *IEEE Open Journal of the Communications Society*, *2*, 334–366. doi:10.1109/OJCOMS.2021.3057679

Joshi, A. P., Han, M., & Wang, Y. (2018, May 1). A survey on security and privacy issues of blockchain technology. *Mathematical Foundations of Computing*, *1*(2).

Kadhim, K. T., Alsahlany, A. M., Wadi, S. M., & Kadhum, H. T. (2020). An overview of patient's health status monitoring system based on internet of things (IoT). *Wireless Personal Communications*, *114*(3), 1–28. doi:10.100711277-020-07474-0

Kafi, M. A., & Akter, N. (2023). Securing Financial Information in the Digital Realm: Case Studies in Cybersecurity for Accounting Data Protection. *American Journal of Trade and Policy*, *10*(1), 15–26. doi:10.18034/ajtp.v10i1.659

Kagermann, H., Wahlster, W., & Helbig, J. (2013). Recommendations for implementing the strategic initiative INDUSTRIE 4.0. *Final report of the Industrie 4.0 working group*. DIN.

Kaliyar, R. K., Goswami, A., & Narang, P. (2019). Multiclass fake news detection using ensemble machine learning. In *Proceedings of 2019 IEEE 9th International Conference on Advanced Computing (IACC)*, (pp. 103-107). IEEE. 10.1109/IACC48062.2019.8971579

Kalkal, A., Kumar, S., Kumar, P., Pradhan, R., Willander, M., Packirisamy, G., Kumar, S., & Malhotra, B. D. (2021). Recent advances in 3d printing technologies for wearable (bio)sensors. *Additive Manufacturing*, *46*, 102088. doi:10.1016/j.addma.2021.102088

Kamarajugadda, K. K., Movva, P., Raju, M. N., Kant, S. A., & Thatavarti, S. (2021, February 2). *IoMT with Cloud-Based Disease Diagnosis Healthcare Framework for Heart Disease Prediction Using Simulated Annealing with SVM.* Springer. doi:10.1007/978-3-030-52624-5_8

Kannadasan, R., Prabakaran, N., Boominathan, P., Krishnamoorthy, A., Naresh, K., & Sivashanmugam, G. (2018). High Performance Parallel Computing with Cloud Technologies. *Procedia Computer Science*, *132*, 518–524. doi:10.1016/j.procs.2018.05.004

Keras. (n.d.). *Keras: the Python deep learning API.* Keras. https://keras.io

Kerin, M., & Pham, D. T. (2019). A review of emerging industry 4.0 technologies in remanufacturing. *Journal of Cleaner Production*, *237*, 117805. doi:10.1016/j.jclepro.2019.117805

Kesavan, M., & Prabhu, J. (2018). A survey, design and analysis of iot security and qos challenges. *International Journal of Information System Modeling and Design*, *9*(3), 48–66. doi:10.4018/IJISMD.2018070103

Kessler, G. C. (2007). *An Overview of Cryptography. 1998*(November 2006), 1–23.

Khan, A., & Turowski, K. (2016). A survey of current challenges in manufacturing industry and preparation for industry 4.0. *Proceedings of the First International Scientific Conference Intelligent Information Technologies for Industry (IITI'16).* Springer.

Khan, I. A., Moustafa, N., Razzak, I., Tanveer, M., Pi, D., Pan, Y., & Ali, B. S. (2022). XSRU-IoMT: Explainable simple recurrent units for threat detection in Internet of Medical Things networks. *Future Generation Computer Systems*, *127*, 181–193. doi:10.1016/j.future.2021.09.010

Khan, S., & Salah, K. (2019). Trust management in edge computing and IoT: A review, taxonomy, and open research challenges. *IEEE Internet of Things Journal*, *7*(6), 4532–4557.

Khan, T., Michalas, A., & Akhunzada, A. (2021, September 15). Fake news outbreak 2021: Can we stop the viral spread? *Journal of Network and Computer Applications*, *190*, 103112. doi:10.1016/j.jnca.2021.103112

Khanghahi, N., & Ravanmehr, R. (2013). Cloud computing performance evaluation: Issues and challenges. *Comput*, *5*(1), 29–41. doi:10.5121/ijccsa.2013.3503

Kim, D., & Lee, S. (2020). Study of identifying and managing the potential evidence for effective Android forensics. *Forensic Science International: Digital Investigation, 33*, 200897.

Kim, D., Hu, J., & Zhang, L. (2020). Trust Management for IoT Devices in Edge Computing with Blockchain. *IEEE Internet of Things Journal, 7*(9), 7562–7573.

Kim, J. H. (2017). A review of cyber-physical system research relevant to the emerging it trends: industry 4.0, iot, big data, and cloud computing. *Journal of industrial integration and management, 2*(3), 1750011.

Kirubakaran, S. S. (2020). Study of security mechanisms to create a secure cloud in a virtual environment with the support of cloud service providers. *Journal of trends in Computer Science and Smart technology (TCSST), 2*(03), 148-154.

Koohang, A., Nord, J. H., Ooi, K.-B., Tan, G. W.-H., Al-Emran, M., Aw, E. C.-X., Baabdullah, A. M., Buhalis, D., Cham, T.-H., Dennis, C., Dutot, V., Dwivedi, Y. K., Hughes, L., Mogaji, E., Pandey, N., Phau, I., Raman, R., Sharma, A., Sigala, M., & Wong, L.-W. (2023). Shaping the metaverse into reality: A holistic multidisciplinary understand-ing of opportunities, challenges, and avenues for future investigation. *Journal of Computer Information Systems, 63*(3), 735–765. doi:10.1080/08874417.2023.2165197

Koteska, B., Karafiloski, E., & Mishev, A. (2017). Blockchain implementation quality challenges: a literature. In *SQA-MIA: 6th workshop of software quality, analysis, monitoring, improvement, and applications.* IEEE.

Kula, S., Choraś, M., Kozik, R., Ksieniewicz, P., & Woźniak, M. (2020). Sentiment analysis for fake news detection by means of neural networks. In V. V. Krzhizhanovskaya, (Eds), *Computational Science – ICCS 2020* (p. 12140). Lecture Notes in Computer Science. Springer. doi:10.1007/978-3-030-50423-6_49

Kumar, N. M., Mohammed, M. A., Abdulkareem, K. H., Damasevi-cius, R., Mostafa, S. A., Maashi, M. S., & Chopra, S. S. (2021). Artificial intelligence-based solution for sorting covid related medical waste streams and supporting data-driven decisions for smart circular economy practice. *Process Safety and Environmental Protection, 152*, 482–494. doi:10.1016/j.psep.2021.06.026

Kumar, R., & Goyal, R. (2019). On cloud security requirements, threats, vulnerabilities and countermeasures: A survey. *Computer Science Review, 33*, 1–48. doi:10.1016/j.cosrev.2019.05.002

Kumar, R., Rani, S., & Al Awadh, M. (2022). Exploring the Application Sphere of the Internet of Things in Industry 4.0: A Review, Bibliometric and Content Analysis. *Sensors (Basel), 22*(11), 4276. doi:10.339022114276 PMID:35684897

Kumar, S., & Singh, S. K. (2017). Privacy Preserving Security using Biometrics in Cloud Computing. *Multimedia Tools and Applications*. Springer. doi:10.1007/s11042-017-4966-5

Kumari, P., & Jain, A. K. (2023). A comprehensive study of DDoS attacks over IoT network and their countermeasures. *Computers & Security, 127*, 103096. doi:10.1016/j.cose.2023.103096

Kumari, S. (2021). The Future of Edge Computing with Blockchain Technology: Possibility of Threats, Opportunities and Challenges. Recent Trends in Blockchain for Information Systems Security and Privacy. CRC Press.

Lacko, J. (2022, April 1). Camera Modes in Multi-user Virtual Reality Applications in Industry 4.0. *Acta Montanistica Slovaca, 27*(2).

Lau, P., Wang, L., Liu, Z., Wei, W., & Ten, C. W. (2021). A coalitional cyber-insurance design considering power system reliability and cyber vulnerability. *IEEE Transactions on Power Systems, 36*(6), 5512–5524. doi:10.1109/TPWRS.2021.3078730

Lee, J., & Kundu, P. (2022). Integrated cyber-physical systems and industrial metaverse for remote manufacturing. *Manufacturing Letters, 34*, 12–15. doi:10.1016/j.mfglet.2022.08.012

Lee, J., Bagheri, B., & Kao, H. A. (2015). A cyber-physical systems architecture for Industry 4.0-based manufacturing systems. *Manufacturing Letters*, *3*, 18–23. doi:10.1016/j.mfglet.2014.12.001

Lee, S., Wang, S., & Liu, M. (2019). Secure Offloading of Computation in Edge Computing using Blockchain-based Smart Contracts. *IEEE Transactions on Mobile Computing*, *18*(6), 1399–1411.

Leng, J., Ruan, G., Jiang, P., Xu, K., Liu, Q., Zhou, X., & Liu, C. (2020). Blockchain-empowered sustainable manufacturing and product lifecycle management in industry 4.0: A survey. *Renewable & Sustainable Energy Reviews*, *132*, 110112. doi:10.1016/j.rser.2020.110112

Leng, J., Sha, W., Wang, B., Zheng, P., Zhuang, C., Liu, Q., Wuest, T., Mourtzis, D., & Wang, L. (2022). Industry 5.0: Prospect and retrospect. *Journal of Manufacturing Systems*, *65*, 279–295. doi:10.1016/j.jmsy.2022.09.017

Li, B., Liu, Q., & Zhang, T. (2020). Blockchain-Enabled Cloud Computing: Towards Secure and Privacy-Preserving IoT. *IEEE Network*, *34*(6), 58–63.

Li, F., & McMillin, B. (2014). A survey on zero-knowledge proofs. []. Elsevier.]. *Advances in Computers*, *94*, 25–69. doi:10.1016/B978-0-12-800161-5.00002-5

Li, J., Han, D., Wu, Z., Wang, J., Li, K. C., & Castiglione, A. (2023). A novel system for medical equipment supply chain traceability based on alliance chain and attribute and role access control. *Future Generation Computer Systems*, *142*, 195–211. doi:10.1016/j.future.2022.12.037

Li, L. (2022). Reskilling and upskilling the future-ready workforce for industry 4.0 and beyond. *Information Systems Frontiers*, 1–16. PMID:35855776

Li, S., Da Xu, L., & Zhao, S. (2015). The internet of things: A survey. *Information Systems Frontiers*, *17*(2), 243–259. doi:10.100710796-014-9492-7

Li, Y., Hu, F., Liu, Y., Ryan, M., & Wang, R. (2023). A hybrid model compression approach via knowledge distillation for predicting energy consumption in additive manufacturing. *International Journal of Production Research*, *61*(13), 4525–4547. doi:10.1080/00207543.2022.2160501

Li, Y., Wang, H., & Chen, F. (2019). An Edge-Blockchain Architecture for Secure Data Sharing in Smart Cities. *Proceedings of the International Conference on Smart City Applications (SCA),* (pp. 87-96). Springer.

Liang, X., Zhang, X., Luo, X., & Shen, X. (2018). Towards open big data analytics in the fog. *IEEE Communications Magazine*, *56*(10), 94–100.

Lim, W. Y. B., Luong, N. C., Hoang, D. T., Jiao, Y., Liang, Y. C., Yang, Q., Niyato, D., & Miao, C. (2020). Federated learning in mobile edge networks: A comprehensive survey. *IEEE Communications Surveys and Tutorials*, *22*(3), 2031–2063. doi:10.1109/COMST.2020.2986024

Lin, G., Fu, D., Zhu, J., & Dasmalchi, G. (2009, March/April). Cloud computing: IT as a service. *IT Professional*, *11*(2), 10–13. doi:10.1109/MITP.2009.22

Lin, Y., Wang, R., Yan, D., Dong, L., & Zhang, X. (2019). *Audio Steganalysis with Improved Convolutional Neural Network*, (August), 210–215. doi:10.1145/3335203.3335736

Lin, Z., Huang, Y., & Wang, J. (2018). RNN-SM: Fast Steganalysis of VoIP Streams Using Recurrent Neural Network. *IEEE Transactions on Information Forensics and Security*, *13*(7), 1854–1868. doi:10.1109/TIFS.2018.2806741

Liu, Q., Yu, F., Wu, S., & Wang, L. (2018). Mining significant microblogs for misinformation identification: An attention-based approach. [TIST]. *ACM Transactions on Intelligent Systems and Technology*, *9*(5), 1–20. doi:10.1145/3173458

Liu, X., Shi, S., & Chen, C. L. P. (2021). Blockchain-Enabled Secure Data Sharing for Fog-Cloud Computing in Industrial Internet of Things. *IEEE Transactions on Industrial Informatics, 17*(12), 8421–8428.

Liu, Y., Gao, Q., He, Y., Wang, W., & Ren, X. (2017). Resource virtualization for cyber-physical systems in cloud manufacturing. *Journal of Intelligent Manufacturing, 28*(5), 1117–1129.

Liu, Y., Kang, Y., Xing, C., Chen, T., & Yang, Q. (2020). A secure federated transfer learning framework. *IEEE Intelligent Systems, 35*(4), 70–82. doi:10.1109/MIS.2020.2988525

Liu, Y., Park, H., & Garcia, M. (2019). Privacy-Preserving Data Sharing in Edge Computing with Blockchain: Challenges and Solutions. *Journal of Edge Computing, 8*(4), 231–243.

Lo, S. K., Lu, Q., Wang, C., Paik, H. Y., & Zhu, L. (2021). A systematic literature review on federated machine learning: From a software engineering perspective. *ACM Computing Surveys, 54*(5), 1–39. doi:10.1145/3450288

Lu, Y., & Yao, Y. (2017). Artificial intelligence in service. *Science China. Information Sciences, 60*(10), 100301.

Lu, Y., Xu, L. D., & Li, X. (2017). Internet of things (IoT) for smart precision agriculture and farming in rural areas. *Computer Networks, 114*, 1–14.

Lu, Y., Zhang, Y., Zhang, Y., & Zhang, D. (2017). AI-Driven Smart Digital Twins for Internet of Things: A Survey. In *2017 IEEE International Congress on Big Data (BigData Congress)* (pp. 154-161). IEEE.

López-Alt, A., Tromer, E., & Vaikuntanathan, V. (2012, May). On-the-fly multiparty computation on the cloud via multikey fully homomorphic encryption. In *Proceedings of the forty-fourth annual ACM symposium on Theory of computing* (pp. 1219-1234). ACM. 10.1145/2213977.2214086

Ma, Y., Sun, Y., Lei, Y., Qin, N., & Lu, J. (2020). A survey of blockchain technology on security, privacy, and trust in crowdsourcing services. *World Wide Web (Bussum), 23*(1), 393–419. doi:10.100711280-019-00735-4

Ma, Y., Zhang, S., & Ye, X. (2021). A Novel Blockchain-Based Data Integrity Protection Mechanism for Cloud-Assisted Healthcare Systems. *IEEE Transactions on Industrial Informatics, 17*(3), 1846–1853.

Maddikunta, P. K. R., Pham, Q.-V., B, P., Deepa, N., Dev, K., Gadekallu, T. R., Ruby, R., & Liyanage, M. (2022). Industry 5.0: A survey on enabling technologies and potential applications. *Journal of Industrial Information Integration, 26*, 100257. doi:10.1016/j.jii.2021.100257

Mahmood, A. N., & Hu, J. (2020). Digital Twins and Artificial Intelligence Models for Internet of Things: A Survey. *IEEE Access : Practical Innovations, Open Solutions, 8*, 23022–23042.

Mahrous, W. A., Farouk, M., & Darwish, S. M. (2021). An enhanced blockchain-based IoT digital forensics architecture using fuzzy hash. *IEEE Access : Practical Innovations, Open Solutions, 9*, 151327–151336. doi:10.1109/ACCESS.2021.3126715

Malik, S., Bansal, R., & Tyagi, A. K. (Eds.). (2022). *Impact and Role of Digital Technologies in Adolescent Lives*. IGI Global., doi:10.4018/978-1-7998-8318-0

Manavalan, E., & Jayakrishna, K. (2019). A review of Internet of Things (IoT) embedded sustainable supply chain for industry 4.0 requirements. *Computers & Industrial Engineering, 127*, 925–953. doi:10.1016/j.cie.2018.11.030

Mapanga, V., Kumar, W., Makondo, T., Kushboo, P., & Chanda, W. (2017). Design and implementation of an intrusion detection system using MLP-NN for MANET. *2017 IST-Africa Week Conference*. IST-Africa. . doi:10.23919/ISTAFRICA.2017.8102374

Marquezan, C. C., Metzger, A., Franklin, R., & Pohl, K. (2014). Runtime management of multi-level SLAs for transport and logistics services. In *Service-Oriented Computing: 12th International Conference, ICSOC 2014, Paris, France, November 3-6, 2014. Proceedings 12* (pp. 560-574). Springer. 10.1007/978-3-662-45391-9_49

Martynov, V. V., Shavaleeva, D. N., & Zaytseva, A. A. (2019). Information technology as the basis for transformation into a digital society and industry 5.0. In *2019 International Conference" Quality Management, Transport and Information Security, Information Technologies"(IT&QM&IS)*, (pp. 539-543). IEEE. 10.1109/ITQMIS.2019.8928305

Mell, P., & Grance, T. (2011). The NIST Definition of Cloud Computing. *National Institute of Standards and Technology Special Publication, 53*, 1–7.

Meola, A. (n.d.). IoT Healthcare in 2023: Companies, medical devices, and use cases. *Insider Intelligence*. https://www.insiderintelligence.com/insights/iot-healthcare/

Mern, J., Hatch, K., Silva, R., Brush, J., & Kochenderfer, M. J. (2021). *Reinforcement learning for industrial control network cyber security orchestration.* arXiv preprint arXiv:2106.05332.

Mian, A. & Khan, S. (2020). Coronavirus: the spread of misinformation. *BMC Medinine, 18*(89).

Micciancio, D. & Regev, O. (2009). Lattice-based cryptography. *Post-quantum cryptography*, 147-191.

Microsoft. (2023). *SEAL*(Release 4.1). Github. https://github.com/Microsoft/SEAL

Midha, S., & Tripathi, K. (2020). Remotely Triggered Blackhole Routing in SDN for Handling DoS. In: Dutta, M., Krishna, C., Kumar, R., & Kalra, M. (eds) *Proceedings of International Conference on IoT Inclusive Life*. Springer, Singapore. 10.1007/978-981-15-3020-3_1

Midha, S., & Tripathi, K. (2021). Extended Security in Heterogeneous Distributed SDN Architecture. In G. Hura, A. Singh, & L. Siong Hoe (Eds.), *Advances in Communication and Computational Technology. Lecture Notes in Electrical Engineering* (Vol. 668). Springer. doi:10.1007/978-981-15-5341-7_75

Midha, S., & Triptahi, K. (2019). Extended TLS security and Defensive Algorithm in OpenFlow SDN. *2019 9th International Conference on Cloud Computing, Data Science & Engineering (Confluence)*, (pp. 141-146). IEEE. 10.1109/CONFLUENCE.2019.8776607

Midha, S., Kaur, G., & Tripathi, K. (2017). Cloud deep down — SWOT analysis," 2017 2nd International Conference on Telecommunication and Networks (TEL-NET), , pp. 1-5, 10.1109/TEL-NET.2017.8343560

Midha, S., Tripathi, K., & Sharma, M. K. (2021, April). Practical Implications of Using Dockers on Virtualized SDN. *Webology., 18*(Special Issue 01), 312–330. doi:10.14704/WEB/V18SI01/WEB18062

Migliano, J. E. B., Demajorovic, J., & Xavier, L. H. (2014). Shared responsibility and reverse logistics systems for e-waste in Brazil. [JOSCM]. *Journal of Operations and Supply Chain Management, 7*(2), 91–109. doi:10.12660/joscmv7n2p91-109

Mir, U., Kar, A. K., & Gupta, M. P. (2022). AI-enabled digital identity–inputs for stakeholders and policymakers. *Journal of Science and Technology Policy Management, 13*(3), 514–541. doi:10.1108/JSTPM-09-2020-0134

Mishra, A., & Sharma, S. K. (2019). Digital Twins: A Comprehensive Survey. *Journal of King Saud University-Computer and Information Sciences.*

Mishra, S., & Tyagi, A. K. (2022). The Role of Machine Learning Techniques in Internet of Things-Based Cloud Applications. In S. Pal, D. De, & R. Buyya (Eds.), *Artificial Intelligence-based Internet of Things Systems. Internet of Things (Technology, Communications and Computing).* Springer., doi:10.1007/978-3-030-87059-1_4

Mitchell, R., & Chen, R. (2013). Effect of intrusion detection and response on reliability of cyber physical systems. *IEEE Transactions on Reliability*, *62*(1), 199–210. doi:10.1109/TR.2013.2240891

Mittal, S., Khan, M. A., Romero, D., & Wuest, T. (2018). A critical review of smart manufacturing & industry 4.0 maturity models: Implications for small and medium-sized enterprises (smes). *Journal of Manufacturing Systems*, *49*, 194–214. doi:10.1016/j.jmsy.2018.10.005

Mohanta, B. K., Jena, D., Panda, S. S., & Sobhanayak, S. (2019, December 1). Blockchain technology: A survey on applications and security privacy challenges. *Internet of Things.*, *8*, 100107. doi:10.1016/j.iot.2019.100107

Mohanta, B. K., Jena, D., Ramasubbareddy, S., Daneshmand, M., & Gandomi, A. H. (2020, July 13). Addressing security and privacy issues of IoT using blockchain technology. *IEEE Internet of Things Journal*, *8*(2), 881–888. doi:10.1109/JIOT.2020.3008906

Mohanta, B. K., Satapathy, U., Panda, S. S., & Jena, D. (2019). A novel approach to solve security and privacy issues for iot applications using blockchain. In *2019 International Conference on Information Technology (ICIT)*, (pp. 394-399). IEEE. 10.1109/ICIT48102.2019.00076

Mohanty, S. N., Ramya, K. C., Rani, S. S., Gupta, D., Shankar, K., Lakshmanaprabu, S. K., & Khanna, A. (2020, January 1). An efficient Lightweight integrated Blockchain (ELIB) model for IoT security and privacy. *Future Generation Computer Systems*, *102*, 1027–1037. doi:10.1016/j.future.2019.09.050

Mohassel, P., & Zhang, Y. (2017). Secureml: A system for scalable privacy-preserving machine learning. 2017 IEEE symposium on security and privacy. IEEE.

Mohtasham-zadeh, V., & Mosleh, M. (2019). Audio Steganalysis based on collaboration of fractal dimensions and convolutional neural networks. *Multimedia Tools and Applications*, *78*(9), 11369–11386. doi:10.100711042-018-6702-1

Mourtzis, D., Vlachou, E., Milas, N., & Xanthopoulos, N. (2017). The paradigm shift towards cloud manufacturing and its impact on job design. *Journal of Manufacturing Systems*, *43*, 184–191.

Mridha, M. F., Keya, A. J., Hamid, M. A., Monowar, M. M., & Rahman, M. S. (2021). A comprehensive review on fake news detection with deep learning. *IEEE Access : Practical Innovations, Open Solutions*, *9*, 156151–156170. doi:10.1109/ACCESS.2021.3129329

Mukherjee, M., Matam, R., Shu, L., Maglaras, L., Ferrag, M. A., & Ahmim, A. (2019). A survey of intrusion detection systems in IoT-based edge computing. *IEEE Internet of Things Journal*, *7*(12), 10274–10289.

Mukhopadhyay, S. C., & Suryadevara, N. K. (2014). *Internet of things: Challenges and opportunities*. Springer International Publishing. doi:10.1007/978-3-319-04223-7

Münch, C., Wehrle, M., Kuhn, T., & Hartmann, E. (2023). The research landscape around the physical internet – a bibliometric analysis. *International Journal of Production Research*, 1–19. doi:10.1080/00207543.2023.2205969

Nagaraj, A. (2021). *Introduction to Sensors in IoT and Cloud Computing Applications*. Bentham Science Publishers. doi:10.2174/97898114793591210101

Nagaraj, A. (2022). Adapting Blockchain for Energy Constrained IoT in Healthcare Environment. In K. Kaushik, S. Tayal, S. Dahiya, & A. O. Salau (Eds.), *Sustainable and Advanced Applications of Blockchain in Smart Computational Technologies* (p. 103). CRC press. doi:10.1201/9781003193425-7

Nair, M. & Tyagi, A. (2023). *Blockchain technology for next-generation society: current trends and future opportunities for smart era.* Blockchain Technology for Secure Social Media Computing. . doi:10.1049/PBSE019E_ch11

Nair, M. (2023). 6G: Technology, Advancement, Barriers, and the Future. In 6G-Enabled IoT and AI for Smart Healthcare. CRC Press.

Nair, M. M. (2023). *Amit Kumar Tyagi, "6G: Technology, Advancement, Barriers, and the Future", in the book: 6G-Enabled IoT and AI for Smart Healthcare*. CRC Press.

Nair, M. M., & Tyagi, A. K. (2021). Privacy: History, Statistics, Policy, Laws, Preservation and Threat Analysis. Journal of Information Assurance & Security, 16(1), 24-34.

Nair, M. M., & Tyagi, A. K. (2022). Preserving Privacy Using Blockchain Technology in Autonomous Vehicles. In: Giri, D., Mandal, J.K., Sakurai, K., De, D. (eds) *Proceedings of International Conference on Network Security and Blockchain Technology*. Springer, Singapore. 10.1007/978-981-19-3182-6_19

Nair, M. M., & Tyagi, A. K. (2023). Chapter 11 - AI, IoT, blockchain, and cloud computing: The necessity of the future. R. Pandey, S. Goundar, S. Fatima, (eds.) Distributed Computing to Blockchain. Academic Press. doi:10.1016/B978-0-323-96146-2.00001-2

Nair, M. M., Fernandez, T. F., & Tyagi, A. K. (2023). *Cyberbullying in Digital Era: History, Trends, Limitations, Recommended Solutions for Future. 2023 International Conference on Computer Communication and Informatics (ICCCI)*, Coimbatore, India, 10.1109/ICCCI56745.2023.10128624

Nair, M. M., Kumari, S., & Tyagi, A. K. (2021). Internet of Things, Cyber Physical System, and Data Analytics: Open Questions, Future Perspectives, and Research Areas. In: Goyal D., Gupta A.K., Piuri V., Ganzha M., Paprzycki M. (eds) *Proceedings of the Second International Conference on Information Management and Machine Intelligence. Lecture Notes in Networks and Systems*. Springer, Singapore. 10.1007/978-981-15-9689-6_36

Nair, M. M., Tyagi, A. K., & Sreenath, N. (2021). The Future with Industry 4.0 at the Core of Society 5.0: Open Issues, Future Opportunities and Challenges. *2021 International Conference on Computer Communication and Informatics (ICCCI),* (pp. 1-7). Springer. 10.1109/ICCCI50826.2021.9402498

Nair, M. N. (2023). 6G: Technology, Advancement, Barriers, and the Future. 6G-Enabled IoT and AI for Smart Healthcare. CRC Press.

Nan, L., Wu, D., Zhu, J., Fan, Y., & Fan, S. (2018). Manufacturing in the age of artificial intelligence: An evolving perspective. *Journal of Manufacturing Science and Engineering*, *140*(4), 040801.

Nelson, M. (2009). Building an Open Cloud. *Science*, *324*(5935), 1656–1657. doi:10.1126cience.1174225 PMID:19556494

Nilaiswariya, R., Manikandan, J., & Hemalatha, P. (2021). Improving Scalability And Security Medical Dataset Using Recurrent Neural Network And Blockchain Technology. In *2021 International Conference on System, Computation, Automation and Networking (ICSCAN),* (pp. 1-6). IEEE.

Nilsson, A., Smith, S., Ulm, G., Gustavsson, E., & Jirstrand, M. (2018, December). A performance evaluation of federated learning algorithms. In *Proceedings of the second workshop on distributed infrastructures for deep learning* (pp. 1-8). IEEE. 10.1145/3286490.3286559

Novaes, M. P., Carvalho, L. F., Lloret, J., & Proença, M. L. Jr. (2021). Adversarial Deep Learning approach detection and defense against DDoS attacks in SDN environments. *Future Generation Computer Systems*, *125*, 156–167. doi:10.1016/j.future.2021.06.047

Nurmi, D., Wolski, R., Grzegorczyk, C., Obertelli, G., Soman, S., & Youseff, L. (2008*). The eucalyptus open-source cloud-computing system.* Proceedings of Cloud Computing and Its Applications, Shanghai, China.

Ogbuke, N. J., Yusuf, Y. Y., Dharma, K., & Mercangoz, B. A. (2022). Big data supply chain analytics: Ethical, privacy and security challenges posed to business, industries and society. *Production Planning and Control*, *33*(2-3), 123–137. doi:10.1080/09537287.2020.1810764

Okamoto, T., & Uchiyama, S. (1998). A new public-key cryptosystem as secure as factoring. In *Advances in Cryptology—EUROCRYPT'98: International Conference on the Theory and Application of Cryptographic Techniques Espoo* (pp. 308-318). Springer Berlin Heidelberg. 10.1007/BFb0054135

Okewu, E., Misra, S., Maskeliunas, R., Damasevicius, R., & Fernandez-Sanz, L. (2017). Optimizing green computing awareness for environmental sustainability and economic security as a stochastic optimization problem. *Sustainability (Basel)*, *9*(10), 1857. doi:10.3390u9101857

Omotunde, H., & Ahmed, M. (2023). A Comprehensive Review of Security Measures in Database Systems: Assessing Authentication, Access Control, and Beyond. *Mesopotamian Journal of CyberSecurity*, *2023*, 115–133. doi:10.58496/MJCSC/2023/016

Oracle. (2009). *Sun Microsystems Unveils Open Cloud Platform.* Oracle. http://www.sun.com/aboutsun/pr/2009-03/sunflash.20090318.2.xml

Osterrieder, P., Budde, L., & Friedli, T. (2020). The smart factory as a key construct of industry 4.0: A systematic literature review. *International Journal of Production Economics*, *221*, 107476. doi:10.1016/j.ijpe.2019.08.011

Ozkan-Ozen, Y. D., & Kazancoglu, Y. (2022). Analysing workforce development challenges in the industry 4.0. *International Journal of Manpower*, *43*(2), 310–333. doi:10.1108/IJM-03-2021-0167

Paillier, P. (1999). Public-key cryptosystems based on composite degree residuosity classes. In *Advances in Cryptology—EUROCRYPT'99: International Conference on the Theory and Application of Cryptographic Techniques Prague*, (pp. 223-238). Springer Berlin Heidelberg. 10.1007/3-540-48910-X_16

Pandey, A. A., Fernandez, T. F., Bansal, R., & Tyagi, A. K. (2022). Maintaining Scalability in Blockchain. In A. Abraham, N. Gandhi, T. Hanne, T. P. Hong, T. Nogueira Rios, & W. Ding (Eds.), *Intelligent Systems Design and Applications. ISDA 2021. Lecture Notes in Networks and Systems* (Vol. 418). Springer. doi:10.1007/978-3-030-96308-8_4

Pardau, S. L. (2018). The california consumer privacy act: Towards a european-style privacy regime in the united states. *J. Tech. L. & Pol'y*, *23*, 68.

Parimala Devi, M., Choudhry, M. D., Nithiavathy, R., Boopathi Raja, G., & Sathya, T. (2022). Blockchain Based Edge Information Systems Frameworks for Industrial IoT: A Novel Approach. In *Blockchain Applications in the Smart Era* (pp. 19–39). Springer International Publishing. doi:10.1007/978-3-030-89546-4_2

Parisa, M. (2023). Determinants of big data analytics adoption in small and medium-sized enterprises (SMEs). *Industrial Management & Data Systems*, *123*(1).

Park, J., Lee, Y., & Wang, B. (2018). Blockchain-based Authentication and Authorization in Edge Computing Networks. *ACM Transactions on Internet Technology*, *21*(2), 16–28.

Patalas-maliszewska, J., Halikowski, D., & Damasevicius, R. (2021). An automated recognition of work activity in industrial manufacturing using convolutional neural networks. *Electronics (Basel)*, *10*(23), 2946. doi:10.3390/electronics10232946

Paulauskas, L., Paulauskas, A., Blazauskas, T., Damasevicius, R., & Maskeliunas, R. (2023). Reconstruction of industrial and historical heritage for cultural enrichment using virtual and augmented reality. *Technologies*, *11*(2), 36. doi:10.3390/technologies11020036

Paulin, C., Selouani, S. A., & Hervet, É. (2016). Audio steganalysis using deep belief networks. *International Journal of Speech Technology*, *19*(3), 585–591. doi:10.100710772-016-9352-6

Peng, M., Garg, S., Wang, X., Bradai, A., Lin, H., & Hossain, M. S. (2020). Learning-based iot data aggregation for disaster scenarios. *IEEE Access: Practical Innovations, Open Solutions*, *8*, 128490–128497. doi:10.1109/ACCESS.2020.3008289

Picone, M., Cirani, S., & Veltri, L. (2021). Blockchain Security and Privacy for the Internet of Things. *Sensors (Basel)*, *21*(3), 892. doi:10.339021030892 PMID:33525636

Plauska, I., & Damasevicius, R. (2014). Educational robots for internet-of-things supported collaborative learning. *Communications in Computer and Information Science*, *465*, 346–358. doi:10.1007/978-3-319-11958-8_28

Pooyan, M., & Delforouzi, A. (2007). LSB-based audio steganography method based on lifting wavelet transform. *ISSPIT 2007 - 2007 IEEE International Symposium on Signal Processing and Information Technology*, (pp. 600–603). IEEE. 10.1109/ISSPIT.2007.4458198

Pradhan, B., Bhattacharyya, S., & Pal, K. (2021, March 19). *IoT-Based Applications in Healthcare Devices. IoT-Based Applications in Healthcare Devices*. Hindawi. doi:10.1155/2021/6632599

Preethi, G. & Cherukuri, A. (2018). Privacy preserving Hu's moments in encrypted domain. *Intelligent Systems Design and Applications: 17th International Conference on Intelligent Systems Design and Applications (ISDA 2017)*. Springer International Publishing.

Priya, V. & Vijay, P. (2021). The Healthy Skin Framework-Iot Based. *Psychology and Education Journal*, *58*(2), 7731-7734.

Qahtan, S., Yatim, K., Zulzalil, H., Osman, M. H., Zaidan, A. A., & Alsattar, H. A. (2023). Review of healthcare industry 4.0 application-based blockchain in terms of security and privacy development attributes: Comprehensive taxonomy, open issues and challenges and recommended solution. *Journal of Network and Computer Applications*, *209*, 103529. doi:10.1016/j.jnca.2022.103529

Rabah, K. (2004). Steganography-The Art of Hiding Data. *Information Technology Journal*, *3*(3), 245–269. doi:10.3923/itj.2004.245.269

Radanliev, P., De Roure, D., Nicolescu, R., Huth, M., & Santos, O. (2022). Digital twins: Artificial intelligence and the IoT cyber-physical systems in Industry 4.0. *International Journal of Intelligent Robotics and Applications*, *6*(1), 171–185. doi:10.100741315-021-00180-5

Radanliev, P., De Roure, D., Page, K., & Jason, R. C. (2020). Cyber risk at the edge: Current and future trends on cyber risk analytics and artificial intelligence in the industrial internet of things and industry 4.0 supply chains. *Cybersecurity*, *3*(1), 1–21. doi:10.118642400-020-00052-8

Radwan, T., Azer, M. A., & Abdelbaki, N. (2017). Cloud computing security: Challenges and future trends. *International Journal of Computer Applications in Technology*, *55*(2), 158–172. doi:10.1504/IJCAT.2017.082865

Rafiee, H. (2019).. . *Presenting a Method for Improving Echo Hiding.*, *2*(1). doi:10.22067/cke.v2i1.74388

Raghuvanshi, A., Singh, U.K., & Joshi, C. (2022). A review of various security and privacy innovations for IoT applications in healthcare. *Advanced Healthcare Systems: Empowering Physicians with IoT-Enabled Technologies*. IEEE.

Ragothaman, K., Wang, Y., Rimal, B., & Lawrence, M. (2023). Access control for IoT: A survey of existing research, dynamic policies and future directions. *Sensors (Basel)*, *23*(4), 1805. doi:10.339023041805 PMID:36850403

Rahman, S., Ahsan, K., Yang, L., & Odgers, J. (2019). An investigation into critical challenges for multinational third-party logistics providers operating in China. *Journal of Business Research*, *103*, 607–619. doi:10.1016/j.jbusres.2017.09.053

Rahman, Z., Khalil, I. Y., & Atiquzzaman, M. (2021). Blockchain-based security framework for a critical industry 4.0 cyber-physical system. *IEEE Communications Magazine*, *59*(5), 128–134. doi:10.1109/MCOM.001.2000679

Raj, S., Sundararajan, S., & Buyya, R. (2022). Trustworthy and Autonomous Federated Learning in the Cloud-Edge Continuum using Blockchain. *Future Generation Computer Systems, 128*, 261–275.

Rajani, D., Menon, S. C., Kute, S., & Tyagi, A. K. (2022). Preserving Privacy of Social Media Data Using Artificial Intelligence Techniques. In A. Tyagi (Ed.), *Handbook of Research on Technical, Privacy, and Security Challenges in a Modern World* (pp. 186–204). IGI Global. doi:10.4018/978-1-6684-5250-9.ch010

Raja Santhi, A., & Muthuswamy, P. (2022). Influence of blockchain technology in manufacturing supply chain and logistics. *Logistics*, *6*(1), 15. doi:10.3390/logistics6010015

Ramgovind, S., Eloff, M. M., & Smith, E. (2010, August). The management of security in cloud computing. In *2010 Information Security for South Africa* (pp. 1-7). IEEE.

Ranchhodbhai P.N, & Tripathi K. (2019). Identifying and Improving the Malicious Behavior of Rushing and Blackhole Attacks using Proposed IDSAODV Protocol. *International Journal of Recent Technology and Engineering*, *8*(3), 6554-6562.

Ratsel. (2023). *A Game-Based Evaluating Tool for the Dyslexic Using Augmented Reality Gamification*. Information and Communication Technology for Competitive Strategies. LNNS.

Ray, P. P. (2018). A survey of IoT architectures. *Journal of King Saud University-Computer and Information Sciences*.

Ray, T. R., Choi, J., Bandodkar, A. J., Krishnan, S., Gutruf, P., Tian, L., Ghaffari, R., & Rogers, J. A. (2019). Bio-integrated wearable systems: A comprehensive review. *Chemical Reviews*, *119*(8), 5461–5533. doi:10.1021/acs.chemrev.8b00573 PMID:30689360

Reddy, H., Raj, N., Gala, M., & Basava, A. (2020, February 18). Text-mining-based fake news detection using ensemble methods. *International Journal of Automation and Computing*, *17*(2), 210–221. doi:10.100711633-019-1216-5

Reddy, K. S., Agarwal, K., & Tyagi, A. K. (2021). Beyond Things: A Systematic Study of Internet of Everything. In A. Abraham, M. Panda, S. Pradhan, L. Garcia-Hernandez, & K. Ma (Eds.), *Innovations in Bio-Inspired Computing and Applications. IBICA 2019. Advances in Intelligent Systems and Computing* (Vol. 1180). Springer. doi:10.1007/978-3-030-49339-4_23

Regev, O. (2009). On lattices, learning with errors, random linear codes, and cryptography. *Journal of the Association for Computing Machinery*, *56*(6), 1–40. doi:10.1145/1568318.1568324

Rehman, M., Sun, W., & Poh, H. L. (2022). Decentralized IoT Security Management System Based on Ethereum Blockchain. *IEEE Internet of Things Journal*, *9*(5), 4074–4084.

Rekha, G., Malik, S., Tyagi, A. K., & Nair, M. M. (2020). Intrusion Detection in Cyber Security: Role of Machine Learning and Data Mining in Cyber Security. *Advances in Science, Technology and Engineering Systems Journal*, *5*(3), 72–81. doi:10.25046/aj050310

Rekha, G., Tyagi, A. K., & Anuradha, N. (2020) Integration of Fog Computing and Internet of Things: An Useful Overview. In: Singh P., Kar A., Singh Y., Kolekar M., Tanwar S. (eds) *Proceedings of ICRIC 2019*. Springer, Cham. 10.1007/978-3-030-29407-6_8

RenY.LiuD.XiongQ.FuJ.WangL. (2019). *Spec-ResNet: A General Audio Steganalysis scheme based on Deep Residual Network of Spectrogram*. 1–12. https://arxiv.org/abs/1901.06838

Romero, D., & Vernadat, F. (2016). Enterprise information systems state of the art: Past, present and future trends. *Computers in Industry, 79*, 3–13. doi:10.1016/j.compind.2016.03.001

Ronald, L. (1978). Rivest, Len Adleman, and Michael L. Dertouzos. 1978a. On data banks and privacy homomorphisms. *Foundations of Secure Computation, 4*(11), 169–180.

Rong, C., Zhang, D., & Yang, A. (2014). Edge computing in the Internet of Things. *IEEE Transactions on Industrial Informatics, 10*(2), 1568–1576.

Rosati, R., Romeo, L., Cecchini, G., Tonetto, F., Viti, P., Mancini, A., & Frontoni, E. (2023). From knowledge-based to big data analytic model: A novel IoT and machine learning based decision support system for predictive maintenance in Industry 4.0. *Journal of Intelligent Manufacturing, 34*(1), 107–121. doi:10.100710845-022-01960-x

Rose, K., Eldridge, S., & Chapin, L. (2015). The internet of things: An overview. *The internet society (ISOC),* 80, 1-50.

Ryalat, M., ElMoaqet, H., & AlFaouri, M. (2023). Design of a Smart Factory Based on Cyber-Physical Systems and Internet of Things towards Industry 4.0. *Applied Sciences (Basel, Switzerland), 13*(4), 2156. doi:10.3390/app13042156

Sah, B., Gupta, R., & Bani-Hani, D. (2021). Analysis of barriers to implement drone logistics. *International Journal of Logistics, 24*(6), 531–550. doi:10.1080/13675567.2020.1782862

Sai, G. H., Tripathi, K., & Tyagi, A. K. (2023). Internet of Things-Based e-Health Care: Key Challenges and Recommended Solutions for Future. In: Singh, P.K., Wierzchoń, S.T., Tanwar, S., Rodrigues, J.J.P.C., Ganzha, M. (eds) *Proceedings of Third International Conference on Computing, Communications, and Cyber-Security.* Springer, Singapore. 10.1007/978-981-19-1142-2_37

Sai, G. H., Tyagi, A. K., & Sreenath, N. (2023). Biometric Security in Internet of Things Based System against Identity Theft Attacks. *2023 International Conference on Computer Communication and Informatics (ICCCI)*, Coimbatore, India. 10.1109/ICCCI56745.2023.10128186

Samuel, P., Jayashree, K., Babu, R., & Vijay, K. (2023). Artificial Intelligence, Machine Learning, and IoT Architecture to Support Smart Governance. In K. Saini, A. Mummoorthy, R. Chandrika, & N. Gowri Ganesh (Eds.), *AI, IoT, and Blockchain Breakthroughs in E-Governance* (pp. 95–113). IGI Global. doi:10.4018/978-1-6684-7697-0.ch007

Samuel, P., Reshmy, A. K., Rajesh, S., Kanipriya, M., & Karthika, R. A. (2023). AI-Based Big Data Algorithms and Machine Learning Techniques for Managing Data in E-Governance. In K. Saini, A. Mummoorthy, R. Chandrika, & N. Gowri Ganesh (Eds.), *AI, IoT, and Blockchain Breakthroughs in E-Governance* (pp. 19–35). IGI Global. doi:10.4018/978-1-6684-7697-0.ch002

Sanchez, M., Exposito, E., & Aguilar, J. (2020). Industry 4.0: Survey from a system integration perspective. *International Journal of Computer Integrated Manufacturing, 33*(10-11), 1–25. doi:10.1080/0951192X.2020.1775295

Sathish Kumar, K., Om Prakash, P., Alangudi Balaji, N., & Damasevicius, R. (2022). Internet of things and big data analytics for smart healthcare. Handbook of Intelligent Healthcare Analytics: Knowledge Engineering with Big Data Analytics. Wiley. doi:10.1002/9781119792550.ch7

Savage, N. (2021, March 12). Fact-finding mission. *Communications of the ACM, 64*(3), 18–19. doi:10.1145/3446879

Schumacher, A., Erol, S., & Sihn, W. (2016). A maturity model for assessing Industry 4.0 readiness and maturity of manufacturing enterprises. *Procedia CIRP, 52*, 161–166. doi:10.1016/j.procir.2016.07.040

Schuster, T., Schuster, R., Shah, D. J., & Barzilay, R. (2020). The limitations of stylometry for detecting machine-generated fake news. *Computational Linguistics, 46*(2), 499–510. doi:10.1162/coli_a_00380

Schwab, K. (2017). *The fourth industrial revolution*. Currency.

Selvaraj, S., & Sundaravaradhan, S. (2019, December 30). Challenges and opportunities in IoT healthcare systems: A systematic review. *SN Applied Sciences*, *2*(1), 139. doi:10.100742452-019-1925-y

Seo, A. L., Razzaque, S. A., & Kim, D. H. (2022). Towards Blockchain-Based Secure and Privacy-Preserving Industrial Internet of Things. *IEEE Transactions on Industrial Informatics*, *18*(1), 739–746.

Sergi, I., Montanaro, T., Benvenuto, F. L., & Patrono, L. (2021). A smart and secure logistics system based on IoT and cloud technologies. *Sensors (Basel)*, *21*(6), 2231. doi:10.339021062231 PMID:33806770

Sethi, R. J., Rangaraju, R., & Shurts, B. (2019, May 30). Fact checking misinformation using recommendations from emotional pedagogical agents. In A. Coy, Y. Hayashi, & M. Chang (Eds.), *Intelligent Tutoring Systems* (pp. 99–104). doi:10.1007/978-3-030-22244-4_13

Shabandri, B., & Maheshwari, P. (2019). Enhancing IoT security and privacy using distributed ledgers with IOTA and the tangle. In *2019 6th International conference on signal processing and integrated networks (SPIN)*, (pp. 1069-1075). IEEE. 10.1109/SPIN.2019.8711591

Shahid, J., Ahmad, R., Kiani, A. K., Ahmad, T., Saeed, S., & Almuhaideb, A. M. (2022). Data protection and privacy of the internet of healthcare things (IoHTs). *Applied Sciences (Basel, Switzerland)*, *12*(4), 1927. doi:10.3390/app12041927

Shakeabubakor, A. A., Sundararajan, E., & Hamdan, A. R. (2015). Cloud computing services and applications to improve productivity of university researchers. *Int. J. Inf. Electron. Eng.*, *5*(2), 153. doi:10.7763/IJIEE.2015.V5.521

Sharifani, K., & Amini, M. (2023). Machine Learning and Deep Learning: A Review of Methods and Applications. *World Information Technology and Engineering Journal*, *10*(07), 3897–3904.

Sharma, K., Qian, F., Jiang, H., Ruchansky, N., Zhang, M., & Liu, Y. (2019, May). Combating fake news: a survey on identification and mitigation techniques. *ACM Transactions on Intelligent Systems and Technology, 10*(3), 1-42.

Sharma, S. R. (2019, June 30). Internet of Things IoT: IoT in Healthcare. *International Journal of Trend in Scientific Research and Development, 3*(Issue-4), 980–982. https://doi.org/ doi:10.31142/ijtsrd23971

Sheth, H. S. K. (2022). Deep Learning, Blockchain based Multi-layered Authentication and Security Architectures. *2022 International Conference on Applied Artificial Intelligence and Computing (ICAAIC)*, (pp. 476-485). IEEE. 10.1109/ICAAIC53929.2022.9793179

Sheth, H. S. K., & Tyagi, A. K. (2022). Mobile Cloud Computing: Issues, Applications and Scope in COVID-19. In A. Abraham, N. Gandhi, T. Hanne, T. P. Hong, T. Nogueira Rios, & W. Ding (Eds.), *Intelligent Systems Design and Applications. ISDA 2021. Lecture Notes in Networks and Systems* (Vol. 418). Springer. doi:10.1007/978-3-030-96308-8_55

Shi, S., He, D., Li, L., Kumar, N., Khan, M. K., & Choo, K. K. (2020, October 1). Applications of blockchain in ensuring the security and privacy of electronic health record systems: A survey. *Computers & Security*, *97*, 101966. doi:10.1016/j.cose.2020.101966 PMID:32834254

Shirali-Shahreza, S., & Manzuri-Shalmani, M. T. (2008). High Capacity Error Free Wavelet Domain Speech Steganography. Computer Engineering Department Sharif University of Technology, Tehran, IRAN Computer Engineering Department Sharif University of Technology.

Silva, M. C., & da Costa, C. A. (2018). Cyber-physical systems and Industry 4.0: A contemporary overview. *Procedia Manufacturing*, *25*, 268–275.

Simaiya, S., Lilhore, U. K., Sharma, S. K., Gupta, K., & Baggan, V. (2020, June 1). Blockchain: A new technology to enhance data security and privacy in Internet of things. *Journal of Computational and Theoretical Nanoscience*, *17*(6), 2552–2556. doi:10.1166/jctn.2020.8929

Singh, K. (2023). Evaluation planning for artificial intelligence-based industry 6.0 metaverse integration. *Intelligent Human Systems Integra-tion (IHSI 2023): Integrating People and Intelligent Systems 69*(69).

Singh, S. K., Rathore, S., & Park, J. H. (2020). BlockIoTIntelligence: A Blockchain-enabled Intelligent IoT Architecture with Artificial Intelligence. *Future Generation Computer Systems*, *110*, 721–743. doi:10.1016/j.future.2019.09.002

Sinha, H. & Sharma, Y. (2021). Text-convolutional neural networks for fake news detection in Tweets. In V. Bhateja, S. L. Peng, S.C. Satapathy, and Y. D. Zhang (eds), Evolution in Computational Intelligence. Advances in Intelligent Systems and Computing. Springer, Singapore.

Sitaula, N., Mohan, C. K., Grygiel, J., Zhou, X., & Zafarani, R. (2020). Credibility-based fake news detection. In K. Shu, S. Wang, D. Lee, & H. Liu (Eds.), *Disinformation, misinformation, and fake news in social media, Lecture Notes in Social Networks* (pp. 163–182). Springer. doi:10.1007/978-3-030-42699-6_9

Sivaranjani, P. (2020, May). Employee Tracking System using Blockchain. *Test Engineering and Management*, *83*, 5154–5156.

Sivathanu, G., Wright, C. P., & Zadok, E. (2005, November). Ensuring data integrity in storage: Techniques and applications. In *Proceedings of the 2005 ACM workshop on Storage security and survivability* (pp. 26-36). ACM. 10.1145/1103780.1103784

Smith, J., Chen, L., & Kim, S. (2021). Blockchain-Enabled Security Framework for Edge Computing: A Comprehensive Review. *International Journal of Blockchain Research*, *5*(2), 89–101.

Snyder, T., & Byrd, G. (2017). The internet of everything. *Computer*, *50*(6), 8–9. doi:10.1109/MC.2017.179

Somisetti, K. T., & Verma, J. K. (2020). Design, Implementation, and Controlling of a Humanoid Robot. *2020 International Conference on Computational Performance Evaluation (ComPE),* (pp. 831-836). IEEE. 10.1109/ComPE49325.2020.9200020

Sotomayor, B., Montero, R., Llorente, I., & Foster, I. (2009). Virtual Infrastructure Management in Private and Hybrid Clouds. *IEEE Internet Computing*, *13*(5), 14–22. doi:10.1109/MIC.2009.119

Sowmia, K. R., Prithi, S., Vijay, K., Eugene Berna, I., & Bhuvaneswaran, B. (2023). *Crop Monitoring System with Water Moisture Level using Arduino.* 2023 5th International Conference on Smart Systems and Inventive Technology (ICSSIT), Tirunelveli, India. 10.1109/ICSSIT55814.2023.10060913

Spindler, G., & Schmechel, P. (2016). Personal data and encryption in the European general data protection regulation. *J. Intell. Prop. Info. Tech. & Elec. Com. L.*, *7*, 163.

Sridhar, S., Hahn, A., & Govindarasu, M. (2011). Cyber–physical system security for the electric power grid. [IEEE.]. *Proceedings of the IEEE*, *100*(1), 210–224. doi:10.1109/JPROC.2011.2165269

Srivastava, J., Routray, S., Ahmad, S., & Waris, M. M. (2022). Internet of medical things (IoMT)-Based Smart Healthcare System: Trends and Progress. *Computational Intelligence and Neuroscience*, *2022*, 7218113. doi:10.1155/2022/7218113 PMID:35880061

Srivastava, S. Anshu, Bansal, R., Soni, G., Tyagi, A.K. (2023). Blockchain Enabled Internet of Things: Current Scenario and Open Challenges for Future. In: Abraham, A., Bajaj, A., Gandhi, N., Madureira, A.M., Kahraman, C. (eds) Innovations in Bio-Inspired Computing and Applications. IBICA 2022. Lecture Notes in Networks and Systems. Springer, Cham. doi:10.1007/978-3-031-27499-2_59

Stamp, J., McIntyre, A., & Ricardson, B. (2009). *Reliability impacts from cyber attack on electric power systems. IEEE/PES Power Systems Conference and Exposition.* IEEE.

Stantchev, V. (2009). Performance evaluation of cloud computing offerings. *2009 Third International Conference on Advanced Engineering Computing and Applications in Sciences.* (pp. 187–192). IEEE. 10.1109/ADVCOMP.2009.36

Stock, T., & Seliger, G. (2016). Opportunities of sustainable manufacturing in Industry 4.0. *Procedia CIRP*, *40*, 536–541. doi:10.1016/j.procir.2016.01.129

Stoyanova, M., Nikoloudakis, Y., Panagiotakis, S., Pallis, E., & Markakis, E. K. (2020). A survey on the internet of things (IoT) forensics: Challenges, approaches, and open issues. *IEEE Communications Surveys and Tutorials*, *22*(2), 1191–1221. doi:10.1109/COMST.2019.2962586

Strozzi, F., & Pozzi, R. (2023). Trend and seasonality features extraction with pre-trained CNN and recurrence plot. *International Journal of Production Research*, 1–12. doi:10.1080/00207543.2023.2227903

Suakanto, S., Supangkat, S., & Saragih, R. (2012). *Performance measurement of cloudcomputing services*. arXivPrepr. arXiv1205.1622.

Subasree, S., & Sakthivel, N. K. (2022). Combining the advantages of radiomic features based feature extraction and hyper parameters tuned RERNN using LOA for breast cancer classification. *Biomedical Signal Processing and Control, 72*. doi:10.1016/j.bspc.2021.103354

Subramanian, B., Nathani, K., & Kumar, S. (2019). IoT Technology, Applications and Challenges: A Contemporary Survey. *Wireless Personal Communications*, *108*(1), 363–388. doi:10.100711277-019-06407-w

Suo, H., Wan, J., Zou, C., & Liu, J. (2012). Security in the Internet of Things: A review. *Internet of Things Journal*, *1*(1), 8–19. doi:10.1109/ICCSEE.2012.373

Susmitha, C., Srineeharika, S., Laasya, K. S., Kannaiah, S. K., & Bulla, S. (2023, February). Hybrid Cryptography for Secure File Storage. In *2023 7th International Conference on Computing Methodologies and Communication* (ICCMC) (pp. 1151-1156). IEEE. 10.1109/ICCMC56507.2023.10084073

Tai, Y., Gao, B., Li, Q., Yu, Z., Zhu, C., & Chang, V. (2021, February 1). *Trustworthy and Intelligent COVID-19 Diagnostic IoMT Through XR and Deep-Learning-Based Clinic Data Access*. PubMed Central (PMC). doi:10.1109/JIOT.2021.3055804

Takeda-Berger, S. L., & Frazzon, E. M. (2023). An inventory data-driven model for predictive-reactive production scheduling. *International Journal of Production Research*, 1–25. doi:10.1080/00207543.2023.2217297

Tan, L., & Neng, W. (2010). Future Internet: The Internet of Things. *International Conference on Advanced Computer Theory and Engineering(ICACTE)*, Chengdu, China,.

Tao, F., Cheng, J., Qi, Q., Zhang, M., Zhang, H., & Sui, F. (2018). Digital twin-driven product design, manufacturing and service with big data. *International Journal of Advanced Manufacturing Technology*, *94*(9-12), 3563–3576. doi:10.100700170-017-0233-1

TensorFlow. (n.d.). *TensorFlow: an end-to-end open source machine learning platform.* TensorFlow. https://www.tensorflow.org

Tien, N. H., Diem, P. T., Van On, P., Anh, V. T., Van Dat, N., Hung, N. T., & Tam, B. Q. (2021). The formation and development of CRM system at Thien Hoa electronics supermarket in Vietnam. *International Journal of Research and Growth Evaluation*, *2*(4), 752–760.

Tiwari, S. (2011). Aruni Singh, Ravi Shankar Singh and Sanjay Kumar Singh, "Internet Security using Biometrics". In D. P. Vidyarthi (Ed.), *Technologies and protocols for Future Internet Design: Reinventing in Web (IGI Global Publishing)*. doi:10.4018/978-1-4666-0203-8.ch006

Trappey, A. J., Trappey, C. V., Govindarajan, U. H., Chuang, A. C., & Sun, J. J. (2017). A review of essential standards and patent landscapes for the internet of things: A key enabler for industry 4.0. *Advanced Engineering Informatics*, *33*, 208–229. doi:10.1016/j.aei.2016.11.007

Tripathi, K., Pandey, M., & Verma, S. (2011). Comparison of reactive and proactive routing protocols for different mobility conditions in WSN. In *Proceedings of the 2011 International Conference on Communication, Computing & Security (ICCCS '11)*. Association for Computing Machinery, New York, NY, USA, 156–161. 10.1145/1947940.1947974

Tyagi, A., Fernandez, T. F., Kumari, K. S., & Tyagi, A. K. (2023). A Survey on Text Processing Using Deep Learning Techniques. In A. Abraham, S. Pllana, G. Casalino, K. Ma, & A. Bajaj (Eds.), *Intelligent Systems Design and Applications. ISDA 2022. Lecture Notes in Networks and Systems* (Vol. 646). Springer. doi:10.1007/978-3-031-27440-4_19

Tyagi, A., Kukreja, S., Nair, M. M., & Tyagi, A. K. (2022). Machine Learning: Past, Present and Future. *NeuroQuantology : An Interdisciplinary Journal of Neuroscience and Quantum Physics*, *20*(8). doi:10.14704/nq.2022.20.8.NQ44468

Tyagi, A. K. & Sreenath, N. (2015). Preserving Location Privacy in Location Based Services against Sybil Attacks. *International Journal of Security and Its Applications, 9*(12), 189-210.

Tyagi, A. K. (2016, March). Article: Cyber Physical Systems (CPSs) – Opportunities and Challenges for Improving Cyber Security. [Published by Foundation of Computer Science] [FCS] [, NY, USA.]. *International Journal of Computer Applications*, *137*(14), 19–27. doi:10.5120/ijca2016908877

Tyagi, A. K. (2019). Building a Smart and Sustainable Environment using Internet of Things (February 22, 2019). *Proceedings of International Conference on Sustainable Computing in Science, Technology and Management (SUSCOM)*. Amity University Rajasthan, Jaipur.

Tyagi, A. K. (2021). Analysis of Security and Privacy Aspects of Blockchain Technologies from Smart Era' Perspective: The Challenges and a Way Forward. In Recent Trends in Blockchain for Information Systems Security and Privacy. CRC Press.

Tyagi, A. K. (2021). Healthcare Solutions for Smart Era: An Useful Explanation from User's Perspective. Recent Trends in Blockchain for Information Systems Security and Privacy. CRC Press.

Tyagi, A. K. (2021, October). AARIN: Affordable, Accurate, Reliable and INnovative Mechanism to Protect a Medical Cyber-Physical System using Blockchain Technology. *IJIN*, *2*, 175–183.

Tyagi, A. K. (2021, October). Aswathy S U, G Aghila, N Sreenath "AARIN: Affordable, Accurate, Reliable and INnovative Mechanism to Protect a Medical Cyber-Physical System using Blockchain Technology". *IJIN*, *2*, 175–183.

Tyagi, A.K. (2022). *Handbook of Research on Technical, Privacy, and Security Challenges in a Modern World.* IGI Global., doi:10.4018/978-1-6684-5250-9

Tyagi, A. K. (2022). SecVT: Securing the Vehicles of Tomorrow Using Blockchain Technology. In A. A. Sk, T. Turki, T. K. Ghosh, S. Joardar, & S. Barman (Eds.), *Artificial Intelligence. ISAI 2022. Communications in Computer and Information Science* (Vol. 1695). Springer. doi:10.1109/ICCCI54379.2022.9740965

Tyagi, A. K. (2022). *Using Multimedia Systems, Tools, and Technologies for Smart Healthcare Services*. IGI Global. doi:10.4018/978-1-6684-5741-2

Tyagi, A. K. (2023). Decentralized everything: Practical use of blockchain technology in future applications. In R. Pandey, S. Goundar, & S. Fatima (eds.), Distributed Computing to Blockchain. Academic Press. doi:10.1016/B978-0-323-96146-2.00010-3

Tyagi, A. K. (Ed.). (2021). *Multimedia and Sensory Input for Augmented, Mixed, and Virtual Reality*. IGI Global. doi:10.4018/978-1-7998-4703-8

Tyagi, A. K., & Abraham, A. (2020). Internet of Things: Future Challenging Issues and Possible Research Directions, *International Journal of Computer Information Systems and Industrial Management Applications*.

Tyagi, A. K., & Bansal, R. Anshu, Dananjayan, S. (2023). A Step-To-Step Guide to Write a Quality Research Article. In: Abraham, A., Pllana, S., Casalino, G., Ma, K., Bajaj, A. (eds) Intelligent Systems Design and Applications. ISDA 2022. Lecture Notes in Networks and Systems, vol 717. Springer, Cham. doi:10.1007/978-3-031-35510-3_36

Tyagi, A. K., & Nair, M. M. (2020). Internet of Everything (IoE) and Internet of Things (IoTs): Threat Analyses, Possible Opportunities for Future. *Journal of Information Assurance & Security*, *15*(4).

Tyagi, A. K., & Sreenath, N. (2023). Fog and Edge Computing in Navigation of Intelligent Transportation System. In *Intelligent Transportation Systems: Theory and Practice. Disruptive Technologies and Digital Transformations for Society 5.0*. Springer. doi:10.1007/978-981-19-7622-3_7

Tyagi, A. K., Agarwal, K., Goyal, D., & Sreenath, N. (2020). A Review on Security and Privacy Issues in Internet of Things. In H. Sharma, K. Govindan, R. Poonia, S. Kumar, & W. El-Medany (Eds.), *Advances in Computing and Intelligent Systems. Algorithms for Intelligent Systems*. Springer. doi:10.1007/978-981-15-0222-4_46

Tyagi, A. K., Chandrasekaran, S., & Sreenath, N. (2022). Blockchain Technology:– A New Technology for Creating Distributed and Trusted Computing Environment. *2022 International Conference on Applied Artificial Intelligence and Computing (ICAAIC)*, (pp. 1348-1354). IEEE. 10.1109/ICAAIC53929.2022.9792702

Tyagi, A. K., Dananjayan, S., Agarwal, D., & Thariq Ahmed, H. F. (2023). Blockchain—Internet of Things Applications: Opportunities and Challenges for Industry 4.0 and Society 5.0. *Sensors (Basel)*, *23*(2), 947. doi:10.339023020947 PMID:36679743

Tyagi, A. K., Fernandez, T. F., Mishra, S., & Kumari, S. (2021). Intelligent Automation Systems at the Core of Industry 4.0. In A. Abraham, V. Piuri, N. Gandhi, P. Siarry, A. Kaklauskas, & A. Madureira (Eds.), *Intelligent Systems Design and Applications. ISDA 2020. Advances in Intelligent Systems and Computing* (Vol. 1351). Springer. doi:10.1007/978-3-030-71187-0_1

Tyagi, A. K., Nair, M. M., Niladhuri, S., & Abraham, A. (2020). Security, Privacy Research issues in Various Computing Platforms: A Survey and the Road Ahead. *Journal of Information Assurance &Security.*, *15*(1), 1–16.

Tyagi, A. K., Rekha, G., & Sreenath, N. (2020). Beyond the Hype: Internet of Things Concepts, Security and Privacy Concerns. In S. Satapathy, K. Raju, K. Shyamala, D. Krishna, & M. Favorskaya (Eds.), *Advances in Decision Sciences, Image Processing, Security and Computer Vision. ICETE 2019. Learning and Analytics in Intelligent Systems* (Vol. 3). Springer. doi:10.1007/978-3-030-24322-7_50

Uckelmann, Harrison, & Michahelles. (2011). An Architectural Approach Towards the Future Internet of Things," in Architecting the Internet of Things. Springer-Verlag.

Vadakkethil Somanathan Pilla, E. S. (2023). *A self-reconfigurable ANN*. https://github.com/sanjaikanth/ANNSelfConfigure

Vadakkethil Somanathan Pillai, E., S. & Hu, W.-C. (2022). *Effective information retrieval for mobile misinformation identification.* In 2022 International Conference on Engineering, Science and Technology (IConEST 2022), Austin, Texas.

Vanderhaegen, F. (2017). Towards increased systems resilience: New challenges based on dissonance control for human reliability in Cyber-Physical&Human Systems. *Annual Reviews in Control*, *44*, 316–322. doi:10.1016/j.arcontrol.2017.09.008

van der Linden, S. (2022). Misinformation: Susceptibility, spread, and interventions to immunize the public. *Nature Medicine*, *28*(3), 460–467. doi:10.103841591-022-01713-6 PMID:35273402

Van Dijk, M., Gentry, C., Halevi, S., & Vaikuntanathan, V. (2010). Fully homomorphic encryption over the integers. In *Advances in Cryptology–EUROCRYPT 2010: 29th Annual International Conference on the Theory and Applications of Cryptographic Techniques*. Springer Berlin Heidelberg.

Varsha, R. (2020, January 1). Deep Learning Based Blockchain Solution for Preserving Privacy in Future Vehicles. *International Journal of Hybrid Intelligent Systems*, *16*(4), 223–236.

Varsha, R., Nair, S. M., Tyagi, A. K., & Aswathy, S. U. (2021). The Future with Advanced Analytics: A Sequential Analysis of the Disruptive Technology's Scope. In Hybrid Intelligent Systems. HIS 2020. Advances in Intelligent Systems and Computing. Springer. doi:10.1007/978-3-030-73050-5_56

Vecchiola, C., Pandey, S., & Buyya, R. (2009). High-performance cloud computing: A view of scientific applications, *in 2009 10th International Symposium on Pervasive Systems, Algorithms, and Networks*, (pp. 4–16). IEEE.

Venckauskas, A., Morkevicius, N., Jukavicius, V., Damasevicius, R., Toldinas, J., & Grigaliūnas, Š. (2019). An edge-fog secure self-authenticable data transfer protocol. *Sensors (Basel)*, *19*(16), 3612. doi:10.339019163612 PMID:31431005

Verma, A., Bhattacharya, P., Madhani, N., Trivedi, C., Bhushan, B., Tanwar, S., Sharma, G., Bokoro, P. N., & Sharma, R. (2022). Blockchain for Industry 5.0: Vision, Opportunities, Key Enablers, and Future Directions. *IEEE Access : Practical Innovations, Open Solutions*, *10*, 69160–69199. doi:10.1109/ACCESS.2022.3186892

Villegas-Ch, W., García-Ortiz, J., & Urbina-Camacho, I. (2023, May 30). *Framework for a Secure and Sustainable Internet of Medical Things, Requirements, Design Challenges, and Future Trends*. MDPI. doi:10.3390/app13116634

Visser, J., Lawrence, J., & Reed, C. (2020). Reason-checking fake news. *Communications of the ACM*, *63*(11), 38–40. doi:10.1145/3397189

Vranken, H. (2017). Sustainability of bitcoin and blockchains. *Current Opinion in Environmental Sustainability*, *28*, 1–9. doi:10.1016/j.cosust.2017.04.011

Waheed, N., He, X., Ikram, M., Usman, M., Hashmi, S. S., & Usman, M. (2020, December 6). Security and privacy in IoT using machine learning and blockchain: Threats and countermeasures. *ACM Computing Surveys*, *53*(6), 1–37. doi:10.1145/3417987

Wang, F. -Y., Yang, J., Wang, X., Li, J., Han, Q. (2023). Chat with chatgpt on industry 5.0: Learning and decision-making for intelligent industries. *IEEE/CAA Journal of Automatica Sinica, 10*(4).

Wang, S., Wan, J., Zhang, D., Li, D., & Zhang, C. (2016). Towards smart factory for Industry 4.0: A self-organized multi-agent system with big data-based feedback and coordination. *Computer Networks*, *101*, 158–168. doi:10.1016/j.comnet.2015.12.017

Wang, S., Wang, D., Su, L., Kaplan, L., & Abdelzaher, T. F. (2014). Towards cyber-physical systems in social spaces: The data reliability challenge. *IEEE Real-Time Systems Symposium* (pp. 74-85). Rome, Italy: IEEE. 10.1109/RTSS.2014.19

Wang, X., Liu, Y., & Chen, Q. (2018). Smart Contract-based Security Mechanisms for Edge Computing Networks using Blockchain. *Journal of Edge Intelligence, 13*(4), 215–226.

Wang, X., Wan, J., & Imran, M. (2017). Internet of things for industrial automation systems: A survey. *IEEE Transactions on Industrial Informatics, 13*(5), 2233-2247.

Wang, X., Wang, B., & Huang, J. (2011). Cloud computing and its key techniques. *2011 IEEE International Conference on Computer Science and Automation Engineering,* (pp. 404–410). IEEE. 10.1109/CSAE.2011.5952497

Wang, X., Zha, X., Ni, W., Ren, P. L., Guo, Y. J., Niu, X., & Zheng, K. (2019). Survey on blockchain for Internet of Things. *Computer Communications, 136*, 10–29. doi:10.1016/j.comcom.2019.01.006

Wang, Y., & Kung, L. (2018). A survey on industrial Internet of Things: A cyber-physical systems perspective. *Journal of Industrial Information Integration, 10*, 28–40.

Wang, Y., Yi, X., Zhao, X., & Su, A. (2019). RHFCN: Fully CNN-based Steganalysis of MP3 with Rich High-pass Filtering. *ICASSP, IEEE International Conference on Acoustics, Speech and Signal Processing*, (pp. 2627–2631). IEEE. 10.1109/ICASSP.2019.8683626

Wang, Z., Li, X., & Ng, K. (2018). A Consensus Mechanism for Edge Computing using Blockchain Technology. *Proceedings of the International Conference on Edge Computing (ICEC),* (pp. 125-134). IEEE.

Warkentin, M., Schmidt, M. B., & Bekkering, E. (2007). Steganography and steganalysis. *Intellectual Property Protection for Multimedia Information Technology*, (January), 374–380. doi:10.4018/978-1-59904-762-1.ch019

Wei, J., Yang, Y., & Xu, L. D. (2017). Industrial Internet of Things-based intelligent energy management system for sustainable machining in Industry 4.0. *Journal of Cleaner Production, 142*, 476–489.

Weintrit, A. (2013). Technical infrastructure to support seamless information exchange in e-Navigation. In *Activities of Transport Telematics: 13th International Conference on Transport Systems Telematics, TST 2013,* (pp. 188-199). Springer Berlin Heidelberg. 10.1007/978-3-642-41647-7_24

Williams, B. D., Roh, J., Tokar, T., & Swink, M. (2013). Leveraging supply chain visibility for responsiveness: The moderating role of internal integration. *Journal of Operations Management, 31*(7-8), 543–554. doi:10.1016/j.jom.2013.09.003

Wogu, I. A., Misra, S., Assibong, P. A., Olu-Owolabi, E. F., Maskeliunas, R., & Damasevicius, R. (2019). Artificial intelligence, smart class-rooms and online education in the 21st century: Implications for hu-man development. *Journal of Cases on Information Technology, 21*(3), 66–79. doi:10.4018/JCIT.2019070105

Wood, A., Najarian, K., & Kahrobaei, D. (2020). Homomorphic encryption for machine learning in medicine and bioinformatics. *ACM Computing Surveys, 53*(4), 1–35. doi:10.1145/3394658

World Health Organization. (2023, June 28). *WHO Coronavirus (COVID-19) Dashboard: Overview*. WHO. https://covid19.who.int/

Wu, D., Rosen, D. W., Wang, L., & Schaefer, D. (2016). Cloud-Based Design and Manufacturing: A New Paradigm in Digital Manufacturing and Design Innovation. *Computer Aided Design, 59*, 1–14. doi:10.1016/j.cad.2014.07.006

Wu, Z., Liu, M., & Zhang, Y. (2021). Towards Trustworthy Edge Computing with Blockchain: A Case Study on Industrial IoT. *Journal of Blockchain Applications, 12*(3), 157–169.

Wurster, M., Exner, Y., Kaiser, J.-P., Stricker, N., & Lanza, G. (2021). Towards planning and control in cognitive factories - a generic model including learning effects and knowledge transfer across system entities. Procedia CIRP, 103, 158 – 163. doi:10.1016/j.procir.2021.10.025

Xamarin. (n.d.). *Cross-platform with Xamarin*. Microsoft. https://dotnet.microsoft.com/en-us/apps/xamarin/cross-platform

Xu, C., Wang, J., Tao, J., Zhang, J., & Zhong, R. Y. (2023). A knowledge augmented image deblurring method with deep learning for in-situ quality detection of yarn production. *International Journal of Production Research*, *61*(13), 4220–4236. doi:10.1080/00207543.2021.2010827

Xu, R., Baracaldo, N., & Joshi, J. (2021). Privacy-preserving machine learning: Methods, challenges and directions. *arXiv preprint arXiv:2108.04417*.

Xu, X., Lu, Y., Vogel-Heuser, B., & Wang, L. (2021). Industry 4.0 and Industry 5.0—Inception, conception and perception. *Journal of Manufacturing Systems*, *61*, 530–535. doi:10.1016/j.jmsy.2021.10.006

Xu, Y., Wu, J., & Kumar, S. (2022). Toward Blockchain-Based Secure and Private Machine Learning in Edge Computing. *IEEE Transactions on Industrial Informatics*, *18*(1), 646–653.

Yaacoub, J. P. A., Noura, M., Noura, H. N., Salman, O., Yaacoub, E., Couturier, R., & Chehab, A. (2020). Securing internet of medical things systems: Limitations, issues and recommendations. *Future Generation Computer Systems*, *105*, 581–606. doi:10.1016/j.future.2019.12.028

Yadav, R., Arora, S., & Dhull, S. (2022). A path way to industrial revolution 6.0. *Int. J. Mech. Eng*, *7*, 1452–1459.

Yan, M., Yu, S., Zhang, Y., & Gjessing, S. (2018). Trust and privacy in edge computing: A review. *IEEE Access : Practical Innovations, Open Solutions*, *6*, 4904–4922.

Yang, A., Liu, Y., & Ran, S. (2021). Blockchain-Based Privacy-Preserving Attribute Matchmaking for Mobile Cloud Computing. *IEEE Transactions on Industrial Informatics*, *17*(7), 5114–5121.

Yang, F., & Gu, S. (2021). Industry 4.0, a revolution that requires technology and national strategies. *Complex & Intelligent Systems*, *7*(3), 1311–1325. doi:10.100740747-020-00267-9

Yang, Z., Cai, H., & Liu, Y. (2021). A Secure and Efficient Data Integrity Verification Scheme for Cloud-Based IoT With Blockchain. *IEEE Internet of Things Journal*, *8*(1), 339–349.

Yao, Y., Lin, X., Huang, K., Liu, Z., & Lu, X. (2020). Digital Twins for IoT-Enabled Smart Cities: A Survey. *IEEE Communications Surveys and Tutorials*, *22*(2), 1511–1555.

Yaqoob, I., Hashem, I., Abaker, T., Ahmed, A., & Kazmi, H. (2019). Internet of things forensics: Recent advances, taxonomy, requirements, and open challenges. *Future Generation Computer Systems*, *92*, 265–275. doi:10.1016/j.future.2018.09.058

Yavari, F., & Pilevari, N. (2020). Industry revolutions development from industry 1.0 to industry 5.0 in manufacturing. *Journal of Industrial Strategic Management*, *5*(2), 44–63.

Yli-Huumo, J., Ko, D., Choi, S., Park, S., & Smolander, K. (2016). Where is current research on blockchain technology?—A systematic review. *PLoS One*, *11*(10), e0163477. doi:10.1371/journal.pone.0163477 PMID:27695049

Yli-Ojanpera, M., Sierla, S., Papakonstantinou, N., & Vyatkin, V. (2019). Adapting an agile manufacturing concept to the reference architecture model industry 4.0: A survey and case study. *Journal of Industrial Information Integration*, *15*, 147–160. doi:10.1016/j.jii.2018.12.002

You, X., Wang, C.-X., Huang, J., Gao, X., Zhang, Z., Wang, M., Huang, Y., Zhang, C., Jiang, Y., Wang, J., Zhu, M., Sheng, B., Wang, D., Pan, Z., Zhu, P., Yang, Y., Liu, Z., Zhang, P., Tao, X., & Liang, Y.-C. (2021). Towards 6g wireless communica-tion networks: Vision, enabling technologies, and new paradigm shifts. *Science China. Information Sciences*, *64*(1), 110301. doi:10.100711432-020-2955-6

Yu, F., Liu, Q., Wu, S., Wang, L., & Tan, T. (2019). Attention-based convolutional approach for misinformation identification from massive and noisy microblog posts. *computers & security, 83*, 106-121.

Yu, Y., Li, Y., Tian, J., & Liu, J. (2018, December). Blockchain-based solutions to security and privacy issues in the internet of things. *IEEE Wireless Communications, 25*(6), 12–18. doi:10.1109/MWC.2017.1800116

Yunana, K., Alfa, A., Misra, S., Damasevicius, R., Maskeliunas, R., & Oluranti, J. (2021). Internet of things: Applications, adoptions and components - a conceptual overview, Advances in Intelligent Systems and Computing 1375 AIST 494 – 504. doi:. doi:10.1007/978-3-030-73050-550

Yunis, A. I. M., Abusharkh, M. E., & Al-Rawi, S. (2022). Blockchain-Enhanced IoT Security for Smart Cities: A Case Study of Smart Waste Management. *IEEE Internet of Things Journal, 9*(3), 2510–2522.

Zeng, W., Hu, R., & Ai, H. (2011). Audio steganalysis of spread spectrum information hiding based on statistical moment and distance metric. *Multimedia Tools and Applications, 55*(3), 525–556. doi:10.100711042-010-0564-5

Zhang, H., Kim, Y., & Wang, S. (2020). A Secure Data Storage Scheme for Edge Devices using Blockchain Technology. *Proceedings of the International Conference on Cloud Computing and Big Data (CCBD),* (pp. 45-54). IEEE.

Zhang, J., Li, C., Ye, J., & Qu, G. (2020, September). Privacy threats and protection in machine learning. In *Proceedings of the 2020 on Great Lakes Symposium on VLSI* (pp. 531-536). 10.1145/3386263.3407599

Zhang, Q., Chen, Y., & Hu, J. (2020). Scalable Blockchain-based Data Provenance for Edge Computing. *Proceedings of the International Conference on Edge Intelligence (ICEI)*, (pp. 78-87). IEEE.

Zhang, Q., Lee, H., & Wang, X. (2020). Decentralized Access Control using Blockchain in Edge Computing Environments. *IEEE Transactions on Network and Service Management, 17*(3), 876–887.

Zhang, Y., Wang, L., Xiang, Y., & Ten, C. W. (2015). Power system reliability evaluation with SCADA cybersecurity considerations. *IEEE Transactions on Smart Grid, 6*(4), 1707–1721.

Zhang, Y., Wang, L., Xiang, Y., & Ten, C. W. (2016). Inclusion of SCADA cyber vulnerability in power system reliability assessment considering optimal resources allocation. *IEEE Transactions on Power Systems, 31*(6), 4379–4394. doi:10.1109/TPWRS.2015.2510626

Zhang, Y., Xiang, Y., & Wang, L. (2016). Power system reliability assessment incorporating cyber attacks against wind farm energy management systems. *IEEE Transactions on Smart Grid, 8*(5), 2343–2357. doi:10.1109/TSG.2016.2523515

Zhang, Z., & Bowes, B. (2023). The future of artificial intelligence (AI) and machine learning (ML) in landscape design: A case study in Coastal Virginia, USA. *arXiv preprint arXiv:2305.02327.*

Zhao, C., Zhao, S., Zhao, M., Chen, Z., Gao, C. Z., Li, H., & Tan, Y. A. (2019). Secure multi-party computation: Theory, practice and applications. *Information Sciences, 476*, 357–372. doi:10.1016/j.ins.2018.10.024

Zhao, F., & Yao, J. (2018). Digital Twin Driven Prognostics and Health Management for Complex Equipment. *Journal of Manufacturing Science and Engineering, 140*(3), 030801.

Zheng, Z., Xie, S., Dai, H., Chen, X., & Wang, H. (2017). An overview of blockchain technology: Architecture, consensus, and future trends. In *In 2017 IEEE international congress on big data (BigData congress)* (pp. 557–564). IEEE. doi:10.1109/BigDataCongress.2017.85

Zheng, Z., Xie, S., Dai, H. N., Chen, X., & Wang, H. (2018). Blockchain challenges and opportunities: A survey. *International Journal of Web and Grid Services, 14*(4), 352–375. doi:10.1504/IJWGS.2018.095647

Zhong, R. Y., Xu, X., Klotz, E., & Newman, S. T. (2017). Intelligent manufacturing in the context of industry 4.0: A review. *Engineering (Beijing)*, *3*(5), 616–630. doi:10.1016/J.ENG.2017.05.015

Zhou, J., Chen, X., & Chen, C. (2020). Digital twin-driven decision-making method for production and maintenance planning in smart manufacturing. *Journal of Manufacturing Systems*, *56*, 238–253.

Zhou, J., Feng, Y., Wang, Z., & Guo, D. (2021). Using secure multi-party computation to protect privacy on a permissioned blockchain. *Sensors (Basel)*, *21*(4), 1540. doi:10.339021041540 PMID:33672175

Zhou, X. & Zafarani, R. (2020, October). A survey of fake news: fundamental theories, detection methods, and opportunities. *ACM Computing Surveys, 53*(5), 109, 1-40.

Ahmed, R. S., Ahmed, E. S. A., & Saeed, R. A. (2021) Machine learning in cyber-physical systems in industry 4.0. In Artificial Intelligence Paradigms for Smart Cyber-Physical Systems, 20–41. IGI Global.

About the Contributors

Lakshmi D, Dr., is presently designated as a Senior Associate Professor in the School of Computing Science and Engineering (SCSE) & Assistant Director, at the Centre for Innovation in Teaching & Learning (CITL) at VIT Bhopal. She has 17 international conference presentations, and 21 international journal papers inclusive of SCOPUS & SCI (cumulative impact factor 31). 3 SCOPUS inee book chapters. A total of 24 patents are in various states and 18 patents have been granted at both national and international levels. One Edited book with Taylor & Francis (SCOPUS Indexed). She has won two Best Paper awards at international conferences, one at the IEEE conference and another one at EAMMIS 2021. She received two awards in the year 2022. She received two awards in the year 2022. She has addressed innumerable guest lectures, acted as a session chair, and was invited as a keynote speaker at several international conferences. She has conducted FDPs that cover approximately ~80,000 plus faculty members including JNTU, TEQIP, SERB, SWAYAM, DST, AICTE, MHRD, ATAL, ISTE, Madhya Pradesh Government-sponsored, and self-financed workshops across India on various titles.

Amit Kumar Tyagi is working as Assistant Professor, at National Institute of Fashion Technology, 110016, New Delhi, India. Previously he has worked as Assistant Professor (Senior Grade 2), and Senior Researcher at Vellore Institute of Technology (VIT), Chennai Campus, 600127, Chennai, Tamilandu, India for the period of 2019-2022. He received his Ph.D. Degree (Full-Time) in 2018 from Pondicherry Central University, 605014, Puducherry, India. About his academic experience, he joined the Lord Krishna College of Engineering, Ghaziabad (LKCE) for the periods of 2009-2010, and 2012-2013. He was an Assistant Professor and Head- Research, Lingaya's Vidyapeeth (formerly known as Lingaya's University), Faridabad, Haryana, India for the period of 2018-2019. His supervision experience includes more than 10 Masters' dissertations and one PhD thesis. He has contributed to several projects such as "AARIN" and "P3- Block" to address some of the open issues related to the privacy breaches in Vehicular Applications (such as Parking) and Medical Cyber Physical Systems (MCPS). He has published over 100 papers in refereed high impact journals, conferences and books, and some of his articles awarded as best paper award.

***

Michael Olaolu Arowolo, PhD, is a renowned research scholar specializing in Bioinformatics, Artificial Intelligence, Deep Learning, Machine Learning, and Data Mining. He currently serves at the University of Missouri, USA. Dr. Arowolo's groundbreaking work involves unraveling complex biological systems through cutting-edge computational techniques. His PhD stands as a testament to his commitment to advancing knowledge. As an inspiring mentor, he cultivates the talents of future scientists. Driven by a passion for innovation, he continues to pioneer solutions that address pressing challenges in his field, making an indelible mark in academia and beyond.

Kiran Bellam holds a Ph.D. in Computer Science from Auburn University and has served as a faculty member at Prairie View A&M University, where she currently holds the position of Associate Dean for the College of Engineering. Dr. Bellam's research has significantly contributed to fields like cloud computing, energy-efficient storage disks, and Engineering education. She secured substantial research grants to support her research. Her work has been widely published and recognized, making her a notable figure in the field of computer science.

Mani Deepak Choudhry pursued a B.Tech.(Information Technology) at SNS College of Technology, Coimbatore and continued Post Graduation in M.E (Software Engineering) at Regional Centre, Anna University Coimbatore. He has 13 years of experience in Teaching and currently working as Assistant Professor/IT at KGiSL Institute of Technology, Coimbatore. He is pursuing PhD in the field of Video Processing in IoRT. He is life member of ISTE. He has published 5 papers in National conferences and 5 papers in international conferences, 4 book chapters and also 10 papers in international journals. His areas of interest are Machine Intelligence, Deep Learning, Internet of Things, Block chain and Image Processing. He is potential reviewer for Neural Processing Letters, CMC, CSSE, IASC, IGI Global journals and book chapters.

Sayani Chattopadhyay holds the position of Assistant Professor at CIMT within Burdwan University. She accomplished her BCA degree at Burdwan University, followed by the attainment of her MCA from IGNOU. Currently, she is actively engaged as a research scholar with a keen focus on the domains of Cyber Security and Data Analytics.

Aswani Kumar Cherukuri is a Professor (Higher Academic Grade) of School of Information Technology & Engineering, Vellore Institute of Technology, Vellore. His research interests are machine learning, information security and quantum computing. In particular, his work is focused on encrypted network traffic analysis, machine learning techniques. Also, he has interests in post quantum cryptography. He published more than 190 research papers and has 3580+ citations and h-index of 29 as per Google scholar. He executed as principal investigator, different research projects of worth 10 million USD from various funding agencies of India. He has guided 8 PhD research scholars and few foreign interns. He is continuously recognized since 2020 as top 2% scientists in India in the area of AI and ML by a study from Stanford University researchers. He has received awards including Young Scientist Fellowship, Inspiring Teacher Award, Educator excellence award, etc. Heis editorial board member of several international journals. He is a member of IEEE, Senior Member of ACM, Vice Chair of IEEE Educational Taskforce on Datamining.

D. Shanthi is currently serving as a Professor in the Department of Computer Science and Engineering at PSNA College of Engineering and Technology, Dindigul, Tamil Nadu, India. She possesses expertise in the fields of Cloud Computing and Blockchain Technology.

Shalbani Das is an ambitious student enrolled at the esteemed Institute of Information Technology, Amity University Kolkata. She is currently pursuing her Master of Computer Applications (MCA) degree, with a projected completion date in 2025. Recognizing her academic excellence, Amity University has bestowed upon her a merit scholarship, acknowledging her outstanding achievements. Shalbani's passion lies in the field of cybersecurity, and she aspires to conduct research in various domains within this rapidly evolving area. Already making strides in her academic journey, she recently presented a paper on Quantum Key Distribution at an esteemed International Conference, showcasing her knowledge and dedication to exploring cutting-edge topics. She has contributed significantly to the academic community, having previously published a chapter with IGI Global, a renowned publisher in the field of information technology and computer science. Her dedication to scholarly pursuits and her contributions to academia exemplify her commitment to expanding the boundaries of knowledge in the realm of cybersecurity.

Sanjaikanth E. Vadakkethil Somanathan Pillai is a Senior Systems Analyst for Visa Inc. with 16 years of industry experience. Sanjaikanth completed his bachelor's degree from The University of Calicut, India, and his Master's in Electrical and Computer Engineering (Software Engineering) from The University of Texas at Austin. He is currently studying toward a Ph.D. in Computer Science at The University of North Dakota. His expertises include application programming, automation, performance optimization, and data research.

Mahmoud Elsisi (Senior Member, IEEE) received the B.Sc., M.Sc., and Ph.D. degrees from the Electrical Engineering Department, Faculty of Engineering (Shoubra), Benha University, Cairo, Egypt, in 2011, 2014, and 2017, respectively.,He worked as an Assistant Professor at the Electrical Engineering Department, Faculty of Engineering (Shoubra), Benha University. From August 2019 to July 2022, he worked as an Assistant Professor with the Industry 4.0 Implementation Center, Center for Cyber-Physical System Innovation, National Taiwan University of Science and Technology, Taipei, Taiwan. He is currently an Associate Professor with the Electrical Engineering Department, National Kaohsiung University of Science and Technology, Kaohsiung, Taiwan. His research interests include studying the machine learning, deep learning, the Internet of Things (IoT), cybersecurity, model predictive control, neural networks, fuzzy logic, Kalman filter, observers, decentralized control of largescale systems, robotic control, autonomous vehicle control, renewable energy, power system dynamics: stability and control, nuclear power plant control, and wind energy conversion systems, faults diagnosis, power transformers.

Wen-Chen Hu received a PhD in Computer Science from the University of Florida. He is currently an associate professor in the School of Electrical Engineering and Computer Science of the University of North Dakota. He is the general chairs of about 20 international conferences and has been the editor-in-chiefs of the Journal of Information Technology Research (JITR) since 2023 and International Journal of Handheld Computing Research (IJHCR) from 2010 to 2017. In addition, he has acted as more than 200 positions like editors and editorial board members of international journals/books and program committee members of international conferences. Dr. Hu has been teaching for more than 25 years at the US universities and about 20 different computer/IT-related courses and advising/consulting more than 100 graduate students. He has published about 200 articles in refereed journals, conference proceedings, books, and encyclopedias, edited more than 10 books and conference proceedings, and solely authored a book. His current research interests include (mobile) data research and applications.

J. Benadict Raja is working as associate professor in the Department of Computer Science and Engineering at PSNA College of Engineering and Technology, Dindigul. He completed his master's degree and PhD degree at Anna University, Chennai and his research interest include medical image processing and parallel computing

Nimish Jain is undergraduate student of School of Information Technology & Engineering, Vellore Institute of Technology, Vellore, India. His research interests are security and machine learning.

Akshya Jothi obtained her bachelor's degree (BE CSE) and pursued her M.Tech (Advanced Computing) in SASTRA University. She completed her PhD in SASTRA University. She is currently working as Assistant Professor, Department of Computational Intelligence, SRM Institute of Science and Technology, Kattankulathur – Chennai.She presented papers in various international conferences and published in SCI, Web of Science and Scopus indexed Journals. She has teaching and research experience of 3 years. Her research areas are Computational Geometry, Graph Theory, Machine Learning, Deep Learning and Artificial Intelligence.

Vijay K. is working as Assistant Professor (SG) in the department of Computer Science and Engineering, Rajalakshmi Engineering College, Chennai, Tamilnadu, India. He is B.Tech., M.E., graduate and pursuing PhD in Anna University, Chennai in the area of Cloud Computing. Having 16+ years of experience in teaching. Received the award, "Active Participation Youth", under CSI Service Award at the CSI Annual Convention 2016. He was awarded with "Inspire Faculty Partnership Level award" in 2017 (Bronze Level) by Infosys. He is a life time member of Computer Society of India, IEI-India. He received Best Faculty Award many times. Presented/published more than 20+ papers in various conferences and journals. His areas of interest include Cloud Computing, Image Processing, IOT and Machine Learning.

Sowmia K.R. is currently working as Assistant Professor [SG] in the Department of Artificial Intelligence and Machine Learning, Rajalakshmi Engineering College. She has 13 years of teaching experience and 2 years of industrial experience .Pursing research in the field of Student learning methodologies using Artificial Intelligence and Machine Learning. She guided more than 10 ME projects and 40 BE projects. As a mentor, her student team participated in different hackathon and bagged prizes. She has several papers published in reputed journal and international conference to her credits. She is instrumental in consultancy and industry projects.

Firuz Kamalov obtained PhD in Mathematics in 2011 from University of Nebraska-Lincoln. While at UNL he was a recipient of prestigious Othmer Fellowship (2005-2008) given to exceptional incoming scholars. Dr Kamalov obtained BA in Mathematics and Economics from Macalester College where he was a recipient of DeWitt Wallace Distinguished Scholarship (2000-2004). Dr Kamalov joined Canadian University Dubai in 2011 where he has taught a wide range of mathematics courses across curricula. He is a recipient of CUD Academic Research Award (2013) and CUD Teaching Award (2013). Dr Kamalov's research interests include C*-algebras, functional analysis, machine learning, and data mining. He is a managing editor of Gulf Journal of Mathematics.

Manivannan Karunakaran is a Professor in the Department of Computer Science and Engineering in JAIN (Deemed-to-be University), Bangalore, India. He has received his B. E., in Computer Science and Engineering from Anna University, Chennai in 2003 and M.E., in Computer Science and Engineering from Anna University, Chennai in 2008. In February 2015, he completed his Ph.D. degree from Anna University, Chennai. With more than 18 years of experience in teaching, his areas of specialization include Machine Learning and Medical image Processing. He has published 3 patents in IPR and has published more than 40 papers in reputed international Scopus/SCI indexed journals, 4 Books and Book Chapter. He has published 10 papers in National and International Conferences and has served as editor/reviewer for Springer, Elsevier, Wiley, etc., He is an active member of ISTE, IACSIT, and IAENG. He has organized several National/International conferences, Workshops and Technical Events. He is regularly invited to deliver lectures in various programs for imparting skills in research methodology to students and research scholars. He has successfully guided 5 PhD scholars in Anna University, Chennai. He has received Rs.40, 000 from Indian council of Medical Research as Seminar Grant for organizing Workshop on Application of i-SMAC Technologies &Tools for Public Health Surveillance to Prevent Epidemic Disease ATAL FDP on Blockchain from AICTE worth of Rs.90000. He has been awarded as a Recognized reviewer of Elsevier Publications in the year 2020.

Shabnam Kumari is working as a Ph.D Research Scholar at SRM Institute of Science and Technology, Chennai, Tamilnadu, India.

Sundarrajan M. obtained his bachelor's degree (BE CSE) from PSV College of Engineering and Technology and pursued his M.Tech (Advanced Computing) in SASTRA University. He was awarded PhD from Periyar Maniammal Institute of Science and Technology, Thanjavur. He is currently working as Assistant Professor/CSE, SRM Institute of Science and Technology, Ramapuram Campus, Chennai. He presented papers in various international conferences and published in SCI, Web of Science and Scopus indexed Journals. He has teaching and research experience of 7 years. His research areas are Data Security, Internet of Things, Mathematical Cryptography and Threat Intelligence.

Ibrahim's M. H. went from Assistant Professor to Head of Information Technology Introduction: Ibrahim's life has been a testament to perseverance, hard work, and a passion for technology. Rising through the ranks from an Assistant Professor to becoming the Head of the Department of Information Technology, this journey is nothing short of inspiring. This biography chronicles the key milestones, challenges, and accomplishments that have shaped my professional career. Ibrahim was born in Tirunelveli, India and from an early age, he showed an aptitude for academics and a keen interest in technology. He excelled in his studies and demonstrated an innate curiosity for understanding how things worked. This led him to pursue a higher education in the field of computer science. After completing my undergraduate studies in computer science, I went on to pursue a Master's degree in the same field. Upon completing my Master's, Ibrahim started an academic career as an Assistant Professor at Sadakathullah Appa College. His teaching style, combined with his practical knowledge of the industry, quickly earned him respect among students and colleagues.

Bireshwar Dass Mazumdar obtained MCA degree from UP Technical University, Lucknow, India in the year of 2005. He did his PhD from Department of Computer Engineering,Indian Institute of Technology, B.H.U; Varanasi India.Currently he is working in capacity of Associate Professor, Bennett University, Greater Noida, UP. His research interest is Multiagent system and its application in e-commerce,Business Intelligence,Cognitive Computing, Machine Learning

Sanjay Misra, a Sr. member of IEEE and ACM Distinguished Lecturer, is a Senior Scientist at the Institute for Energy Technology(IFE), Halden, Norway. Before joining IFE, he was associated with the Computer Science and Communication department of Østfold University College, Halden, Norway, and was a Full Professor (since Jan 2010) of Computer (Software) Engineering at Covenant University (400-500 ranked by THE(2019)) since 2012 yrs. He holds PhD. in Information & Knowledge Engg(Software Engg)from the University of Alcala, Spain & M.Tech.(Software Engg) from MLN National Institute of Tech, India.As per SciVal (SCOPUS- Elsevier) analysis (on 01.12.2021). He has been the most productive researcher (Number 1) in Nigeria since 2017 (in all disciplines), in computer science no 1 in the country & no 2 in the whole of Africa. Total around 700 articles (SCOPUS/WoS) with 500 coauthors worldwide (-150 JCR/SCIE) in the core & appl. area of Software Engineering, Web engineering, Health Informatics, Cybersecurity,Intelligent systems,AI,etc. He has been amongst the top 2% of scientists in the world (published by Standford University) for last 3 years.

Shreyashi Mukherjee is currently pursuing the BCA-MCA integrated course from Amity University Kolkata.

M. Parimala Devi received B.E. (Electronics and Communication) from Bharathiyar University, Coimbatore, M.E. (VLSI Design) from Anna University, Chennai, M.B.A. (Human Resource Management) from Anna University and Ph.D (Information and Communication Engineering) from Anna University, Chennai. Currently, she is Associate Professor in the Velalar College of Engineering and Technology, Erode. She has published 25 papers in national and international journals and conferences. She has been the reviewer for many SCOPUS indexed journals and received best paper awards at international conferences. She has published a book named "Advanced Microprocessors and Microcontrollers" with University Science Press, New Delhi. She is a lifetime member of IETE. Her research interests include VLSI &SoC, IoT, Microprocessor based system design and Nanoelectronics.

Ambika N. is a MCA, MPhil, Ph.D. in computer science. She completed her Ph.D. from Bharathiar university in the year 2015. She has 16 years of teaching experience and presently working for St.Francis College, Bangalore. She has guided BCA, MCA and M.Tech students in their projects. Her expertise includes wireless sensor network, Internet of things, cybersecurity. She gives guest lectures in her expertise. She is a reviewer of books, conferences (national/international), encyclopaedia and journals. She is advisory committee member of some conferences. She has many publications in National & international conferences, international books, national and international journals and encyclopaedias. She has some patent publications (National) in computer science division.

Vijayakumar R. is working as Assistant Professor (SS) in the department of Computer Science and Engineering, Rajalakshmi Engineering College, Chennai, Tamilnadu, India. He is B.Tech., M.Tech., graduate. He is also deputy Controller of Examinations, Rajalakshmi Engineering College. Having 9+ years of experience in teaching. Received the award, "Active Participation Youth", under CSI Service Award at the CSI Annual Convention 2017. He was awarded with "Inspire Faculty Partnership Level award" in 2017, 2018, 2019(Gold Level) by Infosys. He is a life time member of Computer Society of India, IEI-India. He received Best Faculty Award many times. He certified as Wipro certificate Faculty from wipro in 2018. Presented/published more than 10+ papers in various conferences and journals. His areas of interest Cyber security, application development and Algorithms.

Mahmoud Ragab is a Professor at Department of Information Technology, Faculty of Computing and Information Technology, King Abdulaziz University, Jeddah, Saudi Arabia. Also, He is a professor, data Science, Mathematics Department, Faculty of Science, Al Azhar University, Cairo, Egypt. He is currently the head of the Biological Quantum Computing Unit in the Centre for Artificial Intelligence in Precision Medicine, King Abdulaziz University. He is a former Consultant for the Vice Presidency for Graduate Studies and Scientific Research and a former Consultant for Vice President for Development, at KAU as well. In addition, He has been serving as an editorial board member of several reputed journals and working in different research groups at many universities such as the Combinatorial Optimization and Graph Algorithms Group (COGA), Faculty II Mathematics and Natural Sciences, Berlin University of Technology, Berlin, Germany, the British University in Egypt BUE, Arbeitsgruppe Stochastik",Christian Albrechts University at Kiel CAU Kiel, Germany. Moreover, he worked as a research assistant in department of Computer Science and Automation, Integrated Communication Systems Group, Ilmenau University of Technology TU Ilmenau, Thuerengen, Germany. Prof. Dr. Mahmoud Ragab received his B. Sc. in Statistics and Computer Science from Mansoura University, Mansoura, Egypt and M. Sc. Degree in Statistics & operations Research, Faculty of Science, Al Azhar University, Cairo, Egypt. He obtained his Ph.D. degree in Partial Quicksort Algorithms and weighted branching Processes from the faculty of Mathematics and Natural Sciences of the Christian-Albrechts-University at Kiel (CAU), Schleswig-Holstein, Germany. His research focuses on: Artificial intelligence in diseases and biomedical applications, AI techniques for Cancer detection and classification, Deep learning, Sorting algorithms / Efficiency, Optimization, Mathematical Modeling, Data Science / Data analysis, Applied Statistics, Neural Networks, Time series analysis, Quantum computation.

Yadav Krishna Kumar Rajnath is born in Ghazipur in Uttar Pradesh (India) on 10th July 1988. He migrated to Maharashtra (India) during the childhood and received his schooling from Maharashtra State Board. He obtained Bachelor's in Engineering (B.E.) in Mechanical Engineering from K.J. Somaiya College of Engineering, Vidyavihar (Mumbai) in 2010 with First Class with Distinction and completed the Masters of Technology (M.Tech.) in Mechanical Engineering with specialization on Refrigeration, Air-conditioning and Heat Transfer from the National Institute of Technology (NIT) Patna, Bihar (India) in 2014 with First Class with Distinction. In the following year, Dr. Yadav joined as a Junior Research Fellow (JRF) in a Govt. of India sponsored research project on "Flow control in complex duct using synthetic jets" in the Department of Applied Mechanics at the Motilal Nehru National Institute of Technology (MNNIT) Allahabad, Prayagraj (India) and continued in the project till June 2017. He also joined in the Ph.D. programme in the same department in July 2015 and completed Doctor of Philosophy (Ph.D.) in February 2021.

S. Gnanavel is currently working as an Associate Professor in the department of Computing Technologies at SRM Institute of Science and Technology, Kattankulathur, Chennai, India. He Received the B.Tech (IT), M.E (CSE) and Ph.D. degree from Anna University Chennai, India. He has over 14 years of teaching and research experience. He works in the area of Multimedia transmission on Wireless Networks, Internet of Things and cloud security. His current research interests are in Machine Leaning, cyber security and cloud computing. He is a life time member of MISTE, ACM and MIANG. He published many papers in international refereed journals and conferences. He is serving as a reviewer for many journals and conferences.

S. Jeevanandham pursued B.E(CSE) at Coimbatore Institute of Engineering and Technology, Coimbatore and continued Post Graduation in M.E (Computer Science and Engineering) at Akshaya College of Engineering and Technology. He has 13 years of experience in Teaching and currently working as Assistant Professor/IT at Sri Ramakrishna Engineering College, Coimbatore. He is pursuing PhD in the field of Wireless Sensor Networks. He is life member of ISTE. He has published 5 papers in National conferences and 5 papers in international conferences and also 6papersin international journals. His areas of Interest are Wireless Sensor Networks, Cloud Computing, Network Security and Internet of Things.

Aderonke Thompson, PhD FFIN, is a Professor in the Cyber Security Department at the Federal University of Technology, Akure (FUTA)., Nigeria. She has attended many international conferences and presented papers both locally and internationally. She is a member of several professional bodies: including Internet Society; IEEE; ACM; WiCys and Cyber Security Expert Association of Nigeria (CSEAN). She is a Board member at- Nigerian Techsters Women Initiative with Tech4Dev on a Microsoft sponsored Programme for Nigerian Women; Vigi Trust-; Top 50 Women in Cybersecurity Africa 2020; Speaker across 3 Continents and an ISO27001 LI & LA

Shrikant Tiwari (Senior Member, IEEE) was born in Karuwa Village, Maihar, Madhya Pradesh, India in 15th Aug. 1983. He received his Ph.D. in the Department of Computer Science & Engineering (CSE) from the Indian Institute of Technology (Banaras Hindu University), Varanasi (India) in 2012 and M. Tech. in Computer Science and Technology from the University of Mysore (India) in 2009. Currently, he is working as an Associate Professor in the School of Computing Science and Engineering (SCSE), Galgotias University, Greater Noida, Gautam Budha Nagar, Uttar Pradesh-203201 (India). He has authored and co-author more than 50 national and international journal publications, book chapters, and conference articles. He has five patents filed to his credit. His research interests include machine learning, deep learning, computer vision, medical image analysis, pattern recognition, and biometrics. Dr. Tiwari is a FIETE and member of ACM, IET, CSI, ISTE, IAENG, SCIEI. He is also a guest editorial board member and a reviewer for many international journals of repute.

Virendra Kumar Verma is currently working as an assistant professor in Institute of Engineering & Rural Technology (IERT) Prayagraj. His area of interest is Manufacturing Technology, Artificial Intelligence, Optimisation techniques etc.

Ramesh S. Wadawadagi received his M.Tech in Computer Science and Technology from the University of Mysore, India in 2009. He received his Ph. D in Computer Science and Engineering from Visveswaraya Technological University, Belagavi, India in 2021. Currently, he works in Nagarjuna College of Engineering and Technology, Banglore as an Associate Professor in the Department of Information Science and Engineering. His research interest includes Machine Learning, Deep Learning, AI, and Cyber security.

Index

D

E

F

G

H

I

L

M

N

O

P

Q

R

S

T

V

Z

Printed in the United States
by Baker & Taylor Publisher Services